THE KIZILBASH/ALEVIS IN OTTOMAN ANATOLIA

Edinburgh Studies on the Ottoman Empire
Series Editor: Kent F. Schull

Published and forthcoming titles

Migrating Texts: Circulating Translations around the Ottoman Mediterranean
Edited by Marilyn Booth

Ottoman Sunnism: New Perspectives
Edited by Vefa Erginbaş

The Politics of Armenian Migration to North America, 1885–1915: Migrants, Smugglers and Dubious Citizens
David E. Gutman

The Kizilbash/Alevis in Ottoman Anatolia: Sufism, Politics and Community
Ayfer Karakaya-Stump

Çemberlitaş Hamami in Istanbul: The Biographical Memoir of a Turkish Bath
Nina Macaraig

Nineteenth-century Local Governance in Ottoman Bulgaria: Politics in Provincial Councils
Safa Saraçoğlu

Prisons in the Late Ottoman Empire: Microcosms of Modernity
Kent F. Schull

Ruler Visibility and Popular Belonging in the Ottoman Empire
Darin Stephanov

Children and Childhood in the Ottoman Empire: From the Fourteenth to the Twentieth Centuries
Edited by Gülay Yılmaz and Fruma Zachs

edinburghuniversitypress.com/series/esoe

THE KIZILBASH/ALEVIS IN OTTOMAN ANATOLIA

SUFISM, POLITICS AND COMMUNITY

Ayfer Karakaya-Stump

EDINBURGH
University Press

To Laine, *aşk ile*

Edinburgh University Press is one of the leading university presses in the UK. We publish academic books and journals in our selected subject areas across the humanities and social sciences, combining cutting-edge scholarship with high editorial and production values to produce academic works of lasting importance. For more information visit our website: edinburghuniversitypress.com

Edinburgh University Press Ltd
The Tun – Holyrood Road
12 (2f) Jackson's Entry
Edinburgh EH8 8PJ

First published in by hardback Edinburgh University Press 2020

Typeset in Jaghbuni by
Servis Filmsetting Ltd, Stockport, Cheshire

A CIP record for this book is available from the British Library

ISBN 978 1 4744 3268 9 (hardback)
ISBN 978 1 4744 3269 6 (paperback)
ISBN 978 1 4744 3270 2 (webready PDF)
ISBN 978 1 4744 3271 9 (epub)

Published with the support of the University of Edinburgh Scholarly Publishing Initiatives Fund.

Contents

List of Figures vi
Acknowledgements viii
Notes on Transliteration and Terminology xi
List of Abbreviations xiv
Map 1. West Asia in the late medieval and early modern periods xx
Map 2. The Ottoman–Safavid conflict *c.*1500 xxi

Introduction 1
1. The Iraq Connection: Abu'l-Wafa᾿ Taj al-ᶜArifin and the Wafa᾿i Tradition 44
2. The Forgotten Forefathers: Wafa᾿i Dervishes in Medieval Anatolia 89
3. Hacı Bektaş and his Contested Legacy: The Abdals of Rum, the Bektashi Order and the (Proto-)Kizilbash Communities 145
4. A Transregional Kizilbash Network: The Iraqi Shrine Cities and their Kizilbash Visitors 188
5. Mysticism and Imperial Politics: The Safavids and the Making of the Kizilbash Milieu 220
6. From Persecution to Confessionalisation: Consolidation of the Kizilbash/Alevi Identity in Ottoman Anatolia 256

Conclusion 320

Glossary 327
Selected Bibliography 330
Index 365

Figures

I.1	An Alevi document (*ziyāretnāme*) dated 1237/1821 with an illustration of Burak	5
I.2a	Kaygusuz Abdal standing in *dar-ı Mansur*, miniature painting by Levni	6
I.2b	Young Alevis standing in *dar-ı Mansur*, Adıyaman	7
I.3	Hüseyin Dede (Keko Hüseyin) from the *ocak* of Üryan Hızır	15
I.4a	Sample Alevi document in its protective case, private archive of Abuzer Güzel Dede	19
I.4b	Sample Alevi document from the private archive of Muharrem Naci Orhan	20
I.4c	Sample Alevi manuscript (*Buyruk*), undated	21
2.1a	The door of the (presumed) tomb-shrine of Ağuiçen, in the village of Bargını in Hozat-Tunceli, before its restoration in 2014	106
2.1b	The (presumed) tomb-shrine of Ağuiçen, in the village of Bargını in Hozat-Tunceli, after its restoration in 2014	107
2.2	Trademark seals of Alevi documents issued at the shrine of Imam Husayn during and after the sixteenth century	110
2.3	The (presumed) tomb of Dede Kargın, village of Dedeköy in Derik-Mardin	117
2.4a	Burial site of the Kargıni family, village of Bahri in Akçadağ-Malatya	119
2.4b	Burial site of the Kargıni family, picture from inside	120
2.4c	The wooden headstone marking the grave of Yusuf Dede	120
2.5	The (presumed) tomb-shrine of Sultan Sinemil(li), Piran-Elazığ	127
4.1	The Karbala convent (Kerbela Dergâhı) in the shrine complex of Imam Husayn	193

4.2	A section of a *ziyāretnāme* with illustrations dated 1259/1843	204
4.3a	Official note (Ot. *tezkere*; Ar. *tadhkara*) dated 1207/1792 verifying *sayyid*-ship issued by the local *naḳībü'l-eşrāf* in Karbala	206
4.3b–c	The two ends of a scroll that comprises a written genealogy (Ot. *şecere*; Ar. *shajara*) dated 1207/1792 verifying *sayyid*-ship issued by the local *naḳībü'l-eşrāf* in Karbala	207
5.1	Safavi *ḫilāfetnāme* dated 1089/1678	233
6.1	A building with a multi-layer roof signifying the seven heavens (*kırlangıç çatı*)	299
6.2	Alevi document dated 1155/1742	300

Acknowledgements

This project has lasted much longer than I ever imagined it would. It was a fixture of my life for nearly two decades, from its initial research phase through its first rendition as a dissertation in 2008 and its final expansion and transformation into this book. It was made possible by contributions from a multitude of people, all of whom, I am afraid, I am unable to mention here by name. A very special thanks goes to my former supervisor, Cemal Kafadar, who has profoundly shaped my thinking about history with his well-rounded erudition, nuanced understanding of the Ottoman world in its wider context, and sense of historical empathy. I owe him several debts of gratitude for his inspiring guidance, trust in my work and ever-appreciated friendship. I am equally indebted to Carter Findley, my first mentor in the field, who will always serve as a model of assiduous and meticulous scholarship. A heartfelt thanks also goes to the late Şinasi Tekin. The individualised Ottoman language classes that I took with him during the early stages of my research proved to be a lifesaver as I was entering the polyglot territory of Alevi documents and manuscripts. In addition, I am grateful to Ahmet Karamustafa for generously sharing with me his vast expertise in Sufism and his precious insights into Alevi-Bektashi history over the years.

Much of the research for this book would not have been possible were it not for the many Alevi *dede*s and *ocakzade*s who opened their private archives and imparted information and traditions to me concerning their family histories. I am eternally grateful to them and to all other members of the Alevi community who hosted and guided my husband and me during my field trips, helped me acquire copies of documents and manuscripts, and generously shared their knowledge regarding various aspects of Alevi *ocak*s. Among them I should particularly note the late Hasan Çevik Dede, Bektaş Keskin Dede, Mehmet Ekber Çevik,

Hüseyin Keskin and Hüseyin Cahit Kargıner, all from Antep; Hüseyin Doğan Dede, Hayri Doğan Dede, Abuzer Güzel Dede, Mustafa Alkan (Aşık Özeni) and Kazım Acar from Adıyaman; the late (Küçük) Tacim Bakır Dede, the late Mehmet Yüksel Dede, Abuzer Erdoğan Dede, Veyis Erdoğan Dede, Asaf Koçdağ and Mehmet Ocak from Maraş; the late Ali Rıza Kargın Dede and Eşref Doğan from Malatya; Ahmet Mutluay Dede and Hayrettin Kaya from Elazığ; Hamza Özyıldırım Dede and Ali Özgöz Dede from Erzincan; Halil Öztürk, Demir Durgun, Mustafa İyidoğan and Kelime Ata from Sivas; Mustafa Aygün Dede, Çelebi Eken Dede, Haydar Altun Dede, Mustafa Öksel and Hüseyin Karşu from Amasya; the late Muharrem Yanar and Abdülkadir Sel Dede from Tokat; Galip Dedekargınoğlu, İzzettin Doğan, Nurcemal Mola, İbrahim Sinemillioğlu, Muharrem Ercan Dede and Kamil Öksel, who currently reside in Istanbul, and the late Muharrem Naci Orhan, also from Istanbul; Hüseyin Dedekargınoğlu Dede, Hamdi and Hayriye Kargıner, who currently reside in Ankara; İsmail and Aysel Doğan, who currently reside in Izmir; and many others whom I cannot acknowledge due to economy of space. A special thanks also goes to my friend and colleague Ali Yaman and to the late Mehmet Yaman Dede; early on in my research process they both generously shared with me documents and manuscripts from their own libraries, which they had collected from their family members and members of other Alevi *ocak*s.

Numerous other colleagues and friends contributed to this work with their time and labour. Among them I should gratefully acknowledge Himmet Taşkömür and Abdullatif al-Khaiat, who many times over the years provided assistance to me in deciphering documents in Ottoman Turkish and Arabic. I also received help from Nima Shafaieh and Shantia Yarahmadian with some Persian documents and passages. Aimee Dobbs and Shahin Mustafayev helped me acquire a copy of a book from the library of the Academy of Sciences in Baku, and Richard McGregor was kind enough to share with me his copy of the manuscript containing Murtada al-Zabidi's *Rafᶜ niqāb.* Afet Dadashova transcribed some pages for me from Cyrillic into the Latin alphabet. Derrick Wright went over the entire manuscript, editing its language. I would like to extend my heartfelt gratitude to all of them. I am also indebted to the following teachers, colleagues and friends who in different ways and to varying extents helped me along the way: András Riedlmayer, Wolfhart Heinrichs, Bedriye Poyraz, Mark Soileau, Helga Anetshofer, Hakan Karateke, Özer Ergenç, Zeynep Ertuğ, İlhan Başgöz, Edouard Méténier, Irene Markoff, Hülya Taş, Rüya Kılıç, Hülya Canbakal, Amelia Gallagher, Ali Akın, Abdullah Bilgili, Can Delice, Erdem Çıpa, Ethel Sara Wolper, Abir Yousef, Hüseyin Abiba,

Ayhan Aydın, Nabil al-Tikriti and Levent Mete. I apologise to anyone whom I may have inadvertently omitted.

At different stages of this project, I received financial assistance from a number of institutions and foundations, including the American Research Institute in Turkey, the Kirkland Fellowship and the Whiting Dissertation Fellowship from Harvard University, the National Endowment for Humanities and Koç University's Research Center for Anatolian Civilizations. I would also like to acknowledge the financial support of my department and the School of Arts & Sciences of the College of William & Mary in Virginia. Staff of the Vakıflar Genel Müdürlüğü Arşivi in Ankara (The Archive of the General Directorate of Foundations), among them especially Burhan Toy, and of the Başbakanlık Osmanlı Arşivleri (The Ottoman Archives of the Prime Minister's Office) in Istanbul greatly facilitated my research in those archives. I also made extensive use of the collections and interlibrary loan services of Widener Library at Harvard University, İSAM (Center for Islamic Studies) and Boğaziçi University libraries in Istanbul, and the library of the College of William & Mary. I thank all these institutions and their staff for their support, as well as the fellows at William & Mary Center for Geospatial Analysis who prepared the maps. Finally, I would like to thank the series editor Kent Schull and the editorial staff at Edinburgh University Press, including Nicola Ramsey and Eddie Clark, for their expertise, professionalism and cooperation.

No words of appreciation would suffice to express my gratitude to my family. My parents, Melek (Dolar) Karakaya and Delil Karakaya, have always been the greatest source of emotional support and motivation for me in my educational pursuits. They were the ones who inadvertently sparked the initial fire for this project and supplied me with first-hand information on several issues. Their presence and prayers made the writing of this book so much more meaningful than it would have been otherwise. Thanks also to my brothers Abbas Karakaya and Mehmet Ali Karakaya, to my late sister Aysel Karakaya and to my sister-in-law Sibel Tatar for their constant encouragement whenever I needed reassurance and for their help in practical matters. My daughters, Ezgi and Bahar, literally grew up with this book as if it were a third sibling in need of constant undue attention. With their cheerful presence, they made this painful and seemingly unending process of reading, writing and editing much more bearable, and infused my life with a sense of balance. This book, for whatever it is worth, owes the most to my husband Laine Stump, who unswervingly stood by me during this very long journey. I have relied on him in more ways than I can even count.

Notes on Transliteration and Terminology

Transliteration

Given the polyglot nature of the sources, a certain level of inconsistency proved inevitable in the transliteration of non-English words. I have generally deferred to their linguistic and historical context in transliterating proper names, less known technical terms and direct quotations, while choosing a simplified form for more commonly used proper names and words. More specifically:

- In direct quotations of Turkish written in Arabic letters, I have employed a slightly modified version of the transliteration system used in the *İslam Ansiklopedisi*. For Arabic and Persian, I have used the system recommended by the *International Journal of Middle East Studies* with minor variations.
- Less known technical terms used within the text are rendered in Arabic or Turkish transliteration depending on context, although in ambiguous cases both are provided at initial appearance. Words that are found in an unabridged English dictionary are, however, not transliterated (including 'Qur^{c}an', 'Sunni', 'Shi^{c}i', 'Sufi', 'shaykh', 'dervish', 'sultan', 'shah', 'imam', 'ulema', 'fatwa', 'mufti', 'kadi' and 'shari^{c}a').
- Unless they are directly quoted from a written source, regardless of their origin, I have used modern Turkish orthography for specialised Alevi terminology and the proper names of Alevi saintly lineages, considering their primarily oral mode of transmission (for example, '*semah*', rather than '*semā*^{c}', and 'the *ocak* of İmam Zeynel Abidin', rather than 'the *ocaḳ* of Imām Zayn al-^{c}Ābidīn'; but note the exceptions of '*mürşid*', '*talib*', and '*seyyid*', and 'musahib' instead of '*mürşit*', '*talip*', '*seyit*' and '*musahip*').

Pronunciation of modern Turkish letters:

- c j, as in *jet*
- ç ch, as in *chart*
- ş sh, as in *short*
- ı io, as in *fashion*
- ö u, as in *burn*
- ü u, as in *puree*
- ğ unvocalised, lengthens preceding vowel

- For proper names and names of months, unless part of a quotation, book title or longer transliterated phrase, no diacritics are used. ᶜAyn and hamza are retained in both Ottoman and Arabic names except when hamza is the initial letter. The Arabic article is dropped when a surname stands on its own. The transliteration of Arabic compound names is simplified when used within a Turcophone context: for example, Gıyaseddin instead of Gıyas al-Din.
- Names of dynasties and well-known place names are written in their common, Anglicised form. Names of Sufi orders are given according to the Arabic system and without diacriticals (for example, 'Wafaᵓi' rather than 'Vefaᵓi' and 'Naqshbandi' rather than 'Nakşbendi') with the following exceptions, whose influence was largely confined to Turcophone environments: 'Yesevi', rather than 'Yasawi', 'Mevlevi' rather than 'Mawlawi', 'Halveti' rather than 'Khalwati', and 'Zeyni' rather than 'Zayni'. Frequently occuring group names are likewise given without diacriticals and in a simplified form, including 'Alevi' rather than 'ᶜAlevī', 'Bektashi' rather than 'Bektāşī', 'Kizilbash' rather than 'Ḳızılbaş', 'Turkmen' rather than 'Türkmen', 'Abdal' rather than 'Abdāl', and 'Ahi' rather than 'Aḫī' or 'Akhi'. Names of lesser known places in Turkey are rendered according to modern Turkish spelling. Other place names are transliterated upon their initial appearance.
- When referring to a specific document, I first provide the Hijri date and then the Common Era date, the two separated by a slash. For the sake of simplicity, I have chosen to provide only the first Common Era year in which the Hijri year falls, for example, 1299/1881 rather than 1299/1881–1882. When not referring to a specific document, only the Common Era dates are used. I follow the same format with publication dates supplied according to Hijri calender.

Terminology

- I have consistently translated as '(dervish) convent' the following terms, notwithstanding the nuances among them in terms of size, function and so forth: Ot. '*tekye*' or '*tekke*', Ot. '*zāviye*' and Ar. '*zāwiya*', Ot. '*dergāh*' and P. '*dargāh*', P. and Ar. '*khānqāh*', and P. and Ot. '*ās(i)tāne*'.

- On the basis of organisational structures, there are currently three distinct groups that are often conflated under the category of 'the Alevi-Bektashi community'. These are groups attached to: 1) the Bektashiyye's Babagan or Babacı branch, who believe that Hacı Bektaş had no biological offspring and that they themselves are his spiritual descendants; 2) the Çelebi Bektashis, who claim to be the biological descendants of Hacı Bektaş; and 3) the *ocakzade dede*s, whose authority is based on a charismatic lineage traced back to the Twelve Imams. Of these, it is the last group that is the main focus of this book. In this study the terms 'Kizilbash' and 'Alevi' will be used sometimes together and sometimes interchangeably (depending on the historical period and context), to refer to those communities in Anatolia that have been linked to various *dede ocak*s.

Abbreviations

ABS	*Ansiklopedik Alevilik-Bektaşilik Terimleri Sözlüğü*, edited by Esat Korkmaz. Istanbul: Kaynak Yayınları, 2003.
Ar.	Arabic
Aspz	ᶜAşıkpaşazade Ahmed. *Tevārih-i Āl-i Osmān.* Transliteration with facsimile in *Âşıkpaşazâde Tarihi,* edited by Necdet Öztürk. Istanbul: Bilge Kültür Sanat, 2013.
BA	Başbakanlık Osmanlı Arşivi [The Ottoman Archives of the Prime Minister's Office]
Cambridge-Iran-4	*The Cambridge History of Iran.* Vol. 4: *The Period from the Arab Invasion to the Saljuqs,* edited by R. N. Frye. Cambridge: Cambridge University Press, 1975.
Cambridge-Iran-5	*The Cambridge History of Iran.* Vol. 5: *The Saljuq and Mongol Periods*, edited by J. A. Boyle. Cambridge: Cambridge University Press, 1968.
Cambridge-Iran-6	*The Cambridge History of Iran.* Vol. 6: *The Timurid and Safavid Periods*, edited by Peter Jackson and Laurence Lockhart. Cambridge: Cambridge University Press, 1986.
DedeKarkın-Kum	Kum, Naci. *Dedekarkın, Karkınoğulları, Çepniler: Belgeler ve Menkıbeler Üzerine Yapılan Tetkikler*, typescript, 1951, also published as an appendix to *Dede Kargın: Şiirler*, edited by Rahime Kışlalı and Ali Yeşilyurt, 126–201. Mersin: Can Matbaacılık, 1999.

	References will be made to the published version.
DIA	*Türkiye Diyanet Vakfı İslâm Ansiklopedisi.* Istanbul: Türkiye Diyanet Vakfı, 1988– .
EI-2	*The Encyclopaedia of Islam*, 2nd edn. Leiden: Brill, 1960– .
Evliya-Seyahatnâme	Evliyâ Çelebi b. Derviş Muhammed Zıllî. *Evliyâ Çelebi Seyahatnâmesi: Topkapı Sarayı Bağdat 305 Yazmasının Transkripsiyonu-Dizini,* 10 vols, edited by Yücel Dağlı et al. Istanbul: Yapı Kredi Yayınları, 1996–.
FD	Family document(s)
FD/Ferman-DK-1	Copy of an Ottoman *ferman*, 7 Zi'l-hicce 930/1524, embedded in Scroll-DK-1
FD/Ferman-DK-2	Ottoman *ferman*, dated Receb 1131/1719; FD of Ahmet Rıza Kargın. Published under 'Vesika 9' in *Dedekarkın-Kum*, 143, and under 'Vesika 4' in Kargın-Yalçın, 78–80; republished with facsimile in *Garkın-Ocak*, 269–271.
FD/Ferman-DK-3	Ottoman *ferman*, dated 5 Cemaziye'l-ahır 1230/1815; FD of Ahmet Rıza Kargın. Published under 'Vesika 12' in *Dedekarkın-Kum*, 145, and under 'Vesika 3' in Kargın-Yalçın, 80–81.
FD/Ij-AGU-Am	Wafaʾi *ijāza*, dated Muharram 993/1586; FD of Mustafa Aygün.
FD/Ij-AGU-Ma	Wafaʾi *ijāza*, dated Dhu'l-hijja 990/1582; FD of İzzettin Doğan.
FD/AhiIj-DK-Antep	Ahi *ijāza*, dated 14 Şaʿban 775/1374; FD of Hüseyin Cahit Kargıner. Partial Turkish translation published in *Dedekarkın-Kum*, 153–155. A second identical copy in the same collection is undated, but appears to be of more recent making.
FD/Ij-DelBer	Wafaʾi *ijāza*, undated copy of an original from the year 840/1436, and a second identical copy made in Jumada al-awwal 1061/1651; both FD of İsmail Doğan.
FD/Ij-Garkini-DK-1	Garkını *ijāza*, dated 510/1116(?); FD of Ahmet Rıza Kargın. Nearly identical copies embedded in Scroll-DK-3a and Scroll-DK-3a.

FD/Ij-Garkini DK-2	Garkını *ijāza*, date?; FD of Ahmet Rıza Kargın. Similar in content to Ij-Garkini-DK-1, embedded in Scroll-DK-Archive.
FD/Ij-IZA-1	Wafaᵓi *ijāza*, dated Dhu'l-hijja 855/1451; FD of Muharrem Naci Orhan.
FD/Ij-KaraPirBad	Wafaᵓi *ijāza*, dated Safar 916/1520, *ocak* of Kara Pir Bad centred in Divriği-Karageban. Published in Nejat Birdoğan, *Anadolu ve Balkanlar'da Alevi Yerleşmesi* (Istanbul: Mozaik Yayınları, 1995), 223–235.
FD/Ij-Kureyşan	Wafaᵓi *ijāza*, undated, *ocak* of Kureyşan centred in Tunceli; FD of Zülfikar Kureyş Dedeoğlu. Published in Alemdar Yalçın and Hacı Yılmaz, 'Kureyşan Ocağı Hakkında Bazı Bilgiler', *Hacı Bektaş Velî Araştırma Dergisi* 23 (Autumn 2002): 9–24d.
FD/Ij-ShAhm	Wafaᵓi *shajara/ijāza*, dated Muharram 829/1425; FD of Mustafa Tosun. A facsimile of the document is published in Muhammet Beşir Aşan, 'Fırat Havzasında Tespit Edilen Vefâi Silsile-Nâmesi ve Bazı Düşünceler', in *XIV. Türk Tarih Kongresi (9–13 Eylül 2002)* (Ankara: Türk Tarih Kurumu, 2005), 2: 1,517–1,524.
FD/Ij-Wafaᵓi-DK-1	Wafaᵓi *ijāza*, 10 Muharram 905/1499, embedded in FD/Scroll-DK-1.
FD/Ij-Wafaᵓi-DK-2	Second copy of Ij-1-DK, dated Jumada al-awwal 952/1545, embedded in FD/Scroll-DK-2.
FD/Kerbela-Zyrtn-DK	*Ziyaretname* granted at the shrine of Imam Husayn in Karbala, dated Muharram 997/1588; FD of Ahmet Rıza Kargın. Transliteration published under 'Vesika 25' in Kargın-Yalçın, 56–59; republished with a facsimile of the document in *Garkın-Ocak*, 255–266.
FD/Scroll-DK-1	Scroll with mutliple documents; FD of Ahmet Rıza Kargın. An undifferentiated copy of its content is published under 'Vesika 23' in Kargın-Yalçın, 41–47; republished with a facsimile of the document in *Garkın-Ocak*, 195–211.
FD/Scroll-DK-2	Scroll with mutliple documents; FD of Ahmet Rıza Kargın. Partial translation under 'Vesika

	1' in *Dedekarkın-Kum*, 132–34; a more complete version was published under 'Vesika 21' in Kargın-Yalçın, 35–42; republished with a facsimile of the document in *Garkın-Ocak*, 212–224.
FD/Scroll-DK-3a	Scroll with mutliple documents, dated Ramadan 963/1556; FD of Ahmet Rıza Kargın. Partial translation published under 'Vesika 26' in Kargın-Yalçın, 53–56, and under 'Vesika 2' in *Dedekarkın-Kum*, 134–138; republished with a facsimile of the document in *Garkın-Ocak*, 225–241.
FD/Scroll-DK-3b	Scroll with mutliple documents, dated Rajab 971/1564; FD of Ahmet Rıza Kargın. Content nearly identical to Scroll-DK-3. Translated under 'Vesika 22' in Kargın-Yalçın, 47–53; republished with a facsimile of the document in *Garkın-Ocak*, 242–254.
FD/Scroll-DK-Archive	Scroll with mutliple documents, BA, Ali Emîrî, folder no. 1. Facsimile and translation with significant omissions into Turkish published in *Garkın-Ocak*, 154–194.
FD/Scroll-IZA-2	Scroll with multiple documents, dated Rabiʿ al-awwal 984/1576; FD of Muharrem Naci Orhan. A loose and unreliable Turkish translation with some signficant omissions was published in Kureyşanlı Seyyid Kekil, *Peygamberler ile Seyyidlerin Şecereleri ve Aşiretlerin Tarihi* (Köln: Hans und Sigrid Verlag, n.d.), 175–208.
FD/Sj-DK-1	Fragment of a *sayyid* genealogy in prose, undated, embedded in Scroll-DK-3b; FD of Ahmet Rıza Kargın. A second, nearly identical copy embedded in Scroll-DK-3b; a third, even shorter copy embedded in Scroll-DK-1.
FD/Sj-DK-2	*Sayyid* genealogy in prose, copied in Muharram 837/1433 (?); FD of Ahmet Rıza Kargın. Similar in content to FD/Sj-DK-1 but much longer.
Garkın-Ocak	Ocak, Ahmet Yaşar. *Ortaçağ Anadolu'sunda İki Büyük Yerleşimci (Kolonizatör) Derviş Yahut Vefâiyye ve Yeseviyye Gerçeği: Dede Garkın & Emîrci Sultan (13. Yüzyıl)*. Ankara:

	Gazi Üniversitesi Türk Kültürü ve Hacı Bektaş Veli Araştırma Merkezi Yayınları, 2011.
Heritage of Sufism-1	*The Heritage of Sufism.* Vol. 1: *Classical Persian Sufism from Its Origins to Rumi (700–1300)*, edited by Leonard Lewisohn. Oxford: Oneworld Publications, 1999.
Heritage of Sufism-3	*The Heritage of Sufism.* Vol. 3: *Late Classical Persianate Sufism (1501–1750): The Safavid & Mughal Period*, edited by Leonard Lewisohn and David Morgan, 389–414. Oxford: Oneworld, 1999.
IAA	*İslâm Alimleri Ansiklopedisi.* Istanbul: Türkiye Gazetesi Yayınları, 1990–1993.
Karakaya-YK	Karakaya-Stump, Ayfer. 'Yeni Kaynaklar Işığında Kızılbaş Hareketinin Oluşumu ve Anadolu'daki Kızılbaş/Alevi Topluluklarının Safevilerl İlişkileri (İki Safevi Hilafetnamesi: Çeviriyazılı Metin, Günümüz Türkçesine Çeviri, Tıpkıbasım)'. In *Vefailik, Bektaşilik, Kızılbaşlık: Alevi Kaynaklarını, Tarihini ve Tarihyazımını Yeniden Düşünmek,* 79–112. Istanbul: Bilgi University Press, 2015.
Kargın-Yalçın	Yalçın, Alemdar and Hacı Yılmaz. 'Kargın Ocaklı Boyu ile İlgili Yeni Belgeler', *Türk Kültürü ve Hacı Bektaş Velî Araştırma Dergisi*, no. 21 (Spring 2002): 13–87.
MD	Mühimme Defteri
Menāḳıb-Arabic	al-Shabrisi al-Wasiti, Shihab al-Din Abu'l-Huda Ahmad b. ʿAbd al-Munʿim. *Tadhkirat al-muqtafīn āthār uli al-ṣafāʾwa tabṣirat al-muqtadīn bi-ṭarīq Tāj al-ʿĀrifīn Abi'l-Wafāʾ*, MS copied in 878/1473, Bibliothèque Nationale in Paris, no. 2,036.
Menāḳıb-Turkish	*Menāḳıb-ı Seyyid Ebū'l-Vefāʾ*, MS, undated, Süleymaniye Library, Murad Buhari 257. Translation into Ottoman from the Arabic original with an added introduction. Facsimile and transliteration published in Dursun Gümüşoğlu. *Tâcü'l-arifîn Es-Seyyid Ebu'l Vefâ Menakıbnāmesi: Yaşamı ve Tasavvufi Görüşleri*. Istanbul: Can Yayınları, 2006.

MIA	*İslâm Ansiklopedisi. İslâm Alemi Tarih, Coğrafya, Etnografya ve Bibliyografya Lugatı.* Istanbul: Milli Eğitim Basımevi, 1965.
MMAK	Mevlânâ Müzesi Abdülbâkî Gölpınarlı Kütüphanesi [Mevlana Museum Abdülbaki Library]
MNK-Eflaki	al-Aflākī al-ᶜĀrifī, Şams al-dīn Aḥmed (d. 1360). *Manāḳib al-ᶜArifīn*, edited by Tahsin Yazıcı, rev. 2nd edn, 2 vols. Ankara: Türk Tarih Kurumu, 1976–1980.
MNK-Elvan Çelebi-1995	Elvân Çelebi. *Menâkıbu'l-Kudsiyye Fî Menâsıbi'i-Ünsiyye (Baba İlyas-ı Horasânî ve Sülâlesinin Menkabevî Tarihi).* Edited by İsmail E. Erünsal and Ahmet Yaşar Ocak. Ankara: Türk Tarih Kurumu, 1995.
MNK-Elvan Çelebi-2000	Elvân Çelebi. *Menāḳıbu'l-ḳudsiyye fī menāṣıbi'l-ünsiyye.* Edited by Mertol Tulum in *Tarihî Metin Çalışmalarında Usul: Menâkıbu'l-Kudsiyye Üzerinde Bir Deneme.* Istanbul: Deniz Kitabevi, 2000.
Niebuhr-Reise	Niebuhr, Carsten. *Reisebeschreibung nach Arabien und andern umliegenden Ländern.* 3 Vols. 1778; reprint, Frankfurt: Institut für Geschichte der Arabisch-Islamischen Wissenschaften, 1994.
Noyan-Bektâşîlik	Noyan, Bedri. *Bütün Yönleriyle Bektâşîlik ve Alevîlik.* 9 vols. Ankara: Ardıç Yayınları, 1998–2011.
Ot.	Ottoman Turkish
P.	Persian
T.	Modern Turkish
TMA	Topkapı Sarayı Müzesi Arşivi [Topkapı Palace Museum Archive]
TS	Gölpınarlı, Abdülbâkî. *Tasavvuf'tan Dilimize Geçen Deyimler ve Atasözleri*. Istanbul: İnkılap ve Aka, 1977.
Velâyetnâme-Duran	*Velâyetnâme: Hacı Bektâş-ı Veli.* Edited by Hamiye Duran. Ankara: Türkiye Diyanet Vakfı, 2007.
VGMA	Vakıflar Genel Müdürlüğü Arşivi [The Archive of the General Directorate of Foundations]

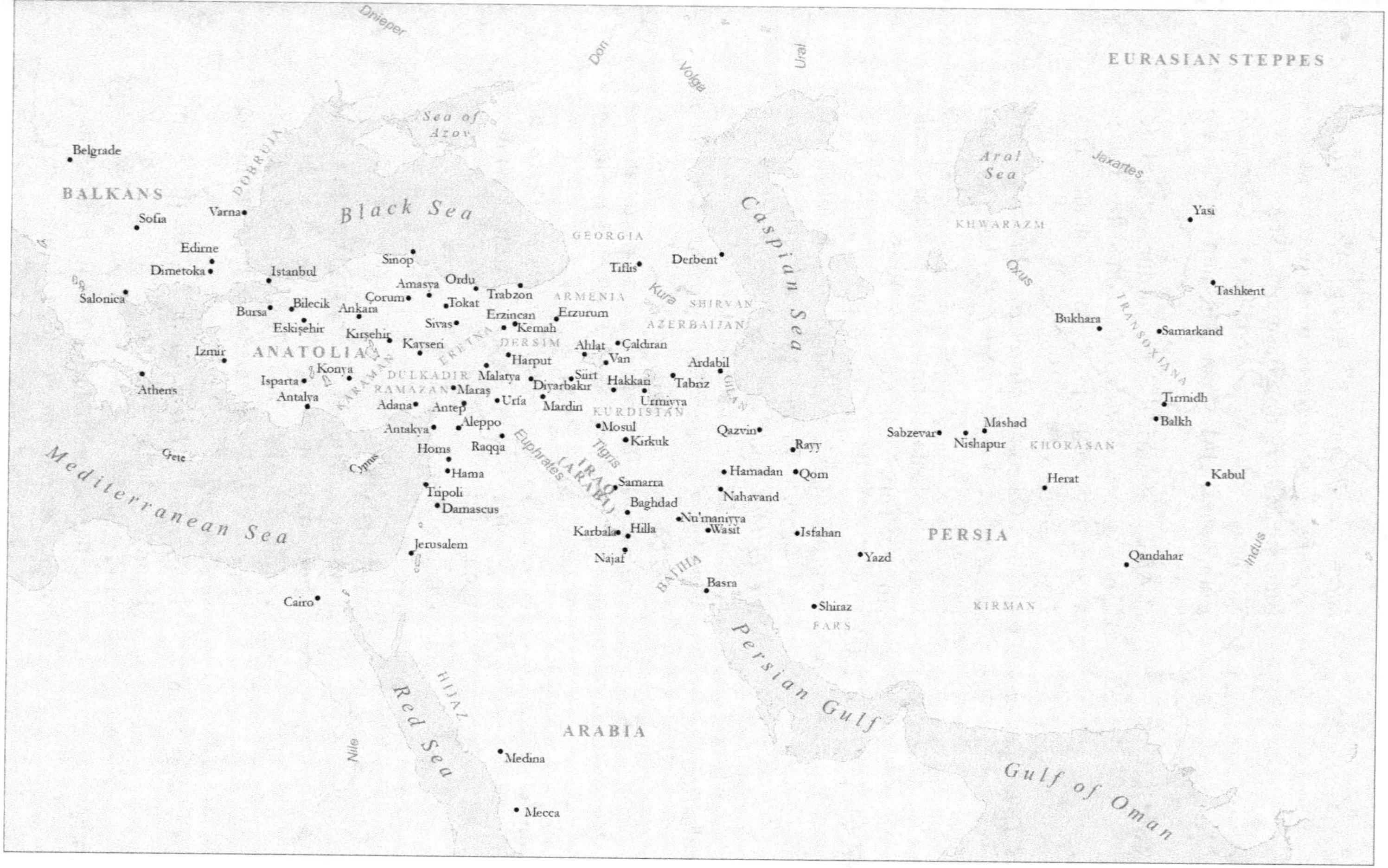

Map 1 West Asia in the late medieval and early modern periods: settlements and geography

Source: William & Mary's Center for Geospatial Analysis.

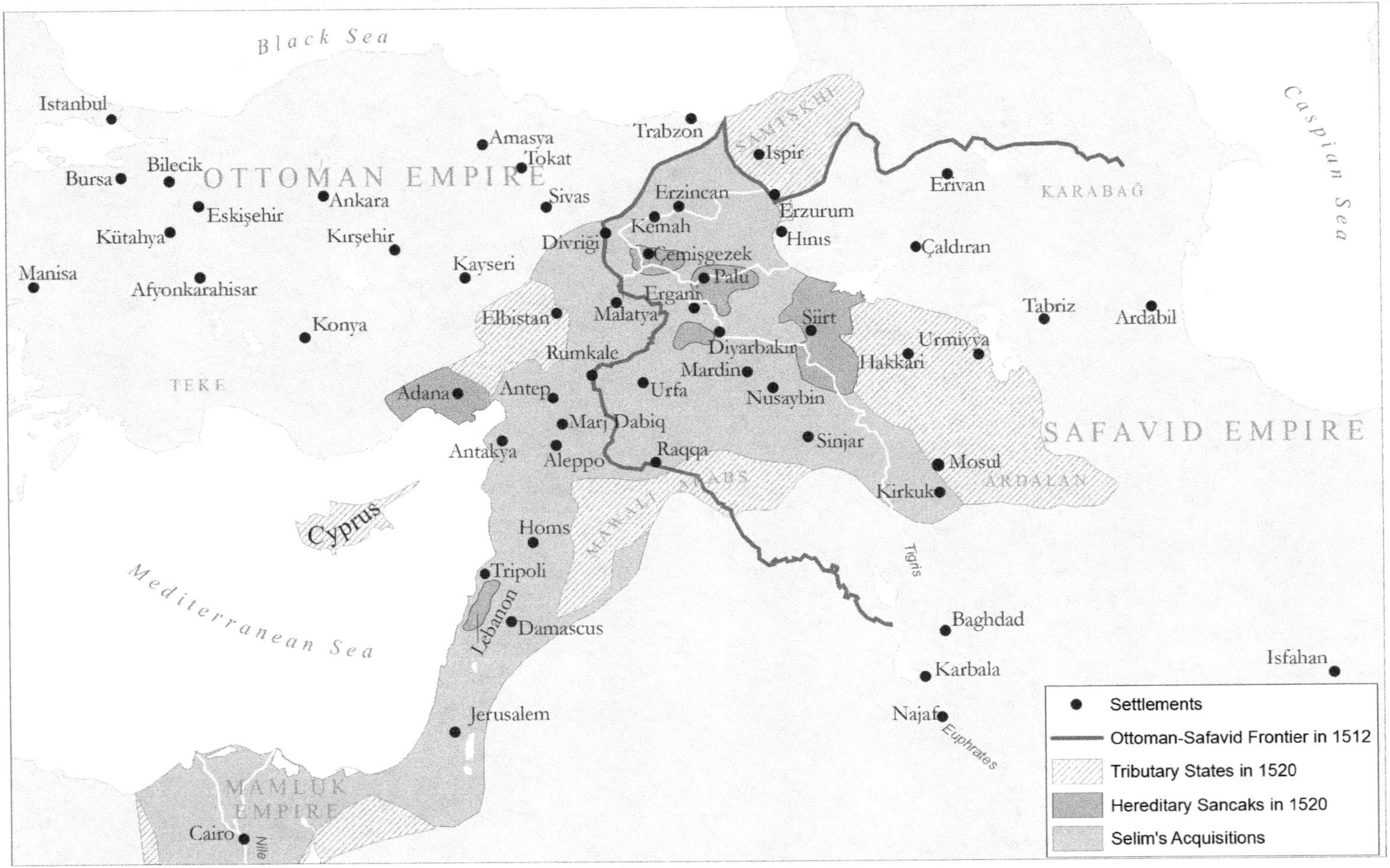

Map 2 The Ottoman–Safavid conflict *c.*1500

Map adapted from 'Map XX' in Donald Edgar Pitcher, *An Historical Geography of the Ottoman Empire from Earliest Times to the End of the Sixteenth Century*

Introduction

I am aware that there is an inherent tension in suggesting that we should acknowledge our position while taking distance from it, but I find that tension both healthy and pleasant. I guess that, after all, I am perhaps claiming that legacy of intimacy and estrangement.

– Michel-Rolph Trouillot, *Silencing the Past: Power and the Production of History*

On 5 October 2002, a grand performance called *Binyılın Türküsü – The Saga of the Millennium* as its organisers translated it – took place in one of the largest indoor stadiums in Istanbul. It was organised by the European Federation of Alevi Associations, bringing together 1,500 *bağlama* players ranging in age from seven to seventy, several hundred *semah* performers and dozens of soloists, most from different parts of Turkey and Europe, but also several from Australia and North America. Every effort was made to publicise the event, parts of which were also broadcast live on a few national television channels in Turkey.

The performance was set up as a stylised Alevi religious ceremony known as a '*cem*', in which the ritual dance of *semah* is performed by groups of men and women, and mystical poems (*deyiş* or *nefes*) are recited, accompanied by the music of the *bağlama*, the sacred lute.[1] However, the performance's sheer size and splendour, its cosmopolitan venue and its inclusion of diverse traditions of music and dance from around the world, as well as its organisers' concerted effort to reach as wide an audience as possible, set *The Saga of the Millennium* in stark contrast to traditional Alevi *cems*, which took place in a village setting with close-knit congregations that were strictly closed to the non-initiated. Alevis would hold their *cems* at night in utmost secrecy to avoid the state authorities and their Sunni Muslim neighbours who viewed them with suspicion because of their non-conformity to shari^ca-centred normative Islam. While most

Alevis live in urban centres and lead secular lives today, with their Alevi heritage more a cultural than a religious affiliation, their community identity is still deeply rooted in a shared sense of being a group persecuted for its beliefs. These collective memories of oppression and resistance were enacted throughout *The Saga of the Millennium*, turning the performance into a celebration of the Alevis' cultural resilience.[2]

The forefathers of the modern-day Alevis were the Kizilbash (T. Kızılbaş), whose story is at the centre of this book.[3] To the extent that the Kizilbash are familiar to historians outside the field of Turkish-Ottoman studies, they are known as the devoted Anatolian followers of Shah Isma^cil (1487–1524) – the hereditary shaykh of the Safavi Sufi order and the founder of the Safavid dynasty – who played a key role in the establishment of the Safavid state in 1501 but whose non-normative teachings and rituals would be quickly abandoned in favour of legalist Imami Shi^cism, which the new state adopted as its official creed.[4] The Kizilbash uprisings against the Ottoman state in the sixteenth century and the many waves of Kizilbash persecution,[5] are also more or less common knowledge for those acquainted with the basics of the Sunni Ottoman and Shi^ci Safavid rivalry that defined the early modern Middle East.[6] What is less recognised is that while Kizilbashism in Safavid Persia assimilated into mainstream Imami Shi^cism over the course of a few generations, it survived in Ottoman Anatolia as a distinct identity and confession despite a hostile political and religious environment.[7] The Kizilbash, today commonly known as Alevis, constitute the second largest faith community in modern Turkey, making up about 15 per cent of the country's population, with smaller pockets or related groups in neighbouring countries, especially in the Balkans.[8]

Existing scholarship in the main views Kizilbashism through two distinct but overlapping frameworks. The first of these, more prevalent within the field of Turkish-Ottoman studies, treats Kizilbashism as an undifferentiated strain within the hazy category of Turkish folk Islam. It points to Turkmen tribal groups, with their largely oral practices and strong Central Asian heritage in the form of shamanism, to account for non-mainstream Kizilbash practices and beliefs.[9] In the fields of Islamic and Iranian studies, on the other hand, the tendency is to bracket Kizilbashism with other popular religio-political movements that proliferated in the late medieval Irano-Turkic world. These movements are perceived as reincarnations of the so-called extreme Shi^ci groups (*Ghulāt*) associated with the initial party of ^cAli who purportedly divinised him.[10] Despite some differences, there is much that is common in the two approaches. Most importantly, both of them relegate Kizilbashism to the world of a timeless syncretism that blended Islam with various foreign elements rooted in some obscure, distant past. As such, neither of them pays sufficient attention to the immediate historical context that spawned the Kizilbash milieu, nor do they have much to say about the period after the early sixteenth century, when the Kizilbash transformed from a proselytising, revolutionary movement into a quietist religious order of closed communities.[11] The present work, in addition to offering an alternative framework for the study of Kizilbash origins, also charts this process of transformation, drawing on a recently surfaced corpus of documents and manuscripts generated within the Kizilbash/Alevi milieu. Combining these internal sources with their conventional literary and archival counterparts, this book recounts how during this period Kizilbash communities developed an elaborate socio-religious organisation centred on a number of charismatic family lineages known as *ocak*s (lit. hearths). Through the case study of the Alevi *ocak* network in eastern Anatolia, the following chapters trace the historical roots of the *ocak*-centred socio-religious organisation of the Kizilbash/Alevi communities to the cosmopolitan Sufi milieu of late medieval Anatolia and neighbouring regions, and account for its evolution roughly up to the nineteenth century when the *ocak*s were increasingly incorporated into the institutional framework of the kindred Bektashi order.

Just a few decades earlier, neither a public performance such as *The Saga of the Millennium* nor a book attempting to explore Alevi history from an internal perspective based on sources from the private archives of *ocak* families would have been conceivable. What made both possible was the Alevi cultural revival of the late 1980s and the early 1990s, which brought an unprecedented visibility to the once isolated and guarded Alevis. Having come into being under the long-term pressures of rural–urban migration during the 1950s and 1960s that progressively shifted the centre of gravity of Alevi culture away from the village,[12] the Alevi cultural revival commenced with a flurry of popular publications on Alevism mostly by first-generation urbanite Alevis.[13] These not only generated an easily accessible pool of valuable information concerning the religious and social aspects of Alevism, but also helped normalise the 'Alevi issue' as a topic of debate and scholarly research. With the relative normalisation of public discourse on the hitherto taboo subject of Alevism, a process facilitated and carried further by the concomitant proliferation of Alevi cultural associations in Turkey's cities and among the Alevi diaspora in Europe, a growing number of Alevis have come to assert their difference openly, something they were previously reluctant to do for fear of stigmatisation and retaliation. The same impetus for greater visibility also facilitated the willingness of members of *ocak* lineages – the *dedes* or *pirs* (lit. elders) – to make available for research purposes their family archives upon which this book primarily relies.

Although generally subsumed under Shiᶜi Islam based on the criterion of the veneration of ᶜAli, the first Shiᶜi imam, and his eleven successors, Alevi beliefs and ritual practices defy Shiᶜi normativity. Alevis typically do not perform formal Islamic obligations such as daily prayers and fasting during the month of Ramadan.[14] Full integration of women into Alevi ritual life, which takes place in separate sacred spaces rather than a mosque, and the permitted use of alcohol are likewise ritual and social practices that contravene Islamic 'orthopraxy'.[15] Clearly formulated dogmas are in general less essential for the constitution of Alevism than ritual practices and socio-ethical norms. Despite this theological fuzziness, Alevi mystical poetry and the rich stock of Alevi religious maxims contain many clues that help to gain an understanding of basic Alevi teachings. At the most fundamental level, these reveal a conception of the Divine that is immanent and all-encompassing, permeating all creation. This monistic ontology complements and informs other more specific Alevi beliefs, such as the idea of the Perfect Man (*insan-ı kamil*) and ᶜAli in particular as the locus of Divinity (*Hakk ademdedir*), the immortality of souls (*ölen tendir, canlar ölmez*) and the possibility of their transmigration from one body to another (*don değiştirmek*), and the kindred notion of cyclical existence (*devir*),[16] all of which run contrary to Islam's normative precepts. Similarly, the Alevi understanding of hell and heaven as metaphors for the relative spiritual condition of the soul renders all but extraneous such core Islamic theological notions as the day of resurrection and the afterlife.[17]

Despite such characteristic Alevi beliefs and practices that are hard to reconcile with canonical Islam, traditional Alevi discourse is clearly located within Islamic systems of reference and betrays an intimate connection to Sufism, a key consideration of this book. To begin with, their very term of self-designation, 'Alevi', is derived from its Arabic cognate *ᶜAlawī*, which in its base meaning refers to the descendants and followers of Imam ᶜAli, the cousin and son-in-law of the Prophet Muhammad.[18] Alevi tradition, however, in a manner reminiscent of the Sufi notion of *nūr Muḥammadī* (the Muhammadan light), unites ᶜAli and Muhammad into one, as two inseparable halves of a cosmic entity emanating from the primordial divine light. It is this idea, it would seem, that underscores the famous Alevi triad of 'Allah (or Hakk), Muhammad, Ali'.[19] Likewise, Alevi communal ceremonies, *cems*, are performed as re-enactments of the prototypical gathering of forty saints (*Kırklar Meclisi*) that Alevis believe took place during the Prophet Muhammad's nocturnal ascent into heaven (T. *Miraç*; Ar. *Miᶜrāj*) (Figure I.1).[20] The central point of the ritual space (*meydan*) where the *cem* ceremony takes place is, moreover, named after the famous tenth-century Sufi martyr, Husayn b. Mansur al-Hallaj (858–922), whom Alevis hold in particularly high-esteem. Known as *dar-ı Mansur* (lit. the gallows of Mansur), a disciple stands on this spot during initiation, facing the *dede* officiating the ritual, with one or both hands crossed on the chest, right toe placed on the left toe and head bowed down, a position that simultaneously alludes to Mansur's execution and signifies the disciple's willingness to make sacrifices on the path to God/the Truth (*Hakk yolu*) (Figures I.2a and I.2b).[21] These and many other features of the Alevi tradition are paralleled in one form or another in Islamic mysticism, even though the particular permutations, ways of articulation and ritualistic enactments of these beliefs amount to a distinctive Alevi religious system.

Alevis, separated in this manner from both Shiᶜi and Sunni Muslims, provide an important example of groups in the Islamic world whom, for lack of a better term, I call 'dissentient religious communities'. These are, broadly speaking, united in their rejection of the legalistic orientation and textual literalism of normative Islam in favour of an esoteric and ethical

Figure I.1 An Alevi document (*ziyāretnāme*) dated 1237/1821 with an illustration of Burak (A. Burāq), the mythical horse that is believed to have transported the Prophet Muhammad to Heaven during his *Miᶜrāj*

Source: Original in the private archive of Hüseyin Temiz Dede, member of the *ocak* of İmam Zeynel Abidin from the village of Karaca, Yazıhan-Malatya. Photograph by the author from a copy in the archive of Cem Vakfı in Yenibosna, Istanbul, 2002.

Figure I.2a Kaygusuz Abdal standing in *dar-ı Mansur*, miniature painting by Levni (d. 1732)

Source: Original in Hacı Bektaş Museum in Nevşehir. Photograph by Taylan Sümer, 2018.

understanding of religion. Other such groups that apparently arose in an Islamic context but have since become more or less autonomous religious bodies with an ambiguous or completely breached relationship to the rest of the Muslim community include, for instance, the Ahl-i Haqq in Iran, the Nusayri Alawites in Syria, the Yazidis in Iraq and Turkey and the Druze in Lebanon and Israel. Lack of sources, save those by hostile or superficially

Figure I.2b Young Alevis standing in *dar-ı Mansur*, Adıyaman
Source: Photograph by Laine Stump, 2002.

informed outsiders, has made the groups in question obscure targets of historical scholarship. There is typically an inadequate understanding of their belief systems and internal structures, and little more than poorly substantiated speculations concerning their origins. Historians often approach these non-conformist religious groups, relegated to the realm of 'heresy' by proponents of normative Islam, as marginal to the larger Islamic history, correlating their emergence to the 'survival' or 'infiltration' of extra-Islamic beliefs and practices. Their treatment as parochial phenomena on the basis of tenuous survival theories not only shrouds the broader Islamic context that generated these communities but also denies them a historical dimension.[22]

The present work moves away from such externalistic and decontextualised approaches as it explores Kizilbash/Alevi history against the backdrop of social and religious developments in Anatolia and the neighbouring regions during the late medieval and early modern era. The Kizilbash as a socio-religious collectivity emerged within the Safavid-led Kizilbash movement[23] over the course of the late fifteenth century and early sixteenth. In that sense, the genesis of a distinct Kizilbash/Alevi identity is the story of how an epithet that had been the name of a radical religio-political movement became the name of an inward-looking religious community with relatively well-defined boundaries. But as a system of religious ideas and liturgical practices, with particular organisational underpinnings, the Kizilbash milieu was far from being an entirely Safavid creation but had an autonomous and prior existence grounded in a cluster of separate but interconnected Sufi and dervish groups and *sayyid* families. These seem to have shared in common a mode of piety marked by a pronounced esoteric and ᶜAlid orientation, and a claim to spiritual authority based on personal and/or genealogical charisma that tacitly rejected the strictly textual authority of legalist Islam. From a longue durée perspective, then, the formation of a distinct Kizilbash/Alevi identity is the story of multifaceted encounters and cross-fertilisations among different Sufi and dervish traditions with certain common religious references and overlapping spheres of influence, and the union of related charismatic family lines and their disciple communities under the spiritual leadership of the Safavi family, or *ocak* (P. *dūdmān*).

Kizilbash Origins, Syncretism and the Köprülü Paradigm

There has been limited scholarly effort to study the history of Kizilbash/Alevi communities in an integrated fashion and with an attitude that takes seriously its socio-religious aspects. If one reason for this failure is the deficiencies of available sources, which at best present a caricature of Kizilbash/Alevi religious ideas and internal structures, a second, related reason is scholars' tendency to treat Kizilbashism/Alevism as a nebulous manifestation of syncretistic folk Islam, a tendency that allows for little of the generalisation necessary for a positive line of historical enquiry. The renowned early twentieth-century Turkish historian Fuad Köprülü set the framework for this approach in his seminal works on the development of Islam in Anatolia, which still form a point of departure for most pertinent scholarly and popular debates.[24] A brief overview of Köprülü's major assumptions and arguments, as well as recent challenges to them, is therefore necessary, both to place the present work within the larger historiography and to set the stage for a discussion of new information and perspectives emerging from recently surfaced Alevi written sources.

Fundamental to Köprülü's construct of Turkish religious and cultural history was a dichotomous framework based on a rigid and hierarchical separation between high Islam and folk Islam. High Islam, represented by established Sunni dogma, was defined by its book-based nature while folk Islam was defined by its orality.[25] The contrast between high and folk Islam was further sharpened in Köprülü's narrative by such overlapping and mutually reinforcing binaries as settled versus nomad, cosmopolitan versus local, pure versus syncretic and, finally, orthodox versus heterodox. The Alevis were integrated into this dualist framework as lay followers of the Bektashi Sufi order, with the two groups together conceived of as the primary locus of 'Turkish folk Islam'. In Köprülü's thinking, Turkish folk Islam was an organic and direct extension of a pre-Islamic Turkish cultural heritage that had been preserved under the cloak of the Yeseviyye, a Sufi order founded by the twelfth-century Turkish mystic Ahmed Yesevi (d. 1166?), and that was transmitted as such from Central Asia to Anatolia more or less intact. The foremost carriers of this supposedly authentic Turkish culture were the illiterate nomadic Turkmen tribes who persisted in their attachment to ancient shamanic beliefs and practices even as they nominally converted to Islam. Köprülü argued that their nomadic lifestyles and orally passed on culture rendered these tribes oblivious to the textual normativity of high Islam and its cosmopolitan culture, thus leaving them open to influences from 'deviant' popular Shiʿi and esoteric (*baṭinī*) currents, designated as 'extreme Shiʿism', or *ghulūw*, in Islamic heresiographies and modern scholarship alike.[26]

Notwithstanding the obvious significance with which Köprülü imbued them, the role played by the Turkmen tribes in this scenario was in fact a passive one. The real agents in the making of Turkish folk Islam were the Turkmen religious leaders, called *baba*s or *dede*s, who, according to Köprülü, combined in themselves both tribal and religious leadership, and were successors to the pre-Islamic shaman-bards (T. *kam-ozan*), but now in a Sufi garment.[27] The thirteenth-century mystic Hacı Bektaş, eponym of the Bektashi order, was one such religious figure and one to whom Köprülü attributed a key role in the transfer of the Yesevi tradition from its Central Asian homeland to Anatolia. In the thirteenth century, a group of these Turkmen *baba*s, most affiliates of the Yesevi order like Hacı Bektaş, instigated the massive Baba'i revolt of 1239–1241 against the Seljuks of Anatolia. For Köprülü, the Baba'i revolt was the seminal event in the development of Anatolian heterodoxies where all the social and religious elements of the heterodox Turkmen milieu came together to sow the seeds of successive heretical movements in the region. Thus, the spiritual legacy of the Baba'is would later be taken over by the itinerant dervish group known as the Abdals of Rum (Ot. Abdālān-ı Rūm), to be passed on eventually to the Bektashis. It was this syncretistic Turkish folk Islam with its timeless shamanic core, Köprülü seems to suggest, that would acquire a sectarian dimension under the influence of the Safavids from the second half of the fifteen century onwards when perennial tensions between the nomadic Turkmens and the centralising Ottoman state became particularly acute.[28]

This brief summary, admittedly, cannot do justice to Köprülü's wider scholarship that had a profound impact in launching the study of Turkish and Islamic history in the Anatolian context on its modern path. However, the two-tiered model of religion and the survival theories that formed the analytical backbone of his approach, while standard items in the conceptual toolkit of religious historians of his time, have come under considerable critical scrutiny since then. Parallel critical reassessments of Köprülü's conceptual framework have been put forward by some leading scholars of Sufism and popular piety in the Anatolian and Central Asian contexts. Most notable among them are Ahmet Karamustafa and Devin DeWeese who, approaching the subject from different geographical directions, have both cast doubt on Köprülü's dualistic model, challenging the idea of a simple dichotomy and an impermeable boundary between 'high' and 'popular' Sufism and calling into question the aggregation of distinct religious movements under the ill-defined and all-inclusive heading of 'folk religion'. The two scholars also have exposed the tenuous nature of approaches that are based on the notion of pre-Islamic survivals, which tend to abstract religious ideas and practices from their historical contexts and impose an undue continuity on them.[29] Cemal Kafadar, similarly, has problematised the categories of 'heterodoxy' and 'orthodoxy', disputing specifically their utility as analytical concepts within the context of late medieval Anatolia. In doing so, he drew attention to the confessional ambiguity that prevailed in the Babaʾi milieu in particular and the broader Sufi environment in contemporary Anatolia in general.[30]

Another aspect of Köprülü's scholarship that has attracted critical attention is its politics, which, at least as much as its conceptual framework, was a product of its times. Making this point, Markus Dressler recently emphasised and scrutinised how the formative concerns of Turkish nationalism shaped and limited Köprülü's thinking.[31] A most conspicuous manifestation of Köprülü's investment in the nascent Turkish nationalist project is his blatantly Turco-centric vision of popular Islam in Anatolia. His depiction of the Alevi-Bektashi communities as embodiments of an unadulterated pure Turkish culture, one that had disappeared almost entirely among the cosmopolitan Ottoman elite, correlates to his representation of Alevism-Bektashism as an exclusively Turkmen phenomenon (by entirely glossing over Kurdish and Zazaki speaking Alevis, for example). This key premise of the Köprülü paradigm, in part a response to American Protestant missionaries' earlier attribution of non-Turkish and Christian origins to the related communities,[32] was crucial in establishing the continuity and permanence of an essential core in Turkish culture even as the latter's geographical locus shifted from Central Asia to Anatolia.

The same concern underpins Köprülü's emphasis on a formative Central Asian connection in the genealogy of Alevism-Bektashism despite his inability to adduce sufficient evidence of a widespread Yesevi presence in medieval Anatolia, as Karamustafa observed earlier.[33]

Notwithstanding its seeming efficacy for the nationalist agenda, Köprülü's narrative also contains a major thread of ideological tension. This is a tension that pulls between his affirmative depiction of the Turkmen tribes as unintentional and passive carriers of a national heritage and his negative portrayal of the same groups, specifically within the context of the Baba'i and the Kizilbash uprisings. Exponents of these uprisings, Köprülü wrote, were ill-intentioned protagonists of 'esoteric currents' that deliberately aimed at 'subverting the fundamentals of Islam and establishing their own domination', an idea clearly echoing the Islamic heresiographical discourse concerning the so-called *Ghulāt* sects.[34] Köprülü often fell back on such essentialist notions as the nomadic Turkmens' innate propensity for heterodoxy and militancy as if to alleviate this tension, but the discord resulting from an uneasy combination in his approach of nationalist priorities and normative religious assumptions (good Turks but problematic Muslims) seems to have remained unresolved.[35]

Despite the difficulties generated by some of its empirical and conceptual assumptions, and certain blind spots arising from its political embeddedness, the Köprülü paradigm continues to be influential in shaping both scholarly and popular perceptions of Alevi-Bektashi communities. Leading contemporary students of Kizilbash/Alevi history Irène Mélikoff[36] and Ahmet Yaşar Ocak[37] have been particularly important in perpetuating and spreading Köprülü's views on the subject. These two well-known scholars have followed in Köprülü's footsteps in treating Kizilbashism-Alevism together with Bektashism as the principal manifestation of Turkish folk Islam. Most of their works on the subject from the second half of the twentieth century are devoted to further expounding Köprülü's basic 'pre-Islamic survivals' thesis by identifying additional traces in Alevi-Bektashi hagiographic literature and lore in the shape of nature cults and miracle motifs presumably associated with shamans in pre-Islamic times. Mélikoff and Ocak, however, differ from Köprülü in so far as both downplay the Shi^ci elements in the makeup of popular Islam in medieval Anatolia, attributing the later palpable Shi^ci manifestation to Safavid influence. Ocak, in addition, sees Anatolian folk Islam as also incorporating elements from sources other than shamanism, in particular the various Iranian and Indian religious traditions, although the latter, at least until recently (see below), have clearly occupied a secondary place in his analysis.

Over the past thirty years, the Köprülü paradigm through the works of Mélikoff and Ocak also attained wide public circulation among Alevis themselves.[38] As a result, the idea of Alevi-Bektashi culture as an outgrowth of the Central Asian Yesevi tradition and a storehouse of pre-Islamic Turkish culture was embraced and internalised as common knowledge by a significant segment of the Alevi community. Since then, a flood of publications by researchers of Alevi background have detected shamanic imprints in their religious and cultural traditions, thereby confirming Alevis' and Alevism's authentic Turkish origins. These researchers have upheld the notion of 'syncretism' as a defining feature of their ancestral belief system, conceiving it as a positive synthesis of national culture and religion that is deemed to be inherently more tolerant and amicable to modern secularism.[39] The popularisation and normalisation of Köprülü's ideas concerning the Central Asian/Turkish origins of Alevism did not, however, go uncontested. Some members of the Alevi community rejected the Central Asia thesis as a fictitious official narrative and a product of the so-called Turk-Islam synthesis cultural policy that was put in place following the 1980 military coup. In an effort to disprove it, and offset its pervasive influence, exponents of this opposing position came to construct their own counter-narratives stressing the non-Turkish – specifically Kurdish and in some cases Zaza – and/or non-Islamic essence of their tradition. This collision resulted in sustained and heated debates, turning Kizilbash/Alevi history into an embattled terrain between groups with contrasting visions of Kizilbashism/Alevism and with divergent political interests and sympathies.[40]

The place and significance of ongoing polemics concerning Kizilbash origins in contemporary Alevi identity politics and their intersectionality with secularising Kurdish and Islamist movements are beyond the scope of this work. What is relevant for the purposes of the present discussion is how these polemics have highlighted some of the gaps in Köprülü's pertinent works, the most glaring of which is the aforementioned disregard for the sizeable Kurdish- and Zazaki-speaking Alevi communities who are typically, but unconvincingly, explained as 'assimilated Turks' by those advocating the Central Asia thesis. Despite their destabilising effect on Köprülü's nationalist metanarrative, however, the many accounts of Kizilbash/Alevi history put forward in recent years as an alternative to that of Köprülü's tend to lack a strong empirical grounding. Neither do any of them truly succeed in providing a substantive and systematic critique of Köprülü's basic conceptual framework based on a flawed notion of syncretism. [41] For instance, those who foreground Kurdish- and Zazaki-speaking Alevis in their works simply invert Köprülü's Central Asia thesis as they seek the roots of Alevi beliefs and ritual practices in ancient Mesopotamian and Kurdish religions. Others, eager to maintain a distance from both types of nationalist narratives, connect Alevism to the various repressed religious traditions of Anatolia or to a set of humanist and socialist values with no religious dimension of any kind.[42] No matter how radical a departure they claim to represent from Köprülü's views, however, all of these critical voices still subscribe to the same imprecise and malleable notion of syncretism, drawing on the same pool of alleged pre-Islamic residues in Alevi beliefs and ritual practices to support their conflicting conclusions. As such, they not only reinforce politically and intellectually suspect preoccupations with primordial essences that characterised Köprülü's thinking but also often commit the methodological fallacy of treating similarities and parallels as evidence of direct transmission and continuity.

These ongoing polemical debates around the question of Kizilbash/Alevi origins and identity are instructive in that they exhibit the pitfalls of ahistorical applications of the concept of religious syncretism. The presence of syncretic processes – that is the fusion of beliefs and ritual practices from various distinct sources – in the making of Kizilbashism/Alevism (as in other religious traditions) is not what is disputed here. Indeed, given the social-temporal space within which it originated and was sustained, it would be surprising if some of the elements of Kizilbash/Alevi tradition were not extensions of pre-Islamic forms of worship and beliefs that prevailed among Turkmen, Kurdish and Zaza communities, or adapted, knowingly or unknowingly, from other religious groups that inhabited the same region. After all, this is the way religious and cultural traditions historically operate. Neither is it my intention to make a case for a complete abandonment of the concept of syncretism in studies of cultural transplantations and cross-fertilisation, and for scrutinising the perceptions and politics surrounding such processes, whether in Alevi studies or elsewhere.[43] Rather, my goal here is to question the utility of syncretism as an explanatory model and, more specifically, its treatment as the defining characteristic of Kizilbashism-Alevism. Methodologically, as put by Eric Maroney, 'calling a religion "syncretistic" is often a way of saying that it is the sum of its parts or of beginning to reduce or dissect it'.[44] The drawbacks of taking apart practices and identities only to trace back their individual constituent components to some imagined pure ethnic and religious generative source are forcefully in evidence in the multitude of publications on Alevism that fail to yield a clear picture of how the greater whole is constituted and has maintained its resilience over the centuries. More than mere analytical concerns are at stake here. There are issues of power involved in singling out certain religious traditions as 'syncretistic' when in reality all religions have composite historical origins. When used as a taxonomic tool to differentiate allegedly 'pure' traditions from their 'decadent' counterparts, the concept of syncretism thus not only loses much of its analytical power; it also turns into an othering term that serves to validate the hegemony of the self-acclaimed custodians of normativity, a tendency that is unfortunately still all too common in Islamic historiography.

Topical Focus and Approach

This work, above all, is an attempt to rescue Kizilbashism/Alevism from the murkiness of a timeless folk Islam and to return it to the status of a historical object in context, not as an anomaly or a historical accident but as a particular manifestation of various religious and social trends in the late medieval and early modern Islamic(ate) world. The framework of analysis that it adopts is one of socioreligious organisation. Its initial point of departure is a pool of information concerning the inner workings of traditional Alevism that has accumulated since the Alevi cultural revival. This new information has dispelled the myth of the Kizilbash/Alevi communities as being a nebulous collection of tribes devoid of any identifiable religious structures.[45] Indeed, one can no longer doubt in the light of the emerging data that the traditional community organisation of the Kizilbash/Alevis developed reasonably clear contours. This was a genealogically based socio-religious organisation centred on a collection of charismatic family lines, the so-known *ocak*s, and sustained through semi-formal and informal social networks and a set of morally sanctioned and quasi-hierarchically structured relationships.[46]

The basic parameters of the *ocak* system reaching to modern times can be summed up as follows. Each Alevi community, whether defined on the basis of a village or a tribe, or as a subsection of either, is attached to a particular *ocak*, or saintly lineage group. Members of these *ocak*s, the *ocakzade*s, owe their elevated spiritual status to their real or imagined *sayyid* (T. *seyit*) ancestry, that is their prophetic descent through the progeny of ᶜAli and the Prophet's daughter, Fatima. Individual *ocak*s are generally concentrated in particular regions and preside over one or a few central villages that may contain a pilgrimage site, or *ziyaret*, associated with that *ocak*. Religious leaders, called *dede*s (or *pir*s), are chosen from among the *ocakzade*s, and fulfil liturgical, judicial and educational functions (Figure I.3). Historically, *dede* families have tended to move from one village to another, often following their migrating disciples (*talib*s, lit. seekers). Such mobility partially explains the historical proliferation of Alevi *ocak*s because a *dede* family moving to a new place may emerge as an independent *ocak* under a new name.[47] In addition to the basic

Figure I.3 Hüseyin Dede (Keko Hüseyin) from the *ocak* of Üryan Hızır with the iconic untrimmed long beard and moustache associated with the *dede*s, 1963

Source: Original in the private collection of Ali Büyükşahin, from the village of Bulam, Çelikhan-Adıyaman.

ocakzade–talib division that underlies Alevi communal structures, there are also regional hierarchies among the *ocak*s themselves, with certain ones recognised as *mürşid* (lit. the one who guides) lines to whom other *dede* families pledge allegiance, although such categorical designations are not always uncontested.

Individual *ocak* communities are conceived in terms of a family model. Intermarriage between members of *dede* families and members of their *talib* communities is therefore traditionally not permitted because their relationship is likened to one between parents and their children. One's *ocak* affiliation is inherited from one's father and forefathers and cannot be shifted from one *dede* lineage to another except under unusual circumstances. *Dede*s are responsible for officiating *talib* initiation ceremonies (T. *ikrar cemi*), as well as at annual *görgü cemi* (lit. ritual of good manners), where any conflicts between community members are resolved and any wrongdoings compensated for or punished. In order to be eligible for initiation, a *talib*, who must ideally be married, is required to pick from among his peers another married man with whom he will form a bond of *musahiblik* (companionship), thereby establishing a fictive kinship between the two married couples who make a lifelong commitment for mutual emotional and physical support. He also has to have a *rehber* (guide), someone knowledgeable about Alevi ritual practices recruited from among the qualified *talib*s, who will symbolically deliver him and his *musahib* to the *dede*. The same set of relationships is replicated at the level of *dede*. Just like a lay follower, a *dede*, too, has to have a *musahib* and a *rehber*, pledge allegiance to a fellow *ocakzade* and pass through *görgü* once a year.[48] The *dede* officiating at an *ocakzade*'s rites of *ikrar* and *görgü* is in turn regarded as the *mürşid*. In matters superseding the authority of the *dede*, a *talib* may have recourse to the mediation of his *mürşid*.

Each *ocak* community, with its local hierarchies, tends to function independently, but in principle all *ocak*s are connected to a convent that serves as their supreme spiritual centre. This function was historically fulfilled by the Safavi convent in Ardabil, albeit evidently with an Abdal-turned-Bektashi convent located in the Iraqi town of Karbala, known as the Karbala convent (*Kerbela Dergâhı*) among the Alevis, acting as the intermediary. However, from the early nineteenth century onward, when relations with the Karbala convent started to break down due mostly to external factors, the Hacı Bektaş convent in Kırşehir gradually emerged as the new institutional focal point for the Alevi communities in Anatolia, and it was to it that the Alevi *dede*s began to appeal for accreditation.

By all appearances, the crystallisation of the *ocak* system was a key aspect of the consolidation of a distinct, overarching Kizilbash/Alevi identity.[49] This decentralised and flexible configuration of authority, binding together saintly families and convents in a loose hierarchy, seems to have generated and successfully sustained a distinct Kizilbash/Alevi collectivity over the centuries. Alevis often depict the resulting matrix of relations in the maxim 'hand to hand, hand to God/Truth' (*el ele, el Hakk'a*), revealing their awareness of a broader Kizilbash/Alevi network beyond the boundaries of their local *ocak* community. It is true that traditional Alevi communal structures have been eroded significantly since the middle of the twentieth century when large-scale migrations into urban centres began; only a limited number of *ocak*s are currently functional in their traditional formats. Yet, the internal definition of the community's external boundaries still rests on the memory of this network of Alevi *ocak*s and their affiliates whose descendants qualify as members of the in-group simply by virtue of being born into an Alevi family irrespective of whether, or to what degree, they embrace and practice the Alevi faith.

The *ocak*s, with their constitutive centrality to Alevi socio-religious organisation and identity, thus provide us with a much more tangible entry point into Kizilbash history than the relatively elusive and historically hard-to-document religious ideas and ritual practices. They not only offer a safer base for the analysis of the generative foundations of Kizilbashism but also of its shifting social boundaries and content over time. Following this line of thinking, the present work uses a group of *ocak* lineages in eastern Anatolia, the region with the highest Kizilbash concentration until recent times, as illustrative case studies to investigate the emergence and development of Kizilbash identity and tradition primarily through the lens of communal structures.

Alevi Sources[50]

Paucity of sources is a perennial problem for historians interested in the study of dissentient minority religious communities who by definition did not have equal access to the means of production of historical narratives as their hegemonic counterparts. Such groups have tended to leave behind few paper trails, and accounts of them by outsiders abound with major gaps, prejudices and misconceptions that place serious limitations on their use. Looked at from this perspective, it is hardly possible to exaggerate the importance of Alevi documents and manuscripts in private hands that have stayed out of the reach of researchers until relatively recently. The tantalising evidence emerging from this new body of written material, which I shorthand as 'Alevi sources', offers at least partial answers to many basic questions about Kizilbash/Alevi history that are still outstanding. It also undermines, refines and enriches our assumptions concerning the wider socio-religious history of Anatolia during the four centuries between the initial arrival of the Seljuk Turks in the late eleventh century and the entrenchment of Pax Ottomanica circa 1500.

Alevi sources consist of documents and manuscripts that have been handed down from generation to generation within Alevi *dede* families as a type of sacred trust and as testimony to the families' *ocakzade* status and *sayyid* descent (Figures I.4a, I.4b, I.4c). In the past, *dede*s carefully guarded their family documents from the gaze of outsiders, including that of lay followers, and some continue to do so. It was only in the wake of the Alevi cultural revival in the early 1990s that individual *dede* families began making their documents available for research purposes. Overall, we still do not have a clear idea as to the full extent of these documents as new ones continue to come forth. While individual examples of Alevi documents have appeared in print, the bulk of them are still unpublished, and they have not so far been systematically examined in their entirety with attention to historical context, mechanisms of production and renewal, audience, as well as content.[51] A similar situation holds true for the more widely known *Buyruk* manuscripts that have become the subject of several articles of varying scope and quality since the beginning of the revival.[52] Nor have Alevi sources been utilised to rethink the broader contours of Kizilbash/Alevi history. The present work sets out to do just that, using the family documents of a select group of Alevi *ocak*s in eastern Anatolia that are unified in their historical affinity to the Wafaᵓiyya – an Iraqi-born Sufi tradition and descent group traced to the eleventh-century mystic Abu'l-Wafaᵓ al-Baghdadi. Given their novelty and some of their unusual characteristics, it would be in order to offer a general overview of the Alevi sources utilised in this work and to describe the nature of evidence they contain.

The greater part of the documents explored here come from families affiliated with the *ocak*s of Dede Kargın, Ağuiçen and İmam Zeynel Abidin (the last also known as the *dede*s of Mineyik), whose private archives were the most comprehensive of all those available in terms of both the number of documents and the length of the time period they spanned. These three *ocak*s are among the most prominent in eastern Anatolia, with the last two also having a claim to *mürşid*-hood. The remaining Alevi sources used in this work are documents that belong to the *ocak*s of Sinemilli, Şeyh Süleyman, Şeyh Ahmed Dede, Şeyh Delil Berhican, Şeyh Çoban, Celal Abbas (aka Şah Ali Abbas), Kara Pir Bad, Kureyşan, Kızıl Deli and Şah İbrahim Veli. The first six of these *ocak*s intersect with the previously mentioned three on the grounds of their historical linkage to the Wafaᵓiyya; disciples of the *ocak*s of Sinemilli and Kureyşan, in addition, recognise the Ağuiçens as their *mürşid*. The Kızıl Deli *ocak* is associated with the well-known Bektashi saint Seyyid ᶜAli Sultan even though its Malatya branch, which is considered here, historically recognises the

Figure I.4a Sample Alevi document in its protective case, private archive of Abuzer Güzel Dede, member of the *ocak* of Ağuiçen from the village of Bulam, Çelikhan-Adıyaman

Source: Photograph by Laine Stump, Adıyaman, 2002.

dedes of Mineyik as the *mürşid* line. The *ocak* of Şah İbrahim Veli, on the other hand, is another very prominent *ocak* with a claim to *mürşid*-hood similar to the Ağuiçens and the *ocak* of İmam Zeynel Abidin; it is, however, unique (with the possible exception of the *ocak* of Celal Abbas) in having a pedigree tracing back to the house of the Safavids.

Compared to their archival counterparts, Alevi documents pose an array of additional challenges to the researcher. First, Alevi documents as a whole are dispersed among dozens, or possibly even hundreds, of *dedes* and their families in different corners of Anatolia and the Balkans. Even in the case of a single *ocak*, they are often scattered unevenly among several *dede* families inhabiting different localities. In general, one or two families possess all or the majority of documents related to their *ocak*, with the rest of the affiliated families holding just a single specimen

Figure I.4b Sample Alevi document from the private archive of Muharrem Naci Orhan, member of the *ocak* of İmam Zeynel Abidin, from the village of Mineyik, Arguvan-Malatya

Source: Photograph by the author, Istanbul, 2006.

Figure I.4c Sample Alevi manuscript (*Buyruk*), undated

Source: Original in the private archive of Hamza Özyıldırım, member of the *ocak* of Celal Abbas from the village of Terkiloh (Kayabaşı), Kemah-Erzincan. Photograph by the author, Erzincan, 2002

or none at all. Identifying the locations of the different branches and offshoots of an *ocak*, seeking out those individuals and families who are in possession of one or more of the documents relating to that *ocak*, and acquiring their consent for studying these documents are tasks that can be difficult and time-consuming, and virtually impossible to accomplish with perfection given the element of chance. Second, with regard to older Alevi documents, only a few are still in their original state. The rest are copies made at later dates, evidently to ensure the preservation of the physically deteriorated originals or to produce additional copies for the individual archives of affiliated *dede* families. During the copying process, multiple documents were occasionally integrated into a single scroll, most likely because it was physically easier to keep a single long sheet than multiple short ones. *Dede*s also had their documents periodically copied as part of a procedure for renewing their legitimacy as *ocakzade*s and for updating their family tree with the inclusion of subsequent generations.

This practice of recurrent copying and recopying, undertaken at times by individuals with limited competence, explains the degenerated state of some of the documents, more so of those originally composed in Arabic. Many of these display copying errors, misspellings and lapses in the flow of the text. In addition to such unintended mistakes, these later copies also frequently include what appear to be intended omissions and revisions that reflect changing religious sensibilities and needs, as well as altered significance and usage of the documents in question. It is thus an extremely tedious job to sort out the initial configurations of documents from their later copies, especially in cases when the extant copies don't always supply original composition dates, instead providing only copying or renewal dates or no dates at all. Further adding to the challenge are: the polyglot character of the documents, which variously use Turkish (at times non-standard or archaic forms), Arabic and Persian, sometimes within the same document; the scattered nature of their chronology, with dates ranging from the late fourteenth to the mid-twentieth century; and their various and at times eclectic genres that have been little studied. All these challenges are aggravated in cases of long scrolls that are compilations of multiple documents, where disentangling the textual layers is particularly onerous because the different parts are not always clearly separated from one another and have uneven styles.

Notwithstanding all these problems and ambiguities, a number of models relatively consistent in form and content can be discerned in the set of documents examined for this research. Excluding some two dozen fragments and entirely illegible documents, I have analysed approximately 150 Alevi documents (several of which were rough replicas of one another) written on separate sheets or scrolls of paper. Of these, about forty concerned commercial transactions, criminal court cases and other such mundane issues, or were from the twentieth century, including a few personal letters. The rest of the dated documents, which are particularly important for the purposes of the present work, have dates between the second half of the sixteenth century and the end of the nineteenth, with five exceptions that bear earlier dates. These largely consist of: (1) Sufi diplomas (Ar. *ijāza*s; Ot. *icāzetnāme*s) of the Wafaʾi order; (2) documents issued or renewed at the Karbala convent in Iraq or by Karbala's *naḳībüʾl-eşrāf* (Ar. *naqīb al-ashrāf*), the local chief of the descendants of the Prophet; (3) Bektashi diplomas conferred by the Çelebis at the Hacı Bektaş convent in Kırşehir; and (4) various documents issued by Ottoman authorities and the kadi courts confirming the holders' status as *sayyid*s and dervishes.

Putting aside what appears to be a sixteenth-century copy of an Ahi (Ot. *Aḫī*; Ar. *Akhī*) *ijāza* dated 14 Şaʿban 775/1374, the oldest layer of Alevi documents consists of *ijāza*s of the Wafaʾi order, all in Arabic. These were the most disappointing in terms of the quality of the extant copies. Of the fifteen dated copies of Wafaʾi *ijāza*s, the oldest four are from the fifteenth century, while another nine date to the sixteenth century and the remining two to the first half of the seventeenth century. A final one, reframed as a *sayyid* genealogy (Ar. *shajara*, Ot. *şecere*) when it was copied in 1265/1848, must have been originally drawn up sometime in the sixteenth century or earlier. An additional group of documents revealing a Wafaʾi affinity includes *sayyid* genealogies reaching back to Abu'l-Wafaʾ, which were issued or renewed by the *naḳībü'l-eşrāf* in Karbala during the eighteenth and nineteenth centuries. In many cases, these *shajaras* in Arabic were bestowed by the *naḳībü'l-eşrāf* on the authority of older documents, some of which may also have been composed initially as *ijāzas*, although such a transition in genre is rarely discernible; one such exception is the aforementioned document dated 1265/1848.

More than three dozen documents originating in Iraq are the second oldest documents. As a whole, they reveal that *dedes* periodically travelled to this region from at least the mid-sixteenth century on. Oral testimonies also confirm that journeys to obtain updated genealogies were made until the middle of the twentieth century. During these travels, it turns out, *dedes* visited various Shiʿi-Alevi pilgrimage sites and a number of Sufi convents that over time, if not originally, came to be associated with the Bektashi order. Of these convents, the one at Karbala appears to be the place where many Alevi documents originated. Notwithstanding the fact that distinctions between different genres seem to be blurred in many cases, Alevi documents from Iraq are basically of three types: above-mentioned *shajaras* in Arabic, *ziyāretnāmes* in Turkish (some in narrative format, others containing, or consisting entirely, of pictorial illustrations) and *ḫilāfetnāmes* in Turkish, respectively confirming the *dedes*' *sayyid* descent, their visits to the Shiʿi-Alevi sacred sites in Iraq and their paying homage to the convent in Karbala.

Of the remaining documents, twenty-seven were issued by Ottoman authorities or the kadi courts, verifying their holders' status as dervishes and *sayyids*. All of these are dated from the seventeenth to the nineteenth centuries, with the exception of a copy of an imperial edict (Ot. *fermān*) dated 930/1524 and ten *icāzetnāmes* granted by the Çelebi Bektashis in Kırşehir during the nineteenth century and early twentieth. I have come across surprisingly few Alevi documents, only two in fact, that are directly traceable to the Safavids. The first, the original of which is extant, is dated 1089/1678. The second, although copied in 1242/1826, must have been initially composed sometime in the early sixteenth century. The explanation of why significantly fewer Safavid-related documents than one would expect have been preserved must lie either in the risk involved in holding on to them or in their growing irrelevance after the Safavids' demise in the early eighteenth century, or more likely both.[53]

In addition to such individual documents, Alevi sources also include manuscripts of literary religious works. A significant portion of these works, emanating from Bektashi, Hurufi and Shiᶜi milieus, are not uniquely Kizilbash/Alevi, although they are important for undoing the common notion of Kizilbash/Alevi communities as being isolated islands with an exclusively orally transmitted tradition and for showing their interconnections with broader Sufi and Shiᶜi literary traditions and networks. In addition to these, there are among Alevi sources a set of more distinctively Kizilbash/Alevi manuscripts known as *Buyruk* (lit. Command) that are held in especially high esteem and that, therefore, deserve special attention. According to tradition, *Buyruk* contains an authoritative account of basic Kizilbash/Alevi beliefs and rituals, and only *dede* families would own a copy of it. The earliest written reference to *Buyruk* is found in a missionary report from 1857,[54] and a *Buyruk* text was published for the first time in Turkey in 1958.[55] Since then, multiple other *Buyruk* manuscripts in private collections and in libraries have become known, with the oldest dating to the early seventeenth century, and a few of these have fully or partially appeared in print.[56] A close examination of these different manuscripts reveal great variations among them, suggesting that '*Buyruk*', rather than being the title of one single work, was the name given to collections of religious treatises originating with the Safavids. *Buyruk* manuscripts are thus particularly significant for revealing previously little-understood aspects of relations between the Safavids and their followers in Anatolia, including first and foremost their continuing contacts well into the late seventeenth century, as well as for offering an emic picture of the spiritual nature of these relations. Also found in the private archives of *dede* families are a special set of rectangular-shaped manuscripts, known as *cönk*, that include collections of Kizilbash/Alevi mystical poetry; while these are of utmost importance for exploring Kizilbash/Alevi teachings and religious ideas, they largely lie outside of the bounds of the present book, which focuses on socio-religious history rather than theology.[57]

Major Findings

One of the most interesting surprises that came from delving into Alevi documents was the discovery of the historical affinity of a sizeable network of Alevi saintly lineages with the Wafaᵓi Sufi tradition. Originating in eleventh-century Iraq, the Wafaᵓiyya was apparently an important component of the late-medieval Anatolian socio-religious landscape, although historians operating with Köprülü's central postulate of Central Asian roots of popular Islam in Anatolia have until recently failed to grant it adequate attention. As early as 1936, Abdülbâkî Gölpınarlı suspected the

Wafaʾi affiliation of a group of important religious and literary figures associated with the Abdals of Rum, a dervish group that existed in Anatolia since at least the fourteenth century. Yet neither he nor any others further pursued this idea, perhaps because it was not in accord with received scholarly notions.[58] The long-standing neglect of historians of a possible Wafaʾi connection in the origins of Anatolian Sufism was first noted in earnest in a brief but seminal article by Ahmet T. Karamustafa, in which the author urged scholars to pursue this line of enquiry.[59] Of late, Ahmet Yaşar Ocak, too, revised his long-standing emphasis on the Central Asia/Yesevi connection by allowing a much greater space for the Wafa'iyya as a constitutive component of 'popular mysticism' in Anatolia and of the Alevi-Bektashi tradition in particular.[60] A systematic investigation of the Alevi documents, which this works sets out to do, further expands and nuances our understanding of the role of Wafaʾi-affiliated Sufi communities and descent groups in the making of the Kizilbash/Alevi milieu. It also offers us the basic parameters of a new narrative of Kizilbash/Alevi history from its early beginnings up to its consolidation, a narrative that calls for a readjustment in focus from pre-Islamic Central Asia to the cosmopolitan Sufi milieu of late medieval Anatolia and the neighbouring regions.

*İcāzetnāme*s granted by the Çelebi Bektashis from the nineteenth century and early twentieth aside, the Alevi documents reveal no evidence of a Yesevi connection. Nor do they validate Köprülü's reductionist view of the Alevis as lay followers of the Bektashi order. While they do confirm the closely intertwined trajectories of the two affiliations, they draw a much more complicated picture of their relationship than is commonly assumed. Among other things, the Alevi documents indicate that Kizilbash–Bektashi relations were primarily forged not in the central Bektashi convent in Kırşehir but across a previously unknown network of convents in the various cities of Iraq that housed the shrines of the Shiʿi Imams and their kinsfolk. The hub of this network was a convent in Karbala that initially belonged to the Abdals of Rum but was eventually incorporated into the Bektashi order. The Karbala convent appears to have maintained a relatively institutionalised relationship with the Alevi *ocak*s, and those of Wafaʾi origin in particular, with its members, it would seem, serving as liaisons between the Safavids and their Kizilbash followers in Anatolia. Many Alevi documents granted to the members of Alevi saintly lineages were issued or renewed there, as mentioned earlier.

A broader conclusion that can be drawn from these two important findings – namely the historical Wafaʾi affinity of a sizeable cluster of Kizilbash/Alevi *ocak*s and their ties to a network of Sufi convents in

Iraq – concerns the question of the underlying dynamics and nature of the Kizilbash movement. The conventional view represents the Kizilbash milieu as a collection of different Turkmen tribes who were directly linked to the Safavids.[61] The Alevi sources significantly modify this common conjecture, for they indicate that in the microcosm of the Anatolian Kizilbash milieu were not individual tribes as such, whether Turkmen or otherwise, but rather various Sufi and dervish circles, and *sayyid* families, each with its own sphere of influence, all of which coalesced under the leadership of the Safavi family, or, using the Alevi terminology, the *ocak* of Ardabil (*Erdebil ocağı*). To the extent that tribal identities and kinship relations were relevant in the configuration of Kizilbash communities, they interfaced with a phenomenon known as 'communal Sufi affiliation'. This phenomenon, which occupies an important but insufficiently examined place in the history of Sufism, developed in tandem with Sufism's diffusion beyond its original urban base into rural and tribal settings from the eleventh century onward, and with the concurrent spread of the genealogical discourse in Islamdom.[62] Current scholarship has typically viewed the popularisation of Sufism as a decline and degeneration of its classical ideals and has, therefore, paid little attention to the long-term social and religious implications of this process.[63] This might explain the common failure to recognise how the dissemination of certain Sufi ideas and institutions paved the way for the formation of alternative religious systems and communities in the Islamic world. The Alevi sources are illuminating in this regard as they allow us to trace the evolution of hereditary Sufi lines into independent *ocak*s within the framework of the Kizilbash movement. Many ideals of Sufism were accordingly translated from the individual to the communal level and put to use as the basis for a new social and moral order.

The Sufi connection in the making of Kizilbash communities should come as no surprise to scholars in the field. Even putting aside the Sufi origins of the Safavids themselves, this connection is in evidence in the distinctively Sufi character of the Alevis' conceptual, ritual and organisational vocabulary, as well as in some of the key tenets of the Alevi belief system that were briefly summarised above. Köprülü, too, was cognisant of such a connection. Yet for Köprülü and most others, Sufism was no more than a thin veneer barely hiding the timeless pre-Islamic (in the case of Köprülü, shamanic) core of Kizilbashism. Disputing this supposition, the present work argues that Sufism was not an added veneer but the very context within which Kizilbash communities formed and developed.

The recovery of the previously undervalued and understudied Sufi context of the Kizilbash movement also sheds a new light on the

Ottoman–Safavid conflict and the process of Sunni confessionalisation that it heralded in the Ottoman empire. Recent studies of Sunni confessionalisation in the Ottoman Empire have highlighted Sufism as a key site of contestation in this process.[64] This new insight is particularly valuable in gaining a better understanding of the causes, experience and long-term consequences of the Kizilbash persecutions in the Ottoman Empire that, among other things, targeted the Sufi infrastructure of the Kizilbash milieu, and in turn catalysed a parallel process of Kizilbash confessionalisation. Additionally, and more specifically, it helps to make better sense of the variegated trajectory of the Wafaʾi tradition in late medieval Anatolia, cutting across social, ethnic and even sectarian divisions. Wafaʾi offshoots that thrived in the region since pre-Ottoman times enjoyed a historical affinity not only with many Alevi *ocak*s but also with a number of prominent Sufi shaykhs and *sayyid* families of Sunni denomination, who were patronised by various dynasties, including the Seljuks and the Ottomans. The Wafaʾi legacy, characterised as it was by a 'metadoxic' outlook, to use Cemal Kafadar's terminology, would, however, not survive the pressures of confessionalisation unleashed by the Ottoman–Safavid conflict, losing its independent identity and assimilating largely into the Kizilbash milieu and/or the Bektashi tradition over the course of the sixteenth century.

Organisation of Chapters

This book is in large measure organised around four major themes that are brought to the forefront by the Alevi documents, presented as much as possible in the order of their chronological relevance. Chapters 1 and 2 address the implications of the historical affinity of some of the most prominent Alevi saintly lineages with the Iraqi-born Wafaʾi Sufi tradition. Chapter 1 presents a selective overview of the life and spiritual legacy of Abu'l-Wafaʾ, based on the hagiography of the saint and other near-contemporary Sufi narratives. This chapter makes the point that the metadoxic outlook of the Babaʾi milieu in medieval Anatolia, as well as many components of Kizilbashism-Alevism, explained on the basis of pre-Islamic survivals in the conventional literature, in fact had their parallels and antecedents in the early Wafaʾi milieu. Chapter 2 proceeds by tracking the various Sufi figures and *sayyid* families who are purported to be spiritual and/or biological descendants of Abu'l-Wafaʾ and who thrived in Anatolia from the late twelfth century or early thirteenth until the mid-sixteenth century. It shows how, from the second half of the fifteenth century onward, most Wafaʾi offshoots in eastern Anatolia came to be assimilated under the common flag of Kizilbashism, gradually losing their group identities and order structures as they evolved into components of the Kizilbash/Alevi *ocak* system. This chapter also argues that the erosion of the Wafaʾi memory, to some extent a natural corollary of the incorporation of the Wafaʾi affiliates into the Safavid-led Kizilbash movement, also involved the conflation and blending of the Wafaʾi legacy with that of the Bektashi tradition as it was configured in the Bektashi hagiographic and oral tradition compiled at about the turn of the sixteenth century.

The second major theme that emerges from the Alevi sources concerns relations between the Kizilbash/Alevi communities and the Bektashi order, an issue that occupied historians for some time. Chapters 3 and 4 take up this multifaceted issue and modify some of the related assumptions of the Köprülü paradigm. Chapter 3 traces the roots of the complex relations between the two affiliations to their common association with the cult of Hacı Bektaş and their shared links to the Abdals of Rum, whose legacy would in large part be absorbed by the Bektashi order. Chapter 4 focuses on the Abdal-Bektashi convent in Karbala, which seems to have served as a link between the Safavids and their Kizilbash followers in Anatolia. The informal networks that developed around this convent throw further light on the entwined histories of the Kizilbash/Alevi communities and the Bektashi order and on the workings of the Alevi *ocak* system.

Teasing out the wider implications of the findings presented in previous chapters, Chapter 5 formulates an alternative account of the Kizilbash movement as a nexus of various mystical circles, dervish groups and *sayyid* families who came together around Safavid spiritual leadership over the course of the late fifteenth century and early sixteenth. This chapter also shows how the Kizilbash communities in Anatolia persisted through the Çaldıran defeat in their attachment to their distant spiritual masters, the Safavid shahs, who in turn appear to have never entirely abandoned their spiritual claims over these communities. Contacts between the Safavids and the Kizilbash communities in Anatolia were maintained not only indirectly through the mediation of the Karbala convent in Iraq but also through other mechanisms. Of the latter, I identify three: the dispatching of religious treatises, the granting of the position of *ḫalīfe* (P. *khalīfa*) to selected Alevi *ocak*s and the mediation of a branch of the Safavid family in southeastern Anatolia that evolved into the Alevi *ocak* of Şah İbrahim Veli.

Another theme brought to the fore by the Alevi documents is relations between the Ottoman state and the Kizilbash communities, which is taken up in Chapter 6. Alevi documents that were issued by Ottoman authorities or the kadi courts recognising related families as Sufi dervishes and/or *sayyid*s form a point of departure of the analysis in this chapter. While such documents might at first sight be interpreted simply as manifestations of Ottoman religious tolerance and administrative pragmatism, this chapter approaches them in the light of the key argument of this book that emphasises the Sufi genealogies of Kizilbash/Alevi saintly lineages. In assessing relations between the Ottoman state and the Kizilbash communities, a special emphasis is placed on the sixteenth-century Kizilbash persecutions and their ruinous impact on the Sufi infrastructure of the Kizilbash milieu. I contend that the persecutory measures employed against the Kizilbash, rather than being viewed within such binaries as tolerance versus intolerance and politics versus religion, ought to be understood in connection to a range of other developments in Ottoman history, including most importantly the process of Sunni confessionalisation that entailed the demarcation of boundaries of acceptable Sufism. Pressures for confessionalisation would also pave the way for Kizilbashism to evolve from a social movement comprising a diverse range of groups and actors into a relatively coherent and self-conscious socio-religious collectivity.

Notes

1. On Alevi ritual practices and expressive culture, and further bibliography on the subject, see Irene Markoff, 'Music, Saints, and Ritual: Samā^c^ and the Alevis of Turkey', in *Manifestations of Sainthood in Islam*, ed. Grace Martin Smith (Istanbul: Isis Press, 1993), 95–110; and Paul V. Koerbin, '"I Am Pir Sultan Abdal": A Hermeneutical Study of the Self-Naming Tradition (*Mahlas*) in Turkish Alevi Lyric Song (*Deyiş*)', (PhD diss., University of Western Sydney, Sydney, 2011).
2. Mirroring this sentiment was a giant banner decorating the concert hall that read, 'We will keep performing *semah* and reciting *deyiş*' (*Semah Dönmeye Deyiş Söylemeye Devam Edeceğiz*).
3. The name 'Kizilbash' (T. *Kızılbaş*), literally meaning 'red-head', was presumably derived from the crimson headgear (*tāj*) with twelve gores representing the Twelve Shi^c^i Imams worn by Safavid followers; for details about the Kizilbash *tāj*, see Willem Floor, *The Persian Textile Industry in Historical Perspective: 1500–1925* (Paris: Éditions L'Harmattan, 1999), 277–290. The original use of the epithet is commonly linked to the Safavid tribal warriors mostly of Turkmen stock; see, for example, Hans R. Roemer, 'The Qizilbash Turcomans: Founder and Victim of the Safavid Theocracy', in *Intellectual Studies on Islam: Essays Written in Honor of Martin B. Dickson*, eds Michel M. Mazzaoui and Vera B. Moreen (Salt Lake City: University of Utah Press, 1990), 27–28. In the wake of Sultan Selim I's ascent to power, the Ottomans began using the term 'Kızılbaş' in an expanded sense as a contemptuous epithet for Shah Isma^c^il's followers in general. It was also embraced by the affiliates of the movement themselves as a self-designation and as a

provocative token of pride. In the following poem, the eighteenth-century Kizilbash poet Derviş Mehmed (1755–1828) reviles those who use the term pejoratively, calling them 'Yazid', the second of the Umayyad caliphs and responsible for the murder of the Prophet's grandchild, Imam Husayn:

Gidi Yezid bize Kızılbaş demiş,
Bahçede açılan gül de kırmızı.
İncinme ey gönül ne derse desin,
Kuran'ı derc eden dil de kırmızı.

(Yezid called us Red-head/The rose blooming in the garden is also red/Oh [my] heart, don't feel sorrow/The tongue reciting the Qur'an is also red.) For the entirety of the poem, see *Alevi-Bektaşi Şiirleri Antolojisi*, ed. İsmail Özmen, 5 vols (Ankara: Saypa Yayın, 1995), vol. 3: 9.

4. Standard works on Safavid origins include Walther Hınz, *Uzun Hasan ve Şeyh Cüneyd: XV. Yüzyılda İran'ın Millî Bir Devlet Haline Yükselişi* (Ankara: Türk Tarih Kurumu, 1992), originally published under the title *Irans Aufstieg zum Nationalstaat im fünfzehnten Jahrhundert* (Berlin: Walter de Gruyter GmbH & Co., 1936); Michel M. Mazzaoui, *The Origins of the Ṣafawids: Šī'ism, Ṣūfism, and the Ġulāt* (Wiesbaden: Franz Steiner Verlag, 1972); Roger M. Savory, *Iran under the Safavids* (Cambridge: Cambridge University Press, 1980), 1–50; Hans R. Roemer, 'The Safavid Period', *Cambridge-Iran-6*: 189–350; M. Masashi Haneda, *Le châh et les Qizilbāš: le système militaire safavide* (Berlin: Klaus Schwarz, 1987); Jean Aubin, 'L'avènement des Safavides reconsidéré (Études Safavides III)', *Moyen Orient & Océan Indien* 5 (1988): 1–130; for a more recent and more nuanced take on early Safavid history, also see Andrew J. Newman, *Safavid Iran: Rebirth of a Persian Empire* (London: I. B. Tauris, 2006), esp. Introduction and Chapter 1.
5. On Kizilbash uprisings and persecutions, see Ahmet Refik, *On altıncı asırda Rafizîlik ve Bektaşilik* (Istanbul: Muallim Ahmet Halit Kitaphanesi, 1932); Hanna Sohrweide, 'Der Sieg der Ṣafaviden in Persien und seine Rückwirkungen auf die Schiiten Anatoliens im 16. Jahrhundert', *Der Islam* 41 (1965), 95–201; C. H. Imber, 'The Persecution of the Ottoman Shīᶜites according to the *mühimme defterleri*, 1565–1585', *Der Islam* 56, no. 2 (July 1979): 245–273; Saim Savaş, *XVI. Asırda Anadolu'da Alevîlik* (Ankara: Vadi Yayınları, 2002).
6. For conventional treatments of the Ottoman–Safavid conflict, see Jean-Louis Bacqué-Grammont, *Les Ottomans, les Safavides et leurs voisins (1514–1524)* (Istanbul: Nederlands Historisch-Archaeologisch Instituut, 1987); Adel Allouche, *The Origins and Development of the Ottoman–Safavid Conflict (906–962/1500–1555)* (Berlin: Klaus Schwarz Verlag, 1983); and M. C. Şehabettin Tekindağ, 'Yeni Kaynak ve Vesikaların Işığı altında Yavuz Sultan Selim'in İran Seferi', *Tarih Dergisi* 17, no. 22 (1967): 49–86.
7. On the decline and disappearance of the Kizilbash milieu in Safavid Iran, see Rula Jurdi Abisaab, *Converting Persia: Religion and Power in the Safavid*

Empire (London: I. B. Tauris, 2004); Kathryn Babayan, *Mystics, Monarchs, and Messiahs: Cultural Landscapes of Early Modern Iran* (Cambridge, MA: Harvard University Press, 2002); Said Amir Arjomand, *The Shadow of God and the Hidden Imam: Religion, Political Order, and Societal Change in Shiᶜite Iran from the Beginning to 1890* (Chicago: The University of Chicago Press, 1984), Chapter 4; and Jean Aubin, 'La Politique religieuse des Safavides', in *Le Shiᶜisme Imamite, Colloque de Strasbourg, 6–9 mai 1968*, ed. T. Fahd (Paris: Presses Universitaires, 1970), 235–244.

8. There are no official statistics regarding the size of the Alevi community in Turkey. Within the wide scope of estimates, 15 per cent of the total population appears to be the most reasonable and common estimate. This figure is corroborated by a relatively recent report on this issue prepared at the direction of Sabahat Akkiraz, member of the Turkish Parliament from 2011 to 2014; the report estimates a decline in the Alevi population from 30 to about 15 per cent since the founding of the Republic in 1923. For the full report, see Hasan Akkiraz, 'Sabahat Akkiraz'ın Hazırlattığı Alevi Raporu', *Alevi Enstitüsü* [blog], 12/19/2012, http://alevienstitusu.blogspot.com/2012/12/sabahat-akkirazn-hazrlattg-alevi-raporu.html.
9. For the use of the term 'Turkish folk Islam' (*Türk halk Müslümanlığı*), see Ahmet Yaşar Ocak, *Türk Sufîliğine Bakışlar*, 5th edn (Istanbul: İletişim Yayınları, 2002), 74 and passim. Fuad Köprülü, whom Ocak cites frequently as the predecessor of his own scholarship, similarly proposes 'folk Sufism' (*halk tasavvufu*) as the proper framework within which to study the Kizilbash and the kindred Bektashi Sufi order; see Fuad Köprülü, 'Introduction', in *Türk Edebiyatında İlk Mutasavvıflar* (1919; reprint, Ankara: Türk Tarih Kurumu, 1993), 1–7. Emblematic cases for this approach also include Irène Mélikoff, 'Le problème ḳızılbaş,' *Turcica* 6 (1975): 49–67, which is still one the most frequently cited works on Kizilbash religion in international scholarship. For details and further literature, see the discussion of the Köprülü paradigm below.
10. For the conceptualisation of Kizilbashism as a latter-day *Ghulāt* movement, see, for instance, Mazzaoui, *Origins of the Ṣafawids*; Arjomand, *Shadow of God,* esp. Chapter 2; Babayan, *Mystics, Monarchs, and Messiahs*, esp. the Preface; and, more recently, William F. Tucker, 'The Kūfan Ghulāt and Millenarian (Mahdist) Movements in Mongol-Türkmen Iran', in *Unity in Diversity: Mysticism, Messianism and the Construction of Religious Authority in Islam*, ed. Orkhan Mir-Kasimov (Leiden: Brill, 2014), 191–192. On *Ghulāt*, see Wadad al-Qadi, 'The Development of the Term *Ghulāt* in Muslim Literature with Special Reference to Kaysāniyya', in *Akten des VII. Kongresses für Arabistik und Islamwissenschaft Göttingen*, ed. Albert Dietrich (Göttingen: Vandenhoeck & Ruprect, 1976), 295–319; Marshall G. S. Hodgson, 'How Did the Early Shi'a Become Sectarian?', *Journal of the American Oriental Society* 75, no. 1 (January–March 1955), 8; and Mushegh Asatryan, *Controversies in Formative Shiᶜi Islam: The Ghulat Muslims and*

Their Beliefs (London and New York: I. B. Tauris, 2017). Some Muslim heresiographers since medieval times have conventionally located the original source of *Ghulāt* in a plot masterminded by an insincere convert aiming to subvert Islam from within by infusing religion with corruptive innovations (*bid*ᶜ*a*); see Abbas Barzegar, 'The Persistence of Heresy: Paul of Tarsus, Ibn Saba', and Historical Narrative in Sunni Identity Formation', *Numen* 58 (2011): 207–231; and Sean W. Anthony, *The Caliph and the Heretic: Ibn Saba and the Origin of Shiism* (Leiden and Boston: Brill, 2011).

11. An important partial exception is Babayan's *Mystics, Monarchs, and Messiahs*, which treats the Kizilbash milieu in Safavid Iran. However, Babayan's thematic focus is the waning of Kizilbashism as a mode of piety and a collective identity as befitting the Iranian context. The present work, in contrast, concerns itself with the formation and resilience of Kizilbash identity in Ottoman Anatolia.
12. On the Alevi Revival, see Krisztina Kehl-Bodrogi, 'Die 'Wiederfindung' des Alevitums in der Türkei: Geschichtsmythos und kollektive Identität', *Orient* 34, no. 2 (1993): 267–281; Reha Çamuroğlu, 'Alevi Revivalism in Turkey', in *Alevi Identity: Cultural, Religious and Social Perspectives,* ed. T. Olsson, et al. (Istanbul: Isis Press, 1998), 79–84; Şehriban Şahin, 'The Rise of Alevism as a Public Religion', *Current Sociology* 53, no. 3 (May 2005): 465–485; Burak Gümüş, *Die Wiederkehr des Alevitentums in der Türkei und in Deutschland* (Konstanz: Hartung-Gorre Verlag, 2007).
13. This initial flurry included, for example, Cemal Şener, *Alevilik Olayı: Bir Başkaldırının Kısa Tarihçesi* (Istanbul: Yön Yayıncılık, 1989); Fuat Bozkurt, *Aleviliğin Toplumsal Boyutları* (Istanbul: Yön Yayıncılık, 1990); Rıza Zelyut, *Öz Kaynaklarına Göre Alevilik* (Istanbul: Anadolu Kültürü Yayınları, 1990); Lütfü Kaleli, *Kimliğini Haykıran Alevilik: Araştırma, Derleme* (Istanbul: Habora Kitabevi, 1990); Nejat Birdoğan, *Anadolu'nun Gizli Kültürü: Alevilik* (Hamburg: Hamburg Alevi Kültür Merkezi, 1990).
14. Alevis' metaphorical approach to religious formalities is reflected nicely in the following excerpt from a poem by the Bektashi poet Rıza Tevfik, which is popularly performed by Alevi musicians:

> Gel derviş, beri gel, yabâna gitme,
> Her ne arıyorsan, inan, sendedir.
> Nefsine bîhûde eziyyet etme,
> Kaʾbeyse maksûdun, Rahman sendedir!.
>
> Çöllerde dolaşıp serâba bakma!..
> Allah Allah!.. deyip sehâba bakma!..
> Tâlib i hak isen kitâba bakma!.
> Okumak bilirsen Kurʾan sendedir!..

(Come, O Dervish, come, don't go afar/Whatever you seek, believe it is in you/Do not torture your soul [*nefs*] in vain/If what you aim for is the Kaᶜba, the All Compassionate is in you.
Do not wander in the desert looking at mirages/Do not look into the air saying

'Allah, Allah'/If you are a seeker of the Truth, do not look for a book/If you know how to read, the Qur᾽an is in you.)
For the full poem, see Rıza Tevfik Bölükbaşı, *Serab ı Ömrüm ve Diğer Şiirleri* (Istanbul: Kenan Matbaası, 1949), 274–275.

15. Alevis have faced charges of sexual immorality by hostile outsiders because of their gender-mixed communal rituals; Imre Adorján, ''Mum Söndürme' İftirasının Kökeni ve Tarihsel Süreçte Gelişimiyle İlgili Bir Değerlendirme', in *Alevilik*, eds İsmail Engin and Havva Engin (İstanbul: Kitap Yayınevi, 2004), 123–136. Such accusations, including regarding the practice of orgies, are among the stock and most crude strategies of othering employed especially against religious minorities. For examples in different historical and religious contexts, see R. M. Grant, 'Charges of Immorality against Religious Groups in Antiquity', in *Studies in Gnosticism and Hellenistic Religions: Studies Presented to Gilles Quispel on the Occasion of his 65th Birthday*, eds R. van den Broek and M. J. Vermaseren (Leiden: Brill, 1997), 161–170; and Richard Shek, 'The Alternative Moral Universe of Religious Dissenters in Ming-Qing China', in *Religion and the Early Modern State: Views from China, Russia, and the West*, eds James D. Tracy and Marguerite Ragnow, reissue edn (Cambridge: Cambridge University Press, 2010), 13–51, esp. 41.
16. The complicated notion of *devir* refers to 'the cycle of existence passing out from the Divine Reality down through the arc of Descent and then back to the godhead in the form of Perfect Man'. John K. Birge, *The Bektashi Order of Dervishes* (1937; reprint, London: Luzac Oriental, 1994), 260. For details and samples of poetry based on this notion, known as *devriye*, see Abdülbâkî Gölpınarlı, *Alevî Bektaşî Nefesleri* (Istanbul: İnkılâp Kitabevi, 1992), 70–82. For a brief discussion of the difference between reincarnation (Ar. *tanāsukh*) and *devir*, see Mustafa Aşkar, 'Reenkarnasyon (Tenasüh) Meselesi ve Mutasavvıfların Bu Konuya Bakışlarının Değerlendirilmesi', *Tasavvuf* 1, no. 3 (April 2000): 85–100, see esp. 99–100.
17. Alevi religious ideas are best reflected in Alevi mystical poetry, the recitation of which to the accompaniment of music played on the *bağlama*, called 'the stringed Qur᾽an' (T. *telli Kuran*) in Alevi parlance, forms a core component of Alevi ritual practices and spiritual experience as well as the transmission of the Alevi tradition. Some of the most important published collections of Alevi-Bektaşi mystical poetry include Gölpınarlı, *Alevî Bektaşî Nefesleri*; İbrahim Arslanoğlu, *Şah İsmail Hatayî ve Anadolu Hatayîleri* (Istanbul: Der Yayınları, 1992); Turgut Koca, ed. *Bektaşi Alevi Şairleri ve Nefesleri* (Istanbul: Maarif Kitaphanesi, 1990); Sadeddin Nüzhet Ergun, *Bektaşi Edebiyatı Antolojisi: Bektaşi Şairleri ve Nefesleri* (Istanbul: Maarif Kitaphanesi, 1944); and Abdülbâkî Gölpınarlı and Pertev Nailî Boratav, *Pir Sultan Abdal* (Ankara: Türk Tarih Kurumu, 1943). Also important are books by members of Alevi *ocak*s; see, for example, Halil Öztoprak, *Kur᾽an'da Hikmet Tarihte Hakikat ve Kur᾽an'da Hikmet İncil'de Hakikat* (1956; reprint, Istanbul: Demos Yayınları, 2012); Başköylü Hasan Efendi, *Varlığın Doğuşu,*

ed. Pirsultan Özcan (Istanbul: Anadolu Matbaası, 1992); Mehmet Yaman, *Alevîlik: İnanç–Edeb–Erkân* (1994; reprint, Istanbul: Demos Yayınları, 2012). A useful work on the Alevi religious tradition in English based on ethnographic research is David Shankland, *The Alevis in Turkey: The Emergence of a Secular Islamic Tradition* (London and New York: Routledge Curzon, 2003). For representative samples of Alevi poetry in English translation, see Koerbin, '"I am Pir Sultan Abdal"'.

18. Markus Dressler, following Irène Mélikoff, notes that the use of the term 'Alevi' in the sense of followers of Ali to designate a specific ethnoreligious community does not reach back any further than the late nineteenth century. This observation is, however, based largely on Ottoman sources and accounts by Western missionaries and travellers and is, thus, more reflective of a shift in the external ascriptions of outsiders rather than on insiders' own self-designation. Moreover, even though its solidification as a standard label indeed seems to be of relatively recent origins, it is not entirely accurate that the term 'Alevi' did not exist as a group name before the nineteenth century. Dressler himself notes occasional instances in pre-nineteenth century sources, including Alevi poetry, where 'Alevi' was employed in connection to the Kizilbash and the affiliates of the kindred Bektashi Sufi order, but dismisses them as exceptional; see Markus Dressler, *Writing Religion: The Making of Turkish Alevi Islam* (New York: Oxford University Press, 2013), 1–2. For further examples, see Sadullah Gültekin, 'Osmanlı Devleti'nde Alevî Sözcüğünün Kullanımına Dair Bazı Değerlendirmeler', *Alevilik Araştırmaları Dergisi*, 6, no. 11 (2016): 27–41. We may add to these one Safavi *ḫilāfetnāme* from the late seventeenth century found among Alevi documents where reference is made to the '*millet-i beyżā*ʾ*-i* ʿ*Alevī*' ('The pure Alevi nation/community'), see my *Vefailik, Bektaşilik, Kızılbaşlık: Alevi Kaynaklarını, Tarihini ve Tarihyazımını Yeniden Düşünmek* (Istanbul: Bilgi University Press, 2015), 87. While admittedly limited in number, these examples nonetheless suggest as a possibility the use of the term 'Alevi' – along with other, more generic ones such as '*mü*ʾ*min*' (believer), '*ehl-i hakk/ hakīkāt*' ('People of God/Truth'), and '*yol ehli*' (people of the Path) that are encountered in Alevi sources – as a self-attribute by the Kizilbash communities already before the nineteenth century, although Ottoman official discourse might have shunned the application of this honorable label to a group charged with religious deviance.

19. Shah Ismaʿil, whose poems written under the pen name Hataʾi (T. Hatayi) are consistently recited in Alevi communal rituals, articulates this belief as follows:

   Hak[k] Muhammed Ali üçü de nurdur
   Birini almasan üçü de birdir

   (God/Truth, Muhammad and ʿAli, all there are (divine) light/(Even) if you don't count one, all three are united/the same)
   For the full poem, see Arslanoğlu, *Şah İsmail Hatayî*, 353–354.

20. The Alevi narrative of the *miraç* is very different and much more elaborate and embellished than its more mainstream versions; for a detailed exposition, see *ABS*, s.v. 'miraç'. There is a particular genre in Alevi-Bektashi poetry, known as *miraçlama* or *miraçname*, thematising the Prophet's *miraç* and his encounter with ᶜAli and the Forty Saints in the heavens; see *ABS*, s.v. 'miraçlama'. For examples of *miraçlama*, see Arslanoğlu, *Şah İsmail Hatayî*, 372–374; and Ergun, *Bektaşi Edebiyatı Antolojisi*, 172–173.
21. *ABS*, s.v. 'Dâr'. Also see Thierry Zarcone, 'La mort initiatique dans l'alévisme et le Bektachisme: de la 'résurrection' de 'Alī à la pendaison de Ḥallāj', in *L'Ésotérisme Shiᶜite, ses racines et ses prolongements*, eds M. A. Amir-Moezzi, et al. (Turnhout: Brepols Publishers, 2016), 781–798.
22. In the conventional literature, these groups are often described with predisposed terms, such as 'heterodox', 'syncretistic', and 'extremist Shiᶜis', the last being a problematic translation of the heresiographical concept of *Ghulāt*; see, for example, Matti Moosa, *Extremist Shiites: The Ghulat Sects* (Syracuse: Syracuse University Press, 1988); and Krisztina Kehl-Bodrogi, Barbara Kellner Heinkele, and Anke Otter-Beaujean, eds, *Syncretistic Religious Communities in the Near East: Collected Papers of the International Symposium 'Alevism in Turkey and Comparable Syncretistic Religious Communities in the Near East in the Past and Present', Berlin, 14–17 April 1995* (Leiden and New York: Brill, 1997).
23. My use of the term 'movement' in connection to the early Kizilbash does not imply a coherent group with homogeneous ideas, orientations, and actions. Rather, I use it in the sense of a 'network of informal interactions between a plurality of groups, individuals and organisations', who are drawn together by common interests, commitments, and goals; see Mario Diani, 'The Concept of Social Movement', *The Sociological Review* 40, no. 1 (1992): 1–25, 8; see also Tim Jordan, 'The Unity of Social Movement', *The Sociological Review* 43, no. 4 (1995): 675–692.
24. Köprülü's ideas concerning the origins of the Alevi-Bektashi communities are scattered throughout his various works; for a summary of them, see Doğan Kaplan, 'Fuad Köprülü'ye Göre Anadolu Aleviliği', *Marife*, no. 2 (Autumn 2003): 143–163. See also Ahmet Yaşar Ocak, 'Babaîler İsyanından Kızılbaşlığa: Anadolu'da İslâm Heterodoksisinin Doğuş ve Gelişim Tarihine Kısa Bir Bakış', *Belleten* LXIV, no. 239 (April 2000): 129–159. The fact that a couple of Köprülü's books were translated into English in the 1990s and 2000s is also testimony to his continuing relevance in international scholarship; for full references see n25.
25. Köprülü's most important and relevant works include *Türk Edebiyatında İlk Mutasavvıflar*, trans. into English by Gary Leiser and Robert Dankoff under the title *Early Mystics in Turkish Literature* with an insightful critical foreword by Devin DeWeese (London: Routledge, 2006); *Anadolu'da İslâmiyet* (1922; reprint, Istanbul: İnsan Yayınları, 1996), trans. into English by Gary Leiser under the title *Islam in Anatolia after the Turkish Invasion*

(Prolegomena) (Salt Lake City: University of Utah Press, 1993); and *Osmanlı Devleti'nin Kuruluşu* (1959; reprint, Ankara: Türk Tarih Kurmu, 1991).

26. Unlike Köprülü, who attributes only a secondary importance to such 'heterodox' Shi^ci movements in the formation of Kizilbashism, historians of Iran and Shi^cism typically consider Kizilbashism to be essentially and primarily a *Ghulāt* sect without, however, rejecting its Turkmen social base and various shamanic influences, as envisioned by Köprülü; for references, see n10 above.
27. Köprülü's understanding of the Turkmen *baba*s is essentially the same as Ernest Gellner's notion of 'tribal holy men' whose connection with mysticism is 'minimal', and who, as such, ought to be separated from 'genuine mystics'; see Ernest Gellner, 'Doctor and Saint,' in *Islam in Tribal Societies: From the Atlas to the Indus*, eds Akbar S. Ahmed and David M. Hart (London and Boston and Melbourne and Henley: Routledge & Kegan Paul, 1984), 21–38, esp. 22.
28. Köprülü's first major work, in which he established a direct connection between Central Asian and Anatolian literary and religious traditions was *Türk Edebiyatında İlk Mutasavvıflar.* In this book, Köprülü questioned the historicity of Bektashi claims to Yesevi ancestry, but later he changed his opinion, treating the Bektashiyye as the primary heir of the Yesevi legacy in Anatolia; see *MIA*, s.v. 'Aḥmed Yesevî' by Köprülü. For his views on shamanic influences on the formation of Yesevi and Bektashi communities, also see 'Bektaşîliğin Menşeleri: Küçük Asya'da İslâm Batınîliğinin Tekâmül-i Tarihîsi Hakkında Bir Tecrübe', *Türk Yurdu* (1341/1925): 121–140; and *Influence du chamanisme Turco-Mongol sur les ordres mystiques musulmans* (Istanbul: Imp. Zellitch frères, 1929).
29. See especially the introductions to Ahmet T. Karamustafa, *God's Unruly Friends: Dervish Groups in the Islamic Later Middle Period 1200–1550* (Salt Lake City: University of Utah Press, 1994) and Devin DeWeese, *Islamization and Native Religion in the Golden Horde: Baba Tükles and Conversion to Islam in Historical and Epic Tradition* (Pennsylvania: Pennsylvania State University Press, 1994); and DeWeese's foreword to Leiser and Dankoff, *Early Mystics in Turkish Literature.* For similar critical observations from the perspective of architectural history, see Ethel Sara Wolper, *Cities and Saints: Sufism and the Transformation of Urban Space in Medieval Anatolia* (University Park: Pennsylvania State University Press, 2003), 4–7.
30. Cemal Kafadar, *Between Two Worlds: The Construction of the Ottoman State* (Berkeley and Los Angeles: University of California Press, 1995), see esp. 76. The term 'confessional ambiguity', which Kafadar does not use, was first coined by John E. Woods to describe the religious outlook of the Turco-Iranian world during the post-Mongol period, *The Aqquyunlu: Clan, Federation, Empire*, 2nd edn (Salt Lake City: The University of Chicago Press, 1999), 1. Kafadar instead coins and uses the term 'metadoxy', which

he defines as 'a state of being beyond doxies, a combination of being doxy-naïve and not being doxy-minded, as well as the absence of a state that was interested in rigorously defining and strictly enforcing an orthodoxy'. In this work, I use both concepts interchangeably.

31. Dressler, *Writing Religion*, esp. Part Two.
32. American Protestant missionaries, whose initial encounters with Kizilbash communities occurred in the mid-1800s in eastern Anatolia, were the first to make such claims, portraying the Kizilbash religion as a syncretistic composite of Christian and pagan elements overlaid with an Islamic veneer. Their ideas would later be taken up by Western travellers and scholars who further elaborated on the missionaries' notions, conflating along the way the question of religious origins with that of the Kizilbash's racial origins. In response to such speculations, a group from within the early Turkish nationalist milieu embarked on the creation of an alternative account of Kizilbash origins that asserted the pure Turkish descent of the communities in question, and posited certain Kizilbash/Alevi beliefs and ritual practices, which Western writers variously connected to Christianity or to pagan traditions of Anatolia, to be vestiges of ancient Turkish religions rooted in Central Asia, specifically shamanism. In many ways, the Köprülü paradigm was the most sophisticated and influential expression of this Central Asia thesis. For details, see my 'The Emergence of the Kızılbaş in Western Thought: Missionary Accounts and their Aftermath', in *Archaeology, Anthropology and Heritage in the Balkans and Anatolia: The Life and Times of F. W. Hasluck, 1878–1920*, 2 vols., ed. David Shankland (Istanbul: Isis Press, 2004), 1: 329–353.
33. Ahmet Karamustafa, 'Yesevîlik, Melâmetîlik, Ḳalenderîlik, Vefâʾîlik ve Anadolu Tasavvufunun Kökenleri Sorunu', in *Osmanlı Toplumunda Tasavvuf ve Sufiler: Kaynaklar–Doktrin–Ayin ve Erkan–Tarikatlar–Edebiyat–Mimari–İkonografi–Modernizm*, ed. Ahmed Yaşar Ocak (Ankara: Türk Tarih Kurumu, 2005), 70. Also see Devin DeWeese, 'The Yasavī Order and Persian Hagiography in Seventeenth-Century Central Asia: ᶜĀlim Shaykh of ᶜAlīyābād and His *Lamaḥāt min Nafaḥāt al-Quds*', in *Heritage of Sufism-3*, 390.
34. Köprülü, *Türk Edebiyatında İlk Mutasavvıflar*, 206 n34.
35. For the empirical unsustainability of 'generalizations about nomad religion and ideology' and hypotheses 'based only on ideas of syncretism or on ecological or cultural variables alone', see Richard Tapper, 'Holier Than Thou: Islam in Three Tribal Societies', in *Islam in Tribal Societies: From the Atlas to the Indus*, eds Akbar S. Ahmed and David M. Hart (London and Boston and Melbourne and Henley: Routledge & Kegan Paul, 1984), 244–251.
36. Of Mélikoff's numerous articles related to the subject, see, for example, 'Le problème ḳızılbaş' and 'Recherches sur les composantes du syncrétisme Bektachi-Alevi', in *Studia Turcologica Memoriae Alexii Bombaci dicata* (Napoli: Instituto Universitario Orientale, 1982): 379–395. For her most recent summation of her findings and arguments, see *Hadji Bektach: un*

mythe et ses avatars: Genèse et évolution du soufisme populaire en Turquie (Leiden: Brill, 1998), published in the same year in Turkish as *Hacı Bektaş: Efsaneden Gerçeğe*, trans. Turan Alptekin (Istanbul: Cumhuriyet Kitapları, 1998). For an insightful critical review, see Hamid Algar, 'Review of Hadji Bektach: un mythe et ses avatars. Genèse et évolution du soufisme populaire en Turquie, by Irène Mélikoff', *International Journal of Middle East Studies* 36, no. 4 (November 2004): 687–689.

37. See, most importantly, his *Bektaşî Menâkıbnâmelerinde İslam Öncesi İnanç Motifleri* (Istanbul: Enderun Kitabevi, 1983); *Babaîler İsyanı: Alevîliğin Tarihsel Altyapısı Yahut Anadolu'da İslâm-Türk Heterodoksisinin Teşekkülü*, revised 2nd edn (Istanbul: Dergâh Yayınları, 1996); *Osmanlı İmparatorluğunda Marjinal Sûfilik: Kalenderîler: XIV–XVII. Yüzyıllar* (Ankara: Türk Tarih Kurumu, 1992); and his collection of essays, *Türk Sufîliğine Bakışlar* (Istanbul: İletişim Yayınları, 1996).
38. The publication in Turkish in 1993 of Mélikoff's collected articles on Alevi-Bektashi religion and communities played a particularly crucial role in bringing about a wide circulation of the idea of Alevism as Islamised shamanism within Turkey; Irène Mélikoff, *Uyur İdik Uyardılar: Alevîlik-Bektaşîlik Araştırmaları*, trans. Turan Alptekin (Istanbul: Cem Yayınevi, 1993).
39. See, for example, Rıza Zelyut, *Türk Aleviliği: Anadolu Aleviliğinin Kültürel Kökeni* (Ankara: Kripto Yayınları, 2009); Cemal Şener, *Aleviler'in Etnik Kimliği* (Istanbul: Etik Yayınları, 2010); İsmail Engin, *Tahtacılar: Tahtacıların Kimliğine ve Demografisine Giriş* (Istanbul: Ant Yayınları, 1998).
40. For a brief overview of competing discourses on Alevism following the Alevi cultural revival, see Karin Vorhoff, 'The Past in the Future: Discourses on the Alevis in Contemporary Turkey', in *Turkey's Alevi Enigma: A Comprehensive Overview*, eds Paul J. White and Joost Jongerden (Leiden: Brill, 2003), 93–108. For a more recent critical discussion of contemporary Alevi identity politics within the broader context of Turkish state's politics of diversity, see Kabir Tambar, *The Reckoning of Pluralism: Political Belonging and the Demands of History in Turkey* (Stanford: Stanford University Press, 2014).
41. For the historical background to the term 'syncretism' and its pitfalls and potentials as a conceptual tool, see the selection of articles in *Syncretism in Religion: A Reader*, eds Anita Maria Leopold and Jeppe Sinding Jensen (New York: Routledge, 2004); and the introduction to *Syncretism/Anti-Syncretism: The Politics of Religious Synthesis*, eds Rosalind Shaw and Charles Stewart (London: Routledge, 1994). Eric Maroney, *Religious Syncretism* (London: SCM Press, 2006) also includes good examples of the application of the term in specific historical contexts.
42. For typical examples of such counter-narratives, see Cemşid Bender, *Kürt Uygarlığında Alevilik* (Istanbul: Kaynak Yayınları, 1991); Faik Bulut, *Ali'siz Alevilik* (Ankara: Berfin Yayınları, 2007); Hüseyin Çakmak, *Dersim*

Aleviliği: Raa Haqi: Dualar, Gülbengler, Ritüeller (Ankara: Kalan Yayınları, 2013); Erdoğan Çınar, *Aleviliğin Gizli Tarihi: Demirin Üstünde Karınca İzleri* (Istanbul: Kalkedon Yayınları, 2007).

43. For example, a more discriminating and nuanced treatment of the question of shamanic influences in the Alevi ritual dance of *semah* is offered by Thierry Zarcone, 'The Bektashi-Alevi "Dance of the Crane" in Turkey: A Shamanic Heritage?' in *Shamanism and Islam: Sufism, Healing Rituals and Spirits in the Muslim World* (London and New York: I. B. Tauris, 2017), 203–216.
44. Maroney, *Religious Syncretism*, xii.
45. No sense of a timeless or unchanging set of beliefs or structures is implied with the term 'traditional'. I use it simply as a heuristic device to refer to Alevism as it was experienced in the village setting before large-scale urbanisation of the communities in question since the mid-twentieth century. Accounts of 'traditional Alevism' as such are based primarily on oral and written reports from contemporary Alevis and in-field observations.
46. *Ocak*, lit. 'hearth', is a metaphor for the home or household in many different cultures, but in the Alevi parlance it specifically refers to a group of saintly lineages whose members, the *ocakzade*s, serve as the religious leaders of their respective disciple communities; see *TS*, s.v. 'Ocak–Ocak-zade'. Needless to say, the use of lineage as a device for organising is not confined to Alevi communities, but is found in various traditions within and without the Islamic context. The Ahl-i Haqq of Iran and the kindred Kakaʾis of Iraq, both of which are religious communities in many ways akin to the Alevis, are similarly organised around a number of charismatic family lines known as *ujāq*s: W. Ivanow, *The Truth-Worshippers of Kurdistan: Ahl-i Haqq Texts*, The Ismaili Society Series A no. 7 (Leiden: Brill, 1953), see esp. the introduction; and C. J. Edmonds, *Kurds, Turks, and Arabs* (London and New York: Oxford University Press, 1957), 182–196. Another example of a similar pattern of communal organisation is found among the Turkmen in Central Asia: V. N. Basilov, 'Honour Groups in Traditional Turkmenian Society', in *Islam in Tribal Societies: From the Atlas to the Indus*, eds Akbar S. Ahmed and David M. Hart (London: Routledge & Kegan Paul, 1984), 220–243. For an enlightening discussion of the symbolism of 'hearth' in Central Asian religious customs, see DeWeese, *Islamization and Native Religion*, 39–50. For an example of the same notion outside of the Islamic context, see Elizabeth Morrison, *The Power of Patriarchs: Qisong and Lineage in Chinese Buddhism* (Leiden and Boston: Brill, 2010).
47. For a list of about two hundred Alevi *ocak*s that have survived to the present, see Ali Yaman, *Kızılbas Alevi Ocakları* (Istanbul: Elips Yayınları, 2006).
48. On *musahiblik*, see Krisztina Kehl-Bodrogi, 'On the Significance of Musahiplik among the Alevis of Turkey: The Case of the Tahtacı', in *Syncretistic Religious Communities in the Near East*, 119–137.
49. Virtually all the components and terminology of the *ocak* organisation, and rituals associated with it, are encountered in the poetry of Shah Ismaʿil/

Hata'i, suggesting that the basic features of it were already in existence or in the process of forming at the time of his writing, that is by the early sixteenth century: see, for example, Arslanoğlu, *Şah İsmail Hatayî*, 353–354, 379, 380; for other, near-contemporaneous Kizilbash/Alevi poets treating similar themes, see Gölpınarı, *Alevî Bektaşî Nefesleri*, 161–170.

50. My discussion of the Alevi sources draws largely on an earlier article of mine, 'Documents and *Buyruk* Manuscripts in the Private Archives of Alevi *Dede* Families: An Overview', *British Journal of Middle Eastern Studies* 37, no. 3 (2010): 273–286.
51. Most of these appeared in non-academic works, and need to be used cautiously; for example, see İsmail Kaygusuz, *Onar Dede Mezarlığı ve Adı Bilinmeyen Bir Türk Kolonizatörü Şeyh Hasan Oner* (Istanbul: Arkeoloji ve Sanat Yayınları, 1983); Mehmet Şimşek, *Hıdır Abdal Sultan Ocağı*, 3rd edn (Istanbul: Can Yayınları, 2004); Nejat Birdoğan, *Anadolu ve Balkanlar'da Alevi Yerleşimleri: Ocaklar-Dedeler-Soy Ağaçları* (Istanbul: Alev Yayınları, 1992); Kureşanlı Seyit Kekil, *Peygamberler ile Seyitlerin Şecereleri ve Aşiretlerin Tarihi* (Köln: Hans und Sigrid Verlag, n.d.). A number of Alevi documents also appeared in various issues of the journal *Hacı Bektaş Velî Araştırma Dergisi* published by Gazi Üniversitesi Türk Kültürü ve Hacı Bektaş Velî Araştırma Merkezi, but these, too, should be used cautiously since they include many reading and translation mistakes; all issues available online at: http://www.hbvdergisi.gazi.edu.tr/index.php/TKHBVD/issue/archive. Also see the following works of mine for selected samples of these documents: 'Sinemilliler: Bir Alevi Ocağı ve Aşireti', *Kırkbudak* 2, no. 6 (Spring 2006): 19–59; 'Kızılbaş, Bektaşi, Safevi İlişkilerine Dair 17. Yüzyıldan Yeni Bir Belge (Yazı Çevirimli Metin-Günümüz Türkçesine Çeviri-Tıpkıbasım)', in *Festschrift in Honor of Orhan Okay*, eds Yücel Dağlı, et al., special issue of the *Journal of Turkish Studies/Türklük Bilgisi Araştırmaları* 30, no. II (2006): 117–130; '16. Yüzyıldan Bir Ziyaretname (Yazı Çevirimli Metin-Günümüz Türkçesine Çeviri-Tıpkıbasım)', in *In Memoriam Şinasi Tekin*, special issue of the *Journal of Turkish Studies/Türklük Bilgisi Araştırmaları* 31, no. II (2007): 67–79; and Karakaya-YK, 79–112.
52. Examples include *Buyruk: Alevî İnanç-İbâdet ve Ahlâk İlkeleri*, ed. Mehmet Yaman (Mannheim: Alevî Kültür Merkezi Dedeler Kurulu Yayınları, 2000); Bisâtî, *Şeyh Sâfî Buyruğu*, ed. Ahmet Taşğın (Rheda-Wiedenbrück: Alevi Kültür Derneği Yayınları, 2003); and Doğan Kaplan, *Şeyh Safi Buyruğu* (Ankara: Diyanet Vakfı Yayınları, 2015). For references to further literature, see 'Introductıon' to Doğan Kaplan, 'Buyruklara Göre Kızılbaşlık', (PhD diss., Selçuk Üniversitesi, Konya, 2008); and my 'Alevi Dede Ailelerine Ait *Buyruk* Mecmuaları', in *Eski Türk Edebiyatı Çalışmaları VII: Mecmûa: Osmanlı Edebiyatının Kırkambar*, eds Hatice Aynur et al. (Istanbul: Turkuaz Yayınları, 2012), 361–379.
53. Ahmet Yaşar Ocak falsely assumes that the written *sayyid* genealogies found in *dedes*' private archives were issued by the Safavids; see Ocak, 'Babaîler

İsyanından Kızılbaşlığa', 150. Earlier in the same article, he makes the contradictory claim that most of these documents were granted by the Ottoman state, and asserts that none of them go back any further than the eighteenth century, ibid., 132. Both of these claims, for which Ocak does not provide any concrete support, are clearly inaccurate.

54. 'But they [the Kizilbash] have a large book, called the Bouyouruk.' 'Letter from Mr. Dunmore, January 22, 1857', *Missionary Herald* 53 (1857): 220. Dunmore was an American Protestant missionary who was engaged in proselytising efforts among the Kizilbash in the Dersim region; see my 'Emergence of the Kızılbaş'.
55. *Buyruk*, ed. Sefer Aytekin (Ankara: Emek Basım-Yayınevi, 1958). Aytekin, however, refrained from commenting on the *Buyruk*'s place in Alevi culture, describing it in the brief introduction simply as a book about 'our peoples' beliefs and traditions'. Ibid., 3. Four years earlier than Aytekin's, another *Buyruk* manuscript appeared in print in Iraq, Ahmad Hamid al-Sarraf, *al-Shabak* (Baghdad: Maṭbaᶜat al-Maᶜārif, 1954). The manuscript for this came from among the kindred Shabak communities in northern Iraq.
56. For examples, see n52 above.
57. For *cönk*s, see M. Sabri Koz, 'Cönk ve Mecmûa Yapraklarında Âşık Aramak', in *Eski Türk Edebiyatı Çalışmaları VII: Mecmûa: Osmanlı Edebiyatının Kırkambar*, eds Hatice Aynur et al. (Istanbul: Turkuaz Yayınları, 2012), 157–200. For more bibliography, see Meltem Yılmaz, 'Türkiye'de Cönkler Üzerine Yapılan Çalışmalara Dair', *Tullis Journal* 1, no. 1 (June 2016): 37–53.
58. Abdülbâkî Gölpınarlı, *Yunus Emre: Hayatı* (Istanbul: Bozkurt Basımevi, 1936). There is little doubt that political concerns also loomed large behind Gölpınarlı's and others' failure to pursue this lead, as manifested among other things by Gölpınarlı's unpersuasive efforts in the same book to disprove Abu'l-Wafaᵓ's Kurdishness (to be discussed in Chapter 1) and to depict the environs of Baghdad as being inhabited mainly by the Turkmen tribe of Bayat during the lifetime of the saint, and thereby to understate as much as possible the extent of Abu'l-Wafaᵓ's Kurdish following; see Gölpınarlı, *Yunus Emre: Hayatı*, 58. Tellingly, in his later work on Yunus Emre, first published in 1961, Gölpınarlı seems to dwell less on Abu'l-Wafaᵓ's Kurdish background, *Yunus Emre ve Tasavvuf*. 2nd edn (Istanbul: İnkılâp Kitabevi, 1992), 46–49. A similar sense of unease concerning the Kurdish background of Abu'l-Wafaᵓ is discernable in the work of Ahmet Yaşar Ocak who, with little convincing evidence, posits that there is a stronger possibility of Abu'l-Wafaᵓ being of Turkmen stock rather than Kurdish, *DIA*, s.v. 'Ebü'l-Vefâ' Tâcü'l-ârifîn Seyyid Muhammed b. Muhammed Arîz el-Bağdâdî'.
59. Ahmet T. Karamustafa, 'Early Sufism in Eastern Anatolia', in *Heritage of Sufism-1*, 175–198.
60. Yaşar Ocak had already noted the presence of Wafaᵓi affiliates in medieval Anatolia in some of his earlier works; see, for example, MNK-Elvan

Çelebi-1995, XXVI–XXVII, XL–XLIII. He later indicated a major shift in his thinking towards attributing a greater role to the Wafaᵓiyya in Anatolian religious history in an article published in English in 2005: 'The Wafa'î tariqa (Wafâiyya) during and after the Period of the Seljuks of Turkey: A New Approach to the History of Popular Mysticism in Turkey', *Mésogeios* 25–26 (2005): 209–248. However, in another book published in Turkish six years later, where he treated Dede Kargın and Emîrci Sultan as respective representatives of the Wafaᵓiyya and Yeseviyye in late-medieval Anatolia, Ocak insisted that the Wafaᵓi connection in the origins of Kizilbashism/Alevism as demonstrated by the *ocak* of Dede Kargın does not render invalid Köprülü's basic narrative and, more specifically, his assumption concerning the place of the Yesevi order in the making of popular Islam in Anatolia. *Garkın-Ocak*, Introduction. However, the evidential basis of Ocak's claim of Emîrci Sultan's Yesevi background appears flimsy. Moreover, while he rightly acknowledges the Wafaᵓi connection of Dede Kargın, he is mistaken in treating him as the primary carrier and disseminator of the Wafaᵓi tradition in Anatolia. As will be shown in Chapter 3, the Wafaᵓiyya seems to have been transported into Anatolia directly from Iraq by successive waves of dervishes from that region, and there is a good chance that Dede Kargın himself came to be associated with the Wafaᵓi order only after his arrival in Anatolia.

61. Vladimir Minorsky, 'Introduction', in *Tadhkirat al-mulūk: A Manual of Ṣafavid Administration* (London: Printed for the Trustees of the 'E. J. W. Gibb Memorial', Pub. by Luzac & Co., 1943), 12–19, 189–195; Faruk Sümer, *Safevi Devletinin Kuruluşu ve Gelişmesinde Anadolu Türklerinin Rolü* (Ankara: Türk Tarih Kurumu, 1992). For a recent articulation of the same perspective, see Rıza Yıldırım, 'Turkomans between Two Empires: The Origins of the Qizilbash Identity in Anatolia (1447–1514),' (PhD diss., Bilkent University, Ankara, 2008), 316–320.
62. The term 'communal Sufi affiliation' was coined by Devin DeWeese, 'Yasavī *Šayḫs* in the Timurid Era: Notes on the Social and Political Role of Communal Sufi Affiliations in the 14th and 15th Centuries', *Oriente Moderno* 76, no. 2 (1996): 173.
63. For a classical articulation of this view, see J. Spencer Trimingham, *The Sufi Orders in Islam* (London: Oxford University Press, 1971), part 3. For a critique of this 'decline model', see the introduction to Nile Green's *Sufism: A Global History* (Chichester and Malden, MA: Wiley-Blackwell, 2012).
64. For Sunni confessionalisation in the Ottoman Empire in its broader Eurasian context, see Tijana Krstić, *Contested Conversions to Islam: Narratives of Religious Change in the Early Modern Ottoman Empire* (Stanford: Stanford University Press, 2011), esp. 12–16; for the centrality of Sufism as a site of contention and negotiation in Sunni confessionalisation, see Derin Terzioğlu, 'Sufis in the Age of State-building and Confessionalization', in *The Ottoman World*, ed. Christine Woodhead (New York: Routledge, 2012),

86–99; Derin Terzioğlu, 'How to Conceptualize Ottoman Sunnitization: A Historiographical Discussion', *Turcica* 44 (2012–2013): 301–338; Derin Terzioğlu, 'Where *ᶜİlm-i Ḥāl* Meets Catechism: Islamic Manuals of Religious Instruction in the Ottoman Empire in the Age of Confessionalization', *Past and Present* 220 (2013): 79–114. Also see Nabil al-Tikriti, 'Kalam in the Service of the State: Apostasy and the Defining of Ottoman Islamic Identity', in *Legitimizing the Order: The Ottoman Rhetoric of State Power*, eds Hakan T. Karateke and Maurus Reinkowski, 131–149 (Leiden: Brill, 2005), 131–149; idem, 'Ibn-i Kemal's Confessionalism and the Construction of an Ottoman Islam', in *Living in the Ottoman Realm: Empire and Identity, 13th to 20th Centuries*, ed. Christine Isom-Verhaaren and Kent F. Schull (Bloomington: Indiana University Press, 2016), 95–107; and Guy Burak, 'Faith, Law and Empire in the Ottoman "Age of Confessionalization" (Fifteenth–Seventeenth Centuries): The Case of "Renewal of Faith"', *Mediterranean Historical Review* 28, no. 1 (2013): 1–23.

1

The Iraq Connection: Abu'l-Wafa' Taj al-ᶜArifin and the Wafa'i Tradition

'Oh shaykh, (tell us) what is Islam?' [said the questioner].
'Whose Islam are you asking about? My Islam or your Islam?' said the shaykh [Abu'l-Wafa'].
'Is your Islam different from my Islam?' said the questioner.
'Yes' said the sayyid [Abu'l-Wafa'].

– Shihab al-Din al-Wasiti, *Menāḳıb-ı Seyyid Ebü'l-Vefā'*[1]

In the mid-eleventh century, a rumour circulated in Baghdad about a Sufi of ᶜAlid descent living in a nearby province. The progeny of the fourth Shiᶜi imam, Zayn al-ᶜAbidin, this shaykh had thousands of followers and, according to the rumour, harboured ambitions for the caliphate. Abbasid caliph al-Qa'im bi-Amrillah (r. 1031–1075) summoned the shaykh, Abu'l-Wafa' (Ot. Ebü'l-Vefa'), to Baghdad for interrogation by forty leading religious scholars who examined him on the meaning of Islam. During the interrogation, the opening of which is partially reproduced in the epigraph above, Abu'l-Wafa' appeared confident as he proceeded to respond to the questions in his accented Arabic. Sitting on a burning hot, iron platform, the shaykh delivered a long and spirited speech contrasting his own esoteric understanding of religion with that of the exoteric jurists who, he contended, were incapable of penetrating the surface of Islam to reach its actual essence. His answers were so elegant that he put to shame the ulema in attendance, who had been quick to dismiss him as ignorant because, having grown up among the Kurds, he spoke broken Arabic. At the end of this trial and several others, all of which he passed with equal success, the caliph was finally convinced of Abu'l-Wafa''s true sanctity and detachment from worldly ambitions, and granted him the income of villages in the vicinity of his dervish convent (Ar. *zāwiya*; Ot. *zāviye*), located in the Qusan district of central Iraq, an offer that Abu'l-Wafa' would, however, decline.[2]

To those members of the present-day Alevi community in Turkey who have some basic acquaintance with Alevi oral traditions, this story of a falsely charged ᶜAlid *sayyid* from the provinces would sound strikingly familiar despite its temporal and spatial distance. Generations of Alevis in Anatolia have recounted similar stories in which cultic figures of the Alevi pantheon endure a series of trials and physical ordeals through which they prove their superior spirituality and deeper understanding of religion to a suspicious ruler, a probing religious rival or a potential convert. Although present-day Alevis lack a direct memory of the protagonist of the above story, one may presume a historical connectedness between the story of Abu'l-Wafa' and its Alevi counterparts, given the many Alevi documents in which Abu'l-Wafa' Taj al-ᶜArifin is frequently named as a familial and/or spiritual progenitor. These Alevi documents – mainly Sufi diplomas (Ar. *ijāza*s; Ot. *icāzetnāme*s) and genealogies (Ar. *shajara*s; Ot. *şecere*s) – contain little information about Abu'l-Wafa' (d. 1107), the eponym of the Iraqi-born Wafa'i Sufi tradition and the related Wafa'i *sayyid*s, beyond his spiritual pedigree and his descent from the family of the Prophet Muhammad.[3] Alevi oral tradition, likewise, seems to have preserved only faint traces of Abu'l-Wafa''s memory, such as the consistently highlighted descent of certain Alevi *mürşid ocak*s from Imam Zayn al-ᶜAbidin, from whom Abu'l-Wafa' allegedly also descended. A brief explanatory note in Turkish that was added in 984/1576 to the end of an older Arabic *ijāza* that was found among the Alevi documents suggests that already in this period the memory of the saint had begun to sink into oblivion among the Wafa'i-cum-Kizilbash *ocak*s. This passage, most likely derived from oral reports, provides an anachronistic account of Abu'l-Wafa''s life, presenting him as a contemporary of the Umayyads whose oppressive policies towards the descendants of the Prophet forced him to leave his native home and take refuge among the Kurds.[4] A version of the story without the Umayyad connection is told in Abu'l-Wafa''s hagiographic vita about his father. Alevi *dede*s traditionally cite the same storyline, stripped of its specific Wafa'i connection, when recounting the initial settlement in Anatolia of ᶜAlid *sayyid*s who are believed to have founded the various Kizilbash/Alevi *ocak*s.

With rare exceptions, one hardly finds any information on Abu'l-Wafa' and his Sufi tradition in the modern histories of Islamic mysticism.[5] The little-known story of the Wafa'iyya begins in eleventh-century Iraq with its eponym, Abu'l-Wafa', who grew up among tribal Kurds in central Iraq where he commanded an ethnically and socially diverse following. His spiritual lineage reaches back to one of the earliest Sufi circles based in Basra and represented an alternative strain within Sufism distinct from that of the norm-setting Baghdadi tradition. Abu'l-Wafaᵓ's spiritual legacy appears to have faded away in its birthplace after several generations, leaving behind few visible imprints. However, various Wafaᵓi offshoots seem to have thrived in Anatolia (as well as Greater Syria, Egypt and Shirvan-Azerbaijan) from no later than the turn of the thirteenth century until about the mid-sixteenth century, evolving in their new home in different religious and political directions and forming, among other things, one of the major building blocks of the Kizilbash milieu across the course of the late fifteenth century and early sixteenth.

Apart from the pertinent Alevi documents, and their archival counterparts indicating a significant Wafaᵓi presence in medieval Anatolia, there are virtually no known literary sources bearing upon Abu'l-Wafaᵓ's life and his Sufi tradition that were produced in the Anatolian context despite the apparently important role of the Wafaᵓiyya in the region's history. Abu'l-Wafaᵓ's hagiographic vita in Turkish (hereafter *Menāḳıb*-Turkish), where the above story is reported, is a partial translation of its two-volume Arabic original (hereafter *Menāḳıb*-Arabic) that was compiled by a certain Shihab al-Din al-Wasiti;[6] the author's *nisba* 'Wāsiṭī' attests to his affiliation to the ancient city of Wasit in central Iraq, one of the focal points of Abu'l-Wafaᵓ's influence during his lifetime.[7] Completed in 777/1376, this work is more than two-and-a-half centuries removed from the lifetime of Abu'l-Wafaᵓ, but apparently the narrative it contains draws on a few earlier compilations, which also explains the multiplicity of versions of some of the stories in it.[8] Although the text includes a significant amount of fictional material, as one would expect of this genre, and presumably reflects to some degree the preferences and 'editing' of later Wafaᵓi tradition in Iraq, it seems to have been built around an authentic historical kernel. This impression stems from the considerable amount of circumstantial details with which some of the stories are presented and specific references to people, places, local conditions and dates that correspond to historical realities of eleventh-century Iraq. Lending further credence to this general impression is the complex religious profile of Abu'l-Wafaᵓ as it emerges from the hagiography, combining a number of seemingly incongruous characteristics. This variegated picture makes sense within this period of transition in the history of Sufism, when officially sanctioned normative Sufism was in the process of being defined but had not yet fully crystallised.

Besides his hagiography, the most extensive information about Abu'l-Wafaᵓ is given in a Sufi biographical dictionary, *Tiryāq al-muḥibbīn*, whose author, Taqi al-Din ᶜAbd al-Rahman al-Wasiti (d. 1343), was likewise from the city of Wasit.[9] Even though Taqi al-Din al-Wasiti's work, dedicated to the Rifaᶜi order, mistakenly claims Abu'l-Wafa' for the broader Rifaᶜi tradition, it does serve to corroborate most details of the saint's biography, while also offering us diverging accounts of certain aspects of his life.[10] Another source of great significance is Murtada al-Zabidi's (d. 1790) *Rafᶜ niqāb*, the author yet again a native of Wasit. Zabidi's work is different from the first two in that it postdates them by more than four centuries and is based on a study of a large number of written genealogies that the author reportedly acquired in Egypt, Jerusalem, Aleppo and other regions in Greater Syria. Zabidi is the main source (aside from the Alevi documents and those located in the Ottoman archives) that provides written documentation of the geographical diffusion of Abu'l-Wafa''s memory and progeny (via his nephews) outside of Iraq.[11] A final source worth mentioning here is the massive encyclopaedic work on Sufi orders by Haririzade Mehmed Kemaleddin, a nineteenth-century Ottoman Sufi writer. Haririzade treats in detail the Wafa'i *silsila*, explaining its connection with other, better-known ones.[12] There are several other Sufi works that mention Abu'l-Wafa' or his immediate disciples, but these add limited concrete information to our knowledge. They are, nonetheless, important as testimony to the enduring memory of Abu'l-Wafa' in Iraq, as well as to the high degree of convergence and entanglement of the early Wafa'i environment and other Iraq-based Sufi traditions, especially the Rifaᶜiyya and the Qadiriyya.[13]

Drawing primarily on these sources, this chapter pieces together the broad contours of the life and spiritual legacy of Abu'l-Wafa' to illuminate the origins of this relatively little-known Sufi tradition as background to its later trajectory in the Anatolian context where it would make a major impact. The overall religious profile of Abu'l-Wafa' and the early Wafa'i milieu emerging from the sources defy easy categorisation within the conventional binaries of Sunni versus Shiᶜi and 'orthodoxy' versus 'heterodoxy'. This complex picture is aptly captured by Cemal Kafadar's analytical concept of 'metadoxy', which he uses to describe the Wafa'i/Baba'i milieu in Anatolia. Kafadar tends to link this metadoxic outlook to the special conditions prevailing in the late medieval Anatolian frontiers, where people enjoyed a relative freedom from the disciplining influence of entrenched political and religious centres.[14] This, however, can only be part of the explanation. Judged by Abu'l-Wafa''s hagiography, it appears that a 'metadoxic' outlook was part-and-parcel of the Wafa'i tradition as it formed and evolved in its original habitat of Iraq. In fact, based on his biography, I argue that Abu'l-Wafa''s own example played a decisive role in its emergence. An additional, more general aim of this chapter is to test the historical efficacy of the Wafa'i origins of several *ocak*s, as suggested by recently surfaced Alevi documents, and to develop the book's central thesis that the basic doctrinal, devotional and organisational features of Kizilbashism/Alevism must be sought within Sufism broadly defined.

Situating Abu'l-Wafa᾽ in Time and Space

Abu'l-Wafa᾽'s lifetime spanned across most of the eleventh century and early twelfth, a period of major religious and political conflicts and realignments in Iraq and the larger Middle East. His childhood coincided with declining control in Iraq of the Shiᶜi Buyid amirs and revival of the Abbasid caliphs' religious influence under caliph al-Qadir bi-llah (r. 991–1031).[15] Qadir was an advocate of Hanbalism, a strict traditionalist school of Sunni jurisprudence espousing a strong opposition to all forms of innovation. Unlike most earlier and later caliphs, who took a more conciliatory approach to Shiᶜism, Qadir was decisively antagonistic against the Shiᶜa and was particularly alert against alleged ᶜAlid claimants to the caliphate. His Hanbali-inspired Sunni vision, enshrined in the epistles collectively known as the 'Qadiri creed', would become the benchmark of the new Abbasid/Sunni orthodoxy that successive caliphs reigning during the life-time of Abu'l-Wafa᾽ upheld and perpetuated. In addition to condemning the rational theologians and the Shiᶜa, the Qadiri creed embraced the literalist position in the interpretation of the Qur᾽an, insisting on the fulfilment of formal prayers as a religious imperative, the neglect of which was now viewed to be tantamount to infidelity. The Qadiri creed was an expression and a product of the alliance formed between the Hanbali religious scholars and the caliphs in Baghdad during the tenth and eleventh centuries.[16] This alliance, in the longer term, would effect a shift in Sunni religious life towards greater homogenisation along the lines of Sunni traditionalism and jurisprudence.[17]

In 1055, when Abu'l-Wafa᾽ was already a mature adult and most likely well advanced on the Sufi path, the Seljuk Turks defeated the Shiᶜi Buyids and took control of Baghdad. The restoration of effective Sunni political dominance in the Abbasid capital not only ended the rule of the Buyids, but also occasioned a general crackdown on the public manifestation of all forms of Shiᶜism on imperial and local levels.[18] New circumstances of heightened Sunni–Shiᶜi antagonism find clear echoes in Abu'l-Wafa᾽'s hagiography. For example, the hagiography alludes to a broader war against the Shiᶜa as the context for the military confrontation between Sayf al-Dawla, the Shiᶜi Mazyadid amir of the city of Hilla (aka Sadaqa b. Mansur, r. 1086–1107), and the Seljuk sultan, Muhammed Tapar (r. 1104–1118, apparently conflated with his son Sultan Mesᶜud in the text).[19]

It is in that same context that the hagiography mentions Abu'l-Wafaʾ's proselytising activities among the local population, the majority of whom it is emphasised showed an inclination towards Shiʿism (*meẕheb-i Rāfż*).[20] The region of Qusan, which was Abu'l-Wafaʾ's birthplace and later location of his lodge, must have been particularly susceptible to ongoing sectarian tensions. Neighbouring the better-known city of Nuʿmaniyya, Qusan was situated in the Shiʿi-majority belt of central Iraq, halfway between Baghdad, the seat of the Sunni caliphate, and Wasit, another Sunni-majority city of great importance for the imperial capital due to the agricultural resources of the surrounding area.[21] Wasit came briefly under the control of the Ismaʿili Fatimids of Egypt shortly before the Seljuk conquest in 1057 and later, towards the end of Abu'l-Wafaʾ's lifetime, was ruled by the Shiʿi Mazyadid ruler Sayf al-Dawla for four years. Mazyadid domination in Wasit and the neighbouring regions eventually ended when the Seljuk sultan Muhammed Tapar defeated and slew Sayf al-Dawla – a turn of events Abu'l-Wafaʾ allegedly predicted with his saintly foresight.[22]

Just to the south of Wasit lay the lower Iraqi marshes, a geographically difficult area to penetrate, which provided a safe haven for various kinds of political and religious non-conformists throughout history.[23] Also known as the region of al-Batiha, this wetland area bordered Kufa in the west, Wasit in the northeast and Basra in the south. Inhabited today almost entirely by Arab Shiʿi tribes, at the time of Abu'l-Wafaʾ it was a true collage of religions, including Mandaeism, Christianity and different Muslim sects. Batiha has a special place in the history of Sufism as being the cradle of the Rifaʿiyya, one of the first and best-known Sufi orders commonly associated with flamboyant ritualistic practices, such as fire-walking, riding on lions and piercing oneself with an iron spike. The order's earlier name, Bataʾihiyya, comes from Mansur al-Bataʾihi, maternal uncle of Ahmad al-Rifaʿi (1118–1182), whose spiritual mantle and circle of followers the latter inherited. Abu'l-Wafaʾ was a contemporary of Mansur al-Bataʾihi, and the two were both initiated to Sufism by Abu Muhammad Talha al-Shunbuki, a Sufi master based in the town of Haddadiyya near Basra.[24] It is the common link of Abu'l-Wafaʾ and Mansur al-Bataʾihi to Talha al-Shunbuki that explains why *Tiryāq al-muḥibbīn* falsely subsumes the entire Shunbukiyya–Wafaʾiyya line under the broader umbrella of the Rifaʿi order, even though the order's eponym Ahmad al-Rifaʿi was still an infant when Abu'l-Wafaʾ died.[25]

The eleventh century carries a special significance in the history of Sufism in that it marks the beginning of the Sufi tradition's diffusion from its original urban base into rural and tribal settings.[26] Abu'l-Wafaʾ was presumably one of the early examples of a Sufi shaykh from a provincial/tribal background whose saintly memory was embraced and promoted by relatively permanent collectivities. His Sufi career predated, or marginally coincided with, those of the famous early eponymic Sufi masters, such as ᶜAbd al-Qadir al-Jilani (1077–1166) and Ahmad al-Rifaᶜi (1118–1182). Abu'l-Wafaᵓ was reportedly known and praised by both, and Jilani is furthermore said to have attended Abu'l-Wafaᵓ's gatherings in his youth.[27] Abu'l-Wafaᵓ is also purported to be the first Sufi to hold the cognomen 'Tāj al-ᶜĀrifīn' (Crown of the Gnostics).[28]

Expansion of Sufi influence at various levels of society from the eleventh century onwards largely correlated with increasing pressures towards a greater alignment with Sunni traditionalism as outlined above. These pressures no doubt played a role in the formulation of a normative Sufism that affirmed active involvement in social life and emphasised scrupulous observation of religious formalities. Demarcation of a normative Sufism as such involved the domestication of some of Sufism's earlier strains deemed antithetical to juristic Islam, or their gradual elimination from the mainstream of Sufism. This compromise, if you will, between juristic and mystical Islam would find its most authoritative articulation in the works of Abu Hamid al-Ghazali (d. 1111), the famous Ashᶜarite theologian and the jurisconsult of the Nizamiyya madrasa. Yet its main outlines were largely worked out in earlier Sufi manuals that were composed from about the turn of the eleventh century onwards by jurist-Sufis, such as Sulami (d. 1021) and Qushayri (d. 1072) who, like Ghazali, were intellectually and politically invested in defining and presenting Sufism in a manner acceptable to the custodians of Islamic law.[29]

If one point of tension between the juristic ulema and the Sufis concerned the boundaries of proper belief and acceptable devotional practices, the other one involved competition for social and political influence. Both groups vied for the same economic favours and privileges allocated by power brokers who, especially during and after the Seljuk era, extended their patronage to Sufi convents and madrasas alike by way of an effort to boost their religious legitimacy and appeal among their subjects. Relations between the political authorities and the Sufis were typically more varied and volatile than with the juristic ulema, however. This was due to the crowd-gathering propensity of popular Sufi shaykhs who were kept under scrutiny for fear that their spiritual prestige among the masses could potentially be converted into oppositional political action. Concerns of this type underscored the time-honoured carrot-and-stick policy vis-à-vis Sufis that entailed selective patronage of those who conformed and the persecution to varying degrees of those who were seen as troublemakers. Such policies no doubt contributed to the 'moderating' pressures on the broader Sufi milieu exerted by the proponents of law and 'orthodoxy', with the Hanbali circles leading the effort during the time period under consideration.[30]

Increased tensions between mystics and their traditionalist adversaries are reflected in the specific details of the above-cited story of Abu'l-Wafa''s heresy trial in Baghdad. It is reported that among the ulema who interrogated Abu'l-Wafa' were two famous Hanbali scholars of eleventh-century Baghdad, Abu'l-Hasan al-Jawzi (d. 1120), father of the famous anti-Sufi Hanbali traditionalist Abu'l-Faraj b. al-Jawzi (d.1200), and Ibn ᶜAqil (d. 1119).[31] These two figures are singled out as the ringleaders of the hostile camp that formed against Abu'l-Wafa'. They allegedly scorned the saint for his poor Arabic and charged him with utter ignorance (*nesne bilmez deyu*) before they were put to shame by Abu'l-Wafa''s erudite answers to their questions.[32] Although not corroborated by other sources, this story appears in two different versions in the hagiography, and represents in several respects the climax of Abu'l-Wafa''s sacred biography. This speaks to the relevance of antagonistic relations between the traditionalist Hanbalis and the Sufi circles of eleventh-century Iraq in shaping Abu'l-Wafa''s religious legacy, at least as it was recollected and presented by the early Wafa'i milieu in Iraq.

Hanbali's animosity against Sufism, rather than being categorical, was based on an assumed differentiation between 'genuine' Sufis, such as 'the Junaids of the past', and 'false Sufis who led a merry life'. This distinction was made in *Talbīs Iblīs* by Ibn al-Jawzi, the aforementioned son of Abu'l-Wafa''s detractor, who became more renowned than his father for his unrelenting attacks against certain segments of the Sufi milieu. Ibn al-Jawzi condemned such Sufi practices as *samāᶜ* (ritual dancing and singing), celibacy, mendacity and the dubbing of juristic Islam as *ᶜilm-i ẓāhir* (exoteric science) as opposed to *ᶜilm-i baṭin* (esoteric science), which Sufis considered to be a higher form of knowledge.[33] While Ibn al-Jawzi did not name any names as examples of those who were on the receiving end of his condemnations, Abu'l-Wafa''s religious profile, according to his hagiography, displays many of the features associated with those whom Jawzi viewed as 'false Sufis'.[34]

The Life and Legacy of Abu'l-Wafa'

A KURD AND A *SAYYID*

Notwithstanding his *nisba*, 'al-Baghdādī', Abu'l-Wafa' (12 Rajab 417/1026–Rabiᶜ al-awwal 501/1107)[35] spent virtually his entire life in central and lower Iraq. He was born and later established his convent in Qalminiyya, which lay southeast of Baghdad between Nu^c^maniyya and Wasit in the region of Qusan. His father, Muhammad al-^c^Aridi, was purportedly a *sayyid* descended from the line of Imam Zayn al-^c^Abidin – this lineage being a major theme of the hagiography – who had settled in Qusan after leaving his native village and his family to escape the persecution of the *sayyids*.[36] In Qusan, he took refuge among tribal Kurds known as Bani Narjis and married a Narji woman named Fatima Umm Kulthum, but he died while she was still pregnant with their son, Muhammad, the future Abu'l-Wafa'.[37]

Abu'l-Wafa' al-Baghdadi, known also by the *nisba* al-Kurdi, was thus partially of Kurdish origin and grew up among tribal Kurds. According to his hagiography, he spoke only Kurdish until one day the Prophet appeared to him in a dream and miraculously taught him Arabic.[38] Local Kurds gave him the title *Kākīs*[39] to express their respect and affection.[40] Abu'l-Wafa''s Kurdish background is another major theme – and source of tension – in his hagiography, which contains accounts of his detractors invoking it in order to question his *sayyid* descent and his competence in religious sciences, as well as to denigrate some of his Sufi practices. For example, one account states that a follower of Abu'l-Wafa' was mocked by a fellow Sufi affiliated with the Rifa^c^iyya for engaging in the *samā^c^* ritual, or the Wafa'i version of whirling, because this practice belonged to the 'sons of Kurd(s)' (*Kürd oğlanları*).[41] Abu'l-Wafa''s initial snubbing by members of the Baghdadi ulema due to his poor Arabic might likewise be read as a veiled reference to his Kurdish and provincial background, and taken as a marker of his relative outsider status vis-à-vis the contemporary urban intellectual milieu and Sufi mainstream.

Indeed, it does not require a great sense of subtlety to notice that among Abu'l-Wafa''s detractors and rivals, as the hagiography portrays them, the term 'Kurd' connoted tribalism, boorishness and irreligiosity. A further impression of this social baggage associated with Kurdish identity comes from the incidental details of a story about a bridge that Abu'l-Wafa' is said to have built with his own hands to aid local Kurds in crossing a ferocious river. In the story, one of Abu'l-Wafa''s close disciples, Majid Kurdi (ironically himself of Kurdish background, as indicated by his *nisba*), queried the master about the appropriateness of this act of benevolence towards the Kurds on the grounds of their 'neglect to perform the daily prayers and their lack of conformity with shari^c^a'.[42] In his apologetic response, Abu'l-Wafa' proclaimed his confidence that there were no sinners (*fāsiḳ*) among the Kurds and that many of them would cross the *ṣirāṭ* (the extremely fine bridge that one must cross to enter paradise) as easily as they would cross the bridge that he built to help them and others.[43]

Interestingly, such anecdotes that depict Abu'l-Wafa' as having a strong sense of compassion for the seemingly 'irreligious' local Kurds are coupled in the hagiography with a consistent effort to rectify what are presented as false rumours about Abu'l-Wafa''s own 'Kurdishness' (obviously stemming from his affinity with the Kurdish tribe of Bani Narjis on his mother's side) despite his *sayyid* descent (on his paternal side). Besides recurring explicit statements to that effect, which punctuate the entire text,[44] the hagiography records numerous stories attesting to Abu'l-Wafa''s genuine *sayyid*-ship because of his displayed, congenital power to work miracles and his profound inborn piety. These qualities were reportedly present in him since childhood, despite his upbringing in a tribal environment where there were people who had never prayed before the arrival of his father (who presumably guided them to the right path). A good example is the hagiography's depiction of events leading to Abu'l-Wafa''s initiation into the Sufi path. Only ten years old at the time, Abu'l-Wafa', or Muhammad as he was then known, was allegedly praying by himself in a remote corner of the forest when he was first spotted by his future shaykh, Shunbuki, who invited him to join his circle of pupils in Haddadiyya. Muhammad agreed only after making sure he had his mother's blessing. In Haddadiyya, he impressed Shunbuki with his miracles from day one and was, therefore, awarded by his shaykh the title 'Tāj al-ᶜārifīn', a title by which he has since become famous.[45]

The hagiography's idealised portrayal of Abu'l-Wafa''s early life starkly contrasts with the corresponding information in *Tiryāq al-muḥibbīn*, which claims he was a highway robber fond of horsemanship and armed confrontations before his conversion to Sufism. In this alternate account, Abu'l-Wafa' converts to Sufism only after a confrontation with Shunbuki, who invites the young Muhammad into his presence after a group of people he robbed near Haddadiyya complain to the shaykh.[46] There is, unsurprisingly, no mention of Abu'l-Wafa''s alleged early life as a bandit in his hagiographic vita. However, there are stories in it, perhaps crafted to counter such reports, that cast a critical light on cultural norms legitimating banditry in the tribal environment within which Abu'l-Wafa' grew up, but to which he always remained aloof. One such story portrays Abu'l-Wafa' as a miracle-worker even while in his mother's womb. In the story, his pregnant mother eats a piece of a melon that one of her fellow tribesmen had picked from a garden without permission. The minute she swallows it, she is hit with a powerful stomach ache that causes her to vomit. Years later, when passing by the same garden, Abu'l-Wafa' reminds his mother of the incident and explains to her that it was he who caused the stomach ache and made her vomit lest she swallow an unlawful morsel (*ḥarām loḳma*).[47]

On the Sufi path: Abu'l-Wafa's dual legacy

After his initiation into the Sufi path, Abu'l-Wafaᵓ takes a trip to Bukhara to study the exoteric religious sciences (*ulūm-i ẓāhir*).[48] The hagiography, however, only refers to this sojourn in general terms, making one wonder if it really reflects part of Abu'l-Wafaᵓ's early life or whether it is merely a later Wafaᵓi tradition aimed at casting the saint as equally knowledgeable about formal aspects of Islam. Even with this caveat in mind, however, the possibility that such a trip occurred should not be rejected out of hand since there is nothing inherently unreasonable about an individual seeking formal education after entering the world of Sufism. Whatever the case may be, the hagiography tells us that after his return from Bukhara, Abu'l-Wafaᵓ embarked upon the life of an itinerant dervish, spending many years wandering in the wilderness and communicating mainly with feral animals. The hagiography explicitly mentions three separate journeys of this type, each sanctioned by his shaykh and lasting several years.[49]

The hagiography of Abu'l-Wafaᵓ provides a surprisingly detailed account of his transformation from a reclusive ascetic dervish to a settled Sufi master.[50] This was apparently not an easy decision for the saint since settling down would entail compromising the principle of absolute poverty that he strictly observed during his earlier hermetic existence. The process is set in motion during Abu'l-Wafaᵓ's third prolonged journey in the wilderness, when he comes upon a village in 'the land of the east' called Kasriyya (presumably a place in western Iran). In this land lived a great shaykh known as Shaykh ᶜAjami, a name too generic to be identified as a historical figure but nonetheless significant for signalling a Persian connection.[51] Upon his arrival in the village, Abu'l-Wafaᵓ joins the crowd for prayer in the *masjid* (small mosque) situated in the front yard of the shaykh's dwelling where, following the shaykh's persistent requests, he subsequently stays as a guest for three consecutive days. The shaykh and the people of the village, unwilling to let Abu'l-Wafaᵓ go, insist that he settle there, get married and have children in accordance with the tradition of his ancestors. But even the shaykh's offer of his daughter's hand in marriage fails to persuade Abu'l-Wafaᵓ; he decides instead to perform *istiḫāre* (the practice of lying down to sleep in order to obtain a sign from heaven) before making up his mind. A divine sign comes but only to refer him to ᶜAli, the Prophet's cousin and son-in-law, for consultation. At ᶜAli's shrine (one that is different from the well-known one in Najaf, as noted in the hagiography) Abu'l-Wafaᵓ is finally given heavenly sanction to marry Shaykh ᶜAjami's daughter, Husniyya. After their wedding in Kasriyya, Abu'l-Wafaᵓ receives from his father-in-law half of his property as a wedding gift, and he and his wife return to his hometown Qalminiyya where they settle down.[52]

Abu'l-Wafa''s marriage would not follow a traditional course, however. Despite his wife's desire to have children and all of her efforts to seduce him, Abu'l-Wafa' remained dedicated to celibacy until the end of his life, never abandoning his belief in the hazards of sensual pleasures and procreation for the seeker of the Divine.[53] This account of Abu'l-Wafa''s half-hearted conversion from a hermetic to a settled life, and more specifically that of his chaste marriage, captures a key duality in his religious legacy. It also marks Abu'l-Wafa' as a transitional figure, someone whose career encompassed the practice and development of two distinct modes of Sufi piety, the earlier ascetic strand and the later world-embracing mysticism.[54] This duality would characterise the Wafa'i tradition throughout its history and become especially pronounced in the late medieval Anatolian context, where Abu'l-Wafa''s spiritual heritage would be claimed by two distinct groups, each of which represented one of his this-worldly and renunciatory orientations.

Abu'l-Wafa''s Spiritual Successor(s)

The story of Abu'l-Wafa''s settling down after years of a hermetic existence is told in a more or less identical fashion in the Arabic original of the hagiography and in its Turkish rendering up to the point of his marriage to Husniyya. Both versions recount that Abu'l-Wafa', having no offspring of his own, decided to adopt a son to appease his wife's desire to have children. There is, however, a significant discrepancy between *Menāḳıb*-Arabic and *Menāḳıb*-Turkish regarding the number of Abu'l-Wafa''s spiritual successor(s), an issue treated as a sequel to the same story. According to *Menāḳıb*-Arabic, Abu'l-Wafa' asks his wife to prepare a dish of milk and bread (or rice) in a bowl in which he earlier had her wash his thobe (*thawb*), which was spotted with a drop of semen. He then declares that whomever of his brother Salim's two sons first comes and eats the prepared dish would become their adopted son and his heir, and we learn quickly thereafter that this lucky adoptee is Sayyid Matar.[55] There is, however, a notable detail, or rather absence, here: the name of Salim's other son is never mentioned, an absence even more intriguing when coupled with the virtual silence on him and his descendants in the remainder of the hagiography (in both its Arabic and Turkish versions alike). This leads us to suspect that the saint's vita was written in part with the aim of explaining and validating Sayyid Matar's succession.[56]

Unlike the Arabic original, which presents Sayyid Matar as Abu'l-Wafaʾ's one and only adopted son, and does not even mention the name of the other potential candidate, the Turkish version of the hagiography identifies six more adoptees in addition to Sayyid Matar through whom the saint's spiritual legacy is allegedly passed down.[57] These, in turn, can be categorised into two groups. The first group includes ʿAbd al-Rahman Tafsunji, ʿAli b. Hayti and Shaykh ʿAskari Shuli, who also appear frequently in the Turkish and Arabic versions of the hagiography as close disciples of the saint. The remaining three, Sayyid Ghanim b. Sayyid Munjih, Sayyid Muhammad b. Sayyid Kamal Hayat and Sayyid ʿAli b. Sayyid Khamis, are presented as both disciples and blood relatives of Abu'l-Wafaʾ on his paternal side. Oddly, however, in contrast to the first three, the members of this second group are virtually invisible in the remainder of the narrative in *Menāḳıb*-Turkish (as well as in *Menāḳıb*-Arabic, where they are not mentioned at all with one exception to be noted below).

Of the second group, Sayyid Ghanim is of particular interest for our purposes, because he turns up in various Alevi documents as the progenitor of several *ocak*s in eastern Anatolia. These documents frequently identify Sayyid Ghanim as Abu'l-Wafaʾ's brother (*aḫūhu*), and claim that his descendants have an exclusive hereditary right to the leadership of the Wafaʾiyya. Other sources differ from the Alevi documents: for example, *Menāḳıb*-Turkish appears to suggest that he was a nephew rather than a brother of Abu'l-Wafaʾ. This reading is verified in a later passage (included also in *Menāḳıb*-Arabic) in which Sayyid Ghanim's name is cited for a second time as the ancestor of a certain Sayyid Rukn al-Din (or Zaki al-Din). This passage clearly identifies Ghanim as Abu'l-Wafaʾ's nephew (T. *ḳardaşı oğlī*; A. *ibn aḫi*).[58] Zabidi's account supplies further support to this claim by showing Sayyid Ghanim as the second son of Sayyid Salim.[59] It is possible, therefore, to cautiously identify Sayyid Ghanim as the brother of Sayyid Matar, whose name the author of *Menāḳıb*-Arabic avoided to mention while recounting the story of Abu'l-Wafaʾ's authorisation of the latter as his heir, but who is conflated with his father Sayyid Salim in the Wafaʾi *ijāza*s.

The remaining two adoptees of Abu'l-Wafaʾ who were also his blood relatives, Sayyid Muhammad b. Sayyid Kamal Hayat and Sayyid ʿAli b. Sayyid Khamis, are harder to track down in other sources. There are no mentions of Sayyid Muhammad b. Sayyid Kamal Hayat in either the Alevi documents or in Zabidi's work. However, mention is made of a certain 'Seyyid Pīr Ḥayāt el-Dīn' in the introduction to *Menāḳıb*-Turkish as the great ancestor of Seyyid Velayet, the commissioner of the Turkish translation of the hagiography, who might possibly be the same person.

The father of Seyyid Velayet, thus a progeny of Seyyid Pir Hayat el-Din, reportedly moved from Iraq to Anatolia and settled in Bursa in 841/1437.[60] As for Sayyid ᶜAli b. Sayyid Khamis: his father, Sayyid Khamis, appears in both the Alevi documents and in Zabidi's *Rafᶜ niqāb*. However, in the Alevi documents he is identified as Sayyid Ghanim's son, while Zabidi calls him the son of Sayyid ᶜAli (thus reversing the generational order), and places him a few generations further down the line among Sayyid Ghanim's descendants.[61] Such inconsistencies, while rendering harder to assess the historical efficacy and relevance of a given genealogical claim, are not unusual in written family trees, which tend to skip lesser known family members, add generic names as placeholders and use shortened or alternative versions of names.

Irrespective of the historicity of the figures involved, and the nature of their real or fictitious kinship ties to Abu'l-Wafa' and to one another, a discrepancy of this magnitude between the Arabic and the Turkish versions of the hagiography calls for further attention and comment. Such a discrepancy could have been generated if the Turkish version was based on a copy of the Arabic original other than the one found in the Bibliothèque Nationale, or if it drew on an entirely different hagiographic work. This, however, appears unlikely given the overlap between the two versions in terms of the sequence and content of the individual stories. A more likely scenario is that the text may have been tampered with during the translation process, with the addition of six extra adopted sons, who would thus be equally legitimate spiritual heirs of the saint. A close and comparative reading of the relevant passages supports this conjecture: in *Menāḳıb*-Turkish, there is an abrupt and conspicuous shift in the narrative following Husniyya's preparation of the milk dish, when Abu'l-Wafa' suddenly decides to perform *istiḫāre* to seek a divine sign for identifying his heir-to-be. In his sleep he has a vision of the Prophet, who directs his descendants Hasan, Husayn and Zayn al-Abidin to present Abu'l-Wafa' with the seven names of Abu'l-Wafa's divinely sanctioned adoptees and spiritual successors, making the milk dish test practically irrelevant to the election process.

Even assuming the translator's modification of the original text, it would be injudicious to write off the six additional heirs as entirely fictitious constructs with no value for an understanding of Wafa'i history. A more sagacious approach must contemplate another possibility: that this amendment reflects alternate Wafa'i traditions that gained particular prominence in medieval Anatolia. The knowledge of these (alleged) collateral Wafa'i lines might have grown faint in the Iraqi Wafa'i milieu with the passing of time, or were deliberately suppressed in the Arabic original of the hagiography.[62] This possibility is buttressed by certain clues in the hagiography that betray internal tensions concerning the issue of Abu'l-Wafaᵓ's rightful successor(s). One such clue is found in another story (included in both *Menāḳib*-Arabic and *Menāḳib*-Turkish) relaying the saint's naming of Sayyid Matar as his successor, this time publicly, but only after a relatively anxious extended wait on the part of Sayyid Matar. It is reported that Abu'l-Wafaᵓ, when he was on his deathbed, distributed his personal belongings to a number of his close associates, but assigned nothing to Sayyid Matar. The hagiography highlights the latter's profound relief, after his disappointment about being excluded, when Abu'l-Wafaᵓ finally names Sayyid Matar as his (financial and) spiritual heir (Ot. *vāris-i ḥālim*; Ar. *wārith mālī wa ḥālī*) in front of his close disciples. Apparently, Sayyid Matar and those around him had feared the possibility that Abu'l-Wafaᵓ would make some 'outsider' (Ot. *ecnebī*; Ar. *ajnabī*) his spiritual heir.[63] While the account contains no direct evidence of who this 'outsider' might have been, it is clear from the amount of attention given to this event that an internal division and a rivalry existed among Abu'l-Wafaᵓ's disciples, possibly based on whether or not they had kinship ties to the master.

A further internal friction, which is of greater relevance in this consideration, seems to have existed concerning the number and identity of Abu'l-Wafaᵓ's familial successors. The first point to remember in this regard is the unnamed second son of Sayyid Salim in the story recounted above. Moreover, at a later place in *Menāḳib*-Arabic, the author raises the issue of Abu'l-Wafaᵓ's other siblings, including a sister named Zaynab, but only to dismiss it as a false claim, and to insist that the Sayyid Salim was the saint's one and only sibling.[64] While these neither establish nor preclude the validity of the contention concerning Abu'l-Wafāᵓ's six other adopted sons, whose names seem to have been inserted into the Turkish version of the hagiography during the translation process, it is evident that there were, presumably already at the time of the compilation of the original Arabic text, other self-defined descent groups tracing themselves to Abu'l-Wafaᵓ besides the one issuing from Sayyid Matar. Such a possibility is particularly strong in the case of the line purportedly issuing from Sayyid Ghanim, whose overall historicity is attested to by multiple sources, even though it is impossible to ascertain with full confidence the true nature of his relationship to Abu'l-Wafaᵓ.

Putting aside for now the question of collateral Wafaᵓi lines that later emerge in Anatolia, the hagiography makes clear that Sayyid Matar's descendants held on to their predominant position among the Wafaᵓi affiliates in Iraq, acting as administrators (*mutawallī*) of Abu'l-Wafaᵓ's convent in Qalminiyya after his death.[65] However, they seem to have begun faltering in that role by the fourth generation after Abu'l-Wafaᵓ's demise, as suggested in a story concerning the collapsing of the dome of Abu'l-Wafa''s tomb. This collapse is said to have resulted from the neglect of the administrator, an unnamed great-grandson of Sayyid Matar, who is described as 'too inclined toward this world'.[66] It is only after one of the dervishes attending his shrine sees Abu'l-Wafa' in a dream that the dome is finally repaired. In the dream, Abu'l-Wafa' not only demands that the collapsed dome be immediately restored but also urges that the dervishes residing in his shrine be given their fair share of the endowment's revenues. While this postmortem saintly intervention allegedly convinced Sayyid Matar's progeny to act more responsibly, the circulation of such a story can be interpreted as a signal of the failure in the leadership of the community that formed around Abu'l-Wafa''s sacred memory in Iraq after just a few generations. Still, given the mention of Abu'l-Wafa''s tomb (P. *mazār*) in an early fourteenth-century work, even if only as a prominent landmark near Nu'maniyya, the Wafa'iyya must have survived in Iraq in later centuries at least as a hereditary shrine community.[67] Evliya Çelebi's *Seyaḥatnāme* also contains a reference to what appears to be Abu'l-Wafa''s tomb-shrine. If so, then the saint's shrine was clearly still standing by the mid-seventeenth century.[68] Sources also record a shrine to the saint in Mosul that survived to the early twentieth century. However, judged by its location this was most likely a shrine different from the one containing Abu'l-Wafa''s actual tomb.[69]

Circle of Disciples and Lay Following

Abu'l-Wafa''s hagiography portrays him as a popular Sufi master leading a large number of disciples and a much larger community of lay devotees. Of his close circle of disciples identified by name, Sayyid Matar, ʿAbd al-Rahman Tafsunji, ʿAli b. Hayti, Shaykh ʿAskari Shuli, Majid Kurdi and Baqa' b. Batu also appear in Sufi biographical dictionaries as Sufi masters in their own rights, some setting up their own convents and training their own pupils in different parts of central and northern Iraq. Another renowned figure who had what resembled a master–disciple relationship with Abu'l-Wafa' was ʿAdi b. Musafir, the central figure in the Yazidi pantheon.[70] Although his convent was based in Hakkari, ʿAdi b. Musafir seems to have maintained an intimate, if sometimes fraught, relationship with Abu'l-Wafa'. It was to ʿAdi b. Musafir that the dying Abu'l-Wafa' bequeathed his garment (*libās*), doing so at the expense of causing some discontent among his other disciples for reasons not fully explained in the hagiography. Still more, Abu'l-Wafa''s will specified that ʿAdi b. Musafir should wash his corpse before burial, an even clearer sign of a special affinity between the two that surely deserves further investigation for an understanding of Yazidi genealogy and its possible historical connections to the Wafaʾi tradition.[71]

Abu' l-Wafaʾ's other disciples mentioned by name in the hagiography have diverse social and geographic origins as well as religious temperaments. Among them are Muhammad Turkmani, allegedly the sultan of Bukhara before becoming a disciple of Abu'l-Wafaʾ;[72] Muhammad al-Misri, who appears as Abu'l-Wafaʾ's liaison with his followers in Egypt and was entrusted with the transfer of large donations (*naẕr*) from that region; ʿAyna Khatun, a penitent prostitute who tried to seduce Muhammad al-Misri during a trip to Egypt;[73] Husayn al-Raʿi, a shepherd turned Sufi whose name later turns up in Anatolia;[74] and Ramadan Majnun, who stood out from Abu'l-Wafaʾ's other more sober disciples with his extended ecstatic states and outlandish behaviour, such as roaming around naked and his active participation in warfare against infidels in a manner recalling the warrior-dervishes of medieval Anatolia.[75] The hagiography also mentions affiliates of Abu'l-Wafaʾ leading extreme ascetic lives in Lebanon,[76] as well as others who settled in Tabriz and Khorasan.[77] But perhaps most notably, it presents Abu'l-Wafaʾ as the forgotten spiritual forebear of the famous Badawiyya order, also known as the Ahmadiyya, based in North Africa. According to the hagiography, Qays al-Badawi was travelling in Iraq when he met Abu'l-Wafaʾ and was initiated by him into the Sufi path; Qays al-Badawi's spiritual legacy was then inherited by his brother's son (or grandson), Ahmad al-Badawi (1199–1276), the eponymous founder of the Badawiyya order.[78]

While the historicity of many of these individuals or their alleged links to Abu'l-Wafaʾ cannot be verified by other sources, there is evidence in the historical record of the presence of self-identified Wafaʾi *sayyid*s and/or dervishes in multiple regions outside of Iraq at various points in time. Different aspects of Abu'l-Wafaʾ's rich and variegated legacy seem to have been appropriated and accentuated within these relatively far-flung Wafaʾi circles. There were, for example, families derived from Abu'l-Wafaʾ who settled in Egypt and different parts of Greater Syria, whose genealogies were extensively studied by Zabidi.[79] One of these was the Jerusalemite Badri family, whose great ancestor Badr al-Din moved to Palestina as early as the first half of the thirteenth century, establishing there a Wafaʾi *zāwiya*. A member of the Badri family gave a copy of Abu'l-Wafaʾ's Arabic vita to Seyyid Velayet while he was travelling in Egypt, which was then translated into Turkish by one of Seyyid Velayet's disciples.[80] In sixteenth-century Aleppo, on the other hand, the Wafaʾi tradition was represented by an antinomian itinerant dervish by the name of Sayyid Abu'l-

Wafa' b. Abu Bakr who claimed a dual spiritual and natural genealogy leading back to Abu'l-Wafa' Taj al-ᶜArifin. He would later settle down and establish one of the most important Sufi lodges in that town.[81] In the same century, in 1526, a *zāwiya* affiliated with the Shunbukiyya-Wafā'iyya was founded in Egypt.[82] Sources also record Wafa'i affiliates in late fifteenth-century Shirvan, where 'a group of ecstatic Sufis who practiced such acts as dancing [*raqṣ*], magic [*shaᶜbada*], and placing of a sword on different parts of the body' were led by someone claiming to be a descendant of Abu'l-Wafa' al-Baghdadi.[83] The Anatolian offshoots of the Wafa'iyya will be discussed in greater detail in the next chapter. Suffice it to say that they similarly followed various discrete and sometimes contrary paths, including sedentary *tarīqa* Sufism and the Qalandari type of dervish piety.

It is not always easy to distinguish between Abu'l-Wafa''s occasional associates and his actual disciples, whose names are aggregated in lists of seventeen, forty and eighty-two in the hagiography.[84] It is also difficult to determine how far his relationship with his close circle of companions (*aṣḥāb*) can be understood to accord with the classical Sufi view of the relationship between the initiate (*murīd*) and spiritual guide (*murshid*). It would seem, however, that Abu'l-Wafa''s following during his lifetime, allegedly reaching tens of thousands, encompassed a sizeable number of laypeople, even if their numbers are likely amplified. Revealing in this regard are stories where Abu'l-Wafa' emerges as a popular preacher who regularly takes trips to proselytise (*daᶜvet-i ḫalḳ içün*).[85] This phenomenon of the 'preacher-master', although shunned by some early Sufi authorities such as Junayd, became a part of the Islamic landscape by the eleventh century in tandem with the wider dissemination of the Sufi tradition. Sufis of the preacher-master type ranked among Islam's most effective proselytisers, especially in such frontier environments as medieval Anatolia.

One of the most theatrical stories in the hagiography that shows Abu'l-Wafa' as a preacher-master in action affords a glimpse into the dynamics of this phenomenon. According to the story, Abu'l-Wafa''s missionary efforts in a village, whose inhabitants were adherents of the Khariji sect, prove futile until the son of the community's aged leader comes to see Abu'l-Wafa' to request his help in curing his father's debilitating illness. 'If you were to cure my father's illness,' the man declares, 'this community would submit themselves to you en masse' (*bu ḳavm cemīᶜan size tābiᶜ olur*). Abu'l-Wafa' agrees to the request and cures the old man on the condition that he and his community abandon their 'wicked sect' (*ḫabīs̱ meẕheb*). When the news of the community's conversion spreads, however, the old man comes under attack from other Khariji leaders who pressure him to retract his decision. Some threaten his life, while others try to convince him that it was God who cured him, not Abu'l-Wafa°, who they claimed was not a genuine *sayyid* since he grew up among the Kurds. The story ends with the old man giving in to the pressure and returning to the 'wicked sect' of his ancestors, after which his illness returns with a vengeance.[86]

This story, notwithstanding the unhappy ending, illuminates the socio-psychological dynamics and the local-level, practical aspects of the popularising process of Sufism by demonstrating the connection between the phenomena of preacher-master and lay Sufi followers. Devin DeWeese articulates this connection with the concept of 'communal Sufi affiliation', which he defines as 'the establishment of formal relations, often described in terms of actual discipleship and initiatory bonds, between Sufi shaykhs and entire communities, both nomadic and sedentary'.[87] DeWeese observes that communal Sufi affiliations were typically coupled with hereditary shaykhhood, which was the most common organisational principle among the Sufis of the Yesevi tradition in the fourteenth and fifteenth centuries. Compared to orders organised around notions of initiation and individual discipleship, those operating on the basis of genealogical succession and communal affiliation had obvious advantages: not only could they reach out to broader collectivities beyond the confines of a typical Sufi order by attracting followers on a communal basis, but they could also form durable bonds with groups of people who had not undergone a full initiatory experience, but who might nonetheless feel attached to a Sufi order or a saintly lineage.[88]

DeWeese demonstrates how, through the agency of the Yesevi shaykhs, hereditary succession and communal Sufi affiliations facilitated Islamisation among non-Muslim nomads in Central Asia. Although 'conversion' was aimed at the sectarian level in the above story, the story likely captures some of the same basic dynamics and processes.[89] Communal Sufi affiliations, whether used as an instrument in converting non-Muslims and sectarians, was a key mechanism in the transformation and growth of Sufism from a mode of spirituality cultivated by a small number of circles to a widespread social presence throughout the Muslim world. It also played a significant role in creating distinctive socio-religious collectivities over a long period of time. If Abu'l-Wafa°'s example represents a general trend, then Sufi shaykhs from provincial backgrounds must have played a particularly important role in both types of processes.

Abu'l-Wafa°'s biography is also demonstrative of tensions concerning Sufism's proper social and doctrinal boundaries brought on by its diffusion into rural and tribal environments. These are echoed in stories in the hagiography implicating Abu'l-Wafa°'s populist outlook as a source of apprehension among some of his close disciples. It is related, for instance, that a close disciple of Abu'l-Wafa' by the name of ᶜAbd al-Hamid Sufi one day reproached his master for indiscriminately admitting into his company people from all walks of life, regardless of social rank, spiritual aptitude or level of religious observance. Abu'l-Wafa''s response was a forceful one, marshaling proof directly from the Qur'an in defence of his seemingly unusual egalitarian and inclusive attitude as a Sufi master. He first had the disciple recite aloud the Qur'an's inaugural chapter, *Sūrat al-Fātiḥa*, which commences with an invocation to God as 'the lord of the universe'. Abu'l-Wafa' then explained that his inclusive attitude was simply a practical application of the Qur'an as declared by the opening verse of its first chapter; that is to say, since God is the lord of all, it was incumbent on Abu'l-Wafa' to lead all to the right path, including the unrighteous, the sinners (*fāsiḳ*), as well as the righteous and pious (*ṣāliḥūn*).[90] Coming from a 'communal' shaykh, to use DeWeese's terminology,[91] it is difficult not to read into this response an implicit critique of the exclusivist and elitist predisposition of contemporary urban Sufis, some of whom, the hagiography contends, were also among Abu'l-Wafa''s ardent opponents.

Expansion of Sufi influence in society meant that charismatic Sufi shaykhs with a large following, as was Abu'l-Wafa' according to his hagiography, could potentially turn into major actors in the political arena as well. In the story of his heresy trial in Baghdad, the hagiography blames Abu'l-Wafa''s envious rivals and enemies for arousing the caliph's suspicion of the saint by falsely accusing him of pursuing a political agenda. On the other hand, there are other anecdotes in the hagiography that portray Abu'l-Wafa' as much more than a disinterested esoteric mystic. These show the saint as a spokesperson for local populations, petitioning rulers on their behalf, and even leading effective acts of protest. In the year 499/1105, for instance, it is said that Caliph al-Mustazhir bi-llah (r. 1094–1118) had planned a large-scale confiscation of pious endowments, but was unable to bring his project to fruition in Qusan. This was thanks to the intervention of Abu'l-Wafa', who saved the people from dispossession by miraculously preventing the departure of the ships loaded with property from the appropriated endowments.[92] The picture of Abu'l-Wafa' emerging from these stories is clearly one of a Sufi shaykh prone to public and political involvement and, as such, foreshadows the proclivity of the Wafa'i/Baba'i circles for political activism in Seljuk Anatolia.

Spiritual Lineage

Different sources give more or less the same initiatic chain (*silsila*) for Abu'l-Wafa'. This chain grounds Abu'l-Wafa' squarely within the Sufi tradition of lower Iraq, reaching back via Talha al-Shunbuki to Abu Bakr b. al-Hawwari al-Bataʾihi, and from him to one of the earliest Sufi communities that formed in Basra around the seminal figure of Sahl al-Tustari (818–896). In the hagiography, Abu'l-Wafaʾ's initiatic chain is as follows:

> *Abū'l-Wafāʾ Tāj al-ʿĀrifīn ←Abū Muḥammad Ṭalḥa al-Shunbukī ←Abū Bakr al-Hawwārī ←Sahl al-Tustarī ←Muḥammad al-Sawwār ←Dhū'l-Nūn al-Miṣrī ←Abū ʿAbdullāh Muḥammad b. Ḥayya ←Jābir al-Anṣārī ←ʿAlī b. Abī Ṭālib.*[93]

The same line of affiliation is also provided in Wasiti's *Tiryāq al-muḥibbīn*, except it does not include Muhammad al-Sawwar, Tustari's uncle and first mentor, and the chain leading from ʿAli b. Abi Talib to Dhu'l-Nun al-Misri is slightly different.[94] The Alevi documents also contain two marginally different variations of the same spiritual genealogy for Abu'l-Wafaʾ.[95] These are identical to each other, as well as to those in the other two sources, from Abu'l-Wafaʾ to Hawwari. After that, the first version inserts Muhammad al-Nahrawani into the chain between al-Hawwari and Tustari, and Hasan al-Basri before ʿAli b. Abi Talib. The second version further interpolates Muhammad Kanjawi into the chain following Muhammad al-Nahrawani.[96] All the other differences between the two versions can reasonably be attributed to spelling mistakes,[97] with one significant exception being the case that gives Taj al-Din as the first name of Abu Bakr b. al-Hawwari, probably a later tinkering reflecting heightened Shiʿi-Alevi sensitivities.[98]

Taken as a whole, the sources are in agreement in connecting Abu'l-Wafaʾ's spiritual lineage to Sahl al-Tustari, a familiar figure in the history of Sufism but whose name is not typically encountered in the initiatic chains of Sufi orders. Many of the better-known chains of spiritual masters, especially in the Iraqi context, proceed through Junayd al-Baghdadi, who was the key personage of Baghdad-centred normative Sufism, which emphasised the necessity of the strict observance of religious formalities. While boundaries between the Baghdadi Sufis and those of the Basran milieu were by no means impervious, the latter possessed certain unique features deriving from the personal example of Tustari and his thought, which did not have clear counterparts among the Sufis in Baghdad, at least those who were contemporaneous with Tustari. These included 'vegetarianism, the proclivity for having "visions," [Tustari's] peculiar "light" cosmology centered on the idea of "the Muhammadan light," and the conviction that [one] could access the "inner meaning" of the Qur'ān'.[99] Nor is Dhu'l-Nun al-Misri – another formative figure in early Sufism, known for contributing to explorations of the inner meaning of the Qurʾan – a *silsila* founder.

He does, however, appear in Sufi primary sources as Tustari's spiritual forebear, the two reportedly having met in Mecca when they were both on pilgrimage. It is, of course, not possible to verify the existence of an unbroken chain of transmission between the people the *silsila* names, but nor is there any obvious anachronism that would justify its debunking as a complete fabrication, at least insofar as it indicates a distinct Sufi tradition that was embraced by the early Wafaᵓi milieu. Looked at from this perspective, and putting aside the question of the historical veracity of its details, what must be emphasised about Abu'l-Wafaᵓ's spiritual pedigree for present purposes is its relative unusualness in comparison with the much more widely known and better institutionalised Sufi initiatic chains typically traced to Junayd al-Baghdadi.[100]

Sahl al-Tustari, the pivotal figure in Abu'l-Wafaᵓ's initiatic chain and one of the two giants of early Iraqi Sufism (the other being Shaykh Junayd), was known for his powerful renunciatory orientation and esoteric (*baṭinī*) approach to Qurᵓanic interpretation. A native of the city of Tustar in southwest Iran, he led an extreme ascetic life in solitude before his emergence as a Sufi master surrounded by a circle of disciples. He was the first mentor of the famous and controversial Mansur al-Hallaj, who later temporarily joined the circle of Junayd al-Baghdadi, and was eventually executed in a gruesome manner allegedly for uttering the phrase 'I am the Truth' (*ana al-Ḥaqq*) at a moment of mystical ecstasy.[101] In terms of his religious thinking, Tustari is recognised first and foremost for his above-mentioned unique 'light' cosmology, which conceived of Muhammad as a cosmic entity composed of pure light (*nūr Muḥammadī*) emanating from the primordial light of God Himself.[102] He was forced to leave his native Tustar, relocating to Basra, in the wake of a controversy arising from his claim to be the 'proof of God' (*ḥujjat Allāh*), a claim most Muslim scholars consider tantamount to the 'heretical' notion of direct communion with the divine and a challenge to the finality of Muhammad's prophethood. Although there is no sign in the historical record of any obvious Shiᶜi affiliation on his part, or of charges thereof against him, the notion of *ḥujjat* – a key term in the Ismaᶜili system of thought – nonetheless implicates an affinity between Tustari's religious ideas and the Shiᶜi conception of the nature of the imam. Another possible source of Shiᶜi influence in his teachings is an earlier Qurᵓan commentary by the sixth Shiᶜi imam, Jaᶜfar al-Sadiq (d. 148/765), which Tustari seems to have had access to but is no longer extant. There are also some oblique signs that Tustari might have entertained sympathies for the cause of the Shiᶜi Zanj, who installed a governor of their own in Basra shortly before Tustari went into exile there.[103]

Mainstream Sufi tradition honours Tustari as one of its formative figures, notwithstanding the controversy that some of his religious and political positions caused during his lifetime. Excepting his forced departure from Tustar, neither he nor his immediate circle of disciples seem to have faced persecution because of their religious ideas or practices. Yet some of the later representatives of Tustari's spiritual legacy were reprimanded for espousing 'heretical' ideas and doctrines. Among the chastised groups was the Tustari-Salimiyya who derived from Tustari's closest pupil, Muhammad b. Salim, and eventually turned into a theologically orientated school; the Salimiyya would in time be consigned to an obscure role as a fringe historical sect in heresiographies, being associated, along with the so-named Hallaji sect, with *ḥull*, or incarnationism.[104] Others from among Tustari's original following in Basra later relocated to Baghdad where they evolved in different directions, some joining the Sufi circles of Junayd and others mixing with the Hanbalis.[105]

Looked at from this perspective, the Wafaʾi *silsila* gains particular significance as possibly the one and only Sufi line claiming an explicit and direct connection to the seminal Sufi figure Sahl al-Tustari. This hitherto little-known line must be the same line that some sources call the Hawwariyya, in reference to Abu Bakr b. al-Hawwari, who is shown in the Wafaʾi *silsila* as the link between Sahl al-Tustari and Abu'l-Wafaʾ's spiritual master, Talha al-Shunbuki. Haririzade Mehmed Kemaleddin's encyclopaedic work on Sufi orders from the nineteenth century is one of the rare sources that mention the Hawwariyya. Haririzade treats the Qadiri, the Rifaʿi, the Abhari and the Suhrawardi orders, along with the Wafaʾi order, as offshoots of the Hawwariyya.[106] Abu'l-Wafaʾ is depicted in the hagiography as asking one of his disciples to visit the tomb of his shaykh Abu Bakr b. al-Hawwari, suggesting a continuing sense of attachment in the early Wafaʾi milieu to the Hawwari line.[107] There are in the hagiography also many stories and pious sayings of Sahl al-Tustari, Dhu'l-Nun al-Misri, Talha al-Shunbuki and Abu Bakr b. al-Hawwari.[108] The spiritual lineage running through these names must have solidified into a relatively more permanent *silsila* under the influence of Abu'l-Wafaʾ, presumably after his death (notwithstanding the hagiographer's references to the path (*ṭarīḳ*) and cloak (*ḫırḳa*) of Abu'l-Wafaʾ in various anecdotes from the saint's lifetime), and re-named accordingly. While the exact timing of this process is difficult to determine, it is clear that by the time the hagiography was composed in the late fourteenth century, a distinctive Wafaʾi *silsila* had already crystallised and was important enough as a component of the larger Wafaʾi identity to be pronounced at the very outset in the hagiography. Its significance and integrity as a *silsila* would be preserved in Anatolia until as late as the middle of the sixteenth century, as evinced by the Wafa'i *ijāzas* found among the Alevi documents.[109]

Overall, the Wafa'i line is set apart in more than one way from other more mainstream Sufi *silsilas* of Iraq origin. First, it does not pass through Junayd.[110] In fact, Junayd is absent not only from the Wafa'i *silsila* but from Abu'l-Wafa''s hagiography altogether. This absence becomes especially noteworthy when one bears in mind the proximity of Qusan to Baghdad, a proximity to which Abu'l-Wafa' must owe his *nisba* Baghdadi. Also noteworthy here is a special spiritual connection that the hagiography posits to have existed between Abu'l-Wafa' and the famous Bayazid Bistami (d. 875?), 'one of the foremost "esotericists" in Islam', whose 'intoxicated Sufism' is often contrasted with Junayd's 'sober Sufism.'[111] The connection is established by a story in the hagiography, according to which Abu'l-Wafa' made twenty of his disciples eternal brothers (Ot. *āẖiret kardaşı*) with twenty Sufis affiliated with Bistami; this was reportedly following a disagreement between the two groups concerning the true affiliation of a fellow Sufi who had recently passed away.[112] Bistami was a Persian mystic from northeastern Iran who is purported to have received a nonphysical initiation in the Uwaysi style by the spiritual presence of Jaᶜfar al-Sadiq. He is renowned, among other things, for being the first Sufi to furnish an esoteric reading of the Prophet's nocturnal ascension, *Miᶜrāj*. Despite the geographical distance, Bistami was also well known to Sufis in Iraq. For the Baghdadi intellectuals, however, Bistami was 'a frontiersman', both in a geographical and a spiritual sense, 'unrestrained by the conventions of the city'.[113] All these considerations combined indicate a deliberate sense of distance and dissonance, temperamentally and/or doctrinally, between the early Wafa'i milieu and the Baghdadi Sufis, and some close (albeit apparently not entirely tension-free) contact with the intoxicated Sufism of the so-called School of Khorasan. Among leading representatives of the latter who were nearly contemporaneous with Abu'l-Wafa' were the famous Abu'l-Hasan al-Kharaqani (d. 1033), an illiterate shaykh, and Shaykh Abu Saᶜid b. Abu'l-Khayr (d. 1048), a jurist-turned-Sufi, whose combination of a (nominal) Sunni identity with anti-legalistic ideas and non-canonical ritual practices are reminiscent of Abu'l-Wafa'.[114]

An even more intriguing feature of the Wafa'i *silsila* that demarcates it from its many better-known counterparts is the distinctive social background of its three consecutive initiatic links, Abu Bakr b. al-Hawwari, Talha al-Shunbuki and Abu'l-Wafa': all three of them, according to *Tiryāq al-muḥibbīn*, were highway robbers before their conversion to the Sufi path.[115] These curious conversion stories recall, and perhaps were modelled after, the famous early Sufi Fudayl b. ᶜIyad (d. 187/803).[116] At the same time, they might also be a reflection of the distinct social milieu of lower Iraq, with its predominantly tribal geography where banditry was probably a routine part of economic life. Abu'l-Wafaᵓ's hagiography indeed affirms his tribal background, although says nothing of his putative early life as a bandit. Abu Bakr b. al-Hawwari was likewise of tribal extraction, with sources linking him to the Kurdish tribe of Hawwar, which apparently is the origin of his *nisba*.[117] Banditry is, of course, not identical with being a member of a tribe; in fact, it is possible that 'banditry' functions in this context as much as a metaphor for tribalism and provincialism as a belligerent economic activity. In any event, at a time when Sufism was still largely an urban-based, middle- and upper-class movement, the provincial/tribal background of Abu'l-Wafaᵓ and of his two most immediate *silsila* predecessors would have clearly distinguished them as atypical Sufi masters. Indeed, one of his Baghdadi detractors, revealing his social bias, remarked woefully that the caliph brought Abu'l-Wafaᵓ, who was until then residing in the backcountry (*yabanda tururken*), to Baghdad (for interrogation) where he was now gaining more followers.[118]

It would be foolhardy, however, to take the provincial/tribal sociocultural geography within which Abu'l-Wafaᵓ and his two immediate forebears apparently originated and grew up as suggesting that the Sufi tradition they embraced and perpetuated was of an inferior character. Worth underscoring here is another context where Sahl al-Tustari, Dhu'l-Nun al-Misri, Bayazid Bistami and Mansur al-Hallaj, whose memories were in different ways and to varying degrees entangled with the Wafaᵓi tradition, come together: the writings of Shihab al-Din Suhrawardi, commonly known as 'Shaykh al-Maqtūl' (the Murdered Master) for having been executed on charges of heresy. Born in Suhravard in northwestern Iran in 1154, Suhrawardi was the founder of the Illuminationist (*Ishrāqi*) philosophy that claimed to draw on the ancient wisdom of Iran, Greece and Egypt. His ideas influenced Iranian Sufism and Shiᶜism and 'found their way . . . sometimes through dim and secret historical channels, even into modern Iranian culture, after their interesting revival in the seventeenth-century School of Isfahan'.[119] In one of his works, Suhrawardi lays out 'a sort of spiritual *silsila*', which brings together Iranian, Greek and Egyptian names with a few Muslim ones, including Dhu'l-Nun al-Misri, Sahl al-Tustari, Bayazid Bistami, Mansur al-Hallaj and the illiterate Abu'l-Hasan al-Kharaqani, as carriers of the same ancient wisdom passed down from one to the other in that order.[120] That one of the most original and sophisticated thinkers of the Islamic world, as Suhrawardi undoubtedly was, staked claim to part of the same spiritual genealogy as Abu'l-Wafaᵓ, a little-known representative of provincial Sufism, is a striking reminder of the difficulty with treating popular and elite Sufism as if they were inherently clashing phenomena that belonged to two entirely different historical narratives. This point is particularly relevant for ideas and practices deemed heretical by the hegemons of Islam, which seem to be exactly the arena wherein popular and elite Sufism tended to converge. For non-conformist streams of Sufism that were pushed beyond the pale could find refuge only in spheres that either were socially peripheral to the urban power centres or lay behind the opaque terminology of learned Sufism.

Religious Metadoxy

Sources concur on Abu'l-Wafaᵓ's Sunni sectarian identity. According to *Tiryāq al-muḥibbīn*, he belonged to the Shafiᶜi school, while the hagiography claims that he did not adhere to any school exclusively, instead choosing to follow one of the four Sunni schools on different issues.[121] The hagiography, in a similar vein, portrays Abu'l-Wafaᵓ as defending what might be called the moderate Sunni position in his exchanges with individual Shiᶜis on the relative status of the Prophet's companions, deploying arguments based on divine providence to justify the legitimacy of the first three caliphs while still upholding the primacy of ᶜAli.[122] An even more pointed confirmation of Abu'l-Wafaᵓ's Sunni identity is a second, esoteric (*bāṭin*) *silsila* that both sources attribute to him. Like his exoteric (*ẓāhir*) *silsila*, it passes through Hawwari but from him reaches back to the first caliph, Abu Bakr al-Siddiq, rather than ᶜAli b. Abi Talib. Hawwari, it is said, received his first initiation in a dream from Abu Bakr, who conferred on Hawwari a coat (*khirqa*) and a cap as tokens of initiation. According to the *silsila*, the coat and the cap were passed on from Hawwari to Shunbuki, who then transmitted them to Abu'l-Wafaᵓ. Subsequently, they were passed to Abu'l-Wafaᵓ's disciple ᶜAli b. al-Hayti and from him to ᶜAli b. Idris al-Baᶜqubi, after which they were lost.[123] While this alternative Bakri *silsila* of Abu'l-Wafaᵓ might appear unusual from the perspective of later, institutionalised *silsila*s, which typically led from ᶜAli, there is, in fact, a powerful strain in early Sufism whose affiliates identified Abu Bakr as their spiritual forebear. One of the most important representatives of this strain was none other than Mansur al-Hallaj, who purportedly identified himself as a '*siddiqi*'.[124] Overall, this Bakri connection in Abu'l-Wafaᵓ's religious profile not only confirms his Sunni denomination but also reinforces his position as a transitional figure in the development of Sufism.[125]

Abu'l-Wafaᵓ's Sunni identity is, however, combined with an unmistakable pro-ᶜAlid disposition. His ᶜAlid orientation is evident in his pronounced commitment to the progeny of the Prophet, particularly the line ensuing from the fourth Shiᶜi imam, Zayn al-ᶜAbidin, to which Abu'l-Wafaᵓ himself allegedly belonged. It is also foregrounded in the hagiography as Abu'l-Wafaᵓ's special personal bond to ᶜAli, whose moral counsel he sought in making seemingly the hardest decision of his life, namely to return to society after years of solitude in the wilderness. It is difficult to determine to what extent this kind of ᶜAlid Sunnism, typically associated with the post-Mongol Sufi milieu, is more a reflection of the sensibilities of fourteenth-century Wafaᵓi circles in Iraq in which the hagiography was produced than Abu'l-Wafaᵓ's genuine religious leanings.[126] However, given the hagiography's overall Sunni slant, as well as the author's connection to the Sunni-dominated city of Wasit, if the hagiography had been subjected to a sectarian fine-tuning, one would expect a retrospective enhancement of Abu'l-Wafaᵓ's Sunni image rather than the other way around. For this reason, it seems more sensible to assume that the ᶜAlid component of the Wafaᵓi tradition was at least in part an imprint of its namesake and not an entirely later accruement.

Scholarship has yet to offer a clear picture of the origins of 'ᶜAlidism' as a suprasectarian adoration of ᶜAli and his progeny. It has been convincingly shown that the trend towards ᶜAlidism gained momentum during the Mongol era with the Ilkhanids' extension of special patronage to the *sayyid*s. For the *sayyid*s' descent-based claims for spiritual legitimacy and social authority provided a more legible model for the Ilkhanids, whose own legitimacy rested on their charismatic lineage from Chinggis.[127] Deeper roots of ᶜAlidism, however, predate the Mongols to roughly between the late ninth and twelfth centuries; one of its early manifestations was the establishment and dissemination of the *niqāba*, or syndicates of the ᶜAlid (or *Ṭālibid*) families, whose job it was to keep genealogical registers to prevent false claims of Prophetic descent.[128] The same appears to be true for the related but more specific phenomenon of various Shiᶜi elements infusing Sufism. While more amplified and pervasive during and after the Mongol era, Shiᶜi influences within Sufism must have had their initial seeds in an earlier period, as suggested by the example of Abu'l-Wafaᵓ, whose ᶜAlid orientation seems to be a direct legacy of Sahl al-Tustari and his Sufi circle in Basra.[129]

Historically, Abu'l-Wafaᵓ's ᶜAlid proclivities might also be linked to the variegated social, political and religious influences that prevailed in eleventh-century Iraq. The region of Qusan, with its strong Shiᶜa demographic and its location between two Sunni-dominated urban centres, must have been particularly propitious for the kind of ᶜAlid Sunnism that Abu'l-Wafaᵓ seems to have espoused. Two points are worth considering in this regard: first, the absence in the hagiography of a pronounced hostility towards the Shiᶜis, despite unequivocal disapproval of their teachings, specifically in regards to their rejection of the first three caliphs; and second, clues therein of frequent and affable day-to-day interactions between Qusan's Sunni and Shiᶜi inhabitants fostered by their physical proximity. Both points are brought home in an anecdote in the hagiography in which Abu'l-Wafa', during one of his sermons, comments on the kind of punishments that awaited the Shiᶜa in the hereafter and then weeps at such a grim prospect for people who, despite all their faults, testify to the oneness of God and the prophethood of Muhammad. Abu'l-Wafa''s remarks, apparently occasioned by the growing inclination of the local people to Shiᶜism, brings one of his servants in the audience to tears out of concern for his Shiᶜi neighbour. Soon after this incident, the neighbour, aided by the prayers and appeals to God of Abu'l-Wafa' and his servant, allegedly repents and abandons Shiᶜism (*meẕheb-i Rāfż*).[130]

Another story indicative of frequent and multifaceted cross-confessional encounters in Qusan during the lifetime of Abu'l-Wafa' alludes to the conflict between the Shiᶜi Mazyadid Sayf al-Dawla and Sultan Mesᶜud (mistakenly substituted for his father, Muhammad Tapar, in the hagiography). It recounts how one of Abu'l-Wafa''s disciples was wounded during the conflict and, pretending to be Shiᶜi, took refuge with a widow in a Shiᶜi (*Rāfiżī*) village. When Sultan Mesᶜud attacked the village, the widow's house was miraculously saved thanks to Abu'l-Wafa''s saintly intervention.[131] These undoubtedly embellished stories, whatever might be their historical core, are not only indicative of the contradictory and vacillating religious and political pressures in the environment in which Abu'l-Wafa' was active, but also reveal the permeability of boundaries between the Sunni and Shiᶜi populations in and around Qusan. Still more, they show that local Shiᶜis, as much as the Sunnis and other groups, were within Abu'l-Wafa''s range of vision as conceivable targets for his religious message. One can conjecture that a Sufism coloured with a strong veneration for the family of the Prophet (*Ahl al-bayt*) would potentially serve as a useful religious and political compromise in such a context of sectarian conflict and coexistence, with the notion of *sayyid*-ship forming an apt bridge between the two confessions, and would thereby enhance a proselytising Sufi master's cross-sectarian appeal.

What renders Abu'l-Wafa''s Sunnism even more unusual than its pro-ᶜAlid orientation is its curious confluence with an antinomian disposition. As noted earlier, Abu'l-Wafa''s spirited responses during his trial in Baghdad expressly posited the superiority of his understanding of Islam over that of the juristic ulema. His Islam, he declared, required no less than the mortification of the individual and the transformation of the self so that one is always mindful of God's presence, while that of exoterist ulema was confined to the profession of the oneness of God, the prophethood of Muhammad and conformity to the externals of religion. Abu'l-Wafaᵓ, in a similar vein, differentiated and established a hierarchy between, for instance, fasting during the month of Ramadan and fasting as a life-long disavowal of worldly desires and remission from all abject moral qualities.[132] Such an emphasis on the symbolic or inner dimensions of religious duties in a Sufi work would be unremarkable in and of itself were it not for the impression conveyed by the rest of the hagiography that, from the point of view of Abu'l-Wafaᵓ, a Sufi adept could forgo the performance of religious formalities in favour of a deeper spirituality and understanding. This is suggested by various other entries in the narrative, showing, for example, Abu'l-Wafaᵓ placing a greater premium on obtaining the favour (*himmet*) of one's shaykh over the actual performance of pilgrimage to Jerusalem or even Mecca.[133]

Moreover, while there are no detailed descriptions of their devotional practices, it seems that Abu'l-Wafaᵓ and his followers were known for certain ritual practices that would elicit ambivalence or outright condemnation by the self-claimed guardians of Islamic normativity. Among these were *samāᶜ* ceremonies involving dance and music, the Wafaᵓi version of which was evidently distinct enough to attract the mockery of other Sufis.[134] Even more noteworthy were their mixed-gender communal rituals and their (alleged) consumption of wine, the two quintessential markers of heresy from the perspective of juristic Islam. These appear as implicit charges against Abu'l-Wafaᵓ and his followers in a story whose cast includes Caliph al-Qaᵓim bi-Amrillah, the same caliph who had summoned the saint to the imperial capital for interrogation. Qaᵓim was known to have embraced and continued the conservative religious ideology of his father, Caliph al-Qadir, and for additionally implementing austere social policies, such as the prohibition of mixed-gender ferries on the Tigris and the eviction from Baghdad of 'singing girls and loose women'.[135] Caliph al-Qaᵓim bi-Amrillah, as the story goes, suspects Abu'l-Wafaᵓ of religious deviance and decides to test his piety. He does so by having one of his servants deliver to Abu'l-Wafaᵓ seven jars of wine with an attached message saying that drinking wine would be most appropriate for his kind of assemblies, in which men and women commingle. Sensing with his saintly foresight what was in them, Abu'l-Wafaᵓ miraculously transforms the contents of the jars from wine into butter and honey before distributing them among his dervishes. In return for the seven jars of wine, he subsequently sends to the caliph a cup containing the following three items: a piece of burning cinder, representing men's lust; some cotton, representing women's sensuality;

and a piece of ice, the ice preventing the cotton from catching fire.[136] This symbolically loaded gift, while clearly meant as a rejection of the caliph's barely veiled accusation of sexual immorality and consumption of wine, conveys a key idea that permeates the entire hagiography, namely the transformative power of a true shaykh, represented here by the piece of ice, that ensures the chastity of his disciples even when men and women are allowed to intermingle in Wafa'i ritual gatherings.[137] Tellingly, the same legend, with only slight variations and separate casts of characters, later circulated among the Wafa'i-Baba'i, Kizilbash and Bektashi circles.[138] This miracle motif, as such, appears as a golden thread that wove its way from the Iraqi Wafa'i milieu to the kindred Sufi and dervish groups in medieval Anatolia.

Just as volatile an issue as the esoteric and antinomian thrust of the hagiography from a standpoint of Islamic normativity is its attribution of saintly powers to Abu'l-Wafa', which included both an ability to cure the sick and foretell the future while alive, and the power to work miracles after death. As the aforementioned story of the collapsed dome demonstrates, Abu'l-Wafa''s spiritual presence sometimes revealed itself and offered guidance to his living followers in their dreams, a common trope in Sufi hagiographical literature. What are more unusual are stories in which Abu'l-Wafa' posthumously appears in corporeal form to physically aid his followers in trouble. For example, in one story he catches the architect who fell while restoring the collapsed dome of his tomb (the same miracle, incidentally, is attributed to Hacı Bektaş in his own hagiography).[139] In another story, Abu'l-Wafa''s spirit appears in full human form to console his disciples who are saddened by his bodily death, and urges them to visit his tomb to seek his help whenever they needed it.[140] Ideas about the immortality of the soul and its possible reincarnation in other bodies, which have been consistently condemned as 'heretical' excesses in normative Sufi texts, are likewise evident in different parts of his hagiography.[141]

Conclusion

Iraq, the original cradle of Sufism, was also the birthplace of the Wafa'i tradition, which recently surfaced Alevi documents show as having close historical ties with several Kizilbash/Alevi *ocak*s in eastern Anatolia. The Wafa'iyya formed around the saintly memory of a little-known enigmatic Sufi master, Abu'l-Wafa' al-Baghdadi, who was in many ways a transitional figure. He was active as a number of trends converged to permanently change the face of Sufism from a small, socially and religiously elitist movement to the most popular expression of Muslim piety. Having grown up in a tribal environment, Abu'l-Wafaʾ seems to have made a successful, if not entirely uncontested, entry into the world of Sufism, which was still largely based in cities at the time, and achieved renown during his lifetime by attracting a sizeable and socially diverse following. Abu'l-Wafaʾ, thus, should be viewed as both an early product and a facilitator of the process of Sufism's gradual penetration into rural and tribal settings from the eleventh century onwards.

Abu'l-Wafaʾ's complex religious profile thwarts the conventional view of sectarian identities – understood in terms of a spectrum that runs from being most Sunni and 'orthodox' to most Shiʿi and 'heterodox' – and appears to have taken shape amidst various contrary social, religious and political dynamics. His powerful renunciatory leanings, which would tone down later in his life but never entirely disappear, as well as his pronounced esoteric approach to Islam, betray the imprint of his roots in lower-Iraqi Sufism, issuing from one of the earliest Sufi communities formed in Basra around the seminal figure of Sahl al-Tustari. The ʿAlid strand in his religious outlook, coexisting with an esoteric Bakri *silsila*, is likewise predicted by the teachings of Tustari, whose thinking apparently absorbed various Shiʿi notions without him actually converting to Shiʿism. The nexus of an explicit Sunni affiliation (albeit in a minimalist sense, espousing the legitimacy of the first three caliphs) with a strong ʿAlid orientation within the persona of Abu'l-Wafaʾ might also be linked at some level to the complex and volatile political and religious conditions convening in eleventh-century Iraq, and more specifically in Qusan and its environs, during the saint's lifetime.

Granted, it is difficult to establish clear divisions between the various strains of early Sufism because of their fluid boundaries and the many cross-fertilisations among them; still, several features of Abu'l-Wafaʾ's complex religious profile set him apart from would-be 'orthodox' Sufis. What renders Abu'l-Wafaʾ's example particularly intriguing is its combination of a Sunni denomination with an antinomian disposition. The non-normative elements marking Abu'l-Wafaʾ's religious profile, including the interiorisation of ritual practice, belief in the eternity of the human spirit and mixed-gender communal ceremonies, are exactly the kind of ideas and practices condemned by tenth- and eleventh-century Sufi manuals as deviations from 'true' Sufism.[142] Their very appearance in this literature, even if only for the purpose of refutation, suggests that they were part and parcel of the broader historical landscape of Sufism. From this perspective, Abu'l-Wafaʾ appears as one of those mysterious characters who epitomised the 'antinomian and nonconformist edge' of Sufism that was increasingly pushed to the margins of Islam.[143]

The broader lesson highlighted by the case of Abu'l-Wafa' is the hazards of reading the early history of Sufism through the prism of the canonical version that later took shape. This tendency has led to the misattribution of various elements in the Kizilbash/Alevi belief system that deviate from normative Sufism to extra-Islamic sources, even though many of those elements were in fact part of historical Sufism, no matter what their distant origins might be. For example, the characteristic Alevi-Bektashi belief in the esoteric unity of Allah, Muhammad and ᶜAli is sometimes likened and connected to the Christian doctrine of the Holy Trinity. However, the parallel between this belief and the Sufi notion of the 'Muhammadan light' (*nūr Muḥammadī*) that originated with Sahl al-Tustari, and that also exists in a somewhat modified form in Shiᶜism, is hard to miss.[144] Similarly, the Alevi ritual dance of *semah*, featuring revolution and rotation, is commonly assumed to be a survival of shamanist ritual practices of pre-Islamic Central Asia. However, considering the historical affinity of many Kizilbash/Alevi *ocak*s to the Wafa'iyya as revealed by the Alevi documents, a link between the Alevi-Bektashi *semah* and the Wafa'i *samāᶜ* that reportedly involved a similar devotional dance appears much more reasonable.[145] Another good example is the institution of *musahiblik*, a spiritual covenant of life-long mutual support established between two Alevi couples. Also known as '*ahiret kardeşliği*' (lit. brotherhood of eternity), this institution is considered to be a sine qua non element of traditional Alevi socio-religious organisation. According to the hagiography, a similar spiritual covenant of brotherhood was established by Abu'l-Wafa' between his own disciples and the descendants of Bayezid Bistami's spiritual lineage. Whether or not one can presume a direct continuity between what appears to be a one-time Wafa'i practice and the routinised Alevi institution of *musahiplik*, it is obvious that such spiritual covenants were not unheard of in the early Sufi milieu of Iraq. These examples of parallel religious notions and practices between the early Wafa'i circles in Iraq and the Kizilbash/Alevi communities in Anatolia are too many and too distinct to be coincidental, especially given the historically demonstrable venues of transmission in the form of saintly lineages between these two milieus, which is the topic of Chapter 2.

Notes

1. 'İslām ne nesnedür, yā Şeyḫ? Ḥażreti Şeyḫ eyitdi: Sizüñ İslāmuñuz mı sorarsın yoḫsa benüm İslāmum mı? Sā'il eyitdi: Senüñ İslāmuñ benim İslāmuñ ġayri midür? Seyyid eyitdi: Neᶜam.' *Menāḳıb*-Turkish, fol. 28a; cf. *Menāḳıb*-Arabic, fol. 49b.

2. *Menāḳıb*-Turkish, fols 27b–29a; for a longer version of the story, see fols 101a–121b.
3. The Iraqi Wafaʾiyya should not be confused with the better known Egyptian Wafaʾi Sufi tradition and *sayyid*s, see Richard J. A. McGregor, *Sanctity and Mysticism in Medieval Egypt: The Wafāʾ Sufi Order and the Legacy of Ibn ʿArabī* (Albany: State University of New York Press, 2004), 52.
4. *FD/Scroll-IZA-2*.
5. An exception is Alya Krupp, *Studien zum Menāqybnāme des Abu l-Wafāʾ Tāğ al-ʿĀrifīn: Das historische Leben des Abu l-Wafāʾ Tāğ al-ʿĀrifīn* (München: Dr. Rudolf Trofenik, 1976). A rare, general work on Sufism that does briefly mention the Wafaʾiyya is Trimingham, *The Sufi Orders in Islam* (London: Oxford University Press), 49 n6.
6. *Menāḳıb*-Arabic. The only extant copy of this two-volume work, dated 878/1473, is in the Bibliothèque nationale in Paris: M. le Baron de Slane, *Bibliothèque nationale, Département des manuscrits: Catalogue des manuscrits arabes* (Paris: Imprimerie nationale, 1883–1895), no. 2,036. In about the late fifteenth century, *Menāḳıb*-Arabic was partially translated into Turkish under the title *Menāḳıb-ı Seyyid Ebü'l-Vefāʾ*, with the addition of a relatively long introduction; see *Menāḳıb*-Turkish. Ayla Krupp is the only researcher so far to have utilised both the Arabic original and the Turkish translation of the hagiography in her *Studien zum Menāqybnāme*. Notwithstanding its value, Krupp's work is a limited one that does not contain a comprehensive analysis of the hagiography's content. Nor does Krupp offer a systematic comparison between *Menāḳıb*-Arabic and *Menāḳıb*-Turkish. Such a task is also beyond the scope of the present study, although even a cursory comparison of the two versions demonstrates that the Turkish translation is based almost entirely on the first volume of *Menāḳıb*-Arabic, with only a limited number of passages from the second volume added to the end. In this work, references to the hagiography will be based primarily on *Menāḳıb*-Turkish. *Menāḳıb*-Arabic will be cited only occasionally to highlight meaningful and particularly relevant divergences between the two versions.
7. Several of Abu'l-Wafāʾ's disciples and associates carried the *nisba* 'Wāsiṭī' or lived in that city; see, for example, 'Şeyḫ Receb b. ʿImrān Wāsiṭī', fol. 57a; 'Ebu'l-Fażl Wāsiṭī', fol. 65b; and 'Ebu Turāb Mekkī', fol. 85a in *Menāḳıb*-Turkish. According to the hagiography, moreover, a governor of Wasit by the name of 'Marjān Ṭāwashī' defended Abu'l-Wafāʾ's shrine and surrounding areas in Qusan against Arab raiders (*ʿArab azğunları*), and established a well-endowed madrasa next to the shrine, *Menāḳıb*-Turkish, fols 74b–75a.
8. Krupp, *Studien*, 21–23; the existence of multiple hagiographic accounts of Abu'l-Wafāʾ's life is confirmed in Taqi al-Din ʿAbd al-Rahman b. ʿAbd al-Muhsin al-Wasiti, *Tiryāq al-muḥibbīn fī ṭabaqāt khirqat al- mashāyikh al-ʿārifīn* (Cairo: Maṭbaʿat al-Miṣr, 1305/1887), 42.

9. Wasiti, *Tiryāq al-muḥibbīn.*
10. Wasiti, *Tiryāq al-muḥibbīn*, 7. Drawing upon this source, Trimingham also counts the Shunbukiyya-Wafa'iyya line under the Rifaᶜi umbrella in his classical work, *The Sufi Orders in Islam*, 281.
11. Murtada al-Zabidi, *Rafᶜ niqāb al-khafā' ᶜan-man intahā ilā Wafā wa- Abī'l-Wafā'*, MS, Dār al-Kutup al-Miṣriyya, Tārīkh Taymūr, no. 2,323.
12. Haririzade Mehmed Kemaleddin, *Tibyān wasā'il al-ḥaqā'iq fī bayān salāsil al-ṭarā'iq*, 3 vols. (1876; reprint, Istanbul: n.p., 1949).
13. See, most importantly, ᶜAbd al-Wahhab al-Shaᶜrani, *al-Ṭabaqāt al-kubrā (or lawāqiḥ al-anwār fī ṭabaqāt al-akhyār)*, 2 vols (Cairo: al-Maṭbaᶜa al-ᶜĀmira al-ᶜUthmānīyya, 1316/1898), vol. 1: 221a–225a; Eyüb Sabri, *Mir'ātü'l-Ḥarameyn* (Istanbul: Baḥriyye Maṭbaᶜası, 1306/1890), 3: 134–136. Also see the multiple references to Abu'l-Wafa' in the collection of hagiographic anecdotes on Ahmad al-Rifaᶜi by Husam Ibrahim b. Muhammad al-Qazaruni, *Ahmed er-Rifâî Menkıbeleri* [*Shifā' al-Asḳām fī Sīrati Ġavs̱ al-Anām*], trans Nurettin Bayburtlugil and Necdet Tosun (Istanbul: Vefa Yayınları, 2008), 17, 24, 56. For an anecdote in which three of the leading disciples of Abu'l-Wafa' – ᶜAli b. Hayti, Baqa' b. Batu, and Majid Kurdi – attend ᶜAbd al-Qadir al-Jilani's circle, see *IAA*, s.v. 'Abdülkâdir Geylânî'. Another one of Abu'l-Wafa''s disciples, ᶜAbd al-Rahman at-Tafsunji, is depicted as a pupil of ᶜAbd al-Qadir al-Jilani; see *IAA*, s.v. 'Abdurrahmân Tafsûncî'.
14. Kafadar, *Between Two Worlds*, 76.
15. Mafizullah Kabir, *The Buwayhid Dynasty of Baghdad* (334/946–447/1055) (Calcutta: Iran Society, 1964), 84–87, 136–144, 201–211; G. Le Strange, *Baghdad during the Abbasid Caliphate: From Contemporary Arabic and Persian Sources* (London: Curzon Press, 1900/1990), 154–155. For Buyid history, also see John J. Donohue, *The Buwayhid Dynasty in Iraq 334H/945 to 403H/1012: Shaping Institutions for the Future* (Leiden: Brill, 2003).
16. For eleventh-century Baghdad, see George Makdisi, *History and Politics in Eleventh-Century Baghdad* (Aldershot: Variorum, 1990); Daphna Ephrat, *A Learned Society in a Period of Transition: The Sunni 'Ulema' of Eleventh-Century Baghdad* (Albany: State University of New York Press, 2000). For the Qadiri Creed, see Eric J. Hanne, *Putting the Caliph in His Place: Power, Authority, and the Late Abbasid Caliphate* (Madison and Teaneck: Fairleigh Dickinson University Press, 2007), 65–82; and Patrick Scharfe, 'Portrayals of the Later Abbasid Caliphs: The Role of the Caliphate in Buyid and Saljūq-era Chronicles, 936–1180' (MA Thesis, The Ohio State University, Ohio, 2010), 28, 39–41.
17. The view in older scholarship of a 'Sunni revival' following the end of Shiᶜi-Buyid rule has been modified in more recent scholarship that prefers the concept of 'Sunni recentering' as a more apt characterisation of the religious developments during the eleventh and twelfth centuries. The new term emphasises the traditionalist ulema rather than the Seljuk state as the

driving force behind changes in Sunni religious life during this period; for an early critique of the 'Sunni revival' thesis, see George Makdisi, 'The Sunni Revival', in *Islamic Civilization 950–1150*, ed. David S. Richards (Oxford: Cassirer, 1973), 155–168. For a discussion of 'Sunni recentering', see Jonathan P. Berkey, *The Formation of Islam: Religion and Society in the Near East, 600–1800* (New York: Cambridge University Press, 2003), 189–201; and Richard Bulliet, *Islam: The View from the Edge* (New York: Columbia University Press, 1995), 126–127.

18. A classical and still useful overview of religion under Seljuk rule is A. Bausani, 'Religion in the Seljuq Period', *Cambridge-Iran-5*, 283–302. For a recent discussion of Shiᶜism under the Seljuks, see A. C. S. Peacock, *The Great Seljuk Empire* (Edinburgh: Edinburgh University Press, 2015), 258–266; also see Berkey, *Formation of Islam*, 191–194.
19. *Menāḳıb*-Turkish, fols 156b–158a. The author of the hagiography seems to be confusing the Seljuk sultan Muhammed Tapar (r. 1105–1118) with his son Sultan (Giyaseddin) Mesᶜud (d. 1134–1152) from the Iraqi branch of the Seljuks, as it was Muhammed Tapar, not his son, who went to war against Sayf al-Dawla, the most famous member of the Mazyadid dynasty; for details, see Mawlawi Fadil Sanaullah, *The Decline of the Saljūqid Empire* (Calcutta: University of Calcutta, 1938), 108–127; Peacock, *Great Seljuk Empire*, 90–91; Seyfullah Kara, *Büyük Selçuklular ve Mezhep Kavgaları* (Istanbul: İz Yayıncılık, 2007), 153–163, 223. For Sayf al-Dawla, also see *DIA*, s.v. 'Sadaka b. Mansūr' by Abdülkerim Özaydın. A list of Mazyadid and Seljuk rulers is provided in Clifford Edmund Bosworth, *The New Islamic Dynasties: A Chronological and Genealogical Manual* (New York: Columbia University Press, 1996). For the dates of the Mazyadids, and the foundation of Hilla, see George Makdidi, 'Notes on Ḥilla and the Mazyadids in Medieval Islam', *Journal of the American Oriental Society* 74 (1954): 249–262.
20. *Menāḳıb*-Turkish, fol. 87b.
21. The Syrian geographer Yaqut (1179–1229) describes Qusan as a district with many villages between Nuᶜmaniyya and Wasit and the population of Nuᶜmaniyya as consisting of mostly 'extremist Shiᶜa' (*Shiᶜat ghāliyya*); see Yaqut b. ᶜAbdu'llah al-Hamawi, *Muᶜjam al-buldān*, 5 vols (Beirut: Dār al-Kuttāb al-ᶜIlmiyya, 1955), 4: 468, 339–340. At one point during Ottoman times, Qusan was an administrative district encompassing Nuᶜmaniyya; see Muhammad Rashid al-Feel, *The Historical Geography of Iraq between the Mongolian and Ottoman Conquests 1258–1534* (Najaf: Al-Adab Press, 1967), Map 18. For the religious and sectarian map of Iraq during the Buyid period, see Heribert Busse, *Chalif Und Grosskönig: Die Buyiden im Iraq (945–1055)* (Beirut: In Kommission bei F. Steiner, Wiesbaden, 1969), Map II. For the history of Wasit, see *EI-2*, s.v. 'Wāsiṭ'. Established in the late seventh century on the Tigris by the Umayyads as their provincial capital in Iraq, Wasit disappeared as a city with the change in the river's course.

22. *Menāḳıb*-Turkish, fols 158a–158b; for a shorter version of the story, see fol. 88b.
23. Ninth-century Batiha became the scene of the biggest slave revolt in the history of Islamdom, the well-known Zanj revolt, led by an alleged descendant of ᶜAli. About a century later it came under the rule of a felon named ᶜImran b. Shahin (d. 369/979) who fled to these marshlands and successfully resisted later Buyid attempts to subjugate him. He and his sons eventually gained official recognition as legitimate amirs of Batiha and maintained control over the whole swamp until the early eleventh century, refusing during this period to turn over fugitives to the Buyid and Seljuk authorities. For the history of Batiha and the biography of ᶜImran b. Shahin, see *DIA*, s.v. 'Batîha' by Hakkı Dursun Yıldız; and s.v. 'İmrân b. Şâhin' by Ali Yardım.
24. Trimingham, *The Sufi Orders in Islam*, 37–40, 49 n6.
25. Indeed, despite the mutual praising of Abu'l-Wafa' and Ahmad al-Rifaᶜi in the hagiography, there are also signs in the text of a rivalry between the followers of the two figures; see n 41 below.
26. Useful surveys of early Sufism include Alexander Knysh, *Islamic Mysticism: A Short History* (Leiden and Boston and Köln: Brill, 2000), especially the first six chapters; Ahmet T. Karamustafa, *Sufism: The Formative Period* (Berkeley: University of California Press, 2007); and Nile Green, *Sufism: A Global History* (Chichester and Malden, MA: Wiley-Blackwell, 2012), esp. Chapters 1 and 2. Also still useful is the classical work, Trimingham, *The Sufi Orders in Islam*. Specifically for the Seljuk period, also see Hamid Dabashi, 'Historical Conditions of Persian Sufism during the Seljuk Period', in *Heritage of Sufism-1*, 137–174.
27. Shaᶜrani, *Al-Ṭabaqāt al-kubrā*, 1: 107; Qazaruni, *Ahmed er-Rifâî*, 56; Zabidi, *Rafᶜ niqāb*, fol. 7a; and *Menāḳıb*-Turkish, fols 141b–144a.
28. Shaᶜrani, *Al-Ṭabaqāt al-kubrā*, 1: 108.
29. Karamustafa, *Sufism*, Chapter 4; and Dabashi, 'Historical Conditions of Persian Sufism', 144–153.
30. Although the image of the orthodox-minded jurist inflicting persecution on the Sufis finds an early precedence and prototype in the ninth-century Hanbali scholar Ghulam Khalil (d. 888), relevant tensions seem to have reached a high point during the eleventh century. For Ghulam Khalil and the persecution of Sufis prior to the eleventh century, see Annemarie Schimmel, 'Abū'l-Ḥusayn al-Nūrī: 'Qibla of the Lights', in *Heritage of Sufism-1*, 59–64; Carl W. Ernst, *Voices of Ecstasy in Sufism* (Albany: SUNY Press, 1985), 97–110; Gerhard Böwering, 'Early Sufism between Persecution and Heresy', in *Islamic Mysticism Contested: Thirteen Centuries of Controversies and Polemics*, eds Frederick De Jong and Bernd Radtke (Leiden: Brill, 1999), 45–67; Karamustafa, *Sufism*, 11–15, 21–23.
31. *DIA*, s.v. 'İbn Akîl, Ebü'l-Vefâ' and s.v. 'İbnü'l-Cevzî, Ebü'l-Ferec', both by Yusuf Şevki Yavuz; *EI-2*, s.v. 'Ibn ᶜAḳil' by G. Makdisi; and İsmail

Cerrahoğlu Abdurrahmân, 'Ibnu'l-Cevzi ve 'Zâdu'l-Mesir Fi İlmi't-tefsir' Adlı Eseri', *Ankara Üniversitesi İlahiyat Fakültesi Dergisi* 29 (1987): 127–134.

32. *Menāḳıb*-Turkish, fol. 29a.
33. Bausani, 'Religion in the Seljuq Period', 300. For relations between the Hanbalis and the Sufis, including a discussion of Hanbali jurists attracted to the ascetic strain of Sufism, see Christopher Melchert, 'Ḥanābila and the Early Sufis', *Arabica* XLVIII, no. 3 (2001): 352–367; and Donohue, *Buwayhid Dynasty*, 318–322.
34. According to another, longer version of the story in the hagiography, both Jawzi and Ibn ᶜAqil later apologised and asked for forgiveness from Abu'l-Wafaᵓ for his interrogation in Baghdad, and became his disciples. In the same place, even Abu'l-Faraj b. al-Jawzi is shown to have come to appreciate Abu'l-Wafaᵓ, and finally initiated into his path by one of his leading successors. However, these stories can be safely rejected as spurious. *Menāḳıb*-Turkish, fols 113a–114a.
35. Wasiti, *Tiryāq al-muḥibbīn*, 41. *Menāḳıb*-Turkish confirms these dates except the month of his death, fol. 6b. Zabidi likewise states that Abu'l-Wafaᵓ died after the year 500, at more than eighty years of age, Zabidi, *Rafᶜ niqāb*, fol. 7a.
36. Wasiti, *Tiryāq al-muḥibbīn*, 41 and *Menāḳıb*-Turkish, fol. 10b trace the genealogy of Abu'-Wafaᵓ back to Imam Zayn al-ᶜAbidin as follows: *Abu'l-Wafāᵓ← Muḥammad← Muḥammad← Muḥammad Zayd← Ḥasan al-Murtaḍā al-Akbar al-ᶜArīḍī ← Zayd←Imām Zayn al- 'Ābidīn*. The Alevi documents give the same basic genealogy, albeit with certain variations in the names and with occasional extra names interpolated into the chain; for example, in the oldest Alevi document that includes the family tree of Abu'l-Wafaᵓ, dated Dhu'l-hijja 855/1452, a certain ᶜAli appears between Muḥammad Zayd and Hasan al-Murtada al-Akbar al-ᶜAridi; *FD/ Ij-IZA-1*. Zabidi, on the other hand, questions the accuracy of this genealogy, proposing an alternative one that runs, after Imam Zayn al- 'Abidin, through Imam Muhammad al-Baqir and Imam Jaᶜfar al-Sadiq, see Zabidi, *Rafᶜ niqāb*, fol. 5b.
37. Wasiti, *Tiryāq al-muḥibbīn*, 41; *Menāḳıb*-Turkish, fols 6b, 12a–14b.
38. *Menāḳıb*-Turkish, fols 14b–15a.
39. *Menāḳıb*-Turkish, fol. 6b; Wasiti, *Tiryāq al-muḥibbīn*, 43.
40. The word *Kākīs* is defined as '*erenler atası*' (father of saints) in *Menāḳıb*-Turkish, fol. 6b, and somewhat similarly as '*Abu al-rijāl*' (father of men) in *Menāḳıb*-Arabic, fol. 5a. In *Ṭabaqat*-Wasiti, 43, the name is likewise spelled *Kākīs*, but no specific Kurdish connection is emphasised. An Alevi document, on the other hand, spells the term as *Bākīs*, translates it as 'shepherd' (Ar. *ar-rāᶜī*; T. *çoban*), and claims that it was a nickname given to Abu'l-Wafaᵓ by his mother. The latter appears a much less likely explanation, however, given the fact that the root *kāk* or *kak* carries the meaning

of 'older brother' in the Kurdish language and is also used as a term of address for men in general. Michael C. Chyet, *Kurdish–English Dictionary/ Ferhenge Kurmancî-Inglîzî* (New Haven: Yale University Press, *c.*2003); personal correspondence with Erdal Gezik. Among Kurdish-speaking Alevis in Anatolia, we also see the use of derivatives of this same root as a term of respectful address for Alevi *dedes*. For an example, see my paper 'The Emergence of the Kızılba in Western Thought: Missionary Accounts and their Aftermath', in *Archaeology, Anthropology and Heritage in the Balkans and Anatolia: The Life and Times of F. W. Hasluck 1878–1920*, ed. David Shankland, 2 vols (Istanbul: ISIS Press, 2004), 2:329–353. This etymology, meanwhile, also raises the intriguing question of a possible connection between Abu'l-Wafa''s spiritual legacy and the Kurdish-speaking Kakaᶜis of Iraq, as the root meaning of this group's label appears to be part of the same semantic universe; see C. J. Edmonds, *Kurds, Turks, and Arabs* (London and New York: Oxford University Press, 1957), 184–185.

41. *Menāḳıb*-Turkish, fol. 84b.
42. 'zīrā ekseri bīnemāzlardan[dur] ve umūr-ı şeriᶜiyyeye riᶜāyet itmezler', *Menāḳıb*-Turkish, fol. 51a.
43. 'bu Kürdlerde fāsiḳ yokdur', *Menāḳıb*-Turkish.
44. See, for example, *Menāḳıb*-Turkish, fol. 15a.
45. *Menāḳıb*-Turkish, fols 6b–10b.
46. Wasiti, *Tiryāq al-muḥibbīn*, 41.
47. *Menāḳıb*-Turkish, fols 13b–14b.
48. *Menāḳıb*-Turkish, fols 15a–16a.
49. *Menāḳıb*-Turkish, fols 16a–18a.
50. *Menāḳıb*-Turkish, fols 18a–19b
51. *Menāḳıb*-Turkish, fol. 18b. In *Menāḳıb*-Arabic, fol. 10a, the shaykh's name is given as 'Shaykh ᶜAli ᶜAjami', but that too is far too unspecific to help us identify him as a historical figure.
52. *Menāḳıb*-Turkish, fols 18a–19b.
53. *Menāḳıb*-Turkish, fols 20a–20b.
54. Christopher Melchert, 'The Transition from Asceticism to Mysticism at the Middle of the Ninth Century C.E.', *Studia Islamica* 83 (1996): 51–70. This was, however, not a seamless transition as projected by the Sufis' own traditional accounts of their origins that treat the early 'Muslim ascetics as the natural forebears of the Sufis'. Green, *Sufism*, 20.
55. *Menāḳıb*-Arabic, fols 10a–11a; cf. *Menāḳıb*-Turkish, fols 20a–22a.
56. Wasiti, *Tiryāq al-muḥibbīn*, similarly, does not mention any of the adopted sons of Abu'l-Wafa' other than Sayyid Matar, whom he presents as Abu'l-Wafā''s primary successor. Ibid., 42.
57. The seven adopted sons of Abu'l-Wafa' are listed as follows: '*ve ol yedi ᶜazīzüñ birisi Seyyid Maṭar'dur ki Seyyid Salim oğlıdur ki Seyyid Ebü'l-Vefā''nuñ ḳardaşıdır ve birisi Seyyid Ġānim'dür ki Erba'īn'de Ebü'l-'Abbās diyü ẕikr olınur ki Seyyid Müncih[?] oğlıdur. Seyyid Müncih [bin?]*

Muḥammed bin Seyyid Zeyd'dür ki Ebü'l-Vefā°'nuñ dedesidür ve birisi Seyyid Muḥammed bin Seyyid Kemāl Ḥayāt ibni Seyyid Muḥammed bin Seyyid Zeyd'dür ve birisi Seyyid ᶜAlī bin Seyyid Ḫamīs'dür ki Seyyid Zeyd oğlıdur, Erba'īn'de ᶜAlī bin Üstād diyü ẕikr olınur. Ḫamīs diyü anuñ içün didiler Seyyid Zeyd'ün beşinci oğlıdur ve birisi ᶜAbdu'r-raḥmān Ṭefsūncī'dür ve birisi Şeyḫ ᶜAlī bin Heyetī'dür ve birisi Şeyḫ ᶜAsker-i Şūlī'dür ki nesebi İmām Ḥasan ᶜAskerī'ye çıkar.' Menāḳıb-Turkish, fol. 21a. Elsewhere in the hagiography, Sayyid Ghanim is more clearly described as a nephew of Abu'l-Wafa°: *'ve birisi seyyid şerīf Ebū'l-Maᶜālī Aḥmed bin Şeyḫ Rükne'd-dīn ki Seyyid Ġānim oğlanlarındandur ki Hażret-i Seyyid'üñ ḳardaşı oğlıdur.*' Ibid., fol. 21a.

58. *Menāḳıb*-Turkish, fol. 155b; cf. *Menāḳıb*-Arabic, fol. 75a
59. Zabidi, *Rafᶜ niqāb*, fol. 7a.
60. *Menāḳıb*-Turkish, fols 5a–5b.
61. Zabidi, *Rafᶜ niqāb*, fol. 7a.
62. The hagiography itself was produced within the Jerusalemite family called Badris, who were descendants of Sayyid Matar, son of Sayyid Salim. The Arabic text was transmitted to Seyyid Velayet by a member of this family while they were both in Egypt; see Jonathan Brack, 'Was Ede Bali a Wafā°ī Shaykh? Sufis, Sayyids, and Genealogical Creativity in the Early Ottoman World', in *Islamic Literature and Intellectual Life in Fourteenth-Century Anatolia*, eds A. C. S. Peacock and Sara Nur Yıldız (Würzburg: Ergon Verlag, 2016), 339–340.
63. *Menāḳıb*-Turkish, fols 35b–36a; cf. *Menāḳıb*-Arabic, 18a.
64. *Menāḳıb*-Arabic, fol. 88a; cf. Krupp, *Studien zum Menāqybnāme*, 28. This note, found in the second volume of *Menāḳıb*-Arabic, is missing in the Turkish version, which is based almost entirely on the first volume.
65. *Menāḳıb*-Turkish, 64b, 73b.
66. *Menāḳıb*-Turkish, fol. 73b.
67. Karl Jahn, *Geschichte Ġāzān-Ḫān's Aus Dem Ta°riḫ-i-mubārak-i-Ġāzānī Des Rašīd Al-Dīn Faḍlallāh B. ᶜImād Al-Daula Abūl-Ḫair* (London: Luzac & Co., 1940), 106.
68. The brief and incomplete note in Çelebi's *Seyaḥatnāme* mentions a tomb-shrine located to the northeast of Wasit that belonged to a certain 'Ḥażret-i Sulṭān Tāj al-ᶜĀrifīn' – the name apparently left incomplete for a later addition that never happened, *Evliya-Seyahatnâme*, 2: 299.
69. *H. 1330/1912 Tarihli Musul Vilayet Salnamesi*, eds Cengiz Eroğlu, Murat Babuçoğlu, and Orhan Özdil. (Ankara: ORSAM, 2012), 398. The genealogical information included in the source leaves little doubt that the person to whom the tomb is dedicated is Abu'l-Wafa° al-Baghdadi.
70. For individual disciples of Abu'l-Wafa°, see related articles in Shaᶜrani, *Al-Ṭabaqāt al-kubrā* and in *IAA*. Sayyid Matar's name appears in these as 'Sayyid Maṭar al-Bādarā°ī'; see, for example, Shaᶜrani, 117.
71. *Menāḳıb*-Turkish, fols 34a–35a, 90b–91b. While Sufi elements in the

Yazidi tradition have been recognised in the historiography, the origin of its founder, ᶜAdi b. Musafir, has so far remained a question; for a brief discussion, see Nelida Fuccaro, 'The Ottoman Frontier in Kurdistan in the Sixteenth and Seventeenth Centuries', in *The Ottoman World*, ed. Christine Woodhead (London: Routledge, 2011), 247–248.

72. *Menāḳıb*-Turkish, fol. 16a.
73. *Menāḳıb*-Turkish, fols 43b–46a.
74. *Menāḳıb*-Turkish, fols 164b–165b.
75. *Menāḳıb*-Turkish, fols 123a, 142a–142b, 37a.
76. *Menāḳıb*-Turkish, fols 92b–93b.
77. *Menāḳıb*-Turkish, fols 163b and 139b.
78. *Menāḳıb*-Turkish, fols 81b–82a.
79. Zabidi, *Rafᶜ niqāb*, fols 5b–13a. Also see McGregor, *Sanctity and Mysticism in Medieval Egypt*, 52.
80. For the Badri family, see Nimrod Luz, 'Aspects of Islamization of Space and Society in Mamluk Jerusalem and Its Hinterland', *Mamluk Studies Review* 6 (2002): 133–154; and Daphna Ephrat, *Spiritual Wafarers, Leaders in Piety: Sufis and the Dissemination of Islam in Medieval Palestine* (Cambridge: Cambridge University Press, 2008), 158–160, 161–165. For the contacts between Seyyid Velayet and the Badri family, see Brack, 'Was Ede Bali a Wafāʾī Shaykh?', 339–343.
81. Heghnar Zeitlian Watenpaugh, 'Deviant Dervishes: Space, Gender, and the Construction of Antinomian Piety in Ottoman Aleppo', *International Journal of Middle East Studies* 37 (2005): 541–542; and Marco Salati, 'An Act of Appointment to the Leadership of the Wafāʾiyya Sufi Order from the Ottoman Court Records of Aleppo (1099/1687)', *Eurasian Studies* XI (2013): 79–84.
82. Trimingham, *The Sufi Orders in Islam*, 281.
83. Kazuo Morimoto, 'An Enigmatic Genealogical Chart of the Timurids: A Testimony to the Dynasty's Claim to Yasavi-ᶜAlid Legitimacy,' *Oriens* 44, nos 1–2, (2016), 154.
84. *Menāḳıb*-Turkish, fols 121b–124b.
85. *Menāḳıb*-Turkish, fol. 53a; in *Menāḳıb*-Arabic, '*li-daᶜwa al-khalq ilā al-khaq*', fol. 27a.
86. *Menāḳıb*-Turkish, fols 53a–54b; cf. *Menāḳıb*-Arabic, fols 27a–27b.
87. Devin DeWeese, 'Yasavī Šayḫs in the Timurid Era: Notes on the Social and Political Role of Communal Sufi Affiliations in the 14th and 15th Centuries', *Oriente Moderno* 76, no. 2 (1996): 173.
88. The concept of 'communal Sufi affiliations' is reminiscent of Trimingham's notion of *ṭāʾifa*s (differentiated from *ṭarīqa*s), with the caveat that he sees the formation of the *ṭāʾifa*s as a degeneration of classical ideals of Sufism, rather than assessing it as an independent and potentially productive socio-religious development. See Trimingham, *The Sufi Orders in Islam*, Chapter 3.

89. A few stories also show Abu'l-Wafa[ʾ] successfully converting Jews and crypto-Christians to Islam, but these are all cases of individual rather than communal conversions; see *Menāḳıb*-Turkish, 62b and 75b–76a.
90. *Menāḳıb*-Turkish, fols 46a–46b.
91. Devin DeWeese, 'The Sayyid Atāʾī Presence in Khwārazm during the 16th and Early 17th Centuries', in *Studies on Central Asian History in Honor of Yuri Bregel*, ed. Devin DeWeese (Bloomington: Research Institute for Inner Asian Studies, 2001), 276.
92. *Menāḳıb*-Turkish, fols 96a–97a.
93. *Menāḳıb*-Turkish, fols 11a–11b.
94. *Dhū'l-Nūn al-Miṣrī ←Isrāfīl al-Maghribī ←Abū ʿAbdullah M. Ḥubaysha at-Tābiʿī ←Jābīr al-Anṣārī' al-Ṣaḥḥābī ←ʿAlī b. Abī Ṭālib*. This same *silsila* is also one of the initiatic chains postulated for Ahmad al-Rifaʿi, which is the one used by Wasiti to connect the Shunbukiyya-Wafaʾiyya line to the Rifaʿiyya order; see Wasiti, *Tiryāq al-muḥibbīn*, 44.
95. These two versions in their complete forms are included in four separate Wafaʾi *ijāza*s, the oldest of which belongs to the *ocak* of Imam Zeynel Abidin and is dated Dhu'l-hijja 855/1452; see *FD/Ij-IZA-1*. Another copy of the same *ijāza*, dated Dhu'l-hijja 990/1582, is virtually identical except for some editing reflecting later Shiʿi-Alevi sensibilities; it is found among the documents of the Tunceli/Malatya branch of the Ağuiçens; see *FD/Ij-AGU-Ma*. The second *ijāza* belongs to the Malatya branch of Dede Kargıns and is similarly extant in two copies, both found in scrolls comprising multiple documents; the first copy, *FD/Ij-Wafaʾi-DK-1*, is dated 10 Muharram 905/1499, while the second, *FD/Ij-Wafaʾi-DK-2*, bears the date Jumada al-awwal 952/1545. The third *ijāza*, dated Safar 916/1520, comes from the *ocak* of Kara Pir Bad centred in Divriği-Karageban; see *FD/Ij-KaraPirBad*. Finally, the fourth *ijāza* comes from the *ocak* of Kureyşan centred in Tunceli; its date is for all practical purposes unknown because only the last two digits of the year are given in the document; see *FD/Ij-Kureyşan*.
96. But Tustari is misspelled as 'Taskari' in *FD/Ij-Wafaʾi-DK-1* and *FD/Ij-Kureyşan*, and Nahrawani is misread and Turkified as 'Nahrulu' in *FD/Ij-KaraPirBad*.
97. In two of the *ijāza*s, for instance, al-Hawwari's *nisba* is misspelled as 'al-Harrawi', an obvious copying mistake caused by an inadvertent change in the order of the letters.
98. *FD/Ij-AGU-Ma*.
99. Karamustafa, *Sufism*, 43. For a discussion of Basran Sufism, also see Alexander Knysh, *Islamic Mysticism*, Chapter 5.
100. For the main *ṭarīqa* lines, see Trimingham, *The Sufi Orders in Islam*, 12, 31–51.
101. Ernst, *Words of Ecstasy*, 10, 43–44, 102–110. The most detailed study on Hallaj was carried out by Louis Massignon; for an abridged English

version of his four-volume majestic work on the subject, see *The Passion of Al-Hallaj: Mystic and Martyr of Islam* (Princeton, NJ: Princeton University Press, 1994).

102. The doctrine of *nūr Muḥammadī* also appears in the writings of al-Hakim at-Tirmidhi (d. 869?) and Ibn al-ᶜArabi, and informs both Sufi and Shiᶜi concepts of sainthood (*walāya*); see 'Nur Muhammadi', *The Oxford Dictionary of Islam*, ed. John L. Esposito (New York: Oxford University Press, 2003).
103. Karamustafa, *Sufism*, esp. 38–43. For more details about Sahl al-Tustari, see Gerhard Böwering, *The Mystical Vision of Existence in Classical Islam: The Qur'anic Hermeneutics of the Ṣūfī Sahl at-Tustarī (d. 283/896)* (Berlin: De Gruyter, 1980), esp. 58–75; and 'Sehl et-Tüsterî', *DIA*.
104. Trimingham, *The Sufi Orders in Islam*, 11; For more information regarding the Salimiyya, see Böwering, *Mystical Vision*, 89–99; Karamustafa, *Sufism*, 104–114. For *ḥulūl* as a category of 'heresy', also see Ernst, *Words of Ecstasy*, 120–123.
105. Böwering, *Mystical Vision*, 75–99.
106. Haririzade, *Tibyān wasā'il*, vol. 3: fols 263a, 263b, 221a. Haririzade gives Abu Bakr b. al-Hawwari's full name as 'Abū Bakr b. Hawāzin al-Hawwarī al-Baṭā'ihī' and reports that he opposed the cooking of meat, including fish, at his shrine (*turba*), implying that he was probably a strict vegetarian, as was his master Sahl al-Tustari.
107. *Menāḳıb*-Turkish, fol. 71b.
108. Most of the relevant passages are in the second volume of *Menāḳıb*-Arabic, esp. fols 92b–93a, 104a–128a, and did not therefore make it to *Menāḳıb*-Turkish.
109. This chronology represents a certain divergence from DeWeese's observation that the *silsila* became the primary 'guarantor of legitimacy' no earlier than the late fifteenth century, see, for example, Devin DeWeese, 'The Legitimation of Bahā' ad-Dīn Naqshband,' *Asiatische Studien/Études asiatiques* 60, no. 2 (2006): 261–262, 268–271.
110. This point is also highlighted as unusual in Wasiti, *Tiryāq al-muḥibbīn*, 44.
111. S. H. Nasr, 'Sufism', *Cambridge-Iran-4*, 457. Trimingham, *The Sufi Orders in Islam*, 4, 12.
112. *Menāḳıb*-Turkish, fols 68b–69b.
113. Green, *Sufism*, 38.
114. For the Sufi Schools of Khorasan and Baghdad, as well as the limits of this categorisation, see Herbert Mason, 'Ḥallāj and the Baghdad School of Sufism', and Terry Graham, 'Abū Saᶜīd ibn Abī'l-Khayr and the School of Khurāsān', both in *Sufi Heritage-1*, 65–82 and 83–136. For Kharaqani and Abu Saᶜid, also see Karamustafa, *Sufism*, 122–124; and Dabashi, 'Historical Conditions of Persian Sufism', esp. 137–138.
115. Wasiti, *Tiryāq al-muḥibbīn*, 41–42.
116. Böwering, 'Early Sufism', 47–48.
117. *IAA*, s.v. 'Ebû Bekr bin Hüvârâ El-Betâihî'.

118. *Menāḳıb*-Turkish, fol. 108a; in *Menāḳıb*-Arabic, '*kāna ba*ᶜ*īdan*', fol. 48b.
119. Bausani, 'Religion in the Seljuq Period', 302.
120. Bausani, 'Religion in the Seljuq Period', 301–302. For Suhrawardi's perception of Sufism, and more specifically of Dhu'l-Nun al-Misri and Sahl al-Tustari, within his broader framework of the ancient wisdom of the East, see John Walbridge, *The Wisdom of the Mystic East: Suhrawardī and Platonic Orientalism* (Albany: State University of New York, 2001), esp. 42–46.
121. al-Wasiti, *Tiryāq al-muḥibbīn*, 41; *Menāḳıb-Turkish*, fol. 11b
122. *Menāḳıb-Turkish*, fols 60b–62a.
123. *Menāḳıb*-Turkish, fols 11a–11b; al-Wasiti, *Tiryāq al-Muḥibbīn*, 42–43.
124. Massignon, *Passion of al-Hallaj*, 273; for Abu Bakr's particularly high standing among early Sufis, also see John Renard, 'Abū Bakr in Tradition and Early Hagiography', in *Tales of God's Friends: Islamic Hagiography in Translation*, ed. John Renard (Berkeley: University of California Press, 2009), 15–29.
125. While one cannot exclude completely the possibility that Abu'l-Wafaᵓ might have been a Shiᶜi masquerading as a Sunni – especially given that the Shafiᶜi *madhab* he reportedly belonged to is the school of religious law that is closest to the Shiᶜa and therefore normally adopted by Shiᶜis practicing *taqiyya* – it would be baseless to make such a claim without any concrete evidence pointing in that direction.
126. I define ᶜAlid Sunnism as the espousal of *tawallā*, or 'adhesion to and support [for the ᶜAlid s]', without the endorsement of *tabarrā*, or 'declaring oneself free [of the opponents of the ᶜAlid s]', the two together constituting the twin principles of Shiᶜi Islam. The translation of the terms has been adopted from Clifford E. Bosworth, 'Bahāᵓ al-Dīn ᶜĀmilī in the Two Worlds of the Ottomans and Safavids', in *Convegno sul tema La Shīᶜa nell'impero ottomano: Roma, 15 aprile 1991* (Rome: Accademia Nazionale dei Lincei, 1993), 99. The same phenomenon was also termed 'Shiᵓi-Sunni syncretism' and described as a characteristic of 'folk Islam'. H. R. Roemer, 'The Safavid Period', *Cambridge-Iran-6*, 192–194.
127. The religious outlook of the Turco-Iranian world during this period has been described as being marked by 'confessional ambiguity'. For the term's first use in this context, see John E. Woods, *The Aqquyunlu: Clan, Federation, Empire*, 2nd edn (Salt Lake City: The University of Chicago Press, 1999), 1. For the Mongol/Ilkhanid impact on the growing salience of *sayyid*-ship as a marker of spiritual authority, and other relevant bibliography, see Judith Pfeiffer, 'Confessional Ambiguity vs. Confessional Polarization: Politics and the Negotiation of Religious Boundaries in the Ilkhanate', in *Politics, Patronage and the Transmission of Knowledge in 13th–15th Century Tabriz*, ed. Judith Pfeiffer (Leiden: Brill, 2013), 129–168. For a conventional view of the growing Shiᶜitization of Sufism in the post-Mongol period, also see A. Bausani, 'Religion in the Post-Mongol Period', *Cambridge-Iran-5*, 538–549.

128. Teresa Bernheimer, *The ᶜAlids: The First Family of Islam, 750–1200* (Edinburgh: Edinburgh University Press, 2013), especially Chapter 4. Also see, idem, 'Genealogy, Marriage, and the Drawing of Boundaries among the ᶜAlids (Eighth–Twelfth Centuries)', in *Sayyid and Sharifs in Muslim Societies: The Living Links to the Prophet*, ed. Morimoto Kazuo (London: Routledge, 2012), 75–76; and Donohue, *Buwayhid Dynasty*, 288, 303–314. For the architectural manifestation of ᶜAlidism in medieval Islamdom, see Stephennie Mulder, *The Shrines of the ᶜAlids in Medieval Syria: Sunnis, Shiᶜis and the Architecture of Coexistence* (Edinburgh: Edinburgh University Press, 2014).
129. The relationship between Sufism and Shiᶜism is an important topic that is still in need of a comprehensive treatment. The most useful existing treatments of the topic include Marshall G. S. Hodgson, *The Venture of Islam: Conscience and History in a World Civilization* (Chicago: The University of Chicago Press, 1977), 2: 369–385, 445–455, 463; Mustafa Kamil Shaybi, *Sufism and Shiᶜism* (Surbiton: LAAM, 1991); Seyyed Hossein Nasr, 'Shiᶜism and Sufism: Their Relationship in Essence and in History', *Religious Studies* 6, no. 3 (September 1970): 229–242; M. A. Amir-Moezzi, *The Divine Guide in Early Shiᶜism: The Sources of Esotericism in Islam*, trans. D. Streight (Albany: State University of New York Press, 1944), 50–51; and Farhad Daftary, 'Ismaili–Sufi Relations in Post-Alamut Persia', in *Ismailis in Medieval Muslim Societies: A Historical Introduction to an Islamic Community*, ed. Farhad Daftary (London: I. B. Tauris, 2005), 183–213.
130. *Menāḳıb*-Turkish, fols 87a–88b.
131. *Menāḳıb*-Turkish, fols 156a–157b.
132. *Menāḳıb*-Turkish, fols 27b–28b.
133. *Menāḳıb*-Turkish, fols 65b–66a, 136a–136b.
134. *Menāḳıb*-Turkish, fol. 84b. For Abu'l-Wafaᵓ's view concerning the appropriateness of *samāᵓ* ceremonies for those with a polished heart, see *Menāḳıb*-Turkish, fol. 30b.
135. Scharfe, *Portrayals of the Later Abbasid Caliphs*, 77.
136. *Menāḳıb*-Turkish, fols 105b–106b.
137. In addition to this story, which implicitly confirms the point, we have other clues in the historiography of mixed-gender Wafaᵓi ritual gatherings. In another story, for instance, the caliph joins under disguise the crowd of Abu'l-Wafaᵓ's followers during a communal ritual, touches a couple women inappropriately as a way of testing them, and gets scolded by them; *Menāḳıb*-Turkish, 105a. There is, however, no other sign of wine drinking in the hagiography that I could identify.
138. The saintly figures supplanting Abu'l-Wafaᵓ in the legend's different derivatives include Geyikli Baba, Shaykh Marzuban, and Abdal Musa; for references and details, see n28 and n43 in Chapter 2. The miracle motif of changing wine into honey is also encountered in varying contexts in the

fifteenth-century hagiography of the most important representative of the Qadiri tradition in late medieval Anatolia, Eşrefoğlu Rumi, and in that of the famous Mevlana Celalleddin Rumi. See Abdullah Veliyuddin Bursevi, *Menâkıb-ı Eşrefzâde (Eşrefoğlu Rûmî'nin Menkıbeleri)*, ed. Abdullah Uçman (Istanbul: Kitabevi Yayınları, 2009), 23–24; *MNK-Eflaki*, 2:885. In *Cevāhirü'l-ebrār min emvāci'l-bihār*, which was compiled at the end of the sixteenth century, the miracle of preventing a piece of cotton from catching fire is attributed to Ahmed-i Yesevi with the same underlining symbolism. Fuad Köprülü in *Türk Edebiyatında İlk Mutasavvıflar* (1919; reprint, Ankara: Türk Tarih Kurumu, 1993), 33–34.

139. *Menāḳıb*-Turkish, fols 74a–74b.
140. *Menāḳıb*-Turkish, fol. 139a.
141. *Menāḳıb*-Turkish, fols 68a–68b and 33b–34a; cf. *Menāḳıb*-Arabic, fols 32a–32b.
142. Karamustafa, *Sufism*, 155–160.
143. Karamustafa, *Sufism*, 176, 166; Green, *Sufism*, 25.
144. Hossein Nasr, 'Shiᶜism and Sufism', 235.
145. This, of course, does not necessarily preclude extra-Islamic influences on Kizilbash/Alevi beliefs and ritual practices (or Sufism for that matter), although taking them as foundational is problematic. The conclusion reached in a recent study by Thierry Zarcone of possible Shamanic influences on the Bektashi-Alevi Dance of the Crane is worth noting in this regards. Zarcone writes: 'To summarise, the Bektashi-Alevi "Dance of the Crane" is, without any doubt, a Mystical/Sufi ceremony and no more, though based on some Shamanic elements which have been reinterpreted over time.' Thierry Zarcone, 'The Bektashi-Alevi 'Dance of the Crane' in Turkey: A Shamanic Heritage?', in *Shamanism and Islam: Sufism, Healing Rituals and Spirits in the Muslim World*, eds Thierry Zarcone and Angela Hobart (London and New York: I. B. Tauris, 2017), 213.

2

The Forgotten Forefathers: Wafaʾi Dervishes in Medieval Anatolia

[A]ny historical narrative is a particular bundle of silences.

– Michel-Rolph Trouillot, *Silencing the Past: Power and the Production of History*

Already during his lifetime, or soon after, Abu'l-Wafaʾ's influence seems to have expanded beyond Iraq, gaining a footing on the eastern and southern edges of Anatolia through his associates and descendants who settled in northern Mesopotamia as far as Hakkari and various localities in the Levant. During the first half of Abu'l-Wafaʾ's Sufi career, Anatolia proper, however, was still part of Byzantine territory, with its southeastern rim forming the frontier between Christendom and Islamdom. Established in the seventh century, this frontier would eventually shift further to the west after the Seljuk commander Alparslan defeated the Byzantine imperial army in the Battle of Manzikert in 1071. With this victory began a new era in the 'lands of Rum' – that is, the 'lands of the Romans' – as Muslims called Anatolia at the time. Recently Islamised Turkmen tribes poured into the region, inaugurating a new chapter in its history with the overarching themes of Turkification and Islamisation. These two mutually reinforcing trends carried further and solidified with the Mongol invasions of the thirteenth century. The latter triggered a second influx from the east that brought a group of people more socially and ethnically diverse than their mostly Turkmen and nomadic predecessors, who had entered Rum with Alparslan's armies less than two centuries prior.[1]

With these successive political and demographic developments, an extraordinarily complex and fluid socio-cultural landscape was established in Anatolia over the four centuries between the initial arrival of the Seljuks and the entrenchment of a pax Ottomanica circa 1500. Muslims of different ethnic and social identities, and religious orientations and temperaments – ranging from madrasa-centred Sunni juridical Islam to normative *ṭarīqa* Sufism and antinomian dervish piety with Shiᶜi-ᶜAlid tinges – commingled and cross-pollinated with an equally heterogeneous indigenous Christian population in this western-most frontier of Islam. Of these diverse social groups, the Sufis and dervishes were arguably the most palpable and ubiquitous representatives of Islam during the period under consideration. The migrant Sufis and dervishes hailing from more established centres of Islam in the east, and their genealogical and spiritual descendants born into the rich socio-cultural mosaic of late medieval Anatolia, exerted a powerful influence among both the immigrant and native populations. As the most effective proselytisers, they were the driving force of Islamisation and, at the same time, also contributed to the development of a literary culture in Western Turkish. In the political arena, too, they were important players, bestowing religious legitimacy on the frontier warriors, the *ġāzīs*, and the many local dynasties that dotted the political map of the region following the waning of Mongol political control.[2]

Among the first Sufis and dervishes to arrive in Anatolia, there were those who traced their spiritual and/or natural genealogies back to Abu'l-Wafaᵓ al-Baghdadi. A few of these have been long known to specialists in the field. These include such thirteenth and fourteenth-century figures as Ede Balı and Geyikli Baba, who are shown in the sources to be within the close circle of early Ottoman rulers; and Çelebi Hüsameddin, the close companion and deputy of the famous Mevlana Celaleddin Rumi. Their Wafaᵓi connection, however, has failed to receive serious and sustained attention in mainstream scholarship.[3] Fortunately, this situation is now changing with the growing realisation that these few renowned personages were only the tip of a larger Wafaᵓi iceberg in medieval Anatolia, the main body of which has hitherto remained mostly buried under the debris of history.[4] Unearthing and bringing into the limelight the broader Wafaᵓi presence in medieval Anatolia, and restoring it to the historical narrative of the region and of the Kizilbash/Alevi communities, in particular, is the main goal of this chapter. I will do so drawing on newly surfaced Alevi documents and overlooked archival and epigraphic evidence that corroborates and complements them. Data in this combination of sources show that, at about the turn of the thirteenth century, familial groups and Sufi communities with a self-conscious attachment to the memory of Abu'l-Wafaᵓ were established at many different levels of Anatolia's Muslim society, cutting across social, political and even sectarian divisions. In its new home, the Wafaᵓi tradition would undergo further diversification and differentiation along both religious and political lines, with a sizeable group of its representatives eventually merging with the Kizilbash milieu.

Shaykh Ede Balı and the Early Ottomans: The Tip of the Wafa'i Iceberg

One of the most popular founding myths of the Ottoman state describes a fateful meeting of its eponym Osman and a saintly shaykh who predicts the splendour of the empire. One night while the young Osman is sleeping at the shaykh's house, he dreams that a moon arises from the breast of the holy shaykh and enters his own, whereupon from his navel springs a magnificent tree with long sweeping branches, shading mountains, rivers and streams and people. After awaking in the morning Osman goes to the shaykh and relates his dream. Recognising the dream as a divine endorsement of Osman's bid for rulership and assurance of the future glory of his line, the shaykh gives the young warrior his glad tidings: 'Osman, my son, congratulations, for God has given the imperial office to you and to your descendants, and my daughter Malhun shall be your wife.'[5] This dream and the sanctified marriage between Osman and the shaykh's daughter launched the heavenly approved Ottoman imperial project in the Muslim frontiers of northwestern Anatolia, or so it was imagined by later Ottoman generations.[6]

This obviously apocryphal dream story, a stock component of Ottoman histories with multiple variants, has been viewed by some historians as little more than an ex post facto legitimation of the house of Osman by Ottoman chroniclers. A closer scrutiny of sources, however, has more recently discovered a verifiable historical core relating to the figure of the saintly shaykh who was in all likelihood a Sufi master affiliated with the Wafa'i tradition.[7] The fifteenth-century Ottoman historian ᶜAşıkpaşazade (d. *c*.1490), to whom we owe one of the first written renderings of the story, identifies this holy figure in his *Tevārīḫ* completed circa 1480 as a Sufi named Ede Balı.[8] ᶜAşıkpaşazade describes Ede Balı as a dervish whose 'dervishliness was located within his interior' (*dervīşlik bāṭınındayıdı*), meaning that Ede Balı was not an ascetic type of dervish – such as the Abdals of Rum who at that time were roaming the same frontier regions in absolute poverty (*faḳr*) – but a sedentary Sufi shaykh in possession of 'worldly wealth, material blessings and flocks of animals'. As a well-off and socially prominent shaykh, Ede Balı's guest house (*misāfirḫāne*) was never vacant, and this was where his future son-in-law, Osman, was staying when he had his famous dream.[9] According to ᶜAşıkpaşazade, Osman allocated to Ede Balı the taxes of the entire town of Bilecik.[10] ᶜAşıkpaşazade also reports Ede Balı's kinship ties to other notable Muslim families of the early Ottoman milieu, including the family of the famous Çandarlı Halil who served as grand vizier under both Murad II and

Mehmed II. The two became brothers-in-law when Ede Balı took as his second wife the daughter of the well-known religious scholar Taceddin-i Kurdi whose other daughter was married to Çandarlı Halil.[11]

The veracity of all the details of ᶜAşıkpaşazade's account of Ede Balı is difficult to confirm. However, the fact that a fairly prominent Sufi shaykh by that name lived in western Anatolia in the first half of the fourteenth century and enjoyed economic favours from the would-be empire's first ruler is corroborated by archival sources. Two entries in the earliest surviving Ottoman land surveys record an 'Ede Şeyḫ' as the beneficiary of an endowment created by Osman that consisted of two villages in Söğüt, the original habitat of the fledgling Ottomans in northwestern Anatolia.[12] While the size of the endowment might be considered too modest to indicate such a close familial connection, a sixteenth-century *mühimme* register, referring to Ede Shaykh as Osman's father-in-law, lends further credence to ᶜAşıkpaşazade's claim that Ede Balı's daughter was one of Osman's two wives, even if it appears unlikely that the dynasty issued from this union.[13] Whatever his exact familial ties with the House of Osman were, what is nearly certain is that a Sufi called Ede Balı arrived in the vicinity of Söğüt before 1300, possibly as part of the initial cohort of Sufis taking up residence in the Ottoman domains, established himself as a respectable religious figure in the area and cultivated a congenial and mutually supportive relationship with the house of Osman, as apparently did his descendants.[14]

Curiously, ᶜAşıkpaşazade does not ascribe any specific Sufi affiliation to Ede Balı. The earliest clue of Ede Balı's association with the Wafaᵓi/Babaᵓi milieu is the mention of his name, together with that of Hacı Bektaş and others, in Elvan Çelebi's *Menāḳıbü'l-ḳudsiyye* from the mid-fourteenth century, where he is implicated to be a deputy (*ḫalīfe*) of Baba Ilyas.[15] A more explicit statement to the same effect is found in the introduction to the Turkish translation of Abu'l-Wafaᵓ's hagiographic vita from a century later; there, Ede Balı is described in plain language as one of the deputies of Taj al-ᶜArifin Sayyid Abu'l-Wafaᵓ. This translation, as noted in the previous chapter, was produced at the behest of ᶜAşıkpaşazade's disciple and son-in-law, Seyyid Velayet (1451–1522).[16] In addition to emphasising Ede Balı's Wafaᵓi affiliation, the translator, one of Seyyid Velayet's own disciples, reproduces ᶜAşıkpaşazade's version of the dream story in the introduction, highlighting Ede Balı's critical contributions to the House of Osman. The same introduction also informs us of Seyyid Velayet's own familial ties to Abu'l-Wafaᵓ, which is what apparently motivated him to commission the translation of the saint's hagiography into Turkish.[17]

While ᶜAşıkpaşazade fails (avoids?) to note Ede Balı's Wafaᵓi affinity, he does refer to a certain Ahi Hasan as Ede Balı's nephew. According to Ottoman chronicler Neşri, Ede Balı's brother (the father of Ahi Hasan) bore the same title, being known as Ahi Şemseddin.[18] Many historians, based on these clues, have conjectured Ede Balı himself to be an Ahi (Ot. *Aḫī*; Ar. *Akhī*) leader as well.[19] The Ahis, in many ways an extension of the Islamic chivalric tradition known as *futuwwa* (Ot. *fütüvvet*), were fraternities of young men and artisans organised along mystical principles. They acted as important social and political players especially, but not only, in the town centres of medieval Anatolia where they are said to have filled the power vacuum at a time of declining centralised rule, from the mid-thirteenth century to the mid-fourteenth.[20] However, in the medieval Anatolian context, as Sara Wolper observes, drawing a boundary between the Sufis and the Ahis was practically impossible. Not only did the two groups occupy the same buildings but the very title 'Ahi' was also one of many others used by the broad category of Sufis.[21] While Wolper does not link her observations to any specific Sufi order(s), an Ahi *ijāza* found among Alevi documents (see below) suggests that the Wafaʾi and Ahi circles in Anatolia shared an intertwined history. This assumption is further buttressed by certain details of the aforementioned Hüsameddin Çelebi's family history: his father, reportedly a descendant of Abu'l-Wafaʾ al-Baghdadi who moved from Urumiye to Anatolia sometime before 1225, served as the shaykh of all Ahis in and around Konya during his life time; Hüsameddin Çelebi was, therefore, known by the nickname 'Ahi Türkoğlu' (Son of Ahi Turk).[22] It thus follows that, if Ede Balı was indeed linked to the Ahis in some capacity, it would strengthen rather than preclude the possibility of him also having a connection to the Wafaʾi tradition.

Ede Balı's probable Wafaʾi connection also casts a new light on ʿAşıkpaşazade's seemingly exaggerated emphasis on his role in the rise of the Ottomans.[23] In the opening lines of his *Tevārīḫ*, ʿAşıkpaşazade traces his own line of descent back to Baba Ilyas, the spiritual leader of the thirteenth-century Babaʾi revolt, whom he expressly identifies as a *ḫalīfe* of Abu'l-Wafaʾ.[24] ʿAşıkpaşazade's illustrious family tree, issuing thus from a Wafaʾi shaykh, included other famed figures such as his great-grandfather, Aşık Paşa, who was the author of the first major Sufi work in Anatolian Turkish, the *Ġaribnāme*. His grandfather's brother, Elvan Çelebi (Aşık Paşa's son), was likewise a renowned Sufi who had a dervish lodge (Ot. *zāviye*; Ar. *zāwiya*) in Mecidözü near Çorum, in addition to being the author of the aforementioned *Menāḳıbü'l-ḳudsiyye*, which recounts the history of the Wafaʾi/ Babaʾi circles from an internal perspective.[25] George of Hungary, a war captive who spent more than two decades in rural central Anatolia in the mid-fifteenth century, counts Elvan Çelebi and his father Aşık Paşa as two of the four most highly venerated saints among the people of the region (the other two being Hacı Bektaş and Seyyid Gazi, about whom more will be said in the next chapter), a clear indication of the powerful impact of Wafaᵓi/ Babaᵓi affiliates in shaping the religious life of Muslims in parts of late medieval Anatolia.[26]

Judged by the significance that ᶜAşıkpaşazade attributed to his family's Wafaᵓi heritage (enough to include it in the opening passage of his book), it is most likely that his purpose in writing the *Tevārīḫ* was more than simply to tell the story of the early Ottomans. Conceivably, at least one of his goals was the recovery of a critical component of that story involving the Wafaᵓi shaykhs that had, however, fallen into oblivion, and the restoration of it to Ottoman historical consciousness. This concern is more clearly evident in his portrayal of Geyikli Baba, who, like Ede Balı, is mentioned in ᶜAşıkpaşazade's chronicle in connection to his support for the House of Osman. Geyikli Baba, ᶜAşıkpaşazade writes, accompanied Osman's son and successor, Orhan, during his siege of the city of Bursa, the first major urban centre to come under Ottoman control, and planted a tree in the yard of Orhan's palace as a sign of his blessings on the new state. ᶜAşıkpaşazade leaves no doubt concerning Geyikli Baba's spiritual genealogy, depicting him as saying, 'I am a disciple of Baba İlyas . . . I am a follower of the order of Abu'l-Wafaᵓ' (*Baba İlyās mürīdiyin . . . Seyyid Ebü'l Vefāᵓ tarīḳindenin*).[27] Later Ottoman sources that mention Geyikli Baba more or less repeat the same information and, additionally, reproduce the story of Abu'l-Wafaᵓ miraculously transforming wine into honey and butter as reported in his own hagiography (see Chapter 1), except here casting Geyikli Baba and Orhan Beg in place of Abu'l-Wafaᵓ and the Abbasid caliph.[28] Ottoman tax registers from the late fifteenth century vouch for a close association between the two figures; they record that Orhan Beg endowed Geyikli Baba with the taxes from a village in Bursa. Two alternative names are given for this village in the registers, the village of Geyikli Baba (Karye-i Geyiklü Baba) and the village of the Babaᵓis (Karye-i Babaᵓī), the double naming offering further proof for Geyikli Baba's Wafaᵓi/Babaᵓi background.[29]

Until the 'discovery' of the Turkish translation of Abu'l-Wafaᵓ's hagiography, which explicitly describes Ede Balı as a Wafaᵓi shaykh, Geyikli Baba was virtually the only figure widely recognised in the Ottoman historiography to have a spiritual affinity with Abu'l-Wafaᵓ al-Baghdadi.[30] Unlike Ede Balı, however, Geyikli Baba was an archetypical ascetic dervish dedicated to a life of voluntary poverty, roaming in the wilderness and communicating with feral animals.[31] Geyikli Baba and Ede Balı as such represented two distinct strains within the Wafaʾi tradition (as well as within late-medieval Anatolian Sufism, in general) that were temperamentally and doctrinally at odds with each other. These two distinct orientations differed in terms of their understanding of the quintessential Sufi notion of poverty (*faqr*), which mainstream Sufis (re)interpreted (primarily) as an internal spiritual state, while their more radical counterparts viewed it as (also) a rejection of all worldly goods and pleasures. They seem to have coexisted within the Wafaʾi tradition from its inception, even if not entirely tension-free, as symbolically encapsulated in the story of Abu'l-Wafaʾ's half-hearted transition from a life of an itinerant dervish to one of a settled Sufi shaykh, and as further demonstrated by the heterogeneity of his close disciples and successors, who included both sober and ecstatic type of dervishes. This temperamental and doctrinal differentiation became polarised in the Anatolian context, and sharpened further along sectarian lines until it developed into a full-fledged Sunni–Shiʿi divide, as will be discussed in Chapter 3.

It is probably no coincidence that the timing of what seems to have been a coordinated effort by ʿAşıkpaşazade and Seyyid Velayet to create a written record of the contributions of Wafaʾi dervishes, both sedentary and itinerant, to the state-building enterprise of Osman's household coincided with the rise of the Bektashi order as the sole representative of the Ottoman frontier ethos. Catalysing the latter development was the near-contemporary compilation of Bektashi hagiographic works from the late fifteenth century onward, which gave the (proto-)Bektashi dervishes the leading Sufi role in the empire's founding drama by casting them in close company and cooperation with the early Ottoman rulers and *ġazīs*.[32] ʿAşıkpaşazade's and Seyyid Velayet's apparent desire to revive the memory of their Wafaʾi ancestors must have been at least in part a response to this pro-Bektashi narrative, which was already on its way to becoming established dogma.[33] This consideration would also go a long way in explicating the polemical remarks in ʿAşıkpaşazade's *Tevārīḫ* about Hacı Bektaş, around whose cult the Bektashi order took shape. Not only did ʿAşıkpaşazade debunk claims that Hacı Bektaş was involved in the creation of the Janissary corps, he also tried to disqualify Hacı Bektaş from being recognised as the founder of the Bektashi order by portraying him as an ecstatic dervish incapable of such an undertaking.[34] However, the efforts of ʿAşıkpaşazade and Seyyid Velayet to set the record straight, as it were, seem to have been mostly ineffective given the remarkable silence surrounding the Wafaʾiyya in later Ottoman sources, which tend to assimilate the few known Wafaʾi figures, or their real or fictitious legacies, into the Bektashi tradition.[35] The depiction of the aforementioned Geyikli

Baba as a Bektashi dervish in the seventeenth-century *Seyaḥatnāme* by the famous Ottoman traveller and litterateur Evliya Çelebi is a clear case in point.[36] Another one, symbolically perhaps even more potent, is the story in the hagiographic vita of Hacı Bektaş in which the latter takes the place of Ede Balı as the Sufi shaykh blessing the foundation of the empire.[37]

ᶜAşıkpaşazade and Seyyid Velayet, notwithstanding their familial Wafaʾi heritage, were themselves members of the Zeyniyye, a Sufi order in the Ottoman Empire whose members were among the most fervent upholders of the Ottoman moral and political order against the ideological threat of the Safavids. The two figures successively headed one of the two major Zeyni convents in Istanbul that were patronised and frequented by the imperial capital's elite. With their religiously and politically centrist stand, ᶜAşıkpaşazade and Seyyid Velayet represented one end of the Ottoman religio-political cultural spectrum; the other end, ironically, was occupied by none other than their distant cousins in the eastern half of Anatolia who claimed the same genealogical pedigree, reaching back to Abu'l-Wafaʾ, but who, along with the kindred Abdals of Rum, would embrace the Kizilbash cause over the course of the late fifteenth century and early sixteenth. If Ede Balı and Geyikli Baba were the tip of the Wafaʾi iceberg in medieval Anatolia, then their genealogical and/or spiritual cousins in the east constituted its main body, as seems to be finally starting to become clear from the sources.

Tracking Wafaʾi Convents and Dervishes in Medieval Anatolia

The basic contours of the broader Wafaʾi presence in medieval Anatolia can be reconstructed on the basis of documents preserved in family archives of Wafaʾi-cum-Kizilbash *ocak*s and a group of archival documents that support and complement them. Saving the discussion of the *ocak*s and their documents for later, I start here with an overview of the Wafaʾi/Babaʾi affiliates who left their imprints on the official record. We encounter these figures primarily in Seljuk-era *waqfiyya*s (endowment deeds; Ot. *vaḳfiyye*s or *vaḳıfnāme*) and various later Ottoman archival sources, which place them in neighbouring provinces of Sivas and Malatya, two of the epicentres of the later Kizilbash movement.

Two such Sufi shaykhs with a likely Wafaʾi connection who made it into the historical record were Shaykh Marzuban (T. Şeyh Merzuban) and Bahlul Baba (T. Behlül Baba). Both had established convents in the province of Sivas, in the districts of Zara and Suşehri, respectively, that were endowed by the Seljuk sultan Giyaseddin Keyhusrev III (r. 1266–1282). The *waqfiyya* recording the endowment for the convent located at Shaykh

Marzuban's tomb-shrine, which is still standing today in the village of Tekke, was composed in Şaᶜban 672/1274. The deed was ratified multiple times over the course of the following two-and-a-half centuries, the last ratification being made by the kadi of Sivas in Muharram 920/1514, the year in which the copy we have today was produced. The full name of Shaykh Marzuban appears in the *waqfiyya* as 'Shaykh Maḥmūd b. Sayyid ᶜAlī al-Ḥusaynī al-Baghdādī', his *nisbas* indicating his descent from Imam Husayn and his Iraqi origins. [38]

Shaykh Marzuban's Wafa'i identity is implicated in two additional *nisbas*, 'al-Wafā'ī al-Ḥanafī', that are attached to his name in another document recording the creation of an additional endowment for the convent in Muharram 943/1536.[39] These extra *nisbas* are crucial pieces of evidence for identifying Shaykh Marzuban as a Wafa'i shaykh. So as to not take it at face value, however, we shall first explore what might account for this amendment. It is not inconceivable that this amendment represents an invented tradition to project externally an 'orthodox' image for the convent's founder, especially given that the date of the document coincides with the high point of Sunni confessionalisation in the Ottoman Empire and the state's repression of the exponents of the Kizilbash milieu. On the other hand, there are considerations that run contrary to such a conjecture. To begin with, there seems to be no obvious rationale for forging a connection with the Wafa'iyya instead of some other, better-known Sufi order of Iraqi origin, unless of course we assume that the knowledge of the Wafa'i order and its Sunni credentials were equally well established in the Anatolian context by the early sixteenth century, which is the ultimate point of the present discussion. Furthermore, the specification of Shaykh Marzuban's *madhab* as Hanafi is noteworthy, for it runs contrary to the sources' depiction of Abu'l-Wafa''s as a Shafiᶜi, or as one with no specific *madhab* preference. A different light is thrown on this point by Zabidi's *Rafᶜ niqāb*, where we encounter among the Wafa'i *sayyids* a certain Shihab al-Din Ahmad who later adopts the Hanafi *madhab*. Shihab al-Din Ahmad's father, Abu Bakr, whose dates Zabidi gives as 799/1396–859/1455, was reportedly the ancestor of the Wafa'i *sayyids* in Aleppo, as well as the namesake of the Wafa'i convent in that city. Shihab al-Din Ahmad would become the leader of the Wafa'iyya after his father, who had inherited the position from his own father. According to Zabidi, Shihab al-Din Ahmad later relocated to the land of Rum, where he was honoured by the sultan (it is not clear which), and died there in 883/1478. Zabidi also adds that Shihab al-Din was the first among his family members (or the Wafa'i *sayyids* at large?) to convert to the Hanafi *madhab*.[40] From this statement, it seems safe to conclude that there were other Wafaʾi *sayyid*s and shaykhs, presumably in Anatolia and/or Aleppo, who embraced the Hanafi *madhab* after Shihab al-Din Ahmad. The latter then might have projected this identity onto their ancestors, as perhaps was the case with Shaykh Marzuban. Shihab al-Din Ahmad's acquired Hanafi identity, coupled with the absence of any apparent reason to attribute to Shaykh Marzuban an imagined Wafaʾi background, thus lead us to believe that the amendment in question cannot be discarded altogether as a fabrication with no connection to historical reality.

Having said that, the addition of the extra *nisba*s, 'al-Wafāʾī al-Ḥanafī', to Shaykh Marzuban's name at this moment in time might still be of special significance in that it possibly represented a deliberate move to magnify and foreground the Sunni credentials of the founder and namesake of the convent, so as to shield its contemporary affiliates from accusations of real or false Kizilbash sympathies.[41] Notably, the same convent is found under the name of 'Merziban Velî Ahioğlu Zâviyesi' in the list of Bektashi convents compiled by Bedri Noyan, the head of the Babagan Bektashis for most of the twentieth century. Noyan also mentions that Shaykh Marzuban is known in local Alevi lore as a descendant of Imam Zayn al-ʿAbidin, and cites a poem by the twentieth-century Alevi poet Aşık Ali İzzet Özkan praising the shaykh. In the poem, Özkan refers to Shaykh Marzuban as '*mürşid*' and '*pir*'[42] and recounts a miracle in which he turns wine sent by the ruler into honey and butter, the same miracle that is attributed to Abu'l-Wafaʾ in his hagiography and to Geyikli Baba in Ottoman sources. A slightly different version of the same legend casting Shaykh Marzuban, a local Armenian who was his foe, and Sultan ʿAlaʾeddin of the Seljuks (see below) has also been recorded as a living tradition in Zara in the second half of the twentieth century.[43]

Giyaseddin Keyhusrev III, the same year that he created an endowment for Shaykh Marzuban's convent, also endowed the convent of Bahlul Baba, which was situated in the district of Suşehri.[44] Unlike Shaykh Marzuban, however, Bahlul Baba was of Khorasani origin, his name given as 'Shaykh Bahlūl Dānā b. Ḥusayn al-Khorāsānī' in the *waqfiyya* of his convent, of which only a nineteenth-century copy has survived. Hüseyin Hüsameddin in his *Amasya Tārīḥi* mentions a certain Behlül Baba who was the son and deputy (*ḫalīfe*) of Baba İlyas Khorasani exiled to Suşehri.[45] Assuming the accuracy of Hüseyin Hüsameddin's claim, and if this was the same person, then we can identify Bahlul Baba as a Sufi shaykh associated with the Wafaʾi/Babaʾi milieu. Evliya Çelebi makes a reference to a Bektashi convent located between Şebinkarahisar and Erzincan affiliated with a certain Behlül Semerkandi; this might possibly be the same convent. Remains of a shrine attributed to a certain Şeyh

Behlül Dana are today situated in the village of Aşağı Tepecik (previously called 'Aşağı Baru') in the modern district of Gölova in the province of Sivas, a location that accords with Evliya's description of the location of Behlül Semerkandi's convent.[46]

According to its *waqfiyya*, Bahlul Baba's convent was originally built by Sultan Rükneddin Kılıçarslan IV (r. 1249–1266), father of Giyaseddin Keyhusrev III. The two *waqfiyya*s also make it clear that by the time Giyaseddin Keyhusrev III established these endowments both Shaykh Marzuban and Shaykh Bahlul Baba had already died, which suggests that they must have been in Anatolia no later than the early thirteenth century. Supporting this inference, at least in the case of Shaykh Marzuban, is a note in one of the late nineteenth-century official annuals (*sālnāme*) for the province of Sivas: according to this note, Shaykh Marzuban's convent was earlier endowed with tracts of land by 'Ṣulṭān ᶜAlāeᵓd-dīn', who is said to have stopped in the village of Tekke (Ot. *Tekye*) on his way to a campaign in the east in 672/1274.[47] Despite the discordant date (which, incidentally, is the same date of the above-mentioned endowment deed), from context we can presume that the sultan in question was the famous sultan ᶜAlaᵓeddin Keykubad I (r. 1220–1237). His reign represents the golden age of the Seljuks of Rum, when many religious scholars, Sufis and literary figures from established centres of Islam are known to have taken up residence in Anatolia.[48] It is, of course, possible for this statement, contained in a nineteenth-century *sālnāme*, to be nothing more than a reiteration of an established local tradition. On the other hand, it does accord with Hasan Yüksel's proposed reading of the date inscribed on the shaykh's mausoleum, 635/1237, which coincides with the last year of Sultan ᶜAlaᵓeddin's reign.[49]

The convent of Shaykh Çoban, yet another convent that appears to have been Wafaᵓi affiliated, was located in the city of Sivas itself. Local tradition holds Shaykh Çoban to be a dervish who had accompanied Shaykh Marzuban on his journey to Anatolia; allegedly both men established their convents at the respective spots where their camels came to a halt.[50] In Sivas today all that remains of Shaykh Çoban's *zāwiya* complex is a fountain and a tomb where he is believed to be buried. When the convent and tomb were first constructed is not clear; however, it must have been before the nearby fountain was erected in the year 723/1323, when Sivas was under Mongol Ilkhanid rule. The *zāwiya* complex included a *masjid* that was still standing as late as the mid-twentieth century. While the original construction date of the *masjid* is likewise obscure, we know it was renovated in 771/1369 when the control of the city passed from the Ilkhanids to the rulers of the Eratne principality, a local Mongol-successor state known for its patronage of Sufi sites. Shaykh Çoban's tomb was restored and renovated multiple times during the Ottoman period, first in 862/1457, just three years after the Ottomans carried out the initial cadastral survey of the city in 1454.[51] According to these survey registers, the convent was located in one of the city's major neighbourhoods named after the shaykh (Ot. Şeyḫ Çoban), and of the nineteen adult men living in the neighbourhood, eight were dervishes. This is a clear sign of the building's prominence as a physical and religious marker for the city in the pre- and early Ottoman period.[52] The tax registers carried out in 1572 likewise mention the convent but not any dervishes residing in the neighbourhood. However, an Ottoman register of endowments dated 1576 shows the tax income of three villages as endowments for the convent, suggesting it was still an active convent at this date.[53] It is not implausible that from 1572 to 1576 the convent changed hands under the pressure of the Ottoman state's ongoing Sunnitisation policies, examples of which I shall discuss in Chapter 6.

Besides Shaykh Çoban's association with Shaykh Marzuban in the local tradition, the possibility of his Wafaʾi affiliation is bolstered by his alternate Arabic name, Husayn Raᶜi; the Arabic word '*rāᶜī*' and the Turkish word '*çoban*' both mean 'shepherd'. Although the earliest inscription on the tomb identifies the saint buried at the site as Shaykh Çoban, a later inscription from the year of 1318/1902 gives his name as Husayn Raᶜi (Ot. Hüseyin Raᶜi), which may have been the name recorded in the original endowment deed of the convent that is no longer extant. Felicitously, the name Husayn Raᶜi appears in the hagiography of Abu'l-Wafaʾ as a direct disciple of the saint who is said to have been a cattle herder before joining the Sufi path, hence his nickname. However, according to the hagiography, Husayn Raᶜi settled in a village called Rahman in the latter part of his life following his shaykh's demise. In this account, Rahman is where Husayn Raᶜi allegedly trained his own disciples and where he is buried.[54] Although the exact location of this village is not revealed, judging by the hagiography's broader context the implied setting is Iraq. Obviously this information contradicts the evidence connecting Husayn Raᶜi to the Anatolian city of Sivas.

Such contradictory evidence raises a variety of possible scenarios, none of which, however, can be conclusively proven. According to one scenario, the hagiography is mistaken in identifying the village of Rahman as the final destination of Husayn Raᶜi, who indeed spent the last part of his life in Anatolia having migrated there sometime in the early twelfth century, that is, within only decades of the Seljuk Turks' arrival in the peninsula. If true, this scenario would push the initial arrival of Wafaʾi dervishes in

Anatolia further back to as early as the twelfth century. That would be the same time period when ᶜAdi b. Musafir (a close associate of Abu'l-Wafa' according to the latter's hagiography, as noted in the previous chapter) and his immediate descendants were visible players in the local politics of eastern Anatolia.[55] Perhaps the convent of Shaykh Çoban in Sivas was not in fact established by Husayn Raᶜi; an alternative scenario suggests that it was founded by one of his disciples who arrived in Anatolia together with, or about the same time as, Shaykh Marzuban. Both of these scenarios assume that Husayn Raᶜi was a direct disciple of Abu'l-Wafa', as asserted by the hagiography, and that the popular narratives showing him as a contemporary of Shaykh Marzuban simply collapsed stories of the two Wafa'i shaykhs into one. However, it is also not beyond the pale to imagine that Husayn Ra'i was not Abu'l-Wafa''s own disciple but a later spiritual descendant, perhaps indeed part of the same cohort as Shaykh Marzuban, who, for some reason, is falsely depicted in the hagiography as having an unmediated relationship with Abu'l-Wafa'.

Whatever the case may be, today people of all confessions visit the tomb of Shaykh Çoban seeking cures for certain illnesses, even though local Alevis regard the saint resting there as one of their own. The latter point acquires a greater significance in view of the Alevi *ocak* bearing the name of 'Şeyh Çoban', two branches of which are today found in the district of Alaca in the province of Çorum (headquartered in the village of Nesimi Keşlik) and in the district of Mazgirt in the province of Tunceli. There is, in fact, in Mazgirt a tomb ascribed to Şeyh Çoban that apparently was part of a convent by the same name that appears in the sixteenth-century Ottoman tax registers of Çemişgezek. According to the registers, the tax income of two villages was an endowment for the convent.[56] A connection between the Shaykh Çoban buried in Sivas and the Alevi *ocak* by the same name, while difficult to prove with complete certainty, is compelling nonetheless in the light of the *ocak*'s family documents that connect them to the Wafa'i order.[57] Yet another, albeit different kind of clue to an actual historical link between Shaykh Çoban, or Husayn Ra'i, and the proto-Kizilbash communities of medieval Anatolia comes from a previously mentioned Alevi document dated 984/1576, in which Abu'l-Wafa's title 'Kakis' (misspelled as 'Bakis') is translated into Turkish as '*çoban*' (shepherd).[58] This wide-of-the-mark translation may well be a conflation of the founder of the order with one of its earliest representatives in Anatolia, given that there is no obvious semantic or phonetic relationship between the two words. Conceivably, an idiom commonly used among the Alevis of central Anatolia, 'faith of a shepherd' (T. *çoban itikadı*), might also be an echo of the memory of Husayn Ra'i. It is used to describe the firm, intuitive faith of an illiterate individual, which is deemed superior to the bookish faith of the learned classes.

Another centre of attraction and early destination for the Wafaʾi dervishes in Seljuk Anatolia was the province of Malatya, lying just south of Sivas. Our information on the Wafaʾi presence in this region comes primarily from later Ottoman official records. For instance, the Ottoman registers of pious endowments compiled in the year 1530 record the existence of a convent bearing the name of 'Şeyḫ Aḥmed-i Ṭavīl' in the village of Şeyh Hasanlu in the district of Muşar; the shaykh to whom the convent is attributed is identified in the registers as a descendant of Abu'l-Wafaʾ. The register notes that the original endowment of the convent, which is no longer extant, was created by Sultan ᶜAlaʾeddin. This time, however, the sultan in question appears to be ᶜAlaʾeddin Keykubat II (r. 1249–1254), the grandson of the above-mentioned Alaʾeddin Keykubat I, whom we have already met as the likely first endower of Shaykh Marzuban's convent.[59] Two other documents from the Ottoman archives, dated 5 Cemaziye'l-evvel 1102/1691 and Rebiᶜü'l-evvel 1117/1705, also mention a convent of 'Sayyid Shaykh Abu'l-Wafāʾ Ḳuṭb al-ᶜĀrīfīn' in the Muşar district of Malatya.[60] These are probably references to the same convent in the village of Şeyh Hasanlu.

The village of Şeyh Hasanlu, according to the sixteenth-century Ottoman land registers, also housed the tomb of Shaykh Ahmed-i Tavil, known locally as Şeyh (or Şıh) Ahmed Dede, which must have been part of the convent.[61] In the 1970s, his tomb was relocated to a nearby spot in order to save it from disappearance under the waters of the Karakaya Dam. Although it does not bear an inscription to help us date its construction, the two other tombs relocated at the same time are respectively inscribed with the dates of 740/1340 and 817/1414. According to an oral tradition kept alive, these two tombs, originally situated close to that of Şeyh Ahmed Dede, hold the remains of his son and wife. The veracity of this tradition, however, would appear rather unlikely if Şeyh Ahmed was indeed alive during or before the reign of ᶜAlaʾeddin Keykubat II in the mid-thirteenth century, when his convent endowment was reportedly established. Another local tradition maintains that Şeyh Ahmed's wife, Güher Ana, was Sultan ᶜAlaʾeddin Keykubat's sister. Even though this tradition also cannot be authenticated with other sources, it is still noteworthy in so far as it fits the pattern of ruling houses forming marriage alliances with major Sufi families, as in the purported marriage between Shaykh Ede Balı's daughter and Osman Beg about a century later.[62]

Alevi lore attributes the name of the village, Şeyh Hasanlu, to Şeyh Ahmed Dede's brother Hasan, whom local tradition maintains to be the common ancestor of a large group of Alevi tribes in the Dersim region. Şeyh Ahmed Dede himself is believed to be the progenitor of an important Alevi *ocak* bearing his name centred in the modern province of Tunceli.[63] The Wafaʾi origin of this *ocak* is borne out by the *ocak*'s family documents, which indeed contain the oldest dated Wafaʾi document that has surfaced to date. Composed (or copied) in the year 829/1425, this *shajara*-cum-*ijāza* derives the family line of the *ocak* from a certain Shaykh Ahmad al-Jammi (spelled as *j-m-ī*) who is identified in the document as one of the forty direct disciples of Abu'l-Wafaʾ.[64] The list in the document of Abu'l-Wafaʾ's forty closest disciples largely matches the list provided in his hagiography, although the latter does not mention Ahmad al-Jammi, unless al-Jammi was another, alternative *nisba* of 'Shaykh Aḥmad Baqlī' who is mentioned.[65] Whatever Jammi's relationship to historical reality, and to Abu'l-Wafaʾ in particular, which is difficult to elucidate at this point, the sources' overall picture of Şeyh Ahmed Dede converges with a common element found in many semi-legendary Alevi oral narratives, which show a 'Sultan Alaeddin' acting as the benefactor of Alevi saintly figures.[66] Curiously, however, a local tradition first documented in the 1970s and still maintained by many today equates Şeyh Ahmed with the eponymous founder of the Yesevi order, Ahmed-i Yesevi, who is said to have come from Khorasan to settle in this part of Anatolia.[67] No doubt facilitated by the common names of the two personages, this obviously anachronistic belief is another illustratation of the fusion of the Wafaʾi legacy in Anatolia with that of the Bektashi order.

The Ottoman register of pious endowments from the year 1530 records another Wafaʾi convent in Hısn-ı Mansur, a district in the province of Malatya where the Babaʾi revolt was first launched. The lead to the Wafaʾi affiliation of the convent is the name under which it was recorded, namely 'zâviye-i Ebü'l-Vefa'. Although the register does not include any information concerning its construction date, the convent apparently existed already before the Ottomans took control of the region from the Mamluks in 1514.[68] Finally, mention should also be made of a local site of pilgrimage (*ziyāret*) attributed to 'Şeyh Ebülvefa' in the eastern Anatolian province of Siirt. The site still exists today though we lack any historical data concerning its origins.[69] There might well be other Wafaʾi affiliated ones among the many Sufi (and Ahi) convents that are recorded in the various early Ottoman registers, whose foundations clearly predated the early sixteenth century.[70] Here, however, we run into a problem of sources, for the order affiliations of these convents are typically not noted in the registers, except in a fraction of cases when a special explanation is added to individual entries. Even so, however, available archival evidence gives us sufficient grounds to assume that a significant Wafaʾi presence began building up in and around Sivas and Malatya from no later than the early thirteenth century.[71] This assumption finds further support in the family documents of Wafaʾi-cum-Kizilbash *ocak*s to which I turn now.

Wafaʾi-Cum-Kizilbash Ocaks *in Eastern Anatolia*

Data provided by in-field observations and family documents of Wafaʾi-cum-Kizilbash *ocak*s show that the historic stronghold of the Wafaʾiyya was in the upper Euphrates basin and its environs. Stretching from Malatya to Erzincan and from Sivas to Elazığ, this geographical spread concurs with the archival evidence laid out above concerning the dissemination of Wafaʾi/Babaʾi convents and dervishes in medieval Anatolia. A sizeable web of Wafaʾi-cum-Kizilbash *ocak*s have concentrated in the region extending northward and eastward from the opposite bank of the Euphrates River, an area inhabited mainly by Kurdish- and Zaza-speaking Alevis. Among the most important of these are the *ocak*s of İmam Zeynel Abidin and Ağuiçen, whose origins can be inferred to be Iraqi in light of their family documents and some patchy oral traditions.[72] Another *ocak* with a historical affinity to the Wafaʾi tradition is the *ocak* of Dede Kargın, whose progenitor purportedly hailed from Khorasan, the place to which most *ocak*s traditionally trace their origins. The Dede Kargıns' area of influence, unlike that of the other two *ocak*s of Wafaʾi background, extended southward from the western side of the Euphrates basin and included a largely Turkmen following.

THE *OCAK*S OF AĞUİÇEN AND İMAM ZEYNEL ABİDİN

The *ocak* of Ağuiçen is one of the most prominent Alevi saintly lineages, both in terms of the geographical reach of its affiliates and its widely recognised *mürşid* status in the broader Dersim region. This region, including the modern province of Tunceli and its environs, is today the only locality in Anatolia inhabited by a predominantly Alevi population. Historically sound evidence is not available concerning the *ocak*'s founding patriarch. According to semi-legendary accounts, the original Ağuiçens were four brothers, one of whom, Köse Seyyid, was a celibate. The existing branches of the *ocak* of Ağuiçen are thus believed to have issued from the remaining three brothers. The youngest of the four brothers, Seyyid Mençek, is said to have performed a miracle in the presence of the sultan of his time, drinking a cup of poison and excreting it from the tip of one of his fingers in the form of honey, hence the name Ağuiçen, 'the poison-drinker'.

An alternative oral tradition links the original Ağuiçen to the figure of Karadonlu Can Baba in the hagiography of Hacı Bektaş, the *Velāyetnāme*. Karadonlu Can Baba, a *ḫalīfe* of Hacı Bektaş, reportedly performed a similar miracle by drinking poison without being harmed. However, this oral tradition, like the one identifying Şeyh Ahmed Dede with Ahmed-i Yesevi, appears to have originated in the relatively recent past, coinciding with the growing influence of the Çelebi Bektashis among the Kizilbash/ Alevi communities from the early nineteenth century onward, an issue to be touched upon in Chapters 3 and 4. This development seems to have given rise to a tendency to conflate various eponyms of eastern Anatolian *ocak*s of Wafa'i origin with different figures in the hagiographic vita of Hacı Bektaş, the *Velāyetnāme*.[73]

The oldest known centres of the Ağuiçens, and several other *ocak*s who recognise them as their *mürşid*, are found mostly dispersed northward and eastward from the eastern bank of the Euphrates. One of the two major branches of the *ocak* is based in the village of Sün in the province of Elazığ, where the most senior of the four brothers, Koca Seyyid, is believed to be buried.[74] The presence of *dede*s affiliated with the Ağuiçens in Sün can be tracked through their family documents as far back as the early seventeenth century, although the date of their initial settlement in the village is obscure.[75] It is told that it was from Sün that the other three brothers later moved to the village of Ulukale in the Çemişgezek district of Tunceli. Köse Seyyid and Seyyid Mençek reportedly remained in Ulukale for the rest of their lives, and still today just outside of this village there is a pilgrimage site (*yatır*) associated with these two brothers. Mir Seyyid, on the other hand, is said to have left Ulukale and settled in the village of Bargını (Ot. Bārginī; modern-day Karabakır) in the neighbouring district of Hozat, where his tomb, known as the *türbe* of Ağuiçen, still stands[76] (Figures 2.1a and 2.1b). There are various smaller branches of this *ocak* in other parts of Anatolia, but most of them seem to have migrated to those areas from their old centres in Elazığ and Tunceli over the course of the nineteenth century. Such relocations of *dede* families often took place at the invitation of their disciple communities, who had migrated earlier as part of a general westward and southward demographic flow from the northeastern provinces of Anatolia. For example, the Adıyaman branch of the Ağuiçens, centred on the village of Börgenek and in the district of Bulam, consists of *dede*s who moved out of Sün. Similarly, there are *dede*s of Sün origin who currently reside as *mürşid*s among the disciples of the *ocak* of Sinemilli in Maraş. The Ağuiçen *dede*s in Göynücek-Amasya, likewise, are historically linked to one of the Tunceli branches of the *ocak*. In all these cases, the related families' relocation to

Figure 2.1a The door of the (presumed) tomb-shrine of Ağuiçen, in the village of Bargıni in Hozat-Tunceli, before its restoration in 2014

Source: Photograph by Suat Baran.

these regions is still part of the remembered past. The same is true of the Ağuiçens in Malatya (known as the family of Doğan Dede), who migrated to the village of Kırlangıç in the Yeşilyurt district as recently as the early twentieth century.[77]

Compared to the Ağuiçens, the *ocak* of İmam Zeynel Abidin, one of the few *ocak*s named after one of the Twelve Imams, is much less dispersed: it is associated primarily with the village of Mineyik (modern-day Kuyudere) in the Arguvan district of Malatya, with the exception of one offshoot that I could identify in the village of Karaca, in Yazıhan-Malatya.[78] Documents in the family archives place the *ocak* in the environs of Malatya from before the late seventeenth century and specifically in Mineyik from before the late eighteenth century. In spite of the apparently localised nature of their sphere of influence in modern times, family members have maintained a claim to *mürşid*-hood over several Kizilbash/Alevi communities in eastern Anatolia.[79] This puts them in opposition to the widely recognised prerogative of the Ağuiçens to that status. There are, however, some oral reports showing the two *ocak*s as distant relatives, which in turn raise the possibil-

Figure 2.1b The (presumed) tomb-shrine of Ağuiçen, in the village of Bargıni in Hozat-Tunceli, after its restoration in 2014

Source: Photograph by İnanç Dolu.

ity that they branched out from the same lineage into separate families at some point in the past.[80] Contextualisation of the two *ocak*s' rival claims in their family documents demonstrates that this course of development was entirely plausible, since their written genealogies link the respective *ocak*s, both by kinship and by *silsila*, to Abu'l-Wafa' via Sayyid Ghanim, the saint's (alleged) brother. Their shared (real or assumed) kinship with Abu'l-Wafa', in turn, helps to elucidate the historical grounds of the two *ocak*s' claims to *mürşid*-hood, which was most likely an extension of their privileged position within Wafa'i circles prior to their assimilation into the Kizilbash milieu.

The lineage of Sayyid Ghanim

The lineage attributed to Sayyid Ghanim, brother of Abu'l-Wafa', from which the *ocak*s of Ağuiçen and Imam Zeynel Abidin purportedly stem, appears to have been the predominant *silsila* among Wafa'i-cum-Kizilbash *ocak*s in medieval Anatolia. With few exceptions, it is this line, passing through Sayyid Ghanim's son, Sayyid Khamis, that is encountered in all the Wafa'i *ijāza*s that have come down to us. Reconstructing a composite *silsila* based on genealogies contained in these *ijāza*s, each of which naturally bring the chain of initiation only up to the time of their composition, is not an easy task due to many, not easily reconcilable inconsistencies among them. Some of these inconsistencies are clearly unintentional errors on the part of the copyists, who, for instance, tend to break down a single name into two, use variously a given name or a nickname, or altogether exclude certain lesser known names from the *silsila*. Others reflect a deliberate tinkering with individual names and titles, presumably in tandem with growing Shiᶜi/Alid sensibilities. Despite such difficulties, a provisional and partial *silsila* comprising the key links cited consistently in all the available Wafaᵓi *ijāza*s can be reconstructed as follows:

> *Sayyid Muḥammad ← Sayyid Ibrāhīm, known as Tāj al-Dīn ← Sayyid Shihab al-Din Aḥmad, known as Sayyid al-Hāshim ← Sayyid Sharaf al-Dīn Isḥāq ← . . . ← Sayyid Sharaf al-Dīn Ḥusayn ← . . . ← Sayyid Sāliḥ ← Sayyid Khāmis (son of Sayyid Ghānim) ← (his uncle) Sayyid Abu'l-Wafāᵓ Tāj al-ᶜArifīn ← . . .*

For our current purposes, what is most significant about this *silsila* is what it represents in different *ijāza*s: unlike those coming from the 'regular' Wafaᵓi-cum-Kizilbash *ocak*s, where this genealogy stands for spiritual descent only, and is often accompanied by a second one indicating the family background of the receiver of the document, the *ijāza*s from the two *mürşid ocak*s of Ağuiçen and İmam Zeynel Abidin typically present it as a combined natural and spiritual descent line. This overlap, befitting for hereditary Sufism, helps to explain the two *ocak*s' claim to the title of *mürşid*, as their past members seem to have risen to the leadership position of the Wafaᵓiyya based on their alleged biological descent from the order's eponym. A few documents from the related *ocak*s repay close examination to illustrate this point.

The first of these documents is a Wafaᵓi *ijāza* embedded in a scroll that was dated Rabiᶜ al-awwal 984/1576, which comes from the *ocak* of İmam Zeynel Abidin.[81] It has been mentioned before in connection with its Turkish appendix offering a brief and historically anachronistic biography of Abu'l-Wafāᵓ. The main body of its text, or the *ijāza* proper, is, however, in Arabic and was copied from an older original that is explicitly described in the text as (physically) worn out (*wathīqa qadīma fāniya bāliya*).[82] We gather from the lines added to the text during the copying process by the local syndic of the descendants of the Prophet (*naqīb al-nuqabāᵓ*) in Karbala that the original, 'worn out' Wafaᵓi *ijāza* was brought to him by a certain Sayyid Ghanim b. Sayyid Qalandar b. Sayyid Muhammad.[83] The latter did so in order to provide written testimony to his descent from Sayyid Ghanim, the brother of Abu'l-Wafaᵓ, and thereby prove his *sayyid-*

ship. The text of the original Wafaʾi *ijāza* as reproduced in the extant copy records a meeting at the Madrasat al-Mustansiriyya of the successors (*khulafāʾ*) and relatives (*aqribāʾ*) of Abu'l-Wafāʾ, which took place in the presence of four kadis representing the four Sunni schools (*madhāhib*; sing. *madhhab*). At this meeting one of the ancestors of the recipient of the original *ijāza* (whose name is not legible) was acknowledged to be a blood relative of Abu'l-Wafaʾ as well as his spiritual heir, and thereupon sanctioned as head of the order (*ṭarīqa*) of Abu'l-Wafaʾ with authority over anyone claiming affiliation with it.[84] What we can deduce from this is that the original *ijāza* was produced within a Wafaʾi milieu that viewed the spiritual leadership of the Wafaʾi order to be a hereditary prerogative of Sayyid Ghanim's progeny.

It is unfortunately impossible to determine the date of the original Wafaʾi *ijāza.*[85] A very rough dating is, however, possible on the basis of some textual evidence. At the top of the extant copy of the document is the seal of the shrine of Imam Husayn, the names of the Twelve Imams and the prayer *Nād-i ʿAlī*, all of which are characteristic of Alevi documents copied or composed in Karbala during and after the sixteenth century; together they are clear clues of a Shiʿi-Alevi affiliation (Figure 2.2). On the other hand, the meeting described in the text of the original document took place at the Madrasat al-Mustansiriyya, which was established in Baghdad in the early thirteenth century and named after the contemporary Abbasid caliph, Mustansır bi-llah. The Mustansiriyya was the first madrasa to be inclusive of all four Sunni *madhab*s, which tallies with the reported meeting of kadis from the four Sunni schools. Based on this information, the date of the original *ijāza* can be placed between the early thirteenth century and the full integration of the Wafaʾiyya into the Kizilbash/Alevi milieu over the course of the late fifteenth century and early sixteenth. By the time the present copy was produced by the syndic in Karbala, however, the original *ijāza* was apparently valued mainly for making a claim to *sayyid*-ship via natural descent from Abu'l-Wafaʾ's paternal line rather than establishing a (privileged) link with the Wafaʾ tradition.

A second Wafaʾi *ijāza*, also from the *ocak* of İmam Zeynel Abidin, confirms that the order's spiritual leadership was derived exclusively from the bloodline of Sayyid Ghanim, while also demonstrating the Wafaʾiyya's dual function as a Sufi order and a family group. Although the copy that has come down to us is clearly a reproduction of an older original that was likewise made at the shrine of Imam Husayn at Karbala, the date it bears, Dhu'l-hijja 855/1451, might still reflect the *ijāza*'s original compilation date.[86] It was issued by Sayyid Khamis Husayni in the name of Sayyid Ibrahim, both figures apparently descendants of Sayyid Ghanim,

Figure 2.2 Trademark seals of Alevi documents issued at the shrine of Imam Husayn during and after the sixteenth century. FD/Scroll-IZA-2

Source: Photograph by the author, Istanbul, 2006

and contains a single genealogy that is a combined natural and spiritual one reaching back to Abu'l-Wafaʾ via his nephew Sayyid Khamis, son of Sayyid Ghanim.[87] In order to elucidate the real significance of this *ijāza*, we shall compare it with another Wafaʾi *ijāza*, this one coming from the *ocak* of Dede Kargın and dated 10 Muharram 905/1499.[88] In terms of both format and language, the two *ijāza*s are very similar with two noteworthy exceptions. First, the Dede Kargın *ijāza* contains a separate family genealogy of the inductee, Shaykh Muhammad, son of Shaykh Hasan el-Kargıni (al-Ġarḳīnī), in addition to the standard Wafaʾi *silsila* traced back to Sayyid Khamis, son of Sayyid Ghanim, and from him to Abu'l-Wafaʾ, indicating that Shaykh Muhammad's link to Abu'l-Wafaʾ pertained to the realm of spirituality alone. This is interesting in so far as it suggests the coexistence of hereditary transmission with the more normative *silsila*-based succession within the Wafaʾi milieu in Anatolia, although the latter mechanism, it seems, was used to establish a master–disciple relationship between two family lines rather than two individuals.

Second, while Shaykh Muhammad, son of Shaykh Hasan el-Kargıni, was appointed simply as *khalīfa* (*qad tawallāhū ᶜalā manṣib khilāfatihī*), Sayyid Ibrahim was appointed as *khalīfa* over all other *khalīfa*s and shaykhs ('*qad tawallāhū ᶜalā manṣib khilāfatihī ᶜalā jamīᶜ al-sādāt al-ashrāf wa'l-khulafāʾ wa'l-mashāʾikh al-kibār al-abrār fī aqṭār al-arḍ jamīᶜan*'). That is to say, Sayyid Ibrahim, unlike Shaykh Muhammad, was not merely an ordinary Wafaʾi *khalīfa*, but the head of the entire order. Furthermore, all descendants of the Prophet (*jamīᶜ al-sādāt al-ashrāf*) were also to be put under the authority of Sayyid Ibrahim. This means that Sayyid Ibrahim, in addition to occupying the leadership position of the order, also served in a capacity similar to that of a *naqīb*, presumably within the framework of his extended family or the Wafaʾi *sayyid*s in general. The dual function conferred on Sayyid Ibrahim is illustrative of the tangled relationship between family groups of *sayyid* descent and hereditary Sufi orders, a pattern that other scholars note in cases of the Yasavi tradition in central Asia[89] and the Egyptian Wafaʾiyya.[90] In the latter two cases, we see members of related families also filling the office of *naqīb al-ashrāf* (*Ot. naḳībü'l-eşrāf*) in different localities. That a similar situation held true for some of Sayyid Ghanim's progeny is suggested by another *ijāza*, this one coming from the Amasya branch of the Ağuiçens. This document, too, is a copy of an older original that was made in Karbala in 993/1586.[91] Unlike the previous two *ijāza*s, however, this one records the simultaneous appointment of its receiver, Sayyid Shihab al-Din Ahmad al-Husayni al-Wafaʾi, as head *naqīb* over all Husayni *sayyid*s in the shrines of Imam ᶜAli and Imam Husayn ('*naqīb al-nuqabā* *ᶜalā jamīᶜ ashrāf al-Ḥusaynī fī al-mashad Imām ᶜAlī wa Imām Ḥusayn*'). We can thus surmise that Sayyid Shihab al-Din Ahmad, purportedly one of the ancestors of the *ocak* of Ağuiçen, served as the official syndic of all descendants of the Prophet in the two shrine cities of Najaf and Karbala sometime prior to the year of 993/1586 when the extant copy was made. Indeed, he is probably the same person as Sayyid Shihab al-Din Ahmad who signed off the above-mentioned *shajara*-cum-*ijāza*, dated Muharram 829/1425, to verify its authenticity.[92]

Over time, a relatively extensive Wafaᵓi network developing under the aegis of the spiritual and hereditary line spawned by Sayyid Ghanim via his son Sayyid Khamis seems to have penetrated deep into rural and tribal settings in eastern Anatolia through numerous appointed Wafaᵓi *khalīfa*s. Many of these Wafaᵓi offshoots, which similarly would follow the principle of hereditary succession within their own family groups, were to form the seeds of a number of future Kizilbash/Alevi saintly lineages. These would continue to perpetuate the internal Wafaᵓi hierarchy among themselves, but within the new framework of the *ocak* system subsequent to their incorporation into the Kizilbash milieu. Consider as an example the Tunceli-based *ocak* of Şeyh Delil Berhican, which recognises the Ağuiçens as their *mürşid*. According to an *ijāza* found among the *ocak*'s family documents, the eponym of the *ocak*, Şeyh Delil Berhican (spelled as 'Shaykh Dalū Balnijān' in the text), was appointed as a *khalīfa* of the Wafaᵓi order specifically with jurisdiction over forty-two Kurdish tribal communities (Ar. *jamāᶜat*) whose names are listed at the end of the document. All signs in the document suggest that Şeyh Delil Berhican was a regular *khalīfa* with no genealogical connection to Abu'l-Wafaᵓ or claim to *sayyid* descent, as befitting the fact that the only title given to him was 'shaykh'. The mention of forty-two Kurdish tribes, moreover, accords with the *ocak*'s traditional following, which field research reveals to be almost exclusively Kurdish speaking. Another noteworthy feature of this document concerns the financial obligations of these tribes vis-à-vis their shaykhs. The said communities, according to the *ijāza*, were obliged to pay their alms and all other religiously sanctioned taxes and charity payments (*zakāt wa'l-ᶜushr wa'l-ṣadaqa wa'l-fiṭr wa'l-ażḥā al-qalīl wa'l-kabīr*) to Shaykh Delil Berhican, and these funds were to be spent on the poor and the needy (*fuqarāᶜ wa'l-masākīn*), the wayfarer and all those in need of charity.[93] This illustrates how bonds formed through communal Sufi affiliations within hereditary Sufi orders could be regularised and institutionalised on the basis of a religiously sanctioned payment in exchange for spiritual leadership. It would not be far off to consider this type of payment as the source of the Alevi notion of *hakullah* (lit. God's due), a monetary compensation of an unfixed amount from their disciples to an Alevi *dede* officiating at religious rites.

Based on their genealogical claims reaching back to Abu'l-Wafa' and their extended close ties to Karbala (as indicated by their family documents that were issued or renewed there), we can assume that the ancestors of the *ocak*s of Ağuiçen and Imam Zeynel Abidin hailed from Iraq, a point also supported by some of the oral traditions as mentioned above.[94] It is, however, difficult to determine when the ancestors of these *ocak*s emigrated to Anatolia, and whether they did so directly from Iraq and all at the same time. Leaving aside the complicated case of Husayn Raᶜi, if the aforementioned Shaykh Marzuban al-Baghdadi belonged to the same line, then Wafa'i-affiliated groups and individuals of Iraqi background must have been in Anatolia no later than the early thirteenth century. On the other hand, if Sayyid Shihab al-Din Aḥmad, whose name is included in multiple documents coming from the Wafaᶜi-cum-Kizilbash *ocak*s, is the same Shihab al-Din Ahmad mentioned by Zabidi who died in Anatolia in 1478, then it might be the case that the ancestors of some of these *ocak*s hailed from Aleppo, rather than directly from Iraq, as late as the mid-fifteenth century.[95]

Moreover, not all Wafa'i-affiliated groups and individuals in medieval Anatolia were necessarily linked to the Sayyid Khamis–Sayyid Ghanim line. For instance, the father of Seyyid Velayet, the commissioner of the Turkish translation of Abu'l-Wafa''s hagiography, is said to have moved from Iraq to Bursa in the year 841/1437. He is presented in the hagiography's introduction as an offspring of Sayyid Pir Hayat al-Din, allegedly another nephew and adopted son of Abu'l-Wafa'.[96] Additionally and more importantly, we have evidence of another Wafa'i line represented among Wafa'i-cum-Kizilbash *ocak*s, but this one with no claimed familial connection to Abu'l-Wafa'. Passing through a certain Shaykh Ahmad al-Jammi, this line is encountered in the previously mentioned Wafa'i document from the *ocak* of Şeyh Ahmed Dede, dated 829/1425, in which Ahmad al-Jammi is asserted to be one of the forty original disciples of Abu'l-Wafa'.[97] But these and other alternative Wafa'i lines seem to have never achieved the same influence as the one issuing from Sayyid Khamis, son of Sayyid Ghanim, who is shown as the distant ancestor of the *ocak*s of Ağuiçen and İmam Zeynel Abidin in their family documents.

THE *OCAK* OF DEDE KARGIN

Of all the *ocaks*, that of Dede Kargın is the one whose history is the best documented as well as most written about in recent years.[98] The *ocak*'s eponym Dede Kargın is assumed to have arrived in Anatolia from Khorasan, presumably in the wake of the Mongol invasions. In addition to a long-standing family tradition that connects the *ocak*'s origins to Khorasan,[99] this supposition more specifically rests on some apparently close ties that existed between Baba İlyas Khorasani and Dede Kargın as described in Elvan Çelebi's *Menāḳıbu'l-Ḳudsiyye.* The Dede Kargıns' likely connection to Khorasan finds additional support in the *ocak*'s family documents discussed below, which also make it clear that the family has been continuously associated with southeastern Anatolia since late medieval times, and with Malatya in particular, since at least the Mamluk period.

Our earliest source to mention Dede Kargın (Dede Ġarḳīn) is the fourteenth-century *Menāḳıbu'l-Ḳudsiyye* by Elvan Çelebi, which places him in Hıns-ı Mansur (modern-day Adıyaman, historically part of the Malatya province) circa 1240. According to Elvan Çelebi, Dede Kargın was an eminent Sufi shaykh with thousands of followers and hundreds of *ḫalīfe*s. He enjoyed the patronage of a contemporary sultan, probably ᶜAlaᵓeddin Keykubat I, who is said to have endowed him with seventeen villages.[100] Elvan Çelebi portrays Dede Kargın as closely associated with Baba İlyas, the leader of the Babaᵓi revolt.[101] The two reportedly held a prolonged meeting in a cave prior to the revolt, and subsequently Dede Kargın commanded a group of his leading *ḫalīfe*s to join Baba İlyas and to remain loyal to him unto death.[102] Dede Kargın's name is also cited by the sixteenth-century Ottoman historian Mustafa ᶜÂli in his famous *Tārīḫ-i Künhü'l-Aḫbar*, in which he speaks of Elvan Çelebi as a prominent Sufi contemporaneous with Osman Beg. ᶜAli, in the same place, describes Dede Kargın (*Şeyḫ Ġarḳīn*) as a saintly shaykh (*meşāyih-i vāṣılīnden*), further noting the existence of a work in Turkish by Elvan Çelebi that contains an exchange of questions and answers relating to Sufism between the author and Dede Kargın.[103] Neither of the sources, however, have any explicit indication of Dede Kargın's Wafaᵓi affinity. It is only through the *ocak*'s family documents that we can verify the family's Wafaᵓi connection, although it is unclear whether this affiliation was acquired before or after their migration to Anatolia.

We can surmise Dede Kargın's real name to be 'Nuᶜmān' since individual members of the *ocak* are described in two separate documents as descendants of 'Sayyid Nuᶜman, known as al-Ġarḳīnī' and of 'Şeyḥ Nuᶜmān Ḳarġınī'.[104] Nineteenth-century Alevi poet Ednai likewise gives the shaykh's real name as Nuᶜman, and confirms 'Dede Kargın' to be his nickname.[105] However, the fact that the name 'Nuᶜman' occurs multiple times in the written pedigrees of the *ocak*, none being explicitly identified as 'Dede Kargın', renders it difficult to discern which of these Nuᶜmans is the one who migrated to Anatolia. Moreover, the origins of the name 'Kargın' is still in need of clarification. Inspired by the Köprülü model, some modern researchers presume an organic relationship between the *ocak* of Dede Kargın and the Oghuz tribe of Karkın, perceiving Dede Kargın as an archetypal Turkmen *baba* unifying in his persona tribal and religious leadership.[106] At first sight, such a connection appears plausible, given the presence of tribal groups and villages with the same name, or its derivatives, in many corners of Anatolia. Moreover, and more importantly, according to a sixteenth-century document, discussed in more detail below, the disciple communities of the *ocak* also included a group from the Karkın tribe. On the other hand, the Karkın tribe is only one of several tribal communities whose names are mentioned in the document, which also includes groups affiliated with the Yağmurlu, Bayındır and Çepni tribes, and the residents of dozens of villages whose ethnic or tribal origins are unidentified. Speculations about a familial link between the *ocak* and the tribe of Karkın are further complicated by the variant spellings of the name Kargın, rendered in the sources as 'Ġarḳīn', 'Ḳarḳīn', or 'Ḳarġın' and by the word's unclear etymology.[107]

Whatever the Dede Kargıns' historical connection to the Oghuz tribe of Karkın may or may not be, the *ocak*'s family documents claim a *sayyid* descent for the family. A revealing piece of evidence in this regard is a document that seems to combine a *sayyid* genealogy with a Sufi diploma. The copy at hand is clearly not the original but a later copy made by someone with poor Arabic skills; its highly degenerated language, unfortunately, prevents full comprehension. It is worth mentioning, however, that the part of the document narrating the family's origins in prose foregrounds a certain Katil (Kattal?) Gazi Kargını (*Ḳātil Ġāzī Ġarḳīnī*), allegedly a *mujahid* fighting alongside the Prophet, as the progenitor of the family, one of whose descendants is claimed to have later married a granddaughter of Imam Jaᶜfar al-Sadiq.[108] The details of this largely mythic story, which seems to attribute the family a *sayyid* descent from the maternal side, need not detain us here. The true value of the document for the present discussion is what it reveals in terms of the family's self-perception as descendants of the Prophet. Of further and related significance is the list of witnesses at the end of the document who attested to its truthfulness. These include four *sayyid*s whose identities suggest Khorasan to be the place where the original document was composed. One of the *sayyid*s who affirmed the veracity of the document was identified as a resident of Balkh (*sākin-i Devlet*[*ā*]*bād-i Balḥ-est*) and two others bore the *nisba* Tirmidhi.[109] Similarly connected to Tirmidh was the syndic (*naqīb*) Haydar, son of Husayn al-Tirmidhi, who granted the *shajara*. The identities of the witnesses suggest that the original document was composed outside of Anatolia, probably in Balkh or Tirmidh – two important cities historically considered part of Khorasan.

Besides validating the commonly assumed Khorasanian origins of the Dede Kargıns and testifying to the family's self-image, as well as recognition by others, as *sayyid*s long before their arrival in Anatolia, this document produces another potentially significant revelation: it indirectly links the ancestors of the *ocak* with the famous Sayyids of Tirmidh, the clue being provided by the title *khānzāde* attached to the names of all four witnesses. This is a title associated with the members of the house of ᶜAlaᵓ al-Mulk who belonged to the Tirmidhi Sayyids. The fame of the Tirmidhi Sayyids is in large part based on their connection to the alternative caliphate established by the Khwarazm-Shahs, a dynasty that competed with other local dynasties for the control of Khorasan following the decline of Seljuk domination in the region. The Khwarazm-Shah Muhammad, declaring the Abbasids as usurpers, proclaimed in the early thirteenth century a Husaynid *sayyid* from among the house of ᶜAlaᵓ al-Mulk as caliph.[110] The Dede Kargıns' affinity with the Tirmidhi Sayyids, if true, would speak to the long-standing elevated social and religious status of the family within their seemingly native Khwarazm before they left the region for Anatolia. It also strengthens the possibility that they did so in the wake of the Mongol destruction of the Khwarazmi state, which purportedly extended its patronage to the family.

The first destination of the Dede Kargıns in Anatolia appears to have been Mardin. Ottoman tax registers dated 914/1518 show that the district of Berriyecik in the province of Mardin encompassed a sizeable village called Dede Kargın, which contained a convent by the same name.[111] The unusual cone-shaped brick building of this convent still stands today, although the date of its construction is obscure (Figure 2.3). However, given that the name of the broader region where the village is situated was recorded as the 'place of Dede Kargın' in a work from 876/1471, one can reasonably assume a well-established presence of the Dede Kargıns in the environs of Mardin going further back than the date of this historical record.[112] It may be of some significance as well that Mardin is mentioned in the hagiography of Abu'l-Wafaᵓ as the hometown of two unnamed visitors to the saint's tomb. This was in the days when Sayyid Yaqub, son of Sayyid Matar, who is highlighted in Abu'l-Wafaᵓ's hagiog-

Figure 2.3 The (presumed) tomb of Dede Kargın, in the village of Dedeköy in Derik-Mardin

Source: Photograph by İlkan Yalvaç, 2017.

raphy as the saint's paternal nephew and primary spiritual successor, was serving as the gatekeeper of the saint's tomb (*türbedār*).[113] Whether these two mysterious individuals were in any way linked to the Dede Kargın family is difficult to determine; if, however, the hypothesis that the family arrived in Anatolia with the second wave of Muslim migrations following the Mongol invasion of Khwarazm in the early thirteenth century is accepted, the possibility of a direct connection would have to be ruled out. Regardless, the story is significant for signalling the presence of Wafa'i-affiliated individuals in the Mardin region, probably the first home of the Dede Kargıns in Anatolia, as early as two generations after the passing of Abu'l-Wafa', that is roughly during the mid- to late twelfth century. I will return to this point below when discussing the timing of the Dede Kargıns' acquisition of a Wafa'i identity.

From circa 1500 onwards, by which time the main branch of the *ocak* had moved from Mardin to the environs of Malatya, the Dede Kargıns come into historical record more clearly. A curious story in the hagiography of Hacı Bektaş compiled in about the late fifteenth century mentions a group of Dede Kargın descendants (*Dede Ġarḳīn oğılları*) who were in a verbal conflict with the Bektashis over the right to wear a particular headgear with a deer horn on both sides. This encounter reportedly took place in the Dulkadirli region, which historically comprised the provinces of Malatya and Maraş and the surrounding areas.[114] The Ottomans took control of the Dulkadirli region from the Mamluks in 1514. By this time, the Dede Kargıns were already long-time residents of the village of Bimare (Bīmāre) located in the Keder Beyt district (modern-day Akçadağ) of the Malatya province. According to an Ottoman imperial decree (*fermān*) dated 1524, copies of which are found both in the Ottoman archives and among the *ocaks*' family documents,[115] descendants of Dede Kargın living in Bimare had enjoyed certain tax privileges during the Mamluk era (*eyyām-ı Çerākise*) as *sayyids* and dervishes attending a convent where they served travellers. These privileges were recorded and endorsed in the very first Ottoman cadastral survey of the region after the conquest, and from then on repeatedly ratified.[116]

By the middle of the sixteenth century, we find the Bimare-centred Dede Kargıns commanding a vast following in and around Malatya. The extent of their sphere of influence is revealed by a list of the Dede Kargıns' affiliated disciple communities that was copied on two different scrolls, one dated Ramadan 963/1556 and the other Rajab 971/1564.[117] In addition to several tribes, the scrolls list more than 125 villages, which for the most part can be cross-checked in the contemporary Ottoman land surveys. The locations of the villages, when mapped, show that the neighbouring districts of Akçadağ, Keder Beyt, Subadra, Arguvan, Kasaba, Pağnik, Muşar and Cubaş made up a relatively well-defined region within the province of Malatya where the Dede Kargıns wielded influence.[118] Of further interest to us is a note in Turkish that follows the list, stating that each of the affiliated communities were obliged to provide annually three okes of butter and three sheep to members of the Dede Kargın family, and invoking curses against those who interfered with the practice.[119] This document as such not only demonstrates the degree of de facto control of Sufi families over rural life in Anatolia, and the vastness of the Dede Kargıns' sphere of influence in particular, it also supplements and reinforces the previously mentioned document of the *ocak* of Delil Berhican in illuminating how communal Sufi affiliations were subjected to a process of routinisation and institutionalisation through regular payment of alms to shaykhly families.

The convent in Bimare, as is usually the case with Sufi convents, also contained a tomb-shrine. Ottoman documents give conflicting information concerning the identity of the person buried at this site, one source identifying him as 'Dede Kargın', another as 'Seyyid Numan son of Seyyid Yusuf son of Kargın Baba'.[120] Although a village by the name of Bimare no longer exists, the probable site of the convent is today part of the village of Bahri, modern-day Akçadağ, where a burial site of the Kargıni family has survived up to the present.[121] While no local tradition concerning the Dede Kargıns has survived to corroborate this among the village population, which today consists mainly of Sunni Muslims, the Alevi inhabitants of the neighbouring village of Bektaşlar confirmed to me the association of the *ziyāret* (site of pilgrimage) with the Dede Kargıns. The site contains dozens of tombs, many inscribed with names bearing the Kargıni family epithet. These are situated inside an adobe and stone building with a wooden roof that comprises multiple courts and a yard encircled by a low concrete wall topped with steel rods. Within the innermost enclosure of the building there is an older tomb overlaid with a wooden coffin; this, according to its undated inscription, is the resting place of a certain 'Yūsuf Dede bin Velī Dede' (Figures 2.4a, 2.4b, 2.4c). The Yusuf Dede buried at this site is most likely to be identified with the individual known in the family oral tradition as 'Sultan Yusuf', the patriarch of the Malatya branch of the *ocak*.[122] It was presumably under the leadership of Sultan Yusuf that the family moved to Malatya from Mardin, where the eponym of the *ocak*, that is, the original Dede Kargın, must be buried. A document fragment from a relatively unexpected source serves to substantiate this conjecture; this fragment found in the family archives of another Alevi *ocak*, that of Güvenç Abdal centred in the modern province of Ordu, includes a clear statement to the effect that Dede Kargın passed away in Mardin.[123]

Figure 2.4a Burial site of the Kargıni family, in the village of Bahri in Akçadağ-Malatya

Source: Photograph by the author, 2006.

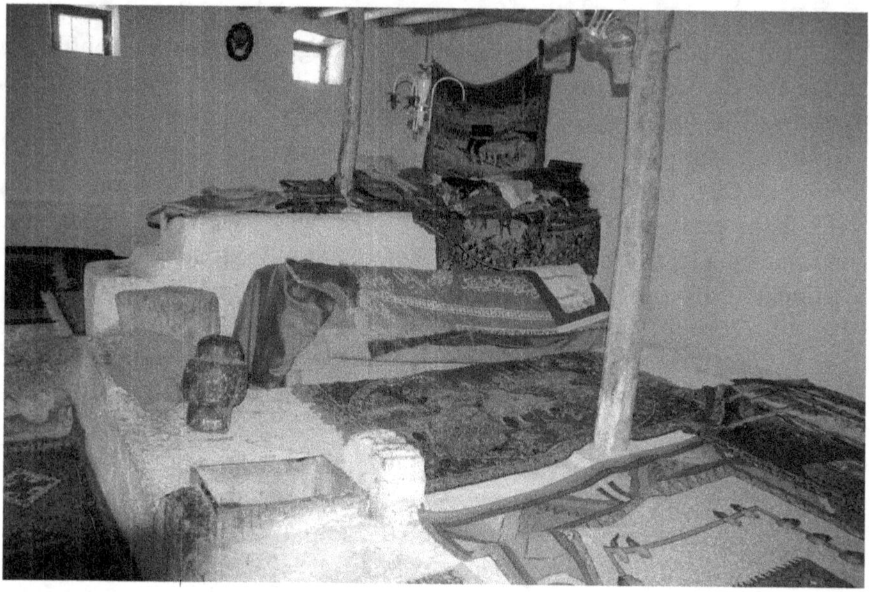

Figure 2.4b Burial site of the Kargıni family, picture from inside

Source: Photograph by the author, 2006.

Figure 2.4c The wooden headstone marking the grave of Yusuf Dede, patriarch of the Malatya branch of the *ocak* of Dede Kargın

Source: Photograph by the author, 2006.

The death in 2011 of the last representative of the *ocak*'s Malatya branch, Ahmet Rıza Kargıner, brought an end to the long history of the *ocak* in that region. However, the line continues elsewhere. Sometime in the nineteenth century a group of Dede Kargıns moved from Malatya to Çorum; the *dedes* associated with this Çorum branch are currently the only active members of the *ocak*. Yet another branch of the Dede Kargın *ocak* inhabits the province of Antep. A traveller's account reporting a sizeable 'Dede Karkın tribe' in the environs of Antep in 1766 is the earliest written source to attest their existence.[124] Unlike the *ocak*'s Malatya branch, whose disciple communities comprised mainly sedentary villagers, the Antep branch appears to have had a primarily (semi-)nomadic following, especially from among the Turkmen tribe of Çepni. While the historical connection between the Dede Kargıns in Malatya and those in Antep is obscure, it is possible that the latter were a group who left Mardin and moved directly to Antep, or alternatively a splinter branch of the Dede Kargıns of Malatya who later settled in Antep.[125]

The Wafa'i connection of the Dede Kargıns

Most concrete evidence of the Dede Kargıns' historical affinity with the Wafa'i order is supplied by a Wafa'i *ijāza* dated 10 Muharram 905/1499. Preserved in the family archives of the Dede Kargıns' Malatya branch, this *ijāza* has come down to us in two copies, the second one being from Jumada al-awwal 952/1545. This *ijāza*, which has already been mentioned above, was granted to Shaykh Muhammad b. Shaykh Hasan al-Kargıni (al-Ġarḳīnī) on the occasion of his elevation to the position of *khalīfa*; the grantee's *nisba* 'al-Ġarḳīnī' affirms his identity as a descendant of Dede Kargın.

While the *ijāza* attests to the Wafa'i connection of the Dede Kargıns, it also raises the question of how far back this affiliation goes, as there is no evidence to that effect in earlier sources. It is true that Abu'l-Wafa''s hagiography identifies Bukhara as one of the areas where the saint's influence had reached during his lifetime, which means that the family might have had a long-standing familiarity or affinity with the Wafa'i tradition when they were still in Khorasan. The existence of other Wafa'i shaykhs of Khorasani background in medieval Anatolia, such as Bahlul Baba and Baba İlyas, also signals that possibility. On the other hand, the *ijāza* under consideration contains the Wafa'i chain of initiation running through Abu'l-Wafa''s paternal nephew Sayyid Khamis (son of Sayyid Ghanim), which is the same Wafa'i line encountered in the family documents of most other Wafa'i-cum-Kizilbash *ocak*s. In other words, the *ijāza* contains no sign of an independent Wafa'i line transmitted from Khorasan to Anatolia.

Furthermore, the above-discussed document exposing the Dede Kargıns' possible links to the Tirmidhi Sayyids mentions 'the noble dervish cloak of the Ġarḳinīyya [order]' (*al-khirḳa al-sharīfa al-Ġarḳiniyya*), a phrase implying the existence of a separate Garkıni (Kargıni) Sufi tradition.[126] Based on this, Ahmed Yaşar Ocak suggests that the Garkiniyya might be an offshoot of the Wafaʾi order.[127] However, the fact that the chain of initiation provided in this document, presumably pertaining to the Garkiniyya, does not include Abu'l-Wafaʾ as one of the links speaks against Ocak's argument; instead it reaches Imam ʿAli through an entirely different succession of names, including Dede Garkın and Salman Farisi, among others.[128] All of this makes it more likely that the incorporation of the Dede Kargıns into the Wafaʾi milieu took place not before but after they took up residence in Anatolia. This may have happened in Mardin, the family's likely first destination in the region, given the existence of individuals associated with the Wafa'i order in that city since the twelfth century, as we are informed by Abu'l-Wafaʾ's hagiography. If so, the Dede Kargıns may have been previously part of a separate, but similarly hereditary Sufi tradition known as the Garkiniyya, the memory of which has been preserved in their family epithet.

The Dede Kargıns' Ahi connection

Another notable aspect of the story of the Dede Kargıns is their likely but hard-to-define ties to the Ahis, the aforementioned urban fraternal communities of artisans and craftsmen. The idea that some close or even organic links existed between the Ahis and the Wafaʾi circles in medieval Anatolia was suggested earlier in our discussion of Ede Balı's and Hüsameddin Çelebi's familial Ahi affinities. Further evidence in support of this idea comes from an Ahi *ijāza* that is half in Arabic and half in Persian. It has come down to us in two copies, both of which have been kept in the private archives of the order's Antep branch.[129] The older of the two copies bears the date of 14 Şaʿban 775/1374, although we can infer from its formal qualities that it is actually a sixteenth-century copy of an *ijāza* whose original was compiled at the given date, which the copier apparently retained. Issued in the name of a certain 'Aḫī Ṭūrsān b. Hābīl', this *ijāza* includes a chain of initiation reaching back to Imam ʿAli via the famous Ahi Evran of the thirteenth century, the patron saint of the Anatolian tanners.[130] Where the *ijāza* was initially composed is not recorded, although a hint is provided by a barely visible *nisba* of 'Hısni' attached to the name of one of the witnesses. This suggests as a possible location of composition Hısn-ı Mansur, modern-day Adıyaman, the place where the meeting of Dede Kargın and Baba İlyas reportedly took place in the days leading up to the Babaʾi revolt. The second, slightly modified copy of the same *ijāza* is undated but appears to be of more recent making. Added to the end of the document is the phrase '*bi-kaza-ı Türkmen-i Haleb*', an Ottoman administrative unit designating nomadic Turkmen populations of the broader Aleppo region. Clearly, the family had the older physically deteriorated *ijāza* reproduced while still keeping the earlier copy. A seemingly small but telling discrepancy in terms of content that exists between the two copies involves the titles of individuals included in the long list of witnesses at the end: in all cases, the title 'Aḫī' was either replaced or supplemented by the title 'Sayyid' in the more recent one. This clearly deliberate modification of the document is similar in significance to what I call the '*sayyid*-isation' of shaykhly families in tandem with their assimilation into the Kizilbash milieu, a topic to which I return below.

The value of this precious Ahi *ijāza* found in the private archives of the *ocak* of Dede Kargın is manifold.[131] First and foremost, it reinforces the proposed entanglement between the Ahi and the Wafaʾi milieus in medieval Anatolia. On a broader level, it also corroborates and complements what is already known of the popularity of the Safavid-Kizilbash cause within *futuwwa* circles in Iran, suggesting that a similar dynamic was at play in the expansion of the Kizilbash influence in the Anatolian context.[132] Indeed, there is at least one Kizilbash/Alevi *ocak* whose founding patriarch Ahi Mahmud Veli, also known as Keçeci Baba (maker of felt), apparently presided over an Ahi convent in the subdistrict of Erbaa in the modern province of Tokat, the building of which has survived to the present.[133] Another Alevi *ocak* with possible historical ties to the Ahis is that of Turabi Baba centred in Çubuk-Ankara. Such a connection is suggested by their family documents, which include what appears to be an Ahi *ijāza* reaching back to Selman Kufi, the patron saint of water bearers (*saḳā*).[134] All this, finally, also helps to explain the circulation of *futuwwa*-related literature among Kizilbash communities in Anatolia and the presence of some conspicuous overlaps between this literature and the Alevi *Buyruk*s in terms of language and content, as aptly observed years ago by Abdülbâkî Gölpınarlı.[135]

The Evolution of the Wafaʾyya in Light of the Wafaʾi **Ijāzas**

The Wafaʾi *ijāza*s, or fragments thereof, found among Alevi documents not only serve to demonstrate the Sufi provenance of the Alevi *ocak* system; they are also revealing in terms of the evolution of the Wafaʾi tradition in medieval Anatolia. Before exploring this point further, it would be worthwhile to comment on the value of these *ijāza*s for such an undertaking. To start with, despite the difficulty in many cases of determining and verifying individual *ijāza*s' original dates of composition, there is no obvious basis to question the broader time frame, namely the fifteenth and sixteenth centuries, within which their current copies are said to have been produced. Nor is there any compelling reason, be it in terms of content, style or context, to doubt the genuineness of this body of widely dispersed documents regarding their stated purpose. Assuming the genuineness of these Wafaʾi *ijāza*s is, of course, not the same as vouching for the historical accuracy of their genealogical claims, specifically relating to the line stemming from the putative nephew of Abu'l-Wafaʾ, Sayyid Khamis, son of Sayyid Ghanim. For one cannot rule out the possibility that these genealogies may be, in full or in part, later constructs, fashioned to provide the pertinent families with a sacred lineage. Even so, the fact remains that these genealogical traditions, leading back to a relatively obscure Sufi master of Sunni denomination, are quite old and reflect a time before the incorporation of the related families into the Kizilbash milieu. Their obvious antiquity is also in accord with what other sources reveal concerning the presence in late medieval Anatolia of familial groups and/or Sufi circles who defined themselves in terms of natural and/or spiritual descent from Abu'l-Wafaʾ.

Taken collectively, these *ijāza*s are indicative of the evolution of a certain strain within the Wafaʾi milieu from a network of loosely connected *sayyid* and shaykhly families into a relatively institutionalised Sufi order. This process must have been underway no later than the early to mid-fifteenth century, from when we have their earliest dated samples.[136] A close examination of all extant *ijāza*s reveals a common inventory of themes and ideas expressed in a shared vocabulary and format, which demonstrate a common milieu of production and circulation. They, for instance, quote the same Qurʾanic verses and Prophetic traditions (*ḥādith*) to illustrate similar ideas. The *ijāza*s are also unified in featuring the same basic Wafaʾi *silsila*, a set of standard Wafaʾi paraphernalia, as well as a distinct Wafaʾi initiation ritual, of which most, if not all, can be linked back to the early Wafaʾi milieu in Iraq as it emerges from Abu'l-Wafaʾ's fourteenth-century hagiography. 'Poverty' (*faqr*) is the dominant Sufi theme in these *ijāza*s, echoing as such the example of Abu'l-Wafaʾ, whose Sufi career featured extreme forms of asceticism. Their introductions consistently cite the Prophetic tradition, 'poverty is my crown', and their texts allude to the Wafaʾiyya as the 'order of poverty' (*ṭarīqat al-faqr*). They also list several 'tokens of poverty' bestowed on the newly appointed Wafaʾi *khalīfa*s, including a pair of scissors (*miqrāḍ*), a (woolen) robe (*khirqa*), a prayer rug (*sajjāda*), a banner (*ʿalam*), a lamp (*qandīl*), a basket (*zanbīl*), and a waistband (*miyān al-basta*). Two of these, scissors and waistband, were apparently used in Wafa'i initiation rituals; as explained in the *ijāza*s, the ritual involved 'running the scissors through the hair of the repentants . . . and wrapping their waists' (*yajriya bi'l-miqrāḍ ᶜalā shuᶜūr al-tā'ibīn . . . wa-yashudda awsaṭahum*).[137] That hair cutting as an act of initiation originated with the early Wafa'i milieu in Iraq can be presumed from the multiple references to Abu'l-Wafa' himself practicing it in his hagiography. On the other hand, we find no mention in the hagiography of the wrapping of the inductee's waist, a practice that may have been a later accretion, possibly adopted from the Ahis; it is an initiation ritual also practiced by the Kizilbash/Alevi communities.[138]

The *ijāza*s also shed light on the assimilation process of these Wafa'i-affiliated family lines into the Kizilbash milieu, which, it seems, entailed various degrees of diluting, recasting or even repressing their Wafa'i past. While pinpointing an exact beginning and ending for this process is difficult, it is possible to infer from the existing evidence that it was most likely completed no later than about the middle of the sixteenth century. A relatively good sign of this is a *ziyāretnāme* dated 995/1548. A formulaic passage from an Arabic Wafa'i *ijāza* inserted into this otherwise Turkish *ziyāretnāme* establishes the Wafa'i affiliation of its recipient, Derviş Hasan b. Derviş ᶜAşıḳ, who was apparently the progenitor or one of the ancestors of the *ocak* of Şeyh Süleyman based in the Arguvan district of Malatya. According to this passage, Derviş Hasan was initiated into the Wafa'i order by Sayyid Muhammad b. Sayyid Ibrahim. The rest of the document records Derviş Hasan's visit to Iraq in the year 995/1548, offering the full itinerary of the journey, which included visitations to various Shiᶜi-Alevi sacred sites but none associated with the Sunnis.[139] Given that Derviş Hasan's initiation was prior to his trip, we can assume that a Wafa'i shaykh by the name Sayyid Muhammad b. Sayyid Ibrahim was still actively issuing Wafa'i *ijāza*s in the environs of Malatya circa the early sixteenth century. Notably, the name Sayyid Muhammad b. Sayyid Ibrahim also appears as the last link in the previously cited composite *silsila* of the line of Sayyid Khamis that emerges from the extant Wafa'i *ijāza*s. If the two Muhammads should be identical, then it would be reasonable to assume that after his death the Wafa'iyya more or less ceased to exist as a separate order, having completed its merger with the Kizilbash milieu. The existing *ijāza*s then became obsolete relics, valued solely as documentation of the *sayyid* descent and/or *ocakzade* status of related *dede* families.

A further indication of this process of assimilation includes the ways that the Wafa'i-related Alevi documents were edited to bring them in line with growing Shiᶜi-Alevi sensibilities. Although most copies of the *ijāza*s at hand were produced after the merger of the Wafaʾiyya with the Kizilbash milieu (oftentimes at the Karbala convent, as seen in previous examples), several of them, nonetheless, bear traces of their pre-Kizilbash past. Putting aside the isolated example of the above-cited document that refers to a meeting involving the Sunni ulema at the Mustansiriyya Madrasa, these traces are most consistently discerned in the *ijāza*s' prologues. In addition to praising God, the Prophet Muhammad, his family and companions, and ᶜAli, some of these prologues pay tribute to the first three Sunni caliphs (Abu Bakr, ᶜUmar and ᶜUthman) as well as to certain major Shiᶜi-sub-Alevi figures, including Imam Husayn, Imam Hasan and the two uncles of the Prophet Muhammad, Hamza and ᶜAbbas. This combination of religious figures, noteworthy for its confessional eclecticism, clearly mirrors the 'moderate' pro-ᶜAlid Sunnism exhibited in Abu'l-Wafaʾ's hagiography. A close comparison of different *ijāza*s also demonstrates efforts to erase traces of past Sunni affiliation and/or sectarian metadoxy in tandem with the intensifying Sunni–Shiᶜi polarisation. Take as examples the Dede Kargın *ijāza* dated 10 Muharram 905/1499 and another from the Malatya branch of the *ocak* of Ağuiçen, copied in Dhu'l-hijja 990/1582. While the earlier one mentions the names of the first three caliphs in its introduction, the later one omits them, instead paying tribute to the Twelve Imams. Similarly, in the Wafaʾi *silsila* contained in the latter copy we see that the name of Sayyid Minaʾ al-Din ᶜUthman is modified to Sayyid Qasim, and the first name of Abu Bakr al-Hawwari changed to Taj al-Din.[140]

Another notable aspect of the assimilation of the Wafaʾi legacy within the Kizilbash/Alevi *ocak* system seems to be what I call the '*sayyid*-isation' of the shaykhly families. This trend is most clearly in evidence in some old Wafaʾi *ijāza*s that were later reframed and reproduced as *sayyid shajara*s at the Karbala convent. The *shajara* of the *ocak* of Sinemilli is a case in point. The Sinemillis pay homage to the Koca Seyyid branch of the Ağuiçens, based in the village of Sün in the modern province of Elazığ. According to their family documents, they originated in nearby Piran and migrated to Maraş and Erzincan at about the turn of the eighteenth century (Figure 2.5).[141] Our knowledge of the Sinemillis' historical Wafaʾi affiliation rests on a fragment of a Wafaʾi *ijāza* embedded in a document from the Erzincan branch of the *ocak*. The text, identified as 'the *shajara* of the *ocak* of Sinemilli' in a side note, explicitly states that the current copy was drawn up in 1265/1848 at the Karbala convent based on an older '*shajara*', a word that came to be used among the Alevis in a generic fashion to mean any written proof of a family's *ocak* status. Notwithstanding the conflated

Figure 2.5 The (presumed) tomb-shrine of Sultan Sinemil(li), Piran-Elazığ
Source: Photograph by Laine Stump, 2003.

terminology, a close examination of the document reveals the current copy to be an abridged and amended version in Turkish of an original Wafaʾi *ijāza* in Arabic, supplemented with an updated genealogy of the owner of the document, Sayyid İbrahim, son of Sayyid Hasan.

The fragment of the original Wafaʾi *ijāza* retained in the document provides the following pedigree for the ancestors of the *ocak*, tracing back to a certain Hayran Abdal as follows:

Sayyid İbrāhīm ←Sayyid Ḥasan ←Shaykh Naẓar ←Shaykh Zennūn ←Ḥayrān Abdāl

No further information is available about the individual names in the pedigree. Nor do we have the original date of the Wafaʾi *ijāza* that is embedded in the document. However, we can make a number of educated guesses based on the changing titles of the successive members of the family. To begin with, the fact that the apparent progenitor of the family is referred to as an Abdal suggests that he may have been one of those itinerant dervishes collectively known as the Abdals of Rum. In the document, Hayran Abdal is stated to be an affiliate of the order of Abu'l-Wafaʾ, initiated into the path by a Sayyid Muhammad (possibly the same Sayyid Muhammad as the one mentioned above) whose spiritual genealogy, as provided in the text, passes through Sayyid Khamis. Today, members of the *ocak* of Sinemilli, like those of Ağuiçen, do not recall any affiliation with the Wafa'i order but recognise the latter as their *mürşid*s. Even though the memory of it appears to have been lost, the relationship between the two families must have been first established with the initiation of Hayran Abdal into the Wafa'i order by one of the ancestors of the Ağuiçen *ocak* while both families were still living in the province of Elazığ. In time, this relationship was apparently recast and perpetuated on the basis of the *mürşid–dede–talib* hierarchy within the framework of the Kizilbash/Alevi *ocak* system.

Hayran Abdal's next two successors are referred to as 'şeyh' (shaykh), possibly indicating their adoption of a sedentary lifestyle. What lends additional weight to this conjecture are references in two separate documents to a convent bearing the name Shaykh Sinemilli (*zāviye-i Şeyḫ Sinemillī*) located in the district of Piran, the family's place of dwelling before they moved to Maraş and Erzincan in about the middle of the eighteenth century.[142] Of further and particular interest to us are the last two names in the pedigree, which bear the title '*sayyid*'. The same title precedes the names of all the subsequent descendants of the *ocak* that were added to the text when it was copied in the year 1265/1848 by way of updating the family genealogy. While examples of the term 'shaykh' being used for '*sayyid*' do exist in the historical record, this shift in titles nonetheless calls for attention, the more so when combined with the fact that the family's descent line as given in the present document is not even traced all the way to the Prophet. This could be a deliberate omission of the copyist, who, for whatever reason, might have left out parts of the original document. Alternately, it could also be interpreted as denoting a non-biological or spiritual descent from the Prophet, based on the idea that 'true kinship with the Prophet is not biological but spiritual', which was a notion not uncommon among the Sufis.[143] Having said that, there is in the family archives of the Maraş branch of the *ocak* a separate *shajara* that was issued by the syndic in Karbala in 1782, which includes a genealogical chart that actually reaches all the way back to the Prophet. However, this was a *shajara* granted not on the basis of an older document, as was the case with the *ocak* of İmam Zeynel Abidin, for instance, but one granted on the basis of witness testimonies attesting to the family's long-established renown as *sayyid*s.[144] These witnesses, more specifically, testified that the family's old *shajara* was lost. It is possible that the reference here is to the old Wafa'i *ijāza* that stayed with the Erzincan branch of the family rather than an actual *sayyid shajara*. If that was indeed the case, then it would be possible to hypothesise that the family's recognition as *sayyid*s postdated their initiation into the Wafa'i order. Put differently, the growing social stature of the family resulting from their acquired affiliation with the Wafa'i order might have augmented their reputation, suggesting a line of a sacred descent or even spawning the need for one; hence the family's acquisition of a written *sayyid* genealogy to enhance their spiritual authority.

Whatever the specific circumstances were with the issuing of the Sinemilli *shajara* by the syndic in Karabala, this shift from shaykh-hood to *sayyid*-ship that we observe in the case of the *ocak* of Sinemilli appears to be part and parcel of a broader process attending the assimilation of the Wafa'iyya into the Kizilbash movement. In this process, *sayyid*-ship seems to have gradually emerged as a key source of spiritual legitimacy and social authority, rendering irrelevant any religious credentials deriving from an affiliation with the Wafa'iyya or any other Sufi tradition. In the longer term, the substitution of sanctity based on initiatic or hereditary transmission from a Sufi saint with descent from the Prophet through ʿAli must have helped to forge a more coherent and homogenous socio-religious system out of a heterogeneous collection of dervish groups and Sufi networks under the banner of Kizilbashism by allowing the different *ocak*s to connect themselves to a common source.

The line of analysis above, meanwhile, leads us to the sensitive question of the authenticity of the Alevi *ocak*s' claims to *sayyid*-ship. From the point of view of the present discussion it matters little whether or not these claims are indeed historically accurate. For it is certain that these families have long been recognised as *sayyid*s by the communities they lived in and are, therefore, *sayyid*s in social terms regardless of the authenticity of their genealogical charts. On the other hand, it is undoubtedly of some significance that we find no *sayyid* genealogies among the family documents of certain *ocak*s, such as the Sinemillis, that are of comparable antiquity as the ones found in the family archives of the *ocak*s of Imam Zeynel Abidin, Ağuiçen and Dede Kargın. It may be more important to note this difference in the dates of pertinent documents than to assess their authenticity. While the antiquity of a *shajara* issued by the *naqib*s and recognised by the state authorities does not automatically establish the historical veracity of particular genealogical claims, it does, at the very least, show that the *sayyid*-ship of some of the *ocak*s gained social and/or official recognition earlier than others. But even in cases of the latter *ocak*s, the official recognition of whose *sayyid* status is dateable to an earlier time, one may speak of a *sayyid*-isation process insofar as their Sufi or more specifically Wafa'i affiliations clearly receded into the background, eventually fading away completely in favour of an exclusive emphasis on their *sayyid* descent. If one factor propelling this process of *sayyid*-isation was these families' coalescence under the leadership of the Safavi family, and the gradual decline in value, or even deliberate repression, of their prior Sufi affiliations, another factor was the Ottoman state's persecutory measures against them over the course of the sixteenth century. Since I will take up this topic again in Chapter 6, suffice it to say at this point that these measures entailed the destruction or confiscation of Sufi/dervish convents that were directly or indirectly associated with the exponents of the Kizilbash milieu, in addition to the better-known physical forms of punishment employed against the Kizilbash. The result was the virtual elimination of the Sufi infrastructure of the *ocak*s, which, in turn, must have increased the pressure on these families to seek alternative sources of spiritual legitimacy and social authority.

Conclusion

Alevi documents, when used in dialogue with archival and epigraphic evidence, reveal a relatively extensive Wafaʾi presence in eastern Anatolia since late medieval times. The first Wafaʾi dissemination into Anatolia proper appears to have begun no later than the opening of the thirteenth century and continued until at least the early fifteenth century. Multiple groups of Sufis, dervishes and *sayyid*s with a Wafaʾi affiliation seem to have entered Anatolia from Iraq and Khorasan, evolving in different directions in their new home in terms of social, political and religious orientations. Among the factors that encouraged the rapid dissemination and proliferation of the Wafaʾiyya in Anatolia were geographical proximity, the patronage that individual Wafaʾi shaykhs received from the Seljuk, Mongol/Ilkhanid and Mamluk rulers, as well as the former's effective translation of Sufism to tribal and rural settings through communal affiliations. The Wafaʾi audience in Anatolia was not, however, exclusively rural; it also included urban populations, as indicated by the existence of Wafaʾi convents in city centres (such as that of Şeyh Çoban in Sivas), not to mention the Ahi connections of certain Wafaʾi shaykhs or their relatives.

A distinct Wafaʾi network that had formed around the spiritual lineage descending from Sayyid Khamis, son of Sayyid Ghanim, the putative brother of Abu'l-Wafaʾ, seems to have remained independently active in and around the upper Euphrates basin as late as the first half of the sixteenth century before fully blending in with the Kizilbash milieu. Although an independent Wafaʾi identity subsequently faded, the communal following and established local hierarchies of the order's various branches were perpetuated and reconfigured within the new framework of the Kizilbash/Alevi *ocak* system. This evolving trajectory of the Wafaʾi legacy is reflected in the later copies of extant Wafaʾi *ijāzas*, which were edited to bring them in line with growing Shiʿi-Alevi sensibilities. It is also suggested by the shifting use of these *ijāzas* as simple genealogical pedigrees of *ocakzade* families, whose source of religious authority was now recast exclusively on the basis of *sayyid*-ship.

In time the memory of the Wafaʾiyya appears to have been erased almost completely among the Wafaʾi-cum-Kizilbash *ocaks*, as well as among the Ottomans in general. This amnesia was as much a corollary of the fusion of the Wafaʾi network in eastern Anatolia with the Kizilbash milieu as it was the result of the Wafaʾi legacy's absorption into the Bektashi tradition through the intermediary of the Abdals of Rum in the west. Further light will be shed on this issue in the following two chapters, in which the intertwined historical trajectories of the Abdals, the Bektashi order and the Wafaʾi-cum-Kizilbash communities will be explored.

Notes

1. Classical works on the Turkification and Islamization processes in Asia Minor include Franz Babinger, 'Der Islam in Kleinasien', *Zeitschrift Der Deutschen Morgenländischen Gesellschaft* 1, no. 1 (1922): 126–152; Fuad Köprülü, *Anadolu'da İslâmiyet* (1922; reprint, Istanbul: İnsan Yayınları, 1996); and Speros Vryonis, *The Decline of Medieval Hellenism in Asia Minor and the Process of Islamization from the Eleventh through the Fifteenth Century* (Berkeley: University of California Press, 1971). For more recent research and scholarly trends on the subject, see Gary Leiser, 'The Madrasah and the Islamization of Anatolia before the Ottomans', in *Law and Education in Medieval Islam: Studies in Memory of Professor George Makdisi*, eds Joseph E. Lowry, et al. (Cambridge: E. J. W. Gibb Memorial Trust, 2004), 174–191; A. C. S. Peacock, 'Islamisation in Medieval Anatolia', in *Islamisation: Comparative Perspectives from History*, ed. A. C. S. Peacock (Edinburgh: Edinburgh University Press), 134–155; A. C. S. Peacock and Sara Yıldız, 'Introduction: Literature, Language and History in Late Medieval Anatolia', in *Islamic Literature and Intellectual Life in Fourteenth- and Fifteenth-century Anatolia*, eds A. C. S. Peacock and Sara Yıldız (Würzburg: Ergon Verlag Würzburg in Kommission, 2016), 19–45; A. Karamustafa, 'Islamisation through the Lens of *Saltuk-name*', in *Islam and Christianity in Mediaeval Anatolia*, eds A. C. S. Peacock, Sara Nur Yıldız, and Bruno de Nicola (Farnham: Ashgate, 2015), 349–364; and other relevant articles in the last two volumes.
2. On the predominance of dervishes and Sufis in shaping the religious and cultural landscape of late medieval Anatolia, see Fuad Köprülü, *Osmanlı Devleti'nin Kuruluşu* (1959; repr. Ankara: Türk Tarih Kurmu, 1991),

83–102; and Cemal Kafadar, *Between Two Worlds: The Construction of the Ottoman State* (Berkeley and Los Angeles: University of California Press, 1995), esp. Chapter 3. For the Sufis' contribution to the process of Islamization and Turkification in Anatolia and the Balkans, also see Ömer Lütfü Barkan, 'Osmanlı İmparatorluğunda Bir İskân ve Kolonizasyon Metodu Olarak Vakıflar ve Temlikler', *Vakıflar Dergisi* 2 (1942): 279–386; and Vryonis, *Decline of Medieval Hellenism*, esp. 351–402. For the eastern half of Anatolia and Northern Mesopotamia, see Osman Turan, *Doğu Anadolu Türk Devletleri Tarihi* (Istanbul: İstanbul Matbaası, 1973), 224–231.

3. Regarding individual Wafaʾi dervishes in early Ottoman society, see Abdülbâkî Gölpınarlı, *Yunus Emre: Hayatı* (Istanbul: Bozkurt Basımevi, 1936), 17–50; Halil İnalcık, 'How to Read ʿĀshıḳ Pasha-zāde's History', in *Essays in Ottoman History* (Istanbul: Eren Yayıncılık, 1998), 31–37; Kafadar, *Between Two Worlds*, 74, 128–129; Ahmet Yaşar Ocak, *Babaîler İsyanı: Alevîliğin Tarihsel Altyapısı Yahut Anadolu'da İslâm-Türk Heterodoksisinin Teşekkülü* (1980; rev. ed., İstanbul: Dergâh Yayınları, 1996), 74–76; *MNK-Elvan Çelebi-1995*, xxvi–xxx. Hüsameddin Çelebi's genealogical link to Abu'l-Wafaʾ al-Baghdadi has attracted even less attention, even though it is stated in the preamble of Rumi's masterpiece, see *Mathnawi of Jalaluddin Rumi*, 5 vols, trans. A. Reynold Nicholson, compiled by Reza Nazari and Somayeh Nazari (1925; reprint, Learn Persian Online Website, 2017), II: 4. It is also mentioned in passing by Fuad Köprülü in *Türk Edebiyatında İlk Mutasavvıflar* (1919; reprint, Ankara: Turk Tarih Kurumu Basımevi, 1993), 226 n63; and in Gölpınarlı, *Yunus Emre: Hayatı*, 56. Gölpınarlı, however, later rejects this connection, Gölpınarlı, *Yunus Emre ve Tasavvuf* (Istanbul: İnkilâp Kitabevi, 1992), 47, n39. For possible political concerns that might have influenced his change of mind, see n58 above in Introduction.
4. Historians' long-standing failure to recognise the importance of the Wafaʾiyya in the origins of Anatolian Sufism was first noted in Karamustafa, 'Early Sufism in Eastern Anatolia', 175–198. An earlier scholar to draw attention to the role of Wafaʾi affiliates in late medieval Anatolia was Abdülbâkî Gölpınarlı, Gölpınarlı, *Yunus Emre: Hayatı*, but he failed to pursue this idea further; see n58 above in Introduction. As testimony to the growing interest in the subject among specialists in the field, see, for example, Ocak, 'The Wafa'î tariqa', 209–248; also see my article 'The Wafā'iyya, the Bektashiyye and Genealogies of "Heterodox" Islam in Anatolia: Rethinking the Köprülü Paradigm,' *Turcica* 44 (2012–2013): 279–300.
5. *Aspz*, 11–13. For the English translation of the relevant paragraph, see Rudi P. Lindner, *Nomads and Ottomans in Medieval Anatolia* (Bloomington: Research Institute for Inner Asian Studies, Indiana University, 1983), 37.
6. For an expanded and better-established version of the story, see Mehmed

Neşri, *Kitâb-ı Cihan-Nümâ: Neşri Tarihi,* 2 vols, eds Faik Reşit Unat and Mehmed A. Köymen (Ankara: Türk Tarih Kurumu, 1995), 1: 80–85. For an overview of its different renderings, see Colin Imber, 'The Ottoman Dynastic Myth', *Turcica* 19 (1987): 20–22; and V. I. Ménage, 'On the Recensions of Uruj's "History of the Ottomans"', *Bulletin of the School of Oriental and African Studies* 30, no. 2 (1967): 317–22.

7. For a sceptical approach to the historicity of this story, and the conventional accounts of Ottoman origins, in general, see Imber, 'Ottoman Dynastic Myth', and Imber, 'Canon and Apocrypha in Early Ottoman History', in *Studies in Ottoman History in Honour of Professor V. L. Ménage,* eds Colin Heywood and Colin Imber (Istanbul: Isis Press, 1994), 134–137. For evidence and arguments to the contrary, see İnalcık, 'How to Read', esp. 39–41, and Kafadar, *Between Two Worlds*, 128–129.
8. This name is frequently transcribed as 'Edebali' in the secondary literature (see, for example, *DIA*, s.v. 'Edebâli', by Kamil Şahin), but 'Ede' appears to be a title of affectionate respect rather than part of the name and, therefore, needs to be written separately. It means 'elder brother', is thus semantically comparable to Abu'l-Wafa''s epithet, 'Kakis'; *Tarama Sözlüğü,* 8 vols. (Ankara, 1963–77), 3:1384. Moreover, I vocalise the name as 'Balı', rather than 'Bali' following the pronouncation of the name among Beydilli Türkmens in rural Sivas, which I personally observed.
9. *Aspz*, 11.
10. *Aspz*, 31.
11. *Aspz*, 13.
12. Ömer Lûtfi Barkan and Enver Meriçli, *Hüdâvendigâr Livâsı Tahrir Defterleri* (Ankara: Türk Tarih Kurumu, 1988), 1: 282, 283.
13. BA.MD.31, h. 985 (/1577), p. 237, cited in Kafadar, *Between Two Worlds*, 129 n26. Kafadar cautions us against treating this register as conclusive evidence, however, since this information might have become accepted dogma by then. Also see, İnalcık, 'How to Read', 42, 46.
14. Ede Balı's son and grandson were appointed by imperial decree as administrators of the endowment created in his name in later centuries, Barkan and Meriçli, *Hüdâvendigâr Livâsı*, 282, 283.
15. *MNK-Elvan Çelebi-2000*, couplets 1985, 1995; also see *MNK-Elvan Çelebi-1995*, LXV.
16. *Menāḳıb*-Turkish, fol. 5a.
17. Seyyid Velayet, the introduction claims, was a progeny of Sayyid Pir Hayat al-Din, allegedly a nephew and adopted son of the saint. *Menāḳıb*-Turkish, fols 5a–5b. Also see İnalcık, 'How to Read', 34–35.
18. Neşri, *Kitâb-ı Cihan-Nümâ*, 1: 130–131; also see ᶜAşıkpaşazade Ahmed, *Die altosmanische Chronik des Āšiḳpašazāde*, ed. Friedrich Giese (Leipzig: O. Harrassowitz, 1929), 28.
19. See, for example, Köprülü, *Anadolu'da İslâmiyet*, 64; Barkan, 'Osmanlı İmparatorluğunda Bir İskân', 301.

20. For a recent, general overview of the significance of Ahi groups in medieval Anatolia and for further bibliography on the subject, see İklil Selçuk, 'Suggestions on the Social Meaning and Functions of *Akhi* Communities and Their Hospices in Medieval Anatolia', in *Architecture and Landscape in Medieval Anatolia, 1100–1500*, eds Patricia Blessing and Rachel Goshgarian (Edinburgh: Edinburgh University Press, 2017), 95–113; and Rachel Goshgarian, 'Futuwwa in Thirteenth-Century Rūm and Armenia: Reform Movements and the Managing of Multiple Allegiances on the Seljuk Periphery', in *The Seljuks of Anatolia: Court and Society in the Medieval Middle East*, eds A. C. S. Peacock and Sara Nur Yıldız (London: I. B. Tauris, 2015), 227–263.
21. Sara Wolper, *Cities and Saints: Sufism and the Transformation of Urban Space in Medieval Anatolia* (University Park: Pennsylvania State University Press, 2003), 77–78. Fuad Köprülü, on the other hand, singles out the Halvetiyye as a Sufi order that had close ties with the Ahis in thirteenth-century Anatolia; see Köprülü, *Osmanlı Devleti'nin Kuruluşu*, 96. For the early phases of the convergence of the *futuwwa* and Sufi traditions, see Muhammad Ja^cfar Mahjub, 'Chivalry and Early Persian Sufism', in *Heritage of Sufism-1*, 549–581. Similar close ties among Sufis, *sayyid*s, and *futuwwa* organizations have been noted in other contexts as well. For example, a Twelver Shi^ci Sufi leader who held the leadership of a *futuwwa* organization is mentioned in Kazuo Morimoto, 'Sayyid Ibn ^cAbd al-Ḥamīd: An Iraqi Shi^ci Genealogist at the Court of Özbek Khan', *Journal of the Economic and Social History of the Orient* 59, no. 5 (2016), 689. For *sayyid*s 'who may have played an important "esoteric" function' in *futuwwa* organizations, see May Farhat, 'Islamic Piety and Dynastic Legitimacy: The Case of the Shrine of Ali al-Rida in Mashhad (10th–17th Century)' (PhD diss., Harvard University, Massachusetts, 2002), 104.
22. See n3 above. Also see *DIA*, s.v. 'Hüsâmeddin Çelebi' by H. Amed Sevgi.
23. İnalcık, 'How to Read', 36, 45–48. ^cAşıkpaşazade's failure to mention Ede Balı's affiliation with the Wafa^ɔi tradition, although intriguing and in need of an explanation, does not in and of itself preclude this as a likely possibility, especially given an explicit statement to that effect in the introduction that was added to the Turkish translation of the Abu'l-Wafa^ɔ hagiography commissioned by his disciple and son-in-law, Seyyid Velayet.
24. ^cAşıkpaşazade himself gives this information as part of his family genealogy: '*Ben ki faḳīr Dervīş Aḥmed ^cĀşıḳīyem ibni Şeyḫ Yaḥya ibni Şeyḫ Süleymān ve ibni Bali sulṭanü'l-^cālī ^cĀşıḳ Paşayam ve ibni mürşidü'l-āfāḳ Muḫliṣ Paşayam ve ibni ḳuṭbü'd-devrān Baba İlyās, ḫalīfetü's-Seyyid Ebü'l-Vefā^ɔ Tācü'l-^cārifīn.*' See *Aspz*, 3, fol. 1b.
25. For Elvan Çelebi and other prominent figures in ^cAşıkpaşazade's family tree, see Semavi Eyice, 'Çorum'un Mecidözü'nde Âşık Paşaoğlu Elvan Çelebi Zâviyesi', *Türkiyât Mecmuası* 15 (1968): 211–246; *MNK-Elvan Çelebi-1995*, 29–69; and Sara Ethel Wolper, 'Khiḍr, Elwan Çelebi and the

Conversion of Sacred Sanctuaries in Anatolia,' *Muslim World* 90, nos 3–4 (Autumn 2000): 309–322.

26. Georgius de Ungaria, *Tractatus de moribus condictionibus et nequicia Turcorum,* first published in 1480 in Latin; pertinent section translated into English in F. W. Hasluck, *Christianity and Islam under the Sultans*, 2 vols (Oxford: Clarendon Press, 1929), 2: 494–499.
27. *Aspz*, 64.
28. Hilmi Ziya Ülken, 'Anadolu'da Dini Ruhiyat Müşahadeleri: Geyikli Baba', *Mihrab Mecmuası*, nos 13–14 (1340/1924), 447. Also see Ahmed Refik, *Bizans Karşısında Türkler* (1927; reprint, Istanbul: Kitabevi Yayınları, 2005), 169–170.
29. Barkan and Meriçli, *Hüdâvendigâr Livâsı*, 1:110.
30. The filtering of the sources through the prism of the Köprülü paradigm may explain why the early sixteenth-century Turkish adaptation of the original Arabic hagiographic vita of Abu'l-Wafa' al-Baghdadi was largely passed over by scholars until relatively recently, even though Turkey's libraries contain many copies. Fuad Köprülü himself was aware of its existence, referencing it in his works at least twice: first, as a source for the biography of 'Aşıkpaşazade's son-in-law, Seyyid Velayet, in *MIA*, s.v. 'Āşık Paşa-zāde', 707; second, in connection to Hüsameddin Çelebi in *Türk Edebiyatında İlk Mutasavvıflar*, 226 n63. Köprülü makes it clear that he had access to two separate copies of the hagiography. Abdülbaki Gölpınarlı also uses Abu'l-Wafa''s hagiography relatively extensively in his *Yunus Emre: Hayatı* and *Yunus Emre ve Tasavvuf*, but never really goes back to it in his later works.
31. Ahmet K. Karamustafa, *God's Unruly Friends: Dervish Groups in the Islamic Later Middle Period, 1200–1550* (Salt Lake City: University of Utah Press, 1994), 70–78.
32. Zeynep Yürekli, *Architecture and Hagiography in the Ottoman Empire: The Politics of Bektashi Shrines in the Classical Ages* (Farnham and Burlington: Ashgate, 2012), 65–68.
33. Jonathan Brack proposes that Seyyid Velayet's motivation in commissioning the translation of Abu'l- Wafa''s hagiography, with an introduction asserting his kinship to the saint, was to reinforce his own credentials as a *sayyid*. This seems unlikely, given the absence of any clues that Seyyid Velayet's noble descent was questioned in the Ottoman capital at the time, as Brack himself also acknowledges; see Jonathan Brack, "Was Ede Balı a Wafā'ī Shaykh? Sufis, Sayyids, and Genealogical Creativity in the Early Ottoman World," in *Islamic Literature and Intellectual Life in Fourteenth-Century Anatolia*, eds A. C. S. Peacock and Sara Nur Yıldız (Würzburg: Ergon Verlag, 2016), 354. Neither does Brack offer any explanation as to why Seyyid Velayet would choose to forge a connection specifically with Abu'l- Wafa' rather than another better-known figure who could serve the same function. For Seyyid Velayet and his high socio-religious standing in the Ottoman capital, see İnalcık, 'How to Read', 31–35.

34. *Aspz*, 307–308. ᶜAşıkpaşazade also claims that, upon arriving in Anatolia, Hacı Bektaş went straight to Sivas to see Baba İlyas, thus implicitly acknowledging the Wafaᵓi shaykh's seniority and eminence. Hacı Bektaş's link to the Babaᵓi milieu and his own possible Wafaᵓi affiliation will be discussed in more detail in Chapter 3.
35. ᶜAşıkpaşazade's history was apparently not a book widely read by the Ottoman literati class, and it would only be discovered by modern historians in the early twentieth century, which might partly explain its limited impact. *MIA*, s.v. "Āşık Paşa-zāde" by Fuad Köprülü, 708.
36. *Evliya-Seyahatnâme*, 2: 26.
37. *Velâyetnâme*-Duran, 538–554.
38. Hasan Yüksel, 'Selçuklular Döneminden Kalma Bir Vefaî Zaviyesi (Şeyh Marzubân Zaviyesi)', *Vakıflar Dergisi* 25 (1995): 235–250.
39. Yüksel, 'Selçuklular Döneminden', 237.
40. Zabidi, *Rafᶜ niqāb*, 12b.
41. For a similar interpretation, see Yüksel, 'Selçuklular Döneminden', 238.
42. *Noyan-Bektâşîlik*, 5: 331–332. The first strophe of the poem is as follows:

    Güzel Sivas Zara Tekke Köyünde
    Şeyh Merziban Velî gibi er yatar
    Hamdolsun yüz sürdüm ocak ayında
    Bu tekkede mürşîd yatar, pîr yatar.

    (In the beautiful village of Tekke [located] in Zara [district] in Sivas/ Rests a hero as Shaykh Merziban, the Saint/ Thankfully [to God], I rubbed my face [at his tomb] in the month of January/ In this convent lays a *mürşid*, a *pir*.)
43. İsmail Hakkı Acar, *Zara Folkloru* (Sivas: Emek Matbaa, 1975), 82–83. This version of the legend, including a non-Muslim in its cast, is also told about Abdal Musa in his hagiography, see *Abdal Mûsâ Velâyetnâmesi*, ed. Abdurrahman Güzel (Ankara: Türk Tarih Kurumu, 1999), 144–146.
44. Hasan Yüksel, 'Bir Babaî (Vefaî) Şeyhi Zaviyesi (Şeyh Behlül Baba)', *Osmanlı Araştırmaları* 21 (2001): 97–107.
45. Hüseyin Hüsameddin, *Amasya Tārīḫi*, 4 vols (Istanbul: Ḥikmet Maṭbaᶜası, 1327–1330/1911–14), 1: 235–236, 2: 395–396, cf. Yüksel, 'Bir Babaî (Vefaî) Şeyhi', 97.
46. *Evliya-Seyahatnâme*, 2: 199.
47. *Ṣalnāme-i Vilāyet-i Sivas*, 1301/1883, 179.
48. *DIA*, s.v. 'Keykubat I' by Faruk Sümer.
49. This represents a revision of the earlier reading of the date as 935/1528, see Yüksel, 'Selçuklular Döneminden', 236 n16.
50. Kutlu Özen, *Sivas Efsaneleri* (Sivas: K. Özen, 2001), 190.
51. BA, TD no. 2: 470, 471.
52. Ömer Demirel, *Osmanlı Vakıf-Şehir İlişkisine Bir Örnek: Sivas Şehir Hayatında Vakıfların Rolü* (Ankara: Türk Tarih Kurumu, 2000), 37–59;

Hikmet Denizli, *Sivas: Tarihi ve Anıtları* (Sivas: Özbelsan A.Ş. Kültür Hizmeti, 1995), 118–21; İsmail Hakkı Uzunçarşılı and Rıdvan Nafiz, *Sivas Şehri*, ed. Recep Toparlı (Sivas: Sivas Ticaret Ve Sanayi Odası, 1997), 161–163.

53. BA, TD no. 14: 15a–b; and BA, no. TD 583: 7b.
54. *Menāḳıb*-Turkish, fols 164b–165b
55. Turan, *Doğu Anadolu Türk Devletleri*, 228–231.
56. The convent of Şeyh Çoban is first mentioned in the tax registers of Çemişgezek dated 1523 and 1541; Mehmet Ali Ünal, *XVI. Yüzyılda Çemişgezek Sancağı* (Ankara: Türk Tarih Kurumu, 1999), 165.
57. This is suggested most importantly by a document in the family archives of Nesimi Dede/Hüseyin Karaca, member of the Çorum branch of the *ocak* of Şeyh Çoban. It is a copy of a Wafa'i *ijāza* that is, however, undated and poorly written.
58. *FD/Scroll-IZA-2*.
59. Ersin Gülsoy and Mehmet Taştemir, eds, *1530 Tarihli Malatya, Behisni, Gerger, Kâhta, Hısn-ı Mansur, Divriği ve Darende Kazâları: Vakıf ve Mülk Defteri* (Ankara: Türk Tarih Kurumu, 2007), 53. The editors seem to have miscalculated the date of the original endowment based on the number of years that had passed since its creation, as given in the register, erroneously placing it during the reign of ᶜAla'eddin Keykubat I; see xxvıı.
60. BA, İbnü'l-Emîn Evkaf, 2,725: '*Ḳażā-i mez̠bure* [i.e., Malatya] *tābiᶜ Muṣār nāḥiyesinde āsūde olan Kuṭbü'l-ᶜArifīn Seyyid Şeyh Ebü'l-Vefā' ḳuddise sırruhu'l-ᶜazīzün zāviye tekiyesinde*'; and BA, Cevdet Evkaf, 6,210: '*Malāṭiya mużāfātından Muṣār nāḥiyesinde vāḳiᶜ āsūde olan Kuṭbü'l-ᶜArifīn Seyyid Şeyh Ebü'l-Vefā' zāviyesinde*.'
61. Yinanç Refet and Mesut Elibüyük, *Kanunî Devri Malatya Tahrir Defteri (1560)* (Ankara: Gazi Üniversitesi, 1983), 103.
62. For oral traditions concerning Şeyh Ahmed, see Nazmi Sevgen, 'Efsaneden Hakikate', *Tarih Dünyası*, no. 21 (1951): 882–883.
63. Sevgen, 'Efsaneden Hakikate', 883.
64. *FD/Ij-ShAhm*.
65. *Menāḳıb*-Turkish, fol. 122a.
66. For a recent recording of this oral tradition, see Gıyasettin Aytaş, ed., *Bingöl, Muş/Varto Yörelerinde Ocaklar, Oymaklar ve Boylarla İlgili Araştırma Sonuçları* (Ankara: Gazi Üniversitesi Türk Kültürü ve Hacı Bektaş Veli Araştırma Merkezi, 2010), 27, 193.
67. This oral tradition was recorded in writing in Mehmet Özdoğan, *Aşağı Fırat Havzası 1977 Yüzey Araştırmaları* (Istanbul: Orta Doğu Teknik Üniversitesi Keban Ve Aşağı Fırat Havzası Projeleri Müdürlüğü, 1977), 64–65.
68. Gülsoy and Taştemir, *1530 Tarihli Malatya*, 291, 293. Also see Mehmet Taştemir, *XVI. Yüzyılda Adıyaman (Behsini, Hısn-ı Mansur, Gerger, Kâhta) Sosyal ve İktisadi Tarihi* (Ankara: Türk Tarih Kurumu, 1999), 244.

69. Abdülkadir Sezgin, 'Eren ve Evliya Kavramının Dini Tarihi Folklorik İzahı ve Eren İnancı Üzerine Düşünceler', in *I. Uluslararası Türk Dünyası Eren Ve Evliyalar Kongresi Bildirileri* (Ankara: Anadolu Erenleri Kültür Ve Sanat Vakfı, 1998), 502.
70. There are in the archives at least fifteen extant *vakıfnāme*s belonging to Ahi convents, with their dates of creation spanning from 1291 to 1514; see Hasan Yüksel, 'Ahi Vakıfları', in *Uluslararası Kurluşunun 700. Yıl Dönümünde Bütün Yönleriyle Osmanlı Devleti Kongresi, 7–9 Nisan 1999*, eds Alâaddin Aköz, et al. (Konya: Selçuklu Üniversitesi, 2000), 157–159.
71. This chronology also fits with the emigration to Jerusalem of the famous Badri family, who were descendants of Sayyid Matar, son of Sayyid Salim, which also occurred in the early thirteenth century; see Brack, 'Was Ede Bali a Wafāʾī Shaykh?', 340.
72. Personal conversations with Muharrem Naci Orhan, member of the *ocak* of İmam Zeynel Abidin, Summer 2002. Also see Orhan Türkdoğan, *Alevi-Bektaşi Kimliği: Sosyo-antropolojik Araştırma* (Istanbul: Timaş Yayınları, 1995), 271–272.
73. Erdal Gezik, *Dinsel, Etnik ve Politik Sorunlar Bağlamında: Alevi Kürtler* (Ankara: Kalan Yayınları), 153–155.
74. In the sixteenth century there were two villages in Harput, called 'Ṣūn-türk' and 'Ṣūn-kürd'; BA, TD 64, 924/1518, 657–658; TD 998, 928–929/1523, 186; Tapu ve Kadastro Genel Müdürlüğü Kuyud-ı Kadime Arşivi, TD 106, 974/1566, 157b, 165a, cited in Zekeriya Bülbül, *XVI. Yüzyılda Diyarbekir*, 2 vols (PhD diss., Selçuk University, Konya, 1999), 387, 388. For sixteenth-century Harput, also see Mehmet Ali Ünal, *XVI. Yüzyılda Harput Sancağı (1518–1566)* (Ankara: Türk Tarih Kurumu, 1989); a list of villages is provided on pages 232–239.
75. The earliest document locating *dede*s affiliated with the Ağuiçens in Harput (Ot. Ḫarbūrt) is a court document dated 1034/1624, and the document that specifically refers to the village of Sün is another court document dated 1062/1651. The documents deal with cases involving inheritance and the sale of property, respectively; FD of Hüseyin and Hayri Doğan, the Adıyaman branch of the *ocak* of Ağuiçen.
76. There are records of both of these villages in the sixteenth-century Ottoman tax registers; see, for example, BA, TD 64, 924/1518, 795, 802, cited in Bülbül, 'XVI. Yüzyılda Diyarbekir,' 451, 469, 470. For sixteenth-century Çemişgezek, see the list of villages in Ünal, *XVI. Yüzyılda Çemişgezek*, 277–297.
77. Hamza Aksüt, *Anadolu Aleviliğinin Sosyal ve Coğrafi Kökenleri* (Ankara: Art Basın Yayın, 2002), 156–157.
78. Mineyik was in the past administratively part of the Arapgir district; see Bülbül, *XVI. Yüzyılda Diyarbekir*, 420.
79. Personal conversation with Muharrem Naci Orhan, member of the *ocak* of İmam Zeynel Abidin, Summer 2002. Also see Türkdoğan, *Alevi-Bektaşi Kimliği*, 407–408.

80. Personal conversation with İzzettin Doğan, member of the *ocak* of Ağuiçen, Summer 2003.
81. *FD/Scroll-IZA-2*.
82. At the end of the document, this fact is reiterated succinctly as follows: '*Nuqila mā fī hādhihi al-wathīqa min al-wathīqa al-qadīma al-aṣlīya bilā ziyāda.*' *FD/Scroll-IZA-2.*
83. The name of the syndic is given as 'Ibrāhīm b. Sulṭān b. Idrīs al-Ḥusaynī, Muḥammad b. Ḥusayn Kammūna(?) al-Ḥusaynī.' *FD/Scroll-IZA-2*.
84. '*jamīʿa al-āʿlām al-dāyira fī sāyir aqṭār al-arḍ al-maḥbūsa bi-ḥaḍrat sayyidinā al-sayyid Abi'l-Wafā' qaddasa'llāhu rūḥahū yataʿallaqu amruhū fī al-āfāq bi-ijāzat hādha al-faqīr wa idhnihī wa ishāratihī wa ʿalāmatihī.*' *FD/Scroll-IZA-2*.
85. The date given in the document, 408/1017, is anachronistic, considering that Abu'l-Wafa' probably had not even been born by this date. Nor did the Madrasat al-Mustanairiyya exist at this time, not being built until the thirteenth century. The most probable explanation for this anachronism would be careless copying. Indeed, later on, in the part concerning Abu'l-Wafa''s biography, the year 408/1017 recurs as the saint's death date. It is possible that this date, which would be more reasonable as the birth date of Abu'l-Wafa', may have been mistakenly written or copied as his death date instead. One might also conjecture that as a result of a misguided inference based on this mistake, the copyist wrote the same date as the year when the original document was put into writing, perhaps assuming that the appointment of a spiritual heir to Abu'l-Wafa' must have happened in the immediate aftermath of his death.
86. *FD/Ij-IZA-1*.
87. The familial/spiritual pedigree from Abu'l-Wafa's grandfather Zayd onward is given as follows in the document: *Imām Zayn al-ʿĀbidīn* → . . . → *Zayd Muḥammad Ghānim, brother of Abu'l-Wafā'* → *Sayyid Khāmis (? could also be read as 'ʿAbbās,' although there appears to be a later tempering in this part of the text perhaps to turn a rather unusual name into a more familiar one)* → *Zakī* → *Ṣāliḥ* → *ʿAbbās* → *Sharaf al-dīn Ḥusayn* → *ʿIzz al-dīn* → *Luqmān* → *Maḥmūd* → *Sayyid Ibrāhīm*. More or less the same cluster of names, extending back all the way to Imam ʿAli, forms the basis of all other *sayyid* genealogies belonging to the *ocak* of İmam Zeynel Abidin and the various branches of the Ağuiçens.
88. *FD/Ij-Wafa'i-DK-1*.
89. Devin DeWeese, 'The Descendants of Sayyid Ata and the Rank of Naqīb in Central Asia,' *Journal of the American Oriental Society* 115, no. 4 (October–December 1995): 612–634.
90. Michael Winter, 'The *Ashrāf* and the *Naqīb Al-ashrāf* in Ottoman Egypt and Syria: A Comparative Analysis', in *Sayyids and Sharifs in Muslim Societies: The Living Links to the Prophet*, ed. Morimoto Kazuo (London and New York: Routledge, 2012), 142–143. Despite their shared name, and a number

of other similarities, the Egyptian Wafaʾiyya is considered to have roots in Maghreb, and is separated as such from the Wafaʾiyya that derived from Abu'l-Wafaʾ al-Baghdadi, whose familial and/or spiritual descendants are, however, also known to have 'traveled to Egypt and the Levant at various points in time', and established a *zāwiya* affiliated with the Shunbukiyya-Wafaʾiyya line in Cairo; see McGregor, *Sanctity and Mysticism in Medieval Egypt*, 52.

91. *FD/Ij-AGU-Am.*
92. *FD/Ij-ShAhm.*
93. *FD/Ij-DelBer.*
94. See n72 above. While oral accounts connecting the *ocak*'s origins to Baghdad are not as widespread as the claim that Khorasan is its initial homeland, examples of the former are particularly valuable exactly because of the dominance of the latter as a semi-mythical tradition among present-day Alevis in Anatolia. The only other recorded tradition that I am aware of connecting the origins of an Alevi *ocak* to Iraq comes from the *ocak* of Yanyatır based among the Tahtacı Alevis in Izmir; the tradition concerns the *ocak*'s purported founding patriarch Durhasan Dede, whose father is said to have hailed from Baghdad. Sinan Kahyaoğlu, 'Durhasan Dede ve Kaz Dağı Tahtacı Türkmenleri', in *Uluslararası Türk Dünyası İnanç Önderleri Kongresi, 23–28 Ekim 2001* (Ankara: Tüksev Yayınları, 2002), 443–444.
95. See n40 above.
96. '*Ḥażret-i Seyyid Velāyet'üñ babası Seyyid Aḥmed [bin] Seyyid İsḥāḳ bin Seyyid ᶜAllāme'd-dīn bin Seyyid Ḫalīl bin Seyyid Cihāngīr ibn Seyyid Pīr Ḥayāte'd-dīn. Ḥażret-i Tācü'l-ᶜārifīn anı oġul edinmişdür ve hem iki ḳardaş ᶜiyālleridür.*' *Menāḳıb*-Turkish, fol. 5a. Oddly, however, this name is not included in the list of the adopted sons of Abu'l-Wafaʾ provided in the main text of the hagiography, the closest name mentioned being 'Muḥammed b. Seyyid Kemāl Ḥayāt'.
97. *FD/Ij-ShAhm.*
98. See, most importantly, *Dedekarkın-Kum*, the introduction to *MNK-Elvan Çelebi-1995*, and *Kargın-Yalçın*. Also see Hamza Aksüt, *Mezopotamya'dan Anadolu'ya Alevi Erenlerin İlk Savaşi (1240): Dede Garkın, Baba İshak, Baba İlyas* (Ankara: Yurt Kitap, 2006); and Sadullah Gültekin, 'Anadolu'da Bir Vefaî Şeyhi: Tahrir Defterleri Işığında Dede Karkın Hakkında Bir Değerlendirme', *Türk Kültürü ve Hacı Bektaş Veli Araştırma Dergisi* 59 (2011): 147–158.
99. For example, in a versified vita of Dede Kargın preserved in an undated manuscript, the nineteenth-century Alevi poet Ednai from Sivas refers to the former as the 'shah of Khorasan', and, additionally, shows him as Hacı Bektaş's travelling companion on his journey to Rum. *Dedekarkın-Kum*, 158–162.
100. *MNK-Elvan Çelebi-1995*, 203.
101. Based on his reading of a particular couplet in *Menāḳıbü'l-Ḳudsiyye*, Ahmet

Yaşar Ocak suggests that Dede Garkın must have been the shaykh of Baba İlyas; however, the couplet is too vague to be a conclusive piece of evidence for such a conclusion; *MNK-Elvan Çelebi-1995*, XLI. The relevant couplet (680, p. 61) reads as follows: '*Dede Ġarḳīn ki cedd-i aʿlādur; Ẕikri anuñ ḳamudan evlādur*' (Dede Garkın is the first ancestor; recollecting his name is better than recollecting anybody else's).

102. *MNK-Elvan Çelebi-2000*, 217–227, couplets nos 155–210.
103. Gelibolulu Mustafa ʿÂli, *Kitābü't-Tārīḫ-i Künhü'l-Aḫbar*, eds Ahmet Uğur, et al., 2 vols (Kayseri: Erciyes Üniversitesi, 1997), I: 66. ʿAli seems to be referring here to an unknown work by Elvan Çelebi.
104. See *FD/Ij-Wafaʾi-DK-1* and *FD/Kerbela-Zyrtn-DK*, respectively.
105. *Dedekarkın-Kum*, 158–162.
106. See, for example, *Kargın-Yalçın*, 13–87. For the Oghuz tribe of Karkın, see Faruk Sümer, *Oğuzlar (Türkmenler): Tarihleri, Boy Teşkilatı, Destanları* (Ankara: Ankara Üniversitesi, 1972) 312, 314.
107. *MNK-Elvan Çelebi-1995*, XL; cf. Mertol Tulum, *Tarihî Metin çalışmalarında Usul: Nâme-i Kudsî (Menâkıbu'l-Kudsiyye)'nin Yayımlanmış Metninden Derlenen Verilerle* (Konya: Çizgi Kitabevi, 2017), 322–323.
108. A similar, fictitious genealogy was attributed in some early sources to the house of Osman, whose founding patrirach was accordingly claimed to be a companian of the Prophet. Imber, 'Canon and Apocrypha', 128.
109. Cf. *FD/ Sj-DK-1* and *FD/ Sj-DK-2*.
110. For the Tirmidhi Sayyids and ʿAlaʾ al-Mulk, see *EI-2*, s.v. 'Tirmidh' by W. Barthold; for the Kharazm-Shahs, and the counter-caliphate that they established, see idem, *Turkestan Down to the Mongol Invasion*, 3rd edn (London: Luzac & Co., 1968), Chapter 3, esp. 372–378.
111. BA, TD, 64, 924/1518, 363; also cited in Bülbül, 'XVI. Yüzyılda Diyarbekir', 121, 142.
112. Abu Bekr-i Tihranî, *Kitab-ı Diyarbekriyye*, trans. Mürsel Öztürk (Ankara: Kültür Bakanlığı, 2001), 38.
113. *Menāḳıb*-Turkish, fol. 64b.
114. *Velâyetnâme*-Duran, 190–193.
115. The *fermān* refers to three individuals – a dervish, a *sayyid*, and a shaykh – who were most likely ancestors of the *ocak* of Dede Kargıns. It reads as follows: '*Ḥāliyā ol vilāyet [Malatya] müceddeden yazılup defter oldukda ḳarye-i Bīmāri'de Baba(?) Ġarḳīn(?) . . . hümāyunuma gelüp Dervīş ʿAlī ve Seyyid Nuʿmān ve Şeyh ʿİsā nām-ı güzīneler ṣāliḥ ve mütedeyyin kimesneler olup ʿaraḳ-ı cebīneleri ile zindegānī idüp āyendeye ve revendeye ḫiẕmet idüp eyyām-ı Çerākiseden fetḥ-i ḫāḳānīye gelinceyek ʿörfler olan yirler ve eger ʿöşr-i şerʿī ve ʿörfīyi edā idüp resm-i çiftden ve ʿādet-i āġnāmdan ve nüzūldan ve . . . ʿavarıż-ı dīvāniyye(?) ve tekālīf-i pādişāhiyyeden <muʿāf> ve müsellemlerine(?) olageldükleri sebebden sābıḳā defter-i cedīd muʿāf ve müsellemlerin ḳayd olundılar.*' *Ferman-DK-1*. Cf. Refet and Elibüyük, *Kanunî Devri Malatya*, 140.

116. There are several documents to that effect in the *ocak*'s family archives from the sixteenth century onwards, see FD of Ahmet Rıza Karginer; see, for example, *FD/Scroll-DK-3a* and *FD/Scroll-DK-3b*. Other published examples of them can be found in *Dedekarkın-Kum*, *Kargın-Yalçın*, and *Garkın-Ocak*.
117. *FD/Scroll-DK-3a* and *FD/Scroll-DK-3b*, respectively.
118. See, for example, relevant sections in Refet and Elibüyük, *Kanunî Devri Malatya*.
119. The relevant part of the documents reads as follows: '*Cümle-i meẕkūrūnlarıñ üçer yaşar ḳurbān ve neẕr-i zekāt evlād-ı evlād ve daḫi her kim bunuñ düşelgesine ṭamaᶜ eyleye laᶜnet ibn-i laᶜnetdür. Ḳānūn-i Dede Ġarḳīnī çırāḳ ve ḳurban . . . her ev başına yılda üç nügi yağ ve üç yaşar ḳurbān ḳadīmü'l-eyyāmdan ilā yevminā hāẕāya dek meẕkūr Dede Ġarḳīn'e ᶜāiddür ve rāciᶜdür, kimesne māniᶜ olmaya*'; see *FD/Scroll-DK-3a* and *FD/Scroll-DK-3b*.
120. *FD/Ferman-DK-3* and *FD/Ferman-DK-2*, respectively.
121. Besides Bimare, families affiliated with the *ocak* of Dede Kargın inhabited several other villages in the same province at various times, including the village of Dede Kargın, which was the *ocak*'s central location in modern times.
122. For Sultan Yusuf, the great ancestor of the Dede Kargıns of Malatya, see *Dedekarkın-Kum*, 119–201, 127, 166. Naci Kum, writing in the mid-twentieth century, suggested the village of Zeyve as the site of Sultan Yusuf's tomb. There is, however, currently no village by that name, although during my fieldwork individuals I consulted identified another village in the same vicinity as the old Zeyve.
123. Coşkun Kökel, *Güvenç Abdal Ocakları: Tarihi Belgeler* (Istanbul: Güvenç Abdal Araştırma Eğitim Kültür ve Tanıtma Derneği Yayınları, 2013), 22–25.
124. *Niebuhr-Reise*, 2: 416.
125. For other, smaller branches of the *ocak* of Dede Kargın in Diyarbakır and Maraş, neither of which seem to have survived to the present, see *Türk Ansiklopedisi* (Ankara: Milli Eğitim Basımevi, 1974), s.v. 'Karkın'. For other related *dede* families in Adana, Sivas and Tokat, see *Dedekarkın-Kum*, 185, 195–201.
126. *FD/Ij-Garkini-DK-1*; *FD/Ij-Garkini-DK-2*.
127. *Garkın-Ocak*, 55–57. The first to raise the possibility of a separate order founded by Dede Kargın was Irène Mélikoff, 'Les Babas Turcomans,' in *I. Uluslararası Mevlâna semineri bildirileri* (Ankara: Türkiye İş Bankası, 1973), 273.
128. While Abu'l-Wafa's name is mentioned in the scroll where the *ijāza* in question is embedded, it is done so in the context of a clearly apocryphal meeting of three saintly figures including, besides Abu'l-Wafaʾ and Dede Kargın, Muhammad Makki and ᶜAbd al-Qadir al-Jilani, and not as a link in

the *silsila*.

129. *FD/AhiIj-DK-Antep*. A translation into Turkish of the *ijāza* drawing on both copies without any differentiation between them and with some omissions was published in Mehmet Akkuş, 'Farklı Bir Ahilik İcazetnamesi', *Hacı Bektaş Veli Araştırma Dergisi* 21 (Spring 2002): 95–100.
130. For Ahi Evran, and traditions about him, see Cevat Hakkı Tarım, *Tarihte Kırşehri-Gülşehri Ve Babailer-Ahiler-Bektaşler*, 3rd edn (Istanbul: Yeniçağ Matbaası, 1948), 58–64; and Mikâil Bayram, *Ahi Evren Ve Ahi Teşkilâtı'nın Kuruluşu* (Konya: n.p., 1991).
131. The only other extant Ahi *ijāza* that I am aware of is one mentioned in Tarım, *Tarihte Kırşehri-Gülşehri*, 65–66. To the extent described by Tarım, there are significant similarities between the content of this Ahi *ijāza* dated 876/1471 and the one coming from the *ocak* of Dede Kargın.
132. For *futuwwa* circles in Safavid Iran, see Babayan, *Mystics, Monarchs, and Messiahs*, Chapter 6. The *futuwwa* circles' religious outlook seems to have exhibited clear ᶜAlid tendencies with nominal Sunni denomination until the circles came under the Shiᶜitization influence of the Safavids. Lloyd Ridgeon, 'ᶜAlī Ibn Abī Ṭālib in Medieval Persian Sufi-Futuwwat Treatises', in *L'Esotérisme Shiᶜite, ses racines et ses prolongements*, ed. M. A. Amir-Moezzi et al. (Turnhout: Brepols Publishers, 2016), 665–685.
133. The convent appears in the Ottoman archival records from the late fifteenth century through the late sixteenth century; see Murat Hanilçe and Melike Tepecik, 'Anadolu'nun Manevi Önderlerinden Bir Eren: Ahi Mahmud Veli (Keçeci Baba)', *Alevilik Araştırmaları Dergisi/The Journal of Alevi Studies* 12, no. 12 (Winter 2016): 141–170. Also see Sabri Yücel, *Keçeci Ahi Baba ve Zaviyesinde Yetişen Ünlü Kişiler* (Istanbul: Can Yayınları, 2003).
134. A transliteration of this document was published in Alemdar Yalçın and Hacı Yılmaz, 'Bir Ocağın Tarihi Seyyid Hacı Ali Türâbî Ocağı'na Ait Yeni Bilgiler', *Gazi Üniversitesi Türk Kültürü ve Hacı Bektaş Veli Araştırma Merkezi* 26 (Summer 2003): 121–140. While the document's facsimile is not provided for verification, it seems the authors mistakenly read the name 'Selmān-ı Kūfī', the famous patron saint of the water bearers, as 'Süleymān Kūfī'.
135. Abdülbâkî Gölpınarlı, *İslam ve Türk İllerinde Fütüvvet Teşkilâtı ve Kaynakları* (Istanbul: Istanbul University, 1952).
136. DeWeese observes that the *silsila* became the primary 'guarantor of legitimacy' no earlier than the late fifteenth century and the sixteenth see idem, 'The Legitimation of Bahāᵓ ad-Dīn Naqshband', *Asiatische Studien/Études asiatiques* 60, no. 2 (2006): 261–270. The case of the Wafaᵓiyya, however, suggests an earlier date.
137. See, for example, *FD/Ij-IZA-1*; *FD/Ij-Wafaᵓi-DK-1*; *FD/Ij-AGU-Ma*; *FD/Ij-AGU-Am*; *FD/Ij-DelBer*; and *FD/Ij-ShAhm*.
138. For Ahi rituals, see Tarım, *Tarihte Kırşehri-Gülşehri*, 64–75; for the Alevi ritual of waist wrapping, see *ABS*, s.v. 'Kemerbest' and 'Tığbent'.

139. For the document, see my '16. Yüzyıldan Bir Ziyaretname (Yazı Çevirimli Metin-Günümüz Türkçesine Çeviri-Tıpkıbasım)', in In Memoriam Şinasi Tekin', ed. George Dedes and Selim S. Kuru, special issue, *Journal of Turkish Studies/Türklük Bilgisi Araştırmaları* 31, no. 2 (2007): 67–79.
140. Cf. *FD/Ij-Wafaʾi-DK-1* and *FD/Ij-AGU-Ma*.
141. For the Sinemillis and their family documents, see my 'Sinemilliler: Bir Alevi Ocağı ve Aşireti,' *Kırkbudak* 2, no. 6 (Spring 2006): 19–59.
142. FD of Erhan Dede, the *ocak* of Derviş Çimli. It is curious that both of these documents are found in the family archives of a lesser-known *ocak* of Derviş Çimli. On the other hand, the two *ocak*s, it would seem, branched out from the same family line, given their shared home in the province of Elbistan-Maraş and some Sinemilli oral traditions to that effect, even though this claim is rejected by members of the *ocak* of Derviş Çimli. Personal correspondence with Erhan Dede, spring 2018.
143. Michael Ebstein, 'Spiritual Descendants of the Prophet: Al-Ḥakim al-Tirmidhī, Ibn al-ᶜArabī and Ikhwān al-Ṣafāʾ on *Ahl al-Bayt*', in *L'Esotérisme Shiᶜite L'Esotérisme Shiᶜite, ses racines et ses prolongements*, ed. M. A. Amir-Moezzi et al. (Turnhout: Brepols Publishers, 2016), 546.
144. While a modern observer may become easily sceptical of the reliability of a process of proof based solely on witness testimonies and communal recognition, it was in fact in keeping with the rules of the shariᶜa courts that prioritised oral testimonies of Muslim witnesses given under oath over any other type of evidence; see Rüya Kılıç, 'The Reflection of Islamic Tradition on Ottoman Social Structure: The Sayyids and the Sharīfs', in *Sayyids and Sharifs in Muslim Societies: The Living Links to the Prophet*, ed. Morimoto Kazuo (London and New York: Routledge, 2012), 131. These testimonies could also be supplied in written form without the witness being personally present. Ţhis is suggested by a *shajara* that was issued by the *nakībü'l-eşrāf* in Najaf based on two letters, one of which was signed by the local kadi. *Shajara* dated 30 Zi'l-kaᶜde 953/1547, FD of Hüseyin and Hayri Doğan, the Adıyaman branch of the *ocak* of Ağuiçen. This document was published, but its date was read incorrectly as 553/1158 in Fevzi Rençber, 'Anadolu Aleviliğinde Şecere Geleneği: Bir Ağuiçen Şeceresi Örneği', *Alevilik Araştırmaları Dergisi* 6 (Winter 2013): 175–180.

3

Hacı Bektaş and his Contested Legacy: The Abdals of Rum, the Bektashi Order and the (Proto-) Kizilbash Communities

Ninety-six thousand elders of Horasan
Fifty-seven thousand saints of Rum
The eminent leader of all of them
Isn't it my master, Hacı Bektaş

– Abdal Musa (fourteenth century)[1]

Of the many Sufi masters who began arriving in Anatolia in the thirteenth century or earlier, few were destined to play such a pivotal role in the socio-religious history of the region as Hacı Bektaş (d. *c.*1270). Hacı Bektaş is not only the eponym of the Bektashiyye, one of the most influential Sufi orders in the Ottoman Empire; he was also a cornerstone of the broader religious matrix from which Kizilbashism/Alevism emerged. In accordance with his historical significance, Hacı Bektaş and his spiritual legacy have received sustained scholarly and popular interest. Despite that, large gaps and many uncertainties exist in our knowledge of Bektashi history. One particularly baffling aspect of this history that concerns us here is the origins and nature of the relationship between the Bektashiyye and the Kizilbash/Alevi communities. The latter share with the Bektashis a common reverence for Hacı Bektaş. The two groups are likewise united in their veneration of ᶜAli and the Twelve Imams, and they are near-identical in the sphere of doctrine and rites. On the other hand, Hacı Bektaş was also the patron saint of the Janissaries, the elite infantry corps of the Ottomans, and the Bektashiyye was an officially recognised Sufi order in the Ottoman Empire. And so, the Bektashis, unlike the Kizilbash/Alevi communities, have lived for the most part a life free of persecution under Ottoman rule, at least until the order's abolition in 1826 (along with the destruction of the Janissaries), when they entered a period of underground existence.

For Fuad Köprülü, as for many others writing in his wake, the difference between the two groups is reduceable to one of separate social environments and organisation, and divergent political evolution in post-sixteenth-century Ottoman society. In this view, the Alevis are simply the 'village Bektashis' who joined ranks with the Safavids, faced repression as a result and mutated into an inward-looking endogamous ethno-religious community. The Bektashis, in contrast, were organised as a formal Sufi order, functioning on the basis of fixed rules for initiation and progression within the order.[2] It is, furthermore, generally assumed that the Bektashis as a whole maintained a pro-Ottoman, or at least a quietist political stance, in contrast to their 'rebellious' cousins who sided with the rival Safavids. This politically conformist bent, together with the prestige arising from its association with the Janissaries, is said to have earned the Bektashiyye official protection despite the order's evident Shiᶜism and anti-nomianism.[3]

In large measure, the view of the Alevis as lay followers of the Bektashi order reflects the way that the Çelebis (T. *Çelebiler*; Ot. *Çelebiyān*) – one of the two branches of the Bektashiyye – visualise their links with these communities. The Çelebi family, whose members have historically headed the central Bektashi convent in Kırşehir, claim to be biological descendants of Hacı Bektaş. This claim is rejected by the Babas (T. *Babacılar*; Ot. *Babagān*), the other branch of the Bektashiyye, who insist that the saint lived a celibate life. The Çelebis maintain that Hacı Bektaş dispatched during his lifetime a number of his deputies, *ḫalīfe*s, to different corners of Anatolia who then formed the nuclei of the various Alevi *ocak*s in their assigned areas. Over time, links between these *ocak*s and the Hacı Bektaş convent in Kırşehir is said to have weakened, and were eventually completely severed, due to geographical distance and other factors, resulting in the creation of the independent *dede* lineages that we have today.[4]

Although appealing in its simplicity and significant for reflecting the current near fusion of Alevi and (Çelebi) Bektashi identities, such a linear and uni-dimensional understanding of Alevi–Bektashi relations does not adequately account for the complexity of data garnered from in-field observations and the Alevi documents. To begin with, the Alevi communities attached to *dede* lineages, although recognising Hacı Bektaş as a saint, do not traditionally apply the appellation 'Bektashi' to themselves, using it instead strictly for those who are directly attached to the Çelebi family. Even in the countryside, the boundaries between the two groups seem to have been relatively well-defined until the nineteenth century, when the Çelebis began to expand their sphere of influence to include a growing number of Kizilbash/Alevi *ocak*s. As a result, a significant number of *dede* families came to turn to the Çelebis to receive written authorisations as confirmation of their *ocakzade* status.[5] This, however, has been neither a seamless nor a fully completed process, as many *dede* families have resented and resisted the Çelebis' claims of supreme spiritual authority over their *ocak*s, viewing the Çelebi family as no more than another *ocak* of equal status.[6] These *dede* families insist that the source of their *ocak* status is to be traced back not to an initial sanction by Hacı Bektaş, as posited by the Çelebis, but to their own *sayyid* descent and to their authorisation by the Karbala or Ardabil convents. Some *dede* families also maintain that the arrival of their ancestors in Anatolia as bearers of a spiritual mission predated that of Hacı Bektaş. These counter-claims appear to be historically anchored when compared to the Alevi documents that lay bare the Wafaʾi provenance of a sizeable group of Kizilbash/Alevi *ocak*s in eastern Anatolia, as discussed in the previous chapter. The Alevi documents, by the absence among them of any *icāzetnāme*s issued at the convent in Kırşehir prior to the nineteenth century, also corroborate the relatively recent origins of the growing Çelebi influence over these *ocak*s. Overall, the Çelebi construct of Alevi–Bektashi relations, and Köprülü's parallel assumptions, appear too neat in view of the much greater complexity of the picture on the ground, and seem to project back into earlier periods realities of a more recent past.

Further complicating the picture of historical Alevi–Bektashi relations are Alevi documents that reveal relatively institutionalised links between the Kizilbash/Alevi *ocak*s and a group of Sufi convents in Iraq well into the nineteenth century, and in some cases even beyond. At the centre of this web of pro-Safavid Sufi convents was the Karbala convent (Kerbela Dergâhı) located in the courtyard of the shrine complex of Imam Husayn. Formerly under the control of the Abdals of Rum (Ot. Abdālān-ı Rūm; T. Rum Abdalları), this convent appears as Bektashi affiliated in sources from the early eighteenth century onwards. It has been also considered an important Bektashi centre by the Babagan branch of the order (but apparently not by the Çelebis). Routinised interactions between the Abdal/Bektashi convent in Karbala and the Alevi/Kizilbash *dede* families in Anatolia bring to light a new front to be taken into account while tracking the variegated course of Alevi–Bektashi relations. In a similar vein, they highlight the importance of going beyond the convent in Kırşehir, and the Çelebi family heading it, for a broader perspective on the subject. This intricate web of previously unknown connections also raises a set of new questions concerning the role of the Abdals as intermediaries between the Bektashi order and the (proto-)Kizilbash milieu.

The present chapter sets out to explore this nexus of the Abdals, the Bektashis and the Kizilbash milieu in an effort to contribute to a better understanding of the historical roots and evolution of the Alevi–Bektashi (dis)entanglement. In Köprülü's reckoning, the Abdals were the primary heirs to the legacy of the mid-thirteenth-century Baba^ᵓi movement, whose exponents spread to different parts of Anatolia following the suppression of their revolt. As such they formed the mediating link between the Babaᵓis and the Bektashis within the larger historical trajectory of 'heterodox folk Islam' in Anatolia. Köprülü's portrait of relations among the Babaᵓis, the Abdals and the Bektashis as fluid and familial in nature appears strikingly perceptive, and it also forms an underlining assumption in what follows. However, his vision of an insular heterodox tradition in Anatolia, one that was inherited by successive heterodox circles within a linear scheme, is problematic in so far as it implies an inevitable and seamless evolution and does not adequately attend to the workings of power and agency. Moreover, when Köprülü wrote of the Abdals as successors to the Babaᵓi movement, he was either unaware of the latter's Wafaᵓi background or overlooked evidence pointing to it. Discussion of Babaᵓi–Abdal connectedness, therefore, remains incomplete without a discussion of the former's links to the broader Wafaᵓi milieu. My analysis aims at restoring this missing piece of the puzzle while rethinking the interlocking histories of the Babaᵓis, the Abdals, the Bektashis and the Kizilbash movement through the lens of the long-term trajectory and diversification of the Wafaᵓi legacy in Anatolia. This proposed framework also sheds new light on the old question of the bifurcated organisation of the Bektashi order, and opens up fresh ways of thinking about its origin.

Hacı Bektaş in Context

We lack sources from Hacı Bektaş's lifetime that mention him. The earliest ones to reference the saint are three endowment deeds (Ot. *vaḳfiyye*) from the late thirteenth century. Such expressions as '*el-merḥūm*' (used usually for someone deceased) attached to his name in these documents dated 691/1291, 695/1295 and 697/1297 suggest that Hacı Bektaş must have died sometime prior to their composition.[7] This evidence is also backed up by a later added note in a manuscript found in the library of the Hacı Bektaş convent, according to which the saint was born in 606/1209 and died in 669/1270.[8] Later narrative sources that speak of Hacı Bektaş likewise place his lifetime within the thirteenth century by showing him in contact with various known figures from the same time period. Two of these sources date from the first half of the fourteenth century, including the *Menāḳıbu'l- ḳudsiyye* by Elvan Çelebi (d. *c.*760/1358), which, as will be recalled from earlier, includes a verse history of Baba İlyas Horasani and his progeny, and the Persian hagiography of the famous Mevlana Celaleddin, *Manāḳib al-ᶜĀrifīn*, by his disciple Eflaki (d. 1360).[9]

The thirteenth century was a particularly eventful and formative period in the history of Anatolia. It witnessed the second major wave of Muslim migrations from the east, triggered by the Mongol invasions in Central Asia and Iran that began in the 1220s. The Anatolian Seljuks, severely weakened by the massive Babaʾi revolt (1239–1241) of a few years earlier, which had brought together discontented tribesmen (presumably mostly Turkmen) under Sufi leadership, experienced a crushing defeat at the hands of the advancing Mongol armies in the Battle of Kösedağ in 1243, as a result of which they had to submit to vassalage.[10] The political vacuum created by the decline and subsequent collapse at about the turn of the fourteenth century of the Anatolian Seljuks would be filled by various independent Turkmen principalities engaged in *ġazāʾ* expeditions into Christian territories. This politically fragmented and highly porous multicultural environment of medieval Anatolia fostered and produced an array of mystics who had an important influence on the religious and cultural history of the Turkish/Islamic milieu in the region. Hacı Bektaş was one of those pioneering religious figures who, like Dede Kargın, presumably migrated to Anatolia from Khorasan in the wake of Mongol conquests in Khwarazm and Iran.[11]

In his new home, Hacı Bektaş would settle down and establish himself as a religious figure of some repute near the central Anatolian town of Kırşehir. We learn from the above-mentioned *vaḳfiyye* dated 697/1297 that the village where he settled and eventually died, Sulucakaraöyük, was already named after him by the end of the thirteenth century. After his death, his tomb in that village would grow into a major shrine complex under the patronage of the Mongol Eratnid dynasty, which is known to have engaged in similar forms of architectural patronage for a number of other Sufi buildings in their realms. Later additions to the shrine were made in the second half of the fourteenth century when the area around Kırşehir was controlled by the Karamanid principality.[12] The aforementioned George of Hungary, who was in Anatolia from 1436 to 1458, observed that the shrine of Hacı Bektaş was one of the four most popular pilgrimage sites in Anatolia at the time, another one being the convent of Seyyid Battal Gazi that belonged to the Abdals and was located in the modern province of Eskişehir, about which more will be said below.[13]

Notwithstanding the earlier popularity of his shrine as a site of pilgrimage, the enduring prominence of the cult of Hacı Bektaş was by no means a foregone conclusion prior to the end of the fifteenth century, when it acquired its final shape and significance as we know it today. It was during this period, when the Ottoman principality was upgraded to an empire with its newly conquered capital of Constantinople, that legends and traditions concerning the saint and other members of the later Bektashi pantheon were first set down in writing in a series of hagiographies, one of which was the *Velāyetnāme* containing the sacred vita of Hacı Bektaş.[14] The *Velāyetnāme* is the primary repository of the Bektashi tradition concerning the order's spiritual master, which was completed presumably sometime between 1481 and 1501.[15] According to the *Velāyetnāme*, Hacı Bektaş was sent from Khorasan to the lands of Rum by his shaykh, Ahmed Yesevi, charged with a rather unusual mandate: to assume command of the local dervishes who were known as the Abdals of Rum. The Abdals' initial reception of the saint was anything but welcoming, however, for they feared that this uninvited outsider might lure the entire population of Rum into following him, thus leaving no room for them. The *Velāyetnāme* is in part the story of this contentious initial encounter of the Abdals of Rum with Hacı Bektaş and their subsequent recognition of the saint's spiritual superiority.[16] It was the same Abdal milieu that would cherish the memory of Hacı Bektaş after his demise and supply the initial constituency of the Bektashi Sufi order.

The Bektashi hagiographic narratives, to varying degrees, echo the values and sensibilities of the nascent Ottoman polity in the frontier regions of Asia Minor. They tend to portray the Bektashi saints as warrior dervishes embodying the *ġazāʾ* ethos of the early Ottomans, for whom waging war against infidels on behalf of Islam was a principle source of identity and legitimacy. The Bektashi warrior dervishes emerge from these narratives as partners in the Ottoman state-building project and as vital sources of spiritual and moral support for the house of Osman.[17] The *Velāyetnāme*, for instance, claims that Hacı Bektaş had blessed Osman, and before him his father Ertuğrul, in the family's bid for rulership.[18] ᶜAşıkpaşazade, however, categorically denies the claim that Hacı Bektaş had contact with early Ottoman rulers, which is indeed hard to substantiate historically given that the definitive absorption of Kırşehir and its environs by the Ottoman state dates to the early sixteenth century.[19] Be that as it may, the Bektashi hagiographies as such testify to the importance of the Anatolian frontier context in forging some of the basic contours of the Bektashi tradition.

The recording of hitherto orally transmitted Bektashi lore was closely followed by the remodelling and expansion in size of the shrine complex of Hacı Bektaş in the first half of the sixteenth century. The patrons of this architectural activity were well-established families of raider commanders based in the Balkans. These families identified themselves with the traditional *ġazāʾ* spirit of the westernmost frontiers of Islam, but were gradually brushed aside with the consolidation of the Ottoman system into a more formal and centralised state. Their patronage of the saint's shrine complex by way of validating themselves, as well as the ethos and praxis of *ġazāʾ* that they espoused, speaks to the growing association during this period of Hacı Bektaş's memory with the early Ottoman enterprise. The first decade of the sixteenth century also witnessed a thorough reorganisation of the Bektashi order with its two distinct branches, namely the Babagans and the Çelebis, when the convent in Kırşehir was under the administration of Balım Sultan, the *pīr-i s̱ānī*, or second grand-master, of the Bektashi order. It is no doubt of some significance, as will be elaborated later, that Balım Sultan was appointed in 1501 as head of the Hacı Bektaş convent by the then reigning sultan, Bayezid II. [20]

A Yesevi or a Wafaʾi Dervish?

The *Velāyetnāme* presents Hacı Bektaş as a *sayyid* through the line of the seventh of the Twelver Shiʿi Imams, Musa al-Kazim (745–799). His father is identified as a certain Ibrahim Sani, the sultan of Khorasan, and his mother as Hatem Hatun, allegedly the daughter of a major religious scholar from the city of Nishapur. Hacı Bektaş is thus purported to be not only a *sayyid* but also someone of royal blood who refused the throne to become a Sufi – a relatively familiar theme in Sufi literature. He is said to have received his education in religious sciences from Lokman Perende (Loḳmān Perende), an ecstatic Sufi and disciple of the founder of the Yesevi order, Ahmed Yesevi. The *Velāyetnāme* tells us that it was Ahmed Yesevi who dispatched Hacı Bektaş to the lands of Rum after giving him a ceremonial haircut, a set of spiritual accoutrements (*emānetler*) and a written authorisation (*ijāzetnāme*), which implies a shaykh–disciple relationship between the two. Like the *Velāyetnāme*, other Bektashi hagiographies and the numerous Çelebi *icāzetnāme*s granted to the Alevi *dede*s from the nineteenth century onwards connect Hacı Bektaş's spiritual pedigree to Ahmed Yesevi. The various chains of initiation given for Hacı Bektaş in all the Bektaşi sources, and in most of the non-Bektashi sources almost without exception, trace back to this renowned Central Asian Sufi shaykh, although some do so indirectly through Lokman Perende. There are also variations among the different Bektahi *silsila*s concerning the individual links beyond Ahmed Yesevi as well as, in some versions, in the additional names inserted between Lokman Perende and Ahmed Yesevi.[21]

Sources earlier than the *Velāyetnāme*, however, do not speak of Hacı Bektaş's Yesevi affiliation, rather associating him with the Wafaʾi/Babaʾi circles in Anatolia. Rumi's hagiographer, Eflaki, is the one most explicit on this matter, describing Hacı Bektaş as a leading deputy (P. *khalīfa-i khāṣ*) of Baba İlyas.[22] An association between the saint and Wafaʾi/Babaʾi circles is also hinted at in Elvan Çelebi's verse hagiography of Baba İlyas Horasani and his progeny, in which Hacı Bektaş's name is respectfully mentioned in two couplets.[23] ᶜAşıḳpaşazade's *Tevārīḫ*, composed at about the same time as the *Velāyetnāme*, also contains some interesting information about the saint that aligns with these two earlier sources. Hacı Bektaş, ᶜAşıḳpaşazade relates, was accompanied by his brother named Menteş on his trip from Khorasan to Anatolia; once in Anatolia, the two allegedly went straight to Sivas to see Baba İlyas. Menteş would soon be killed under unexplained circumstances, while Hacı Bektaş would settle down in the village of Sulucakaraöyük.[24] Could Menteş have joined the Babaʾis and been killed during the revolt, as hypothesised by some?[25] We do not know. Still, the meeting of Hacı Bektaş and his brother with Baba İlyas, unless a complete fabrication by ᶜAşıḳpaşazade, is significant in reinforcing the evidence found in other sources of some entanglement between Hacı Bektaş and the Wafaʾi/Babaʾi circles.[26]

Interestingly, Köprülü was the first modern historian to express caution about the authenticity of the well-entrenched Bektashi tradition that linked Hacı Bektaş to Ahmet Yesevi. In his first book, *Türk Edebiyatı'nda İlk Mutasavvıflar*, Köprülü observed that a master–disciple relationship between the two figures was chronologically impossible given that Hacı Bektaş had not yet been born when Ahmed Yesevi died in 562/1166. He proposed that Hacı Bektaş was more likely an ecstatic Qalandari (Ot. Ḳalenderī) dervish and that the *silsila*s linking him to Ahmed Yesevi were invented later to draw on the popularity of this famous Central Asian mystic whose fame, Köprülü believed, was carried into Anatolia by the multitude of Yesevi dervishes entering this region in the wake of the Mongol invasions.[27] At a more fundamental level, Köprülü's reluctance to accept the authenticity of the *silsila*s linking Hacı Bektaş to Ahmed Yesevi was connected to the latter's firm credentials as a shariᶜa-abiding Sufi master, and one whose spiritual genealogy, moreover, intersected with that of the emphatically Sunni Naqshbandi order. This 'ortho-prax' picture of Ahmed Yesevi must have been hard to reconcile with a 'hetero-prax' successor such as Hacı Bektaş, who is portrayed in multiple sources as a charismatic mystic with clear antinomian tendencies. Eflaki, for instance, portrays him as having an enlightened heart but not conforming to the shariᶜa, not even performing the daily prayers.[28] Elvan Çelebi, likewise, but in a more affirmative tone, characterises Hacı Bektaş as a saintly figure not bound by the externals of religion.[29] The *Velāyetnāme* indirectly corroborates these two sources by presenting Hacı Bektaş as one who is censored by the shariᶜa-minded for not outwardly performing religious formalities.[30] Even the Ottoman-era sources that cast Hacı Bektaş as a shariᶜa-abiding Sufi squarely within the Sunni fold, in their explicit efforts to disassociate the saint from the 'tainted' reputation of his 'heterodox' followers, indirectly confirm Hacı Bektaş's reputation for religious non-conformism.[31]

Before long, however, Köprülü would change his mind on this matter and defend a position that was diametrically opposed to his original one. Expressing certitude in a historical link between Ahmed Yesevi and Hacı Bektaş, Köprülü later argued that the 'orthodox' image of Ahmed Yesevi was probably nothing but a construct of the Naqshbandi sources, and that Yesevi's true religious outlook was in fact closer to that of a Turkmen *baba* on the model of Hacı Bektaş.[32] This radical shift in Köprülü's thinking, striking as it may be, makes better sense when one bears in mind his paramount concern, which was to establish a line of unbroken cultural continuity between Central Asian and Anatolian Turks. In his first book, *Türk Edebiyatı'nda İlk Mutasavvıflar*, he tried to establish this link through literature by drawing parallels between the poetry of Ahmed Yesevi and Yunus Emre, the first important poet to write in Western Turkish. Whether or not Hacı Bektaş individually had a historical connection to Ahmed Yesevi was, therefore, less important for Köprülü at that stage of his scholarship than the overall formative influence of Ahmed Yesevi on popular culture in Anatolia. In his subsequent works, however, where his focus shifted from literature to popular religion as the primary conduit of cultural transmission (a shift, one suspects, prompted in part by the tenuous evidential underpinnings for the alleged influence of Ahmed Yesevi on Yunus Emre's poetry, as shown early on by Abdülbaki Gölpınarlı[33]), the issue would acquire greater significance. His radical rethinking of the sources when looked at from this angle appears as a necessary move to show the plausibility of a historical tie between Ahmed Yesevi and Hacı Bektaş, hence between the Yeseviyye and the Bektashi orders, as primary expressions of popular Sufism in Central Asia and Anatolia, respectively.

Recent scholarship lends further circumstantial support to the Bektaşi tradition portraying Hacı Bektaş as a deputy of Ahmed Yesevi, which is also the position later adopted by Köprülü. Devin DeWeese's finding that Ahmed Yesevi probably died about a quarter of a century later than the hitherto accepted date of 1166, while not proving it, renders a master–disciple relationship between Ahmed Yesevi and Hacı Bektaş at least chronologically plausible.[34] Building in part upon this finding, Ahmet Karamustafa has recently argued for the conceivability, or even likelihood, of such a connection. Simultaneously, however, Karamustafa called into question Köprülü's broader assumption of a Yesevi omnipresence in medieval Anatolia by drawing attention to the lack of compelling evidence in that direction, save for Hacı Bektaş himself. It is true that Evliya Çelebi, on whose seventeenth-century *Seyahatname* Köprülü relied heavily, attributes Yesevi identity to several other, near-contemporary Anatolian Sufi figures of the medieval era, such as the aforementioned Geyikli Baba. This, however, ought to be viewed as symptomatic of the pertinent Bektashi tradition that was already well-established at the time. The fragile evidential basis of the supposition of a widespread Yesevi presence in pre-Ottoman Anatolia, in turn, strengthens, rather than undermines, the probability of an actual connection between Hacı Bektaş and Ahmed Yesevi by eliminating the raison d'être (i.e., the popularity of the Yesevi tradition in medieval Anatolia) for feigning such a link within the later Bektashi tradition.

Where would Hacı Bektaş's Yesevi background, assuming its historicity, leave us with regard to sources earlier than the *Velāyetnāme* that say nothing of this affiliation, and instead associate the saint with Baba İlyas and the Wafaʾi/Babaʾi circles in medieval Anatolia? The explanation of this seeming discrepancy may be as simple as the non-exclusive nature of Sufi affiliations, which must have been particularly the case during the thirteenth century when the different Sufi traditions were still in a state of flux and not fully institutionalised into distinct orders. It is, in other words, entirely possible that Hacı Bektaş came to Anatolia with some kind of Yesevi affiliation under his belt but received a second initiation from Baba İlyas, or at least intermingled with the Wafaʾi/Babaʾi circles in his new home.

Indeed, a close examination of the *Velāyetnāme* supports the idea of Hacı Bektaş's changing Sufi environments. It is telling in this regard that Hacı Bektaş is associated in his hagiography with the 'Sufi saints of Khorasan' (*Horasan Erenleri*), while his shaykh, Ahmed Yesevi, is described as the master of the 'Sufi saints of Turkistan' (*Türkistan Erenleri*) who, in turn, mandates Hacı Bektaş to take charge of the 'Sufi saints of Rum' (*Rum Erenleri*). These three distinct groups of saintly dervishes, and in particular the Sufi saints of Khorasan and Rum, are frequently conflated in Alevi lore. They are also lumped together in the secondary literature, presumably as part of the same ill-defined proto-Alevi tradition (read as 'Turkish folk Islam' within the context of the Köprülü paradigm).[35] Yet, beyond their implied spiritual communion as saints transcending time and space, it is not clear what temporal links existed among these three distinct groups of dervishes who are consistently identified in the *Velāyetnāme* by their geographical origins only. Nor is it obvious in what capacity Ahmed Yesevi allegedly bestowed Hacı Bektaş with authority over the far-off 'Sufi saints of Rum'. While the *Velāyetnāme* raises more questions than answers on this issue, pertinent episodes in it leave little doubt that Hacı Bektaş was viewed as a rival outsider by the 'Sufi saints of Turkistan' and the 'Sufi saints of Rum' alike, and was initially received poorly by both groups. It is, therefore, reasonable to read these stories as reflective of Hacı Bektaş's changing Sufi environments in tandem with his voluntary emigration or forced displacement from his original home in Khorasan, first to Turkistan and then to Anatolia. The *Velāyetnāme* focuses specifically on Hacı Bektaş's encounter with the Abdals of Rum, presenting it as a watershed moment of sorts in his saintly career. The prominence that the narrative gives to this encounter indicates the greater formative impact of the thirteenth-century western Anatolian frontier context than Hacı Bektaş's probable Central Asian and Yesevi origins in shaping the content of his real or imagined spiritual legacy. Further exploration of the intertwined histories of the Abdals of Rum and the Bektashi order will throw this point into greater relief.

Hacı Bektaş and the Abdals of Rum

Hacı Bektaş, if we are to believe the *Velāyetnāme*, would have been a mature adult and a relatively established Sufi when Ahmed Yesevi dispatched him to Anatolia. Even so, the driving elements behind the incipient development of the Bektashiyye appear to have come less from his life prior to his arrival in Anatolia and more from an encounter and cross-fertilisation between the saint's cult and a core early community of the Abdals of Rum.

This is how the *Velāyetnāme* recounts this initial encounter and the events immediately following it, which together constitute a discernable peak in the hyperbolic narrative of the hagiography: when Hacı Bektaş arrives at the border of the land of Rum, he spiritually salutes the Abdals from afar, but only a saintly woman named Fatima Bacı, who was preparing food for an ongoing gathering of the Abdals, stands up in respect and returns his greetings. Being thus informed of the coming of Hacı Bektaş, and alarmed by it, the 57,000 Abdals try to prevent him from entering their territory by blocking the road with their 'wings of sainthood' (*velāyet kanadları*), but to no avail. Hacı Bektaş immediately transforms himself into a dove and flies over the barrier, landing on a rock in Sulucakaraöyük. Still unwilling to let him in, one of the Abdals by the name of Hacı Tuğrul (Ḥācī Togrul) transforms himself into a hawk and flies to Sulucakaraöyük to pounce upon the saint. Before Hacı Tuğrul has a chance to overpower him, however, Hacı Bektaş returns to human form, grabs the hawk by the neck and squeezes until he loses consciousness. When Hacı Tuğrul comes back to his senses, Hacı Bektaş reproaches him, saying that he came in the form of the mildest (*maẓlūm*) creature he could find, but that the Abdals in their turn confronted him in the form of a cruel (*ẓālim*) creature. Notwithstanding this initial antagonism, the Abdals, beginning with Hacı Tuğrul, come to acknowledge the superiority of Hacı Bektaş's sanctity and pay homage to him.[36]

The *Velāyetnāme* makes clear that it took some members of the Abdal community longer than others to come to terms with what they viewed as Hacı Bektaş's encroachment into territories under their spiritual dominion. For example, in the succeeding episode, when the Abdals are getting ready to go as a group into Hacı Bektaş's presence in order to pledge their allegiance, one of them declines to join them on the grounds that he had not seen anyone named Hacı Bektaş in the *dost dīvānı* ('initial assembly of the friends of God'), where all the saints received their 'rightful share' (*naṣīb*). This obstinate Abdal was none other than Taptuk Emre, the spiritual master of the famous poet Yunus Emre. The competitive thrust of the story of Hacı Bektaş's initial encounter with the Abdals reaches its finale with Taptuk Emre's eventual acceptance of the saint's holiness, and the latter's subsequent reception of his nickname, Taptuk, meaning 'we have bowed down/submitted'. This happens after Hacı Bektaş shows Taptuk a green mole on the palm of his hand, thereby proving that he was the re-embodiment of ᶜAli's mystery (*sırr*), and, more specifically, that he was in the initial assembly, not as a receiver, but as the very distributor of all the other saints' rightful shares.[37]

The *Velāyetnāme*, where these stories are narrated, clearly presumes the pre-existence of a well-entrenched Abdal presence in Anatolia prior to Hacı Bektaş's arrival in the region from Khorasan. There is no sign of a group of followers, whether tribal or otherwise, accompanying Hacı Bektaş; rather the storyline is one of a newly arrived Sufi overcoming the animosity of rival Sufis in his new home and eventually establishing his superiority over them. It would be futile to try to recover the precise historical context of this dramatic story. But given everything else we know about Hacı Bektaş's biography, and assuming the narrative was woven around a historical core, we can roughly date it to the middle of the thirteenth century when a second wave of Muslim migrants fleeing the Mongol armies poured into Anatolia. It would thus seem that this early community of Abdals represented an older dervish/Sufi presence in Anatolia, one that predated the Mongol invasions. This initial circle would later be joined by a second group of dervishes hailing from Khorasan (broadly defined) to escape the destruction of the Mongol invasions in Central Asia and Iran. Hacı Bektaş must have belonged to this latter group, who collectively came to be called 'the saints of Khorasan' in part to be distinguished from the indigenous Abdals of Rum. The Abdals most likely included various Wafaᵓi and/or Wafaᵓi-related groups of Iraqi background who were already in Anatolia from no later than about the turn of the thirteenth century, as shown in the previous chapter.

It was within this erstwhile hostile Abdal milieu that the cult of Hacı Bektaş would take hold and flourish prior to its institutionalisation under the rubric of the Bektashi order. This is demonstrated by the many members of the Bektashi pantheon bearing the title 'Abdal', including among others the famous Abdal Musa who is credited with nothing less than the initial dissemination of the cult of Hacı Bektaş among the *ġāzīs* of the western frontiers of Islam.[38] Who were these Abdals who formed the nucleus of the would-be Bektashis and a major component of the later Kızılbash movement? What was the point at which Abdals and Bektashis came to be differentiated? And how can we elucidate the decline of the Abdal identity and its eventual incorporation within the institutionalised Bektashi order? While the present state of knowledge does not allow for definitive answers to all these questions, an informed engagement with them needs to take into account the course of development of the Wafaᵓi/Babaᵓi tradition in medieval Anatolia, and the role of the Abdals of Rum as a connective tissue between the Bektashi order and the Kizilbash/Alevi communities.

In the Sufi lexicon, *abdāl* (lit. substitutes; sing. *budalāᵓ*) is a rank within the hierarchy of saints.[39] In its more specific sense used here, however, it refers to a group of renunciatory dervishes indigenous to Anatolia. While their origins are often traced back to such thirteenth-century figures as Geyikli Baba, it is unclear whether or to what degree these individual itinerant dervishes roaming the western Anatolian frontiers since at least the fourteenth century were a discrete social entity prior to the fifteenth century, when sources begin talking of them in such terms. ᶜAşıkpaşazade counts the 'Abdālan-ı Rūm' as one of the three mobile groups (*ṭā'ife*) active in early Ottoman Anatolia but does not give any further information about them.[40] A more detailed description of the Abdals as one of eight 'deviant' dervish bands is provided in *Menāḳıb-i Ḫvoca-i Cihān ve Netīce-i Cān*, composed in 929/1522 by Vahidi, an orthodox-minded Sufi of the Zeyni order. Vahidi was particularly disparaging of six of those groups, including, in addition to the Abdals, the Qalandaris, the Haydaris, the Jamis, the Bektashis and the Şems-i Tebrizis. Karamustafa has argued that most of these groups, whom Vahidi treated as distinct collectivities, would eventually merge together under the broader Bektashi umbrella through the course of the sixteenth and seventeenth centuries.[41]

Vahidi portrays the Abdals as having mostly naked bodies and shaved facial hair and heads, and as embracing such renunciatory practices as voluntary poverty, celibacy and itinerancy. The Abdals were distinguished from other 'deviant' dervish groups by their unique attire and paraphernalia, as well as by the tattoos and self-inflicted wounds on their bodies. Many elements in their appearance were symbolic of their Shiᶜi-ᶜAlid penchant. These included pictures of ᶜAli's sword engraved on their chests and a hatchet, named after Abu Muslim Khorasani, the leader of the Abbasid Revolution against the Umayyads, that they carried as an emblem of their hostility against Imam ᶜAli's enemies. The Abdals, Vahidi wrote, believed in divine incarnation in human form (*ḥulūl*), as well as metempsychosis (*tenāsüh*) and the cycle of existence (*devir*). They considered themselves released from prescribed religious observances, practicing in their stead the ritual of *semāᶜ* and consuming ecstasy-inducing substances like hashish. The leading centre of the Abdals was the convent of Seyyid Battal Gazi in the province of Eskişehir in northwestern Anatolia. Finally, according to Vahidi, the Abdals deemed Sultan Şüca (Sultan Şücāᶜ) of the fourteenth century and Otman Baba (Oṭman Baba) of the fifteenth century to be important masters of their path.[42]

The hagiography of Otman Baba, which was written just a few years after Otman Baba's death, in 1483, by one of his disciples named Köçek Abdal, largely confirms Vahidi's picture of the Abdals. It additionally attests the Abdals' self-identification with the traditional *ġāzī* ethos and praxis, if only by showing in a bad light the contemporary sultans for not holding up this early Ottoman tradition. Otman Baba's hagiography as such is also testimony to the volatile relations between the antinomian dervishes and the fledgling Ottoman Empire. This volatility is most conspicuous in the apparent contrast between Otman Baba's personal contact with Mehmet II, where he blessed the sultan's campaign for the conquest of Istanbul, and his later interrogation in the same city on charges of heresy.[43] Relations between the Ottoman state and the Abdals, as well as presumably other dervish bands mentioned by Vahidi, would begin to deteriorate with the rise of the Kizilbash movement that seems to have drawn many of these groups into its orbit, about which more will be said later.

Although indigenous to Anatolia, the Abdals of Rum ought to be treated as part and parcel of a broader trend of renunciatory dervish piety that marked Islamdom during the late medieval era. According to Karamustafa, renunciatory dervish piety emerged from within the broader world of Islamic mysticism, representing a reaction to institutionalised *tariqa* Sufism that displayed a greater proclivity to social, religious and political conformism. It was in many ways reminiscent of the severe ascetic tradition of the early Sufi masters, whose physical understanding of poverty it reinvigorated and embraced. With their dedication to a life in voluntary poverty, the renunciatory dervishes stood apart from the more mainstream Sufis who under various social, religious and political pressures domesticated this key notion of Sufism by translating it into an inner-worldly state, while retaining physical poverty only as an occasional exercise of self-discipline. However, one feature of the renunciatory dervishes of the late medieval era clearly differentiated them from the early ascetic salvation seekers: while the latter regarded retreat from society to be a prerequisite for achieving union with the divine, the former combined a radical understanding of poverty with an active defiance of social and religious norms. Socially shocking behaviour, such as going around naked or shaving facial hair, as was adopted by the Abdals, were among the most visible and common expressions of the anarchist thrust of this second wave of renunciatory dervish piety, which was an integral part of the Anatolian socio-religious landscape during the thirteenth, fourteenth and fifteenth centuries.[44]

The sparsity of written sources makes it difficult to trace the genealogies of distinct dervish groups that come under this rubric, as they were less likely than mainstream Sufis to leave behind a paper trail. This is particularly the case for the Abdals of Rum who, unlike the more transregional Qalandaris and Haydaris, have no single identifiable founding master. Reconstructing the origins of the Abdals must therefore rely mostly on conjecture. According to Köprülü, the Abdals were successors of the Baba'i dervishes who spread to different parts of Anatolia following the suppression of the Baba'i revolt (1239–1240). Köprülü believed that dervishes of pre- and early Ottoman Anatolia bearing titles such as *abdāl*, *baba* and *dede* all belonged to this group.[45] The proposition of an organic link between the Abdals and the Baba'is acquires an even greater appeal in the light of the Wafa'i connection of the Baba'i leadership, more specifically of Baba İlyas. It is, of course, conceivable that the Abdals, and even their presumed predecessors the Baba'is, comprised affiliates of diverse provenance. In that sense they might have represented an ad hoc coalition of dervishes with similar religious values and temperaments that over time coalesced into a distinct collectivity of which we, indeed, have some sporadic indications.[46] But even allowing for a certain level of diversity in its make-up, there is, I believe, reasonable grounds to hypothesise that the Wafa'i heritage as mediated by the Baba'is was one of the primary constitutive components of the religious nexus out of which emerged the Abdal identity.

A good point of departure for reconstructing a plausible course of development that ties together the Wafaʾiyya with the Abdals would be the apparent duality between its this-worldly and renunciatory orientations, both presumably deriving from the example of Abu'l-Wafaʾ himself, as will be remembered from Chapter 1. It seems that the same duality was reproduced by the exponents of the Wafaʾi tradition in late medieval Anatolia, with Shaykh Ede Balı and Geyikli Baba respectively epitomising its world-embracing and world-rejecting threads. This twofold spiritual heritage of Abu'l-Wafaʾ would progressively unravel under the combined pressure of internal dynamics and external socio-political circumstances of late medieval Anatolia to the extent that they would no longer be reconcilable within the same group. The resulting polarisation between the two distinct modes of Sufi piety was in all likelihood a primary dynamic that underscored the differentiation of the Wafaʾiyya into various communities subsequent to its implantation in the western Anatolian context through the intermediary of the Babaʾis. If so, one may conjecture that the Abdals, whose ranks Hacı Bektaş would later join, were the distant heirs of the world-rejecting strain of the Wafaʾi tradition in the Anatolian context that was kept alive by such Babaʾi dervishes as Geyikli Baba.

Even with all these considerations, however, there are certain issues with this line of analysis that call for further deliberation. The most important one of these is the glaring absence in the above-mentioned literary sources from the Ottoman era of any mention of a Wafaʾi–Babaʾi connection to any individual (proto-)Abdal other than Geyikli Baba and Hacı Bektaş. The only partial exception to this is Hacı Tuğrul, who confronted Hacı Bektaş in the form of a hawk to prevent the saint's entry into Abdal territory; he is identified in the *Velāyetnāme* as a pupil of Bayezid Bistami from Iraq. While this rare detail is significant in so far as it points to an Iraqi link, the birthplace of the Wafaʾiyya, and reminds us of the portrayal of relations between Bistami's spiritual descendants and Abu'l-Wafaʾ as particularly close in the latter's hagiography, it obviously does not amount to proof of a Wafaʾi connection. How then can we explain the lack of any references to Abu'l-Wafaʾ in such sources as the *Velāyetnāme* or Vahidi's *Menāḳıb-i Ḫvoca-i Cihān*, the two most extensive sources on the Abdals of Rum, if we are to make a case for the historical interconnectedness of the Wafaʾi tradition and the Abdals?

A reasonable explanation for this problem lies in the strong pro-ʿAlid/Shiʿi character of the Abdals, which stood in contrast to the more temperate ᶜAlid Sunnism of Abu'l-Wafa᾽ and the early Wafa᾽i/Baba᾽i circles in Anatolia. It will be remembered that the order's would-be Kizilbash Anatolian offshoots in the east espoused a similar kind of ᶜAlid Sunnism, until their merger with the Kizilbash milieu when their adherence to Shiᶜi/ᶜAlid elements deepened. One can easily imagine that the Wafa᾽i/Baba᾽i-turned-Abdal dervishes in the west went through a similar process, and that this sectarian transformation is precisely the moment when a distinct and self-conscious Abdal identity was defined. A number of considerations could account for this shift in sectarian outlook. On a macro-level, such a transformation is fully in tune with the spirit of the Mongol era, with its broader Shiᶜitising trend within Sufism. It was during this period that the growing tide of Sufi–Shiᶜi rapprochement reached its peak, with some existing Sufi traditions, such as the Safaviyya, being thoroughly infused with Shiᶜi elements and others, such as the Nurbakhshiyya and Niᶜmatullahiyya, emerging directly out of this confluence of Shiᶜism and Sufism.[47] Within such an environment, and in so far as religious sensibilities are concerned, it must have been a fairly small step for the (proto-) Abdals to move from espousing *tawallā* to also embracing *tabarrā*, thus reinforcing their love for ᶜAli and the *Ahl al-bayt* by combining it with an express hostility against those considered to be their enemies. It is also not hard to see how this shift in sectarian sensibilities might have buttressed the (proto-)Abdals' renunciatory agenda, and in the longer term served as an ideological rallying point for opposition to the emerging imperial mentality of the house of Osman.[48]

A related but harder question to answer would be the timing of this sectarian shift. Given the pronounced Shiᶜi-ᶜAlid penchant of the late fifteenth-century hagiography of Otman Baba, one of the great masters of the Abdals, it could very well be that the metadoxic outlook of their Wafa᾽i/Baba᾽i legacy began crumbling among the (proto-)Abdals even earlier than their cousins in the east, eventually being replaced by a thoroughly Shiᶜi-ᶜAlid outlook. This may have happened independently of the confessionalisation pressures unleashed by the Safavids' rise to power in 1501. The *Velāyetnāme* claims that it was Hacı Bektaş who disseminated the teaching of love for the Prophet's family (*ahl al-bayt*) in the lands of Rum, a claim that might be taken as a clue to some significant role played by Hacı Bektaş in this transformation. This idea, of course, could as well be a projection back in time of Hacı Bektaş's later acquired prominence among the Abdals. It would, anyway, be more logical to assume that the process of Shiᶜitisation was the cumulative result of multiple factors, developing over a longer period of time rather than coming about under the influence of one individual or as a result of one formative moment.

On the other hand, it is by no means beyond the realm of possibility that Hacı Bektaş's influence – or rather the encounter and cross-pollenisation of the Abdals of Rum and the Saints of Khorasan – served as a catalyst of some sort in the deepening of the (proto-)Abdals' Shi^ci-^cAlid identity. A further point worth remembering here is the Bektashi view of Hacı Bektaş as the re-embodiment of the mysterious essence (*sırr*) of ^cAli, the source of all esoteric teachings. The *Velāyetnāme* uses this key element of Shi^ci esotericism to account for the Abdals' eventual recognition of Hacı Bektaş's superior spiritual standing, as such insinuating, once again, an association between him and the growing Shi^ci-^cAlid character of the Abdal milieu. If it is indeed true that the Shi^citisation of the (proto-)Abdal tradition predated the inception of the Kizilbash movement under the leadership of the Safavi family from about the mid-fifteenth century, this could lend credence to the idea that the Safaviyya's own Shi^ci turn was driven, at least in part, by the 'strong Shī^cī tendencies among supporters of the Ardabīl order or among sections of the population which [Junaid] hoped to win over'.[49]

Whatever its exact timing and connection to Hacı Bektaş, the change in the (proto-)Abdals' sectarian sensibilities towards a more unequivocally Shi^ci identity was obviously complete by the time that Otman Baba's hagiography was put into writing towards the end of the fifteenth century. The hagiography demonstrates beyond any doubt that the Abdal milieu represented by Otman Baba had detached themselves entirely from their presumed metadoxic roots in the Baba^ɔi/Wafa^ɔi tradition and embraced a thoroughly Shi^ci/^cAlid identity. The answer to the question with which we started this section, namely the absence of any explicit traces of the Wafa^ɔiyya in the sources that mention the Abdals of Rum, may lie precisely here, namely in the difficulty of reconciling an explicit Shi^ci/^cAlid identity with a figure such as Abu'l-Wafa^ɔ who was of Sunni denomination. The problem posed by his Sunni identity, even if tempered by an ^cAlid orientation, might thus be the main reason behind Abu'l-Wafa^ɔ's eclipse from the pantheon of the Abdals.

Carrying our analysis further, we may assume a correlation between the eclipse of Abu'l-Wafa^ɔ's memory from the Abdals' imagination and the rise of Seyyid Battal Gazi as their (new) spiritual patron in tandem with the (proto-)Abdals' increasing association with the Christian-Muslim frontiers in western Anatolia. Seyyid Battal was an eighth-century Arab warrior of *sayyid* descent struggling against 'infidels' on the Arab-Byzantine frontier in southeastern Anatolia. His once long-lost grave is said to have been miraculously rediscovered through a dream of Sultan ^cAla^ɔeddin's mother at the beginning of the thirteenth century. At this site, which is located in the western Anatolian province of Eskişehir, was later built a convent that served as the central Abdal institution until its eventual incorporation into the Bektashi milieu.[50] It bears noting that the legendary account of Seyyid Battal's feats, known as the *Baṭṭalnāme*, is set in Malatya, one of the first hubs of the Wafaʾiyya in Anatolia and the religious epicentre of the Babaʾi movement. It is likely that the legend of Battal Gazi, after circulating orally for centuries among Muslims in the Muslim-Byzantine frontiers in southeastern Anatolia, was carried westward by Babaʾi/Wafaʾi dervishes before it was eventually recorded in Turkish for a new Turcophone audience.[51] The rise to prominence of the cult of Seyyid Battal Gazi among the Abdals, and his eventual substitution for Abu'l-Wafaʾ, makes better sense when one bears in mind the frontier environment within which the (proto-)Abdals took refuge after the suppression of the Babaʾi uprising and subsequently flourished. What better way to attach yourself more firmly to the frontier ethos and to boost your prestige in such an environment than to associate yourself with the memory of one of the earliest *ġāzī*s in the larger Anatolian context?

If it is true that the emergence of a distinct Abdal collectivity from the renunciatory strain of the Babaʾi/Wafaʾi tradition entailed the convergence of Shiᶜism with the radical strand of the Wafaʾi tradition within the frontier context of Anatolia, and the replacement of Abu'l-Wafaʾ with Seyyid Battal Gazi as the foundational figure, as is hypothesized here, then it is not necessarily surprising that the *Velāyetnāme* and Vahidi's *Menāḳıb-i Ḫvoca-i Cihān* written several decades after the hagiography of Otman Baba would carry no traces of Hacı Bektaş's or other Abdals' ties to the Wafaʾi tradition. For the Wafaʾiyya, and more specifically Abu'l-Wafaʾ himself, was presumably still linked with Sunnism, given that 'not all heirs of the Babaʾi-Wafaʾi tradition went through the [same] radicalization', and remained within the Sunni fold.[52] Yet an alternative explanation for this silence, proposed by Zeynep Yürekli in connection to the absence of Baba İlyas in Bektashi hagiographies, might be the close association between the Wafaʾi/ Babaʾi circles and the Karamanid dynasty, the main rival of the Ottomans for the control of central Anatolia during the fifteenth century.[53] Thus, whether due to changing sectarian sensibilities or new political realities, or possibly both, the Wafaʾi past of the groups in question might have been deemed undesirable, and accordingly repressed in the Ottoman-era sources. Additionally, and more simply, this silence could also be a sign of the withering of the Wafaʾi memory with the passing of time, which ᶜAşıkpaşazade and Seyyid Velayet apparently tried, but largely failed, to revive.

The Abdals and the Proto-Bektashis

Ahmet Yaşar Ocak, taking Köprülü's vision of a reified heterodox tradition flowing seamlessly between successive groups to its apparently logical conclusion, conceptualised the Abdals of Rum as the 'first Bektashis, even though they were not yet called such'.[54] While there is more than sufficient reason to believe that the Abdals formed the core of the early Bektashiyye, it is wrong to assume that all Abdals were Bektashis or were destined to become so. Indeed, evidence suggests that the grafting of the cult of Hacı Bektaş onto pre-existing Abdal structures and the eventual absorption of the latter by the Bektashi Sufi order were both gradual and contested processes.

The implied co-identity of the Abdals and the Bektashis in Ocak's perception is called into question first and foremost by the separate treatment of the two groups in Vahidi's work.[55] Despite the *Velāyetnāme*'s claim that Hacı Bektaş quickly established his prominence among them, Vahidi's early sixteenth-century account of the Abdals does not even mention Hacı Bektaş; it rather foregrounds the *ocak* of Seyyid Battal Gazi (Seyyid Baṭṭāl Ġāzī Ocağı), calling it the Abdals' ka^caba (*ka^cbe*). The lamps the Abdals carried, Vahidi tells us, were symbolic of this attachment.[56] In other words, unlike the Bektashis who, according to Vahidi, claimed to model themselves strictly according to the example of Hacı Bektaş, the Abdals viewed themselves as successors to the spiritual legacy of Seyyid Battal Gazi.

Although Vahidi's description of the Abdals omits Hacı Bektaş, Otman Baba's hagiography written about a half a century earlier confirms the Abdals' reverence for Hacı Bektaş as a true saint (*ṣāḥib-i velāyet*) and as the *ḳuṭb* (chief saint of the age).[57] But while the *Velāyetnāme*, the main repository of the Bektashi tradition, elevates Hacı Bektaş to the unmatchable stature of the *serçeşme* (fountainhead) of ^cAli's esoteric teachings, there is no sign that Hacı Bektaş occupied a comparably high position in the Abdal pantheon. It is noteworthy in this regard that Otman Baba himself is portrayed in his hagiography in terms no less haughty than those used for Hacı Bektaş. The hagiography speaks of Otman Baba variously as the *ḳuṭb* of his own time;[58] the embodiment of Divine Truth (*Ḥaḳḳ*); the bearer of the secret mystery, *sırr*, of the four major Prophets, Adam, Moses, Jesus and Muhammad;[59] as well as the embodiment of various earlier saints, including Sarı Saltuk and Hacı Bektaş.

Equally telling, when viewed from the other end, is the absence of any mention of Seyyid Battal Gazi in Vahidi's description of the Bektashis in the same work. He is, however, mentioned in the *Velāyetnāme*. It is related that Hacı Bektaş's visit to the alleged burial site of Seyyid Battal, which had been discovered by Sultan ᶜAlaᵓeddin's mother through a dream, removed any doubts regarding the site's genuineness. The details of the visit are worthy of notice. When he arrives at the site, Hacı Bektaş greets Seyyid Battal by saying, 'Peace be upon you, O my fountain head,' to which Seyyid Battal replies, 'And peace be upon you, O my city of knowledge.' Following this exchange of greetings, Hacı Bektaş transforms into a limitless ocean and Sayyid Battal's grave floats on that ocean as if it were a boat. Then there is a reversal in roles: Seyyid Battal's grave assumes the form of a boundless ocean on which Hacı Bektaş floats like a boat.[60] This legendary anecdote is significant not only for establishing a special affinity between the two saints beyond the confines of temporality but also for its attribution to Seyyid Battal of a spiritual position on par with Hacı Bektaş, a clear sign of the persisting clout of earlier Abdal icons among the intended audience of the *Velāyetnāme* at the time when the text was first set in writing. One may also read this anecdote as retrospectively legitimising the incorporation of the Hacı Bektaş cult into pre-existing Abdal lore and as validating the nascent Bektashi identity.

All in all, Vahidi's clear-cut separation of the Abdals and Bektashis, when juxtaposed with the picture emerging from the two earlier sources, namely the hagiography of Otman Baba and the *Velāyetnāme*, both of which depict the boundary between the two groups as fuzzy and porous, suggests that the emergence of a separate Bektashi identity was attended by a gradual process of Bektashi-isation of the earlier Abdal pantheon. This was a process that entailed a refashioning of the Abdal spiritual hierarchy with Hacı Bektaş as the central cult figure. Conversely, we can conjecture that the persistence of a distinct Abdal identity was predicated upon a continuing attachment to the seemingly more egalitarian Abdal pantheon and an opposition to its reconfiguration as a unipolar hierarchy with Hacı Bektaş at its top.

Digging yet a little deeper, we see that the dynamics underscoring the differentiation between the Abdal and Bektashi identities and their eventual disentanglement involved divisions even more foundational than a contested spiritual hierarchy. In demonstrating this point, Otman Baba's hagiography is once again a key piece of evidence. Several episodes in it reveal that even though the two groups were united in their esteem for Hacı Bektaş, and circulated within the same spiritual and temporal universe, their relations were fraught with tensions nonetheless. For example, the various Bektashi *baba*s with whom Otman Baba comes in contact consistently fail to recognise his eminence as the *ḳutb* of his time.[61] Otman Baba, in his turn, regards these Bektashi *baba*s as his spiritual inferiors, if not as essentially charlatans. But even more striking than his strained relations with the Bektashi *babas* is Otman Baba's outright animosity against the shaykh of the Hacı Bektaş convent, Mahmud Çelebi. In one story, for instance, when Mahmud Çelebi comes to visit him with his dervishes, Otman Baba bars his Abdals from showing any respect to the uninvited guest and insults Mahmud Çelebi with sarcastic comments about his turban and robe.[62]

In all likelihood, Mahmud Çelebi was one of the ancestors of the Çelebi family whose hereditary right to administer the Hacı Bektaş convent in Kırşehir as the biological descendants of the saint was also recognised by the Ottoman state.[63] Given the significance of the turban and the robe as markers of sedentary Sufis, it appears that Otman Baba's irritation with Mahmud Çelebi and the other Bektashi *babas* was an extension of his larger aversion as a world-renouncing dervish to institutionalised Sufism.[64] It is not surprising that Otman Baba's particular targets in this regard were the Bektashis because, from his perspective, they were guilty of unduly co-opting a major icon of the Abdals, namely Hacı Bektaş, into *tariqa* Sufism.

By looking at the opposition between Otman Baba and the Çelebis as a particular manifestation of broader tensions between different modes of Sufi piety that were particularly acute in late medieval Islamdom, we also gain a new perspective on the future bifurcation within the Bektashiyye itself between its Babagan and the Çelebi branches. The apparent point of contention between the two branches is the question of whether or not Hacı Bektaş fathered any children. While the Çelebis claim to be the saint's natural descendants through his marriage to Kadıncık Ana, the Babagans emphatically reject the idea that Hacı Bektaş ever had any children. The Babagans maintain that Kadıncık Ana was the wedded wife of İdris, in whose house Hacı Bektaş stayed when he first arrived in Sulucakaraöyük, and that their relationship was purely spiritual. The *Velāyetnāme*, projecting a certain vagueness on the subject, shows Kadıncık Ana as İdris's wife who is nonetheless said to have become pregnant after drinking the water with which Hacı Bektaş performed his ablution and into which had fallen drops of blood from the saint's nose.[65] The historical roots of this lingering dispute, in other words, lie directly in the more fundamental question of whether the saint lived a married or celibate life, which, in turn, is tied into broader tensions between world-affirming and world-renouncing modes of Sufi piety. The Babagans clearly upheld the image of Hacı Bektaş as a true Abdal practicing sexual abstinence.[66] A dramatic demonstration of this point is an anecdote in the *Velāyetnāme* involving Hacı Bektaş and İdris's brother, Saru İsmaᶜil, who reportedly suspected Hacı Bektaş of having an eye for Kadıncık Ana. In the anecdote, Hacı Bektaş, sensing the problem, invites Saru İsmiᶜil to go apple picking with him. When Hacı Bektaş climbs up the apple tree, Saru İsmaᶜil sees that Hacı Bektaş has two roses in place of his genitals and understands that he has completely mortified his animal soul. Saru İsmaᶜil subsequently repents and apologises to Hacı Bektaş for having questioned his true intentions.[67]

The fully desexualised portrayal of Hacı Bektaş as a saint dedicated to celibacy clearly echoes the ideals of the world-renouncing Abdals such as Otman Baba who, like Hacı Bektaş, is said to have had roses in place of genitals.[68] This picture stands in sharp contrast to the image of the saint implicated by his alleged paternity of the Çelebis, which assumes a life in conformity with the mainstream Islamic norms of marriage and reproduction. For Otman Baba, the idea of a true Abdal like Hacı Bektaş having biological offspring must have been anathema, thus his aversion to Mahmud Çelebi and his admonishment of 'those who come out as the "son of so and so Çelebi," and gather people around themselves'. In another place in his hagiography, Otman Baba openly reprimands one of the Bektashi *baba*s for having a wife.[69]

So where do these reflections take us in terms of the origins of the bifurcation within the Bektashi order? This split is typically viewed as the creation of Balım Sultan, who, as mentioned earlier, was appointed by the Ottoman sultan Bayezid II as head of the central Bektashi convent in Kırşehir. However, existing scholarship fails to offer a clear motivation for doing so on the part of Balım Sultan who is said to have created – for no obvious reason – a separate branch for the celibate Bektashi dervishes, the Babagans, alongside the already present Çelebis. Based on the foregoing discussion, and contrary to received wisdom, I contend that the roots of the Babagan–Çelebi division predated Balım Sultan, reaching all the way back to the original Abdal–Bektashi differentiation. Thus, rather than causing the bifurcation, Balım Sultan's restructuring of the order was probably meant as a way to accommodate under the same banner two alternative conceptions of the cult of Hacı Bektaş so as to facilitate the integration of the Abdals into the institutional framework of the Bektashi order. Such an integration must have been deemed desirable and necessary to ensure greater state supervision over these 'unruly' dervishes whose predisposition to Kizilbash sympathies was not lost on Ottoman officials. To make better sense of this point, a brief discussion of relations between the Ottoman state and the Abdal-Bektashi circles in the wake of Safavids' rise to power is in order here.

The Ottoman State and the Abdal-Bektashi Circles

One of the long-term effects of the Ottoman state's transformation from a frontier principality into a centralist autocracy was the marginalisation, both politically and religiously, of various groups who were partners in the early Ottoman enterprise, but who later came to be viewed as real or potential loci of resistance against the domineering control of the imperial administration. Among these overlapping groups were the frontier warlord and warriors, the *ġāzīs*, as well as such dervish groups as the Abdals of Rum, whose hands-on blessing for the practice of *ġazāʾ* was an integral component of the frontier ethos. A discordance between these frontier actors, whose economy and status depended on frontier warfare, and the ruling political establishment were in the making since at least the reign of Mehmet II (1451–1481), when the main institutional pillars of the 'classical' Ottoman imperial order were put in place, as a result of which 'the etiological pact between the dervishes and the House of Osman' was also severely fractured.[70]

The already precarious relationship between the centrifugal and the centripetal forces within the early Ottoman polity would take a turn for the worse in the wake of the Safavids' ascent to power in neighboring Persia. The latter functioned as a vortex, pulling in many of the same groups who had earlier contributed to the Ottomans' state-building process but were now alienated from the burgeoning imperial order. To this ideological challenge, the Ottoman state seems to have responded within the framework of a two-tiered policy. The policy combined active persecution, as will be discussed in greater detail in Chapter 6, with efforts to tame 'heterodox' circles under the Bektashi umbrella as cast, or recast, by Balım Sultan. Hacı Bektaş at this point was already venerated as a saint by many groups in the frontier environment. However, his cult appears to have taken on a new meaning during this period, with the Bektashiyye emerging as a relatively sheltered space within the reconfigured Ottoman polity for groups pushed to the fringes who were nonetheless willing to reconcile themselves to the new imperial administration.[71]

Ottoman central authorities were, of course, keenly aware of the continuing susceptibility to oppositional political activism – not necessarily or directly driven by the Safavids, as will be argued in Chapter 6 – of the dervishes and communities linked, at varying levels, with the cult of Hacı Bektaş, despite Balım Sultan's reforms, which aimed to unite and neutralise them under the institutional umbrella of the Bektashi order. This is most vividly demonstrated by the famous Kalender Çelebi uprising of the late 1520s.[72] An alleged descendant of Hacı Bektaş, Kalender Çelebi had replaced Balım Sultan as the head (*postnişīn*) of the Hacı Bektaş convent before the uprising, and his grave is said to be located in its courtyard.[73] According to Bektashi tradition, the convent was closed down after the Kalender Çelebi uprising to be re-opened a couple of decades later under the leadership of Sersem ᶜAli Baba, previously an Ottoman vizier.[74] Although the Kalender Çelebi uprising was the only anti-Ottoman uprising that involved the upper echelons of the Bektashi order, it was not the last to implicate the central convent in Kırşehir. The so-called Düzmece Shah İsmaᶜil uprising of 1577, led by a messianic figure claiming to be Safavid Shah Ismaᶜil, was initiated with a ritual sacrifice performed at the shrine of Hacı Bektaş. Unlike the uprising led by Kalender Çelebi, which was fuelled more by local dynamics, this one seems to be more directly connected to Safavid inspiration, at least in its rhetoric. A *mühimme* entry from the same year suggests that the Bektashis in Kırşehir were investigated in connection with the revolt, as the entry notes 'the absence of any Kizilbash united with Iran in the environs of Kırşehir'.[75] That such an investigation even took place implies that the affiliates of the central Bektashi convent were not altogether cleared of suspicion of pro-Safavid sympathies and activities even at this later date. But assuming that what was reported was accurate, the same *mühimme* entry can also be read as a sign of the Ottomans' success in keeping the convent in Kırşehir free of anti-Ottoman activities in general. The lack of any evidence of official repression targeting any major Bektashi convent in the *mühimme* records from the period from 1560 to 1585, which witnessed a second wave of Kizilbash persecutions, after those under Sultan Selim I, corroborates the supposition that overall the Bektashi order remained on relatively good terms with the Ottoman authorities.[76]

But the same was not true for the community of dervishes associated with the convent of Sayyid Gazi, the central gathering place of the Abdals of Rum. Although the shrine of Sayyid Gazi continued to be visited by the Ottoman sultans prior to military campaigns as a display of their reverence to this early *ġāzī* warrior, and was occasionally granted financial favours for its upkeep,[77] the Abdals residing at the convent came under a sweeping investigation following Kanuni's third and last campaign against the Safavids (1553–1555). As a result, the convent was taken away from the Abdals and given to the administration of a Naqshbandi shaykh, and a madrasa was also built next to it.[78] A *mühimme* record from 1572 shows that the Abdals were later allowed to return to the convent but only on the condition that they abandoned their antinomian practices.[79] It seems that the Ottoman authorities' persistent efforts to ensure the 'orthodoxy' of the Abdals at the Seyyid Gazi convent were still far from successful as late as

1591, when the local judge appealed to the sultan on behalf of his Muslim constituency to ban the annual festival at the convent, known as *maḥyā*, where numerous forms of mischief allegedly took place.[80]

Evliyaᵓ Çelebi, who visited Sayyid Gazi in the mid-seventeenth century, described it as a Bektashi convent and the dervishes in it as fully within Sunni orthodoxy (*ehl-i sünnet ve'l-cemāᶜat*).[81] Evliyaᵓ's latter claim should, of course, be taken with a pinch of salt considering that he portrayed in similar terms the dervishes inhabiting the various other Bektashi convents within Ottoman realms he visited. To the extent they aimed at assimilating the Bektashi order, and the larger Bektashi-Abdal milieu, into the fold of Sunni Islam, the Ottoman state's policies seem to have been only partially successful. This is reflected in the persistence of tensions between normative Sunni sensibilities and the ostensible 'heterodoxy' of the affiliates of the Bektashiyye[82] and in the pains the contemporary Ottoman intellectuals took in their writings to disassociate the patron saint of the order from the tainted reputation of his 'heterodox' followers.[83] Despite all efforts, however, there is little sign that such an 'orthodox' image of Hacı Bektaş as cultivated by the political and cultural elites ever took root among the saint's followers, notwithstanding instances when the Bektashis outwardly adopted a Sunni identity as a form of *taqiyya* to avoid official censorship, which might well have been the strategy they used during their encounters with Evliyaᵓ.

Also noteworthy for our purposes is Evliyaᵓ's depiction of Sayyid Gazi as a Bektashi convent. This fits with the larger historical pattern of the Abdals' gradual absorption into the Bektashi order, as previously observed by Köprülü. Many Abdals took on the Bektashi identity over the course of the sixteenth and seventeenth centuries to elude official persecution, having been pushed in that direction by the state's carrot-and-stick policy. We see the stick part of the policy becoming more dominant from about the turn of the seventeenth century onwards, at which point large-scale Kizilbash persecutions had largely subsided. Suraiya Faroqhi rightfully considers this to be the result of a conscious policy choice involving the establishment of an administrative mechanism to increase central control over the larger Bektashi milieu by conferring to the Çelebi shaykhs in Kırşehir sole authority over all affiliated convents. Documents surviving from the first half of the seventeenth century reveal that this prerogative was granted to the Çelebis for the first time in 1019/1610 and subsequently ratified multiple times. [84] The language used in describing the scope of the prerogative is revealing: it states that the leaders of 'those convents referred to in the common speech of the people with the title of *baba, dede, abdāl, dervīş, sulṭān*' were to be appointed upon the recommendation of the current shaykh of the Hacı Bektaş convent.[85] The rather nebulous and inclusive classification of the convents placed under direct authority of the Çelebi family testifies to the motivation underpinning this administrative measure, which, in all likelihood, was to expand the reach of the institutional framework of the Kırşehir-centred Bektashi order by formally bringing under its umbrella all those communities and convents affiliated with the cult of Hacı Bektaş. The Abdals were undoubtedly the primary target of this measure, given that the first three appellations, namely *baba*, *dede* and *abdāl*, were most typical of this milieu.

When looked at from a longer-term perspective, then, the establishment of a separate Babagan branch appears to have served both as a facilitator and a product of this gradual process of the Abdals' incorporation into the institutional framework of the Bektashi order. This conclusion is congruent with Köprülü's observation that the Abdals, when they eventually were assimilated, did so specifically into the celibate Babagan branch of the Bektashi order. While Köprülü did not fully explain his grounds for this assertion, it appears that the practice of celibacy was a major consideration for him in this regard.[86] Even though this practice had largely lapsed among the Bektashis, the Babagans retained its memory as an ideal and a high stage of mystical development. 'The station of celibacy' (*mücerretlik makamı*), as it is known, is the fourth of a total of five ranks within the Babagan spiritual hierarchy. A dervish reaching this rank must go through a rite of passage in which he takes a vow of celibacy and receives a haircut.

Interestingly, the only three places other than the central Bektashi convent in Kırşehir where this special rite could be carried out was the Karbala convent in Iraq, about which more will be said in Chapter 4.[87] Suffice it to say at this point that the convent in Karbala – which, by the way, the Wafa'i-cum-Kizilbash *ocak*s considered as their spiritual centre and visited periodically well into the twentieth century – is the only documented Abdal convent other than the one situated within the shrine complex of Seyyid Battal Gazi in Eskişehir.[88] Both of these convents would later acquire a Bektashi identity in tandem with the general trend of the Abdals' incorporation under the Bektashi umbrella.

The Karbala convent, as such, emerges from the sources as the physical nexus of the Wafa'i-cum-Kizilbash *ocak*s, the Abdals and the Bektashis. This observation, in turn, gives rise to another important question: was this intriguing convergence of the Wafa'i-cum-Kizilbash *ocak*s with the Abdals of Rum at the Karbala convent the result of socio-religious and political contingencies that took shape within the context of the Kizilbash movement or is it a sign of some earlier links that can be traced back to the two groups' common Wafaʾi heritage pre-dating the Safavids? While this question is difficult to answer with any degree of certainity, it is sensible to assume that both dynamics worked together in producing this result. Whatever the details of this complex and multifaceted process, which will be discussed in the next chapter, the Karbala convent brings our analysis full circle by tying these distinct but overlapping traditions to the same sacred space.

Judged by these historical links, it would not be too far-fetched to assume celibacy to be one aspect of Abu'l-Wafaʾ's spiritual legacy that resonated through the Abdals down to the Bektashi tradition. Further examination allows us to draw several other parallels between the Wafaʾi and the Bektashi traditions, which, considered collectively, strengthen the possibility of a certain degree of transmission and cross-fertilisation between them, with the Abdals as likely brokers. Besides some obvious commonalities, including their esoteric disposition and antinomian practices, such as communal rituals attended by both genders and involving music and the *semah* dance, a possible Wafaʾi imprint on the Bektashi tradition may be detected in the recurrence of several relatively isolated miracle motifs, found both in the *Velāyetnāme* and in the broader Bektashi lore, which are reminiscent of those encountered in Abu'l-Wafaʾ's hagiography. [89] The story of Abu'l-Wafaʾ's postmortem miracle of catching mid-air the architect who fell while fixing the collapsed dome of his shrine is one such example that is told about Hacı Bektaş in the *Velāyetnāme* with little variation.[90] Similarly, the instantaneous transfer of a tray of food to somebody on pilgrimage in Mecca, a motif found in Abu'l-Wafaʾ's hagiography in an episode concerning his disciple, Husayn Raʾi, is attributed to Hacı Bektaş in the *Velāyetnāme*.[91] Mention should be made also of the fascinating story of ᶜAyna Khatun's seduction of Abu'l-Wafaʾ's disciple, Muhammad al-Misri, during a trip to Egypt; the same story, with minor differences, is recounted in the *Velāyetnāme* about Güvenç Abdal, who falls in love with an unnamed woman in India, where he was sent by Hacı Bektaş to collect a donation (*naẕr*).[92] Further examples of miracles performed by both Hacı Bektaş and Abu'l-Wafaʾ include, for instance, praying in the air and rescuing sinking ships from afar.[93] This common stock of miracle motifs, at the very least, implies a case of intertextual connectivity between the two traditions that successively flourished in some of the same places.

A possible indirect Wafaʾi influence on the development of the Bektashi tradition is also suggested by the shared paraphernalia of the two orders. According to the Wafaʾi *ijāza*s found among the Alevi documents, a Wafaʾi dervish elevated to the status of *khalīfa* would be bestowed the following previously cited 'tokens of poverty': a pair of scissors (*miqrād*), a robe (*khirqa*), a prayer rug (*sajjāda*), a banner (*ᶜalam*), a lamp (*qandīl*), a basket (*zanbīl*) and a waistband (*miyān al-basta*). Virtually all of these are also well-known physical symbols of the Bektashi order. The inclusion of a pair of scissors among the paraphernalia of both orders suggests that hair cutting as an initiatic act – which Abu'l-Wafaᵓ himself reportedly practiced in his own lifetime and is also performed by the Babagan Bektashis in the rite of passage associated with the station of celibacy – might have been carried through a chain of transmission from the Wafa'i/Baba'i circles to the Abdals, to then become part of the Bektashi tradition. Granted none of these elements is exclusive to the two traditions, and virtually all can be found in various other Sufi orders. Nevertheless, they do acquire a special significance when considered together with all other historical evidence tying Wafaᵓi/Babaᵓi circles to the Abdals, and the Abdals to the Bektashis, both temporally and spatially.

Of course, neither the Abdals nor the Bektashis were closed communities, and both most likely incorporated – the latter especially in tandem with their growing influence within the Ottoman order – many members and aspects of other, pre-existing dervish groups who probably shared some similar features. The Bektashis, moreover, did not simply refashion and transmit what they inherited from the existing Abdal tradition but formed their own. Indeed, the full-fledged formation of the classical Bektashi order was a process that unfolded over a prolonged period of time, which was probably not completed before the seventeenth century.[94]

The Safavids and the Abdals of Rum

As noted, the Ottomans' policy of promoting the Bektashi order as the sole representative of the communities affiliated with the cult of Hacı Bektaş had only limited success in keeping the Abdals outside of the Safavids' sphere of influence. Indeed, many Abdal circles, rather than attaching themselves to the Bektashi order, appear to have maintained their independence and eventually integrated into the Kizilbash/Alevi network in rural Anatolia and the Balkans as founders of *ocak*s or simply as local saints. Their traces are easily discernable in such *ocak* names as Cemal Abdal, Hıdır Abdal, Üryan Hızır (Hızır the naked), Şücaeddin Veli Baba and Seyyid Battal Gazi, as well as in the names of such Alevi saints as Koyun Abdal and Ali Baba, whose shrines are still venerated and visited by modern-day Alevis, not to mention those whose names have long been forgotten and are recoverable only from Alevi documents, such as Hayran Abdal, the aforementioned patriarch of the *ocak* of Sinemilli.[95]

The Abdals' important place in the making of the Kizilbash movement is also attested by Shah Isma^cil's poems, written under the pen name Hata'i. These contain ample indications of the early Safavids' allure among those associated with the religious and military ethos of the Anatolian *ġāzī* milieu in general, and the Abdals in particular. A couplet from his *dīvān* reads as follows:

> Those who avowed attachment to the sons of the Shah
> Were the Sufis, the *ġāzī*s and the Abdals.[96]

With regard to the Abdals of Rum specifically, we see Shah Isma^cil paying homage to them in a number of other poems as well. For example, in his well-known *Naṣīhatnāme*, a long poem in the genre of *mes̱nevī*, he implores God to forgive his sins for the sake of 'Urum Abdāllari', in addition to various other icons of the Kizilbash circles and of Shi^ci Islam in general.[97]

Unlike the Abdals, however, there are no references to Hacı Bektaş in Shah Isma^cil's poems, except in those of suspect authenticity.[98] As will be discussed in greater detail in the next chapter, the earliest copies of *Buyruk* manuscripts that include religious treatises generated by the Safavids for their Kizilbash followers in Anatolia, similarly, do not mention the saint despite multiple allusions to the Abdals. Can we take the absence of Hacı Bektaş as such in the earlier Kizilbash/Alevi texts as a sign of Safavid indifference to the saint's legacy? The answer is probably 'no', for it is only reasonable to assume that the Safavids must have associated themselves with the legacy of the saint at least to the extent that it was part of the Abdal heritage. Several lines of evidence, albeit scattered, corroborate this view. One such piece of evidence is a note of ownership found in the oldest extant copy of *Buyruḳ*, dated 1021/1612, identifying the owner to be a descendant of Hacı Bektaş.[99] Although the note does not clarify whether the issue here is of biological or spiritual descent, it suffices to show the circulation of *Buyruk* manuscripts among certain 'Bektashi' groups. Another, even more compelling, set of evidence concerns the presence of dervish circles affiliated with the spiritual legacy of Hacı Bektaş in Safavid territories. These have been unearthed by an Azerbaijani scholar, Meshedikhanim Ne^cmet, who, based on primarily epigraphic evidence, has demonstrated the region of Shirvan to be an area where 'Bektashi' dervishes were active during the Safavid period.[100] (This is the same region, incidentally, where sources record a group of Abdal-like Wafa'i dervishes in the late fifteenth century.[101]) Of particular interest here is an inscription found on the mausoleum of a certain Baba Samit (Baba Ṣāmit) in the village of Şıhlar located in the region of Sabirabad in modern-day Azerbaijan. In the text of the inscription, Baba Samit is identified as a *sayyid* from the line of Imam ᶜAli and as a son of Hacı Bektaş (*Ḥażret-i Sultan ᶜAlī oğlu Ḥażret-i Ḥācī Bektaş oğlu . . . Ḥażret-i Baba Ṣāmit*). The inscription further states that the mausoleum over Baba Samit's tomb was built in the month of Dhu'l-qa'da in the year 993/1585 by ᶜAbdullah Khan, the Safavid governor of Shirvan during the reign of Shah Tahmasp. The date given in the inscription is problematic, however, considering that Shah Tahmasp died in 1576.[102] This inconsistency, unless the result of a misreading of the inscription, may cast some doubt on the dating of the building or alternatively suggest that the inscription was a later addition to the mausoleum. Be that as it may, the existence of a Safavid *fermān* from 1704–1705 concerning the appointment of *khalīfa*s over various dervish groups in Shirvan, including those of Baba Samit (*Baba Ṣāmit dervīşleri*), confirms that a certain Baba Samit lived around Shirvan sometime before this date and that there was a community of dervishes formed around his memory who were part of the Safavi-led Kizilbash network.[103]

Further evidence pointing to a notable 'Bektashi' presence within Safavid realms is provided by Evliyaᵓ Çelebi. Evliyaᵓ records the existence of Bektashi convents and dervishes in Persia and in Iraq when he visited the region in 1065/1655. Most importantly, he writes of a major Bektashi convent (*tekye-i Bektaşiyān*) attached to a *maqām* of Imam Ridaᵓ, located somewhere between Urmiya and Tabriz. This was quite a sizeable convent, housing 300 'barefoot, bare-headed' dervishes of various and sometimes little-known orders (*Zırtıl ve Cevellākī ve Ḳalenderī ve Vāḥidī ve Yesevī ve Faḫrī ve Bozdoğanī*). In the kitchen of the convent was a cauldron donated by Shah Tahmasp; the cauldron, Evliyaᵓ claims, was so huge that one would need a five-step ladder to reach its bottom. The eighty cooks of the convent would cook the meat of thirty large-sized animals all at once in this cauldron on the day of *ᶜAşūre* to serve to the poor. In the larger shrine complex, moreover, there were thousands of chandeliers bestowed by the Safavid shahs and the local governors (*her biri birer şāhın ve ḫānın yādigārıdır*).[104]

Even leaving room for exaggeration on the part of Evliyaᵓ in describing its grandeur, it is of great significance that there was a Bektashi convent so big and so lavishly patronised by the Safavids. Evliyaᵓ's description of the convent as a Bektashi convent is, of course, interesting when considering the array of orders to which the dervishes residing in it belonged; this might indicate that while the convent was primarily the domain of Bektashi dervishes, it also facilitated temporary or prolonged lodging for dervishes of other, probably like-minded, orders, as well as housing other visitors to the shrine. Also noteworthy is Evliyaᵓ's emphasis that the dervishes residing in the convent were not of the Sunni fold (*ammā Ehl-i Sünnet değillerdir*); this stands in contrast to Evliyaᵓ's consistency in alleging the fully Sunni character of the Bektashi convents in the Ottoman territories. Besides the one located in the shrine complex of Imam Ridaᵓ, Evliyaᵓ records the existence in Hamedan of eleven other Bektashi convents of which he gives the names of only three (*'tekye-i Genç Yār, tekye-i Imam Taḳī, tekye-i 'Arab Cebbārī ve . . . Şāhruḫ tekyesi*').[105] Without giving any details, Evliyaᵓ also mentions multiple Bektashi convents in the city of Nahavand, along with convents belonging to the Haydaris, Qalandaris and Vahidis (*'ve altı tekye-i dervişān-ı Ḥayderī ve Bektaşī tekyeleri ve Ḳalenderī tekyeleri ve Vāḥidī tekyeleri vardır*').[106] Evliyaᵓ, finally, makes an incomplete note about another Bektashi convent in Qazwin (*'Ābādān-ı tekye-i Bektaşiyān*').[107]

Although we are in complete darkness as to the nature of the formal relations, or the lack thereof, between the Bektashis in the Ottoman Empire and those in Safavid territories, there is little doubt that the latter were beyond the formal institutional network of the Hacı Bektaş convent in Kırşehir. Notwithstanding their description as 'Bektashi' by Evliyaᵓ, these were most likely convents inhabited by successors of those Abdal circles who, according to Köprülü, came to join in with the Kizilbash movement. That in the mid-seventeenth century Evliyaᵓ already spoke of them simply as 'Bektashis' supports the picture of an increasingly more blurred boundary between the two identities, especially from the perspective of the Ottoman establishment.

Conclusion

If we are to unravel the complex and multifaceted relations among the Abdals of Rum, the Bektashi order and the Kizilbash/Alevi communities, we need to reach back to the Wafaᵓi/Babaᵓi milieu in medieval Anatolia and take account of how Abu'l-Wafaᵓ's spiritual legacy underwent diversification and differentiation into various streams and communities along religious/sectarian lines, as well as to bring into our analysis political pressures that came to bear on related dervish communities in the wake of the Ottoman–Safavid conflict. A major differentiation over the proper practice of poverty seems to have occurred within the Wafaᵓi/Babaᵓi circles subsequent to their transplantation to the western frontiers. This differentiation evolved into a sectarian divide between, on the one hand, those who tried to tread a middle ground between mysticism marked with ᶜAlid tinges and state-backed Sunni traditionalism (and who presumably assimilated in the long run into other religiously and politically conformist Sufi orders, such as the Zeyniyye[108]) and, on the other, those who embraced an understanding of poverty based on a complete renunciation of this world, as well as amplified Shiᶜi/ᶜAlid sensibilities. The Abdals of Rum crystallised as a distinct dervish band out of this latter stream representing the convergence between a radical understanding of poverty and Shiᶜi esotericism that was further impregnated with the *ġazā* ethos of the Ottoman frontiers.

The Bektashiyye, in its turn, emerged from within this early Abdal tradition. The two identities coexisted side by side for centuries despite their highly fluid boundaries, with the cult of Hacı Bektaş forming a major connecting tissue between them. However, their differing memories of the saint and competing conceptions of his spiritual legacy fuelled the two groups' eventual disintegration and became markers of their distinctive identities. The Abdals, adhering to a memory of Hacı Bektaş in alignment with their ideal of non-conformity to societal norms, resisted the co-optation of the saint into the institutional framework of *ṭarīqa* Sufism by the Çelebis. The tension between the two camps crystallised around the question of whether Hacı Bektaş lived a married or a celibate life; to this day the dispute underlines the divide between the Babagan and Çelebi branches within the Bektashi order. Recognising the cult of Hacı Bektaş at once as a connective tissue and as a contested terrain between the Abdals and the Çelebis thus paves the way for a new perspective on the twofold structure of the Bektashi order as a reproduction and institutionalisation of this early division, which was underpinned by an opposition between renunciatory and world-embracing modes of Sufi piety.

Looking at it from this angle, Balım Sultan's reforms at about the turn of the sixteenth century, rather than causing the bifurcation of the Bektashiyye, were most probably an attempt to contain these two alternative conceptions of the cult of Hacı Bektaş under a common rubric. Accordingly, the coincidence of these reforms with the rising the Safavid challenge ought to be viewed as part and parcel of the Ottoman policy to promote the Bektashi order as the one and only legitimate custodian of Hacı Bektaş's spiritual heritage, in the interest of taming and bringing under state control communities affiliated with the saint's cult whose susceptibility to Kizilbash sympathies was proven time and again. But the Ottomans achieved only partial success with these policies, at least in the short run, since many Abdal circles remained in the orbit of the Safavids. In fact, together with their Wafaʾi cousins in the east, who seem to have largely operated within the framework of a hereditary Sufi order, the Abdals were a key constituent of the Kizilbash milieu. Alevi documents originating from Iraq provide further evidence for this conjecture, suggesting that the Abdals inhabiting the convent in the shrine complex of Imam

Husayn in Kabala mediated relations between the Safavid shahs and their Kizilbash followers (more specifically those attached to various Wafaʾi-cum-Kizilbash *ocak*s) under Ottoman rule. A more detailed reconstruction of this intricate web of relations is presented in the next chapter.

Notes

1. Doksan altı bin Horasan pîrleri
Elli yedi bin de Rum erenleri
Cümlesinin serfirazı serveri
Pîrim Hacı Bektaş Velî değil mi?

For the rest of the poem, see Musa Seyirci, *Abdal Musa Sultan* (Istanbul: Der Yayınları, 1994), 71.
2. See Fuad Köprülü; for instance, 'Bektaşiliğin Menşeleri: Küçük Asya'da İslâm Batınîliğinin Tekâmül-i Tarîhisi Hakkında Bir Tecrübe', *Türk Yurdu* 7 (1341/1925): 121–140. Also see works by Irène Mélikoff, including 'Bektaşiler Tarikatı ve Hacı Bektaş'a Bağlı Zümreler: Probleme Toplu Bakış', in *Uyur İdik Uyardılar: Alevilik-Bektaşilik Araştırmaları* (Istanbul: Cem Yayınevi, 1993), 21–27. Among the first to use the term 'village Bektashis' (*köy Bektaşileri*) were Besim Atalay, *Bektaşilik ve Edebiyatı* (1922; reprint, Istanbul: Ant Yayınları, 1991), 34; and John Kingsley Birge, *The Bektaşi Order of Dervishes* (1937; reprint, London: Luzac Oriental, 1994), 211. For a general overview of the relevant literature, and for further references, see Suraiya Faroqhi, 'The Bektashis: A Report on Current Research', in *Bektachiyya: Études sur l'ordre mystique des Bektachis et les groupes relevant de Hadji Bektach*, eds Alexandre Popovic and Gilles Veinstein (Istanbul: Isis Press, 1995), 9–28.
3. For relations between the Ottoman state and the Bektashi order, see Irène Mélikoff, 'Le problème ḳızılbaş', *Turcica* 6 (1975): 49–67; and Suraiya Faroqhi, 'Conflict, Accommodation and Long-Term Survival: The Bektashi Order and the Ottoman State', in *Bektachiyya: Études sur l'ordre mystique des Bektachis et les groupes relevant de Hadji Bektach*, eds Alexandre Popovic and Gilles Veinstein (Istanbul: Isis Press, 1995), 171–184.
4. For the Çelebi perspective on this issue, see A. Celâlettin Ulusoy, *Hünkâr Hacı Bektaş Veli ve Alevî-Bektaşî Yolu*, 2nd edn (Hacıbektaş–Kırşehir: n.p., 1986), 194–198. The author himself is a member of the Çelebi family.
5. This division between the Kizilbash attached to the *dede ocaḳ*s and the Bektashis was earlier noted in *MIA*, s.v. 'Kızılbaş', by Abdülbâkî Gölpınarlı. Gölpınarlı writes that the Kizilbash in Anatolia identify themselves as affiliates of the *'Şeyh Safi Süreği'* (Tradition of Shaykh Safi); in a similar vein, the Bektashis identify the Kizilbash as affiliates of *'Sofu Sürekleri'* (Sufi Traditions). Gölpınarlı furthermore remarks that those Kizilbash communities who had recently attached themselves to the Çelebis are referred to as

'dönük' (lit. one who turned), while the ones who remained loyal to the *dede ocak*s are called *'purut'* (lit. one who is resolute).

6. The earliest recorded relevant anecdotes are found in Nuri Dersimi, *Kürdistan Tarihinde Dersim* (1952; reprint, Diyarbakır: Dilan Yayınları, 1992), 92–96. Some indirect evidence of this conflictual process also exists in American missionary records from the second half of the nineteenth century; see my 'The Emergence of the Kızılbaş in Western Thought: Missionary Accounts and their Aftermath', in *Archaeology, Anthropology and Heritage in the Balkans and Anatolia: The Life and Times of F. W. Hasluck, 1878–1920*, ed. David Shankland (Istanbul: ISIS Press, 2004), 344–346.
7. For the three *vakfiyye*s, see Hilmi Ziya (Ülken), 'Anadolu'da Dini Ruhiyat Müşahedeleri', *Mihrab Mecmuası* 15/16 (1340/1924); and Birge, *Bektashi Order*, 41. A recent, concise discussion of sources relating to the biography of Hacı Bektaş is provided in Mark Soileau, *Humanist Mystics: Nationalism and the Commemoration of Saints in Turkey* (Salt Lake City: The University of Utah Press, 2018), 149–153.
8. Introduction to *Vilâyet-nâme: Manākıb-ı Hünkâr Hacı Bektâş-ı Velî*, ed. Abdülbâkî Gölpınarlı (Istanbul: İnkılâp Kitapevi, 1990), xxiii–xxiv.
9. *MNK-Elvan Çelebi-2000*, 632–635, couplets 1994, 1995, and 2003; *MNK-Eflaki*, 1: 381, 1: 498. Slightly predating these two well-known sources is the *Tiryāq al-muḥibbin* by Wasiti (1275–1343), which was mentioned previously as one of the main sources for Abu'l-Wafa's biography and that also includes a long entry on Hacı Bektaş. Based on the fact that Wasiti mentions Hacı Bektaş without adding '*rāḍī Allāh 'anhū*' after his name, Spencer Trimingham concludes that the saint was still alive in about 1320; Trimingham, *The Sufi Orders in Islam* (London: Oxford University Press), 81. However, the *vakfiyye*s mentioned above do not support this conclusion. More recently, Devin DeWeese has shown that this entry, which is found in the nineteenth-century published version of the work, is missing in the one and only known manuscript copy of it. This means that the entry on Hacı Bektaş may be a later addition not found in the original work as composed by Wasiti. Ahmet Karamustafa, 'Yesevîlik, Melâmetîlik, Kalenderîlik, Vefâ'îlik ve Anadolu Tasavvufunun Kökenleri Sorunu', in *Osmanlı Toplumunda Tasavvuf ve Sufiler: Kaynaklar-Doktrin-Ayin ve Erkan-Tarikatlar-Edebiyat-Mimari-İkonografi-Modernizm*, ed. Ahmed Yaşar Ocak (Ankara: Türk Tarih Kurumu, 2005), n29.
10. On the Baba'i revolt, see Ahmet Yaşar Ocak, *Babaîler İsyanı: Alevîliğin Tarihsel Altyapısı Yahut Anadolu'da İslâm-Türk Heterodoksisinin Teşekkülü* (1980; reprint, İstanbul: Dergâh Yayınları, 1996). Ocak has shown that the revolt's leader, referred to as 'Baba Resul' in the sources, was in fact Baba İlyas himself.
11. Ahmet Karamustafa, 'Early Sufism in Eastern Anatolia', in *Heritage of Sufism-1*, 186–190.

12. *DIA*, s.v. 'Hacı Bektāş-ı Velī Külliyesi', by M. Baha Tanman; Zeynep Yürekli, *Architecture and Hagiography in the Ottoman Empire: The Politics of Bektashi Shrines in the Classical Age* (Farnham: Ashgate, 2012), 101–110.
13. Georgius de Ungaria, *Tractatus de moribus condictionibus et nequicia Turcorum,* first published in 1480 in Latin; pertinent section translated into English in Hasluck, *Christianity and Islam under the Sultans*, 2 vols (Oxford: Clarendon Press, 1929), 2: 494–499.
14. Although '*velāyetnāme*' is a common tag for all Bektaşi hagiographies, when one talks about 'the Velāyetnāme' it is commonly understood to be the *menāḳib* of Hacı Bektaş. Gölpınarlı, *Vilâyet-nâme*. For a more recent edition, see *Velâyetnâme*-Duran. For its verse form, see Bedri Noyan, ed., *Hacı Bektaş-Veli Manzum Vilâyetnamesi* (Istanbul: Can Yayınları, 1996). Other major Bektashi hagiographies include the *menāḳıbs* of Hacım Sultan, Otman Baba, Seyyid ᶜAli Sultan, Abdal Musa and Şücaeddin Veli; for their modern editions, see Rudolf Tschudi, ed., *Das Vilâjet-nâme des Hâdschim Sultan* (Berlin: Mayer & Müller, 1914); Şevki Koca, ed., *Vilayetname-i Şahi: Gö'çek Abdal: Odman Baba Vilayetnamesi* ([Istanbul]: Bektaşi Kültür Derneği, 2002); Bedri Noyan, ed., *Seyyid Ali Sultan (Kızıldeli Sultan) Vilayetnamesi* (Ankara: Ayyıldız Yayınları, n.d.); Abdurrahman Güzel, ed., *Abdal Mûsâ Velâyetnâmesi*; *Kaygusuz Abdal (Alâeddin Gaybî) Menâkibnâmesi* (Ankara: Türk Tarih Kurumu, 1999); Şükrü Elçin, ed., 'Bir Seyh Sücâüddin Baba Velâyetnâmesi', *Türk Kültürü Arastirmalari* 22, no. 1 (1984): 199–208.
15. Introduction to Gölpınarlı, *Vilâyet-nâme*, xxiii–xxix. There is both a prose and a verse version of it, as well as one that is a mixture of prose and verse; the oldest extant copy (in prose) is dated 1034/1624. The different versions are interrelated and contain similar content. All three versions appear to be based on the same original compilation.
16. *Velāyetnāme*-Duran, 165–186.
17. Yürekli, *Architecture and Hagiography*, 65–73.
18. *Velāyetnāme*-Duran, 534–554.
19. *Aspz,* 307. For the political history of the region, see *DIA*, s.v. 'Kırşehir', by Ilhan Şahin.
20. For a detailed discussion of these converging developments, see Yürekli, *Architecture and Hagiography*, esp. Chapters 1 and 2.
21. In the nineteenth-century Çelebi *icāzetnāmes*, the spiritual *silsila* of Hacı Bektaş is directly traced to Ahmed Yesevi, son of Muhammad Hanafi, son of Imam ᶜAli; for a published example, see Mehmet Akkuş, '19. Asırdan Bir Bektaşî İcâzetnâmesi', *Tasavvuf* 1, no. 1 (August 1999): 27–39. For alternative *silsilas* of Hacı Bektaş, see Fuad Köprülü, *Türk Edebiyatında İlk Mutasavvıflar* (1919; reprint, Ankara: Türk Tarih Kurumu Basımevi, 1993), 53 n60, 110 n42; and M. Tevfik Oytan, *Bektaşiliğin İçyüzü* (1945; reprint, Istanbul: Demos Yayinları, 2007), 344–345.

22. *MNK-Eflaki*, 1: 381.
23. *MNK-Elvan Çelebi-2000*, 632–635, couplets no. 1994, 1995 and 2003.
24. *Aspz*, 307.
25. Ahmed Yaşar Ocak, 'Anadolu Heterodoks Türk Sûfîliğinin Temel Taşı: Hacı Bektaş-ı Velî el-Horasânî (?–1271)', in *Türk Sufīliğine Bakışlar* (Istanbul: İletişim Yayınları, 1996), 160–180.
26. Contrary to Köprülü, who depicted the leader of the Baba'i revolt, Baba İlyas, as a typical Turkmen *baba* of Qalandari affiliation, Abdülbaki Gölpınarlı was the first scholar to identify the order of the Baba'is as Wafa'iyya and portrayed Hacı Bektaş as a member of the Wafa'i order; cf. Köprülü, 'Bektaşiliğin Menşeleri', 74, and Abdülbaki Gölpınarlı, 'Bektaşilik', in *Türk Ansiklopedisi* (Ankara: Milli Eğitim Basımevi, 1953). Ahmet Yaşar Ocak, on the other hand, was more reluctant to fully dismiss the Yesevi link and tried to resolve, or rather further complicate, the issue by suggesting that Hacı Bektaş was in fact a Haydari dervish. Ocak, following Köprülü, defined Haydariyya (Ot. Ḥayderiyye) as a fusion Qalandariyya (Ot. Ḳalenderīyye) and Yeseviyye, with the former being the main ingredient. He did, however, also suggest that subsequent to his arrival in Anatolia, Hacı Bektaş joined the Baba'i/Wafa'i path, which in Ocak's estimation was yet another offshoot of the larger Qalandari movement. Ahmet Yaşar Ocak, *Osmanlı İmparatorluğu'nda Marjinal Sûfîlik: Kalenderîler: XIV–XVII. Yüzyıllar* (Ankara: Türk Tarih Kurumu, 1992); see especially 205–215.
27. Köprülü, *Türk Edebiyatında İlk Mutasavvıflar*, 48–59, 110–118.
28. '*Ḥājī Bektaş mardī būd ᶜārif-dil u rūshan-darūn ammā dar mutābaᶜat nabūd', MNK-Eflaki, 1: 381*; '*ū aṣlā dar riᶜāyat-i ṣūrat nabūd va mutābaᶜat nadāsht va namāz namīkerd'*, *MNK-Eflaki*, 1: 498.
29. *MNK-Elvan Çelebi-2000*, 632–635, couplets no. 1994, 1995 and 2003.
30. For a nuanced reading of the *Velāyetnāme* emphasising the text's presumably deliberate ambiguity on this issue as a '*taqiyya*-tinged defense of Bektashi non-conformity', see Mark Soileau, 'Conforming Haji Bektash: A Saint and His Followers between Orthopraxy and Heteropraxy', *Die Welt des Islams* 54 (2014): 423–459.
31. See, for example, ᶜAbdurrahman Cami, *Nefeḥātü'l-üns min haḍarāti'l-ḳuds*, trans. Lāmiᶜī Çelebi (Istanbul: Marifet Yayınları, 1980), 691–692; Hoca Saᶜdeddin Efendi, *Tācü't-Tevārīḫ*, vol. II (Istanbul: Tabᶜḫāne-i ᶜĀmire, 1279–1280/1862–1863), 410; Taşköprizade Ebulhayr İsameddin Ahmed Efendi, *Şaḳā'iḳ-i Nuᶜmāniyye ve Ẕeyilleri: Ḥadā'iḳu'ş-Şaḳā'ik*, trans. Mecdi Mehmed Efendi, ed. Abdükadir Özcan, 5 vols (Istanbul: Çağrı Yayınları, 1989), 1: 44; Gelibolulu Mustafa ᶜÂli, *Kitābü't- Tārīḫ-i Künhü'l-Aḫbar*, eds Ahmet Uğur et al., 2 vols (Kayseri: Erciyes Üniversitesi Yayınları, 1997), I: 88–97. Also see, Yürekli, *Architecture and Hagiography*, 63.
32. *MIA*, s.v. 'Ahmed Yesevî', by Fuad Köprülü. A similar shift in Köprülü's thinking occurred in relation to Hacı Bektaş's purported authorship of a

group of religious treatises, including a work entitled *Maḳālāt*. Köprülü initially rejected *Maḳālāt*'s attribution to Hacı Bektaş on the grounds that an ecstatic mystic (*meczūb*), as Hacı Bektaş was depicted by ᶜAşıkpaşazade, would be unable to produce a work that projected such a sober character and level of competence in learned Sufism. Later, he changed his position, accepting as almost certain Hacı Bektaş's authorship of *Maḳālāt*, arguing that it showed Hacı Bektaş's sobriety, contrary to ᶜAşıkpaşazade's portrayal of him as incapacitated by ecstasy, as well as his relative proficiency in religious sciences. The tension between the vision of Hacı Bektaş as an unlearned Turkmen *baba* and his authorship of *Maḳālāt*, which promotes a relatively mainstream view of Sufism – and, one may also add, betrays no shamanist influences – was probably not lost on Köprülü either. Rather than problematising this glaring contradiction, however, Köprülü seems to have tried to muffle it; see Köprülü, 'Bektaşiliğin Menşeleri', 75; and 'Anadolu'da İslâmiyet' (1922; reprint, İstanbul: İnsan Yayınları, 1996), 47–52. This dormant fault line in Köprülü's thinking would be activated in the 1980s with the publication of the critical edition of *Maḳālāt* by Esad Coşan, which elicited an impassioned debate on the subject; Hacı Bektaş Velî, *Makâlât*, ed. Esad Coşan (Ankara: T. C. Kültür Bakanlığı, 1996). Ironically, the most severe rebuttal to Coşan's thesis came from Köprülü's two most prominent followers, Irène Mélikoff and Ahmed Yaşar Ocak, who posited the attribution of the *Maḳālāt* to Hacı Bektaş as entirely spurious; see, for example, Ocak, 'Anadolu Heterodoks Türk', 160–180; and Irène Mélikoff, *Hacı Bektaş: Efsaneden Gerçeğe* (Istanbul: Cumhuriyet Kitap Kulübü, 1998), 99–106. An earlier challenge of these books' attribution to Haci Bektaş is found in Abdülbâkî Gölpınarlı, *100 Soruda Türkiye'de Mezhepler ve Tarikatler* (Istanbul: Gerçek Yayınevi, 1969), 272–274. Needless to say, what on the surface appears to be a discussion of the authorship of the *Maḳālāt* is in actual fact a debate on the religious profile of Hacı Bektaş with strong political undertones; for critical overview of this debate, see Soileau, 'Conforming Haji Bektash'. Mark Soileau rightly posits that Coşan's argument is 'essentially a recapitulation of the 16th-century orthopraxy saint/hierocrat dervishes thesis'. Conversely, however, the unduly rigid position embraced by Mélikoff and Ocak betrays a concern to salvage the model of Turkmen *baba*, one of the signature categories of the Köprülü paradigm. This, ironically, required the abandonment Köprülü's final, more ambivalent stand on the issue in favour of his original position in the interest of analytical consistency.

33. Abdülbâki Gölpınarlı, *Yunus Emre: Hayatı* (Istanbul: İkbal Kitabevi, 1936), 100–102.
34. Karamustafa, 'Yesevîlik, Melâmetîlik', 61–88, 70. Also see Devin DeWeese, 'The Yasavī Order and Persian Hagiography in Seventeenth-Century Central Asia: 'Ālim Shaykh of 'Alīyābād and His Lamaḥāt min nafaḥāt al-quds', in *Heritage of Sufism-3*, 390.

35. See, as an example, Halil İnalcık, *Osmanlı İmparatorluğu Klâsik Çağ (1300–1600)* (1973; rev. edn. Istanbul: Yapı Kredi Yayınları, 2004), 194–195.
36. *Velāyetnāme*-Duran, 174–185.
37. *Velāyetnāme*-Duran, 185–186.
38. *Aspz,* 308. On Abdal Musa, see also *DIA*, s.v. 'Abdal Mûsâ', by Orhan F. Köprülü; for his hagiographic vita, see Güzel, *Abdal Mûsâ Velâyetnâmesi.*
39. For a discussion of the meaning of *abdāl* in the Sufi lexicon and further references, see Michael Ebstein, *Mysticism and Philosophy in al-Andalus: Ibn Masarra, Ibn al-Arabi and the Ismaili Tradition* (Leiden and Boston: Brill, 2013), 125–132.
40. The others being the 'Ġāziyān-ı Rūm' and the 'Baciyān-ı Rūm'; see *Aspz*, 307–308.
41. Ahmet Karamustafa, 'Ḳalenders, Abdâls, Hayderîs: The Formation of the Bektâşîye in the Sixteenth Century', in *Süleyman the Second and His Time*, eds Halil İnalcık and Cemal Kafadar (Istanbul: Isis Press, 1993), 121–129.
42. Ahmet Karamustafa, ed., *Vāḥidī's Menāḳıb-i Ḫvoca-i Cihān ve Netīce-i Cān*, Sources of Oriental Languages and Literatures 17, ser. eds Şinasi Tekin and Gönül Alpay Tekin (Cambridge, MA: Harvard University, 1993), fols 41a–47a; also see pages 7–8 for a summary of the relevant entry in English. For a more detailed account of the Abdals of Rum based on Vahidi and Western travellers' reports, see Ahmet Karamustafa, *God's Unruly Friends: Dervish Groups in the Islamic Later Middle Period, 1200–1500* (Salt Lake City: University of Utah Press, 1994), 46–49 and 70–78.
43. Gö'çek Abdal, *Odman Baba*, 33–54; Halil İnalcık, 'Dervish and Sultan: An Analysis of the Otman Baba *Velāyetnāmesi*', in *The Middle East and the Balkans under the Ottoman Empire: Essays on Economy and Society* (Bloomington: Indiana University, 1993), 27–31.
44. Karamustafa, *God's Unruly Friends*, passim.
45. Köprülü, 'Bektaşiliğin Menşeleri', 75; 'Anadolu'da İslâmiyet', 47–52; 'Abdāl', in *Edebiyat Araştırmaları*, 2 vols (1935; reprint, İstanbul: Ötüken Yayınları, 1989), 1: 384.
46. For example, a follower of Muhammad Nurbakhsh, the eponymous founder of the Nurbakhshi order, by the name of Muhammad Samarqandi, is said to have ended up in Anatolia as one of the Abdals in that region. Shahzad Bashir, *Messianic Hopes and Mystical Visions: The Nūrbakhshīya between Medieval and Modern Islam* (Columbia: University of South Carolina Press, 2003), 69.
47. Alessandro Bausani, 'Religion under the Mongols', in *Cambridge-Iran-5*, 545–547.
48. Karamustafa, *God's Unruly Friends*, 21–22.
49. H. R. Roemer, 'The Safavid Period' *Cambridge-Iran-6*, 205; Roemer borrows this idea from Vladimir Minorsky, 'Sheikh Bālī-efendi on the Ṣafavids', in *Medieval Iran and Its Neighbours: Collected Studies* (London: Variorum Reprints, 1982), 439.

50. For the architectural history of Sayyid Battal's shrine complex, see Yürekli, *Architecture and Hagiography*, 39–46, 79–101.
51. Pertev Naili Boratav, 'Battal', in *İslam Ansiklopedisi* (Istanbul: Maarif Matbaası, 1940–1988). The legend of Seyyid Battal Gazi is preserved in the Turkish-language *Baṭṭalnāme*, edited in Yorgos Dedes, *Battalname: Introduction, English Translation, Turkish Transcription, Commentary and Facsimile*, 2 vols (Cambridge, MA: Harvard University, 1996). The earliest surviving copy of *Baṭṭalnāme* is dated 1436–1437, suggesting it was set into writing sometime before this date; see ibid., 13.
52. Kafadar, *Between Two Worlds*, 144.
53. Yürekli, *Architecture and Hagiography*, 61.
54. *DIA*, s.v. 'Hacı Bektâş-ı Velî', by Ahmet Yaşar Ocak; idem, *Babaîler İsyani*, 174–177.
55. Karamustafa, *Vāḥidī's*, 5–14.
56. Karamustafa, *Vāḥidī's*, 8.
57. Gö'çek Abdal, *Odman Baba*, 53.
58. Gö'çek Abdal, *Odman Baba*, 65, 185.
59. Gö'çek Abdal, *Odman Baba*, 134, 159.
60. *Velâyetnâme*-Duran, 349.
61. Gö'çek Abdal, *Odman Baba*; see, for example, 85 and 105; a Bektashi *baba* named Mü'min Derviş, in fact, tries to win over the Otman Baba's *abdāl*s into his own circle of disciples. Ibid., 140.
62. Gö'çek Abdal, *Odman Baba*, 239–40.
63. Aside from his epithet 'çelebi', the fact that he was the shaykh of the convent of Hacı Bektaş – a position officially occupied by the Çelebis during the Ottoman era – indicates that Mahmud Çelebi was indeed one of the ancestors of the Çelebi line. Otman Baba's condemnation in his *Menāḳıb* of those who gather people around themselves as the 'son of so and so Çelebi' (*fulān oğlu fulān Çelebi*) is further indirect evidence supporting this inference. Gö'çek Abdal, *Odman Baba*, 52. 'Aşıḳpaşazade also mentions a descendant of Hacı Bektaş named Mahmud Çelebi, son of Resul Çelebi (*bu Ḥācī Bektāş-oğlı Maḥmūd Çelebi kim ol Resūl Çelebi'nüñ oğlıdur*), who must be the same individual, *Aspz*, 206.
64. Karamustafa, *God's Unruly Friends*, 25–31.
65. *Velâyetnâme*-Duran, 284–285. For the Çelebi position on the issue, see Ulusoy, *Hünkâr Hacı Bektaş*, 29–39; and for the Babagan perspective, see *Noyan-Bektâşîlik*, 1: 24–27.
66. Hacı Bektaş is indeed referred to as a 'naked Abdal' (*ʿüryān Abdāl*) in the *Velāyetnāme*; see, for example, *Velâyetnâme*-Duran, 125.
67. *Velâyetnâme*-Duran, 250–253.
68. Gö'çek Abdal, *Odman Baba*, 38.
69. Gö'çek Abdal, *Odman Baba*, 52, 141.
70. Hüseyin Yılmaz, *Caliphate Redefined: The Mystical Turn in Ottoman Political Thought* (Princeton: Princeton University Press, 2018), 270.

71. For the frontier milieu and its relationship with the early Ottoman state, and its gradual marginalisation under the classical Ottoman order, see Kafadar, *Between Two Worlds*, 138–150. For the emergence of the Bektashiyye as an internal locus of religious identification for the frontier elements, see Yürekli, *Architecture and Hagiography*, esp. 113–133.
72. For details about the revolt, see A. Haydar Avcı, *Alevi Tarihinde Bir Kesit: Kalender Çelebi Ayaklanması* (Ankara: AAA Yayınları, 1998); and Jean-Louis Bacqué-Grammont, 'Un rapport inédit sur la révolte anatolienne de 1527', *Studia Islamica* 62 (1985): 155–171.
73. Yürekli, *Architecture and Hagiography*, 33. The Çelebis believe that Kalender Çelebi was a descendant of Hacı Bektaş and a brother of Balım Sultan. Ulusoy, *Hünkâr Hacı Bektaş*, 78. But the Babagans reject Kalender Çelebi's, as well as Balım Sultan's, biological descent from the saint. *Noyan-Bektâşîlik*, 1: 123–125. Ottoman sources also talk of Kalender Çelebi as a spiritual descendant of Hacı Bektaş; for example, see, Peçevi İbrahim Efendi, *Tarîh-i Peçevî*, eds Fahri Ç. Derin and Vahit Çabuk (Istanbul: Enderun Kitabevi, 1980), I: 120. Peçevi introduces Kalender Çelebi as such: '*Ḥācī Bektaş-ı Velī evlādından yaᶜnī Ḳadıncıḳ Ana'dan burnı ḳanı ṭamlasıyla nefes oğlı olan Ḥabīb Efendi evlādından ol ṭāᵓifenüñ iᶜtiḳādı mucebince Ḳalender ibni İskender ibni Bālım Sulṭān ibni Resūl Çelebi ibni Ḥabīb Efendi'dür.*'
74. Remzi Gürses, *Hacıbektaş Rehberi* (Ankara: Sanat Matbaası, 1964), 44, cited in Suraiya Faroqhi, 'The Tekke of Hacı Bektaş: Social Position and Economic Activities', *International Journal of Middle East Studies* 7 (1976), 185; and Ahmed Rıfᶜat, *Mirātü'l-Maḳāṣıd fī Defᶜi'l-Mefāsid* (Istanbul: İbrāhīm Efendi Maṭbaᶜası, 1293/1876), 189. Aso see, Yürekli, *Architecture and Hagiography*, 35–36.
75. BA.MD.31:218 (12 Cemaziye'l-evvel 985/1577), cited in Bekir Kütükoğlu, *Osmanlı-İran Siyâsî Münâsebetleri (1578–1612)* (Istanbul: Istanbul Fetih Cemiyeti, 1993), 11.
76. Faroqhi, 'Conflict, Accommodation', 173–174.
77. Yürekli, *Architecture and Hagiography*, 43, 98.
78. Köprülü, 'Abdāl', 376–378; also see Suraiya Faroqhi, 'Seyyid Gazi Revisited: The Foundation as Seen through Sixteenth and Seventeenth-Century Documents', *Turcica* 13 (1981), 92.
79. Ahmet Refik, *Onaltıncı Asırda Rafızîlik ve Bektaşilik* (Istanbul: Muallim Ahmet Halit Kitabhanesi, 1932), 32, doc. no. 42.
80. BA.MD.73: 302: 681 (19 Zi'l-kaᶜde 999/1591), cited in Yürekli, *Architecture and Hagiography*, 46.
81. *Evliya-Seyahatnâme*, 3: 12.
82. Reflective of these persisting tensions are the jokes and humorous stories circulating among the Bektashis (*Bektaşi Fıkraları*), which often poke fun at the conservative Sunni ulema. For examples, see Battal Pehlivan, *Alevi-Bektaşi Fıkraları: Derleme* (Istanbul: Alev Yayınları, 1993); for a study of

Bektashi jokes from this perspective, see Jonas Svendsen, 'Bektaşi Demiş: Orthodox Sunni, Heterodox Bektasian Incongruity in Bektaşi Fıkraları', (PhD diss., The University of Bergen, Bergen, 2012).

83. For example, sixteenth-century Ottoman historian Hoca Sa[c]deddin Efendi writes, '*ve ba*[c]*żı melāḥide nisbet-i kāẓiyye ile ona intisāb da*[c]*vasın iderler.*' *Tācü't-Tevārīḫ*, II: 410.
84. Faroqhi, 'Conflict, Accommodation', 179.
85. '*Memālik-i maḥrūse-i şāhānemde vāḳ*[c]*i baba ve abdāl ve dervīş ve sulṭān nāmiyle elsine-i nāṣda meẕkūr nażargāh ve tekye ve hānḳāh ve zāviyelerde* . . .' Quoted from a document dated Zi'l-hicce 1143/1731, in appendix to Ulusoy, *Hünkâr Hacı Bektaş*, doc. no. 1. The original document is in the private archives of the Çelebi family.
86. Köprülü, 'Abdāl', 384.
87. *Noyan-Bektâşîlik*, 5: 266.
88. Karamustafa, *God's Unruly Friends*, 74–75.
89. Abdülbâki Gölpınarlı is the first scholar to direct attention to the commonly shared miracle motifs in both hagiographies. Gölpınarlı, *Yunus Emre: Hayatı*, 57.
90. *Velâyetnâme*-Duran, 638–641; cf. *Menāḳıb*-Turkish, fols 74a–74b.
91. *Velâyetnâme*-Duran, 85–86; cf. *Menāḳıb*-Turkish, fols 164b–165b.
92. *Velâyetnâme*-Duran, 314–321; cf. *Menāḳıb*-Turkish, fols 43b–46a.
93. *Velâyetnâme*-Duran, 90, 58; 293, 313, 322; cf. *Menāḳıb*-Turkish, fols 17a–17b; 42b–43a.
94. Although the Bektashi tradition asserts that the order took its final shape, as we know it today, under Balım Sultan, Karamustafa argues that 'classical' Bektashi institutions had emerged only by the seventeenth century with the fusion of various 'renunciatory' dervish groups, among them the Abdals, the Haydaris and the Qalandaris, under the Bektashi umbrella. Karamustafa, 'Ḳalenders, Abdâls, Hayderîs', 121–129.
95. For a list of Alevi *ocak*s, see Ali Yaman, *Kızılbaş Alevi Ocakları* (Istanbul: Elips Kitapları, 2006). For Koyun Abdal, see Muzaffer Doğanbaş, ed., *Koyun Baba Velâyetnamesi* (İstanbul: Dört Kapı, 2015); for Ali Baba, see Saim Savaş, *Bir Tekkenin Dini ve Sosyal Tarihi: Sivas Ali Baba Zaviyesi* (Istanbul: Dergâh Yayınları, 1992).
96. '*Şāhuñ ôlādına iḳrār édenler / Ṣūfīler, ġāzīler, abdāllar oldı.*' *Şah İsmail Hatâ'î Külliyatı*, eds Babek Cavanşir and Ekber N. Necef (Istanbul: Kaknüs Yayınları, 2006), 225, poem no. 110. In another version of this couplet, the 'Ṣūfīs' are replaced by the 'Aḫīs'. Shah Isma[c]il Hata[ɔ]i, *Il Canzoniere di Šāh Ismā*[c]*īl Ḫaṭā*[ɔ]*ī*, ed. Tourkhan Gandjeï (Naples: Istituto Universitario Orientale, 1959), 15, poem no. 13. For the *ġāzī* background of the Safavids, see also Michel M. Mazzaoui, 'The Ghāzī Background of the Safavid State', *Iqbāl Review* 12, no. 3 (1971): 79–90.
97. '*Urūm abdālları ṣidḳi ḥaḳıçün/ Ḫorāsān pīrleri lütfi ḥaḳıçün . . . Kebūl ét bu du*[c]*ānı yā ilāhī.*' *Şah İsmail Hatâ'î Külliyatı*, 661–662 couplets no. 159, 170.

98. This observation was made earlier by Irène Mélikoff, 'Hatayî', in *Uluslararası Folklor Ve Halk Edebiyatı Semineri Bildirileri: 27–29 Ekim, 1975* (Konya: Konya Turizm Derneği Yayınları, 1976), 317. The question of the authenticity of poems referring to Hacı Bektaş attributed to Shah Isma[c]il is also dealt with in Ibrahim Arslanoğlu, *Şah İsmail Hatayî ve Anadola Hatayîleri* (Istanbul: Der Yayınları, 1992), 248. Arslanoğlu argued against Sadeddin Nüzhet Ergun who earlier treated such poems that he found in Alevi manuscripts as authentic. Sadeddin Nüzhet Ergun, *Hatayî Divanı: Şah İsmail-i Safevi, Hayatı ve Nefesleri* (Istanbul: Maarif Kitaphanesi, 1956), 24–25.
99. '*Paşa Aġazāde Meḥmed [c]an evlād-ı Ḥācī Bektaş Velī, ḳaddesa'llāhu sırrahu'l-celī ve'l-ḫafī, 2 Teşrīn-i s̱ānī sene 20.*' Bisâtî (?), *Şeyh Sâfî Buyruğu*, ed. Ahmet Taşğın (Rheda-Wiedenbrück: Alevi Kültür Derneği Yayınları, 2003), fol. 27b; a shorter version of the same note without the date is also found on fol. 17b.
100. Meshedikhanim Ne[c]met, *Azerbaycan'da Pirler* (Sosyal-İdeolojik İktisadi-Siyasi Merkezler) [in Cyrillic alphabet] (Baku: Azerbaycan Dovlet Neşriyyatı Polikrafiya Birliyi, 1992), 57–63.
101. Morimoto, 'An Enigmatic Genealogical Chart', 154.
102. Ne[c]met, *Azerbaycan'da Pirler*, 58.
103. Ne[c]met, *Azerbaycan'da Pirler*, 63.
104. *Evliya-Seyahatnâme*, 4: 193.
105. *Evliya-Seyahatnâme*, 4: 209.
106. *Evliya-Seyahatnâme*, 4: 205.
107. *Evliya-Seyahatnâme*, 4: 218.
108. Yürekli, *Architecture and Hagiography*, 62–63.

4

A Transregional Kizilbash Network: The Iraqi Shrine Cities and their Kizilbash Visitors

'. . . how relatively easy it was for a widely flung faith to sustain a network of interlocking and interrelating communities with a shared sense of identity and purpose.'

– Alistair McGrath, *A History of Defending the Truth*[1]

A rapidly diminishing number of members of the Alevi community can still remember *dede*s' visits to Karbala, or at least hearing stories about them.[2] According to oral testimonies, some *dede*s were making the journey to Karbala to have their *ocak*'s genealogical charts (A. *shajara*s; T. *şecere*s) updated until as late as the mid-twentieth century. While these testimonies offer little detail on the exact itineraries of these journeys, gaps in them can now be filled thanks to the recently surfaced Alevi documents of Iraq origin. These include primarily *ziyāretnāme*s and *ḫilāfetnāme*s in Turkish, and *shajara*s in Arabic, spanning the second half of the sixteenth century and the late nineteenth, respectively recording the *dede*s' visits to the Shiᶜi/Alevi sacred sites in Iraq, certifying their attachment to the convent in Karbala and confirming their *sayyid* descent. Collectively they point to some intimate and relatively routinised relations between the Kizilbash/Alevi *ocak*s – specifically those of Wafaᵓi background in eastern Anatolia that this work focuses on – and a web of *sayyid* families and Sufi convents in the Iraqi shrine cities.

This hitherto little recognised transregional Kizilbash network linking the Kizilbash/Alevi *ocak*s in Anatolia to a group of evidently pro-Safavid *sayyid* and Sufi circles in Iraq, while surprising at first sight, becomes more explicable when one keeps in mind the region's critical position in the Ottoman–Safavid rivalry. Beginning in the early sixteenth century, Iraq became a militarily and ideologically contested zone between the two empires. Although the Ottomans and the Safavids agreed to put an end to fighting and to accept each other's legitimacy under the Treaty of Amasya in 1555, several more wars occurred along the Iraqi frontier prior to the Treaty of Kasr-ı Şirin in 1639. Since the end of Akkoyunlu rule in the region in 1508, Iraq was mostly under Ottoman control except for the two prolonged intervals, 1508–1534 and 1624–1638, when it was politically dominated by the Safavids.[3] Besides the region's geopolitical importance as a buffer against the rival Ottomans and its large Shiᶜi population, Iraq had additional significance for the Safavids due to its shrine cities, including Najaf, Karbala, Samarra and Kazimiyya, that housed the tombs of the kinsfolk of the Prophet Muhammad.[4] These shrines, also honoured and patronised by the Sunni Ottomans, would become key sites of the ideological competition between the two empires.[5]

Many records in the *mühimme defterleri* preserved in the Ottoman archives reveal Iraq to be one of the main targets of Kizilbash persecutions during the late sixteenth century, suggesting an extensive presence of pro-Safavid elements in the region even when under Ottoman rule.[6] Safavid influence was particularly strong in the shrine cities that largely remained outside the direct control of Baghdad, the regional capital of Ottoman political and military administration. Real power in these holy cities rested in the hands of a network of *sayyid* families who both held the office of *naqib* as a hereditary right and oversaw the administration of the generously endowed shrines. The Ottoman central authorities suspected the shrines in Karbala and Najaf to be retreats for pro-Safavid groups,[7] and dispatched orders for the punishment of a number of '*seyyid*s, *nakīb*s, and *mütevellī*' at the peak of the second wave of Kizilbash persecutions during the second half of the sixteenth century.[8] Sympathisers of the Safavid/Kizilbash cause were not confined to the shrines' personnel or nearby Sufi residents, however; they also included members of the local Ottoman bureaucracy, such as Hoca Selman (Ḫoca Selmān), a large fief holder (*zuᶜemādan*), and a certain Süleyman who was a translator in the council of the local governor in Baghdad (*Baġdād dīvānında tercümān*).[9] No similar *official* documentation from the post-sixteenth-century era exists that ascertains the continued presence of pro-Safavid elements in Iraq, but this, by itself, is not proof of their total eradication. On the contrary, the *beylerbeyi* of Baghdad reported in 1577 that there was 'no end to the heretics and misbelievers' (*bed mez̲heb ve rāfiżīnin nihāyeti olmayup*) in his region,[10] making it more likely that Iraq remained home to a significant number of groups and individuals affiliated with the Safavid order and/or actively promoting the Safavid cause.

The picture of Iraq as a Kizilbash stronghold is thrown into further relief by an intriguing fact concerning the Safavid governors of Baghdad. At least two of them concurrently carried the title of *khalīfat al-khulafā*, meaning that they also functioned as deputies of the Safavid shahs in their capacities as Sufi masters.[11] One may deduce from this that Iraq during the two intervals when it was under Safavid rule served as an important communication zone between the Safavids and the Kizilbash/Alevi communities in Anatolia. Could it be, then, that a network of pro-Safavid *sayyid*s and Sufis in the 'bridge zone' of Iraq served as liaisons between the Safavid shahs and their followers in Anatolia, even when the former were not politically in charge of the region? Alevi documents of Iraq origin argue for the likelihood of this scenario, and help to reconstruct the inner workings of this transregional Kizilbash network. Links between the *ocak*s and certain Sufi convents in Iraq, as brought to light by the Alevi documents, also have direct implications for the interlocking histories of the Kizilbash/Alevi communities and the Abdal/Bektashi circles, foundational aspects of which were discussed in Chapter 3. They most importantly reveal a previously unrecognised dimension of the symbiosis between the two groups centred on a cluster of convents in Iraq that emerge as Bektashi-affiliated in later sources, including first and foremost the convent in Karbala, a clear hub connecting the two milieus together.

Bektashi Convents in Iraq: An Overview

There were a dozen or more Bektashi convents in Iraq that had survived into the early twentieth century.[12] These convents fell into two groups based on their location. The first group consisted of those situated inside the shrine complexes of the Shi^{c}i imams: that of Imam Husayn in Karbala, Imam ^{c}Ali in Najaf, Imam Musa al-Kazim in Kazimiyya and Imam Hasan al-^{c}Askari in Samarra. The second group comprised those that were structurally independent of any major Shi^{c}i sanctuary, including the convents of Gürgür Baba and Hızır İlyas in Baghdad, and those in and around the region of Kirkuk. Another important Bektashi convent in Iraq, whose exact location I could not determine, is called Şahin Baba in the Alevi documents; this could have been a separate convent in Baghdad or its suburb of Kazimiyya, or just another name for the Hızır İlyas convent.

Available evidence concerning the origins of the individual Bektashi convents is unfortunately sparse and sketchy. It appears, however, that only some of these convents were created after the establishment of the Ottoman rule in the area and were Bektashi-affiliated from the beginning. Among these are: the Gürgür Baba convent, the convent in Kazimiyya, presumably the ones in and around Kirkuk and possibly the one in Samarra. The origins of the rest of the convents are much less straightforward, especially those in Karbala and Najaf, and the Hızır İlyas convent in Baghdad, which were evidently set up before the Ottomans and inhabited by dervishes affiliated with such groups as the Abdals and the Hurufis who were distinct from the Bektashi order but would in time be absorbed by it.

While the details of the initial spread of Bektashi dervishes in Iraq and the Bektashi-zation of the convents in the second group are hard to reconstruct in any satisfactory manner, we are able to trace the presence of individuals in the region with some sort of a Bektashi affiliation as far back as the early seventeenth century. The earliest evidence of dervishes in Iraq associated with the memory of Hacı Bektaş is a letter that comes from the family archives of the *ocak* of Dede Kargın. It appears to have been written in 1624 following the (re)conquest of Baghdad by the Safavid shah, ᶜAbbas I.[13] Composed in Turkish, the letter was sent to Seyyid Yusuf, a member of the *ocak* of Dede Kargın, relaying as good news the Safavids' victory in Baghdad. The letter, additionally, informs its addressee of a ritual of initiation that was carried out in his name and of a *ḫilāfetnāme* that would subsequently be put together and sent for him via a certain Sevindik Sufi. What is of particular relevance for us here is the identity of the sender of the letter, Seyyid Baki, who was apparently a Sufi based in a convent in Iraq, presumably the Karbala convent; he signed his name as a descendant of Hacı Bektaş (*Bende-i Şāh-ı Velāyet, Seyyid Bāḳī, Evlād-ı Ḳuṭbüʾl-ᶜĀrifīn Sulṭān Ḥācī Bektaş-ı Velī*).[14]

The *Seyāḥatnāme* of the seventeenth-century Ottoman traveller Evliyaʾ Çelebi and the travelogue of the German traveller and scientist Carsten Niebuhr, who visited the region a little over a century after Evliyaʾ in the second half of the eighteenth century, constitute the next oldest sources that speak of Bektashi dervishes and convents in Iraq.[15] Together they confirm an entrenched Bektashi presence in different parts of Iraq during the seventeenth and eighteenth centuries. Despite a temporary interruption caused by the abolition of the Bektashi order in 1826, some of the Bektashi convents in the region were later revived, with the one in Karbala in particular remaining functional well into the twentieth century. Two works from the early twentieth century, ᶜAli Suᶜad's *Seyāḥatlerim* and A. Rıfki's *Bektaşī Sırrı*, are particularly informative about the state of Bektashi convents in Iraq during this period.[16] Little documentation exists concerning the fate of the Iraqi Bektashis and their convents after the middle of the twentieth century, by which time *dede*s' trips to Iraq had also come to a permanent halt.

Alevi *dede*s were clearly selective in their associations with the (would-be) Bektashi convents in Iraq: the itineraries of their visits to the region included only the convents in Karbala and Najaf, and the Şahin Baba convent. The convent in Karbala, in particular, appears to have had a central importance for them as all the Alevi documents originating from Iraq, except those granted by the local *naḳībü'l-eşrāf* (Ar. *naqīb al-ashrāf*), were obtained or renewed at this convent. Both types of document were then also ratified by dervishes from the other two convents. Given their particular significance for the purposes of the present discussion, a closer and individual look at these Sufi convents in Iraq is in order.

Sufi Convents in Iraq that Were Part of the Kizilbash/Alevi Network

The Convent in Karbala

The tomb of Husayn, 'the martyr of martyrs' in the view of Shiᶜi-ᶜAlid groups, had long been a leading site for the display of love and grief for the Family of the Prophet (*Ahl al-bayt*), but it was after the tenth century that pilgrimage (Ar. *ziyāra*; Ot. *ziyāret*) to Husayn's shrine, as to those of other Imams and their descendants, was to become institutionalised with established ritual protocols that came to be codified in special guides.[17] Visiting the shrines of the descendants of the Prophet was not an exclusively Shiᶜi tradition, however; it also formed a key component of the religious life of many Sufis. It is, therefore, not surprising to find Sufi convents in and near these shrine complexes. These convents functioned as lodges for dervishes who spent part or most of their lives at these holy sites, while also offering accommodation for visitors. The convents in question, and more generally the shrine cities, were therefore spaces where *sayyid*s and different types of Sufis and dervishes commingled presumably more intensely than anywhere else.

The Karbala convent, located in the courtyard of the tomb complex of Imam Husayn, was one such space that operated both as a Sufi convent and as a guesthouse for pilgrims to the shrine (Figure 4.1). It was also the focal point for the Kizilbash/Alevi *dede*s visiting Iraq and the source of many documents preserved in the private archives of the *dede* families. Its endowment deed (Ot. *vaḳfiyye*; Ar. *waḳfiyya*) shows it to be a convent affiliated with the Abdals of Rum in the mid-sixteenth century. The existence of Alevi documents from about the same period composed in Turkish supports this finding. The earlier Alevi documents, however, make only general references to the dervishes residing in the shrine complex of Imam Husayn, identifying them as '*tekkenişīn-i Imām Ḥüseyin*' without specifying any order affiliation.[18] Its sixteenth-century endowment deed likewise refers to it as the 'Ḥusayniyya' convent, in reference to the adjacent tomb of Imam

Figure 4.1 The Karbala convent (Kerbela Dergâhı) in the shrine complex of Imam Husayn, Karbala-Iraq, circa late nineteenth century. Original in the archive of the first Albanian American Bektashi Teqe in Detroit, Michigan

Source: Photograph received via Hüseyin Abiba.

Husayn, noting that it was also known as the *maydān* (Ot. *meydān*). The earliest instance of the convent in Karbala being identified as Bektashi is in an *ḫilāfetnāme* granted to an Alevi *dede* on 20 Cemaziye'l-ahir 1170/1757 (on which more later). The same convent appears in the archival records from the nineteenth century onwards as the ᶜAbdülmüᵓmin Baba convent (ᶜAbdüᵓl-müᵓmin Baba Zāviyesi),[19] and is referred to in Arabic and German sources from the early twentieth century simply as the convent of the *dede*s (*dadawāt*), in both cases with an explicit Bektashi identification.[20]

Part of the explanation for these ambiguities and shifts in naming must lie in the convent's special location where a convent (*zāwiya*) existed as early as 1326–1327 when Ibn Battuta visited Karbala.[21] While we lack data from the intervening years, the Sufi convent in Imam Husayn's shrine complex apparently came to be dominated by the Abdals of Rum soon after the Ottoman conquest of the region. Its aforementioned endowment deed, recorded under the name of the convent of ᶜAbdülmüᵓmin Dede in the archives, demonstrates this point. Originally composed in Safar 962/1554, during the reign of Sultan Süleyman, aka Kanuni (the Lawgiver), the endowment deed states that a certain Sadık Dede came to the region at an unspecified date with his belongings, his men and his children, settling near the Sulaymaniyya River with permission from the local authorities. One can infer from context that Sadık Dede was assigned a plot of a land in freehold (*temlīk*) on the condition that he develop it. According to the deed, Sadık Dede endowed his entire estate and everything on it, including two houses with all the items and animals in them, for the upkeep of his disciples and children and their children, as well as to the married or celibate Abdals of Rum and (other?) dervishes from Anatolia residing in the 'Ḥusayniyya' convent, but not the Abdals from Persia (*ᶜAcem*). Two points grab one's attention here: an explicit reference to 'married or celibate' Abdals and the explicit exclusion of the Persian Abdals from the groups who could benefit from the income of the endowment, points to be returned to later. Furthermore, the endowment deed stipulates that the future trustee of the foundation would be the most mature of the children of Sadık Dede who would be responsible for spending the income from the endowment for the benefit of the visitors to the tomb of Imam Husayn as well as the aforementioned residents of the convent.[22]

The Karbala convent seems to have acquired an explicit Bektashi identity no later than the early eighteenth century, most likely in tandem with the Abdals' full assimilation under the Bektashi umbrella. In a letter written to A. Rıfki by an Ottoman bureaucrat, named Hazım Agah, who served in Iraq in the 1880s and 1890s, the convent in Karbala is described as belonging to the 'Abdals of Rum, meaning the Bektashis' (*Rūm Abdāllarına, yaᶜnī Bektaşilere maḫṣūṣ*).[23] The conflation of the two identities as such vouches for the gradual shift in the convent's affiliation from Abdal to Bektashi. The Babagan Bektashis, likewise, refer to this convent as both the convent of the Abdals of Rum (Tekke-i Abdâlân-ı Rum) and as the Müᵓmin Dede convent (Müᵓmin Dede Dergâhı), further reinforcing the proposed gradual Bektashi-isation.

Unlike the Çelebis, who seem to have no memory of the Karbala convent, the Babagan Bektashis count the Karbala convent among the four major Bektashi convents (*dergâh*s) where the initiation ritual for the celibate dervishes (*mücerred erkânı*) was carried out in the past.[24] This trajectory of the Karbala convent supports the idea that the Abdals, when they finally did so, integrated specifically into the Babagan wing of the Bektashi order.[25] This does not, however, mean that the Karbala convent was necessarily the exclusive domain of the (celibate) Abdals prior to its Bektashisation, or that of the Babagans afterwards. The ambiguity of the term '*evlād-ı . . Ḥācī Bektaş-ı Velī*' that is used in the aforementioned letter dated 1634, which can signify both biological or spiritual descent, and by extension an affinity with either of the two branches of the Bektashiyye, is the first piece of evidence that needs to be taken into account here. Even more telling is the earlier noted reference to 'celibate as well as married Abdals'. This curious phrase of 'married Abdals' might well be a reference to the Çelebi Bektashis. It is possible, therefore, that the celibate Abdals/Babagans might have wrested exclusive control of the Karbala convent only after a period of cohabitation, possibly in the post-Safavid era, by ousting from the convent the 'married Abdals'. Such a setup, if true, might also help to explain why some Alevi *dede*s came to appeal to the Çelebis rather than the Babagans after the transregional Kizilbash network that connected Anatolia to Iraq was disrupted.

Further details of the Babagan Bektashi tradition concerning the Karbala convent are found in ᶜAli Suᶜad's *Seyāḥatlerim*, which records a conversation between the author and ᶜAbdülhüseyin Dede, the last *postnişin* of the convent who served in the early twentieth century. According to ᶜAbdülhüseyin Dede, the convent in Karbala was founded about 500 years ago by a Bektashi shaykh named ᶜAbdülmüᵓmin Dede, hence its name. The famous poet Fuzuli attached himself to this shaykh, serving under him in the post of *çerāğcı* (candle lighter), and both are said to be buried on the convent's grounds.[26] The Babagan Bektashis also claim that ᶜAbdülmüᵓmin Dede met with the contemporary Ottoman sultan, identified as Sultan Süleyman. ᶜAbdülmüᵓmin Dede, it is said, went to Iraq sometime about the mid-sixteenth century and began spreading the Bektashi order while living in a tent near the tomb of Imam Husayn. During their encounter ᶜAbdülmüᵓmin Dede reportedly asked Sultan Süleyman to build canals to transfer water from the River Euphrates into Karbala. The sultan complied, with difficulties in the construction process being overcome by ᶜAbdülmüᵓmin Dede's prayers, adding to his fame and to the spread of the Bektashi order.[27] This Babagan Bektashi tradition appears to have a historical basis to it when compared with the endowment deed of the Karbala convent. We can indeed assume that ᶜAbdülmüᵓmin was another name for Sadık Dede, given that Sultan Süleyman indeed visited the tomb of Imam Husayn during his military expeditions to the region at about the same time when Sadık Dede was there and did have canals dug to bring water into Karbala, even though there is no sign in non-Bektashi sources of Kanuni's encounter with a Bektashi dervish or an Abdal.[28] The aforementioned, rather unusual injunction in the deed explicitly excluding the Abdals from Iran as beneficiaries of Sadık Abdal's endowment may likewise be read as an indirect indication of the Ottoman rulers' patronage of the convent and of their acuity in keeping it free of pro-Safavid elements.

Be that as it may, it is evident from the Alevi documents that the central government's efforts on that front were not entirely effective. This was owing to the fact that the shrine cities functioned as autonomous entities under the local *sayyid* families and were thus mostly shielded from external interference. Meir Litvak in his study of the ulema of Najaf and Karbala during the Ottoman period describes these local *sayyid* families as having formed a religious elite distinct from both the Sunni and the Shiᶜi ulema in Iraq whose power rested on their control of the shrines and the local post of the *naḳībü'l-eşrāf*.[29] An example in point is the famous Darraj (Darrāj) family of Karbala; individual members of this family (as understood from their family epithet) make multiple appearances in the Alevi documents, beginning in the early seventeenth century, both as keepers of the shrine of Imam Husayn and as local *naḳībü'l-eşrāf*s.[30] In their latter capacity, individuals from this family issued *shajara*s for Kizilbash/Alevi *dede* families that contain their signatures and seals. One such *shajara* is dated Muharrem 1196/1781, and additionally bears the signatures and seals of two witnesses identified as Mehmed Dede from the Bektashi convent (most likely the convent in Karbala) and Halil Dede from the Bektashi convent in Baghdad (most likely the Şahin Baba convent).[31] Another Alevi document, dated Safar 1263/1847, appears to be a combination of the *ziyāretnāme*, *shajara* and *ḫilāfetnāme* genres, and was likewise granted by a *naḳībü'l-eşrāf* with the family name Darraj, and was similarly signed off as witnesses by the *postnişīn*s of the Karbala and Şahin Baba convents. As local notables, the same *sayyid* families also served in other official capacities. Such was the case, for instance, with the Milali (Milālī) family in Najaf whose members not only functioned as keepers of the shrine of Imam ᶜAli but also as governors of Najaf and as tax-farmers.[32] The religio-political dominance and relative autonomy of the local *sayyid*s would largely diminish, however, starting in the 1830s, when the government in Istanbul reasserted its imperial control in the provinces as part of a broader trend towards centralisation. During this process the Ottoman state sought to undermine the power base of the local *sayyid* families by replacing them with members of the Sunni and Shiᶜi ulema as keepers of the shrines and as local *naḳībü'l-eşrāf*s.[33]

After 1826, when the Bektashi order was abolished and many Bektashi convents were destroyed, the convent in Karbala remained untouched, apparently for fear of adverse popular reaction because it was structurally part of the shrine of Imam Husayn. It was, however, taken away from the Bektashis and its endowment was partially confiscated. Later, during the reign of Sultan ᶜAbdülmecid (r. 1839–1861), the convent was revived by a certain Taki Baba.[34] A record in the archives dated 22 Cemaziye'l-ahır 1265/1859 confirms that Seyyid Mehmed Taki Dede was officially appointed as the keeper (*zāviyedār*) of the ᶜAbdülmüᵓmin Baba convent.[35] The availability of Alevi documents issued at the Karbala convent from the same period suggests that, despite some possible temporary interruptions, relations between the convent and the *dede*s from Anatolia continued. In one such Alevi document, Mehmed Taki Dede is given the title *postnişīn*,[36] and in another, dated 28 Muharrem 1265/1848, he is additionally identified as the son of Seyyid Ahmed Dede,[37] who other documents from the 1840s indicate was the previous *postnişīn* of the convent in Karbala.[38] Evidently, at least in the period under consideration, the position of the *postnişīn* at the Karbala convent was inherited within the same family, and Mehmed Taki Dede was already serving in that capacity before his official appointment as the keeper of the convent. After Taki Dede died on 26 Muharrem 1316/1898, his son Seyyid ᶜAbbas was officially installed in his position. Two years later, when Seyyid ᶜAbbas also died on 3 Rebiᶜü'l-evvel 1318/1900, leaving behind four young children in the convent, Selim Dede was officially installed to serve until the son of Seyyid ᶜAbbas, Seyyid Hüseyin, came of age.[39] It is most likely that Seyyid Hüseyin was ᶜAbdülhüseyin Dede with whom ᶜAli Suᶜad had long conversations in the second decade of the twentieth century. He appears to have remained *postnişīn* of the Karbala convent until his death in Mashhad in 1948.[40] Given the absence of Alevi documents issued or ratified at the Karbala convent after the middle of the twentieth century, one can safely date the permanent disruption of connections between the *ocak*s in Anatolia and the Karbala convent to the death of Seyyid Hüseyin at about the same time.

It is interesting to note that ᶜAli Suᶜad identified ᶜAbdülhüseyin Dede as a Naqshbandi shaykh while still acknowledging the Bektashi affiliation of the Karbala convent. This is because, like the other Bektashi convents, the one in Karbala was officially handed over to the Naqshbandi order after 1826. Indeed, archival records reveal that Seyyid ᶜAbbas was appointed as its keeper, on the condition that he practice the rites of the Naqshbandiyya in the convent ('*mez̲kūr zāviyedārlık cihetini āyīn-i Naḳşbendiyye icrā . . . olmak üzere*'). Taki Dede also appears in the official records as a member of the Naqshbandiyya order (*ṭarīḳat-ı ᶜaliyye-i Naḳşbendiyyeden es-Seyyid Meḥmed Taḳī Dede*).[41] There is little doubt, however, that this official requirement had little significance in practice and that the dervishes at the Karbala convent continued their attachment to the Bektashi path, as demonstrated by all other available sources from the twentieth century that identify the convent, and the dervishes residing there, as Bektashi affiliated.[42]

The Convent in Najaf

It is once again Ibn Battuta who offers us the first testimony of a Sufi convent in the vicinity of Imam ᶜAli's burial site in Najaf, which was apparently in existence as early as in the early fourteenth century.[43] After Ibn Battuta, the next earliest sources to make references to this convent in Najaf are the Alevi documents. These speak of the dervishes residing in the convent simply as '*tekkenişīn-i Necefü'l-Eşref*' or '*tekkenişīn-i İmām ᶜAlī*' in reference to the convent's location, which was structurally attached to the adjacent shrine as was the case with the Karbala convent. The only clue to the order affiliation of the dervishes residing at the convent prior to its Bektashi-sation comes from the alternative name given to it in twentieth-century Bektashi sources, according to which the convent was also known as the Virani Baba convent (Virani Baba Dergâhı)[44] after the famous Hurufi/Bektashi poet of the late sixteenth century and early seventeenth who reportedly served for a period as the convent's *postnişīn*.[45] Iraqi historian ᶜAzzawi confirms this association, noting that the turban of Virani Baba was preserved in this convent and treated with much respect as late as the early twentieth century.[46]

An alternative narrative for the origins of the convent in Najaf is offered by Hazım Agah, whose letter to A. Rıfki was mentioned above. Agah alleges that the convent in Najaf was founded and assigned to the celibate Bektashi dervishes by the Ottoman sultan Selim I (r. 1512–1520).[47] It is, however, difficult to bear out Hazım Agah's claim, since it was under Sultan Süleyman that Iraq really became a part of the empire, despite an earlier military expedition that was carried out in the region during the reign of Selim I. Hazım Agah notes the existence of some verses in Persian inscribed above the door of the convent praising the Bektashiyye and affirming the convent's Bektashi affiliation as evidence; yet he fails to address the dating of this inscription, which may well be of more recent origin than he assumed.[48] We can thus posit, with due caution, that the convent in Najaf had been affiliated in some form or another with the Hurufiyye prior to the latter's merger with the Bektashi milieu. Such a picture also parallels the evident trajectory of the convent in Karbala whose Abdal heritage was in time submerged within the Bektashi identity.

The convent in Najaf, like the one in Karbala, was not physically destroyed after 1826, although its endowments were partially confiscated. During the reign of ᶜAbdülmecid (r. 1839–1861), Sükuti Baba revived it and served as its *postnişīn* until his death, after which the governor of Baghdad, Namık Paşa, reportedly took the convent from the Bektashis and appointed someone of Indian origin (some kind of a Sufi?) to administer it.[49] Namık Paşa was governor of Baghdad twice, with his first tenure in 1851 lasting less than a year and his second tenure covering seven years from 1861 to 1868. It was most likely during his second term that Namık Paşa removed the Bektashis from the convent, although it is not known for what purpose the convent building was used after this date. At any event, this incident seems to have marked the end of the Alevi *dede*s' contacts with the convent in Najaf, given the absence of Alevi documents after this date bearing the signature of dervishes associated with it.

The Şahin Baba Convent/The Hızır İlyas Convent

The Şahin Baba convent, located in Baghdad, was one of the three Bektashi convents in Iraq – along with those in Karbala and Najaf – regularly visited by the Alevi *dede*s. With the exception of Hazım Agah's letter mentioned above, its name is only encountered in Alevi documents. An additional Bektashi convent that was likewise located in Baghdad was called Hızır İlyas. There is, however, confusion as to whether Şahin Baba and Hızır İlyas were one and the same convent, or two separate structures.

Judged by Hazım Agah's description of its location, Şahin Baba seems to be the same convent as Hızır İlyas, both located on the shores of the River Tigris in western Baghdad.[50] The latter appears in Ibn Battuta's early fourteenth-century travelogue as a convent (*zāviya*) housing dervishes who were caretakers of a nearby hermitage (*inziva kulübesi*) associated with Hızır İlyas.[51] Evliyaᵓ Çelebi's seventeenth-century *Seyāḥatnāme* speaks of it as '*tekye-i Ḥażret-i Ḫıżır İlyās*'. Other sources similarly call it the Hızır İlyas convent,[52] while one source designates it simply as the convent of *dede*s in Baghdad.[53] The Hızır İlyas convent was originally constructed as a *ribāṭ* in the twelfth century, and had been known as the *ribāṭ* of Selçuki Hatun, in reference to the nearby tomb of the wife of the ᶜAbbasid caliph al-Nasir who was also a daughter of the Seljuk sultan, Kılıçarslan I. It was later used as a convent and was finally converted into a Bektashi convent sometime after the establishment of Ottoman rule in the region. While the exact date of this transformation is not known, in view of Evliyaᵓ Çelebi's description of it as a Bektashi convent, it must have taken place sometime before the mid-seventeenth century.[54] A different type of affirmation of the site's acquired Bektashi affiliation is a local tradition kept alive into the modern period, which holds the site of the convent to be Hacı Bektaş's burial place.[55] This tradition, while hard to substantiate historically, is nonetheless significant as a sign of a well-entrenched Bektashi presence in and around the convent. The Hızır İlyas convent was closed down in 1826, but its building was preserved for use as a religious school.[56] Next to it was built a mosque by the same name during Davud Paşa's governorship of Baghdad from 1817 to 1831.[57] According to Uluçam, a major flood of the Tigris ruined the building in 1831,[58] but considering that on 7 Muharrem 1304/1886 a certain Ahmed Efendi was assigned there as *müderris* to give religious instruction according to the teachings of the Hanafi school of jurisprudence (*mezheb*; Ar. *madhab*), the building must have continued to be utilised even after the flood.[59]

On the other hand, some doubt is cast on the co-identity of the two convents by an Alevi document dated Muharrem 1259/1843, which was signed (among others) by a certain Zeynal Dede (Zeynāl Dede) who is described both as the keeper (*türbedār*) of the Şahin Baba convent and a resident of Baghdad, and as the custodian (*emīn*) of the tomb of Imam al-Kazim ('*Şāhīn Baba Dergāhıʾnda türbedār Dede Zeynāl, sākin-i medīne-i Baġdād ve emīn-i İmām Kāẓım*').[60] The first point to be noted here is the incongruency between the document's composition date of 1843 and our lack of evidence that the Hızır İlyas convent was reopened after 1826. Furthermore, the double duty of Zeynal Dede as keeper of the Şahin Baba convent and as the custodian of the tomb of Imam Kazim raises the possibility that the former might have been located not inside the city of Baghdad but near the tomb of Imam Musa al-Kazim in Kazimiyya, where the shrines of Imam Musa al-Kazim and Imam Muhammad al-Jawad are located.[61] There was indeed a Bektashi convent in the courtyard of the shrine complex of Imam Masa al-Kazim, but according to Hazım Agah it was built in 1299/1881 and hence could not have been the same convent where Zeynal Dede served as custodian a few decades earlier. All in all, while there is no doubt that Şahin Baba was a convent in Baghdad, its exact location remains an open question.

Other Bektashi Convents in Iraq: An Internal Rift?

Besides the three (would-be) Bektashi convents that appear in the Alevi documents on a regular basis, which evidently served as important nodes of the transregional Kizilbash network, there were others in Iraq that seem to have been linked to the Bektashi order from the beginning; these, however, were evidently avoided by the Alevi *dede*s during their visits to Iraq.

Of the convents that were not part of the Kizilbash network, two were located in or near the shrines of Imams in Samarra and Kazimiyya. The former is described by Noyan in connection with the shrine complex of Imam Hasan al-ᶜAskari (İmâm Hasan-ül-Askerî Âstânesi), suggesting that its building was within or near the same complex.[62] Evliyaᵓ Çelebi, without explicitly mentioning the existence of a convent, writes of Bektashi dervishes residing around the sanctuary (*maḳām*) of Imam Mahdi and living off the donations of visitors.[63] Imam Mahdi's sanctuary is likewise located in Samarra near the tombs of Imam al-ᶜAskari and Imam al-Naki. Judged by reports that the sixteenth-century Bektashi poet ᶜAskeri from Edirne (Edirneli Askeri) served for a while at this convent as *postnişīn*, the convent in Samarra must have been founded before or soon after the establishment of Ottoman rule in the region.[64] There was also a convent in the courtyard of the shrine complex of Imam Musa al-Kazim in 1299/1881 in Kazimiyya, as mentioned above. Interestingly, however, its construction was sponsored by Mirza Farhad, the uncle of the Iranian shah, Nasr al-Din, in the name of Hacı Hüseyin Mazlum Baba who had earlier revived the Gürgür Baba convent. Hüseyin Mazlum Baba subsequently appointed a celibate Bektashi dervish by the name Seyyid Veli to head this convent, the latter serving in that capacity until he died in 1313/1895. Hazım Agah claims that after this date the convent was taken over by some Iranians and Arabs and that all of the items in it were looted.[65] But according to Noyan, Selman Cemali Baba, a well-known celibate Bektashi dervish of Albanian origin who apparently was still alive in the early twentieth century, served as *postnişīn* of the convent in Kazimiyya.[66] If this is true, then the convent must have remained operational for some time after Sayyid Veli.

Perhaps the most important Bektashi convent outside of the shrine cities, as well as the Kizilbash network, was that of Gürgür Baba, whose history is best known of all the convents considered here. Although situated in Baghdad, it took its name from a dervish who is believed to have worked miracles in connection with the oil reserves in Kirkuk, which are apparently so close to the surface in some places that they can spontaneously break into flames. One such spot in Kirkuk was given the name of this otherwise unknown dervish, suggesting that he was either originally from Kirkuk or that he at least spent some time in that region.[67] According to ᶜAzzawi, Gürgür meant 'the shining one' (Ar. *nūrānī*), a nickname that must have its origins in Gürgür Baba's miracles involving these oil reserves.[68]

The Gürgür Baba convent and the adjacent mausoleum of its namesake were located in the Maydan district of central Baghdad. The mausoleum was built in 1670 by al-Haj Muhammad al-Daftari b. ᶜAbdullah, who also created an endowment for its upkeep. The Daftaris were a leading Baghdadian family whose members served in the higher echelons of the local Ottoman bureaucracy.[69] Sources give slightly differing accounts concerning the founding dates of the convent and the mosque next to it known by the same name. Abdüsselâm Uluçam suggests that the convent was built by the same individual at the same time as the tomb, but was later converted into a mosque following the abolition of the Bektashiyye in 1826.[70] On the other hand, according to Iraqi historians, al-Haj Muhammad al-Daftari was the patron of both the tomb and the mosque, and it was after his death that the site was turned into a Bektashi convent. We also learn from them that, in line with the conditions established in the endowment deed, the trusteeship (Ot. *tevliyet*; Ar. *tawliyya*) of the endowment was later handed over to the kadi of Baghdad when all of the biological heirs of al-Haj Muhammad al-Daftari died out.[71]

The Gürgür Baba convent was closed down after 1826, but later revived by Hacı Hüseyin Mazlum Baba who had been encouraged to go to Iraq by the contemporary Bektashi *postnişīn* Türabi Dedebaba.[72] Darraji informs us that Dede Hüseyin b. Ahmed b. Mustafa was appointed as the trustee (Ot. *mütevellī*; Ar. *mutawallī*) of the Gürgür Baba convent on 19 Ziᵓl-hicce 1297/1880 by the mufti and deputy kadi of Baghdad.[73] Hüseyin Mazlum Baba was a member of the Babagan branch of the Bektashiyye and, considering that Noyan referred to him as 'Laz Hüseyin Baba', was most likely originally from the Black Sea region.[74] Before settling at the Gürgür Baba convent, he served for seven years as the *ḳahveci* (lit. server of coffee) in the Najaf convent under *postnişīn* Sükuti Baba. He died in 1302/1884 and was buried in the courtyard of the tomb complex of Imam Musa al-Kazim.[75] Shortly before his death in 1300/1882, Hüseyin Mazlum Baba was removed by the kadi of Baghdad from his post as *mütevellī*, and after his death all the Bektashi dervishes were forced out of the Gürgür Baba convent. In his place a Naqshbandi shaykh named ᶜAbdurrahman Efendi from Karadağ[76] was appointed as *mütevellī* and *müderris*, after which the building of the convent was used as a religious school.[77]

Gürgür Baba's probable hometown of Kirkuk itself was the site of a number of Bektashi convents. According to Noyan, there were fifteen Bektashi convents in the region of Kirkuk. ᶜAzzawi also mentions one Bektashi convent in Kirkuk named Merdan ᶜAli and another in the nearby region of Daquq named Caᶜfer Dede; this latter was apparently operational until at least the mid-twentieth century.[78] After mentioning the convent of Merdan ᶜAli in Kirkuk, ᶜAzzawi states that in the regions of Talafar and Sinjar there were also people similarly from the group of *babas* (Ar. *babawāt*) but does not provide further details on the subject. We can deduce from this statement that the Bektashis in Kirkuk were also known as the *babas*. This conclusion acquires greater interest in view of ᶜAzzawi's description of the convent in Karbala, and of another author's referral to the Hızır İlyas convent, as the convent of the *dedes* (Ar. *dadawāt*). While it would be misguided to make broad generalisations solely on this basis, this differentiation in terminology coupled with the apparent selectiveness with which the *dedes* associated with the Bektashis in the region can well be an indication of two distinctive Bektashi groups in Iraq that appealed to different clientele, presumably with dissimilar political inclinations within the framework of the Ottoman–Safavid conflict. However, further research is needed before anything definitive can be said regarding this supposed rift between different Bektashi groups within Iraq, as well as their relations with one another and the Bektashis in Anatolia and the Balkans.

Dedes' *Visits to Iraq*

To the extent reflected in the Alevi documents, the Kizilbash/Alevi *dedes*' periodic visits to Iraq had three related purposes. One was pilgrimage to sacred Shiᶜi/Alevi sites. We gather this from the *ziyāretnāmes* that have survived in the *dede* families' private archives. While some of these *ziyāretnāmes* are exclusively in narrative form, others include, or consist primarily of, illustrations of places visited (Figure 4.2). In both cases, they bear the signature and the seal of individuals who self-identify as *sayyid* and/or *dede*, and who were residents of the shrine complex of Imam Husayn or the adjacent convent. The narrative type of *ziyāretnāmes*, in particular, is characterised by an introduction that highlights the importance of visiting the tombs of the Twelve Imams and other saints, and subsequently supplies a list of sites their grantees visited in order to fulfil this religious obligation. The earliest and most detailed of the available *ziyāretnāmes* that has surfaced so far is dated Muḥarrem 995/1548 and was earlier (in Chapter 2) cited with respect to its receiver's Wafaᵓi background. The name of the receiver – presumably one of the ancestors of the Malatya-based *ocak* of Şeyh Süleyman in whose family archives the document is preserved – was Dervish Hasan b. Dervish Aşık. According to the itinerary included in the *ziyāretnāme*, Dervish Hasan made dozens of stops at the Imams' shrines and other holy sites associated with various saintly and prophetic figures in Najaf, Karbala, Samarra, Kazimiyya,

Figure 4.2 A section of a *ziyāretnāme* with illustrations dated 1259/1843. Original in the private archive of Abuzer Güzel Dede, member of the *ocak* of Ağuiçen from the village of Kurudere, Bulam-Adıyaman

Source: Photograph by Laine Stump, Adıyaman, 2002.

Kufa, Hilla and Baghdad, and performed the appropriate rites and rituals at each place.[79]

Another purpose of these visits, the one that is typically emphasised in the Alevi oral tradition, was the periodic renewal and confirmation of the *dede* families' *shajara*s as documentation of their *sayyid* descent. This process could take different forms. In some cases, the travelling *dede* would bring along an older document, typically a *shajara*, as proof of his family's *sayyid* genealogy, and have it copied at the Karbala convent with the addition to the genealogical chart of the younger male members of the family. This new, updated copy would then be notarised as authentic by one or more of the dervishes of the Karbala convent and of those at the convent in Najaf and the Şahin Baba convent, as well as by the local *naḳībü'l-eşrāf*. In the absence of an older document, that is, if the older *shajara* were lost or destroyed, a *dede* could also prove his noble pedigree by the written or oral testimonies of at least two witnesses. Such was the case, for instance, with Bektaş Dede from the *ocak* of Sinemilli who, as previously mentioned in Chapter 2, visited Karbala from the province of Maraş in the year 1207/1792 with two other *sayyid*s in his company. The two *sayyid*s testified to Bektaş Dede's descent from the family of the Prophet and his reputation as such in the community, and also vouched for Bektaş Dede's claim that his family's written *shajara* was lost.[80]

The significance for the *ocak* families of having written *shajara*s in their possession was manifold. To better understand this point, it is important to look further into the details of Bektaş Dede's trip to Iraq and its aftermath. A point of particular interest in this regard is that Bektaş Dede obtained two separate documents attesting to his *sayyid* descent while in Iraq. One of these was a relatively brief and plain official note (Ot. *teẕkere*; Ar. *tadhkara*) from the local *naḳībü'l-eşrāf*, Murtada al-Musawi al-Husayni, certifying Bektaş Dede's *sayyid* genealogy. The other one was a longer *shajara* written on a highly ornamented scroll that was additionally signed and stamped by Haydar Dede from the convent in Karbala and by ᶜAbdülgafur Dede from the convent in Najaf (Figures 4.3 a, b, c).[81] Although with varying levels of detail, both of these documents charted and affirmed Bektaş Dede's pedigree reaching back to the Prophet and were written in Arabic; the only meaningful difference between them was that the former was ratified solely by the local *naḳībü'l-eşrāf*, while the latter was also signed by two dervishes residing at the Karbala and Najaf convents.

The question is: why did Bektaş Dede need two documents that seemingly served the same purpose? Some useful pointers that help to answer this question are provided in other documents preserved in the *ocak*'s family archive. These show that, upon his return from Iraq, Bektaş Dede

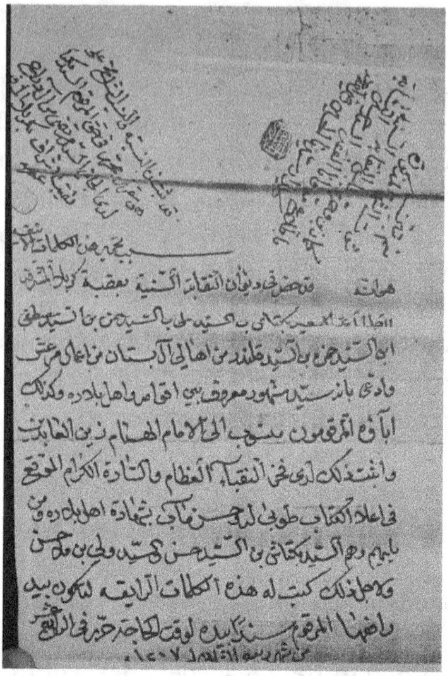

Figure 4.3a Official note (Ot. *tezkere*; Ar. *tadhkara*) dated 1207/1792 verifying *sayyid*-ship issued by the local *naḳībü'l-eşrāf* in Karbala. Original in the private archive of (Küçük) Tacim Bakır Dede, member of the *ocak* of Sinemilli from the village of Kantarma, Elbistan-Maraş

Source: Photograph by the author, Maraş, 2002.

submitted the short official note from the *naḳībü'l-eşrāf* to the kadi courts in Maraş and the nearby subprovince of Darende to have himself officially recorded as a *sayyid*. This was no doubt to ensure the recognition of the family's prophetic descent by local authorities, which would allow them to benefit from the tax-related privileges accorded to their status. At least as important, however, was the confirmation of the family's *ocakzade* status in the eyes of the Kizilbash/Alevi community itself, which must have required something more than a mere certificate of *sayyid*-ship, namely an endorsement and authorisation by the Karbala convent.[82] Therein must lie the explanation for the double documentation: the short and plain note from the *naḳībü'l-eşrāf* of Karbala was clearly meant for the attention of the official Ottoman authorities, more specifically the local kadi courts, while the long, ornamented scroll – also signed and sealed by dervishes from the Karbala and Najaf convents – was intended exclusively for internal consumption. The latter as such must have served as documentation for the family's *ocakzade* status within the Kizilbash socio-religious hierarchy.

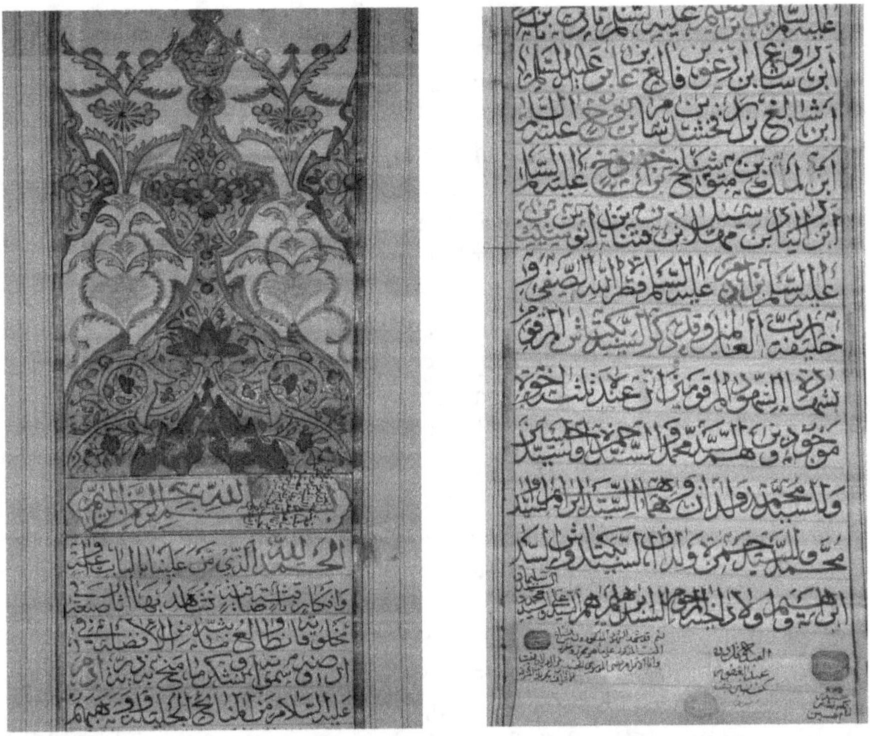

Figures 4.3b and 4.3c The two ends of a scroll that comprises a written genealogy (Ot. *şecere*; Ar. *shajara*) dated 1207/1792 verifying *sayyid*-ship issued by the local *naḳībü'l-eşrāf* in Karbala, and authenticated by dervishes at the Bektashi convents in Karbala and Najaf. Original in the private archive of (Küçük) Tacim Bakır Dede, member of the *ocak* of Sinemilli from the village of Kantarma, Elbistan-Maraş

Source: Photograph by the author, Maraş, 2002.

There is yet another interesting detail concerning the story of Bektaş Dede that deserves attention. Shortly before his visit to the kadi courts in Darende and Maraş, Bektaş Dede apparently deemed it necessary to acquire a fatwa (Ot. *fetvā*) from the local mufti that would affirm that an official note from a *naḳībü'l-eşrāf* attesting to one's *sayyid*-ship would be valid.[83] This seemingly redundant fatwa acquires significance in the context of the imperial government's intensifying attempts to monitor claims of *sayyid*-ship from the middle of the seventeenth century onwards. From 1658 to 1695, an unprecedented five general inspections were carried out with the ostensible goal of weeding out the imposters, or *müteseyyid*s, that had allegedly penetrated the ranks of true *sayyid*s through forged genealogies. Given that the most comprehensive of these inspections coincided with the prolonged and costly wars with the Habsburgs (1683–1699), fiscal emergency was probably a major driving force behind the imperial government's increased vigilance against alleged usurpers of the title of *sayyid.* Hülya Canbakal has shown that these inspections focused primarily on regions with a high concentration of Kizilbash/Alevi communities and nomadic populations; indeed, the highest number of *sayyid*s who lost their green turbans were from the province of Sivas, one of the strongholds of Kızılbashism/Alevism, both in the past and in modern times.[84] Thus, judged by the geographical distribution of data, it may well be that the escalated official surveillance of (pseudo-)*sayyid*s targeted in particular those of suspected Kizilbash affinity, or at least was applied to them with special vengeance. A further, indirect evidence validating this inference comes from imperial orders dispatched to the provincial authorities urging them not to recognise any *sayyid* genealogies that were issued or certified by somebody other than the *naḳībü'l-eşrāf* in Istanbul. The impact of this measure must have been felt particularly strongly by the Kizilbash/Alevi *dede*s whose *shajara*s were obtained almost invariably from the local *naḳībü'l-eşrāf* in Karbala rather than the one in the imperial capital. It is, therefore, entirely possible that Bektaş Dede sought this fatwa and submitted it to the kadis in Darende and Maraş along with his *shajara* issued in Karbala, lest the latter was dismissed in accordance with the imperial orders to only recognise *shajara*s issued in Istanbul. That Bektaş Dede's appeal to the local *mufti* bore fruit is a measure of the limited effect that the imperial orders had in overruling provisions of shariᶜa law in at least certain locales, as well as the successful strategising of the Kizilbash/Alevi *dede*s within the given parameters of the Ottoman system.

Besides pilgrimage to ᶜAlid shrines and the acquisition and/or updating of *shajaras*, another purpose of *dede*s' trips to Iraq was to procure a written authorisation from the Karbala convent, which many *ocak*s in eastern Anatolia viewed as their spiritual centre. This took the form of Sufi diplomas, or *ḫilāfetnāmes*, that were granted to the *dede*s by the dervishes at the Karbala convent. The earliest reference to this practice is in the above-mentioned letter from 1624 that was sent to the *ocak* of Dede Kargın to inform its recipient, Seyyid Yusuf, of a *ḫilāfetnāme* that was put together in his name. Since the actual *ḫilāfetnāme* is missing, however, we cannot tell anything certain about its content, including the order in whose name it was issued. All extant *ḫilāfetnāmes* that were issued at the Karbala convent, at least the three examples that this author had access to, date from a period when the convent had already taken on an unambiguous Bektashi identity. The first part of these *ḫilāfetnāmes* reads much like a *ziyāretnāme* both in content and in language but differs on two significant points. First, while the *ziyāretnāme*s generally refer to the shrine complex (*āsitāne*)[85] of

Imam Husayn, the *ḫilāfetnāmes* specifically mention the Bektashi convent (*tekke*) located in that complex. Second, the *ḫilāfetnāme*s also indicate the holder's acceptance into the order and his appointment as *ḫalīfe* following the completion of the necessary services and rituals in that convent.

The oldest available example of the *ḫilāfetnāmes* originating from the Karbala convent comes from the *ocak* of Kızıl Deli based in Malatya and is dated 20 Cemaziye'l-ahır 1170/1757. Written half in Arabic and half in Turkish, it was issued in the name of Dervish ᶜAli Dede, who is identified in the text as *aşçı* (cook) at the Bektashi convent located in Karbala (*Kerbelāʾ-ı muᶜallāda vāḳiᶜ olan Ḥācī Bektaş-ı Velī –ḳuddise sirruhuʾl-ᶜazīz– tekyesinde*), to record his initiation into the path of the saints (*ṭarīḳ-i evliyāʾ*) and the subsequent conferral on him, along with the *ḫilāfetnāme* document, of a set of fixed paraphernalia signifying his order affiliation (*yedine ṣofra ve çerāġı ve zeng [ve] tīġ ve ᶜalem ve icāzet ve ināyet virildi ve ḫalīfelik ṣafā-naẓar ve himmet olundı*). The *ḫilāfetnāme* bears the seal of Şeyh Mehmed Dede, who is described as a dervish residing in the shrine complex of Imam Husayn (*tekyenişīn-i İmām Ḥüseyin*) in the main text and as the head cook of the Karbala convent (*aşçıbaşı Kerbelāʾ-ı muᶜallā*)[86] in his signature. The document was also ratified by other dervishes from the same convent, by ᶜAli Dede from the convent in Najaf (*tekyenişīn-i Bektaşī fīʾn-Necefüʾl-eşref*) and by İsmaᶜil Dede from the Şahin Baba convent (*tekyenişīn-i Şāhīn Baba*). This *ḫilāfetnāme* also happens to be the oldest document that has surfaced to date in which the three convents in question appear with an explicitly Bektashi identity.[87]

Unlike the *ḫilāfetnāme* belonging to the *ocak* of Kızıl Deli, the other two *ḫilāfetnāmes* that have reached us are briefer and written exclusively in Turkish; they also contain no indication that their grantees served in any specific capacity or for any prolonged period of time at the Karbala convent. One of these two *ḫilāfetnāmes* comes from the *ocak* of Imam Zeynel Abidin and, although undated, must have been composed sometime in the 1780s.[88] The other one comes from the *ocak* of Sinemilli and was granted to the above-mentioned Seyyid Bektaş in 1792.[89] We gather from their texts that these *ḫilāfetnāmes* were granted solely upon the one-time completion of certain specific rites according to set conventions involving ritual slaughter and the subsequent cooking of a ritual meal, a financial donation and the *çerāġ* (candle), without requiring any long-term service at the convent.[90]

All extant *ḫilāfetnāmes*, as already noted, postdate the Bektashisation of the Karbala convent. Despite that, intriguingly, a comparison of the *ḫilāfetnāmes* at the Karbala convent with the *icāzetnāme*s conferred on the Alevi *dede*s by the Çelebi Bektashis reveal a noteworthy difference in terms of content: the *icāzetnāme*s in the latter group include a chain of initiation tracing back to Ahmed Yesevi, eponym of the Yesevi order, which we don't find in the *ḫilāfetnāme*s issued at the Bektashi convent in Karbala. While establishing a connection between this and the debates concerning the original order affiliation of Hacı Bektaş, that is whether he was a Wafaʾi or a Yesevi dervish, would probably amount to an over-interpretation of data, we can at the very least surmise that the Karbala and Kırşehir convents used two different textual conventions to compile Bektashi diplomas. Another noteworthy difference between the two types of Bektashi diplomas is the time period they cover: All the *icāzetnāme*s granted by the Çelebis in Kırşehir that have surfaced so far are from the nineteenth and twentieth centuries and are thus of more recent origin than the *ḫilāfetnāme*s and other documents issued at the Karbala convent.[91] This affirms that the Alevi *ocak*s' relations with the Bektashi convents in Iraq predated their connections to the Çelebis, which, in turn, lends further credence to the belief common among the Alevi *ocak*s in central and eastern Anatolia that their affiliation with the Çelebis is of relatively recent origin.

Relations between Sayyids and Sufis in Iraqi Shrine Cities and Kizilbash/Alevi **Dedes** *in Anatolia: A General Assessment*

While the exact nature of the relationship between the *sayyid*s in charge of the shrine cities and the dervishes residing in the nearby convents eludes us, that it was a close one is indisputable. This point is validated by the Alevi documents discussed above, in particular *shajara*s, bearing the signatures and seals of individuals from both groups. Dozens of other such documents exist in the private archives of Alevi *dede* families that demonstrate that individuals from the two groups acted as authorities in granting written *sayyid* genealogies to the *dede*s and as witnesses testifying to the documents' truthfulness.

Outside of the context of these documents, the *sayyid*s and the Sufi dervishes seem to have also worked together and shared personnel in the day-to-day management of the shrines. For example, I noted above that a certain Zeynal Dede served both as the *türbedār* of Şahin Baba and as the *emin* of the shrine of Imam Musa al-Kazim. Sources also reveal that the shaykhs of the Karbala convent fulfilled the function of the *çerāġcı* for the entire shrine complex of Imam Husayn within well-established ritual conventions. The protocol of the *çerāġ* ritual is reported by ᶜAbdülhüseyin Dede in his conversation with ᶜAli Suᶜad as follows: every day before the evening prayers, the shaykh of the convent would go with the special *çerāġ* in his hand to the tomb of Imam Husayn. The *sayyid*s (presumably keepers of the shrine) waiting for the shaykh at the gate would light their candles from the flames of this *çerāġ* before following the shaykh into the tomb, where they would place the candles on candlesticks and pray. No lighting would be allowed in the complex before the completion of this ritual.[92] ᶜAbdülhüseyin's testimony is largely confirmed by the aforementioned undated *ḫilāfetnāme* from the *ocak* of Imam Zeynel Abidin. Most likely composed towards the end of the eighteenth century, the *ḫilāfetnāme* details the journey of a Kizilbash/Alevi *dede* by the name of Seyyid İbrahim from Malatya to Iraq where he first visited the sacred sites in and around Baghdad, before Halil Dede from the convent of Şahin Baba joined him to go to Najaf and then to Karbala. At the Bektashi convent in Karbala, Seyyid İbrahim carried out all the rituals expected from a *ḫalīfe*, including apparently the *çerāġ* ceremony largely fitting that described by ᶜAbdülhüseyin Dede.[93]

The most obvious conclusion to be drawn from all these pieces of evidence is the existence of some deeply rooted and interlocking webs of *sayyid* and Sufi circles connecting Anatolia to Iraq, whose inception most likely predated the Safavids' rise to power, but that later came to serve as conduits of Safavid influence. A clear case in point here are the Wafaᵓi-cum-Kizilbash *ocak*s of Iraq origin discussed in Chapter 2 who must have sown the early seeds of this transregional network and maintained its vitality over generations through ongoing contacts with the shrine cities in that region, particularly Karbala. In time, this network was probably further expanded and reinforced via new connective threads spun by such dervish groups as the Abdals of Rum in tandem with their assimilation into the Kizilbash milieu. It is also possible that Iraq progressively assumed a greater significance as a bridge between the Safavid shahs and the Kizilbash/Alevi communities due to Ottoman state efforts to prevent border crossings into Persia, thereby disrupting direct lines of communication between Anatolia and Ardabil. Whatever the case may be, the persistence of this network long after the demise of the Safavids helps to explain the resilience of the Kizilbash identity down to modern times. It was only through the course of the nineteenth century, when the policies of the Ottoman state undermined the powerbase of the local *sayyid* families and abrogated the institutional identity of the convents, that this long-standing transregional network began to lose its vibrancy and eventually collapsed. This, in turn, heralded a process whereby the Kizilbash/Alevi milieu gradually lost its transregional character and came to be confined largely to Anatolia, a process that would finally be sealed with the establishment of new national boundaries.

Conclusion

Links between the *dede* families in Anatolia and a web of convents and *sayyid* families in Iraq as revealed by Alevi sources suggest that Iraq served as a connective zone between the Safavid shahs and their followers in Anatolia, with the Karbala convent serving as the main intermediary. This conclusion is also supported by the many *mühimme* registers that implicate Iraq, and more generally its shrine cities, as breeding grounds for the partisans of the Kizilbash movement. While the roots of this transregional Kizilbash network are to be found in some well-entrenched Sufi and *sayyid* circles whose inception predated the Safavids, the network itself clearly came to function as a channel of Safavid influence following the assimilation of these circles and their lay following into the Kizilbash milieu. The process of assimilation no doubt entailed the submergence of the latter's earlier Sufi affinities under the Safavid spiritual leadership, which also explains why the Alevi documents obtained at the Karbala convent consistently obscure the order affiliation of the dervishes ratifying them. It was only after the mid-eighteenth century, when the Safavids had already become a story of the past, that these dervishes and their convents came to recast their identities and identify themselves as Bektashi.[94]

Notes

1. Alister McGrath, *A History of Defending the Truth: Heresy* (New York: HarperCollins Publishers, 2009), 75.
2. Parts of this chapter are derived from my article 'The Forgotten Dervishes: The Bektashi Convents in Iraq and Their Kizilbash Clients', *International Journal of Turkish Studies* 16, nos 1 & 2 (2011): 1–24.
3. For a history of Iraq under Ottoman rule, see Stephen Hemsley Longrigg, *Four Centuries of Modern Iraq* (Oxford: Clarendon Press, 1925). On Ottoman-Safavid competition in the region, see Rudi Matthee, 'The Safavid-Ottoman Frontier: Iraq-ı Arab as Seen by the Safavids', in *Ottoman Borderlands: Issues, Personalities and Political Changes*, eds Kemal H. Karpat and Robert W. Zens (Madison: Center for Turkish Studies, University of Wisconsin, 2003), 157–173.
4. For details, see Matthee, 'The Safavid-Ottoman Frontier'.
5. A notable instance of this rivalry involved replacing the Persian carpets in the shrines of Imam ᶜAli and Imam Husayn with carpets from Anatolia in 1571; see C. H. Imber, 'The Persecution of the Ottoman Shīᶜites according to the *mühimme defterleri*, 1565–1585', *Der Islam* 56, no. 2 (July 1979), 246; and Cemal Şener, *Osmanlı Belgelerinde Aleviler-Bektaşiler* (Istanbul: Karacaahmet Sultan Derneği Yayınları, 2002), 64–65.

6. Imber, ‘Persecution’, 246; Kütükoğlu, *Osmanlı-İran Siyârî Münâsbetleri* (1578–1612) (İstanbul: Istanbul Fetih Cemiyeti, 1993), in particular the introduction.
7. For a report submitted to the imperial *dīvān* in 1573 that people in these shrines were suspected of receiving stipends from the Persians, see Imber, ‘Persecution’, 246–247. For a *mühimme* record concerning suspicious individuals from Iran residing in the shrine complex of Imam Musa al-Kazim, see Şener, *Osmanlı Belgelerinde*, 73.
8. Imber, ‘Persecution’, 246.
9. BA.MD.31:142:52 (4 Cemaziye’l-evvel 985/1577) and BA.MD.31:696:313 (15 Receb 985/1577), respectively, both cited in Kütükoğlu, *Osmanlı-İran*, 11 n35; the former also cited by Imber, ‘Persecution’, 248; for further examples and discussion, see Imber, ‘Persecution’, 246–250.
10. BA.MD.31:142:52 (4 Cemaziye’l-evvel 985/1577), cited in Imber, ‘Persecution’, 246; and Kütükoğlu, *Osmanlı-İran*, 11 n35.
11. Following his conquest of Baghdad in 1508, Shah Isma^{c}il appointed Khadim Beg Talish, who bore the title *khalīfat al-khulafā*, as governor (*ḥākim*) of Baghdad. See James J. Reid, *Tribalism and Society in Islamic Iran 1500–1629* (Malibu: Undena Publications, 1983), 85–87, 155; and Roger M. Savory, ‘The Consolidation of Safawid Power in Persia’, *Der Islam* 41 (1965), 77. The next Safavid governor of Baghdad, Zuʾl-Faqar Khan, known for his sending of the city’s keys to the Ottoman sultan, Kanuni, carried the same title. See Joseph von. Hammer-Purgstall, *Geschichte Des Osmanischen Reiches*, 10 vols (1828; reprint, Graz: Akademische Druck-u. Verlagsanstalt, 1963), 3: 142 and footnote f on the same page. For information on the Safavid institution of *khalīfat al-khulafā*, see Roger M. Savory, ‘The Office of Khalîfat al-Khulafâ under the Safawids’, *Journal of American Oriental Society* 85, no. 4 (1965): 497–502; and Willem Floor, ‘The Khalifeh al-kholafa of the Safavid Sufi Order’, *Zeitschrift der Deutschen Morgenlandischen Gesellschaft* 153, no. 1 (2003): 51–86.
12. Works that contain information on the Bektashi convents in Iraq include *Noyan-Bektâşîlik*, vol. 5, *Dergâhlar*; and F. W. Hasluck, ‘Geographical Distribution of the Bektashi’, *The Annual of the British School at Athens* 21 (1916): 84–124. Also important are the following works in Arabic: ^{c}Abbas al-^{c}Azzawi, *Tārīkh al-^{c}Irāq bayna iḥtilālayn*, 5 vols (Baghdad: Maṭba^{c}at Baghdād, 1935–1949); Hamid Muhammad Hasan al-Darraji, *al-Rubuṭ wa al-takāyā al-Baghdādiyya fī al-^{c}ahd al-^{c}Uthmānī (941–1336 h./1534–1917 m.): Takhṭīṭuhā wa ^{c}imāratuhā* (Baghdad: Dār al-Shuʾūn al-Thaqāfiyya al-^{c}Āmma, 2001); ^{c}Uthman bin Sanad al-Waʾili al-Basri, *Maṭali^{c} al-Su^{c}ūd: Tārīkh al-^{c}Irāq min sanat 1188 ilā sanat 1242 h. /1774–1826 m.*, eds ^{c}Imad ^{c}Abd al-Salam Raʾuf and Suhayla ^{c}Abd al-Majid al-Qaysi (Baghdad: al-Dār al-Waṭaniyya, 1991); and Abdüsselâm Uluçam, *Irak’taki Türk Mimari Eserleri* (Ankara: Kültür Bakanlığı, 1989).
13. For the transcribed text and a facsimile of this letter, as well as for its

dating, see my 'Kızılbaş, Bektaşi, Safevi İlişkilerine Dair 17. Yüzyıldan Yeni Bir Belge: Çeviriyazılı Metin-Çeviri-Tıpkıbasım', in 'Festschrift in Honor of Orhan Okay', eds Yücel Dağlı et al., special issue, *Journal of Turkish Studies/Türklük Bilgisi Araştırmaları* 30, no. 2 (2006): 117–130.

14. I have rendered the word '*evlād*' as 'descendant' in the sense of either biological or spiritual descent, although I am inclined to understand it in the former sense given the author's self-identification as a *sayyid*. This is potentially a highly significant nuance to determine whether the Bektashis affiliated with the Karbala convent were linked to the Babagan or the Çelebi branch of the order because the former believe that Haci Bektaş had only spiritual descendants (*yol evladı*), thus denying the Çelebis' claim to be his biological offspring (*bel evladı*).
15. *Evliya-Seyahatnâme*, 4: 256, 4: 359; *Niebuhr-Reise*, 2: 299–300 and table XLIII, 339.
16. ᶜAli Suᶜad, *Seyāḥatlerim* (Istanbul: Ḳanāᶜat Maṭbaᶜası, 1332/1916), also published in the modern Turkish alphabet by N. Ahmet Özalp (Istanbul: Kitabevi Yayınları, 1996), page citations are to this later edition; A. Rıfki, *Bektaşī Sırrı* (Istanbul, 1325–1328/1907–1910), which includes four separate works: the first two are the two volumes of the original work with the same title and by the same author, the third one is a response to it written by Ahmed Cemaleddin Efendi and the fourth volume is a rejoinder by Rıfki.
17. For example, the first extant guide for the visitation ritual of the tomb of Karbala by Ibn Qulawayh (d. 367/977), entitled *Kāmil al-ziyārat*, was written in the tenth century; for this and other information concerning the development of the practice of *ziyāra* to the Imams' shrines, see see May Farhat, 'Islamic Piety and Dynastic Legitimacy: The Case of the Shrine of ᶜAlī B. Mūsá al-Riḍā in Mashhad (10th–17th century)' (PhD diss., Harvard University, 2002), especially 17–19.
18. *Tekkenişīn*, or *tekyenişīn*, literally 'one who dwells in a Sufi convent'. It can also refer to a person in a position of leadership in a particular convent; see *ABS*, s.v. 'Tekkenişin'.
19. VGMA, register no. 166 (Esas 3/1), entry no. 933. There are also records concerning this convent in register no. 816 (Tafsil-i Arabistan), entry no. 287; register no. 888 (Hülasa Defteri), entry no. 1,096; and register no. 419 (Erzurum Asker), entry no. 1,054.
20. ᶜAzzawi, *Tārīkh al-ᶜIrāq*, 5: 152; and Arnold Nöldeke, *Das Heiligtum al-Husains zu Kerbela* (Berlin: Mayer & Müller, 1909), 11.
21. Ebû Abdullah Muhammed İbn Battûta Tancî, *İbn Battûta Seyahatnâmesi*, ed. A. Sait Aykut, 2 vols (Istanbul: Yapı Kredi Yayınları, 2002), I: 313. Also see EI, 'Karbala', 637.
22. The relevant part of the original Arabic-language *vaḳfiyye* (VGMA, register no. 166 (Esas 3/1), entry no. 933), which includes a number of grammatically unclear parts and some spelling mistakes, reads as follows: '*lammā jāʾa mafkhar al-fuqarāʾ wa al-masākīn Ṣādiq Dada li-shuᶜbatihi al-sharqiyya*

al-māʾkhūdha min nahr al-sharīf al-Sulaymānī bi-mālihi wa rijālihi wa awlādihi wa dhālika bi-maʿrifat Muḥammad Bek Nabī-zāda wa bi-mūjib tadhkirat Jaʿfar Bek wa bi-mūjib amr ʿAlī Bāshā – yassaraʾllāh mā yashāʾu – wa-hum Ḥusayn Qulī wa ʿAbbās Qulī wa Pīr Aḥmad Dada wa Walī Dada wa Ḥusayn Dada wa Muḥammad Dada wa Darwīsh ʿAlī wa Ḥusayn Abdāl wa ghayruhum . . . waqafa wa ḥabasa wa taṣaddaqa bi-jamīʿ al-shuʿbatihi al-madhkūra al-maḥdūda bi-ḥudūd arbaʿ. . . bi-jamīʿ ḥudūdihā wa sāyir [sic] ḥuqūqihā wa ahwārihā wa arāḍīhā wa mazāriʿihā wa shuʿabihā wa sawāqīhā wa masāqīhā wa jamīʿ al-baytayn . . . ʿalā awlādihi al-mansūbīn ilayhi bi-al-murīdiyya wa awlādihi wa ʿalā awlādi awlādihi wa hakādha al-kāʾinīn fī takiyatihi al-ḥaḍrat al-sharīfa al-Ḥusayniyya – ʿalā musharrifihā al-taḥiyya – al-musammāt bi-al-Maydān min ʿabādīl [sic] (1) al-Rūm al-mujaraddīn wa al-mutāʾahhilīn wa lā min ʿabādīl [sic] (2) al-ʿAjam [. . .] (3) ʿalā darāwīsh al-Rūm al-ṣunūf al-mujarradīn wa al-mutāʾahhilīn wa yunfiqu al-mutawallī liʾl-waqf maḥṣūl dhālika ʿalā awlād al-mawqūf ʿalayhim wa ʿalā al-mutaraddidīn min zuwwār al-ḥaḍrat al-sharīfa . . .' 1–2). The word '*ʿabādīl*', misspelled with the letter ayn, is clearly used here as the plural of the word '*abdāl*'. 3) We see a two-letter word or suffix here that appears as '*bin*' or '*īn*' but in either case does not make sense. It is possible that 'al-ʿAjamīn' was used as the plural of 'al-ʿAjam', although such a plural does not exist in Arabic.

23. Rıfki, *Bektaşī Sırrı*; the letter is at the end of the second volume from page 150 to page 160.
24. *Noyan-Bektâşilîk*, vol. 5: 266; later this ritual came to be carried out only in the *dergâh* of Hacı Bektaş in Kırşehir.
25. Fuad Köprülü, 'Abdâl', in *Edebiyat Araştırmaları*, 2 vols (1935; reprint, İstanbul: Ötüken Yayınları, 1989), 1: 384.
26. Suʿad, *Seyāḥatlerim*, 88–89. For differing opinions on claims that connect Fuzuli to the convent in Karbala, see Bülent Yorulmaz, 'Kerbela ve Fuzuli'ye Dair', in *I. Uluslararası Hacı Bektaş Veli Sempozyumu Bildirileri* (Ankara: Hacı Bektaş Anadolu Kültür Vakfı, 2000), 371–401.
27. Muhammed Movako, 'Arnavutluk'ta Bektaşi Edebiyatı', trans. Mürsel Öztürk, *Hacı Bektaş Veli Araştırma Dergisi* 10 (Summer 1999): 51–60; the name of the Bektashi dervish is given here as 'Baba Abdüʾl-Mümin'. For a slightly different version, see *Noyan-Bektâşilîk*, vol. 5: 266.
28. Nasûhüʾs Silâhî (Matrâkçî), *Beyân-ı Menâzil-i Sefer-i ʿIrâkeyn-i Sultân Süleymân Hân*, ed. Hüseyin G. Yurdaydın (Ankara: Türk Tarih Kurumu, 1976), 243–250; Longrigg, *Four Centuries of Modern Iraq*, 25. The first water canals to Karbala were constructed during the Mongol-Ilkhanid period. *EI-2*, 'Karbala'; Ahmed Zeki Velidi Togan, *Umumi Türk Tarihine Giriş* (Istanbul: İsmail Akgün Matbaası, 1946), 308. Hazım Agah goes one step further and asserts that Kanuni was the founder of the convent in Karbala, claiming that the *vakfiyye* he saw recorded the Sultan's creation of a major endowment for its upkeep. As noted earlier, however, there is in the VGM

archives a copy of a *vakfiyye* belonging to the convent of ᶜAbdülmüᵓmin Dede, which was composed in Safar 962/1554, during the reign of Kanuni, but it identifies the convent's endower as Sadık Dede.

29. Meir Litvak, *Shiᶜi Scholars of Nineteenth-century Iraq: The ᶜUlemaᵓ of Najaf and Karbalaᵓ* (Cambridge: Cambridge University Press, 1998), Chapter 6. The politically and administratively dominant and autonomous position of the *nakībü'l-eşrāf* in Najaf, which apparently did not have a separate governor, was noted already in the early fourteenth century by Tancî, *İbn Battûta Seyahatnâmesi*, I: 253.
30. Sayyid Darraj, who at the time of the conquest of Baghdad by Shah ᶜAbbas in 1624 was serving both as the keeper of the shrine of Imam Husayn and as the local *nakībü'l-eşrāf* in Karbala, reportedly saved the lives of many Sunnis by registering them as Shiᶜis. Hammer-Purgstall, *Geschichte*, 5: 15, where his name is transcribed as 'Seid Dürradsch'. For the Darraj family and their place in the history of Karbala, see Litvak, *Shiᶜi Scholars*, 125–126; and Muhammad 'Ali al-Qasir, *Buyūtāt Karbalāᵓ al-qadīmah: wa-sharḥ wa-taḥqīq lum'ah tārīkhīyah fī buyūtāt Karbalāᵓ wa-al-Ghāḍirīyah* (Beirut: Muᵓassasat Al-Balāgh Lil-Ṭibāᵓah Wa-al-Nashr Wa-al-Tawzīᶜ, 2011), 128–133.
31. A Turkish translation of this Arabic document was published in Kureyşanlı Seyit Kekil, *Peygamberler ile Seyitleri Secereleri ve Aşiretlerin Tarihi* (Köln, n.d.), 184–185, but with some significant omissions, including the signature of the *nakībü'l-eşrāf* 'al-Sayyid Murtaḍā al-Darrāj'; the original is in FD of Muharrem Naci Orhan, *ocak* of Imam Zeynel Abidin.
32. Litvak, *Shiᶜi Scholars*, see especially 122–125.
33. Litvak, *Shiᶜi Scholars*, Chapters 6 and 7; these local *sayyid* families, rather than the local Shiᶜi ulema, reacted most strongly against the reassertion of Ottoman central authority in Iraq. Ibid., 139.
34. Rıfki, *Bektaşī Sırrı*, 159–160.
35. VGMA, register no. 166 (Esas 3/1), entry no. 933.
36. *Postnişīn*, literally 'one sitting on the [sheep]skin', means the head of a convent; it appears to be in this context a synonym of *tekkenişīn*.
37. See 'Erzincan-İcazetname' in my 'Sinemilliler: Bir Alevi Ocağı ve Aşireti' *Kırkbudak* 2, no. 6 (2006): 19–59; among the ratifiers of this document, dated 28 Muharrem 1265/1848, is 'Meḥmed Taḳī b. es-Seyyid Aḥmed Dede, postnişīn-i İmām Ḥüseyin'.
38. For example, a *ḫilāfetnāme* dated Ziᵓ l-hicce 1258/1843 bears the seal of '*Eş-Şeyh el-Ḥācī Aḥmed Dede, sākin-i Kerbelāᵓ-ı Muᶜallā Ḥażret-i İmām Ḥüseyin*'; in an undated copy of the same document, '*Seyyid Aḥmed Baba*' is cited with his title '*postnişīn*'. The originals of both of these documents are in FD of İzzettin Doğan, *ocak* of Ağuiçen.
39. VGMA, register no. 166 (Esas 3/1), entry no. 993.
40. ᶜAzzawi, *Tārīkh al-ᶜIrāq*, 5: 152.
41. VGMA, register no. 166 (Esas 3/1), entry no. 933.
42. I have recently learned that some descendants of ᶜAbdülhüseyin Dede,

carrying the last name 'Aldadah', currently live in the United States, and one of them orally confirmed to me that the family has always considered itself as affiliated to the Bektashi order. Meanwhile, interestingly, I have also encountered a *dede* family in Anatolia with the last name 'Aldede', which made me wonder of a possible connection with the Aldadahs. Members of the Aldede family, however, have no recollection of an Iraq connection in their own history.

43. Tancî, *İbn Battûta Seyahatnâmesi*, I: 250.
44. Noyan, *Bütün Yönleriyle Bektaşilik*, 5: 298.
45. For more information on Virani Baba, see *Âşık Virani Divanı*, ed. M. Hâlid Bayrı (Istanbul: Maarif Kitaphanesi, 1959).
46. ^{c}Azzawi, *Tārīkh al-^{c}Irāq*, 5: 153; Virani Babaʾs name is given here as '*al-Hāj al-Sayyid Aḥmad Vīrānī Sulṭān*'.
47. Rıfki, *Bektaşī Sırrı*, 159, 154.
48. Rıfki, *Bektaşī Sırrı*, 158.
49. Rıfki, *Bektaşī Sırrı*, 157.
50. Hazım Agah, who does not mention the Hızır İlyas convent as such, describes the location of Şahin Baba as follows: '*Elyevm yeri yurdu belirsiz bir halde olup, Baġdād'ıñ ḳarşı yaḳasında, Dicle nehri kenarında ġayet dilgüşā bir mevḳi^{c}de vaḳtiyle bulunmuş olan Şāhīn Baba dergāhıyla Gürgür Baba dergāhı öyle ^{c}atebāt-ı sa^{c}ādetden ṣaḥn-ı şerīf derūnunda olmadıklarından 1241 vuḳū^{c}ātında taḫrīb edilmişlerse de.*' Rıfki, *Bektaşī Sırrı*, 155.
51. Tancî, *İbn Battûta Seyahatnâmesi*, I: 271.
52. ^{c}Azzawi, *Tārīkh al-^{c}Irāq*, 5: 153; Uluçam, *Irak'taki Türk*, 225.
53. Basri, *Maṭali^{c} al-Su^{c}ūd*, 367.
54. ^{c}Azzawi, *Tārīkh al-^{c}Irāq*, 5:153–154; al-Basri, *Maṭali^{c} al-Su^{c}ūd*, 367 n313; *Niebuhr-Reise*, 2: 299–300, table XLIII; Uluçam, *Irak'taki Türk*, 222, 225.
55. Basri, *Maṭali^{c} al-Su^{c}ūd*, 367 n313.
56. ^{c}Azzawi, *Tārīkh al-^{c}Irāq*, 5: 153–154; al-Basri, *Maṭali^{c} al-Su^{c}ūd*, 367 n313; Uluçam, *Irak'taki Türk*, 225.
57. VGMA, register no. 166 (Esas 3/1), entry no. 597.
58. Uluçam, *Irak'taki Türk*, 222, 225.
59. VGMA, register no. 166 (Esas 3/1), entry no. 597. According to a corrective note added to the record, the real name of this *müderris* was ^{c}Abdurrahman.
60. Zeynal Dede appears as one of this document's ratifiers. The original, which includes a poem in Persian describing a trip to Karbala, is in FD of Abuzer Güzel Dede, the Adıyaman branch of the *ocak* of Ağuiçen.
61. Tancî, *İbn Battûta Seyahatnâmesi*, I: 319.
62. *Noyan-Bektâşîlik*, 5: 54.
63. *Evliya-Seyahatnâme*, 4: 359.
64. *Noyan-Bektâşîlik*, 5: 54.
65. Rıfki, *Bektaşī Sırrı*, 155–157. Mirza Farhad, a maker of tiles, also replaced the tiles in the rest of the shrine complex of Imam Masa al-Kazim with the permission of the Ottoman authorities; see Uluçam, *Irak'taki Türk*, 37 n5.

66. *Noyan-Bektâşîlik*, 5: 54.
67. *Niebuhr-Reise*, 2: 339.
68. ᶜAzzawi, *Tārīkh al-ᶜIrāq*, 5: 103–104.
69. Ibrahim ᶜAbd al-Ghani al-Durubi, *al-Baghdādiyūn: Akhbāruhum wa Majālisuhum* (Baghdad: Dār al-Shuʾūn al-Thaqāfiyya al-ᶜĀmma, 2001), 100–103.
70. Uluçam, *Irak'taki Türk*, 210.
71. ᶜAzzawi, *Tārīkh al-ᶜIrāq*, 5: 104; al-Darraji, *al-Rubuṭ wa al-takāyā*, 94–95. al-Darraji, furthermore, gives detailed information on the architecture of the convent and the adjacent mosque, and provides pictures of their inscriptions, 94–98, 426, 452.
72. Rıfki, *Bektaşī Sırrı*, 151.
73. Darraji, *al-Rubuṭ wa al-takāyā*, 94–95.
74. *Noyan-Bektâşîlik*, 5: 54.
75. Rıfki, *Bektaşī Sırrı*, 151, 154.
76. Ibid.,156; Karadağ was a subprovince of the district of Sulaymaniyya in Iraq.
77. Darraji, *al-Rubuṭ wa al-takāyā*, 95; Rıfki, *Bektaşī Sırrı*, 156.
78. *Noyan-Bektâşîlik*, 5: 267; and ᶜAzzawi, *Tārīkh al-ᶜIrāq*, 5: 154.
79. For the transcribed text and a facsimile of this document, see my '16. Yüzyıldan Bir Ziyaret name' (Yazı Çevirimli Metin-Günümüz Türkçes ne Qeviri-Tıpkıbasım)! In *In Memoriam Şinasi Tekin*, edited by George Dedes and Selim S. Kuru, special issue of the *Journal of Turkish Studies/Türklük Bilgisi Araştırmaları* 31, no. II (2007), 67–79.
80. For the Sinemillis and their family documents, see my 'Sinemilliler: Bir Alevi', document no. 9.
81. Karakaya-Stump, 'Sinemilliler', documents no. 8 and no. 9.
82. Karakaya-Stump, 'Sinemilliler', documents no. 11 and no. 13.
83. Karakaya-Stump, 'Sinemilliler', documents no. 12.
84. Hülya Canbakal, 'The Ottoman State and Descendants of the Prophet in Anatolia and the Balkans (c. 1500–1700)', *Journal of the Economic and Social History of the Orient* 52 (2009): 542–578.
85. *Āsitāne*, literally 'threshold', can refer to the shrine of an important religious personality or to a major dervish convent located adjacent to the shrine of a prominent figure of the order in question; see *TS*, s.v. 'Âstan' by Abdülbâki Gölpınarlı.
86. Dervishes serving in the *aşevi* (kitchen) of the Bektashi convents are called '*aşçı*' (cook), and their head is called '*aşçı baba*', which is most likely the sense in which the word *aşçıbaşı* was used here. *Aşevi* is the most important of the twelve *evs* (lit. house) that make up a major Bektashi convent. See ibid., 'Aşçı' and 'Aşevi'.
87. The original of this unpublished *ḫilāfetnāme* is in FD of Mustafa İyidoğan, the Sivas-Yıldızeli branch of the *ocak* of Kızıl Deli. For a less elaborate example, see my *Sinemilliler*, document no. 10.
88. FD of Muharrem Naci Orhan, *ocak* of Imam Zeynel. The document was ratified by Seyyid Mehmed Dede, the *tekkenişīn* of the Karbala convent, and

by Halil Dede, the *tekkenişīn* of the undated Şahin Baba convent; based on other Alevi documents sealed by the same individuals, we can deduce that this document was composed sometime in the 1780s. The third ratifier of the document was the *tekkenişīn* of another convent in Baghdad ('*ḫādimü'l-fuḳarā' Şeyh İsmāʿīl(?) tekyenişīn-i Bağdād-ı bihişt-ābād*'), but it is not clear which convent is meant here. We do not come across this convent in other documents that are almost always ratified by the *tekkenişīn* of the Najaf convent, in addition to the *tekkenişīn*s of the Karbala and Şahin Baba convents.

89. Karakaya-Stump, 'Sinemilliler', document no. 10.
90. For example, the relevant part in the undated *ḫilāfetnāme* reads as follows: '*Es-Seyyid İbrāhīm Bağdād-ı bihişt-ābād'a gelüp anda vāḳiʿ olan Şāhīn [Baba ve İmām] Mūsā ve İmām Muḥammed el-Cevād – rażiya'llāhu ʿanhumā – Ḥażretleri'niñ ḳabr-i şerīfleriñ ziyāret ve [neẕirlerin edā idüp] ḥaḳīḳatlü Ḫalīl Dede ile beraber İmām ʿAlī – rażiya'llāhu teʿālā ʿanhu ve kerremu'llāhu vechehu – Ḥażretleri'niñ mübārek şerīfleriñ ziyāret idüp ve ḳurbānlarıñ ve neẕirleriñ edā eyledikten soñra Şāh-ı Kerbelā İmām Ḥüseyin – rażiya'llāhu [ʿanhu] – Ḥażretleri'niñ ziyāretlerine müşerref olup baʿdehu tekye-i Ḥācı Bektaş-ı Velī – ḳuddise sirruhu'l-ʿazīziñ – tekyesinde āyīn-i ṭarīkat ve erkān üzere ḳurbānların boğazlayup ve ḫalīfe ḳazanını āyīn-i dervīşān üzere ḳaynadup cümle dervīşāna neẕirlerin virüp ve Ḳırḳbudaḳ çerāğı rūşen idüp ve Seyyidü'ş-şühedā' ve İmām ʿAbbās Āsitāneleri'nde bal mumların yandurup baʿdehu ṭarafımızdan kendine bīʿat ve iẕinnāme vir[ildi].*' The shrine complex of Imam ʿAbbas mentioned in the document is in Karbala near the shrine of Imam Husayn. FD of Muharrem Naci Orhan.
91. For a published example, see Mehmet Akkuş, '19. Asırdan Bir Bektaşi İcazetnamesi', *Tasavvuf* 1 (August 1999): 27–39.
92. Suʿad, *Seyāḥatlerim*, 90.
93. See n90 above.
94. The last Safavid shah, Shah ʿAbbas III, reigned until 1736 and was killed by Nadir Shah in 1740, along with a number of other members of his dynasty.

5

Mysticism and Imperial Politics: The Safavids and the Making of the Kizilbash Milieu

The texts of the heterodox sects make no overt references to sedition and rebellion, yet why is it that members of these sects invariably end up becoming rebels? The cause of rebellion lies in the assembly of large numbers of people.
– Huang Yubian, *Poxie xiangbian*[1]

The Safavids emerged onto the historical scene as a Sufi order of Shaykh Safi al-Din Ishaq (1252–1334) in the town of Ardabil in Iranian Azerbaijan at the height of Mongol/Ilkhanid power. The heads of the order are purported to have engaged strictly in contemplative Sufism within the Sunni fold with no ostensible signs of political activism or Shiᶜism for the first four generations. This religiously normative and politically muted demeanour, combined with their widespread following in regions as far-flung as Azerbaijan, Anatolia and Transoxiana, earned the order the esteem and patronage of many contemporary ruling authorities, including the early Ottomans who would send the Safavi shaykhs yearly donations under the name of *çerağ akçesi* (lit. candle money).[2] The turning point in Safavid history came at about the middle of the fifteenth century. This is when the Safaviyya would be transformed from a conventional Sufi order into a radical religio-political enterprise with messianic overtones that exerted a powerful attraction over people well beyond the limits of its traditional following. This new grouping would be designated – pejoratively by its detractors, and with approbation by its affiliates – as the Kizilbash (T. *Kızılbaş*; P. *Qizibash*).[3]

This chapter offers a revisionist reading of the formative period and nature of the Kizilbash milieu that highlights its pre-Safavid socio-religious underpinnings. It does so primarily in the light of Safavid-related Alevi sources, and by expanding on discussions in the previous chapters concerning the Wafaᵓi origins and Abdal/Bektashi affinities of a large number of Kizilbash/Alevi *ocaks*. I propose that the early Kizilbash milieu, contrary to its conventional perception as a nebulous collection of (Turkmen) tribes, is best thought of as a complex and dynamic network of overlapping dervish and Sufi circles, and sayyid families, all with their own tribal and nontribal clientele, which flourished in late medieval Anatolia and the neighboring regions. This coalition of like-minded dervishes, Sufis and sayyids, who coalesced under the spiritual leadership of the Safavi household, played a constitutive role in the formation of the incipient Kizilbash movement. It is only by recognising such deeply entrenched pre-Safavid roots of Kizilbash-ism that we can come to grips with its socioreligious reality, and be able to explain its remarkable growth and resilience as a collective identity.

The Making of the Safavids' Kizilbash Constituency in Anatolia

The stereotypical narrative of the formative phase of the Kizilbash milieu goes as follows:[4] Junayd, the first shaykh of the order to exhibit political ambitions, laid the foundations of the initial movement during several years of exile in Anatolia following his banishment from Ardabil on orders from the contemporary Karakoyunlu ruler of Azerbaijan, Jihan Shah. It was during this time that Junayd travelled among the Turkmen tribes, many of whom were already disciples of the Safavi order, recruiting supporters for his militant cause. As simple people, whose conversion to Islam was relatively recent and mostly superficial, and whose religiosity was shaped by a mixture of elements from the Sufi form of popular Shiᶜism and pre-Islamic shamanic cults, these uncouth and gullible tribesmen were innately susceptible to Junayd's messianic claims and propaganda. Junayd succeeded in building an organised force of *ġazīs* out of these Turkmen tribesmen who were easily swayed by his crude messianic claims; with their participation he then carried out *ġazāʾ* expeditions against the Christian enclave of Trebizond and the Georgians along the Caucasus frontier. As a sign of his desire to combine in his person both spiritual and temporal authority, Junayd assumed the titles of both 'shaykh' and 'sultan', thereby breaking away from the tradition of his ancestors whose sole preoccupation as genuine Sufis was spiritual and otherworldly matters. When he died during an expedition in the Caucasus, his son Haydar, born into Junayd's marriage with the sister of the Akkoyunlu ruler, Uzun Hasan, succeeded him as the head of the order. Haydar followed in his father's footsteps in pursuing political ambitions under the guise of Sufism. He reinforced the familial alliance between the Safavids and the Akkoyunlu dynasty by marrying Uzun Hasan's daughter, further promoted his father's policy of engaging in *ġazā*ᵓ activities in the Caucasus and like his father died on the battlefield. Haydar was the one to require his followers to wear a distinctive red headgear with twelve folds, known as the *tāj-i Ḥaydarī*, from which the name Kızılbaş, literally meaning 'red-head', was derived. The Kizilbash movement eventually reached its climax and fulfilled its political aspirations with Junayd's grandson, Ismaᶜil. Barely fourteen years old at the time of his coronation, Ismaᶜil had eradicated the power of the Akkoyunlus and the various petty rulers of Iran with the help of his Kizilbash troops who viewed him as nothing less than God. Yet, following his capture of the Akkoyunlu capital Tabriz in 1501, and his subsequent crowning as shah of Persia, he proclaimed Twelver Shiᶜism as the official religion of the new state, thereby, ironically, also marking the beginning of the end of Kizilbash dominance within Safavid domains.

There are several problems with this conventional narrative of the making of the Kizilbash milieu that hinder a clear and accurate understanding of its underlining socio-religious dynamics. The first problem is one of sources, for the standard account of the Safavids' rise to power largely draws on external sources, including chronicles of rival Sunni dynasties and European travellers' accounts.[5] These tend to depict the Kizilbash as zealous fanatics and their mode of religiosity as naïve and unsophisticated. A scandalised tone is often used in these accounts when describing the strong devotion of the Kizilbash armies to the Safavid shahs. For example, one of the best-known sources for the period is *Tārīkh-i ᶜĀlam-ārā-i Amīnī* by Fazl-Allah b. Ruzbihan Khunji, the official Akkoyunlu chronicler and an indignant enemy of the Safavids, who had to flee to Transoxiana following the advent of Shah Ismaᶜil. Like the many Ottoman chronicles after him, Khunji pays tribute to the early shaykhs of the Safavi order as true mystics and aloof from politics, and condemns Junayd and Haydar for their worldly ambitions and alleged claims to divinity, referring to them with terms such as 'despicable devil' (*shayṭān-i ẓalīl*) and 'bandits' (*ashqiyā*), and to their Anatolian followers as 'the ignorant ones of Rūm' (*cuhhāl-i Rūm*).[6] Khunji reports that upon Junayd's death his followers called him 'God' (*ilāh*) and his son Haydar 'the son of God' (*ibn-Allāh*). His followers praised him, saying 'he is the Living One, there is no God but he' (*huwa al-ḥayy lā ilāh illā huwa*),[7] and immediately murdered anybody who spoke of him as dead.[8] The dedication of his followers to the 'Great Sufi' also excited the interest of some European visitors to the early Safavid court who reported observations somewhat similar to those of Khunji, except without the emphatically vilifying tone. For example, according to an oft-quoted anonymous Italian merchant who was in Tabriz in about 1508, the Kizilbash soldiers would go into battle without armour, believing that their master Shah Isma^cil would protect them.[9]

It is rather surprising to see the degree to which some modern historians are inclined to reproduce the biases and superficial perspectives of these external sources in their treatment of the Kizilbash and their religious ideas. Many of them not only fail to subject such outsiders' accounts to sufficient criticism but also tend to filter even internal sources through the same alienating lens. A case in point is the idea of the Safavid shahs' crude pretensions to divinity, which is frequently used to highlight the oddity and eccentricity of the Kizilbash experience. Such claims by Khunji and the like are to a large extent taken at face value, and reiterated by many specialists in the field with additional proofs allegedly found in Shah Ismaᶜil's own poetry. The claim that Shah Ismaᶜil's poems exhibit with unabashed openness his self-view as God incarnate was first put forward by V. Minorsky and later adopted by many others without further testing.[10] Minorsky supports his assertion on the basis of various couplets in Shah Ismaᶜil's *divān* where the poetic voice simultaneously identifies himself with such heroic figures of ancient Persian history as Khusraw, Jamshid and Zohak, while also writing of himself as 'the living Khidr and Jesus, son or Mary', and as 'the pir of the Twelve Imams', as well as, more pointedly, 'God's mystery'.[11] The verses in question are taken by Minorsky as evidence of Shah Ismaᶜil's self-deification, even though the poet's voice shifts radically in other couplets, sometimes within the same poem, taking the form of the conventional self-depreciating discourse of the Sufis; Shah Ismaᶜil writes, for example: 'I am Khataʾi [the Sinner], the Shah's slave full of shortcomings. At thy gate I am the smallest and the last [servant].' Minorsky's misinterpretation of the couplets in question reflects in part his absorption of the biases of the traditional primary sources. At the same time, it also demonstrates his failure to take sufficient stock of the couplets' mystical underpinnings, and, more specifically, of the particular poetic genre utilised in this and similar poems by Shah Ismaᶜil. Known as *devriye* (Ar. *dawriya*), this genre is associated with the mystical notion of *devrān* (Ar. *davrān*) that conceives of creation as a circular process.[12] Shah Ismaᶜil was neither the first nor the last Sufi poet to produce poetry within this genre, which is particularly popular among Alevi-Bektashi poets. Ahmet Karamustafa, correcting related misconceptions in the scholarship, has recently pointed out that 'the verses in which Hatayi seemingly identifies himself as God . . . are really to be read as poetic articulations of monism'.[13]

In addition to its limited and biased source base, traditional scholarship's treatment of the Safavids' rise to power as if it was 'a unique phenomenon' is a product of inadequate contextualisation.[14] Granted, it has long been recognised by specialists in the field that the Kizilbash movement that carried the Safavids to power was, at some level, the cumulative and most effective expression of certain late medieval and early modern trends that had previously given rise to such short-lived religio-political formations as the Sarbidars and the Mushaᶜshaᶜ, who were headed similarly by *sayyid*-Sufi families.[15] However, such messianically tinged religio-political currents are typically associated in the literature with popular Sufism, which was purportedly infused with 'extremist Shiᶜi' ideas during this period. Fortunately, this erroneous belief is now being remedied by a growing body of scholarship showing that messianism had become a rather common feature of Sufi piety by the fifteenth century, pervading elite and popular classes alike, and had gained particular momentum with the approaching end in 1591/1592 CE of the first Islamic millennium. The picture of the Safavids emerging from these recent works is, in fact, more similar to than different from those of other contemporary dynasties insofar as they seem to have operated in the same discursive realm, and competed for control of the same symbolic, human and material resources. Their dynastic ideology – steeped in Sufi notions and imagery, and overlaid with a dose of apocalyptic fervour, as it was, which for a long time was perceived as setting the Safavids apart from their rivals – is now recognised to be very much in tune with the prevailing trends in the post-Mongol Turco-Iranian world and the larger early modern Eurasia. This was a world brimming with amplified millenarian hopes and eschatological predictions of the imminent rise of a universal sovereign as harbinger of the End Times. Many competing sovereigns of this era accordingly staked a claim to the status of sacral kingship, enshrined in the notion of *ṣāhib-ḳırān* (master of the conjunction), which was modelled on such great conquerors as Chingiz Khan and Alexander the Great, and more immediately on Timur, who was the first to adopt that title. *Sāhib-ḳırān* was not an Islamic concept but it would soon assume an Islamic garb with the substitution of Chingizid genealogical claims with claims of ᶜAlid descent, and it would become fortified with millenarian and messianic ideas derived from the Islamic and the larger Abrahamic traditions.[16]

The Safavids' use of the Sufi idiom and institutions in organising their forces, and their promotion of a hallowed image of themselves as part of their legitimating apparatus did not, in other words, represent a breach of prevailing political and cultural trends. On the contrary, messianic notions and grandeur informed and shaped the political vision of many other contemporary Muslim rulers, including the Ottomans who championed Sunni normativity against the Safavids. Imperial ideologues of the dynasty, keeping up with the political and cultural zeitgeist, were eager to craft and cultivate a quasi-messianic image of the Ottomans as a dynasty serving a heavenly mission given by God. Sultan Selim I (r. 1512–1520) and Sultan Süleyman I (r. 1520–1566) accordingly assumed such grandiose and universalist titles as *ṣāhib-ḳırān*, *müceddid* (renewer of religion) and even Mahdi,[17] and imitated the Safavids by 'model[ing] their courts on the pattern of Sufi orders', as did the contemporary Mughal emperor Mirza Babur (1483–1530).[18] European dynasties of the period, including especially the Habsburgs under Charles V, similarly made claims to universal monarchy by invoking or alluding to various Christian messianic images and apocalyptic and millennial symbols.[19]

Neither was the content of Safavid messianism qualitatively much different, or necessarily cruder or more rigid than those of other contemporary dynasties. Although many of Shah Isma^cil's poems that circulated among his followers in Anatolia are permeated with a marked messianic flavour, making references to the imminent arrival of the Mahdi, there is no real sign in his poetry or elsewhere that he claimed or asserted an explicit messianic role for himself.[20] This does not rule out the possibility, or even likelihood, that most of his followers and sympathisers understood Shah Ismaᶜil's swift rise to power in the context of ᶜAlid messianism. Given the temper of the times, it is also more than probable that the Safavid shahs themselves encouraged and to a degree internalised such popular perceptions of their divinely assigned objective. Even so, the available sources reveal the messianic component of the Safavids' multi-layered ideological discourse to be much more imprecise and circumspect than is often assumed. For example, an anonymous history in Persian that presumably records Turkmen oral traditions concerning early Safavid history includes a long passage filled with many images of an earthly paradise where Shah Ismaᶜil is depicted not as the Mahdi proper but as his forerunner.[21] Not infrequently, poems by Kizilbash/Alevi dervish poets also allude to the notion of Mahdi-hood, without, however, establishing any specific links between this belief and the Safavids.[22] Recently surfaced Alevi sources, on the other hand, rarely invoke messianic themes, let alone ascribe to the Safavid shahs any overtly messianic (or divine) qualities. They instead connect the Safavid shahs' spiritual legitimacy as *mürşid-i kāmil*s (perfect spiritual guides) primarily to their ᶜAlid genealogy and Sufi credentials.[23] A partial exception to this pattern is a letter from among the Alevi documents that was apparently written in the aftermath of Shah ᶜAbbas's conquest of Baghdad in 1624. The language used in this letter, speaking of Shah Abbas as the long-awaited military commander (*şāhsuvār*) who rose to avenge the blood of the house of the Prophet (*ḥānedān-ı Muḥammed*), is reminiscent of redemptive Mahdism of the Shiᶜi tradition.[24]

Besides their vagueness and less-than-commonly accepted bearing in Safavids' overall legitimacy claims, another, even more intriguing, aspect of the Safavids' messianic pretentions is an often-overlooked fact about the so-called Kizilbash revolts in sixteenth-century Ottoman Anatolia: the local leaders of some of the most important ones of these revolts were messianic figures in their own right who made claims to combined political and religious dispensation. This runs counter to the idea that these revolts, which shook the Ottoman Empire in the early sixteenth century, were necessarily carried out in the name of the Safavid shahs, as will be further discussed in the next chapter. It accordingly and more importantly pushes against the notion that the Safavi household was an exclusive and fixed locus of messianic expectations within the broader (proto-)Kizilbash milieu. At some level, the evident multiplicity and flexibility of messianic possibilities within the sixteenth-century Kizilbash milieu can be viewed as a natural corollary of the fluidity and many uncertainties marking the messianic eschatological mindset. At another level, however, it is an indication and confirmation that the Safavids did not introduce messianic ideas and expectations where there were none before, but offered a powerful unifying locus for them. In either case, it would appear that the Safavids were far from being able to maintain a full and permanent monopoly even within the bounds of the (proto-)Kizilbash milieu over such messianic attributions that, by their very own nature, must have always been subject to a certain degree of competition and negotiation.

Traditional historiography's over-emphasis on Safavid messianism and the shahs' alleged claims to divinity as explanation for their remarkable popular support in Anatolia, in turn, obscures various other socio-religious dynamics of early Kizilbash-Safavid history. One of these, which likewise puts the Safavids into the mix with many other contemporary or near-contemporary Islamic dynasties, was their promotion of the idea and practice of *ġazāʾ* – a common currency among many aspirants of political power in post-Mongol Islamdom. Historians have long known that Junayd and his son Haydar led their own army of *ġazī*s into holy warfare against Christians in the Caucasus. It was under their watch, it is believed, that the Safavi order became militarised, transforming into a political project that could no longer be recognised as a proper Sufi order. Contemporary Armenian sources, however, complicate this picture, revealing the likelihood that Junayd's father, Shaykh Ibrahim, had previously accompanied the Karakoyunlu ruler, Jihan Shah, on *ġazāʾ* raids into Georgia in a fashion reminiscent of Sufi dervishes joining Ottoman warriors in their wars of conquest in western Anatolia and the Balkans right around the same time period.[25] Starting with Junayd, the Safavi family seems to have taken a relatively small but highly effective step away from this more familiar pattern, uniting in themselves spiritual leadership with military command. This move was no doubt encouraged by their deteriorating relations with Jihan Shah, and further facilitated by the political vacuum left behind by the declining Timurids who were among their greatest patrons.[26] Whatever the historical reasons behind it, the Safavi shaykhs association with the ideology and practice of *ġazāʾ* seems to have predated Junayd, and continued to play a crucial role as a means to recruit and mobilise followers into action under his successors. Indeed, Shah Ismaᶜil regularly refers to his community of followers as '*ġazī*s' in his poems.[27] In one of Shah Ismaᶜil's couplets discussed in the previous chapter, the *ġazīs* are counted among those 'who pledged allegiance to the son of the Shah' together with the Sufis (in another version, 'Ahis') and the Abdals. All of these groups were also major players in the initial state-building process of the Ottomans. This striking overlap of the socio-religious groups on whose shoulders they rose to power was no doubt part of the ideological threat that the Ottoman state perceived in the face of the fledgling Safavid dynasty, a topic returned to in Chapter 6.

Where do all these caveats and considerations lead us in terms of the making of the Kizilbash milieu in Anatolia? To begin with they show that the traditional accounts of it, which tend to explain the appeal of the Safavid cause in the region in terms of such essentialising notions as the Turkmen tribes' long-standing tradition of religious heterodoxy and inherent militant temper – two qualities that supposedly rendered them particularly gullible with regard to the early Safavid shahs' claims to divinity – are too simplistic to do justice to a much more complex process. Second, and more specifically, they highlight the deeply entrenched Sufi traditions and structures upon which the Kizilbash milieu arose and operated. This, in turn and more broadly, calls into question the perception of the Kizilbash movement as a virtual replica of the previous Turkmen tribal confederations, namely the Akkoyunlu and Karakoyunlu dynasties who ruled parts of Iran and eastern Anatolia prior to the rise of the Safavids. The view of Kizilbashism that confines it to the Safavids' tribal following largely stems from the prominence in the early Safavid political and military establishment of several Turkmen tribes, such as the Tekelü, Şamlu and Ustaclu, who were also bound to the Safavids spiritually.[28] It is true that the Safavids drew their fighting men almost entirely from their tribal disciples, most (although not all) of whom were of Turkmen stock. However, the building blocks of the larger Kizilbash milieu in Anatolia were not merely or primarily tribal formations, but various shaykhly and *sayyid* families with their own lay followings that comprised a much wider spectrum of social groups, including tribal and non-tribal rural communities, townsmen and even individuals from within the Ottoman military and bureaucracy.[29]

This point finds solid support in the family documents of Kizilbash *ocak* families. These documents, as shown in previous chapters, reveal various Wafaʾi communities and connected Ahi circles, as well as segments of the Abdal/Bektashi milieu, to be among the core constituencies of the Kizilbash movement in eastern Anatolia. Preliminary research exposes additional components of the Kizilbash milieu that fit the same pattern. For example, family documents of a *dede* lineage centred in the southeastern province of Antep, known as the *ocak* of Imam Musa Kazım, reveal the family to be historically affiliated with the Nurbakhshiyya Sufi order. While no other Alevi *ocak* from a Nurbakhshi background has so far emerged, the particular case of this family is consistent with the close relations that existed between certain branches of the Nurbakhshi Sufi order and the Safavids.[30] There are likewise compelling indications concerning the historical connectedness of some of the Kizilbash communities in the Balkans with the Bedreddinis who were followers of Şeyh Bedreddin (d. 1420), a religious scholar and Sufi master, and the leader of the first major popular uprising against the Ottoman state.[31] It is only to be expected that new research will confirm some of these other suspected links, and unearth new ones, between pre-existing Sufi communities and dervish groups and the Kizilbash milieu.

The multiplicity of the constitutive layers of the Kizilbash milieu is also echoed and succinctly expressed in the opening passage of a *Buyruk* manuscript that can be dated roughly to the end of the seventeenth century based on the list of Safavid shahs included in it. Presented as predictions of Shaykh Safi for the future and written as if coming directly out of the shaykh's mouth, this long passage starts out by naming in a chronological order all the Safavid shahs up to Shah Sulayman (r. 1666–1694). It then goes on to list, in two separate but parallel categories, groups that rallied around the spiritual leadership of the Safavi household. The first category includes names of several Sufi figures, including that of Abu'l-Wafa, Hacı Bektaş and Shah Niᶜmatullah Wali, among others, who are praised by Shaykh Safi as 'the light of my eyes, soul of my body' (*gözlerimde nūrum, cesette cānım*). The second category, on the other hand, is more like an inventory of the Safavids' tribal base. It contains a list of tribes, most of them well-known Kizilbash tribes, whom Shaykh Safi describes as 'the fruit in my garden, the bread on the table, and the sheep in my herd' (*bağımda yemişim, ṣoframda etmegim, sürümde koyunum*).[32] Given the dating of the manuscript, this passage might be more reflective of the different segments of the Safavids' social base towards the end of the seventeenth century than those of the earlier periods. Even so, it is still significant as an expression of the internal diversity of the broader Kizilbash milieu that included direct tribal followers of the Safavi order and various other Sufi communities. This point also aligns with James Reid's observation that 'the term "qizilbāsh" did not initially refer to a certain grouping of tribes but to a distinct class of initiates belonging to the mystical order headed by the Safavid family'. 'In the late fifteenth century,' Reid writes, 'as the Safavid Order became more involved in politics, many tribal chieftains were attracted into Safavid service and there rose to the position of qizilbāsh.'[33]

Taken together, these findings and considerations suggest that there was already a complex network of Sufi and dervish circles in the region with shared religious and temperamental affinities and a long history of political and militant activism when Junayd appeared on the Anatolian scene in search of new supporters for his religiopolitical mission. Junayd's success rested primarily on his ability to create a gravitational field that would, over time, pull these groups into its orbit, and establish a unifying spiritual authority over them. In other words, Junayd, and later his son Haydar, laid the foundation of the Kizilbash milieu not just by mobilising the long-standing tribal following of the Safavi order, but by linking up with a number of already well-established Sufi and dervish groups who had their own lay following and deeply rooted structures predating the Safavid state. With this new perspective on the subject, we can now account more easily for the surprisingly rapid expansion of the Kizilbash milieu and its transformation into a mass movement and, more importantly, for the often little-recognised resilience of the Kizilbash/Alevi identity in Ottoman Anatolia.

The Safavid Shahs and their Anatolian Followers in the Post-Çaldıran Period

Shah Isma^cil's coronation in 1501 and his proclamation of Twelver Shi^cism as the official religion of his realm, ironically, sowed the seeds of a protracted decline for the Kizilbash within Persia. Subsequent policies that gradually undermined the clout of the Kizilbash in Safavid territories had two key components: one, shari^ca-based Twelver Shi^cism was imposed while Kizilbash religious and cultural norms were suppressed, and, two, tribally organised Kizilbash military units were replaced by troops of slave soldiers. As a result of these policies, the zenith of which coincided with the reign of Shah Abbas I (r. 1588–1629), the Kizilbash within the realms of the Safavid Empire were almost completely assimilated into Imami Shiᶜism by no later than the end of the seventeenth century.

The role that the Kizilbash tribal military elite played in early Safavid Iran, as well as their internal quarrels and eventual decline from prominence, is well chronicled by Safavid sources and, therefore, also covered relatively extensively in Safavid historiography.[34] Surprisingly, however, the same Safavid sources display little interest in the main Kizilbash population in Anatolia. This curious silence of the contemporary Safavid chronicles on the fate of the Anatolian Kizilbash in the centuries following the Battle of Çaldıran has given rise to a widespread, although recently challenged, idea in Safavid historiography that Sufism was no longer politically expedient for the Safavids once they achieved their imperial ambitions.[35]

Despite the silence of their Safavid counterparts, the Ottoman sources leave no doubt about the continued existence of the Kizilbash communities in Anatolia and their contacts with the Safavid shahs which persisted through the Ottoman victory at Çaldıran and the waves of Kizilbash persecutions on its eve and after. Dozens of records from the *mühimme defterleri* of the second half of the sixteenth century include summary entries of imperial orders to punish the Kizilbash for, among other things, their real or imagined pro-Safavid activities via the intermediary of Safavi *ḫalīfe*s operating in Anatolia.[36] The endurance of spiritual ties between the Safavids and their Anatolian followers as late as the beginning of the seventeenth century is also suggested by a report from 1619 concerning the Kizilbash communities (*ṭā'īfe-i melāhid*) in Anatolia and the Balkans that was prepared by a leading member of the Ottoman ulema, Çeşmi Efendi, for the Ottoman sultan ᶜOsman II. This report noted in particular the Kizilbash communities' unceasing recognition and honouring of the reigning Iranian shah, ᶜAbbas I, as their '*mürşid*'.[37]

The picture of the nature and workings of relations between the Safavid shahs and the Kizilbash in Anatolia, especially after Çaldıran, is further elaborated and nuanced by the Safavid-related Alevi documents that offer us a uniquely internal perspective. To begin with, these confirm the endurance of contacts between the Safavids and the Kizilbash/Alevi *ocak*s at least into the late seventeenth century, if not later. They also uncover two major mechanisms through which Safavids continued to exercise spiritual authority and exert religious influence over the Anatolian Kizilbash: the conferral of *ḫilāfetnāme*s to select Alevi *ocak*s, and the dispatch of religious treatises preserved in the *Buyruk* manuscripts. Pertinent Alevi sources additionally demonstrate how, despite the Safavids' official sponsorship of Shiᶜi normativity within their realm subsequent to their consolidation of power, Sufi discourse remained relevant and primary for them in their continuing rapport with the Kizilbash/Alevi communities in Anatolia.

Appointment of Safavi Deputies

Appointment of deputies (Ot. *ḫalīfe*s; P. *khalīfa*) invested with written authorisation was the primary instrument used by Sufi orders for expansion and for internal control. The Safaviyya was no exception to this. But following the creation of the Safavid state, this function was relegated to the special office of the *khalīfat al-khulafāʾ*, which acted on behalf of the shahs in matters involving Sufi affairs. It was through this office supervising *ḫalīfe* appointments that contacts between the Safavids and the Anatolian Kizilbash were largely maintained.[38] Although no exact data are available, the number of Safavi deputies in Anatolia must have been quite substantial. For example, Maᶜasum Beg Safavi, a Kizilbash who served for sixteen years as the vizier of Shah Tahmasp I (r. 1533–1576), is said to have at one time issued 100 imperial orders for the appointment of *ḫalīfe*s in Anatolia.[39] While the Ottoman *mühimme* registers offer no indication of their overall numbers, those from the second half of the sixteenth century contain many references to Safavi *ḫalīfe*s collecting alms and other pious donations from their followers in Anatolia on behalf of the Safavid shahs, as well as conveying to them *ḫilāfetnāme*s, letters and 'heretical books' from Iran.[40]

Despite its apparent extensiveness and importance for Kizilbash history, very few documentary traces of the Safavi *ḫalīfe* network in Anatolia seem to have survived into the present. Thus far, only two such documents have surfaced from among the Alevi sources. Both of these documents are composed in Turkish and are directly related to *ḫalīfe* appointments in Anatolia; they are therefore precious as sources, especially for illuminating the backgrounds of the Safavi *ḫalīfe*s in the region and the roles they were expected to play among their followers. One of these is from 1089/1678 and was found among the family documents of the *ocak* of Imam Zeynel Abidin. The other one, coming from the *ocak* of Şah İbrahim Veli, despite being dated 1842, appears to be at least partially a copy of an early sixteenth-century original.[41]

Although both of the documents in question would be classified as *shajara*s in Safavid diplomatics, I choose to designate them with the term '*ḫilāfetnāme*' due to their content and in accordance with the usage in the Ottoman *mühimme* registers. *Shajara*s are formally differentiated from other types of Safavid imperial decrees (*farmān*s) by a stylised genealogical tree, written in gold and red colours and placed on the distinctively wide right-hand margin, extending from the Prophet to Imam Musa al-Kazim, Shaykh Safi and the subsequent heads of the Safavi order, eventually ending with the issuing shah. Having fortunately reached us in its original, the first of the documents under consideration here, dated Şevval 1089/1678, displays all the characteristics of other extant *shajara*s in Persian, externally as well as in terms of its content.[42] Henceforth it will be called '*ḫilāfetnāme-1*' (Figure 5.1).

Both its date and the genealogy it contains reveal *ḫilāfetnāme-1* to have been officially issued in the name of Shah Sulayman, also known as Safi II (r. 1666–1694). It concerns the appointment of Seyyid Muhammed Tahir, son of Mahmud Halife, to the position of *ḫalīfe* of the Kavi (Kāvī) community residing in the Akçadağ district of the province of Malatya. Seyyid Muhammed Tahir is said to have travelled to the Safavid's 'world-sheltering *dergāh*' (*dergāh-ı cihān-penāhıma gelüp*), meaning most likely the Safavid convent in Ardabil, to procure this written authorisation. The text begins with the invocation of God and praises to the Prophet Muhammad and Imam ᶜAli, followed by a statement emphasising the necessity of appointing *ḫalīfe*s to different parts of the world to guide the common people onto the right path. The specific purpose of the document is subsequently explained: Seyyid Muhammed Tahir, who is referred to as 'one of our disciples in the land of Rūm' (*Rūm vilāyetinde olan ṭāliblerimizden*), was therewith appointed upon his own request to the position of *ḫalīfe* of the Kavi community previously occupied by his late father.[43] Seyyid Muhammed Tahir's own disciples (*ḫalīfe-i mezbūr ṭālibleri*) and all the Sufis in the land of Rum attached to the Safavi family (*ve ol vilāyetde olan bu ḫānedān-ı velāyet-nişān ṣufileri*) are then urged to recognise his status as *ḫalīfe* and to obey his authority without expecting an annual renewal of the written authorisation.[44]

Ḫilāfetnāme-1 is significant on multiple accounts. First and foremost, it is the first incontrovertible evidence of the Safavid shahs' continuing appointment of deputies among the Anatolian Kizilbash as late as the last quarter of the seventeenth century and of trips to Ardabil by Kizilbash/Alevi *dede*s during the same period. While it is difficult to gauge the frequency of these trips, or to make an assumption about the incidence of *ḫalīfe* appointments, on the basis of such limited number of documents, the fact remains that there was a certain level of direct contact between the Safavids and some, even if not all, of the Kizilbash/Alevi *ocak*s in Anatolia at least into the reign of Shah Sulayman. This finding is corroborated by the second *ḫilāfetnāme* and by religious texts in *Buyruk* manuscripts dateable to the same period, both to be discussed below.[45]

Another noteworthy feature of *ḫilāfetnāme-1* is a long section in it that is devoted to describing Seyyid Muhammed Tahir's duties as *ḫalīfe*.

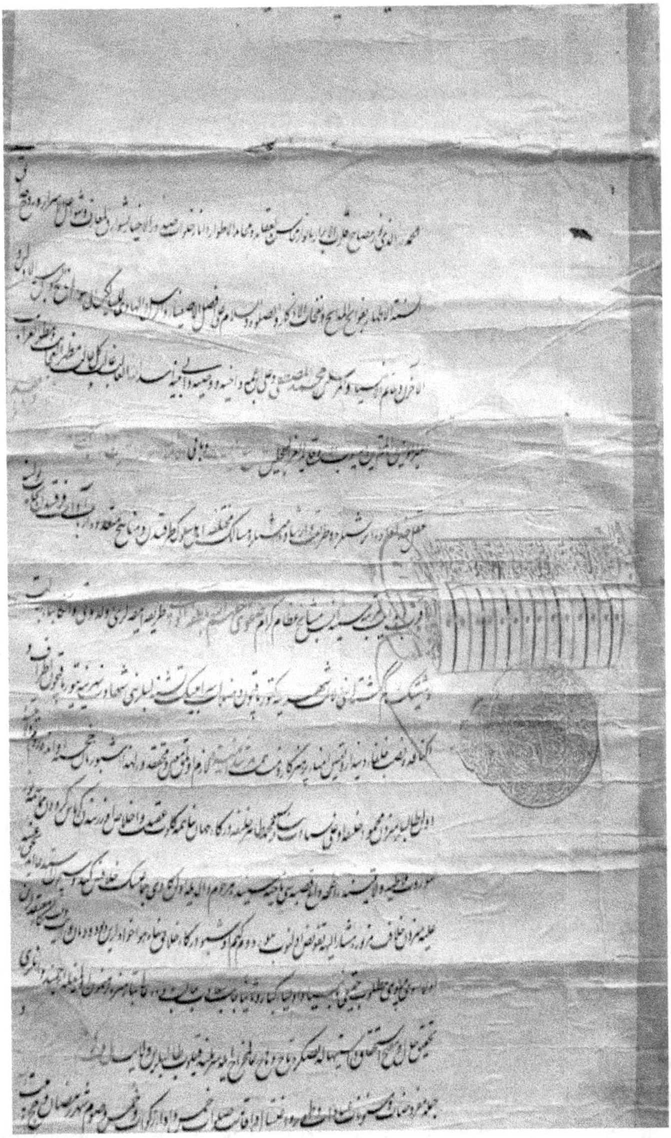

Figure 5.1 Safavi *ḫilāfetnāme* dated 1089/1678. Original in the private archive of Muharrem Naci Orhan, Istanbul, member of the *ocak* of İmam Zeynel Abidin, from the village of Mineyik, Arguvan-Malatya

Source: Photograph by the author, Istanbul, 2006.

According to the detailed list given here, Seyyid Muhammed Tahir was expected to demand good morals and refined manners in his disciples (*mekārim-i aḫlāḳ ve meḥāsin-i eṭvār*) and to enjoin them to carry out, in addition to the more typically Sufi religious service of *ẕikr* (*devām-ı eẕkār*), all prescribed ritual observances of canonical Islam, including the five daily prayers (*ṣalavāt-ı ḫams*), payment of alms (*edā'-i zekevāt u ḫums*), fasting during the month of Ramadan (*savm-ı şehr-i Ramażān*) and pilgrimage to the Ka^{c}ba (*ḥacc-ı beytü'llāhi'l-ḥarām*), and to enforce such shari^{c}a proscriptions as the ban on drinking wine (*şurb-ı ḫumūr*). The conspicuously 'orthoprax' perspective promoted in the document is striking, and exposes Safavids' efforts to push the Kizilbash in Anatolia towards greater congruence with the conservative Imami Shi^{c}i doctrines. Given the dearth of documentation from earlier periods, it is difficult to know how far back such explicit efforts to recast the Anatolian Kizilbash within a shari^{c}a-based Imami framework go, or whether they were, for whatever reason, stepped up during the reign of Shah Sulayman. What is clear, however, is that, despite such efforts – which, by the way, seem largely to have come to naught – relations between the Safavid shahs and their Anatolian followers continued to be conceived of, and articulated, primarily in a Sufi idiom.

Ḫilāfetnāme-1 is also enlightening in terms of the configuration and inner workings of the Kizilbash spiritual hierarchy within the Anatolian context. The *ocak* of Imam Zeynel Abidin, in whose family archive *ḫilāfetnāme-1* was discovered, is one of the Alevi *ocak*s of Wafa'i origin with claims to *mürşid*-hood, as covered extensively in Chapter 2. Their example shows how the Safavid deputies were elected not randomly but from within charismatic family lines with an established *mürşid* status, which was inherited from their past Sufi affiliations (in this case the Wafa'iyya) whose spiritual authority over their own disciples was thereby preserved. If this appointment is typical of a general pattern, we can then assume that the Safavid shaykhs/shahs simply superimposed themselves upon existing hierarchies of Sufi and dervish groups rather than dismantling the latter's entrenched internal structures. These deeply rooted Sufi structures predating the Safavids served as conduits for the spiritual influence exerted by the Safavid shahs over their Anatolian followers; at the same time, however, they seem to have set limits to this influence by filtering out some of its 'innovative' elements. This process of selective mediation goes a long way in rendering explicable the apparent immunity of the Anatolian Kizilbash to the Safavids' efforts – as indicated by the normative content of the *ḫilāfetnāme-1* – to bring them into the fold of shari^{c}a-based Imami Shi^{c}ism.

The second Safavid-related document to be discussed here, henceforth *ḫilāfetnāme-2*, exhibits a set of highly meaningful differences from *ḫilāfetnāme-1* and poses extra challenges to the researcher in its decipherment and interpretation. In terms of its external features, the most obvious variations in *ḫilāfetnāme-2* are in the absence of the stylised design in the right-hand margin that is regarded as an earmark of the *shajara* genre in Safavid diplomatics, and the placement of the Safavi genealogy within the main text. *Ḫilāfetnāme-2* is further differentiated from the first document by its more strictly Sufi discourse, as well as by a set of archaic features in its content and language that appear chronologically out of place in view of its recorded date, Cemaziye's-sani 1242/1826. These points will be subjected to further deliberations below in connection to the question of dating.

The text of *ḫilāfetnāme-2* commences with a short introduction that contains an invocation of God and praises to the Prophet, his family and the saints (*evliyāʾ*), followed by a passage thematising some key concepts of Sufism that include: the four levels of religious experience (*şerīᶜat, ṭarīḳat, maᶜrifet* and *ḥaḳīḳat*); the explanation of the purpose of creation with reference to a well-known hadith much favoured by the Sufis, according to which God created the world because he desired to be known; and the role of the prophets and the saints in leading the people along the right path.[46] Next comes a statement concerning the prominent place of the descendants of the Prophet as saints and spiritual guides, among which, it is said, the Safavi household occupies an eminent place. At this point, the document provides a detailed Safavid genealogy that extends from Imam ᶜAli up to Shah Ismaᶜil I.[47]

Ḫilāfetnāme-2 was granted to a certain Seyyid Süleyman, purportedly one of the ancestors of the *ocak* of Şah İbrahim Veli, centred in the village of Mezirme in Arguvan-Malatya, who apparently migrated to Sivas at some point in the remembered past. According to the genealogy contained in the document, Seyyid Süleyman was a descendant of Shaykh Ibrahim (Safavi) (d. 851/1447), father of Shah Junayd, hence the *ocak*'s name.[48] This genealogy connects Seyyid Süleyman and his family to the Safavid dynasty, and as such is congruent with the family's oral tradition concerning its origins. The *ocak*'s members accordingly regard themselves to be the quintessential representatives of the tradition of Ardabil (*Erdebil süreği*) in Anatolia and, on that basis, claim for themselves the status of *mürşid*-hood over all the Kizilbash/Alevi *ocak*s. The *ocak*'s familial ties to the Safavids appears credible, among other things, by virtue of the rarity and specifity of the related family tradition. Şah İbrahim Veli is the only Alevi *ocak* (with the possible exception of the *ocak* of Celal Abbas) that claims a consanguineous relationship with the Safavi household. All other Alevi *ocak*s for the most part subscribe to the rather imprecise tradition of linking their family origins to Khorasan. Moreover, it is well attested in Safavid historiography that Shaykh Ibrahim's descendants (born to a mother different from that of Junayd), called the 'Shaykhāvand', were one of the two renowned side branches of the royal Safavid family, the other one being the 'Pīrzāde' (kin of Shaykh Safi's shaykh, Zahid Gilani). Both of these clans were affluent landowners in and around Ardabil, and their members held important positions in the Safavid bureaucracy.[49] The family line that Seyyid Süleyman belonged to was presumably an offshoot of the Shaykhavand clan that purportedly migrated to Anatolia at some point in the past where it evolved into one of the major Kizilbash/Alevi *ocaks*. It is not clear when this move might have happened, but another group of *sayyid*s in Aleppo claiming descent from Shaykh Ibrahim Safavi is recorded in the sources as early as the middle of the fifteenth century.[50] While the exact relationship between the two families is difficult to establish, it is possible that the ancestors of the *ocak* of Şah İbrahim Veli emigrated from their hometown of Ardabil prior to the establishment of the Safavid state, like those Safavi *sayyid*s who ended up in Aleppo, settling in Malatya possibly as local representatives of the Safavi family and Sufi order.

According to *ḫilāfetnāme-2*, Seyyid Süleyman travelled from Anatolia (*memleket-i Rūm*) to Ardabil and visited several tombs belonging to his Safavid ancestors, praying and offering sacrifices at each site. Like Seyyid Muhammed Tahir, Seyyid Süleyman also received a document certifying his appointment as *ḫalīfe* when he was in Ardabil. However, there are some telling differences between *ḫilāfetnāme-1* and *ḫilāfetnāme-2*, most conspicuously in terms of what they say were the duties expected from a Safavi *ḫalīfe*. The list in *ḫilāfetnāme-2* is much shorter compared to that in *ḫilāfetnāme-1*, including only tasks pertaining to the spiritual guidance of disciples and the performance of communal religious rituals (*ḥalḳa-i ẕikr*). It does not, in other words, mention any of the normative ritual observances or other shariᶜi injunctions that are so emphasised in *ḫilāfetnāme-1*.[51]

To explain this contrast in assigned duties, we need first to rethink the dating of *ḫilāfetnāme-2*, which records the year of Seyyid Süleyman's trip to Ardabil as 1242/1826. While it is perfectly possible that Alevi *dede*s, especially those affiliated with the *ocak* of Şah İbrahim Veli, might have continued visiting the Safavi convent in Ardabil long after the dynasty's downfall, some of its archaic textual details and linguistic qualities suggest that *ḫilāfetnāme-2* was fully or partially copied from an older document.

To begin with, the Safavi genealogy it contains does not go any further forward than Shah Isma^cil I. Second, *ḫilāfetnāme-2* has a remarkably anachronistic concluding passage: following a reminder concerning the importance of showing proper respect to the saints, the *sayyid*s and the dervishes to ensure the permanence of temporal authority, the sultans and emperors of Rum (*selātīn u ḳayāṣire-i Rūm*) are admonished to honour Seyyid Süleyman on account of his eminent descent and to provide him the appropriate relief from taxes in accordance with his status.[52] Such an appeal to the rulers of Rum, presumably the Ottomans, is obviously obsolete for the early nineteenth century; historically and politically, it would only be relevant to the first decade of the sixteenth century when both Bayezid II and Shah Isma^cil were trying to maintain relatively congenial relations between the two states despite some tensions.

This anachronism in the content of the document is thrown into further relief by the curious admixture of various elements in its language that are archaic and/or from Eastern Turkish (Chaghatay) and Azeri Turkish. By way of examples, the ablative suffix is consistently written as '-dīn' (as in '*icād-ı 'ālemdin*'), '–n' is used as a combinative letter (as in '*Ṣafīyeddīn Erdebīlī'ni . . . ziyāret itdi*'), the gerund '–up' for a reported past tense (as in '*oluplar*'), and one encounters in the text such obsolete words as '*özi*', '*içre*', and '*ilen*'. These linguistic features tally perfectly with what is known about the Turkish used in the early Safavid royal milieu, which, although based on the Azerbaijani dialect, also exhibited Chaghatay influences.[53] All this evidence taken together gives us a sound basis to conclude that the present copy of *ḫilāfetnāme-2* was at least in part copied from a much older document that must have been composed no later than the early sixteenth century. This conjecture also serves to explain the reasons for the formal differentiation of *ḫilāfetnāme-2* from other *shajara*s, especially in regards to its inclusion of the Safavid genealogy within the main body of the text rather than as an ornamented seal on the side; the latter, one can assume, could only be produced by the authorised professional scribes of the Safavi court that no longer existed when Seyyid Süleyman paid a visit to Ardabil in the year 1242/1826.

Who, then, was the person who signed off the document as 'el-'Abd el-ḫādim el-faḳīr Seyyid Mīr Niẓām Erdebīlī' and stamped it with his seal? He was most likely one of the dervishes taking care of the old Safavi convent long after the dynasty disappeared from the historical scene. He must have put together the present *ḫilāfetnāme* for Seyyid Süleyman – both as a record of Seyyid Süleyman's visit to Ardabil and as a way of renewing his status as *ocakzade* – by drawing on an older family document that the latter most probably brought along with him. Such a scenario would be fully in line with similar processes of duplication or partial copying of older documents belonging to Alevi *ocak*s at the Karbala convent. It is, furthermore, conceivable that Sayyid Mir Nizam Erdebili himself was also a member of the Safavi family line, given that that he refers to Seyyid Süleyman's relatives back in Anatolia – that is, the members of the *ocak* of Şah İbrahim Veli – as his cousins (*benī aᶜmām*) in a personal note at the end of the document where he sends them his regards.

Seyyid Süleyman's visit to Ardabil as late as 1242/1826, rather than being an indication of a general pattern, appears to be symptomatic of the particularly intimate connections between the Safavids and the *ocak* of Şah İbrahim Veli. This point finds further validation by in-field observations that demonstrate the special role played by the members of the *ocak* in preserving and perpetuating the memory of the convent in Ardabil as the historical spiritual centre of the Kizilbash/Alevi milieu. As a corollary to that, *dede*s affiliated with this *ocak* have also served as the loci of resistance against the expanding influence, noted in Chapter 4, of the Çelebi Bektashis among the Kizilbash/Alevi communities since the nineteenth century. Not surprisingly, they have categorically opposed the latter's depiction of Hacı Bektaş as the *serçeşme* (lit. fountain-head) of all the Alevi *ocak*s in Anatolia, a claim that indirectly and unduly demotes the role of the Safavids in Kizilbash/Alevi history.

The Dispatch of Religious Treatises: The *Buyruk* Manuscripts

Another mechanism of contact between the Safavids and the Kizilbash communities in Anatolia operated through the transmission of religious texts that were generated within the Safavid milieu specifically for the consumption of their Turcophone Kizilbash followers. These religious treatises were collected in manuscripts known as *Buyruk* (lit. Command), although the title *Buyruk* is not encountered as such in the manuscripts themselves.[54] While our lack of knowledge about the way these texts were meant to be read or used limits our ability to understand their full significance and function, tradition holds that *Buyruk*s contain an authoritative account of the basic Alevi beliefs and rituals.[55] Typically, only *dede* families would own a copy of this quasi-sacred text, and it would have been carefully protected from the gaze of outsiders. Several *Buyruk* manuscripts have come to the surface in recent years, and many more are probably kept in the family archives of *dede* families, along with an array of other better-known religious texts dealing with Sufi and Shiᶜi themes that are beyond the scope of our current discussion.

Even though both are deemed as equally authoritative by Alevi *dede*s and clearly draw on a common pool of texts, a broad differentiation is made between two types of *Buyruk*s, attributed respectively to Shaykh Safi and Imam Jaᶜfar (*Şeyh Şafi Buyruğu* versus *İmam Cafer Buyruğu*), depending on who is cited as the main authoritative source of the ideas in it.[56] The relevant texts are accordingly titled as the *Menāḳıb* (or sometimes the *Risāle*) of one or the other of these two religious personages. But virtually all published and unpublished *Buyruk* manuscripts considered in this research contain multiple other treatises of varying size and contents, or excerpts from them, in addition to the main *Menāḳıb* texts, as well as long sections of poetry typically at the end. At one level, then, *Buyruk* can be understood as a generic name for collections of some key Alevi religious texts, while at a stricter level only the *Menāḳıb* texts may be considered as proper *Buyruk*s that were in time expanded and enriched with further accretions.

Having said that, the two types of *Menāḳıb* texts themselves are not internally uniform, either, and contain multiple textual layers that are not always easy to disentangle. While some sections exhibit clear structural or textual markers separating them from the ones preceding and/or following them, others do not. Furthermore, a treatise that appears as an independent text in one *Buyruk* copy may be chopped up and integrated into the main text of the *Menākīb* in another copy. These variations to a great extent reflect the preferences of and editing by individual copyists, presumably Alevi *dede*s of successive generations, who seem to have copied freely in their own writings a set of available texts, reworking them via selective omissions and interpolations of new material.

Notwithstanding all these variations, however, there is a great deal of overlap between the different *Buyruk* types in terms of issues covered and language used. Rather than containing hagiographic stories, as would be implicated by the word '*Menāḳıb*' in their titles, both types of *Buyruk*s typically focus on the basics of the path, drawing on the authority of Şeyh Safi or Imam Jaᶜfar in addition to other significant religious authorities such as Imam ᶜAli and Bayezid Bistami. More specifically, they elaborate on the principles that should govern relations between a disciple and his spiritual master, and between a disciple and his *musahib*, as well as on standards of good morals and appropriate social behaviours, all of which is articulated in a distinctively Sufi idiom. They also describe the various stages of communal *cem* rituals and related aspects of Alevi beliefs and cosmology.[57]

Given the particular dynamism and intimacy of connections between the transmission of oral and textual teachings within the Kizilbash milieu, a systematic comparison of different *Buyruk* manuscripts can offer us pathways for an understanding of the changing parameters of the Kizilbash/Alevi identity and internal organisation. A closer look at the chronological evolution of *Buyruk* manuscripts with that goal in mind reveals that *Buyruk*s attributed to Shaykh Safi represent an older layer of the genre than those attributed to Imam Jaᶜfar. It is noteworthy in this regard that of all the extant Imam Jaᶜfar *Buyruk*s that this author is aware of none date back any further than the nineteenth century.[58] On the other hand, there are two dated copies of Shaykh Safi *Buyruk*s from the early seventeenth century,[59] and a few others that are dateable to the reign of Shah Tahmasp based on textual evidence including most importantly the Safavid genealogies they include.[60]

In terms of content, one of the most salient differences between the two types of *Buyruk*s concerns the extent to which the Safavids and Hacı Bektaş figure in each. There seems to be a reverse correlation between the two: while Shaykh Safi *Buyruk*s almost never mention Hacı Bektaş, they abound in direct or indirect references to the Safavids. In addition to their very title, the Shaykh Safi *Buyruk*s almost always contain genealogies of Safavid shahs, as well as long sections that are organised in a question-and-answer format with the second shaykh of the Safaviyya, Shaykh Sadr al-Din, asking the questions and the eponym of the order, Shaykh Safi, giving the answers. This stands in contrast to *Buyruk*s attributed to Imam Jaᶜfar, in which the Safavids, save poems by Hataᵓi, are hardly ever explicitly brought up, but Hacı Bektaş and his convent in Kırşehir appear prominently, albeit more so in some copies than in others. Overall, the declining presence of the Safavids seems to correlate with the growing prominence of Hacı Bektaş within the broader trajectory of the evolution of the *Buyruk* manuscripts. One can reasonably interpret this shift as a reflection of two interconnected processes, namely the erosion of Safavid memory and the correlating growth of Bektashi influence among the Kizilbash/Alevi communities in Anatolia in the post-Safavid era.

Looking at it from this perspective, the Shaykh Safi *Buyruk*s emerge as particularly relevant and valuable for an assessment of the nature and trajectory of Safavid–Kizilbash relations. A detailed description of the content of one such manuscript in its entirety would be in order here to illustrate some relevant points. The manuscript under consideration comes from the province of Erzincan (hereafter *Buyruk-Erzincan*), its original belonging to a *dede* family affiliated with the *ocak* of Ağuiçen, one of the *ocak*s of Wafaᵓi origin discussed earlier.[61] It was copied in 1825, although textual evidence suggests that different portions of it were compiled originally during the reigns of Shah Tahmasp and Shah ᶜAbbas. The existence of other *Buyruk* manuscripts that overlap almost fully or partially with

Buyruk-Erzincan is a measure of the fact that it is a relatively common copy.[62] *Buyruk-Erzincan* is 237 pages long according to its original pagination and includes the following works/treatises:

- The first seventeen pages of the manuscript include the treatise entitled '*Hāẕā Kitāb-ı Ḫuṭbe-i Duvāz[deh] Imām raḍiya'llāhu 'anhu*', which comprises a prayer in Arabic thematising the Twelve Imams and an introduction in Turkish about the prayer's uses and benefits.
- Pages 17–139 include '*Kitāb-ı Maḳām-ı Menāḳıb-ı Şerīf-i Kuṭb'ül-'Arifīn Ḥażret-i Şeyḫ Seyyid Ṣafī*', or the *Buyruk* proper. It provides the fundamentals of the path (*ṭarīḳ*) on the authority of Shaykh Safi (often portrayed responding to questions posed by his son Shaykh Sadr al-Din) and occasionally on the authority of Imam Jaᶜfar and Imam ᶜAli. It also includes a Safavid genealogy that goes back as far as Shah Tahmasp, who is referred to as 'Şāh Dehmān b. Seyyid Şāh İsmāᶜī l'; this is followed on pages 58–59 by a poem praising him ('Medḥ-i Şāh Dehmān'). 'Dehmān' is a corrupted form of the name Tahmasp that is used in *Buyruk* manuscripts as well as in Alevi poetry.[63]
- Pages 139–142 include the text of what is identified in the relevant subheading as a letter (*mektūb*) sent by a certain Seyyid ᶜAbdülbaki ('*Dergāh-ı ᶜālīde Seyyid ᶜAbdülbāḳī Efendi'nin Evliyā'ya muḥibb olan muᵓmin-i pāk-iᶜtiḳādlara gönderdügi mektūbdur*'), which covers some of the same issues in the preceding section, albeit in a different format.[64] The following two sections, that is D and E, may or may not be appendices to the letter.
- Pages 142–147 are an untitled section that includes sayings of religious personages beginning with a saying by Imam ᶜAli about good and moral behaviour; the same treatise is given in another *Buyruk* manuscript (ms. no. 181 in MMAK, cited in n59 above) under the heading '*Der Beyān-ı Çehār Kelām*'.
- Pages 147–180 include an untitled text that appears both in terms of its content and format to be a continuation or a different version of '*Kitāb-i Maḳām-ı Menāḳıb-i Şerīf Kuṭb'ül-'Arifīn Ḥażret-i Şeyḫ Seyyid Ṣafī*'.
- Pages 180–182 include a short piece recounting when each of the Twelve Imams died and where each is buried; it is entitled '*Bu Beyān-ı Dūvazdeh İmām'ı Bildirir*'.
- Beginning on page 182 is Hataᵓi's *Naṣiḥatnāme*, a long poem in the genre of *mesnevī*, followed in pages 189–195 by a selection of poems by various other well-known Alevi poets.
- Pages 195–224 include a work entitled '*Hāẕā Kitāb-ı Fütüvvetnāme*'.

- The manuscript ends with a second group of poems and a long prayer to be recited at funerals (‘*Dār Çekmek Du’āsı*’).

Of these various textual segments, it is the *Kitāb-ı Maḳām-ı Menāḳıb-ı Şerīf Kuṭb’ül-’Arifīn Ḥażret-i Şeyḫ Seyyid Ṣafī* in section B that is the longest, and it can be regarded as *Buyruk* proper. It specifies in a relatively systematic way the rules of conduct for the disciples of ‘the path of Muḥammed ᶜAli’, a common emic designation for the Kizilbash/Alevi faith. The compilation date of all or part of it is traceable to the reign of Shah Tahmasp (r. 1524–1576). We infer this from the Safavid genealogy it includes, which ends with Shah Tahmasp, and from other references to him in the text, such as the prayer to be recited during the initiation ceremony of the disciples in which he is referred to as the reigning shah (‘*pādişāh-ı cihān*’) and the current *mürşid* (‘*mürşid-i zamānü’ṭ-ṭarīḳ-i ḥāżirān ve’l-ġā’ībān*’).[65] In another rather unusually theatrical passage, Shah Tahmasp appears as the *mürşid* in action. This passage describes what may or may not be a real-life exchange between the shah and three of his *ḫalīfe*s concerning an issue that apparently came up during an earlier ritual gathering. Upon hearing of the conflict, Shah Tahmasp explains that if forty apples are brought as *loḳma*, or sacred morsel, to a ritual gathering attended by forty individuals, they must be distributed equally among the attendees so that each gets one apple regardless of rank since among the disciples of the path no hierarchy based on social rank is acceptable.[66]

On the other hand, the next section of the manuscript, which includes ‘*Dergāh-ı ‘ālīde Seyyid ‘Abdülbāḳī Efendi’nin Evliyā’ya muḥibb olan mu’min-i pāk-i’tiḳādlara gönderdügi mektūbdur*’, seem traceable to the reign of Shah ᶜAbbas I. This is suggested by the striking overlap in content and duplication of individual phrases between the first part of the letter by Seyyid ‘Abdülbaki included in section C of *Buyruk-Erzincan* and a letter already mentioned in previous chapters that was sent to a member of the *ocak* of Dede Kargın in the immediate aftermath of the conquest of Baghdad by Shah ᶜAbbas I in 1624.[67] That the name of the sender of this second letter was also ‘Seyyid Bāḳī’ provides further support to this conclusion. In both, Shah ᶜAbbas is referred to as the long-awaited military commander ready to avenge the blood of the descendants of the Prophet.[68] Most likely, multiple letters similar in content were sent out to the leaders of the Anatolian Kizilbash at about the same time period to mobilise them in support of Shah ᶜAbbas’s military campaigns of the early seventeenth century, which aimed at regaining territories earlier lost to the Ottomans; a copy of these letters must eventually have found its way into this and other *Buyruk* manuscripts. The Mahdi-like image invoked for Shah ᶜAbbas in this letter is noteworthy as it diverges from the overall picture of the Safavid shahs in the *Buyruk*s where they appear primarily as serene Sufi masters.

Another aspect of *Buyruk-Erzincan* that is worth highlighting is the inclusion of a treatise on *futuwwa* in the section entitled '*Hāẕā Kitāb-ı Fütüvvetnāme*', which structurally and in terms of content stands relatively apart from the rest of the sections. Be that as it may, this is clear testimony to the circulation of *futuwwa*-related literature among Kizilbash/Alevi communities, and is as such congruent with our earlier deliberations concerning certain Alevi *ocak*s' historical ties with the Ahi fraternities. This point, as will be recalled from Chapter 2, was made specifically in connection to the *ocak*s of Dede Kargın, Keçeci Baba and Turabi Baba. It is within this framework, as well as the Safavids' well-known spiritual influence over *futuwwa* circles in general, that the circulation of such literature among Kizilbash communities in Anatolia ought to be understood.

Overall, given their content and traditional secrecy surrounding them, there is little doubt that the *Buyruk*s had their origins in the religious books and letters that were, according to the Ottoman *mühimme* registers, clandestinely transferred from Iran to Anatolia by the Kizilbash *ḫalīfe*s, specifically for the consumption of their followers in Anatolia.[69] This conclusion is also in line with a cautionary note found in *Buyruk-Erzincan*, which clearly states that the work at hand, referred to as 'Menāḳıb-ı Şerīf' in the text, is intended exclusively for 'the disciples of the path of the saints' (*muḥibb-i evliyā olan ṭālibler*), that is the Kizilbash/Alevi communities, and that it should not be recited in the presence of others, or given or even shown to just anybody (*degme kişilere*).[70]

The *Buyruk* manuscripts, together with the two *ḫilāfetnāme*s discussed above, demonstrate the religious/spiritual dimensions of relations between the Safavid shahs and their Kizilbash followers in Anatolia. They also corroborate the permanence of these spiritual bonds over the centuries. Two other separate copies of the *Shaykh Ṣafī Buyruk* reinforce the latter point. The original composition of one of them can be traced to the reign of Shah ᶜAbbas (r. 1587–1629), with its current copy at hand, entitled *Risāle-i Şeyh Ṣāfī*, having been copied in 1021/1612 by a certain 'Meḥemmed b. Ḥabīb in livā-ı Ṣaruḫān' (the modern province of Manisa in western Anatolia). In some ways it is the most coherent and well-organised *Buyruk* manuscript and includes a Safavid genealogy that begins with 'Hāẕā Sulṭān Şāh ᶜAbbās ibni Sulṭān Şāh Ṭahmāsb'. The name of Shah ᶜAbbas also appears in the wording of the vow a disciple is expected to take during the initiation ritual in which he promises to abide by the rules of the path.[71] This stands in comparison to the mention of the name of Shah Tahmasp in *Buyruk-Erzincan* in a prayer to be recited during the initiation of disciples, although the phrasing in the two cases is dissimilar. Altogether, while there are significant commonalities between *Buyruk-Erzincan* and the *Buyruk* copy dated 1021/1612, there are also sufficient differences between them, especially in terms of language and organisation, to suggest that the latter *Buyruk* copy is either an entirely new compilation or a thoroughly reworked version of the former. No messianic undertones similar to those in the above-mentioned letter are, however, detected in the text.

Finally, mention should be made of another *Buyruk* copy, entitled *Kitāb-ı Maḳām-ı Menāḳıb-ı Ḳutbü'l-ᶜArifīn Ḥażret-i Şeyh Seyyid Ṣāfī*, in which Shah Sulayman (r. 1666–1694) appears as the reigning shah. This manuscript was described in detail by Gölpınarlı, who drew attention to the prayer (*gülbāng*) that concludes the work; in it all the Safavid shaykhs/shahs as a group are praised and honoured on account of the spiritual path they have promoted, but with only Shaykh Safi, Shah Ismaᶜil (under his pen name 'Ḫaṭāʾī') and Shah Sulayman as the current shah and *mürşid* being mentioned by name.[72] No *Shaykh Ṣafī Buyruks* post-dating the reign of Shah Sulayman have surfaced; this may well be an indication of waning connections, if not their virtual breakdown, between the Anatolian Kizilbash and the Safavi *dūdmān*, who had already entered a period of decline during this period and who would disappear completely from the historical scene within the next half a century or so. Still, the Alevi/Kizilbash communities in Anatolia seem to have continued to look to Ardabil as (one of) their distant spiritual centre(s) and to especially cherish the memory of Shah Ismaᶜil under his pen name Hataʾi (T. Hatayi) despite the corrosion of the Safavids' memory among them otherwise. The status of Hataʾi as the leading Kizilbash/Alevi poet has not diminished even today among contemporary Alevis in different parts of Anatolia and the Balkans who routinely and unfailingly recite his poems (or those attributed to him) in their communal rituals.[73]

Conclusion

By and large, unexpectedly few Safavid-related documents have been found among the Alevi sources presently at hand. This is a case that is unlikely to be a mere coincidence. Most probably it is a reflection of both the growing irrelevance of the Safavi family for the Anatolian Kizilbash in the wake of the dynasty's decline and eventual demise, and of the high risk associated with preserving such documents. However, even these few documents that have survived, when considered together with the *Buyruk* manuscripts, offer a hitherto unavailable internal perspective on the nature of the religious/spiritual bonds between the Safavids and their Kizilbash followers in Anatolia that were clearly conceived of and articulated in a Sufi idiom. These bonds seem to have been kept alive until at least the reign of Shah Sulayman during the second half of the seventeenth century (notwithstanding possible ups and downs in their intensity over the centuries) through the appointment of *ḫalīfe*s and the dispatching of religious texts.

The primarily Sufi framework of the links between the Safavid shahs and the Kizilbash/Alevi communities in Anatolia, as it emerges from the Safavid-related Alevi sources, in turn, calls into question the impression created in the mainstream historiography that the Safavi *ḫalīfe*s in Anatolia were docile extensions of the Safavid state with no agency of their own, if not full-fledged spies. Treating them as such leads to a serious distortion of their identities and functions among their followers. Instead, we may be better off viewing them as genuine Sufis with entrenched local roots and independent spheres of influence, and with a penchant for forming coalitions with like-minded Sufi and dervish groups to further a particular religio-political agenda under suitable conditions. This way, we can also avoid conflating them with the fully dependent Kizilbash fighters of the Safavid shahs, and make better sense of the seemingly limited and even negotiated nature of the Safavid influence over the Alevi/Kizilbash communities in Anatolia, as well as of the latter's resilience up to the present. More will be said about this last point in the next chapter, where I will explore how a series of distinct but intersecting groups gathered around individual masters or saintly lineages would coalesce into a more coherent religious movement and identity in the course of the sixteenth century under growing pressures toward confessionalisation.

Notes

1. Huang Yubin was a magistrate of the Qing dynasty in China (1644–1912) 'who zealously hunted down sectarian groups and confiscated their scriptures in the nineteenth century'. The quote is from his *Poxie xiangbian* [Detailed refutation of heterodoxy], cited in Richard Shek, 'The Alternative Moral Universe of Religious Dissenters in Ming-Qing China', in *Religion and the Early Modern State: Views from China, Russia, and the West*, eds James D. Tracy and Marguerite Ragnow (Cambridge: Cambridge University Press, 2004), 37.
2. Walther Hinz, *Uzun Hasan ve Şeyh Cüneyd: XV. Yüzyılda İran'in Millî Bir Devlet Haline Yükselişi*, trans. Tevfik Bıyıklıoğlu (Ankara: Türk Tarih Kurumu, 1992), 7.
3. For the etymology of the word, see n3 in Introduction.

4. Some of the well-known and oft-cited works on the origins and the early history of the Safavids include: Michel M. Mazzaoui, *The Origins of the Ṣafawids: Šī 'ism, Ṣūfism, and the Ġulāt* (Wiesbaden: Franz Steiner Verlag, 1972); Jean Aubin, 'L'avenèment des Safavides reconsidéré (Études Safavides III)', *Moyen Orient et Océan Indien* 5 (1988): 1–130; Roger Savory, *Iran under the Safavids* (Cambridge: Cambridge University Press, 1980), 1–29; H. R. Roemer, 'The Safavid Period', *Cambridge-Iran-6*, 189–350; Said Amir Arjomand, *The Shadow of God and the Hidden Imam: Religion, Political Order, and Societal Change in Shiᶜite Iran from the Beginning to 1890* (Chicago: The University of Chicago Press, 1984), 66–82; and Adel Allouche, *The Origins and Development of the Ottoman–Safavid Conflict (906–962/1500–1555)* (Berlin: Klaus Schwarz Verlag, 1983), 30–64.
5. An overview of these sources on the early Safavid history is provided in Mazzaoui, *Origins of the Ṣafawids*, 15–21.
6. Fadlullah b. Ruzbihan Khunji-Isfahani, *Tārīkh-i ᶜĀlam-ārā-yi Amīnī*, ed. John E. Woods, with abridged English translation by Vladimir Minorsky (London: Royal Asiatic Society, 1992), 255, 272–273.
7. This is an exact phrase from the Quran (40:65). Khunji thus charges the Kizilbash with deforming a Quranic phrase by applying the '*huwa*', which refers to God, to Junayd.
8. Khunji-Isfahani, *Tārīkh-i ᶜĀlam-ārā-yi*, 272.
9. 'The Sufi is loved and reverenced as a god especially by his soldiers many of whom enter into battle without armor expecting their master Ismail to watch over them in the fight. Others go into battle without armor, being willing to die for their monarch, crying "Sheikh, Sheikh." The name of God is forgotten throughout Persia and only that of Ismail remembered. Everyone, and particularly his soldiers, considers him immportal.' Quoted in Palmira Brummett, 'The Myth of Shah Ismail Safavi: Political Rhetoric and "Divine" Kingship', in *Medieval Christian Perceptions of Islam: A Book of Essays*, ed. John V. Tolan (New York: Garland, 1996), 337. In the rest of the article, Brummett offers a useful, critical reading of this and other, similar Western accounts concerning Shah Ismaᶜil.
10. V. Minorsky, 'The Poetry of Shāḥ Ismāᶜīl I', *Bulletin of the School of Oriental and African Studies* 10, no. 4 (1942): 1,006–1,053. For some brief but important critical comments regarding the simplistic nature of this line of analysis, see Sanjay Subrahmanyam, 'Turning the Stones Over: Sixteenth-Century Millenarianism from the Tagus to the Ganges', *The Indian Economic and Social History Review* 40, no. 2 (April–June 2003): 140–141.
11. For the English translation of the poem, see Andrew J. Newman, *Safavid Iran: Rebirth of a Persian Empire* (London: I. B. Tauris, 2006), 13–14.
12. On the genre of *devriye*, see Abdülbâkî Gölpınarlı, *Tasavvuf'tan Dilimize Geçen Deyimler ve Atasözleri* (Istanbul: İnkılap ve Aka Kitabevleri, 1977), 93–95; and *DIA*, s.v. 'Devriyye' by Mustafa Uzun; and John K. Birge, *The Bektasi Order of Dervishes* (1937; repr. London: Luzac Oriental, 1994), 260.

13. Ahmet T. Karamustafa, 'In His Own Voice: What Hatayi Tells Us about Şah İsmail's Religious Views', in *L'Ésotérisme Shi^cite: Ses Racines et Ses Prolongements/Shi^ci Esotericism: Its Roots and Developments*, ed. Mohammad Ali Amir-Moezzi (Turnhout: Brepols Publishers, 2016), 608–609.
14. Allouche, *Origins and Development*, 1.
15. Arjomand, *Shadow of God,* Chapter 2.
16. A. Azfar Moin, *The Millennial Sovereign: Sacred Kingship and Sainthood in Islam* (New York: Columbia University Press, 2012), esp. the first two chapters. Although millenarian and messianic reckonings and the promise of imminent salvation have been constantly present in the history of Islam, a proliferation of messianic themes within Sufism from the thirteenth century onwards has been attested by scholars of Islamic mysticism. These scholars have variously attributed it to the influence of Shi^ci messianic doctrines on Sufi thinking or to developments internal to Sufism related to the 'intercessory claims of Sufi communities', two explanations not necessarily exclusive of each other. See, respectively, Shahzad Bashir, 'Messianism', in *The Princeton Encyclopedia of Islamic Political Thought*, ed. Gerhard Böwering (Princeton: Princeton University Press, 2013), 338; and Devin DeWeese, 'Intercessory Claims of Ṣūfī Communities during the 14th and 15th Centuries: "Messianic" Legitimizing Strategies on the Spectrum of Normativity', in *Unity in Diversity: Mysticism, Messianism and the Construction of Religious Authority in Islam*, ed. Orkhan Mir-Kasimov (Leiden: Brill, 2014), 198–199.
17. Cornell H. Fleischer, 'The Lawgiver as Messiah: The Making of the Imperial Image in the Reign of Süleymân', in *Soliman le Magnifique et son temps: Actes du colloque de Paris, Galeries nationales du Grand palais, 7–10 mars 1990*, ed. Gillès Veinstein (Paris: La Documentation française, n.d.), 159–177; Barbara Flemming, 'Sāhib-kırān und Mahdī: Türkische Endzeiterwartungen im ersten Jahrzehnt der Regierung Süleymāns', in *Between the Danube and the Caucasus: A Collection of Papers concerning Oriental Sources on the History of the Peoples of Central and South-Eastern Europe*, ed. György Kara (Budapest: Akadémiai Kiadó, 1987), 43–62; Kaya Şahin, *Empire and Power in the Reign of Süleyman: Narrating the Sixteenth-Century Ottoman World* (Cambridge: Cambridge University Press, 2013), esp. 74-87; H. Erdem Çıpa, *The Making of Selim: Succession, Legitimacy, and Memory in the Early Modern Ottoman World* (Bloomington: Indiana University Press, 2017), Chapter 5; and Hüseyin Yılmaz, *Caliphate Redefined: The Mystical Turn in Ottoman Political Thought* (Princeton, NJ: Princeton University Press, 2018), 267–268.
18. Moin, *Millennial Sovereign*, 2 and passim; Fleischer, 'The Lawgiver as Messiah', 164.
19. See, for example, John M. Headly, 'The Habsburg World Empire and the Revival of Ghibellinism', and Franz Bosbach, 'The European Debate on Universal Monarchy', both in *Theories of Empire, 1450–1800*, ed. David Armitage (Aldershot: Ashgate, 1998), 45–79, 81–98; and Geoffrey Parker,

'Messianic Visions in the Spanish Monarchy, 1516–1598', *Calíope: Journal of the Society for Renaissance and Baroque Hispanic Poetry* 8, no. 2 (2002): 5–24. For a general assessment of sixteenth-century millenarianism in Eurasia, see Subrahmanyam, 'Turning the Stones Over'.

20. Karamustafa, 'In His Own Voice', 608–609. Assumptions to the contrary, according to Karamustafa, represent 'a distortion of the evidence of Hatayi's poems'. While Karamustafa rejects the presence of any messianic pretensions in Shah Ismaᶜil's poetry, he also acknowledges possible gaps between Shah Ismaᶜil's self-presentation in his poetry and his followers' perception of him.
21. Erika Glassen, 'Schah Ismāᶜīl, ein Mahdī der anatolischen Turkmenen?' *Zeitschrift der Deutschen Morgenländischen Gesellschaft* 121, no. 1 (1971): 61–69.
22. For samples of Alevi/Bektashi poetry, see Sadeddin Nüzhet Ergun, *Bektaşi Edebiyatı Antolojisi: Bektaşi Şairleri ve Nefesleri* (Istanbul: Maarif Kitaphanesi, 1944); and Abdülbâki Gölpınarlı, *Alevî Bektâşî Nefesleri* (Istanbul: İnkılâp Kitabevi, 1992).
23. *Sayyid* genealogy of the Safavids may have been a later fabrication, as argued by two separate historians who independently reached the conclusion that the Safavids were descended from Iranised Kurds but forged a *sayyid* genealogy for themselves following the establishment of the Safavid state: Ahmad Kasravi, 'Shaykh Ṣafī va Tabārash', in *Kārvand-i Kasravī*, ed. Yaḥyā Zakā (1926–1927; reprint, Tehran: Shirkat-i Shihāmī-i Kitābha-i Jībī, 1974); Zeki Velidi Togan, 'Sur l'origine des Safavides', in *Mélanges Louis Massignon*, vol. 3 (Damascus: Institut Français de Damas, 1957): 347–357; both cited and summarised in Appendix B to Allouche, *Origins and Development*. But even if it were a fabrication, new research reveals that the Safavids had a written genealogy depicting them as *sayyids* already in the middle of the fifteenth century, that is before the establishment of the Safavid state. Kazuo Morimoto, 'The Earliest ᶜAlid Genealogy for the Safavids: New Evidence for the Pre-dynastic Claim to *Sayyid* Status', *Iranian Studies* 43, no. 4 (2010): 447–469. The Ottomans, too, before the advent of Selim I, recognised the Safavids as *sayyids*. Allouche, *Origins and Development*, 77. This is indirectly also supported by *Ḫilāfetnāme-2*, as discussed below.
24. For the letter and its analysis, see my 'Kızılbaş, Bektaşi, Safevi İlişkilerine Dair 17. Yüzyıldan Yeni Bir Belge: Çeviriyazılı Metin-Çeviri-Tıpkıbasım', in 'Festschrift in Honor of Orhan Okay', ed. Yücel Dağlı et al., special issue, *Journal of Turkish Studies* 30, no. 2 (2006): 117–130.
25. Thomas A. Carlson, 'Safavids before Empire: Two 15th-Century Armenian Perspectives', *International Journal of Middle East Studies* 49, no.2 (2017): 283–285.
26. Michel M. Mazzaoui, 'The Ghāzī Background of the Safavid State', *Iqbāl Review* 12, no. 3 (1971): 79–90.
27. Karamustafa, 'In His Own Voice', 609.
28. For these tribes and their role in the establishment and sociopolitical order

of the early Safavid Empire, see Faruk Sümer, *Safevî Devletinin Kuruluşu ve Gelişmesinde Anadolu Türklerinin Rolü* (Ankara: Türk Tarih Kurumu, 1992); and James J. Reid, *Tribalism and Society in Islamic Iran, 1500–1629* (Malibu, CA: Undena Publications, 1983).

29. On Kurdish- and Zaza-speaking Alevis, see Gezik, *Dinsel, Etnik ve Politik*, esp. Part I. The social diversity of the Kizilbash was alluded to in Chapter 4 within the context of Iraq; for evidence from the *mühimme defterleri*, see n9. Evidence for the same point in the Anatolian context can similarly be found in the various *mühimme* records cited in C. H. Imber, 'The Persecution of the Ottoman Shīᶜites according to the Mühimme Defterleri, 1565–1585', *Der Islam* 56, no. 2 (July 1979): 245–273; Bekir Kütükoğlu, *Osmanlı-İran Siyâsî Münâsebetleri (1578–1612)* (Istanbul: İstanbul Fetih Cemiyeti, 1993), esp. 8–18; and Saim Savaş, *XVI. Asırda Anadolu'da Alevilik* (Ankara: Vadi Yayınları, 2002), esp. 36–39.

30. FD of Hasan Çevik Dede, *ocak* of İmam Musa Kazım. For relations between the Safavids and the Nurbakhsi order, see Newman, *Safavid Iran*, 20.

31. According to ᶜAşıkpaşazde, some followers of Şeyh Bedreddin attached themselves to Shaykh Junayd, *Aspz*, 331. For a *mühimme* register dated 1022/1613 concerning Bedreddinis who joined the ranks of the Kizilbash, see BA.MD. 80/19/49, quoted in *Alevilik ile İlgili Osmanlı Belgeleri*, ed. Baki Öz (Istanbul: Can Yayınları, 1995), 73–74. Also see Mehmet Beytullah, *Alevilik Keşmekeşliği ve Bulgaristan Kızılbaşlığı* (Sofia: Svetlik Yayınevi, 1999), 48–50; and Michel Balivet, *Şeyh Bedreddin: Tasavvuf ve İsyan* (Istanbul: Tarih Vakfı Yurt Yayınları, 2000), originally published under the title *Islam mystique et révolution armée dans les Balkans Ottomans vie du Cheikh Bedreddin le 'Hallâj des Turcs' (1358/59–1416)* (Istanbul: Isis Press, 1995), 104–108.

32. The relevant passage reads as follows: '*Şeyḫ Ṣāfī . . vaḳfiyyesinde mübārek nefesiyle buyurmuşdur ki . . . ve daḫi Rūm vilāyetinde Şeyḫ Nasır Ṣūlṭān Velī bin Emīr Ḥamza ve Şāh Şeyḫ Ḥasan Velī bin Nūre'd-dīn Ḥamza Şāh Niᶜmetu'llah Velī ve daḫi Hācī Bektāş Velī bin Gözcī Hācī Bayrām Ṣūlṭān bin Hidāyetu'llah ve Seyyid Ebü'l-Vefāᵓ Muḥammed bin Seyyid Muḥammed ve daḫi Emīr Süleymān Ṣūlṭān Muḥammed bin ᶜAbdu'llah ve ᶜAbdu'llah Ḫorāsānī bin Muḥammed ve daḫi Ḫalīl ve Dīvāne bin Muḥammed Cihāngir ve Şeyḫ Muḥammed Bedeḫşānī ve Seyyid Aḥmed Kübra ve daḫi Seyyid Ṣelāḥe'd-dīn Muḥammed Ekberānī ve Seyyid Cemāle'd-dīn [. . .] Ebü'l-Ḥüseyin gözlerimde nūrum, cesetde cānım cümle karındaşlarımdır ve daḫi Ẕu'l-ḳadīrli cemāᶜati, Ḳara İmānlī cemāᶜati ve Ustaclu cemāᶜati ve Ḳaçār cemāᶜati ve Ḫarmāndalu cemāᶜati ve [. . .] cemāᶜati ve Afşar cemāᶜati ve Begdili cemāᶜati ve Begceğizli cemāᶜati ve Gündeşlü cemāᶜati ve Hācī Ḥasanlu cemāᶜati ve Ağkoyunlu cemāᶜati ve Cihānbeglü cemāᶜati ve Şādlu ve [. . .] cemāᶜati bağımda yemişim, ṣoframda etmegim, sürümde koyunum buyurmuşlar.*' *Menāḳıb-ı Şeyḫ Seyyid Ṣafī ve Imām Ca'fer-i Ṣādıḳ*, MS, private library of Mehmet Yaman, fols 1b–3b.

33. Reid, *Tribalism and Society*, 2.
34. On the decline of the Kizilbash in Iran, see, for example, Hans R. Roemer, 'The Qizilbash Turcomans: Founder and Victim of the Safavid Theocracy', in *Intellectual Studies on Islam: Essays Written in Honor of Martin B. Dickson*, eds Michel M. Mazzaoui and Vera B. Moreen (Salt Lake City: University of Utah Press, 1990): 27–39; Jean Aubin, 'La Politique religieuse des Safavides', in *Le Shiᶜisme Imamite, Colloque de Strasbourg, 6–9 mai 1968*, ed. T. Fahd (Paris: Presses Universitaires, 1970), 235–244. For a more recent and nuanced treatment of the subject, see Kathryn Babayan, *Mystics, Monarchs, and Messiahs: Cultural Landscapes of Early Modern Iran* (Cambridge, MA: Harvard University Press, 2002).
35. The enduring importance for the Safavid shahs of their Sufi credentials is most explicitly argued in Newman, *Safavid Iran,* see esp. 9–10, 19–20. Newman, however, does so mainly within the framework of Iranian internal politics without much regard for the implication of this assertion vis-à-vis the Alevi/Kizilbash communities in Anatolia.
36. Fariba Zarinebaf-Shahr, 'Qizilbash 'Heresy' and Rebellion in Ottoman Anatolia during the Sixteenth Century', *Anatolia Moderna/Yeni Anadolu* 7 (1977): 1–15; Savaş, *XVI Asırda Anadolu'da Alevilik*, 62–66.
37. A copy of this report is published in M. A. Danon, 'Un interrogatoire d'hérétiques Musulmans (1619)', *Journal Asiatique* (April–June 1921): 281–293. The report was prepared following a comprehensive investigation of the Kizilbash as result of which several individuals were persecuted, Andreas Tietze, 'A Document on the Persecution of Sectarians in Early Seventeenth-Century Istanbul', in *Bektachiyya: Études sur l'ordre mystique des Bektachis et les groupes relevant de Hadji Bektach*, eds Alexandre Popovic and Gilles Veinstein (Istanbul: Isis Press, 1995): 165–170.
38. Roger M. Savory, 'The Office of Khalîfat al-Khulafâ under the Safawids', *Journal of American Oriental Society* 85 (1965): 497–502; for an extended and more nuanced discussion of the nature and functions of the office, see Willem Floor, 'The Khalifeh al-kholafa of the Safavid Sufi Order', *Zeitschrift der Deutschen Morgenlandischen Gesellschaft* 153, no. 1 (2003): 51–86.
39. Zarinebaf-Shahr, 'Qizilbash "Heresy" and Rebellion', 10.
40. Savaş, *XVI. Asırda Anadolu'da Alevilik*, 39–42.
41. Both of these documents have been published in my *Karakaya-YK*.
42. Floor, 'The Khalifeh al-kholafa', 60. For further details about the genre of *shajara*, as Safavi *ḫilāfetnāme*s are called in Safavid diplomatics, and a published example from the reign of Shah ᶜAbbas I, see Jahangir Qaᵓim-maqami, *Muqaddama-ī bar shinākht-i asnād-i tārīkhī* (Tehran: Anjuman-i Ās̱ār-i Millī, 1350/1971), 90–95; for three *shajara*s promulgated by Shah Sultan Husayn, see T. M. Musavi, *Orta-asr Azerbaycan Tarikhina Dair Fars-dilli Sanadlar (XVI–XVIII Asrlar)* [in Cyrillic alphabet] (Baku: n.p., 1977), documents nos 18, 19 and 20; and for a *shajara* by Shah Tahmasp, see H. Mir-Jaᶜfari and M. Hashami Ardkani, 'Farman-i Shah Tahmāsp Ṣafavī ba Mavlānā Rażī

al-Dīn Muḥammad', *Barrasīhā-i tārīkhī* 9 (1352/1973): 95–110. For the historical development and formal characteristics of the *shajara* genre, also see Qāʾim-maqāmī, *Muqaddama-ī bar shinākht-i asnād*, 90–93; and Bert G. Fragner, 'Farmān', in *Encyclopaedia Iranica* (New York: Bibliotheca Persica Press, 1999).

43. '*Li-hāẕā işbu meāl-i ḥüccete evānda Rūm vilāyetinde olan ṭāliblerimizden Maḥmūd Ḫalīfe oğlı siyādet-penāh Seyyid Meḥmed Ṭāhir Ḫalīfe dergāh-ı cihān-penāhıma gelüp ᶜaḳīd ü iḫlāṣ üzerinden kirpās gerdūn-ı hümāyūnuma yüz sürüp Malāṭiyya vilāyetinde Ağçadāġ ḳāṣabası nāḥiyesinde merḥūm vālidiyle olan Kāvī cemāᶜatinün ḫilāfetin kendüsi-çün istidᶜā idicek ᶜatabe-i ᶜaliyyemizden ḫilāfet-i meẕbūre müşārün-ileyhe tefvīż olunup.*' *Ḫilāfetnāme-1*, FD of Muharrem Naci Orhan published in *Karakaya-YK*.

44. '*Ḫalīfe-i meẕbūr ṭālibleri ve ol vilāyetde olan bu ḫānedān-ı velāyet-nişān ṣufīleri mūmā-ileyhi cānib-i şerīfimizden manṣıb-ı ḫilāfete manṣūb ve riᶜāyet ve murāḳabesin ḫāṭır-ı ḫidīvānemize merġūb bilüp evāmir ve nevāhī-i meşrūᶜasına muṭiᶜ ve münḳād olalar ve her ᶜām şecere-i müceddede lāzım bilmeyüp ᶜalāmet-i şerīfe ᶜitimād ḳılalar.*' *Ḫilāfetnāme-1.*

45. It is of course possible that Safavid efforts to revive and reinforce their ties with the Kizilbash in Anatolia intensified during this period, but there is no obvious political reason why this might have been the case given Shah Sulayman's pacifist foreign policy vis-à-vis the Ottomans; see Rudi Matthee, 'Iran's Ottoman Diplomacy during the Reign of Shāh Sulaymān I (1077–1105/1666–94)', in *Iran and Iranian Studies: Essays in Honor of Iraj Afshar*, ed. Kambiz Eslami (Princeton: Zagros Press, 1998), 148–165.

46. '*Ammā ba'd şerī'at aṣḥābınun mir'āt-ı ḳalbine ve ṭariḳat erbābınun mişkāt-ı żamīrine bu beyżā żiyalı olan ma'rifet kelimātı ḥaḳīḳat maḳāmına ẓāhir ve bāhirdür kim ki ġarażı-i aṣlī icād-ı 'ālemdin ve 'illet-i ġā'ī tekvīn-i beni Ādemdin ma'rifet-i ilahī ve ru'yet-i ḥaḳā'ikü'l-eşyā' kemā-hiyedür ki küntü kenzen maḫfiyyen fe-aḥbebtü en ᶜurafe fe-ḫalaḳtu'l-ḫalḳa likey ᶜurafe. Pes Ḥażret-i Rabb-i vedūd maḥż-ı cūd ilen 'ālemi hicāb-ı 'ademdin mevcūt bulup ve ol cümledin Ḥażret-i insanı mir'at (. .) envār-ı cemāl-i cemīl kılup ve min beynihim enbiyā-ı 'iẓāmı ḳulūb-i ṣāfiyye ṣāḥib kılmış ve evliyā-ı kiramı enfās-ı ḳudsiyye ile muṣāḥib itmiş ẕalika fażlu'llāhi yu'tihī men yaşāu' ta ki ḥaḳḳ bendelerine cādde-i şerī'at nişān virüp ve ṭālibin-i rāh-ı hüdātı ṭarīḳat menzilinde ḥaḳīḳat ma'arifetinun bāde ve şarābın içürüp maḳām-ı ḳurba vuṣūl bulsunlar raḥīk-i taḥḳīḳi sāḳi-i ḥaḳḳ elindin ḥuṣūl ḳılsunlar.*' *Ḫilāfetnāme-2*, FD of the Sivas branch of the *ocak* of Şah İbrahim Veli published in *Karakaya-YK*.

47. '*ki cenāb-ı seyyidü'n-nebīyin ve ḥātemü'l-enbiyā' ve'l-mürselīn Ḥazret-i Muḥammed . . . ol Ḥażretün evlād-ı emcādı ilā yevmü'l-ḳıyama evliyā'-ı rāşidīn ve hüdāt-ı dīn-i mübīn abdāl-ı ḥaḳḳ ve aḳṭāb-ı ḥalḳ ve evtād-ı 'ālem ve erkān-ı benī Ādem oluplar ḫuṣūsen silsile-i ᶜAliyye-i ṣafiyye-i 'aleviyye ve sülāle-i ṣāfiyye-i ḥaliyye-i Ṣafaviyye bu rüzgārda bāde-i ḳurb-i ḥaḳḳdin seyrāb ve neş'e-i(?) viṣāl-i raḥmet-i ilahidin kāmyāb olmış ol silsile-i*

ᶜaliyyenun ensāb-ı ṭāhirin bu tertīb ilendür: Ebū'l-muẓaffer Sulṭān Şāh İsma'īl bin Sulṭān Ḥaydar bin Sulṭān Cüneyd bin Sulṭān Şāh İbrahīm bin Sulṭān Ḫ(v)āce 'Alī bin Şeyḫ Ṣadre'd-dīn bin ḳıdvetü'l-evliyā' fī'l-āfāḳ şeyḫ Ṣafīye'd-dīn İsḥaḳ.' Ḫilāfetnāme-2.

48. *'es-Seyyid Süleymān ki ḥażret-i sulṭanü'l-evliyāᵓ ve burhānü'l-aṣfiyāᵓ, el-ᶜāşıḳu'ş-ṣāfī es-selīm Sulṭān Şāh İbrāhīm nesebinde mensubdur.' Ḫilāfetnāme-2.*
49. Husayn ibn Abdal Zahidi, *Silsilāt al-nasab-i Safavīyah* (Berlin: Chāpkhānah-i Īrānshahr, 1343/1924), 65, cited in Kishwar Rizvi, 'Transformations in Early Safavid Architecture: The Shrine of Shaykh Safi al-Din Ishaq Ardabīli in Iran (1501–1629)' (PhD diss., Massachusetts Institute of Technology, Massachusetts, 2000), 138, 141.
50. Morimoto, 'The Earliest ᶜAlid Genealogy for the Safavids', 456, 459.
51. *'Ve bu iki dergāh-ı ḫalāyıḳ-penāḥdın izin buldı ve muraḫḫaṣ oldı ki Rūm memleketinde ṭālib ve muḥibb ve mü'min ve ṣāfī olan eşḫāṣa irşād kılsun ve özini onlara ḫalīfe bulsun, ḥaḳīḳat ve ṭarīḳat 'aḳd u nikāḥı mü'minlere ve mü'mināta icrā itsün ve ḥalḳa-i ẕikr ḳuranda mecmū'-ı ehl-i ẕikr ser-ḥalḳa ve mürşid olsun, mürīdlere murād olsun ve sālikine irşād ḳılsun.' Ḫilāfetnāme-2.*
52. *'Ve selāṭīn u ḳayāṣire-i Rūma ve ümerā-i ol merz u būma lāzım ve evlādır kim ecdādı ḥürmetine onı muḥterem bulup mecmū'-ı ṣādırāt ve sālgūnāt-i sulṭānī ve tekellüfāt ve teklifāt-ı dīvānīdin mu'āf ve müsellem ḳılup belki muvaẓẓaf bulsunlar ki evliyā ve sādāt ve fuḳarāya mürā'āt itmek beḳā-i devlet-i ebed-müddet-i sulṭāniye sebeb-i nūr-ı ḫüdā-ı Ḥażret-i Ḥaḳḳa bā'iṯ olacaḳdur.' Ḫilāfetnāme-2.*
53. Minorsky characterised the language of Shah Ismaᶜil's *dīvān* as a 'Southern Turkish (Turcoman) dialect associated with the so-called 'Āzarbāyjān Turkish', while also noting the various Chaghatay elements in it. Minorsky, 'Poetry of Shah Ismāᶜīl I', 1,010. Reid suggests that Chaghatay Turkish gradually became the lingua franca of the polyglot Kizilbash ruling elite in Iran. Reid, *Tribalism and Society*, 22. For two other early Safavid documents in Turkish, see L. Fekete, 'İlk Sefevî Şahlarının Türkçe Çıkartılmış İki Senedi', *Philologia Orientalis* 3 (1973): 290–293.
54. The name '*Buyruk*' was presumably inspired by the texts' frequent use of the Turkish verb *buyurmak* meaning 'to order, to command' and was used to express the idea of a direct quotation from a prominent Alevi religious figure.
55. The only work that I am aware of focusing on the place of the *Buyruk* in the daily experience of Alevi religion and identity is David Shankland, 'The Buyruk in Alevi Village Life? Thoughts from the Field of Rival Sources of Religious Inspiration', in *Syncrétismes et hérésies dans l'Orient seldjoukide et ottoman (XIV–XVIII siècle), Actes du Colloque du Collège de France, octobre 2001*, ed. Gilles Veinstein (Paris: Peeters, 2005), 311–323.
56. No systematic studies on the sources of the *Buyruk* manuscripts in general, or of the *Menākıb*s in particular, have been carried out until today. It should be noted, however, that Gölpınarlı very early on discerned major overlaps between the *fütüvvetnāme* literature and the *Buyruk*s in terms of common

rituals and stories. Abdülbâkî Gölpınarlı, *İslam ve Türk İllerinde Fütüvvet Teşkilâtı ve Kaynakları* (Istanbul: Istanbul University, 1952). Furthermore, a link between the *Buyruk*s and the sixteenth-century recension of *Ṣafwat aṣ-Ṣafā*, a hagiographic account of the life of Shaykh Safi, was aptly proposed in Z. V. Togan, 'Londra ve Tahrandaki İslâmî yazmalardan bazılarına dair', *İslâm Tetkikleri Enstitüsü Dergisi* 3, nos 1–2 (1959–1960), 152.

57. For example, compare the contents of the various copies of Imam Cafer *Buyruk*s published in *Buyruk*, ed. Sefer Aytekin, with the Shaykh Ṣafī *Buyruk*s published in *Buyruk: Alevî İnanç-İbâdet ve Ahlâk İlkeleri*, ed. Mehmet Yaman (Mannheim: Alevî Kültür Merkezi Dedeler Kurulu Yayınları, 2000); and *Bisâtî, Şeyh Sâfî Buyruğu*, ed. Ahmet Taşğın (Rheda-Wiedenbrück: Alevi Kültür Derneği Yayınları, 2003).

58. The three dated copies of Imam Cafer *Buyruk*s that I know of are *Risāle-i Ṭarīkat-ı Imām Caᶜfer-i Ṣādıḳ*, MS dated 19 Muharrem 1292/1875, private library of Yesari Gökçe; *Menāḳıb-ı Imām Caᶜferü's-Ṣādıḳ*, MS dated 1308/1890, private library of Yesari Gökçe; and *Menāḳıb-ı Imām Caᶜferü's-Ṣādıḳ*, MS dated Şevval 1323/1905, private library of Mehmet Yaman. The first two of these are cited in Doğan Kaplan, 'Aleviliğin Yazılı Kaynaklarından Buyruklar ve Muhtevaları Üzerine' (Paper presented at the International Symposium on Bektashism and Alevism, 28–30 September 2005, Isparta.) All other Imam Cafer *Buyruk*s that I am aware of, including the copies used by Aytekin, are undated and include no obvious textual or linguistic indications of a date earlier than the nineteenth century. This picture may change, however, with further research.

59. *Macmūᶜa*, MS dated 1017/1608, MMAK, no. 181; *Menākıbü'l-Esrār Behcetü'l-Aḥrār*, MS dated 1021/1612, Mevlânâ Museum Ferid Uğur Collection, no. 1,172, transcription and facsimile published in Bisâtî, *Şeyh Sâfî Buyruğu*.

60. Part of MS no. 181 in MMAK, cited in n59 above and the undated MS no. 198 located in the same collection (the content of which is similar to that of MS no. 181) may both be traced to the reign of Shah Tahmasp; see the relevant entries in Abdülbâkî Gölpınarlı, *Mevlânâ Müzesi Abdülbâkî Kütüphanesi Yazma Kitaplar Kataloğu* (Ankara: Türk Tarih Kurumu, 2003). Other examples of *Buyruk* manuscripts partially compiled during the reign of Shah Tahmasp will be discussed below.

61. *Buyruk-Erzincan*, MS dated 1241/1825–1826, private library of Mehmet Yaman.

62. For example: i) *Buyruk-Erzincan-2*, MS dated 1261/1845, private library of Hamza Özyıldırım, is identical to *Buyruk-Erzincan*, except that the first three folios of *Buyruk-Erzincan-2* include the opening *sūra* of the Koran, *al-Fātiḥa*, and a section entitled '*Hāẕā Ṣalavat-ı Sofiyān*'; ii) the Shabak *Buyruk* published by al-Sarraf is an almost identical copy of the first thirty-six pages of *Buyruk-Erzincan*, the sole difference being that the prayer '*Ḫuṭbe-i Duvāzde Imām*' is placed at the end rather than at the beginning as in the *Buyruk-*

Erzincan; and iii) MS no. 181 in Mevlânâ Müzesi Abdülbâkî Kütüphanesi cited in n605 is virtually identical to the first 147 pages of *Buyruk-Erzincan*; the most significant difference between these two manuscripts is that the part titled '*Kitāb-ı Maḳām-ı Menāḳıb-i Şerīf Kuṭb'ül-'Arifīn Ḥażret-i Şeyḫ Seyyid Ṣafī*' in *Buyruk-Erzincan* is titled '*Menāḳıbü'l-Esrār Behcetü'l-Aḥrār Ḥażret-i İmām Nāṭıḳ Ca'fer-i Ṣādıḳ aleyhi's-selām, te'līf Es-Seyyid Ḫaṭā'ī*' in the other.

63. Fuad Köprülü, 'Abbas (Abbas I)', in *Türk Halk Edebiyatı Ansiklopedisi: Ortaçağ ve Yeniçağ Türklerinin Halk Kültürü Üzerine Coğrafya, Etnografya, Etmoloji, Tarih ve Edebiyat Lugatı*, fasc. 1 (Istanbul: Burhaneddin Basımevi, 1935), 14.
64. Abdülbâkî Gölpınarlı calls this text the '*Küçük Buyruk*', meaning the Short *Buyruk*, based on its content, which bears similarities to that of the *Menākib* text; however, there is nothing in the manuscript or in Alevi oral culture to warrant such a designation. Gölpınarlı, *Tarih Boyunca Islâm Mezhepleri ve Şîîlik* (İstanbul: Der Yayınları, 1987), 178.
65. The relevant section of the prayer, which includes a supplication to God on behalf of the Prophet, the Twelve Imams, the Fourteen Innocent Ones and all believers in addition to Shah Tahmasp, reads as follows: '*Sırr-ı Aḥmed Şāh ve āḫirü'z-zamān ve ṣāḥibü'z-zamān ve Duvāzdeh Imām ve Çıhārdeh Maᶜṣūm-ı Pāk ḥuccetü'l-ḳayyūmü'r-raḥmān ve delīl-i hādī'l-burhān ḳuṭb-i meşāᵓīḫ-i zamān ibnü's-sulṭān Şāh Dehmān cān pādişāh-ı cihān ve mürşīd-i zamānü't-ṭarīḳ-i ḥāżirān ve'l-ġāᵓibān ve li-külli'l-mūᵓminīn ecmaᶜīn bi-raḥmetike yā erḥame'r-rāḥimīn.*' *Buyruk-Erzincan*, 62–63.
66. '*Üstād-ı nefes iᶜmān-ı ṭarīkat erkān-ı meşāyiḫ Şāh Dehmān-ı Ḥüseynī buyurur kim ṭāliblere ve muḥiblere maᶜlūm olsunkim Şāh-ı ᶜĀlem-penāh eşiginde ġāziler ḫalḳa-i ṣoḥbet ḳurup tevḥīd iderlerdi. Nāgāh bir müşkil ẓāhir oldı. ᶜAlī Ḫalīfe ve İbrāhīm Ḫalīfe ve Ebū'l-ġār Ḫalīfe ol ṣoḥbetde ḥāżīr idi. Bunlar ayaḳ üzere peymānçe yirine geçüp naẓara ṭurdılar. Şāh-ı ᶜĀlem-penāh ḥażretine ol müşkili āgāh itdiler. Ḥażret-i Şāh buyurdukim bir ṣoḥbetde ḳırḳ kişi cemᶜ olsa ve ol ṣoḥbete ḳırḳ dane elmā gelse vācib oldur ki cümlesine bir bir virüp ḳısmet ideler eger maᶜsūm olsun ve eger kāmil olsun dügeli beraber göreler baḫş ideler zirā kim yol içinde büyük küçük olmaz. Her ḳardaşıñ rıżāsı ḥāṣıldur. Ḫaḳḳın tanımış ḳardaş niyāzmend olur.*' *Buyruk-Erzincan*, 84.
67. For this letter, see my 'Kızılbaş, Bektaşi, Safevi İlişkilerine Dair 17'.
68. Cf. the two following passages: '*siz erenler munca zamāndan beri vaᶜde virüp intiẓārın çekdigiñiz şāhsüvār-ı merd-i meydān ḥālā meydānda ḥāżır olup muḥibb-i ḫānedānıñ murādın virüp ve düş[menān-ı] [ḥā]nedān-ı āl-i Muḥammed'iñ [neseb] ü zürriyātın rūy-ı zemīnden maḥv itmege ẓāhir olmuşdur.*' Karakaya-Stump, 'Kızılbaş, Bektaşi, Safevi İlişkilerine Dair 17', 119. '*Göñli gözi bu dergāh-ı ᶜālīde olup müştāḳ-ı dīdār olanlar . . . müjdegān ve beşāretler olsun kim bir niçe zamān vaᶜde virüp gelür diyü intiẓārın çekdükleri şāhsüvār-ı meydān-ı feṣāḥat ve gevher-i kīmyā-yı kelam-ı*

belāġat tīġ-i ẕū'l-feḳār-ı şecāᶜat çeküp evlād-ı Muḥammed ᶜAlī düşmanlarına mahābet ve ṣalābet gösterüp devlet ve (?) fetḥ u nuṣret ḳılıcın çalup ehl-i beyt-i resūl hiẕmetine dāmen dermeyān ḳılup cevlān üzeredür.' Buyruk-Erzincan, 139–140.

69. For example, concerning an accusation involving thirty-four heretical books ('*rāfıżī kitablar*') brought from Iran by Kizilbash *ḫalīfe*s, see BA.MD.28:349:883 (19 Ramazan 984/1576); full text provided in Savaş, *XVI. Asırda Anadolu'da Alevîlik*, 206.
70. '*İmdi evliyānuñ edebin ve erkānın biz bu kitāb içinde yazdıḳkim muḥibb-i evliyā olan ṭālibler oḳuyup ᶜamel ideler . . . amma erkān erenleri bu Kitāb-i Menāḳıb-ı Şerīf'i her kimüñ öñünde gerekse okumayalar ve degme kişilere virmeyeler ve göstermeyeler.' Buyruk-Erzincan*, 142.
71. '*Tevbe ḳıldım cemīᶜ-i menāhīden hāẕā Şāh ᶜAbbās ibni Şāh Tahmās elinden tevbe itdim, bu ḥāẓır erenler ṭanıḳlıġıyle eğer dönersem mālım telem ve cān ve başım cümle erenler meydānındadır.*' Bisâtî (?), *Şeyh Sâfî Buyruğu*, 25 (fol. 17b).
72. '*Ve Erdebil'de yatan Şeyḫ Seyyid Ṣāfī ve Sulṭan Ḫaṭāʾī pādişāhıñ ve sürdükleri yollarıñ ve erkānlarıñ tevḥīdleriñ ve ulū ᶜaẓīm cemᶜiyyetlerinin ẕevki ve ṣafāsınıñ ve cümle taḫta geçen evlādlarınıñ ve mürşid-i kāmil Süleymān-ı zamāñ şahımızıñ dem-i devleti ve dem-i devrānı ḥürmeti ḥakkıçün gerçeğe hū.*' Cited in Gölpınarlı, *Mevlânâ Müzesi Abdülbâkî*, 203–204.
73. During my interviews with various members of the Alevi community in rural Anatolia, I discovered that they generally did not recognize the name Shah Ismaᶜil; only after mentioning his pseudonym 'Hatayi' did they identify him as a great Alevi poet. While there was a relatively more widespread recognition of Ardabil (T. Erdebil), it was typically identified as an important Alevi *dergāh* comparable to the Hacı Bektaş convent in Kırşehir. However, this situation is rapidly changing as more and more Alevis learn their histories from books with a greater recognition of the Safavids.

6

From Persecution to Confessionalisation: Consolidation of the Kizilbash/Alevi Identity in Ottoman Anatolia

That which you call Persecution, I translate Uniformity

– Roger L'Estrange, *Toleration Discussed*[1]

The focus in this book so far has been on recovering the Sufi genealogies of the Kizilbash movement as they emerge from recently surfaced Alevi documents and other sources. This new framework overturns the conventional narratives of 'otherness' and 'parochialism' heaped upon the Kizilbash subject and allows us to re-envision the Kizilbash milieu as a transregional network of convents, dervish groups and *sayyid* families, all with their own constituencies of diverse socio-cultural backgrounds, who rallied around Safavid leadership on the basis of a set of Sufi ideas and institutions. The same framework will be used in this chapter to examine the transformation of Kizilbashism from a proselytising, revolutionary movement into a quietist religious order of closed communities with a distinct confessional identity, a process I conceptualise as Kizilbash confessionalisation.

The concept of confessionalisation, in the sense of elite-driven processes of confessional boundary-making and identity enforcement, was originally coined and employed by historians of Reformation Germany. More recently, a group of Ottomanist historians have used it to study in a more integrated fashion the widely recognised but imprecisely defined nexus of changing Ottoman imperial discourse and Sunnitisation policies during the sixteenth century and beyond.[2] These historians have therewith sought to capture the closely intertwined nature of various political and religious developments in the early modern Ottoman context, which they discerned to have unfolded in parallel to Shiᶜitisation in Iran under the Safavids,[3] as well as to analogous developments within Europe.[4]

The present chapter builds and expands on these recent efforts to explore the applicability of the concept of confessionalisation for a better and more nuanced understanding of the Ottoman state's policies vis-à-vis the Kizilbash communities. It argues, first, that the Ottoman state's persecutory impulse against the Kizilbash, persisting as it did even when the latter's early political radicalism had largely ebbed, cannot be reduced to a direct and inevitable outcome of the Ottomans' rivalry with the nascent Shiᶜi Safavid state. Instead, it has to be understood in the broader context of imperial confessional politics, which involved Sufism as a key site of conflict and negotiation. Persecution of 'heretics', or the promotion of the idea of persecution, served in this setting as a most palpable articulation and affirmation of the boundaries of Sunni normativity – the cornerstone of the Ottoman state's legitimating ideology during the period under consideration. In terms of its consequences, too, the repressive measures advocated and implemented against the Kizilbash had significance beyond the immediate confines of the Ottoman–Safavid conflict. Most importantly, they contributed to the cultural and religious uniformity of the empire's Muslim subjects at large by effecting a vigilance at the popular level for the observance of shariᶜi injunctions. The surveillance and punishment of the Kizilbash, carried out with the close cooperation of the local kadis and bureaucrats, moreover, strengthened Ottoman centralisation by enhancing the state's ability to intervene at the local level. As a result, central authority was shored up especially in the provinces and the newly conquered areas.

Second, and more importantly for the purposes of the present work, this chapter demonstrates that the Kizilbash communities were not simply victims of the confessional age, but were – in their own way – also engaged in confessionalisation. Within this context, the historical experience of persecution, or the threat thereof, served as a unifying force binding closer together the diverse groups who made up the Kizilbash/Alevi milieu, thus strengthening group cohesiveness and internal solidarity as well as intensifying their differentiation from the rest of the Islamic polity. The government's persecutory policies targeting the Sufi infrastructure of the Kizilbash milieu also worked as a catalyst in the *sayyid*-isation process of the shaykhly families who were exponents of the Kizilbash movement (briefly outlined in Chapter 2), thus facilitating the emergence of a more homogenous and egalitarian *ocak* system among them.

Before embarking on a discussion of developments in Ottoman Sunnism and Kizilbashism during the early modern period, a few clarifications regarding the utility of the concept of confessionalisation in both contexts would be in order. One cannot treat Kizilbashism (or for that matter Sunnism and Shiᶜism) as confessions in the same way in which one can treat Christian denominations that are based on written statements of doctrine and formal church structures. It is also true that the original confessionalisation theory as proposed by Heinz Schilling and Wolfgang Reinhard links it to processes of state-building in the early modern period; they argue that the official promotion and enforcement within a given territory of a particular denomination helped produce overlapping religious and political domains, and served as an instrument of social discipline, religious homogenisation and political centralisation.[5] However, Schilling and Reinhard's original confessionalisation model has been challenged and reshaped on various fronts. Among other things, critics have faulted the model for its state-centric, top–down focus and lack of attention to non-state actors in promoting confessional self-discipline.[6] This point has particular relevance for minority groups, such as the Kizilbash, who seem to have gone through similar confessionalization processes independently or in opposition to political authorities.[7] Here, I employ the concept of confessionalisation in connection to the Kizilbash in the looser sense of the development of internally coherent and externally exclusive confessional communities through social disciplining, without the original theory's emphasis on written confessions of faith and state building.

Moreover, even when applied to describe developments within Ottoman Sunnism and Safavid Shiᶜism, in which case the state-building component of the original confessionalisation model is clearly relevant, one needs to make a number of qualifications and adjustments to the concept as it was formulated by Schilling and Reinhard. To begin with, the Islamic world did not experience a schism akin to the Reformation that produced the Protestant denominations and modern territorial churches; Islam was multi-confessional already before the sixteenth century with the two rival branches, namely Sunnism and Shiᶜism, having been present in the Middle East since the very inception of the new religion. The novelty of the early modern period for the region, thus, resided not in the proliferation of confessions as such but rather in the emergence of a powerful Shiᶜi polity in an otherwise Sunni-dominated environment, which, in turn, was both a result and a driving force of the escalating polarisation between the two confessions. This polarisation represented a break from the past only insofar as it followed a period of relative confessional rapprochement within the framework of Sufism, as indicated by the growing preponderance of ᶜAlidism as a suprasectarian orientation in post-Mongol Islamdom. It is, therefore, not surprising that Sufi ideas and institutions were key sites of contestation at the height of confessionalisation processes in the Sunni Ottoman and Shiᶜi Safavid empires alike.[8] While the Safavids repressed all rival Sufi elements, along with aspects of Kizilbash piety that potentially blurred the Sunni–Shiᶜi boundaries (such as the high esteem with which the Kizilbash held Abu Muslim, the leader of the Abbasids' revolutionary armies against the Umayyads), the Ottomans sought to curtail and domesticate, rather than totally eradicate, the Sufi milieu by labelling and repressing its undesirable elements as 'Kizilbash'.[9]

Finally, unlike church–state relations in the European context (and to a large extent in Safavid Persia despite the more hierarchical organisation of the Shiᶜi ulema), conditioned by the presence of two distinct and often rival institutional structures, the higher echelons of the religious classes in the Ottoman Empire were in large measure structurally integrated and subordinate to the state apparatus since especially the reign of Mehmed II (r. 1451–1481), which saw the initial creation of the Ottoman imperial ethos and centralised bureaucracy.[10] In that sense, the sixteenth century did not mark a real departure from the past. What was remarkable in the Ottoman context was not the close collaboration of the religious and political elites per se, but rather the particularly intense and penetrating form that this collaboration took, and the vigour and systematic nature with which the state came to supervise religion. This process entailed a concerted effort on the part of secular and religious authorities to (re)define the boundaries of proper Sunnism and impose it on the subject populations, which accords with the confessionalisation model. It manifested itself perhaps most vibrantly in the endorsement and authorisation of a set of legal rulings (Ot. *fetvā*) by the famous *şeyhü'l-islām* Ebussuᶜud as dynastic law (*ḳānūn*) by Sultan Süleyman, the Lawgiver (*Ḳānūnī*). This was a practice not seen before.[11] It needs to be acknowledged, however, that 'the sheer geographical scope' of the Islamic empires during the early modern era, especially in the case of the Ottomans, 'made the imposition of a single confession logistically difficult'.[12] Despite this important caveat, one can still speak of a growing territorialisation of Sunni and Shiᶜi confessions, and greater levels of confessional homogeneity on both sides of the Ottoman–Safavid border, even though, unlike in Safavid Iran where Sunnism was largely wiped out, sizeable Kizilbash, as well as Shiᶜi, communities continued to live in Ottoman territories.

A key claim underscoring the present discussion is that the official sanction and implementation of persecutory measures against the Kizilbash was both a necessary condition for, and an outcome of, a 'confessional turn' in Ottoman politics that coincided with Selim I's reign, and the ensuing process of Sunni confessionalisation under his successors. The perspective on Kizilbash persecutions adopted here departs from the mainstream approach to the subject, which tends to confine them, both in terms of their causes and consequences, to an essentially political narrative centred around the Ottoman–Safavid conflict. That it was in some way natural or understandable, or at any rate inevitable that the Ottomans should seek to suppress by force the Kizilbash, who after all colluded with the rival Safavids, has come to be accepted as a matter of course by most historians. This logic of inevitability fails to make adequate room for historical contingencies and human agency, especially as they relate to tensions and power struggles within the Ottoman elite. Of particular relevance here is the intra-dynastic rivalry and the civil war between different contenders for the Ottoman throne in the years and months leading up to Selim I's ascent to power in 1512, a critical moment in Ottoman history that saw a major reconfiguration of Ottoman dynastic self-identification and imperial politics. To be clear, the purpose here is not to trivialise or dismiss the link between the Ottoman–Safavid imperial rivalry and the Ottoman state's hardening Sunni identity and its persecution of the Kizilbash. It is rather to emphasise the need to explore how underlying external conditions interacted with internal dynamics in producing and shaping confessional politics in the empire, which, in turn, not only prepared the necessary background for the Kizilbash persecutions but, more importantly, had broader and enduring ramifications for the Ottoman polity at large.

The widespread tendency to treat Kizilbash persecutions as an unmediated and self-explanatory outcome of the Ottomans' rivalry with the burgeoning Safavid state is in part related to a general inclination within recent scholarly literature to portray the Ottoman policy makers as inherently flexible, pragmatist and religiously tolerant. This approach necessarily foregrounds considerations of political expediency and efficacy in shaping the Ottoman 'politics of difference' at the expense of religious factors and changing ideological needs of the empire that this chapter aims to highlight.[13] To speak of the role of religion in Kizilbash persecutions is, of course, not to say that they can be understood with reference to nothing but religion. It is rather a way of stressing the implications of the linkage of Ottoman rule to Sunni normativity for the dissenting insiders insofar as it narrowed possibilities of inclusion in the polity and provided blueprints for the latter's treatment. This is clearly evident in the official Ottoman stance vis-à-vis groups designated as Kizilbash which was one of zero tolerance, and framed squarely in religious terms. In their numerous *fetvā*s, members of the Ottoman ulema in the sixteenth century, starting with Sarı Gürz Hamza Efendi (d. 1514), declared the Kizilbash to be 'infidels and enemies of the faith' and ruled their destruction to be 'a religious duty incumbent on the Muslim community'.[14] Similar *fetvā*s, with few nuances among them, were issued by such high-profile *şeyhü'l-islām*s as Kemalpaşazade and Ebussuᶜud, and were to be rehashed and repeated by their successors over the centuries.[15] One cannot dismiss this continuous chain of *fetvās* simply as doctrinal or legal rhetoric, or as superficial bureaucratic manoeuvres with no real or significant impact on the ground. On the contrary, they were enacted in the form of various punitive measures to varying degrees in different time periods and places throughout Ottoman history.[16] Even when the more extreme measures against the Kizilbash were largely replaced by milder and more discriminatory forms of imperial disciplining and control around about the turn of the seventeenth century, however, a vilifying discourse of exclusion harking back to medieval heresiographical literature was maintained at the formal level, pressuring the communities in question to dissimulate and lead an underground religious life. This intermediate state of formal suppression and informal accommodation defined the precarious existence of the Kizilbash/Alevi communities on the margins of the imperial polity for most of Ottoman history after the sixteenth century, with the potential for aggression against them lurking in the social background.

Those who posit pragmatism and tolerance as the norm in Ottoman politics do not necessarily deny the persecutory measures inflicted on the Kizilbash, which are well attested in the official sources. They rather present these instances as localised and historically particular exceptions to the norm and as propelled essentially by political motivations.[17] It must be granted, as emphasised by the proponents of the Ottoman pragmatism thesis, that the Ottomans had few qualms implementing situational toleration when deemed politically and economically expedient, even though such administrative pragmatism, at least on its surface, ran counter to the forceful and bitter verbal attacks by the Ottoman religious establishment against the Kizilbash. However, this de facto pluralism and tolerance ought not be confused with a principled commitment to the toleration of religious difference. Like other persecuting states, the Ottomans were ready and capable to employ coercive power whenever they felt it necessary to secure external religious conformity. Nor should one forget that persecutory measures do not have to be universal or end in extermination to be effective. Just the threat or fear of persecution, so long as it is periodically validated and reinforced by actual acts of violence, would often suffice to control people's behaviour. That the Ottoman state shifted and combined various strategies, ranging from persecution to informal accommodation and assimilation, in their long-term management of the 'Kizilbash problem' is thus only confirmation that 'tolerance' and 'intolerance' are not mutually exclusive categories, but often coexist and even require each other to be meaningful.[18]

All in all, talking about confessionalisation in the early modern Ottoman empire opens new vistas for reassessing Kizilbash persecutions within their appropriate social and political context. It enables us to move beyond false binaries, such as religious versus political motivations and persecution versus toleration, that plague current treatments of the subject. By offering us an analytical middle ground, it both provides a remedy against the logic of inevitability and helps to explore the relevance of religion in terms of the aims, experience and consequences of Kizilbash persecutions without falling prey to essentialist assumptions.

From 'Sufis of Ardabil' to 'Kizilbash': The Confessional-turn in Ottoman Politics

On the eve of Shah Isma^cil's enthronement in July 1501, an imperial decree by the Ottoman sultan Bayezid II (r. 1481–1512) was dispatched to the governor of Sivas to affirm an earlier one. The original decree, which is no longer extant, ordered the capture and execution of those 'Sufis of Ardabil' (Erdebīl Ṣūfīleri) who were trying to cross the border to go to Iran, and authorised the appropriation of their goods by whomsoever did the capturing. The later decree reiterated this original order, and additionally reprimanded Ottoman border guards who were apparently willing to spare the lives of those captured in exchange for a monetary payment fixed at 400 *akçe*s for a Sufi and 2,000 *akçe*s for a *ḫalīfe*.[19] The significance of this decree, one of a small group of precious documents concerning Safavid followers in Anatolia from the pre-Selim era, is manifold. Especially meaningful for our current purposes is its employment of the term 'Sufi' for groups affiliated with the Safavi order, a term that was in use virtually in all Ottoman state documents before the advent of Selim I when this familiar and neutral term would be supplanted with the exclusionary and politically charged appellation 'Kizilbash'.[20] Far from being a minor detail or a simple legal device, this sharp and deliberate shift in terminology marks a critical juncture in Ottoman politics, what I choose to call a 'confessional turn'. It represents the discursive dawn of a substantial transformation in the very constitution of the Ottoman polity, one that was predicated on the construction of a Sunni Muslim social base for the empire that was more homogenous in its religious outlook and ideologically more closely integrated with the state. This transformation both required and enabled the criminalisation of a segment of the population that included not only the long-standing disciples of the Safavi order but also various non-conformist Sufi/dervish circles with real or imagined Safavid sympathies, and resulted in their physical or symbolic erasure from the polity.

A combination of internal and external, as well as short-term and long-term, dynamics underscored the confessional turn in Ottoman history that coincided with the advent of Selim I, also known as Yavuz, as the ninth Ottoman sultan. Yavuz Selim is hailed as one of the greatest Ottoman sultans for having doubled the size of the Ottoman domains by annexing former Akkoyunlu territories in eastern and southeastern Anatolia, and for establishing Ottoman control over most of the Arab Middle East. Having acquired the Holy Cities of Mecca and Medina, he also became the first Ottoman sultan to carry the honourable title of 'Servant of the Two Holy Cities' (*ḫādimü'l-Ḥaremeyn*), hitherto belonging to the Mamluks. Yet Yavuz Selim was also the one and only Ottoman sultan to force his father off the throne, a major transgression of Ottoman dynastic principles, before eliminating in a prolonged civil war his two brothers and several nephews to consolidate his grip on power. Later Ottoman sources tried hard to redeem Selim I's dishonourable treatment of his father by depicting Bayezid II as an aged and feeble sultan who was unduly accommodating in his dealings with Shah Isma^c^il, and by presenting Yavuz Selim as the only Ottoman prince who had the foresight and courage to sense the imminence and gravity of the Safavid threat against Ottoman domains, and to take on the Kizilbash challenge decisively.[21]

Mainstream modern historiography tends to agree with this assessment, using as evidence for it a series of uprisings in the sixteenth century that involved Shah Isma^c^il's followers and sympathisers.[22] Especially the first one of these so-called Kizilbash uprisings, the Şahkulu Uprising of 1511, which was particularly destructive, has been commonly viewed by modern historians as a moment of truth that would tip the balance in favour of Selim in the Ottoman civil war. It is alleged that the uprising of Şahkulu demonstrated beyond any doubt the Safavids' use of their followers in Ottoman territories as a fifth column in the service of their expansionist ambitions over Anatolia (Rum), thereby proving the deftness of Selim's proactive policies.[23] This reading, however, fails to attend to the reality in all its complexity as revealed in the documentary evidence, which most importantly highlights the uprisings' local character. While it is true that the leader of the uprising, Şahkulu, was a Safavi *ḫalīfe*, as was his father Halife Hasan, there is no conclusive sign in the sources of any direct cooperation, let alone an operative command structure, between Şahkulu and the Safavid court on the eve of or during the uprising. In fact, we learn from the Ottoman sources that the uprising was carried out not in Shah Isma^c^il's name but in the name of Şahkulu himself, who reportedly had a large sphere of influence expanding westwards into Rumelia, and was hailed as a messianic figure in his own right by his followers.[24] According to these sources, Şahkulu came to arrogate to himself temporal as well as spiritual authority concomitantly with his growing self-confidence and the rapidly increasing number of his supporters beyond his immediate circle of disciples.[25]

A closer look at the social base of the uprising reinforces the idea that local dynamics were a primary driving force behind it. Available sources unfortunately do not allow the participants of the uprising to speak for themselves directly, but they do include sufficient indications of the complex mixture of socio-economic and religious dynamics that drove the participants into action. Judged by their description in the Ottoman sources as 'bums . . who spent their lives on foot' (*piyāde-revün ᶜömrin geçüren . . bīkārlar*) and 'bareheaded and barefoot demons' (*ser-[ā]-pā berhene nekbetīler*),[26] it is easy to imagine that the fighters in Şahkulu's army came primarily from the lower classes in the countryside most vulnerable to the deteriorating economic circumstances during the period under consideration. They almost certainly represented much the same social environment as that of those who had earlier migrated from Teke to Iran and who were denigrated by contemporary Ottoman writers as low-lifes seeking and obtaining undeserved respect and dignity at the court of Shah Ismaᶜil.[27] The latter, undoubtedly, were pulled in the direction of the Safavid territories at least in part by Shah Ismaᶜil's reputation for generosity in distributing the booty and wealth among his followers.[28] Apart from the underprivileged countryside folk, including nomadic tribesmen or peasant villagers,[29] another group responding to Şahkulu's revolutionary message was the disgruntled low-ranking members of the Ottoman military class. These were middle- and lower-ranking provincial cavalrymen, or timariots (*tımarlı sipahi*), composed largely of local elements who saw their fiefs shrinking in size or being lost to government appointees of *devşirme* origin in tandem with the creation of a centralist autocracy from the mid-fifteenth century onwards.[30] Many of these timariots readily abandoned the rebel ranks upon restoration of their former land grants, which also paved the way for the unravelling and suppression of the uprising.[31]

That the Şahkulu uprising served as an outlet for growing popular discontent and frustration with Ottoman rule does not mean that religion played a purely instrumentalist role. Rather, the culmination of an accumulated resentment against the increasingly more formal and authoritarian state and its confluence with the appeal of Şahkulu's religious message is probably what conspired to create a fertile environment for such a powerful grassroots mobilisation. It seems that Şahkulu's messianically tinged message gained further traction thanks to several natural disasters, including a massive earthquake that in September 1509 hit a vast region extending from central Anatolia to the Balkans, levelling many buildings and causing thousands of deaths in Istanbul alone. Still more, this devastating earthquake coincided with ongoing dynastic infighting in the years leading up to the revolt.[32] The rumoured death of Bayezid II amidst this political chaos and natural disaster was in all likelihood viewed as a divine sign that the rule of the Ottoman family had come to an end and that the time was ripe for a new dispensation, as reportedly preached by Şahkulu.[33]

There is, of course, little doubt that Şahkulu was emboldened and inspired by the advent of Shah Ismaᶜil, to whom he allegedly made references in his propaganda. This does not, however, change the fact that Şahkulu's rebellion represented for the most part a local reaction rather than being an undertaking authorised externally. Shah Ismaᶜil's ill treatment of the 'Sufis of Teke', who made it to Iran with their families in the aftermath of the uprising, is a clear testimony to his disapproval of Şahkulu's action, at the very least the form or timing of it.[34] The picture of Şahkulu thus emerging from the available evidence is one of a local religious figure that is all too familiar among the many socially activist dervishes and Sufi masters of the past whose real source of power was his individual charisma and following. This picture, as such, calls into question Şahkulu's treatment as little more than an obedient agent and auxiliary force of the Safavid court who was incited into action by Shah Ismaᶜil. Indeed, barring the revolt led by Nur Ali Halife, about which more will be said below, none of the so-called Kizilbash revolts in Anatolia can be conclusively shown to have been part of an elaborate Safavid plan under the direct orders of, or with explicit sanction from, the Safavid shahs.[35]

The overstatement of Safavid involvement in the contemporary revolts in Anatolia serves to justify another problematic tendency in the conventional literature, namely the common perception of state's repressive measures against real or imagined sympathisers of the Safavid shahs as a natural and automatic answer to the Kizilbash uprisings, in general, and the Şahkulu revolt, in particular.[36] While there is no denying that Ottoman religious policies toughened considerably in the aftermath of the Şahkulu uprising, it is also a fact that the above-mentioned imperial decree from 1501 predated the uprising by almost exactly a decade. This indicates that Ottoman surveillance and punishment of the Anatolian disciples of the Safavi order had already begun during the reign of Bayezid II, when relations between the Ottomans and the Safavids were formally still on friendly terms.[37] Several other decrees with similar content from the same period leave no doubt that Bayezid II was keenly aware of the fledgling new state on the empire's eastern border and its leader's utilisation of his disciples and *ġāzīs* in Anatolia as a pool of manpower. To render this pool inaccessible to the young shah, Bayezid II issued successive orders banning movement across the border for anyone travelling to Safavid territories. This was not Bayezid II's only pre-emptive measure: even more radically, he exiled thousands of lay followers of the Safaviyya and their families in 1502 to recently conquered areas in the west (mainly Modoni and Koroni in southern Greece) as a way of dispersing them from their traditional strongholds in Anatolia.[38] It is, therefore, probably no coincidence that the first so-called Kizilbash insurgence led by Şahkulu broke out in the provinces of Teke and Hamid (present-day Antalya and Isparta), whose inhabitants were among the first and primary targets of Bayezid II's mass deportations. They were targeted, not because of any open rebellion or insurrection, but because of their inclination to leave Ottoman territories for Iran, whether out of religious sentiments, to join Shah Ismaᶜil's forces or to simply seek better socio-economic prospects.[39]

Despite such harsh measures, however, Bayezid II's approach to the Sufis of Ardabil largely remained within the framework of a quasi-ecumenical moderate Sunnism befitting a frontier state that hitherto drew its legitimacy primarily from its expansion into infidel territories. His policies, accordingly, were not exclusively 'stick-based' but came with various familiar 'carrots' attached that aimed at domesticating and accommodating groups that were potentially receptive to the Safavids' religious appeal. We have already seen in Chapter 3 that one of these policies involved the reorganisation of the Bektashi order under Balım Sultan, his appointed administrator of the central Bektashi convent in Kırşehir, which resulted in the creation of a separate Babagan branch. Many Abdals, if not all, would in time take refuge under the protective institutional umbrella of the Babagan Bektashis to avoid punishment. Bayezid II also utilised his special patronage of the Halveti Sufi order as a rival ideological force against the Safaviyya. His choice of the Halvetis for this task of counter-propaganda, rather than some other Sunni order such as the Naqshbandis and Zeynis, presumably had a significance beyond his well-known personal allegiance to the order that was centred in Amasya already before the sultan's princely residence there. For, although self-professedly Sunni, the Halvetis had issued from the same *silsila* as the Safaviyya and espoused a strong ᶜAlid orientation in a fashion reminiscent of the metadoxy that seems to have prevailed in the Sufi environments of medieval Anatolia in general, and the Wafaᵓi/Babaᵓi circles in particular.[40] Such commonalities, the sultan might have reasoned, would help to keep at bay the powerful attraction exerted by the Safavid enterprise over many of his Muslim subjects by more effectively neutralising the religious appeal stemming from their (widely accepted, albeit possibly forged) ᶜAlid descent and prestigious Sufi genealogy.

Bayezid II's relative accommodation of the Safavids and their Anatolian followers – compared to what was to come under his son and successor, Selim I – makes further sense when contextualised within the immediate contours of his reign and vision for the empire. Unlike his father Mehmed II, whose thirty years of ceaseless conquest not only strained the fiscal resources of the empire but also alienated many whose private properties and pious endowments were unlawfully confiscated to fund those campaigns, Bayezid II seems to have prioritised internal consolidation over further territorial expansion.[41] Among those hit hard by Mehmed II's economic policies were the Sufis whose goodwill Bayezid II had successfully restored by returning their properties and by implementing various other measures beneficial to them. In return, he was able to enlist the Sufis' support against his brother, Cem, who contested Bayezid II for the Ottoman throne.[42] Bayezid II's favourable policies towards the Sufis, combined with his personal image of a pious sultan, gained him the epithet 'Velī', or 'friend of God', which is normally reserved for great Sufi masters. Bayezid II would try to use his personal charisma and connections among the Sufis to pull closer to the imperial centre the various alienated Sufi and dervish groups, whose influence extended far and wide in the Ottoman polity, rather than pushing them further away at a time when the Safavids, now a political rival, were expanding and reinforcing their spiritual clout over them.

In stark contrast to his father, however, Prince Selim pursued an openly and decisively hostile policy towards Shah Isma^{c}il from the beginning. As prince-governor of Trabzon, he gave shelter at his court to members of the Akkoyunlu elite, who were escaping Safavid conquests and the attending persecution of Sunni Muslims. These Sunni émigrés from Iran would later emerge as key agents in the process by which a vicious anti-Kizilbasah progranda was engineered and promoted in the empire.[43] Selim also carried out unprovoked raids into former Akkoyunlu territories that had recently come under Safavid control. As early as 1505, Shah Isma^{c}il protested to Bayezid II about Selim's assaults on Erzincan, which had been Safavid territory since 1503. It was thanks to Bayezid II's efforts of reconciliation that a possible acceleration of the conflict between the two was prevented for the time being.[44] A similar complaint about Prince Selim's attacks would be filed with Bayezid in 1508, demanding the return of Safavid armaments that Selim's forces had captured in Erzincan. While this request was ignored, Bayezid II, who was apparently distressed by Prince Selim's belligerence, ordered his son multiple times to desist from further attacks on Safavid-held territories, as well as raids into Christian Georgia.[45]

It is difficult to explain Prince Selim's implacable hostility towards Shah

Isma^c^il solely on the basis of defensive concerns, and his allegedly more perceptive and accurate assessment of the threat posed against the Ottomans by this new, neighbouring power. Those who view Selim's antagonism as being rooted in a well-justified fear for the survival of the empire presuppose an existentialist Safavid menace to its integrity due to Shah Isma^c^il's territorial ambitions over Rum, which he purportedly tried to achieve with the help of his followers scattered in that region.[46] The cogency of this supposition is, however, debatable. For even if we allow for the possibility that Shah Isma^c^il's followers and sympathisers, who presumably saw in him a messianic conqueror, or even Shah Isma^c^il himself, harboured such dreams, there is no clear indication that he planned his military and diplomatic moves according to a consciously articulated goal of conquering the land of Rum.[47] On the contrary, Shah Isma^c^il seems to have expended all his energy on taking over the former Akkoyunlu territories in the west and Khorasan in the east, concurrently '[seeking] peaceful relations with the Ottomans as a requirement of realpolitik'.[48]

Nor can the leaders of the so-called Kizilbash revolts be viewed as tightly controlled instruments of the Safavid court who acted on direct orders of the Safavid shahs, as already noted. Even in cases where the leader of a revolt can be ascertained to be an actual Safavi *ḫalīfe*, as in the case of Şahkulu, the insurgents' connection to the centre of the order or the Safavid court was apparently rather loose or non-existent.[49] The only exception to this is the revolt of Nur Ali Halife, which took place in Tokat in 1512, either right before or right after Selim's enthronement. All the signs about this revolt, contrary to the one led by Şahkulu, indicate direct involvement and orchestration on the part of the Safavid court. To begin with, unlike Şahkulu, Nur Ali Halife was an outsider to the province of Tokat, the centre of the revolt, and was almost certainly sent there by the shah. After taking control of the city with the help of forces he had recruited locally, Nur Ali Halife immediately and tellingly had the *ḫuṭbe* read in the name of Shah Isma^c^il. That Nur Ali Halife was acting on direct orders from Shah Isma^c^il, or at least with his approval, is also supported by his flight to the Safavid court after the event, where he would be awarded with the governorship of Erzincan. Nur Ali Halife would later serve as one of the Safavid commanders in the Battle of Çaldıran of 1514, and eventually meet his death fighting the Ottoman army near Erzincan in 1515.[50]

In assessing Shah Isma^c^il's apparent firsthand involvement in the Nur Ali Halife revolt, one has to bear in mind its timing, which coincided with the last phase of the Ottoman civil war that had been prompted by Selim's pre-emptive bid for the Ottoman throne about a year prior.[51] This was a prolonged intra-Ottoman conflict in which the Safavids had a high stake and took a clear side in supporting Prince Ahmed, Bayezid II's favourite candidate, against their arch-enemy Selim. Shah Isma^cil's instigation of a revolt among his Anatolian followers via Nur Ali Halife was, thus, more likely a last-minute effort to undermine Selim and boost the forces of Prince Ahmed rather than being part of a grand Safavid strategy to expand into Anatolia. Further support for this scenario is supplied by the actions of Prince Murad, son of Prince Ahmed, who reportedly put on the Kizilbash headgear and joined Nur Ali Halife's forces during the revolt in Tokat. According to Ottoman historian Celalzade, Prince Murad's donning of the Kizilbash *tāj* was meant to garner support from the local Kizilbash to continue his father's fight against Selim. Prince Murad was to seek asylum at Shah Isma^{c}il's court following the suppression of the revolt.[52]

That defensive concerns alone are inadequate to explain Prince Selim's anti-Safavid policies is also corroborated by contemporary Ottoman sources that show that the real bone of contention between Shah Isma^{c}il and Prince Selim was not the land of Rum per se. Territorially speaking, the sticking point was the former Akkoyunlu territories, or what is presently considered eastern Anatolia. By reason of his familial ties to the Akkoyunlu dynasty, Shah Isma^{c}il staked a claim to this region, many of the inhabitants of which were, moreover, linked to him by spiritual ties. Bayezid II, who pursued a policy of containment against this new neighbouring state, in effect recognised the validity of the young shah's political claims, even if perhaps grudgingly, by congratulating him on his conquests in Persia and Azerbaijan.[53] Prince Selim, on the other hand, flatly rejected Shah Isma^{c}il's royal pretensions in any form and shape, and specifically as they related to former Akkoyunlu domains that he claimed for the house of Osman.

Prince Selim's expansionist vision for the empire, which diverged from that of his father, is clearly reflected in the Ottoman sources that highlight his intense anger upon hearing of the Safavid troops' capture of the city of Erzincan in 1503. Şükri Bidlisi contains one of the more detailed accounts of Selim's reaction, showing him as saying that now that the Akkoyunlus (Bayındur) were gone, their territories should belong to the Ottomans:

> Who is Shah Isma^{c}il that he dares to capture a place so close to my domain?
>
> . . .
>
> I am the worthy one; how dare the Kizilbash speak [on this matter]. He better stand guard over his throne in Tabriz. The Akkoyunlu is gone, it is now my turn of fortune. That region must submit to Rum.[54]

Şükri Bidlisi's account, assuming its relative accuracy, demonstrates that Selim's antagonism towards Shah Isma^{c}il was not driven as much by a concern to guard the integrity of the existing Ottoman domains as by his vision of a more forceful and expansionist foreign policy in the east. In that sense, his rejection of the Safavids' claim to the Akkoyunlu heritage signified above all his defiance of Bayezid II's policy of reconciliation and containment vis-à-vis the nascent Safavid state. To make better sense of this divergence between father and son, a closer scrutiny of the interplay between the internal politics of the empire and its external conditions is necessary.

Most immediately and from the perspective of internal dynamics, Selim's defiance of his father's policy choices vis-à-vis the Safavids can be linked to the domestic situation in the empire, which was dominated by intradynastic competition over succession. Prince Selim, it seems, realised early on the utility of the Safavid card as leverage in the impending rivalry for the Ottoman throne following the expected death of his aged father whose heir apparent was Selim's older brother, Ahmed.[55] Selim was the youngest and least likely candidate for the throne. Bayezid II worked hard to keep his ill-tempered and ambitious youngest son at a safe distance from Istanbul so as to ensure the succession of Ahmed, who had been appointed to the prestigious governorship of Amasya in relative proximity to the imperial capital. Selim, in contrast, had been sent to Trabzon, the province furthest away from the capital, located in the empire's northeastern corner. Aware of his minimal chances of winning the crown under these circumstances and the apparently high stakes involved, Selim seems to have adopted – and successfully implemented – a deliberate strategy to turn the tide in his favour. This strategy entailed, among other things, the dissemination of an exaggerated sense of the Kizilbash threat and the cultivation of his reputation as the only candidate to the throne capable and ready to tackle it. In that sense, the rise of the Shiᶜi Safavids on the empire's eastern front might be viewed as a turn of fortune for Prince Selim, insofar as it facilitated the fulfilment of his political ambitions by providing a foil against which he could redefine the terms of his candidacy, and promote it even if he did not enjoy his father's endorsement.[56]

Selim's raids into Georgia as prince-governor acquire a new significance when assessed from this angle, throwing into sharper relief the eventual confessional turn in his self-legitimation. His forays into Christian Georgia, the same area raided by Shah Ismaᶜil's holy warriors from Anatolia, was Selim's way of reclaiming on behalf of the Ottoman dynasty the banner of *ġazāʾ*, which, he asserted, his father failed to own adequately due to his underactive foreign policy.[57] In the past, the Ottomans were the indisputable champions of the title of supreme *ġāzī*. Besides supplying the house of Osman with ideological legitimacy, their conquests in Christian territories also had significant socio-economic benefits. These not only created a steady flow of wealth into the central treasury but also kept within the system large numbers of ambitious young men willing to fight for economic and otherworldly gains. One consequence of tapering off the empire's drive for further conquests was a growing surplus population that could no longer be absorbed by the empire's war machine. This demographic pressure was further compounded by the progressive increase in taxes, which were imposed to compensate for the fiscal deficit the central treasury had been suffering since the reign of Mehmed II, as a result of which peasants, unable to afford their payments, had begun abandoning their lands. An additional factor augmenting the economic and political discontent was the declining fortunes of the aforementioned local *tımar* holders, who were losing ground to individuals of *devşirme* background in the Ottoman military-administrative system as a byproduct of the empire's growing drive for centralisation.[58]

All this rendered Anatolia a most fertile ground of manpower for Shah Isma^{c}il to build up his army, as well as of Safavid sympathisers who did not necessarily have a prior spiritual bond to the Safavi order. Prince Selim, like his father, was aware of the resulting human flow from Anatolia to Iran. Unlike his father, however, who focused on rendering this pool inaccessible for Shah Isma^{c}il, Selim sought to harness and redirect the energies of these young men in support of a promise that his candidacy held for a renewed expansionist momentum in Ottoman foreign policy. Particularly illuminating in this regard is a long speech given by Prince Selim to his fighting men in the aftermath of one of their raids into Georgia. In this speech, as reported by Celalzade, Selim openly acknowledged the concerns of the common folk (*merdüm-zāde*) who had been turning towards the Kizilbash due to their diminishing hopes for an official position within the Ottoman system, where individuals of *devşirme* (or *ḳul*) origin had far better opportunities. He promised the young fighters in the audience better prospects for the future, and called on them to urge their fellow countrymen 'to stop loving the Kizilbash' once they were back in their hometowns.[59] Selim's raids into Georgia, when interpreted in the light of this remarkable speech, point to a different, perhaps earlier strategy to expand and solidify support for his candidacy by reclaiming the banner of *ġazā*ʾ that was now effectively contested by the Safavids. Selim's efforts to lure into in his army politically and economically malcontent young inhabitants in the provinces with a promise of renewed military expansionism achieved only limited success, however, being more effective in Rumelia than Anatolia, since the latter was the stronghold of his older brother and main rival, Prince Ahmed.[60] It would thus seem that the confessional turn in Selim's ideological discourse was in part precipitated by the limited success of his original strategy. This strategy, at least in the sense of raids into infidel territories, would soon lose much of its bearing and relevance as Selim's bid for the throne became increasingly framed in confessional terms, presenting what was essentially a dynastic rivalry with the Safavids over Akkoyunlu territory as a legitimate war against 'heresy'.

Confessional Politics and Interdynastic Competition

Even if intradynastic competition provided the initial impetus for the confessional turn in Selim's legitimacy claims for his candidacy, his anti-Kizilbash agenda would outlive the civil war preceding his consolidation of power, and establish a firm basis for future developments in the empire's history by shaping the tenor and content of the new Ottoman imperial ideology. A complex set of religious, structural and external factors accounted for the lasting relevance and preponderance of confessional politics in the empire. To begin with, the immediate efficacy of Selim's strategy owed much to its ready alignment with the political realities on the ground, which were conducive to such a shift in the Ottoman imperial discourse. One thing worth remembering here is that Selim found some of his strongest ideological allies among Akkoyunlu émigrés from Iran who personally suffered under Shah Isma^cil's persecutory policies against the Sunnis. These Iranian émigrés presumably saw in Selim a capable, or even godsent, opponent against their arch-enemy. One such figure was Khawaja Mulla Isfahani, who sent Selim a versified letter at about the time of the Battle of Çaldıran in 1514, in which he addressed the sultan as the Alexander (Dhū'l-qarnayn) of Islam, urging him to conquer the land of Persia from the Safavids.[61] Another one, Husayn b. ᶜAbdullah al-Shirvani, wrote polemical epistles against the Kizilbash in which he depicted Selim as 'the sultan of the East and the West' (*sulṭānü'l-meşārıḳ ve'l-meġārib*) sent (*ersele*) by God.[62] It is not hard to imagine how all these expectations and incitations might have bred and nourished in Selim a genuine sense of being the bearer of a divine mission as a world conqueror and the saviour of the true faith. This feeling, once planted, would have only grown further with his victories on the battlefield, which he and those around him most likely took as proof that God was on their side.

Such grandiose attributions to Selim were also fully in tune with the chiliastic fever of the early sixteenth century that manifested itself in the political arena as competing claims of universal rulership. [63] The widespread sense of the immanency of the apocalypse, which influenced the political vision and rhetoric of virtually all great empire-builders in

Eurasia at the time, must have not only facilitated the authentication and internalisation of the religious mission attributed to Selim by his supporters, but also created a persisting need to project and promote an imperial Sunni cult. This new self-acclaimed image would serve the Ottoman sultans as a powerful instrument of legitimacy against the empire's external rivals, above all the Shiᶜi Safavids, as it earlier did against Selim I's internal opponents. To understand better the underlying dynamics of this development, it is important to recall Cornell Fleischer's observation that Ottoman legitimacy, even as late as the early sixteenth century, was not a given as it is often made out to be in the conventional literature. From early on, the Ottomans shifted and combined different legitimacy claims, variously drawing on *ġazāʾ* ideology, their (alleged) Oghuz-Kayı genealogy, and their links to the Seljuks, whose heir and successor they claimed to be. But even all of these combined would not, from a legitimacy point of view, meet the evolving ideological needs of the dynasty. It is true that the conquest of Constantinople in 1453 imbued the Ottomans with further prestige and promoted them from the status of a frontier state to that of an empire. Still, the Ottomans were neither of Qurayshi descent, the Prophet's clan, which would have invested the dynasty with Islamic legitimacy, nor of Chingizid pedigree, as were some of the contemporary Turco-Mongol dynasties, whose political legitimisation rested on Central Asian political traditions.[64]

The mismatch between the Ottomans' relatively frail religious and genealogical claims to dynastic legitimation and their grand imperial ambitions would only be amplified by the appearance on their eastern front of the Safavid dynasty with its threefold claims as Sufi, *sayyid* and (partial) royal descent duly covering both dynastic and religious grounds. The Ottomans, therefore, had good reason to perceive this vibrant new dynasty as a formidable ideological rival, regardless of the latter's actual or potential encroachments on Ottoman lands. Although the particular trajectory that the rivalry followed was not predestined, owing its shape in large part to the contingencies of the prolonged intra-dynastic rivalry, the Safavids' rise to power would inevitably affect the ideological and political calculus of the Ottomans, the more so given the prevailing political temperament and culture of the times marked by millenarian and universalist impulses. The meteoric political rise of the Safavids as an ᶜAlid family amidst such an atmosphere must have, predictably enough, challenged the sense of immutability and permanence of the Ottoman order, inducing fear about the impending demise of the status quo on the part of the ruling Ottoman elite, just as it inspired and emboldened the empire's alienated subjects to seek change by force. It is against this backdrop of a complex blend of ideological and religio-psychological dynamics that Selim's new mission of defending 'orthodoxy' against 'heresy' evolved into an enduring feature of the Ottoman imperial discourse, serving to negate and counter the Safavids' own claims to a universal Islamic monarchy, and, in the longer term, supplied a new raison d'être for the House of Osman.

An important game changer in this process was no doubt the conquest of Mamluk territories and the Ottomans' subsequent assumption of the honourable title 'servant of the Two Holy Cities'.[65] This victory provided compelling support for Ottoman claims to the leadership of the Islamic world, bolstering their political self-confidence and prestige. Even though neither Selim I nor his son and successor Süleyman were able to fulfil their original objective of permanently and completely removing the Safavid 'heresy', their resounding military victories and conquests in the east provided a relatively solid foundation for the Ottoman sultans' own universalist religious and political assertions. The same universalist claims, and titles suitable to them, would be used to offset similar pretensions among the Catholic Habsburgs, with whom the Ottomans competed for control over Eastern Europe.[66]

The new messianically enriched image of the house of Osman, which began to take shape already under the relatively brief reign of Yavuz Selim himself, would reach its real peak during the first part of the longer reign of Sultan Süleyman, who, more than his father, came to be extolled as the embodiment of classical Ottoman imperial ideals informed by Islamic unversalism. Gradually, however, the messianic ardor of the earlier decades would subside with the emergence of a stalemate between the Ottomans and two of their most immediate and formidable rivals, namely the Habsburgs in the west and the Safavids in the east.[67] One of the decisive moments in the declining importance and growing irrelevance of universalist religious and political ideologies, in tandem with the establishment of a new Eurasian political order based on regional empires, was the signing of the Amasya Treaty in 1555 which meant that 'after half a century of religious, political and cultural tensions, frontier warfare and devastating invasions, the Ottomans and the Safavids settled around the acknowledgement of each other's dynastic and religious identities'.[68] This was also precisely the time when Sunni confessionalisation in the empire came into its own. Two related developments underscored this process. First, the Ottoman ruling elite's attention turned towards internal ideological and administrative consolidation, and second, the emphasis in their legitimation discourse accordingly shifted on the Ottoman sultan's role as the mainstay of order and dispenser of justice based on Islamic law.[69]

It is untenable to assume the continuation and even expansion of punitive campaigns against the Kizilbash during this period to be exclusively or primarily the result of some lingering Safavid political and military threat, or the perception thereof, which, to the extent it existed, was effectively eliminated with the resounding Ottoman victory in the Battle of Çaldıran in 1514, and the annexation of the Mamluk territories a few years after. In this context, the persecution of the Kizilbash represented something more than pre-emptive security measures, operating as a convenient device to foreground and validate the Ottomans' new self-image as the foremost beacon of Sunni Islam. The official condemnation and punishment of 'heretics', more specifically, helped mediate the state's commitment to uphold the rule of shari^{c}a, initially as the basis of a universalist imperial ideology and later, parallel to the declining practical relevance of this claim, as the main pillar of the new Ottoman order, and the linchpin of moral and political unity in the empire.

Kizilbash Persecutions under Selim I

Although Selim formally took his father's place in April 1512, he had to fight a civil war for almost a full year with his brother, Ahmed, who kept briefly under his control the Anatolian provinces as his share of the inheritance. It was only after having killed all of his brothers and nephews (except Murad, who had escaped to Iran) that Selim was firmly established on the Ottoman throne. In less than a year he was ready to march eastward to take on Shah Isma^{c}il. While camping with his army in Fil Çayırı on the outskirts of Istanbul, Selim sent multiple letters to the shah threatening him with war unless he repented and returned 'to the path of Sunna' and considered his 'lands and their people part of the well-protected Ottoman state'.[70] The two armies eventually faced each other on the plains of Çaldıran near Van in August 1514, where the Ottomans with their powerful artillery emerged victorious. Selim subsequently marched on and conquered Tabriz but had to retreat to Rum due to the Janissaries' unwillingness to spend the winter there. Despite this setback, Selim soon resumed his military expeditions and was able to capture from the Safavids southeastern and much of eastern Anatolia over the next two years, not least because of his success in winning to his side the local Sunni Kurdish tribes.[71]

On the eve of Çaldıran, presumably while camping in Fil Çayırı, Selim convened a group of high-ranking ulema to seek their endorsement for his pending attack against another power that professed to be Muslim. It is from this point onwards that we see the production of a series of *fetvās* and polemical writings by members of the Ottoman ulema charging the

Safavids and their followers with 'unbelief' (*küfr*) whose blood could be legitimately shed.[72] This was not only the onset of an intense propaganda campaign against a heterogeneous collection of individuals and groups who had real or imagined ties to, or sympathies towards, the Safavids, all of whom were now designated with the same catch-all category of Kizilbash; it was also the prelude to a persecutory process that would continue with varying intensity all the way into the early seventeenth century.

Mainstream scholarship tends to assess the scope and impact of the Kizilbash persecutions chiefly on the basis of the number of people directly targeted by these punitive measures. Ottoman chronicles claim that Selim, after obtaining *fetvās* for the persecution of the Kizilbash as 'heretics', sent out orders to provincial governors to create registers of those with Kizilbash affinity, whose numbers reportedly reached 40,000, including women, children and the elderly; all were to be executed.[73] Historians in general tend to doubt the figure of 40,000, suggesting that it was probably used symbolically to indicate a high number and that the number of those who were actually killed was probably far less. Although the scope and details of the Kizilbash persecutions under Selim I's watch are largely beyond historical reconstruction because few state documents have survived from this period, this assumption is not unreasonable in and of itself, especially given the evidence that suggests a selective use of capital punishment against those indicted for being Kizilbash, not to mention the physical difficulty and economic liability of eliminating masses of people.[74]

On the other hand, the fragments of two registers that have survived from the first years of Selim I's reign suggest that a relatively systematic persecution against his internal opponents was clearly within the bounds of the Ottoman authorities' imagination and technical capability. One of these fragments includes the names of individuals in parts of the province of Rum, especially Amasya, Çorum and their environs, who were partisans of Selim's rivals during the Ottoman civil strife, including his brothers Korkud and Ahmed, and his nephew Murad, and/or those suspected of Kizilbash affiliation.[75] A note inserted into the document confirms that the list was prepared on the orders of Selim, presumably on the eve of the Çaldıran war.[76] This list is evidence of the relative methodicalness with which Selim I carried out a witch hunt against his opponents as well as the inseparableness, during this early phase, of the 'Kizilbash problem' from the intradynastic conflict preceding his ascent to the throne. Most of the names in the registers belong to individuals who appear to be more than ordinary tax-paying subjects (*re^cāyā*) in the countryside, as they are referred to by such titles as '*bey*', '*çelebi*', and in one case as '*şeyḫ*'.

Several of them, moreover, are identified as '*çericibaşı*' (commander of troops), '*nişāncıbaşı*' (chief chancellor) and '*defterdār*' (keeper of financial records), suggesting membership in the local Ottoman bureaucracy. However, the second fragment, presumably from another register, shows that the regular *reᶜāyā* in the countryside were not spared from these punitive campaigns either.[77] The names included in this second list carry no distinguishing titles and all belong to residents of villages located in a few subprovinces of Amasya and Çorum. Notably, charges levelled against the latter were much more specific in nature, including participation in campaigns or battles, presumably on the side of one of Selim I's rivals to the throne or in Shah Ismaᶜil's army. The second list, unlike the first, also makes clear that those included in it were all executed (*ḳatl*).[78] Together, these two fragments convey a level of discrimination in the application of capital punishment, possibly reserved exclusively for those considered to be ringleaders or capable of significant political and social influence. While they do not provide sufficient grounds to reach a judgement concerning the full scope and nature of the Kizilbash hunt during this period, they do render it reasonable to assume that similar registers had been produced for other regions that have either been destroyed or still await discovery.[79] That such registers of the Kizilbash not only existed but also continued to be used and produced is illustrated by a sultanic order dated 880/1572 that was sent to the kadi of Niksar (a subprovince of Tokat) concerning a group of individuals whose investigation was required to confirm their Kizilbash affinity. The order notes that the brother of one of these individuals had been earlier executed because his name was recorded in the 'Kizilbash register' (*sürhser defteri*).[80]

Measuring the impact of Kizilbash persecutions solely on the basis of the number of actually executed is misleading, because it obscures the very real implications of the much broader socio-psychological impact of these policies. Regardless of the exact number of those actually killed during the first wave of Kizilbash persecutions under Selim I, there are powerful indications that these putative campaigns involved a large-scale mobilisation. The above-mentioned *fetvā* by Sarı Gürz Hamza Efendi, issued on the eve of Çaldıran and the first of its type that would set the tone and content of all future anti-Kizilbash propaganda, deserves particular attention here. Hamza Efendi declared the Kizilbash to be unbelievers and heretics (*kāfir ve mülḥid*) on account of the following charges: scorning the Koran, undermining the shariᶜa, divinising their leader Shah Ismaᶜil (hence committing the great sin of *shirk*, or 'setting up partners to God') and cursing the first three caliphs and the Prophet's wife, ᶜAᵓisha. This set of prosaic accusations would be repeated almost verbatim in virtually all future *fetvā*s and polemical writings against the Kizilbash. The same goes for Sarı Gürz Hamza Efendi's verdict, which would be upheld with only minor differences by successive generations of the Ottoman ulema and form a key premise of the official Ottoman discourse towards the Kizilbash. According to Hamza Efendi, the annihilation of the Kizilbash was not just licit (*mübāḥ*) but incumbent (*vācib ve farż*) on all Muslims. Their men were to be killed without the captured being given a chance to repent, their women and children to be enslaved and their properties confiscated as spoils of war. As apostates, marriages among them, as well as their marriages to others, were null and void and there could be no inheritance from and to them. While Hamza Efendi's verdict of capital punishment for *küfr* (unbelief) followed the consensus among classical legal scholars, his calling for the death penalty even for those who had repented, was the severest possible option that had precedence in Islamic legal tradition.[81]

Apart from its vicious tone and stern verdict, Hamza Efendi's *fetvā* deserves attention for what it reveals about the level of popular mobilisation entailed in the anti-Kizilbash campaign during this period. Noteworthy in this regard is the format and language of this one-page seminal document: it does not follow the conventional Ottoman *fetvā* form of question and answer, but rather 'uses plain Turkish prose and addresses all of the Muslim faithful: "O Muslims! Know and beware!"'[82] The intended audience of Hamza Efendi's *fetvā* was clearly not only the sultan and the Ottoman ruling elite; it was also, or perhaps more so, the sultan's commoner subjects. In fact, '*fetvā*' is probably a misnomer; rather it appears to be a propaganda pamphlet that was obviously put together for widespread dissemination and circulation, presumably to be read out in public during Friday sermons and on other occasions. Hamza Efendi's emphasis on the collective obligation of all Muslims to obliterate the 'heretical' Kizilbash (*cemīᶜ müslümānlara vācib ve farżdır*), as much as it was the duty of the sultan of Islam, is also worthy of note here.[83] This call on all self-professed Muslims for active cooperation in the fight against the Kizilbash amounted to a vision of total mobilisation of the populace and was symptomatic of the powerful disciplinary forces this persecutory process unleashed on the entire society. According to Hamza Efendi, you did not have to be a Kizilbash to be denounced as an unbeliever: 'those who sway toward them [that is, the Kizilbash] and who accept and help their invalid religion' would also be considered as one and punished accordingly.[84] Even eating the meat of an animal slaughtered by a Kizilbash was no longer acceptable because it would be considered impure in accordance with the religious provisions concerning apostasy. It is not difficult to imagine how the criminalisation of even the day-to-day mundane interactions with those branded as Kizilbash would increase the social distance between groups and enhance the confessional consciousness of the Sunni Muslims who would feel ever more pressure to display all the external trappings of their confessional identity.

Of course, neither religio-political uprisings nor persecutions on religious grounds were unknown in earlier Ottoman history. The first such popular uprising, which transpired in 1416 in western Anatolia and the Balkans, was inspired by the scholar and mystic Şeyh Bedreddin (d. 1420), and would end with the public execution of its leader and his close associates. Interestingly, however, while Şeyh Bedreddin's followers, known as Bedreddinis, would later be denounced by *şeyhü'l-islām* Ebussu^c^ud Efendi for their unbelief and shown to be in collusion with the Kizilbash in Ottoman sources from the sixteenth and seventeenth centuries, Şeyh Bedreddin himself was executed not as a religious 'heretic' but as a rebel, hence still a Muslim. There is, moreover, no sign in the historical record of any systematic and sweeping purge of his followers in the aftermath of the revolt. A rare and perhaps best-known case of an openly religious persecution before the sixteenth century was that of the madrasa-trained scholar Molla Lütfi, who was charged with unbelief (*küfr*) and tried by a group of high ulema before being executed in 1494.[85] What differentiated the punishment of the Kizilbash from these earlier examples was that it was simultaneously religious and collective in nature, at least as envisioned by Sarı Gürz Hamza. He wrote:

> *If the people of a town belong to this group*, the sultan of Islam, may God exalt his helpers, can kill the men among them, and distribute their property, women, and children among holy warriors [*ghāzī*] of Islam [as booty] . . . He can also kill those from this country [Ottoman territory] who are known to follow their path or are caught on their way to join them.[86] (emphasis added)

From the standpoint of Hamza Efendi, membership in a group whose beliefs were deemed heretical was clearly sufficient legal justification for one's elimination without proof of any specific crime. The hardline position taken by Hamza Efendi against the Kizilbash, while unprecedented in Ottoman history, echoed the views of a group of earlier Sunni scholars, such as Abu Hamid Muhammad al-Ghazali (1058–1111) and Ibn Taymiyya (1263–1328), who advocated collective punishment and summary executions against the Ismailis and the Nusayri Alawites. This was a more severe position than that taken by some of the even earlier authorities of Islam, who tended to stress individual responsibility and allowed religious deviants to be offered a chance to repent.[87] The idea that heretics were worse than unbelievers (*kuffār*) and that, therefore, fighting against them was the greatest holy war is likewise traceable to Ghazali and his patron Nizam al-Mulk, the famous vizier of the Seljuks.[88] This was exactly the idea that invested the persecution of the Kizilbash, or the public acclaim of its legitimacy, with special symbolic and ideological significance in the defence of Sunni 'orthodoxy'. In the earlier days, the Ottomans' right to rule rested primarily on their implementation of a holy war in Christian lands. However, with Sarı Gürz Hamza Efendi's *fetvā* and others that followed it, the scope of holy war was officially expanded to include war against 'internal dissidents', not to mention other self-professedly Muslim rulers: in fact, holy war against 'heretics' came to be viewed as the greatest holy war of all. Kemalpaşazade, the famous military judge of Anatolia under Selim I, and the first *şeyhü'l-islām* of Selim's son and successor, Süleyman, articulated this idea laconically in one of his *fetvā*s:

> *Question*: Is the killing of the Kizilbash permissible [*ḥelāl*], and would those who fight against them be considered as holy warriors [*ġāzī*s], and those who die at their hands martyrs [*şehīd*]?
> *Answer*: Yes, it is the greatest of holy wars and a glorious martyrdom [*ġazā-i ekber ve şehādet-i ᶜaẓīme*].[89]

The level of actual enactment of this and similar *fetvā*s most likely did not reflect their harsh tone, as many historians would argue. Be that as it may, the novelty of the idea they conveyed should not be underestimated, insofar as it rendered the persecution of religious dissidents, and the Kizilbash in particular, a necessary function for the promotion of the Ottoman sultan's image as the champion and protector of Sunni Islam, the empire's new ideological raison d'être. From this point onwards, warring against 'heresy' was considered equivalent in significance to fighting the infidels, at least at the discursive level. One notable repercussion of this fundamental shift in the Ottomans' imperial legitimacy claims can be observed in the sphere of architecture. Unlike earlier sultanic mosques that were erected in connection with military successes in Christian lands, the construction of the most important dynastic monument of the sixteenth century, the Süleymaniye complex in Istanbul, started in 1548, just before Süleyman left the capital for a campaign against Shah Tahmasp; according to Gülru Necipoğlu, the Süleymaniye complex was 'an architectural expression of the triumph of Sunni Islam'.[90] A comparison between Mehmet II's mosque complex built during the second half of the fifteenth century and that of Süleymaniye in terms of their foundation inscriptions is also enlightening in this regard. While 'Mehmed's inscription stresses his role as conqueror,' Necipoğlu remarks, the Süleymaniye's foundation inscription, prepared by Ebusuᶜud Efendi, emphasises 'the sultan's divine right to rule as revealed in the Koran and his role as protector of orthodox Islam and of the Shariᶜa against heterodoxy'.[91] What better testimony to the fact that religious wars against infidels were supplemented, if not fully replaced, by confessional wars against 'heretics' and the guardianship of 'orthodoxy' as the prime ideological mission of the Ottoman state?

In addition to demonstrating the sultan's commitment to Sunnism as a benchmark of the new Ottoman political and moral order, the persecution of the Kizilbash, at a more practical level, served to achieve higher levels of confessional uniformity as a means of producing a greater integration of state and society. In the European context, the building of strong confessional identities that transcended local particularities and loyalties helped transform medieval feudal monarchies into modern states. Religion played a similar integrative role in the Ottoman context, revealing itself, for example, in the strong political alliance that was formed between the Ottoman state and the Kurdish tribes in eastern Anatolia, among whom 'being an Ottoman subject was closely identified with Sunni Islam'.[92]

Kizilbash Persecutions after Selim I

The scope and nature of the persecutory measures implemented against the Kizilbash under Selim I's three immediate successors, namely Süleyman I (1520–1566), Selim II (1566–1574) and Murad III (1574–1595), are much better documented thanks to the extensive *mühimme defterleri* from this period that include copies of imperial orders sent to the provincial governors and judges.[93] These abound with dozens of sultanic orders concerning the investigation, capture and punishment of groups or individuals from all walks of life – peasants, nomadic tribesmen, lower-ranking bureaucrats, cavalrymen, local notables, artisans and shopkeepers, as well as Sufis and dervishes – for being Kizilbash. Charges levelled against them included failing to attend Friday prayers, not observing the fast of Ramadan, and drinking wine; cursing Islam and the Muslims, the rightly guided caliphs, and the Prophet's wife ᶜAᵓisha; and attending Kizilbash rites where men and women intermingled in unlawful ways (all acts contrary to shariᶜa); as well as possessing heretical books and links to the Safavids, either as their *ḫalīfe*s or through sending them alms.[94] For example, a sultanic decree dated 1584 ordered the investigation and imprisonment of four individuals in Çorum upon 'hearing that they were not of the people of Sunna [*ehl-i Sünnet*]' and had defamed the three Sunni caliphs and Muslims, with no further accusations against them.[95] Another imperial order sent three years earlier, in 1581, to Amasya required a more general investigation in several towns and villages (*kaṣabāt ve ḳurā*) whose inhabitants revealed themselves to be Kizilbash on account of the following allegations: defaming the Sunni caliphs; calling (Sunni) Muslims 'Yezid' (the Umayyad caliph responsible for the murder of the Prophet's grandchild and the second Shiᶜi imam, Husayn, and thus the ultimate Shiᶜi/Alevi insult to Sunnis); holding immoral, gender-mixed gatherings at night; forgoing the obligatory five daily prayers and the Ramadan fast; and never giving their children the names of the first three caliphs, namely Ebubekir, Ömer and Osman. Additionally, it is reported that two of them were Safavi *ḫalīfe*s who maintained connections with the Safavids, circulating among their followers boots and pieces of clothing of the Shah as sacred artefacts.[96] While the destination of these two imperial orders was the province of Rum, which also seems to have been the focus of the Kizilbash persecutions during the reign of Selim I, similar orders were also dispatched to other parts of the empire's core territories, from Varna in the Balkans to Trabzon on the Black Sea, to Maraş in southeastern Anatolia, and to Mosul and Baghdad in Iraq.[97] The dates on many (but not all, see examples below) of these orders coincide with the long war against the Safavids from 1578 to 1590, a time when security concerns regarding Anatolian followers and sympathisers of the Safavids might have been particularly high. On the other hand, neither was this the first, or the only, prolonged war with Safavid Iran, nor do the pertinent reports establish a direct connection between the war efforts and the investigation and persecution of the Kizilbash, which notably, was not confined to border regions as one would expect if they were indeed driven by some immediate security concerns. Moreover, by this time, that is, the second half of the sixteenth century when all these official registers were kept, the Kizilbash uprisings had largely come to an end with perhaps one exception of any significance, that is the Düzmece Şah Ismaᶜil revolt that took place in 1578 in and around Malatya.[98] Those accused of being Kizilbash – sometimes by their own family members and neighbours – were, therefore, mostly individuals who were clearly religious non-conformists but not instigators of, or participants in, any uprising or any other overt anti-Ottoman activity.

Sufism and Ottoman Confessionalism

The persistence of the repressive impulse against the Kizilbash – all the way into the second half of the sixteenth century, and in some cases even the early seventeenth century[99] – cannot be understood in isolation from the broader process of Sunni confessionalisation in the Ottoman empire, which seems to have gained its real momentum following the signing of the Amasya Treaty in 1555. The Amasya Treaty, as noted earlier, was tantamount to the Ottomans' de facto recognition of the Safavid state, signalling the triumph of regional political claims over universal ones. This development resulted in an increasingly greater focus on achieving higher levels of integration of the Ottoman dynasty and the empire's Muslim subjects through confessional unity. Within the framework of this protracted Ottoman self-definition and imperial consolidation, the Kizilbash were perceived as an internal threat to social cohesion, and a key signifier of otherness. In many ways, they represented the antithesis of the 'true' Islam for which the Ottomans claimed to stand, and were as such instrumentalised as a negative point of reference in the delineation of the otherwise overlapping and diffused religious boundaries that had existed in Anatolia since medieval times.

A pivotal figure in this process of Sunni confessionalism in the Ottoman empire was the above-mentioned Ebussuᶜud Efendi, who served as *şeyhü'l-islām* from 1545 to 1574, a period spanning the second half of Süleyman's reign and that of his son, Selim II, when the power of the office of *şeyhü'l-islām* as the chief mufti reached its peak.[100] Ebussuᶜud's *fetvā*s carried an authority that was unprecedented in Ottoman history. Unlike those issued by earlier *şeyhü'l-islām*, his various proclamations collected under the title *Maᶜrużāt* would be submitted to the sultan for endorsement, and thereby endowed with the force of law. There was, indeed, a direct connection between Ebussuᶜud's pertinent *fetvā*s and confessional policies that were inaugurated during Süleyman's reign, such as the compulsory building of a *masjid* in every village, and the enforcement of daily prayers under threat of official retribution.[101]

Through his thousands of *fetvā*s that were issued on a wide variety of topics Ebussuᶜud in effect redefined and crystallised the boundaries of Ottoman Sunnism that would serve as the main pillar of the new imperial identity.[102] In terms of content, one of the most remarkable aspects of Ebussuᶜud's *fetvā*s is their preoccupation with Sufism, manifested as an intense effort to differentiate 'legitimate' Sufism from its 'heretical' counterparts. Drawing a line encircling the 'true' Sufis but leaving out the 'imposters', as Ebussuᶜud sought to do, was not an easy task given the heterogeneity of Sufi beliefs and practices that prevailed in Ottoman territories, and the fact that the Ottoman ruling classes, including the ulema, themselves were often immersed in the Sufi tradition.[103] It is, therefore, not surprising to see Ebussuᶜud spilling much ink on such perennially controversial issues as Sufi ritual dance (*devrān*) that blurred the boundaries between 'devious' and normative Sufism, and engaging in 'hairsplitting discussions about how it is "better" to practice *ẕikr* sitting down rather than standing up, and, if standing up, then at least not to move one's waist and head, and, if moving one's waist and head, then at least not to move the feet'.[104]

This seemingly pedantic attention to detail in Ebussuᶜud's *fetvā*s starts making better sense when one recognises their implicit references to the Sufi and dervish groups associated with the Kizilbash milieu, operating as a foil in articulating the boundaries of 'wholesome' Sufism. For example, in his various *fetvā*s, Ebussuᶜud reprimanded those holding Sufi circles (especially in the *masjid* of a convent), chanting, engaging in ecstasy-inducing dances, and reciting mystical Turkish poetry.[105] Though obviously not confined to it, these were all components of the "Kizilbash rite" (*Kızılbaş āyīni*) which the *mühimme* registers mention as a manifest sign of 'heresy'.[106] Ebussuᶜud also declared as blasphemy the idea that the Prophet himself performed a dance (*raḳṣ*) when he ascended to heaven, a core aspect of Kizilbash/Alevi theology that underpins the *cem* ritual, saying it was based on the misinterpretation of an otherwise reliable (*ṣaḥīḥ*) Prophetic tradition (*ḥādiṡ*).[107] It is likewise probably no coincidence that several historical figures on whom Ebussuᶜud felt obliged to pass a verdict in his *fetvā*s, obviously because they were subjects of popular debate at the time, were mainly Sufi figures, including Şeyh Bedreddin, Hallac-ı Mansur (Mansur al-Hallaj) and Yunus Emre – each of whom is claimed by the Kizilbash/Alevi communities as their own but has also been revered by other Sufis. In all three cases, Ebussuᶜud's verdict was more or less the same: the religious views and specific utterances of these figures were tantamount to unbelief (*küfr*), and those who followed or condoned them deserved punishment accordingly.[108]

Ebussuᶜud's insistence on a clear separation between canonical worship and Sufi rituals is another important point worthy of attention. A Sufi ritual (*ẕikr*), Ebussuᶜud declared, would indicate unbelief (*küfr*) and apostasy (*irtidād*) if it was conceived of as worship (*ᶜibādet*) that could be a substitute for canonical obligations, a deviation of which the Kizilbash were clearly guilty. He expressed this idea in one of his *fetvā*s, without specifically mentioning the Kizilbash, as follows:

> *Question*: If Zeyd who is a Sufi engages in *devrān* while doing *ẕikr* and regards the *devrān* as worship [*ᶜibādet*], would his marriage be valid and the animal he slaughters licit [to eat]?
> *Answer*: One who regards *devrān* as worship is an apostate [*mürted*], can never marry a Muslim or *ẕimmī* [Christian or Jewish] woman, and the meat of the animal he slaughters is foul. However, he would not be an apostate if he does not regard *devrān* as worship but believes that it is permissible [*mübāḥ*].[109]

Ebussu^{c}ud's categorical separation of canonical worship from Sufi *ẕikr*, and the relegation of the latter to a subordinate position, would find its material reflection in the rapid decline in the Ottoman landscape of the T-type convent-mosque, which had historically accommodated both modes of piety, and the rapid spread of neighbourhood *masjid*s and Friday mosques in the urban centres owing to a systemic state-sponsored campaign. The villages, too, were under the purview of this campaign: for example, an imperial decree issued in 944/1537 ordered the construction of mosques in every village.[110] During this process, most of the multifunctional convents were converted into Friday mosques, which became the foremost mode of architectural patronage for the royal family and the Ottoman ruling classes at large. According to Gülru Necipoğlu, the changing fortunes of the T-type convent-mosque was a direct response to 'fatwas that condemned sufi rituals practiced in these multifunctional edifices as unorthodox forms of worship too similar to the rites of the Safavid order centered on eating, chanting, and dancing'.[111]

In comparison to his fastidious attention to matters relating to Sufism, Ebussu^{c}ud displayed surprisingly little direct interest in the Sunni–Shi^{c}i division and showed no obvious anxiety about the strong Shi^{c}i-^{c}Alid tendencies of such popular orders as the Halvetiyye, Mevleviyye and even Bektashiyye. One explanation for this initially puzzling neglect is that Ebussu^{c}ud did not consider the Kizilbash as part of proper Shi^{c}ism, instead depicting their religion as a new heresy combining various malignant elements from different sects with their own deviant innovations.[112] More importantly and relatedly, he was likely well aware of the groundedness of the Kizilbash 'heresy' in what he considered 'deviant Sufism' rather than Shi^{c}ism. That is why Ebussu^{c}ud was fighting his real battle on the terrain of Sufism, with the Sunni–Shi^{c}i bifurcation being of only secondary relevance and significance for him. In other words, what was at stake in Sunni confessionalism spearheaded by Ebussu^{c}ud was not so much the definition and standardisation of the Sunni creed as it was the elimination of the grey areas within Sufism that contradicted Sunni normativity. Sufism, cleansed of its 'heretical excesses' as such, was not only acceptable, but also necessary and desirable as an ideological instrument against the shaykh-cum-shah Safavids. Hüseyin Yılmaz congruently argues that the Ottomans promoted and cultivated 'Ibn Arabism as a spiritual paradigm' around which the pro-Ottoman Sufis of Sunni orientation could be mobilised 'to defeat the Safavids at the spiritual and ideological level'. It should, therefore, come as little surprise that many in the vanguard of the Ottomans' fierce ideological fight with the Safavids, such as the abovementioned ^{c}Abdullah al-Shirvani, were themselves mystics.[113]

This is not to say that the Ottomans were not concerned about distinguishing themselves from the Shiᶜi Safavids. On the contrary, they sought to do so in various ways. For example, the Ottoman elite's intense patronage during this period of great Friday mosques, established in every urban centre with the direct permission of the sultan, was meant to mediate the centrality for them of the canonical congregational Friday prayers. This was critical for accentuating the empire's Sunni identity in contradistinction to the Safavids, who were reluctant to observe the Friday prayer during the occultation of the hidden Imam.[114] The Ottoman state also made a serious effort to draw more sharply than before the sectarian lines on the social level, with the official ban on marriages between Sunnis and Shiᶜis being perhaps the best example.[115]

How then can we explain the relative absence of themes relating to Shiᶜism in Ebussuᶜud's *fetvās*? Rather than a sign of toleration or indifference, Ebussuᶜud's relatively limited engagement with Shiᶜism in his *fetvās* was more likely, and additionally, a reflection of the fact that the theological grounds of the Sunni–Shiᶜi differentiation had been already well established and did not need further elaboration. Divisions between Sunnism and Shiᶜism were overall much less vague than divisions within Sufism between its 'deviant' and 'normative' forms. Even for what is called ᶜAlid Sunnism that prevailed in many Ottoman Sufi orders, a clear boundary of 'orthodoxy' was easily drawn on the basis of the legitimacy of all the four first (Sunni) caliphs: that is to say, one could still remain within the Sunni orbit while elevating and honouring ᶜAli above all the other caliphs, so long as one did not openly reject or defame the other three. The Ottoman state was no doubt vigilant in enforcing this fundamental boundary that was a sine qua non of the Sunni creed. Contrary to assumptions otherwise, the Bektashi order was not an exception to this mandate, for its official toleration was in fact conditioned on its members' nominal embrace of the Sunni confession, even if only externally.[116] A reflection of this premise is the contemporary Ottoman writers' insistence on portraying Hacı Bektaş as a Sufi fully within the fold of normative Sunnism. Evliya Çelebi from the seventeenth century similarly depicts all Bektashi convents in Ottoman territories as adhering to the Sunni denomination. This consideration, finally, might also elucidate the absence of *tabarrā*, that is the cursing of the first three Sunni caliphs, in Hacı Bektaş's *Velāyetnāme*, which otherwise embraces *tawallā,* never failing to praise ᶜAli and the *Ahl al-bayt*.

All these considerations together indicate that Ottoman Sunnism was scaled along two axes of polarisation: Sunni versus Shiᶜi and shariᶜa-observant versus antinomian, the latter being particularly crucial in differentiating between legitimate Sufis and the alleged imposters. For Ebussuᶜud, as for all other Sunni ulema, adherence to the shariᶜa was the ultimate arbiter of the authenticity of Sufism and of (Sunni) Islam in general.[117] The foregrounding of shariᶜa-boundness as the quintessential identity marker for the Sunni/Islamic community had clear implications for the relationship between religion and the state since it rendered the enforcement of Islamic law as the ultimate glue wedding the two together. From this point onwards, a mere profession of the Islamic faith was no longer sufficient for full membership in the Ottoman-Muslim polity; it had to be verified by external conformity to the shariᶜa to be valid.

The idea of the inseparableness of matters of religion and matters of state, or '*dīn ü devlet*' as used in Ottoman parlance, rested on the dual premise that the shariᶜa needed the coercive power of the state for its implementation, and that rulers needed religion to govern justly and with divine sanction. With this twin-notion, then, 'any challenge to the tenets of orthodoxy became, in effect, a challenge to the legitimacy of Ottoman rule'.[118] Being an enemy of both religion and the state, a common topos in the Ottoman anti-Kizilbash propaganda, was another formulation encapsulating the same idea. With this idea, 'religious deviance' was upgraded to 'heresy', threatening simultaneously the foundations of religion and the state. This conflation of religious and political loyalty, or lack thereof, is expressed by Ebussuᶜud as follows:

> *Question*: Is the killing of the Kizilbash licit because they are rebellious and hostile against the Sultan of the people of Islam . . . or are there other reasons for that?
> *Answer*: They are both rebels and are unbelievers [*kāfir*] on multiple accounts.[119]

While exact numbers are impossible to determine, judged by the multitude of pertinent *mühimme* registers that survived from the second half of the sixteenth century, one can easily see that scores of people charged with Kizilbash 'heresy' suffered punishments that took different forms, ranging from exile to Cyprus and forced labour on galleys, to summary executions and being secretly drowned in a river, to even being publicly stoned to death.[120] Even those who 'rehabilitated' themselves from their 'heresy' years ago (*menhiyātdan tevbe it[mek]*) were not necessarily let off the hook by state authorities, who seem to have kept an eye on them in case they relapsed.[121]

But just as important for the longer term was a deliberate and sustained policy of Sunnitisation, institutionalised during the unusually long reign of Kanuni Süleyman, spanning more than four decades. A key point to recognise here is that the Kizilbash were not the only ones on the receiving end of these policies; they also affected those who were nominally Sunni Muslims. It was during this period that the state for the first time began enforcing under threat of retribution the performance of the five daily congregational prayers. Ebussu^cud issued multiple *fetvās* sanctioning the punishment of those who showed delinquency in observing their communal prayers, authorising the execution of those who routinely neglected them or disavowed their necessity of performing them. The same was true of individuals who failed to fast during Ramadan; those who asserted that the Ramadan fast was not really obligatory would be especially worthy of capital punishment, according to Ebussu^{c}ud.[122] All this was by no means mere talk. The state was actively implementing the necessary measures to ensure compliance with Islamic 'orthopraxy' as envisioned by Ebussu^{c}ud, including forcing villagers to build mosques in their villages and sending '*namāzcıs*', a kind of religious police, to those areas where the population insisted on disregarding obligatory daily prayers.[123]

The persecution of the Kizilbash and the attending 'orthodoxisation' campaign were closely related and mutually reinforcing policies in so far as they both served to achieve higher levels of religious and political conformity and confessional homogeneity. *Mühimme* registers are full of cases of people who were observed as forsaking the formalities of religion, whether by failing to perform the communal Friday prayers or by not fasting during the month of Ramadan, and were investigated for a possible Kizilbash connection. It is, therefore, not difficult to imagine how the Kizilbash surveillance and persecutions must have effected a vigilance at the popular level for the observance of the shari^{c}a, as much to avoid being mistaken for a Kizilbash as being discovered to be one. Indeed, the moral and religious passion of the Kizilbash hunt was so high and so all-encompassing that it created among the general populace a mass hysteria analogous to the one caused by the witchcraft craze in sixteenth- and seventeenth-century Europe, as perceptively noted by Fariba Zarinebaf-Shahr.[124] People accused their neighbours, friends and even husbands of being Kizilbash, and groups of local notables got together to write petitions reporting and complaining about nearby Kizilbash villages or communities.[125] Given the atmosphere, it is not surprising that some would make deliberately false accusations, sometimes slanderously for revenge but more often for some worldly gain.[126] One of the most interesting of such cases that is recorded in the *mühimme* registers took place in Baghdad, where a group of criminals secretly sneaked into people's houses to place a Kizilbash *tāj* and subsequently loot all their belongings.[127] Another register records state officials who frightened people into giving them money while carrying out a Kizilbash inspection (*Kızılbaş teftīşi*), or pretending to.[128] Sometimes, people would confuse 'real' Sufis with the 'heretics' because of their similar outlooks and rites, even attacking them directly.[129]

Apart from contributing to the overall religious uniformity of the Muslim polity, the targeting of the Kizilbash for communal persecution also facilitated the Ottomans' state formation process, which entailed beefing up the central authority's control in the provinces. In assessing this point, one has to bear in mind that the imperial centre had to work in close cooperation with the provincial governors and the local kadis, to whom virtually all relevant imperial orders were addressed, in identifying, investigating and punishing those suspected of being Kizilbash. This traffic both required and generated much greater bureaucratic control in provincial towns and their rural hinterlands, resulting in increased state penetration down to the level of villages that otherwise might have little interaction with the imperial government aside from the payment of taxes. Moreover, their cooperation and vigilance, or lack thereof, in the fight against 'heresy' also served as a loyalty test for the local officials and security forces whose ranks were by no means free of Kizilbash affiliates and sympathisers. Those who slacked or showed negligence in carrying out the orders of the central government in detaining and punishing the Kizilbash, or offered them help or protection, would not only lose their positions but would also be severely penalised (as was common practice according to Ottoman criminal justice procedure[130]). For example, an imperial decree sent to the governor of Amasya and the kadi of Merzifon in the year 978/1570 ordered the arrest and dispatch to Istanbul of three individuals whose Kizilbash affinity was proven by the testimonies of a group of reliable Muslims. The decree ends with a warning to the security personnel who would be accompanying them to the imperial capital that they would receive the same punishment as the three indicted Kizilbash if they showed 'any negligence or softness' towards them or allowed them to escape.[131] Likewise, a fortress guard in Hırsova (in modern-day Romania), who allegedly allowed a Kizilbash named Şehsüvar to escape from prison in exchange for a monetary bribe, was ordered to be executed unless he captured and brought back the former.[132] Conversely, those who were particularly diligent in the fight against the Kizilbash would be applauded and receive extra social and economic rewards.[133]

The Socio-economic Implications of Kizilbash Persecutions

The anti-Kizilbash policies of the state were not limited to physical forms of punishment. At least as important was their socio-economic dimension, a hitherto largely neglected topic in the historiography.[134] One of several components of this process was the systematic expulsion of the Kizilbash from the timariot class and from official positions in general. With political loyalty defined in confessional terms, the state insisted on Sunnism as a criterion for social advancement and made a deliberate effort to dispossess anybody with suspect religious affinities of their land grants. For example, in the year 984/1576, the central government ordered the state treasury to confiscate the *zeᶜāmet* (a medium-sized land grant) of a certain Kara Beg in Karaman upon being informed of the latter's heresy (*ilḥād*). No indication of any other accusation or of any Kizilbash connection is included in the two pertinent *mühimme* registers.[135] Another example is a sultanic order dated 976/1569 that was sent to the governor of the province of Bozok (modern-day Yozgat and its environs) for the retraction of the land grant of the military commander (*alaybeği*) Ferhad, who reportedly provided shelter to a group of his relatives who were accused of theft by the local people while serving as cavalry soldiers in the nearby subprovince of Selmanlu. Upon being asked, many people complained that Ferhad was a person of evil deeds and innovations (*ehl-i şenāᶜat ve bidᶜat kimsenelerdür*) and that his family members and children carried such names as Tahmasp, Mirza and Sultan Ali, indicative of Kizilbash sympathies. As in other similar cases, the decree ordered Ferhad's execution following an investigation concerning the reliability of these allegations. We neither know the result of the investigation nor the fate of Ferhad; however, if he were found guilty, there is little doubt that none of his children would have inherited his *tımar*. In fact, it is very likely that members of Ferhad's extended family would likewise be denied an official position in the future, or removed from it if they already had one. We can conjecture this from the warning in the imperial order that the investigation was not to be limited to Ferhad alone but include others like him (*anuñ gibilerüñ*) whose *tımar*s were likewise to be retracted.[136]

Revoking one's land grant was only one of the ways that the state could effect social demotion and economic dispossession of religious dissidents. Another one with a generalised impact was the destruction or confiscation of Sufi/dervish convents directly or indirectly associated with the Kizilbash milieu. As early as the eve of Çaldıran in 1514, a certain Ali b. Abdülkerim prepared a detailed report for Selim I concerning the Kizilbash threat and ways of dealing with it. In this report he advised the new sultan to eradicate these groups and to turn their convents into mosques.[137] The destruction and desertion of scores of dervish convents during the reign of Selim I and the conversion of others into madrasas over the course of the sixteenth century might be a practical manifestation precisely of such advice as that of Ali b. Abdülkerim. Certainly not all convents associated with the Kizilbash were destroyed or confiscated; however, those spared from the onslaught faced a very real risk of being transferred to somebody else if those in charge were shown to be, or suspected of being, Kizilbash. This possibility is exemplified by a *mühimme* register dated 980/1572 that records a petition to the sultan by a certain Seyyid Mustafa via the local kadi requesting for himself the position of keeper of a convent (*zāviyedār*) in Niksar-Tokat, alleging that the current *shaykh* of the convent was Kizilbash as were others in his company.[138]

Paired with these punitive measures was selective government patronage that likewise served to ensure the transfer of convents from the control of Kizilbash affiliates to those who (nominally) subscribed to the Sunni creed. Such transfers sometimes occurred within the same shaykhly family. A good case in point here is the Ali Baba convent in the city of Sivas. Very little is known about Ali Baba as a historical figure, except that the plot of land where the convent was founded was granted to him as private property by past sultans (*selāṭīn-i māżiyye*). Local Alevi lore holds that Ali Baba was the *musahib* of the celebrated sixteenth-century Kizilbash/Alevi poet Pir Sultan Abdal. This oral tradition, combined with his title 'baba' and what is reported about his desire to remain a celibate in his youth, suggest that Ali Baba was probably a non-conformist Abdal-type dervish connected to the Kizilbash/Alevi milieu. However, Ali Baba's descendants would in time branch out into two subdivisions, one Sunni and the other Alevi/Bektashi, both sides claiming the position of keeper of the convent as their hereditary right. The most plausible explanation for this intriguing division in the family is that the former branch most likely embraced the Sunni confession to gain or keep in their hands the formal control of the convent. This proposition finds concrete support in the convent's endowment deed. The endowment was created in the mid-sixteenth century by the Ottoman vizier Rüstem Paşa, who in two separate places in the deed stipulated as a condition for the endowment that its administrators be Sunni. This unusual condition may have propelled the (nominal?) conversion of one branch of the family to Sunnism or was perhaps meant to ensure their permanent control of the convent. This also renders explicable why the convent appears as Qadiri in the nineteenth-century Ottoman documents although its building is today commonly recognised as an Alevi-Bektashi sacred site.[139]

Sixteenth-century *mühimme* registers are full of similar cases that reveal the close surveillance of convents inhabited by non-conformist dervishes, called '*ışık*' in the Ottoman sources, many of whom were presumably affiliates or sympathisers of the Kizilbash movement. One of many examples is the convent of Saruyatar (Saruyatar Zāviyesi) in Denizli, about which a report was submitted to the sultan by the local authorities. According to the report briefly summarised in a *mühimme* register dated 975/1567, the dervishes (*ışıklar*) residing in the convent were 'innovators and deviants' (*bidᶜat ve dalālet üzere olup*) who spent their days and nights engaged in such sinful activities as playing music and chanting (*sāz ve söz ile fısḳ u fücūr idüp*) and did not observe the obligatory daily prayers. They also displayed acts of animosity against the Sunni population by preventing people with names of Ömer and Osman from visiting the shrine unless they changed their names. The central government ordered a thorough investigation into the matter and the imprisonment of those found guilty of 'heresy'.[140] Another *mühimme* register from the year 968/1561 informs us of an investigation concerning the convent of Akyazılı Baba in Varna, which revealed the *ışık*s residing there to be growing grapes to produce wine. One of the most noteworthy aspects of this case is the additional complaint filed by a group of dervishes inhabitating the same convent concerning a fellow dervish who was allegedly engaging in criminal activities; interestingly, while the document identifies those who filed the complaint as Sunni dervishes (*tekye-i mezbūrede Ehl-i Sünnet ve Cemāᶜat vazᶜı üzere olan dervīşler*), it refers to the accused one as '*ışık*'.[141] This record is an elegant testimony to the Ottoman authorities' discursive differentiation between 'legitimate' dervishes, that is those (externally) remaining within the Sunni fold, and their 'deviant' counterparts, just as they excluded the Sufis of Ardabil from the fold of true Sufism by branding them as Kizilbash.

The goal and result of such relatively systematic and long-term policies was the substantial erosion, if not total eradication, of the institutional foundations of the Kizilbash communities in the Ottoman domains. Conceivably, the seeming disappearance from the records after the sixteenth century of scores of older convents was linked to this broader development, reflecting a change of control in administration and personnel, and/or religious identity, or possibly total desertion and destruction.[142] Needless to say further research in the form of specific case studies would be needed to verify and elaborate on this proposition.

The Invisibility of the Kizilbash from the Seventeenth Century Onwards

The Ottoman state's repressive measures against the Kizilbash in the form of physical persecution and socio-economic marginalisation seem to have continued relatively methodically into the early seventeenth century. After this point, the Kizilbash virtually vanish from Ottoman archival documents (before they re-emerge in the late nineteenth century). At first sight, the disappearance of the Kizilbash from the official records could be viewed as confirmation of a notion that is especially popular among contemporary Alevi authors, namely that the Kizilbash/Alevi communities could survive only by taking refuge in the most isolated and remote parts of Anatolia beyond the reach of the state's machinery. However, even if it may be valid for certain regions and periods, a generalisation of this claim appears untenable given the existence among the Alevi sources of dozens of Ottoman imperial decrees and documents issued by the kadi courts during and after the sixteenth century.[143] While some of these deal with such mundane issues as commercial transactions and criminal court cases, others are documents confirming *dede* families' status and privileges as *sayyid*s and dervishes, often but not always on the basis of similar documents from earlier periods. In light of these, it would be unreasonable to take the virtual absence of the Kizilbash in the official Ottoman sources after the sixteenth century as an indication of the Kizilbash/Alevi communities' insular existence and complete freedom from the control of state authorities.

A more reasonable explanation would have to take into account two important observations. One is that the Ottoman officials, as a general pattern, refrained from identifying an individual or a group as 'Kızılbaş' in their documentation except strictly for purposes of incarceration and persecution. The other is the shifting emphasis in Ottoman policy towards the Kizilbash from hot pursuit to informal accommodation around about 1600 when the latter were no longer at the top of the list of major concerns for the state. The reasons for this change in priorities were surely manyfold. Most importantly, Sunni confessionalisation in the empire had by then reached a point of maturation, and the Eurasian continent, as mentioned before, had gradually settled to a new status quo based on regional empires with more-or-less overlapping confessional and territorial boundaries. Apart from the resultant ebb of ideological concerns regarding the Kizilbash, another probable cause for the shift in the state's priorities away from the Kizilbash was the growing difficulty of keeping a large enough population of taxpayers in rural Anatolia due to population decline, which was caused by widespread peasant unrest and the climatic changes associated with the so-called Little Ice Age.[144] Whatever the exact political and socio-economic causes for the Kizilbash slipping in the Ottomans' list of priorities, the two observations combined make it readily obvious why the Kizilbash as such would vanish from the official Ottoman sources after the sixteenth century when the Ottoman state ceased to pursue an active anti-Kizilbash campaign.

During routine interactions, such as payment of taxes or use of kadi courts, the Ottoman bureaucrats would treat the Kizilbash as regular Muslims. The ideological reasoning for this practice is clear: the state, with its self-obliged commission to establish and guard a Sunni Islamic public order, could not ideologically countenance the existence of 'heretics' in its territory. This practice, which essentially amounts to *taqiyya* (religious dissimulation), entailed an unwritten but mutually understood condition that members of the community would refrain from publicly articulating their true religious beliefs and identities during their encounters with state officials. This must have been the name of the game, particularly for the Alevi *dede*s if they wanted to navigate and survive within the Ottoman system without losing their privileges as *sayyid*s. It is of course difficult to know whether the state officials would always be aware of someone's real confessional identity; however, it is probable that local governors and officers would be mostly cognisant of the Kizilbash tribes and villages in their regions, especially in rural areas. Hence, the informal accommodation of the Kizilbash seems to have required the performance of a particular form of *taqiyya*, one that was both expected and reciprocated by state officials, much like a 'don't ask don't tell' policy.

While this policy helps to explain the virtual invisibility of the Kizilbash in the official sources after the sixteenth century, there is, of course, no reason to assume that similar cases of situational tolerance were entirely absent in earlier periods. Indeed, it is more likely than not that instances of informal accommodation of the Kizilbash were widespread especially at the local level even during the sixteenth century, whether due to socio-economic exigencies or simply thanks to the individual inclinations of local officials. But whatever its spatial or temporal scope and the specific local dynamics driving it, the Ottomans' use of a 'don't ask, don't tell' policy vis-à-vis the Kizilbash was far from mere pragmatism, if by pragmatism we understand something entirely separate from religious considerations. This seemingly pragmatist posture, insofar as it still entailed the symbolic erasure of the Kizilbash from the Ottoman polity, did not lack a religious component and rationale to it. To understand this point, we need to turn to Ebussuᶜud's *fetvā*s concerning the punishment of the Kizilbash, which revised those of Sarı Gürz Hamza Efendi and Kemalpaşazade on two points. First, while Ebussuᶜud was in full agreement with his predecessors that Kizilbash men deserved capital punishment, he took a more flexible position in regards to the question of repentance. Unlike Hamza Efendi and Kemalpaşazade, who insisted that the Kizilbash had to be eliminated without being offered a chance to repent, Ebussuᶜud acknowledged the existence of divergent positions on this issue between different Sunni legal schools. Without weighing in on one side or the other, he allowed the sultan to choose whether to grant or deny those discovered to be Kizilbash a chance to repent. Second, and more importantly, he declared that those ordinary tax-paying subjects of the empire who kept their Kizilbash affiliation to themselves ought to be left alone, 'as long as their lies were not made explicit'.[145] It is not hard to discern in Ebussuᶜud's *fetvā*s an underlining concern for the preservation of the producing and tax-paying populations in the imperial domains, and, more broadly, an effort to expand the secular authorities' room for manoeuvre in dealing with the Kizilbash.[146]

On the other hand, a religious justification was not lacking for this apparently more flexible position adopted by Ebussuᶜud. For it echoed and relied on the famous, eighth-century Muslim jurist Muhammad ibn Idris al-Shafiᶜi's (d. 820) distinction between inner disbelief or clandestine apostasy and a public break from Islam. Unlike Ghazali and Ibn Taymiyya, Shafiᶜi held that, of these two legal offences, only the latter, namely a public break from Islam, was liable to capital punishment.[147] It was this line of thinking that extended a religious basis and justification to the informal accommodation of the Kizilbash, which, however, still required the latter's public and official invisibility.

Kizilbash Confessionalisation

The Ottomans' persecutory measures against the Kizilbash and their Sunnitisation policies worked together to alter the socio-religious complexion of Anatolia, and to a lesser extent other parts of the empire, in ways more significant than is often assumed. First and foremost, these policies seem to have taken a demographic toll on the Kizilbash communities, whether through physical elimination or religious assimilation.[148] While assigning a number to the size of those involved is impossible, according to the estimate given in a Venetian embassy report from 1514, about four-fifths of the Anatolian population had Shiᶜi-ᶜAlid leanings.[149] Even if this may be an overly inflated number, contemporary Ottoman sources supply additional testimony to the substantial Kizilbash population, especially in the Anatolian provinces and Iraq. Chronicler Hoca Saᶜdeddin Efendi, for instance, describes the size of Shah Ismaᶜil's followers (e*ḥibba*ᵓ) to be 'uncalculable and uncountable' (*ḥesābdan efzūn ve ḥad ve ᶜadedden bīrūn*) thanks to deputies (*ḫulefā*ᵓ) of his ancestors scattered in the lands of Rum.[150] Moreover, as late as 985/1577, the governor of the province of Rum requested a change in an earlier order from the central government by remarking on the difficulty of employing the death penalty on all the Kizilbash due to their sheer number (*Kızılbaş nāmına olanların* *ḥaḳlarından gelinürse küllī telef-i nefs olmak lāzım gelür*), upon which the verdict was revised from capital punishment to exile to Cyprus for all except the Safavi *ḫalīfe*s who were still to be killed.[151] In the same year, the governor of Baghdad made a similar observation about his own region where, he observed, there was 'no end to the heretics and misbelievers' (*bed mez̲heb ve rāfiżīnin nihāyeti olmayup*).[152]

Apart from an overall decline in numbers, another direct result of state repression seems to have been a progressive confinement of the Kizilbash identity to the rural milieu. This meant an increasingly limited demographic presence in urban centres, where it was much harder to preserve a non-conformist religious identity due to higher levels of official and popular pressure to conform. This social and spatial marginalisation no doubt made an impact on a range of other spheres, including levels of literacy and connectedness to the broader Sufi religious and literary traditions on the part of the Kizilbash communities. Symptomatic of this development might be the deteriorating linguistic quality over time of the documents and manuscripts in the family archives of the Alevi *ocak* families, whose copiers must have had less access to formal education than their predecessors. The same dynamic might have also invited a growing reliance on oral forms of transmission of the Kizilbash/Alevi tradition, although writing and the written record never lost its relevance entirely.

On the flip side of it, the historical experience of persecution, or the lingering threat thereof, seems to have served as a unifying force binding closer together the diverse groups who made up the Kizilbash/Alevi milieu, thus increasing group cohesiveness and internal solidarity as well as deepening external differentiation from the rest of the Muslim polity. This 'push factor' seems to have worked together with the 'pull factor' of the institutional reframing afforded by the Safavid spiritual leadership in driving the process of Kizilbash confessionalisation. Internally, this process entailed higher levels of homogenisation of belief and ritual practices. The corpus of (proto-)'Kizilbash' beliefs and ritual traditions was hardly as amorphous as some historians would like us to believe, with the groups constituting the broader Kizilbash milieu bearing a 'family resemblance' on account of their devotion to ᶜAli, a set of esoteric teachings and ritual practices, and the use of sacred lineage as a device for organising. Yet Kizilbashism/Alevism per se was still in formation during the course of the sixteenth century. A most distinctive trademark of Kizilbashism/Alevism in this early period, as in the present, was the gender-mixed communal *cem* ritual, which is mentioned in the contemporary Ottoman sources as 'Kızılbaş *āyīni*'. The basic components of it, known as the 'twelve services' (*oniki hizmet*), are described in *Buyruk* manuscripts in a fashion very similar to how they have been performed in the modern period among the far-flung Kizilbash/Alevi communities from the Balkans to eastern Anatolia. The *cem* ritual bears a clear Safavid stamp in its requirement for the recitation of Hataʾi's poetry at key intervals, and in the use for initiation ceremonies of the sacred stick, *tarik*, an artefact that was also part and parcel of devotional practices at the Safavid court.[153]

The Safavids seem to have also exerted a Shiᶜitising influence on their followers in Anatolia following their establishment in power, as a result of which the Shiᶜi-ᶜAlid thrust of Kizilbashism was augmented. A manifestation of this, to which I drew attention in Chapter 2, was the substitution of such names as ᶜUthman and Abu Bakr with others that were more in harmony with enhanced Shiᶜi-ᶜAlid sentiments, as new copies of older Wafa'i *ijāzas* were produced, in full or in part, roughly from the second half of the sixteenth century onwards.[154] Apart from in-person encounters during visits to Ardabil and Shiᶜi sacred sites in Iraq, the primary mechanism for the spread of this Shiᶜitising influence involved the circulation of religious treatises targeting a Turcophone Kizilbash audience. These included religious texts that are collected in the *Buyruk* manuscripts discussed in Chapter 4, as well as more generic Shiᶜi works. An illustrative example for the second category is the famous *Risale-i Hüsniyye*, a Shiᶜi polemical work that originally appeared in Persian in Safavid Iran most probably in the sixteenth century. Its Turkish rendition was also widely read in Anatolia among the Kizilbash/Alevi communities, as attested by the many copies of it in the private libraries of *ocak* families.[155]

The recognition of Safavid agency in Kizilbash confessionalisation should not, however, obscure the equally important bottom–up dynamic of the process, initiated by local religious leaders, the *dede*s and *pir*s, and Alevi dervish poets (*aşık*s), whose mobility among widely dispersed Alevi communities was surely an important mechanism in the standardisation and consolidation of Kizilbash/Alevi cultural and symbolic codes. Although much harder to trace historically, a striking uniformity among the different Alevi communities is conspicuous in their rich corpus of oral lore, including poems, hymns, myths, parables and the like; shared social mores and cultural values; as well as specific religious beliefs often expressed in various distinctly Alevi maxims, such as 'control your hands, loins and tongue' (*eline, beline, diline sahip ol*). One can also speak of a relatively early trend of canonisation of Alevi sacred poetry, as seen in the common talk of seven great Sufi poets of the Alevi tradition, including Hataʾi (Hatayi), Fuzuli, Virani, Nesimi, Yemini, Kul Himmet and Pir Sultan Abdal, selections of whose poems, in addition to other, more local Kizilbash/Alevi dervish-poets, are typically found as appendices in *Buyruk* manuscripts. Local Alevi religious leaders also seem to have played a major role in simultaneously mediating and tempering the Safavids' religious influence, especially their Shiᶜitising efforts, over their disciple communities. This filtering of the Safavid influence is reflected emblematically in the continued copying and circulation within the Anatolian Kizilbash/Alevi milieu of the legends of Abu Muslim al-Khorasani (d. 755), the leader of the Abbasid armies that toppled the Umayyad dynasty, compiled under the title of *Ebā Müslim-nāme*, which were systematically repressed in post-revolutionary Safavid Iran.[156]

In the absence of a state power backing their authorities, the *dede*s and *pir*s relied for their leadership on their genealogical charisma and moral authority. By way of exerting religious and social discipline over their disciple communities, they employed peculiar moral instruments of control based on strict socio-religious codes and the institution of *düşkünlük*, a form of excommunication to be imposed temporarily or permanently on those who transgress these norms.[157] One such norm that seems to have cemented the social boundaries of the increasingly inward-looking Kizilbash identity was the practice of marrying only within one's confessional community. This practice, more than anything else, seems to have effected the transformation of the Kizilbash/Alevi identity into one that could only be transmitted by descent and, in the longer term, the evolution of the Kizilbash/Alevis into a semi-ethnic community.

At the level of socio-religious organisation, Kizilbash confessionalisation entailed the gradual eclipse of the specific and heterogeneous origins of individual *ocak*s in the wider cosmopolitan Sufi milieu and the emergence of an internally more uniform *ocak* system based exclusively on the notion of *sayyid*-ship. In Chapter 2, I commented on the internal dynamics of this process, also briefly noting the effect of the Ottoman state's repressive policies in furthering it. One can discern a two-fold impact of state policies on this process. The first is the destruction or confiscation of Sufi and dervish convents associated with the Kizilbash milieu, or their transfer to others embracing the Sunni confession. The resulting erosion of their institutional infrastructure as Sufis and dervishes seems to have fostered the *sayyid*-isation trend among Kizilbash/Alevi shaykhly families who wanted to maintain their social status by acquiring *sayyid* genealogies if they did not already have them or, if they already had pertinent documentation, to stress their *sayyid* background over their Sufi affiliations in their interactions with state authorities. Moreover, it appears that with the loss of their control over many of their formal convents, the Kizilbash/Alevi communities from early on began to use private homes as places for religious congregation. These 'home convents', as they may be called, would deepen

Figure 6.1 A building with a multi-layer roof signifying the seven heavens (*kırlangıç çatı*) used for *cem* gatherings in the past, Zara-Sivas

Source: Photograph by Umut Kaçan, 2013.

the separation of the Kizilbash/Alevi communities from the Muslim polity by increasing their spatial isolation, on the one hand, and by further eroding in memory and in practice their roots anchored in the medieval Sufi context of the original Kizilbash movement, on the other. These home convents may be viewed as precursors of the present-day *cemevi*s for which Alevis currently seek legal recognition as their houses of worship (Figure 6.1).[158]

It is difficult to establish at what point the *ocak* system crystallised out of a relatively heterogeneous collection of Sufi and dervish circles that made up the backbone of the early Kizilbash milieu in Anatolia. On the other hand, a sense and self-awareness of a broader Kizilbash/Alevi community organised horizontally around *ocak*s is visible in a late eighteenth-century document stemming from the family archives of the *ocak* of Celal Abbas. This unusual document, both in terms of content and appearance, is dated 1155/1742 (Figure 6.2). It mentions dozens of Kizilbash/Alevi *ocak*s dispersed throughout various parts of Anatolia and the Balkans, linking them together through a series of master–disciple relationships (the verb used in the document being '*eyvallah etmek*', lit. to express one's acceptance of something, or submission to someone) that had been established at some unidentified point in the past.[159] While we do not know by whom

Figure 6.2 Alevi document dated 1155/1742. Original in the private archive of Fethi Erdoğan, member of the *ocak* of Celal Abbas (aka Şah Ali Abbas) from the village of Mığı, Elazığ

Source: Photograph by the author, Istanbul, 2003.

and for what purpose this document was put together, the fact that its date coincides with the immediate aftermath of the Safavids' demise makes one wonder if its production may have been prompted by them, as though someone wanted to create a written record of all the communities wedded spiritually to the memory of the Safavi household. That it was found in the private archives of one of only, to the best of my knowledge, two Alevi *ocak*s with a family tradition that ties its own genealogical origins to the Safavids lends further support to this conjecture. Whatever the case may be, enshrined in this late eighteenth-century document is as much a sense of a unified Kizilbash collective identity as an acute awareness of its inner plurality.

Conclusion

While most treatments of the sixteenth-century Kizilbash persecutions see them as a minor side issue, an attempt has been made in this chapter to show that they were indeed central to a range of broader developments in Ottoman history. The repressive measures against the Kizilbash emerged not as simple security measures but rather as a factor in Sunni confessionalisation and as a performance of Sunni hegemony, whose very possibility was conditioned upon a fundamental ideological and structural shift in the Ottoman Empire, conceptualised here as a confessional turn. The confessional turn in Ottoman politics unleashed a process of Sunni confessionalisation that came into its own during the second half of the sixteenth century, playing itself out primarily in the realm of Sufism. The othering of the Kizilbash and their exclusion from the Ottoman polity – whether through active persecution or through erasure from the official record – was key to the consolidation and perpetuation of the empire's shariᶜa-centred Sunni identity upon which the Ottoman dynasty came to recast its legitimising ideology.

Pressures for confessionalisation would also pave the way for Kizilbashism to evolve from a social movement comprising a diverse range of groups and actors into a relatively coherent and self-conscious socio-religious collectivity. In spite, or perhaps because, of being physically and symbolically repressed during this process, the Kizilbash/Alevis in the Ottoman realms would experience greater internal consolidation and fortified external boundaries, going through a process of confessionalisation of their own and on their own terms. This was a process driven as much by bottom–up dynamics as Safavid influence, with clear ramifications in a multitude of spheres, ranging from naming practices to literary conventions to ritual procedures, various facets of which are still in need of more focused studies.

It remains a question as to how far the confessional turn in Ottoman politics was directly motivated by religious concerns and how far by the dictates of realpolitik, or if such a differentiation is even possible. However, in terms of their results, the ensuing and mutually reinforcing processes of Sunni and Kizilbash/Alevi confessionalisation had undeniably profound socio-religious ramifications. Most obviously, they divided the empire's Muslim population along confessional lines much more rigidly than before, resulting in the permanent peripheralisation of a large segment of society who did not religiously conform by rendering confession the test for political loyalty and social advancement. If one long-term effect was a greater moral integration of Sunni Muslims with the Ottoman state, another was an amplified confessional polarisation and animosity at both official and popular levels.

Notes

1. Sir Roger L'Estrange (1616–1704) was an English journalist and pamphleteer who supported the Royalist cause during the English Civil War (1642–1651) and the Commonwealth period (1649–1660). The quote is from his *Toleration Discussed* (1663) cited in John Coffey, *Persecution and Toleration in Protestant England, 1559–1689* (Harlow and New York: Longman, 2000), 37.
2. The confessionalisation theory as articulated by Heinz Schilling and Wolfgang Reinhard represents a fusion and expansion of the older ideas of confession formation and social disciplining. The former (*Konfessionsbildung*) was developed by Ernst Walter Zeeden during the 1950s and 1960s, see Ernst Walter Zeeden, *Die Entstehung der Konfessionen: Grundlagen und Formen der Konfessionsbildung im Zeitalter der Glaubenskämpfe* (Munich: Oldenbourg, 1965); idem, *Konfessionbildung: Studien zu Reformation, Gegenreformation und katholischer Reform* (Stuttgart: Klett-Cotta, 1985). For the concept of social disciplining (*Sozialdisziplinierung*), developed by Gerhard Oestreich in the 1960s, see Winfried Schulze, 'Gerhard Oestreichs Begriff "Sozialdisziplinierung in der frühen Neuzeit"', *Zeitschrift für historische Forschung* 20 (1987): 265–302; and Gerhard Oestreich, *Neostoicism and the Early Modern State* (Cambridge: Cambridge University Press, 1982). For a brief overview of the development of the confessionalisation theory on the basis of these two notions, see the introduction to Ronnie Po-Chia Hsia, *Social Discipline in the Reformation: Central Europe 1550–1750* (London: Routledge, 1989).
3. See, especially, Tijana Kristic, *Contested Conversions to Islam: Narratives of Religious Change in the Early Modern Ottoman Empire* (Stanford, CA: Stanford University Press, 2012), esp. 12–16; and Derin Terzioğlu, 'Sufis in the Age of State-building and Confessionalization', in *The Ottoman World,*

ed. Christine Woodhead (New York: Routledge, 2012), 86–99; idem, 'How to Conceptualize Ottoman Sunnitization: A Historiographical Discussion', *Turcica* 44 (2012–13): 301–338. For other references, see n64 in Introduction.

4. For an application of the concept to early modern Europe at large, see Heinz Schilling, 'Confessional Europe', in *Handbook of European History, 1400–1600: Late Middle Ages, Renaissance and Reformation*, eds Thomas A. Brady et al. (Leiden and New York: Brill, 1995), 641–675. For its application to the Orthodox Christian/Eastern European context, see Serhii Plokhy, *The Cossacks and Religion in Early Modern Ukraine* (Oxford and New York: Oxford University Press, 2002). A useful critique of the latter work is found in Alfons Brüning, 'Confessionalization in the *Slavia Orthodoxa* (Belorussia, Ukraine, Russia)? – Potential and Limits of a Western Historiographical Concept', in *Religion and the Conceptual Boundary and Eastern Europe: Encounters of Faiths*, ed. T. Bremer (London: Palgrave MacMillan, 2008), 66–97.
5. Wolfgang Reinhard, 'Gegenreformation als Modernisierung? Prolegomena zu einer Theorie des konfessionellen Zeitalters', *Archiv für Reformationgeschichte* 68 (1977): 226–252; Reinhard, 'Reformation, Counter-Reformation, and the Early Modern State: A Reassessment', *The Catholic Historical Review* 75 (1989): 383–404; Heinz Schilling, *Konfessionskonflikt und Staatsbildung* (Gütersloh: Gütersloher Verlagshaus, 1981); Schilling, 'Confessionalization in the Empire: Religious and Societal Change in Germany between 1555 and 1620', in *Religion, Political Culture and the Emergence of Early Modern Society: Essays in German and Dutch History*, ed. Heinz Schilling (Leiden: Brill, 1992), 205–245.
6. For a helpful overview of the latest arguments for and against this theory of confessionalisation, see, for example, Thomas A. Brady, Jr., 'Confessionalization: The Career of a Concept', and Heinz Schilling, 'Confessionalization: Historical and Scholarly Perspectives of a Comparative and Interdisciplinary Paradigm' both in *Confessionalization in Europe, 1555–1700: Essays in Memory of Bodo Nischan*, eds John M. Headley et al. (Aldershot: Ashgate, 2004), 1–20, 22–35.
7. Studies of the confessionalisation of religious minorities in the European context include, for example, Michael Driedger, *Obedient Heretics: Mennonite Identities in Lutheran Hamburg and Altona during the Confessional Age* (Aldershot: Ashgate, 2002); Raymond A. Mentzer, 'The Huguenot Minority in Early Modern France', in *Religion and the Early Modern State: Views from China, Russia, and the West*, eds James D. Tracey and Marguerite Ragnow (Cambridge: Cambridge University Press, 2004), 185–206; Hans-Jürgen Goertz, 'Kleruskritik, Kirchenzucht und Sozialdisziplinierung in den täuferischen Bewegungen der Frühen Neuzeit', in *Kirchenzucht und Sozialdisziplinierung im frühneuzeitlichen Europa*, ed. Heinz Schilling (Berlin: Duncker & Humblot, 1994), 183–198; and Yosef Kaplan, 'Confessionalization, Discipline and Religious Authority in the

Early Modern Western Sephardic Diaspora', in *Religious Movements and Transformations in Judaism, Christianity and Islam*, ed. Yohanan Friedmann (Jerusalem: The Israel Academy of Sciences and Humanities, 2016), 83–108.

8. For the Ottoman context, this observation was made earlier by Derin Terzioğlu, see especially her 'Sufis in the Age of State-building and Confessionalization'.
9. For the Safavid case, see Babayan, *Mystics, Monarchs, and Messiahs*, 121–160; and Colin P. Mitchell, *The Practice of Politics in Safavid Iran: Power, Religion, and Rhetoric* (London: I. B. Tauris, 2009), 19–67. For the process of conversion to Imami Shi^cism in Iran, also see Said Amir Arjomand, *The Shadow of God and the Hidden Imam: Religion, Political Order, and Societal Change in Shi^cite Iran from the Beginning to 1890* (Chicago: The University of Chicago Press, 1984); and Rula Jurdi Abisaab, *Converting Persia: Religion and Power in the Safavid Empire* (London: I. B. Tauris, 2004). More specifically for the decline of Sufism in Safavid Iran, see Ata Anzali, 'Safavid Shi^cism, the Eclipse of Sufism and the Emergence of ^cIrfān' (PhD diss., Rice University, Texas, 2012).
10. Ahmet Yaşar Ocak, *Osmanlı Toplumunda Zındıklar ve Mülhidler (15.–17. Yüzyıllar)* (Istanbul: Türk Tarih Vakfı Yurt Yayınları, 1998), 92–96; Cornell H. Fleischer, *Bureaucrat and Intellectual in the Ottoman Empire: The Historian Mustafa Âli (1541–1600)* (Princeton: Princeton University Press, 1986), 265. For a study of the development of the Ottoman religious hierarchy in general, see R. C. Repp, *The Müfti of Istanbul: A Study in the Development of the Ottoman Learned Hierarchy* (London: Oxford University, 1986).
11. Pehlul Düzenli, ed., *Ma^crûzât: Şeyhülislâm Ebussuûd Efendi* (Istanbul: Klasik, 2013), 27–29, 33–34. For the *Ma^crûzât*, and its significance, also see Colin Imber, 'Süleyman as Caliph of the Muslims: Ebû's-Su^cûd's Formulation of Ottoman Dynastic Ideology', in *Soliman le Magnifique et son temps: Actes du colloque de Paris, Galeries nationales du Grand palais, 7–10 mars 1990*, ed. Gillès Veinstein (Paris: La Documentation française, n.d.), 180–182.
12. Kaya Şahin, *Empire and Power in the Reign of Süleyman: Narrating the Sixteenth-Century Ottoman World* (Cambridge: Cambridge University Press, 2013), 209. Şahin rightly points out that, despite some interesting parallels between the peace treaties of Augsburg and Amasya, both of which were signed in 1555 between the Catholic Habsburgs and the Lutheran princes and the Ottomans and Safavids, respectively, the notion of *Cuis regio, eius religio,* which the former established as the governing principle of relations between Catholic and Lutheran rulers, was not part and parcel of the vision enshrined in the Treaty of Amasya, which did not 'address the state of Alevis and Shiites who live[d] under Ottoman rule, or the Sunnis under Safavid rule'. Ibid., 136.
13. See, for example, Karen Barkey, *Empire of Difference: The Ottomans in Comparative Perspective* (New York: Cambridge University Press, 2008);

and Kemal Karpat and Yetkin Yıldırım, eds, *The Ottoman Mosaic* (Seattle: Cune Press, 2010). For a favourable comparison of the classical Ottoman order with the contemporary Habsburgs on this matter, also see Fikret Adanır, 'Religious Communities and Ethnic Groups under Imperial Sway: Ottoman and Habsburg Lands in Comparison', in *The Historical Practice of Diversity: Transcultural Interactions from Early Mediterranean to the Postcolonial World*, eds Dirk Hoerder et al. (New York: Berghahn Books, 2003), 54–66. The works in question, however, seem prone to an optical illusion in their overall vision of the Ottomans' politics of difference due to their focus on the non-Muslim subjects of the empire at the expense of such dissenting insiders as the Kizilbash. Unlike Jews and Christians whose incorporation into the Ottoman polity was facilitated by provisions of Islamic law, which extended them a protected, albeit subordinate, status as 'people of the book', the latter lacked any formal protection and were designated as apostates deserving capital punishment from a Sunni legal perspective. Yet another troubling feature of these works is their tendency to favour pragmatism as an explanation for various policy choices and practices of the Ottoman state. By replacing religious fervour with political pragmatism as a timeless operational principle and defining characteristic of Ottoman rule, they thus substitute one type of essentialism with another, and establish a false binary between matters of religion and matters of state. For a general critique of the increasingly more popular use of pragmatism as an explanatory category in Ottoman historiography, see Murat Dağlı, 'The Limits of Ottoman Pragmatism,' *History and Theory* 52 (May 2013): 194–213.

14. Three separate copies of Hamza Efendi's *fetvā* are preserved in the TMA. E. 5960, E. 6401 and E. 12077, cited in Abdurrahman Atçıl, 'The Safavid Threat and Juristic Authority in the Ottoman Empire during the 16th Century', *International Journal of Middle East Studies* 49 (2017), n24. The text of Sarı Gürz Hamza's *fetva* was first published in Şehabettin Tekindağ, 'Yeni Kaynak ve Vesikaların Işığı Altında Yavuz Sultan Selim'in İran Seferi', *Tarih Dergisi* 17, no. 22 (1967): 54–55.
15. For Hamza Efendi's and Kemalpaşazade's views on the Kizilbash, see Atçıl, 'Safavid Threat', 301–304. Also see, Nabil al-Tikriti, 'Kalam in the Service of the State: Apostasy and the Defining of Ottoman Islamic Identity', in *Legitimizing the Order: The Ottoman Rhetoric of State Power*, eds Hakan T. Karateke and Maurus Reinkowski (Leiden: Brill, 2005), 131–149; and İsmail Safa Üstün, 'Heresy and Legitimacy in the Ottoman Empire in the Sixteenth Century' (PhD diss., University of Manchester, Manchester, 1991), 35–68. For Ebussu^{c}ud's relevant *fetvā*s, see Ertuğrul Düzdağ, *Kanuni Devri Şeyhülislam Ebussuud Efendi Fetvaları* (Istanbul: Kapı Yayınları, 2012), 135–140. For similar *fetvā*s after the sixteenth century, see, for example, Yenişehirli Abdullah Efendi, *Behcetü'l-Fetâvâ*, eds Süleyman Kaya et al. (Istanbul: Klasik Yayınları, 2012), 189, #1004 and #1005; and Şeyhülislam Feyzullah Efendi, *Fetâvâ-yı Feyziye*, ed. Süleyman

Kaya (Istanbul: Klasik Yayınları, 2010), 129–131. Also see Ekke Eberhard, *Osmanische Polemik gegen die Safawiden im 16. Jahrhundert nach arabischen Handschriften* (Freiburg: Klaus Schwarz Verlag, 1970), 104–110.

16. For the multitude of imperial orders concerning the persecution of the Kizilbash, copies of which are preserved in the *mühimme* registers (*mühimme defterleri*) in the Ottoman archives, see Ahmet Refik, *Onaltıncı Asırda Rafızîlik ve Bektaşilik* (Istanbul: Muallim Ahmet Halit Kitaphanesi, 1932); Colin Imber, 'The Persecution of the Ottoman Shi^c^ites according to the Mühimme Defterleri, 1565–1585', *Der Islam* 56, no. 2 (1979): 245–273; Saim Savaş, *XVI. Asırda Anadolu'da Alevilik* (Ankara: Vadi, 2002); Ahmet Hezarfen and Cemal Şener, eds, *Osmanlı Arşivi'nde Mühimme ve İrade Defterleri'nde Aleviler-Bektaşiler* (Istanbul: Karacaahmet Sultan Derneği Yayınları, n.d.). Also see Hanna Sohrweide, 'Der Sieg der Safaviden in Persien und seine Rückwirkung auf die Schiiten Anatoliens im 16. Jahrhundert', *Der Islam* 41 (1965): 95–223. A more specific demonstration of the practical relevance of these *fetvās* is the Ottomans' differing treatment of Mamluk women and Kizilbash women: while the latter were frequently enslaved, the former often escaped that fate. B. Lellouch, 'Osmanlı Sultanının İktidar ve Adaleti: Iran ve Mısır Cephelerinde Gerçekleştirilen Kıyımlar', in *Bir Allame-i Cihan: Stefanos Yerasimos*, eds Edhem Eldem et al., 2 vols (Istanbul: Kitap Yayınevi, 2012), I: 413.
17. See, for example, Barkey, *Empire of Difference,* 175–178; Savaş, *XVI. Asırda Anadolu'da Alevilik*; Feridun M. Emecen, *Yavuz Sultan Selim* (Izmir: Yitik Hazine Yayınları, 2011), 95–100; Stefan Winter, *The Shiites of Lebanon under Ottoman Rule, 1516–1788* (Cambridge and New York: Cambridge University Press, 2010), 7–20. For a recent reiteration of this approach bordering on an apologia for the Ottomans' persecutory measures against the Kizilbash, see Ayşe Baltacıoğlu-Brammer, 'The Formation of Kızılbaş Communities in Anatolia and Ottoman Responses, 1450s–1630s', *International Journal of Turkish Studies* 20, nos 1 and 2 (2014): 21–48.
18. For case studies of persecuting societies in the early modern era that highlight the shortcomings of the persecution–toleration binary, see, for example, Coffey, *Persecution and Toleration*; and Alexandra Walsham, *Charitable Hatred: Tolerance and Intolerance in England, 1500–1700* (Manchester: Manchester University Press, 2006). For an example from the medieval period, see Robert I. Moore, *The Formation of a Persecuting Society: Authority and Deviance in Western Europe, 950–1250* (Oxford and New York: B. Blackwell, 1987).
19. İlhan Şahin and Feridun Emecen, eds, *Osmanlılarda Dīvān-Bürokrasi-Ahkām. II. Beyazıd Dönemine Ait 906–1501 Tarihli Ahkām Defteri* (Istanbul: Türk Dünyası Araştırmaları Vakfı, 1994), 8, decree 27.
20. The absence of the term 'Kızılbaş' in earlier official documents including imperial orders is also noted in Feridun M. Emecen, *Osmanli Klasik Çağında Siyaset* (Istanbul: Timaş Yayınlar, 2009), 329; the relevant docu-

ments from Şahin and Emecen, *Osmanlılarda Dīvān*, have been conveniently reprinted in ibid., 338–344. Also see Ömer Faruk Teber, 'Osmanlı Belgelerinde Alevilik İçin Kullanılan Dinî-Siyasî Tanımlamalar', *Dinî Araştırmalar* 10 (May–August 2007): 19–38, esp. 28–29. Contemporary narrative sources, most importantly the chronicle of ᶜAşıkpaşazade, likewise designate as 'Erdebīl Ṣūfīleri' the adherents of the Safavi shaykhs. *Aspz*, 330. The few known exceptions include Kemalpaşazâde who, in the part of his history that he submitted to Bayezid II, uses the term 'Kizilbash' to refer to Shah İsma'il (but not his followers). İbn Kemâl, *Tevârîḫ-i Âl-i Os̱mân, VIII. Defter*, ed. Ahmet Uğur (Ankara: Türk Tarih Kurumu, 1997), 231, 232, 234, 243. Two other exceptions are letters sent by Bayezid II to a local Kurdish amir in the east and to the Akkoyunlu ruler Elvend Mirza presumably during the first years of the 1500s; in these the term 'Kizilbash' is evidently employed as a group name (*'ṭāʾife-i bāġīyye-i Kızılbaşiyye'*). See Feridun Bey, *Münşeāt-ı Selāṭīn*, 2 vols (Istanbul: n.p., 1274–75/1858), I: 351–354, cited in Emecen, *Osmanlı Klasik Çağında Siyaset*, n25. Also see Teber, 'Osmanlı Belgelerinde Alevilik', 28; and Oktay Efendiyev, 'Sultan II. Bayezid ve Şah İsmail', in *XIII. Türk Tarih Kongresi: Ankara, 4–8 Ekim 1999: Kongreye Sunulan Bildiriler* (Ankara: Türk Tarih Kurumu, 2002), 90. However, there seems to be some uncertainty about the dating of these letters. All in all, even these possible exceptions do not change the overall pattern, specifically in regard to official state documents.

21. An entirely new genre, known as *Selīmnāme*, emerged to serve this propagandist's purpose; for a description of this genre, see M. C. Şehabeddin Tekindağ, 'Selim-nâmeler', *İÜEF Tarih Entitüsü Dergisi* 1 (October 1970): 197–230; and Ahmet Uğur, *The Reign of Sultan Selīm I in the Light of the Selīm-nāme Literature* (Berlin: Klaus Schwarz Verlag, 1985).
22. See, for example, Çağatay Uluçay, 'Yavuz Sultan Selim Nasıl Padişah Oldu?' *İstanbul Üniversitesi Edebiyat Fakültesi Tarih Dergisi* 6, no. 9 (March 1954): 53–90; 7, no. 10 (September 1954): 117–142; 8, nos 11–12 (September 1955): 185–200; and Selahattin Tansel, *Sultan II. Bâyezit'in Siyasî Hayatı* (Istanbul: Milli Eğitim Basımevi, 1966), 227–310. For a recent critical treatment of relevant sources and historiography, see H. Erdem Çıpa, *The Making of Selim: Succession, Legitimacy, and Memory in the Early Modern Ottoman World* (Bloomington: Indiana University Press, 2017), 132–175. For individual uprisings, also see İsmail Hakkı Uzunçarşılı, *Osmanlı Tarihi*, 6th edn, vol. 2 (Ankara: Türk Tarih Kurumu, 1995), 253–278, 345–361; and Sohrweide, 'Der Sieg der Ṣafaviden in Persien'.
23. Uluçay, 'Yavuz Sultan Selim Nasıl'; M. C. Şehabettin Tekindağ, 'Şah Kulu Baba Tekeli İsyanı', *Belgelerle Türk Tarihi Dergisi* 3–4 (1967): 34–39, 54–59; Allouche, *Origins and Development*, 94–96.
24. For the details of the Şahkulu uprising, see Sohrweide, 'Der Sieg der Ṣafaviden in Persien', 145–164; and Feridun M. Emecen, ''İhtilalci Bir Mehdilik' Hareketi mi? Şahkulu Baba Tekeli İsyanı Üzerine Yeni

Yaklaşımlar', in *Ötekilerin Peşinde Ahmet Yaşar Ocak's Armağan*, eds Mehmet Öz and Fatih Yeşil (Istanbul: Timaş Yayınları, 2015), 521–534. Elsewhere, Emecen makes the valuable observation of a meaningful difference in Kemalpaşazade's presentation of the revolt in the versions of his chronicle completed before and after Selim I's ascent to the throne; it is only in the latter version, Emecen notes, that Kemalpaşazade openly links the revolt to Shah Isma[c]il. Ibid., 323–325.

25. If what it conveys is accurate, a report sent to Istanbul by the *sancakbeyi* of Filibe – which includes statements by Pir Ahmed, allegedly a 'spy' (*cāsūs*) of Şahkulu – is revelatory concerning the extent of the latter's sphere of influence beyond Teke, for it speaks of dozens of letters that Şahkulu sent to other *ḫalīfes* in Rumelia prior to his revolt. The document does not clarify, however, whether the addressees of the letters were Şahkulu's own *ḫalīfes*, or those of the Safavid shahs, nor does it say anything about the content of the letters. Despite that, a common assumption among historians is that the letters in question were sent to other Safavi *ḫalīfes* by way of preparing them for the revolt. For the document and its mainstream interpretation, see Uluçay, 'Yavuz Sultan Selim Nasıl', 62–63; for its facsimile, also see Tekindağ, 'Şah Kulu Baba Tekeli İsyanı', 36.
26. Hoca Sa[c]deddin Efendi, *Tācü't-Tevārīḫ*, vol. II (Istanbul: Tab[c]ḫāne-i [c]Āmire, 1279–1280/1862–1863), 164–166.
27. This is how Kemalpaşazade describes the refugees from Teke who were pouring into Safavid territories: '*Tekelü Etrâkinüñ dike burun füttâklerinden yanına varanlar taḳaddümle taḳarrüb bulup, Kızılbaş içinde merdânelik ve yoldaşlığ ile meşhûr oldular, [c]ömrinde tîmar yimeyen, diyârında kendüye kimse âdem dimeyen, bi-kârlar tümen beğleri olup, ḥadden ziyâde i[c]tibâr buldılar.*' Quoted in Uğur, *The Reign of Sultan Selīm*, 43. Also see Irène Beldiceanu-Steinherr, 'Le règne de Selīm ler: *Tournant* dans la vie politique et religieuse de l'Empire Ottoman', *Turcica* 6 (1975): 34–48.
28. For this observation by an anonymous Italian merchant, see *A Narrative of Italian Travels in Persia, in the Fifteenth and Sixteenth Centuries*, trans. and ed. Charles Grey (London: Printed for the Hakluyt Society, 1873), 194. Also see Sydney N. Fisher, *The Foreign Relations of Turkey 1481–1512* (Urbana: University of Illinois Press, 1948), 91.
29. Faruk Sümer, 'XVI. Asırda Anadolu, Suriye ve Irak'ta yaşayan Türk aşiretlerine umumi bir bakış', *İstanbul Üniversitesi İktisat Fakültesi Mecmuası* XI (1952), 515; Rudi Paul Lindner, *Nomads and Ottomans in Medieval Anatolia* (Bloomington: Indiana University Press, 1960), 51–63; Irène Beldiceanu-Steinherr, 'A propos des tribus Atčeken (XVe–XVIe siècles)', *Journal of the Economic and Social History of the Orient* 30, no. 2 (1987): 122–195, esp. 159–161.
30. For the deteriorating impact of Ottoman centralisation policies on small fief-holders who had connections with landed and/or military aristocracy from pre-Ottoman times, and their participation in rebellious movements,

see Mustafa Akdağ, 'Tımar rejiminin bozuluşu', *Ankara Üniversitesi Dil ve Tarih Coğrafya Fakültesi Dergisi* 4 (1945): 419–431; Oktay Özel, *The Collapse of Rural Order in Ottoman Anatolia: Amasya 1576–1643* (Leiden: Brill, 2015), Chapters 2 and 3.

31. Hoca Sa^{c}deddin, *Tācü't-Tevārīḫ*, II: 162–163; Tekindağ, 'Şah Kulu Baba Tekeli İsyanı', 35–36; Uluçay, 'Yavuz Sultan Selim Nasıl', 61–74.
32. Sohrweide, 'Der Sieg der Ṣafaviden in Persien', 139–141. The 1509 earthquake, whose aftershocks continued for a month, was preceded by a widespread plague, and followed first by a prolonged famine and then a major flood due to heavy rainfall that also impacted the territories of Rum during the last decade of the fifteenth century. For details about the 1509 earthquake, see Nicholas Ambraseys, *Earthquakes in the Mediterranean and the Middle East: A multidisciplinary Study of Seismicity to 1900* (Cambridge and New York: Cambridge University Press, 2009), 422–433.
33. Richard F. Kreutel, *Haniwaldanus Anonimi'ne Göre Sultan Bayezid-i Velî (1481–1512)*, translated into Turkish by Necdet Öztürk (Istanbul: Türk Dünyası Araştırmaları Vakfı, 1997), 48–49.
34. Hoca Sa^{c}deddin, *Tācü't-Tevārīḫ*, II: 181–182. Hasan-ı Rumlu's account of the incident confirms that of Hoca Sa^{c}deddin; see Hasan-ı Rumlu, *Ahsenü't-Tevārih*, abridged and translated into Turkish by Cevat Cevan (Ankara: Ardıç Yayınları, 2004), 155.
35. Another exception here might be the Şah Veli (b. Şeyh Celal) uprising that took place in Tokat in 1520. However, accounts of the revolt given by different sources are not always easy to reconcile with one another. Most importantly, Ottoman chronicles depict the leader of the revolt as an extremely popular shaykh who was hailed as Mahdi by his followers, so much so that his fame overshadowed that of Shah İsma'il. See, for example, Şükrî-i Bitlisî, *Selîm-Nâme*, ed. Mustafa Argunşah (Kayseri: Erciyes Üniversitesi, 1997), 297–298. On the other hand, according to an Ottoman spy report, Şah Veli was in communication with Shah İsma'il and was encouraged by him to revolt. Overall, while a Safavid connection in the revolt is a strong possibility, the exact nature of this connection is not fully clear. For more details, and the relevant primary sources, see Jean-Louis Bacqué-Grammont, 'Études Turco-Safavides, III, Notes et documents sur la révolte de Şâh Veli b. Şeyh Celâl', *Archivum Ottomanicum* 7 (1982): 5–69.
36. Roemer, for instance, writes: 'The reason for the persecution [of the Anatolian Qizilbash] was the repeated revolts of the Qizilbash and their connection with the Safavids – not their Shī^{c}ī faith, even though this conflicted with the dominant Sunnī creed of the Ottoman empire.' Hans R. Roemer, 'The Safavid Period', *Cambridge-Iran-6*, 222.
37. The friendly nature of relations, at least on the surface, is indicated by letters exchanged between Bayezid II and Shah Isma^{c}il, which are reproduced in Feridun Beg, ed., *Münşe'ātü's-selāṭīni'l-Osmaniyye* (Istanbul: Darüttıbattil'āmire, 1265/1849) 1: 345–348.

38. Roemer, 'The Safavid Period', 219; Gilles Veinstein, 'Les premières mesures de Bâyezîd II contre les Kızılbaş', in *Syncrétismes et hérésies dans l'Orient seldjoukide et ottoman (XIV–XVIII siècle), Actes du Colloque du Collège de France, octobre 2001* (Paris: Peeters, 2005), 227.
39. Hoca Sa[c]deddin, *Tācü't-Tevārīḫ*, II: 127, 162–63. Kemâl, *Tevârîh-i Âl-i Os̱mân*, 233; Solak-zâde Mehmed Hemdemî Çelebî, *Solak-zâde Tarihi*, ed. Vahid Çabuk, 2 vols (Ankara: Kültür Bakanlığı, 1989), 428–429. It appears that these deportations were not readily understandable and acceptable for the larger Ottoman public either, and required a special explanation and justification. We gather this from the manner in which they are reported by [c]Aşıkpaşazade in his *Tevārīḫ*, following the self-posed question as such: 'These were themselves Sufis. They were disciples of Shaykh Safi. In their mystical path they followed the shari[c]a of Muhammad, may Allah send blessing and peace upon him. Why then were they declared as unbelievers?' In the answer to his own question, [c]Aşıkpaşazade then goes on to explain how Safaviyya, once a respectable Sufi order, slipped into 'heresy' starting with Shaykh Junayd, *Aspz*, 330–331.
40. Terzioğlu, 'Sufis in the Age of State-building and Confessionalization', 93; B. G. Martin, 'A Short History of the Khalwati Order of Dervishes', in *Scholars, Saints, and Sufis: Muslim Religious Institutions in the Middle East since 1500*, ed. Nikkie R. Keddie (Berkeley: University of California Press, 1972), 282–285; Yusuf Küçükdağ, 'Osmanlı Devleti'nin, Şah İsmail'in Propagandacılarına Halvetîye ile Karşı Koyma Politikası', in *XIII. Türk Tarih Kongresi: Ankara, 4–8 Ekim 1999: Kongreye sunulan bildiriler* (Ankara: Türk Tarih Kurumu, 2002), 435–444. For the Halveti order, also see John Curry, *The Transformation of Muslim Mystical Thought in the Ottoman Empire: The Rise of the Halveti Order 1350–1650* (Edinburgh: Edinburgh University Press, 2010).
41. Halil İnalcık, 'Mehmed the Conqueror and His Time', *Speculum* 35, no. 3 (1960): 426; Tansel, *Sultan II. Bâyezit*, 4–6; Feridun Emecen, *İmparatorluk Çağının Osmanlı Sultanları I: Bayezid II, Yavuz, Kanûnî* (Istanbul: İSAM Yayınlari, 2011), 45.
42. Emecen, *İmparatorluk Çağının Osmanlı Sultanları*, 26–27.
43. For members of the Akkoyunlu elite who relocated to the Ottoman Empire, see M. Tayyib Gökbilgin, 'XVI. Asır Başlarında Osmanlı Devleti Hizmetindeki Akkoyunlu Ümerâsı,' *Türkiyat Mecmuası* 9 (1951): 35–46. For the contribution of Iranian émigrés to anti-Safavid polemics, see Eberhard, *Osmanische Polemik*, 52–61; and Hüseyin Yılmaz, 'İran'dan Sünnî Kaçışı ve Osmanlı Devleti'nde Safevî Karşıtı Propagandanın Yaygınlaşması: Hüseyin b. Abdullah el-Şirvânî'nin Mesiyanik Çağrısı', in *Uluslararası Diyarbakır Sempozyumu, 2–5 Kasım 2016*, eds Ufuk Bircan et al. (Diyarbakır: T. C. Diyarbakır Valiliği, 2017), 299–310; and idem, *Caliphate Redefined*, 257–267.
44. Fisher, *The Foreign Relations*, 94. Selim's attacks against the Safavid army in Erzincan are covered relatively extensively in the *Selîmnâme* literature

in a triumphant language; see, for example, Celâl-zâde Mustafa, *Selim-nâme*, eds Ahmet Uğur and Mustafa Çuhadar (Ankara: Kültür Bakanlığı, 1990), 273–274; Şükrî-i Bitlisî, *Selîm-Nâme*, 66–70. Allouche thinks that Selim's attacks in Erzincan were a response to the 1507 incident, but this is clearly wrong because Selim's attacks started before that. Allouche, *Origins and Development*, 90. For border skirmishes between Prince Selim and the Safavid forces, also see Namiq Musalı, 'Safevîler'in Diyarbakır Beylerbeyi Muhammed Han Ustaclu ve Anadolu'daki Faaliyetleri', in *Uluslararası Diyarbakır Sempozyumu, 2–5 Kasım 2016*, eds Ufuk Bircan et al. (Diyarbakır: T. C. Diyarbakır Valiliği, 2017), 510–511.

45. Fisher, *The Foreign Relations*, 96; Celâl-zâde Mustafa, *Selim-nâme*, 273–274; For a more detailed discussion and further references, see Yasin Arslantaş, 'Depicting the Other: Qizilbash Image in the 16th Century Ottoman Historiography' (PhD diss., Bilkent University, Ankara, 2013), 59–61.
46. Emecen, for example, argues, without any real evidence, that Konya was Shah Isma[c]il's original choice of centre for his revolution but that he had to eschew it in favour of Tabriz thanks to government measures that effectively cut off his lines of communication with his disciples. Emecen, *İmparatorluk Çağının Osmanlı Sultanları*, 40.
47. An episode construed by some as an omen of Shah Isma[c]il's 'hidden intention . . . to enter Anatolia' was his summoning of his adherents to Erzincan (at the time a province bordering Ottoman-controlled territories) before his march to Shirvan and then to Tabriz in 1501. Allouche, *Origins and Development*, 79. However, this appears to be little more than an effort to recruit new soldiers for his war efforts elsewhere, as also implied by contemporary Ottoman historians; see, for example, Hoca Sa[c]deddin, *Tācü't-Tevārīḫ*, II: 126–127. Ghulam Sarwar reasonably argues that Erzincan was chosen because it was a place where Shah Isma[c]il's followers would have easier access to him. Ghulam Sarwar, *History of Shah Ismail Safawi* (Aligarh: Muslim University, 1939), 33. Another episode highlighted as a sign of Shah Isma[c]il's ambitions towards Rum is his crossing of Ottoman territories on his way to a campaign against the Dulkadirli principality in 1507, Allouche, *Origins and Development*, 89–90. While sources contradict one another on this issue (Sohrweide, 'Der Sieg der Safaviden in Persien', 142), it is well known that Shah Isma[c]il made sure to convey to Bayezid II his peaceful intentions towards the Ottomans on the eve of this campaign. While this assurance did not dissuade Bayezid II from ordering the reinforcement of the empire's eastern borders as a precaution, the incident did not undermine the external congeniality of relations between the two rulers, which lasted until the end of Bayezid II's reign. İbn Kemâl, *Tevârîḫ-i Âl-i O̱smân*, 343; Efendiyev, 'Sultan II. Bayezid ve Şah İsmail', 89–95; Efendiyev, 'Çaldıran Savaşı'na Kadar Osmanlı-Safevi İlişkilerine Kısa Bir Bakış', *Uluslararası Sosyal Araştırmalar Dergisi/The Journal of International Social Research* 26 (Winter 2009): 126–135.
48. J. R. Walsh, 'The Historiography of Ottoman–Safavid Relations in the

Sixteenth and Seventeenth Centuries', in *Historians of the Middle East*, eds Bernard Lewis and P. M. Holt (Oxford: Oxford University Press, 1962), 203. This does not, of course, exclude the possibility of genuine fear of Safavid expansionism and suspicion thereof among the Ottoman rulers and the common folk in the empire; see, for example, İbn Kemâl, *Tevârîḫ-i Âl-i Os̱mân*, 243; and Urs Gösken and Nabil al-Tikriti, 'The 1502–1504 Correspondence between Şehzade Korkud and the Knights of St. John of Jerusalem', *Mediterranea – Ricerche Storiche* 12, no. 34 (2015), 414. Nor does it by any means guarantee that his followers and sympathizers in Ottoman territories did not harbour any such dreams or expectations at certain times and places; see Kreutel, *Haniwaldanus Anonimi'ne Göre*, 4.

49. For an early observation of the limited nature of Safavid influence over the so-called Kizilbash revolts in general, see Walsh, 'The Historiography of Ottoman–Safavid Relations', 202. He writes: 'It is wrong to regard these various local insurrections as being provoked by Safavid propagandists; that they are presented as such by the Ottomans arises from the concern to give their repressive measures against Muslims the allure of counter-heretical activity. Safavid proselytism in the area was at best disorganized and erratic, undertaken on the initiative of local shaykhs whose religious views are rarely susceptible of definition.'
50. Hasan-ı Rumlu, *Ahsenü't-Tevārih*, 164–165, 177–178, 190; Uluçay, 'Yavuz Sultan Selim Nasıl',127–134; Tekindağ, 'Yeni Kaynak ve Vesikaların', 51–52; Allouche, *Origins and Development*, 96–97.
51. For the last phase of the civil war, see Uluçay, 'Yavuz Sultan Selim Nasıl', 117–142.
52. Celâl-zâde Mustafa, *Selim-nâme*, 328. It is of course possible that Prince Murad's conversion was a genuine one, as suggested by Uluçay, 'Yavuz Sultan Selim Nasıl', 127–131, and not mere opportunism as implied by Mustafa, who might not have wanted to tarnish the reputation of the house of Osman as a beacon of correctness. While it is not easy to determine the exact blend of religious and political motivations of Prince Murad, what is clear is the difficulty of separating the 'Kizilbash problem' from the intra-dynastic conflict preceding Selim I's ascension to the throne (see the below discussion of the two registers of Selim I's opponents who were punished).
53. Fisher, *The Foreign Relations*, 94, 102; Efendiyev, 'Sultan II. Bayezid ve Şah İsmail', 91–92.
54. Şāh İsmāʿil kimdür kim gele/ Men dururken mülkümüñ ḳurbın ala

    . . .

    Men sezā-vāram ne söyler sürḫa-ser/ Eylesün Tebriz taḫtından ḥaẓer
    Gitti Bayındur menümdür rūz-gār/ Rūma rām olmaḳ gerekdür ol diyār.

    Şükrî-i Bitlisî, *Selîm-Nâme*, 67. Cf. Celâl-zâde Mustafa, *Selim-nâme*, 274.
55. *EI-2*, s.v. 'Selim I', by Halil İnalcık.
56. For a similar line of analysis, see Çıpa, *The Making of Selim*, 48. Çıpa

writes: 'What hurt Korḳud and Aḥmed politically benefited their brother Selīm, who played the Ḳızılbaş card successfully.'

57. Çipa, *The Making of Selim*, 36–37.
58. My brief description of the declining socio-economic conditions of the common folk in the empire at about the turn of the sixteenth century relies on Mustafa Akdağ's much more detailed, multi-volume analysis of the Anatolian economy over the long durée since Seljuk times. Akdağ observes a gradual decline of the Seljuk socio-economic system centred on the Konya–Sivas–Kayseri triangle over the course of a century and a half from 1300 to 1453, which he believes culminated in a major economic crisis at about the early sixteenth century, hitting particularly hard the peasantry and the local *timar*-holders in Anatolia. Mustafa Akdağ, *Türkiye'nin İktisadi ve İçtimai Tarihi*, 2 vols (1453–1559) (1959; reprint, Istanbul: Cem Yayınevi, 1995), 316–328. For the growing population in the provinces, in particular of single, young men, also see Huricihan İslamoğlu, *Osmanlı İmparatorluğu'nda Devlet ve Köylü*, 2nd edn (Istanbul: İletişim Yayınları, 2010), 217–224.
59. Celâl-zâde Mustafa, *Selim-nâme*, 284–285. For an English translation of the most pertinent part of Selim's speech, as well as a discussion of the nuances of the term '*merdüm-zāde*', see Çipa, *The Making of Selim*, 85–90.
60. Çipa, *The Making of Selim*, Chapter 2.
61. İdrîs-i Bidlîsî, *Selim Şah-nâme*, ed. Hicabi Kırlangıç (Ankara: Kültür Bakanlığı, 2001), 126.
62. Yılmaz, 'İran'dan Sünnî Kaçışı', 305. Although Shirvani wrote his epistles after Selim I's death, it still helps shed light on the latter's perception by the Iranian Sunni émigrés.
63. Cornell H. Fleischer, 'The Lawgiver as Messiah: The Making of the Imperial Image in the Reign of Süleymân', in *Soliman le Magnifique et son temps: Actes du colloque de Paris, Galeries nationales du Grand palais, 7–10 mars 1990*, ed. Gillès Veinstein (Paris: La Documentation française, n.d.), 160.
64. Fleischer, *Bureaucrat and Intellectual in the Ottoman Empire*, 273–283, 286–289. For the changing legitimacy claims of the Ottoman dynasty over the centuries, also see Colin H. Imber, 'Ideals and Legitimation in Early Ottoman History', in *Süleyman the Magnificent and His Age: The Ottoman Empire in the Early Modern World,* eds M. Kunt and C. Woodhead (London and New York: Longman, 1995), 139–153.
65. For Shirvani, the Ottomans' acquisition of the Holy Cities was the clearest sign of their divinely sanctioned role to restore God's order in the world. Yılmaz, 'İran'dan Sünnî Kaçışı', 306.
66. Fleischer, 'The Lawgiver as Messiah', and Barbara Flemming, 'Sāhib-kırān und Mahdī: Türkische Endzeiterwartungen im ersten Jahrzehnt der Regierung Süleymāns', in *Between the Danube and the Caucasus: A Collection of Papers concerning Oriental Sources on the History of the Peoples of Central and South-Eastern Europe*, ed. György Kara (Budapest: Akadémiai Kiadó, 1987), 43–62.

67. Fleischer, *Bureaucrat and Intellectual,* 288–289.
68. Şahin, *Empire and Power in the Reign of Süleyman*, 123.
69. Fleischer, 'The Lawgiver as Messiah', 164–169; Şahin, *Empire and Power in the Reign of Süleyman*, 187–193.
70. For a translation of the full text of Selim I's letter, and Shah Isma^cil's response to it, see *The Islamic World*, eds William H. McNeill and Marilyn Robinson Waldman (Chicago: The University of Chicago Press, 1983), 338–344.
71. For Selim's relations with the (Sunni) Kurdish tribes, see Ebru Sönmez, *İdris-i Bidlisi: Ottoman Kurdistan and Islamic Legitimacy* (Istanbul: Libra Kitap, 2012).
72. Nabil al-Tikriti suggests that the content of these *fetvā*s largely mirrored, and possibly drew on, Prince Korkut's views concerning belief and apostacy, which Korkut articulated in his *Ḥāfız el-İnsān* that was, according to Tikriti, conceived by no later than 1508, see al-Tikriti, 'Kalam in the Service of the State', 146–149.
73. The original source of this information was İdris Bidlisi, the deal-breaker between Selim and Kurdish tribes, see İdrîs-i Bidlîsî, *Selim Şah-nâme*, 130, 136. It would also be repeated by later Ottoman chroniclers, see, for example, Gelibolulu Mustafa ᶜÂlī Efendi, *Kitâbü'l-Târīḫ-i Künhü'l-Aḫbâr*, eds Ahmet Uğur et al. (Kayseri: Erciyes Üniversitesi, 1997), 1,076–1,077; and Hoca Saᶜdeddin, *Tācü't-Tevārīḫ,* II: 245–246.
74. Tabib Ramazan, a physician at the Ottoman court who wrote two of the earliest accounts of Sultan Süelyman's reign, believed that 'eliminating the Kizilbash sedition would only be possible by mass killings of their supporters but such an undertaking would never be feasible because both Persia and the Ottoman realm were full of such people'. Yılmaz, *Caliphate Redefined,* 253–254.
75. TMA. D. 10149, cited in Uluçay, 'Yavuz Sultan Selim Nasıl,' 8, nos 11–12 (September 1955), 192 n68; and is published with its facsimile in Jean-Louis Bacqué-Grammont, '1513 Yılında Rum Eyaletinde Şüpheli Tımar Sahiplerine Ait Bir Liste', in Ord. Prof. Ömer Lütfi Barkan'a Armağan, *İstanbul Üniversitesi İktisat Fakültesi Mecmuası* 44, nos 1–2 (1985), 173–176; republished also in Rıza Yıldırım, 'Turkomans between Two Empires: The Origins of the Qizilbash Identity in Anatolia (1447–1514)', (PhD diss., Bilkent University, 2008), 554–559.
76. '*Südde-i saᵓādetden ḥükm-i cihān-muṭāᶜ vārid olub mażmūn-ı şerīfinde şöyle emrolunmuş ki vilāyet-i Rūm'da Sulṭān Aḥmed'e varan varmıyan ṭāᵓifenüñ . . . anıñ gibi kimesneleri ᶜarżınla irsāl idesin deyu.*' Bacqué-Grammont, '1513 Yılında Rum Eyaletinde', 176. In addition to whether or not he joined Prince Ahmed's forces, the document notes for each individual name whether he was a Kizilbash or not (pertinent phrases used in the document are '*Kızılbaş olmak*' and '*Kızılbaşa gitmek*').
77. TMA. D10149, published in Yıldırım, 'Turkomans between Two Empires', 561–562.

78. For example, a certain Divane Yakub was executed due to the following charges: *'Kadurga seferine ve Torul (Hurhul / Turhal) cengine ve Erzincan'a varduğundan.'* Yıldırım, 'Turkomans between Two Empires', 561.
79. Bacqué-Grammont, '1513 Yılında Rum Eyaletinde', 164–165.
80. Refik, *On altıncı Asırda Rafızilik*, 88.
81. Of the classical Sunni scholars, Malik ibn Anas (d. 795) in particular sanctioned apostates to be given time to rethink their apostasy and return to Islam. Majid Khadduri, *War and Peace in the Law of Islam* (Baltimore: The Johns Hopkins Press, 1955), 149–152.
82. Atçıl, 'Safavid Threat', 299.
83. The part of the document reads as follows: *'fetvā virdük ki ol ẕikr olınan ṭāʾife kāfirler ve mülḥidlerdür ve dahi her kimse kī anlara meyl idüp ol bāṭıl dīnlerine rāżı ve muᶜāvin olalar, anlar dahi kāfirler ve mülḥidlerdür, bunları kırup cemāᶜatlerin dağıtmak cemīᶜ müslümānlara vācib ve farżdır.'* Tekindağ, 'Yeni Kaynak ve Vesīkaların', 55; 80, Vesika I/a.
84. Atçıl, 'Safavid Threat', 300.
85. For Şeyh Bedreddin and Molla Lütfi, as well as other cases of persecution of religious dissidents in the Ottoman Empire, see Ahmet Yaşar Ocak, *Osmanlı toplumunda zındıklar ve mülhidler (15.–17. yüzyıllar)* (Istanbul: Tarih Vakfı Yurt Yayınları, 1998). Also see Michel Balivet, *Şeyh Bedreddin Tasavvuf ve İsyan* (Istanbul: Tarih Vakfı Yurt Yayınları, 2000).
86. Atçıl, 'Safavid Threat', 300.
87. Frank Griffel, 'Toleration and Exclusion: Al-Shafi'i and al-Ghazali on the Treatment of Apostates', *Bulletin of the School of Oriental and African Studies* 64, no. 3 (2001): 339–354; Yaron Friedman, *The Nusayri-'Alawis: An Introduction to the Religion, History and Identity of the Leading Minority in Syria* (Leiden and Boston: Brill, 2010), 175–222.
88. Üstün, 'Heresy and Legitimacy', 61.
89. Üstün, 'Heresy and Legitimacy', 58–59.
90. Gülru Necipoğlu, *The Age of Sinan: Architectural Culture in the Ottoman Empire* (London: Reaktion, 2005), 64–65.
91. Gülru Necipoğlu, 'The Süleymaniye Complex in Istanbul: An Interpretation', *Muqarnas* 3 (1985): 108–109.
92. Nelida Fuccaro, 'The Ottoman Frontier in Kurdistan in the Sixteenth and Seventeenth Centuries', in *The Ottoman World*, ed. Christine Woodhead (London: Routledge, 2011), 239–240.
93. The *mühimme* registers concerning Kizilbash persecutions during the second half of the sixteenth century have been relatively extensively studied, and the texts of most of them have been published in transliteration and facsimile. For references, see n16 above.
94. For examples, see Savaş, *XVI. Asırda Anadolu'da Alevîlik*, Appendices, especially documents no. 1, no. 12, no. 16, no. 22, no. 31, no. 32, no. 50, no. 56, no. 65, no. 80, no. 90, no. 91, no. 99, no. 104. These contain

the following sultanic orders: BA.MD.3/172/473; BA.MD.6/422/897; BA.MD.7/120/312; BA.MD.7/754/2067; BA.MD.10/189/279; BA.MD. 12/302/619; BA.MD.28/340/859; BA.MD.29/96/231; BA.MD. 30/132/319; BA.MD.36/140/393; BA.MD.42/160/514; BA.MD.42/251/781; BA.MD. 53/145/419; BA.MD.69/223/445. Also see Şener, *Osmanlı Belgeleri'nde*, 17, 21, 39, 119.

95. BA.MD.53/145/ 419, published as document no. 99 in Savaş, *XVI. Asırda Anadolu'da Alevîlik*, 225–226; also published in Hezarfen and Şener, *Osmanlı Arşivi'nde*, 197.
96. BA.MD.42/123/429, published as document no. 89 in Savaş, *XVI. Asırda Anadolu'da Alevîlik*, 221–222, and in Hezarfen and Şener, *Osmanlı Arşivi'nde*, 147.
97. See, for example, BA.MD.3/172/473; BA.MD.5/429/1142; BA.MD.5/513/ 1401; BA.MD.6/324–325/686; BA.MD.6/422/897; BA.MD.29/209/488, published as documents no. 1, no. 9, no. 10, no. 11, no. 12, no. 57 in Savaş, *XVI. Asırda Anadolu'da Alevîlik*, Appendices.
98. For the basic facts of the uprising, see Faruk Söylemez, 'Anadolu'da Sahte Şah İsmail İsyanı', *Sosyal Bilimler Enstitüsü* 17 (2004): 71–90.
99. M. A. Danon, 'Un interrogatoire d'hérétiques Musulmans (1619)', *Journal Asiatique* (April–June 1921): 281–293; Andreas Tietze, 'A Document on the Persecution of Sectarians in Early Seventeenth-Century Istanbul', in *Bektachiyya: Études sur l'ordre mystique des Bektachis et les groupes relevant de Hadji Bektach*, ed. Alexandre Popovic and Gilles Veinstein (Istanbul: Isis Press, 1995), 165–170.
100. For Ebussu[c]ud's life and significance in Ottoman history, see Colin H. Imber, *Ebu's-Su'ud: The Islamic Legal Tradition* (Stanford: Stanford University Press, 2009).
101. Düzenli, *Ma[c]rûzât*, 59–60.
102. For Ebussu[c]ud's various *fetvā*s, see Düzdağ, *Şeyhülislām Ebu's-Su[c]ud*; and Düzenli, *Ma[c]rûzât*.
103. A particularly instructive case here is that of the Halveti order, which was patronized by Bayezid II in part to neutralize Safavid influence, but that came under close supervision during the reign of Selim I. See Martin, 'Short History', 282–285; Curry, *The Transformation*, 68–77.
104. Terzioğlu, 'Sufis in the Age of State-building and Confessionalization', 95.
105. Düzdağ, *Şeyhülislām Ebu's-Su[c]ud*, Mesele no. 349, 85–86, and Mesele no. 353, 87.
106. See, for example, BA.MD.30/207/488, published as document no. 66 in Savaş, *XVI. Asırda Anadolu'da Alevîlik*, 212.
107. Düzdağ, *Şeyhülislām Ebu's-Su[c]ud*, Mesele no. 349, 86. Cf. *ABS*, s.v. 'miraç'.
108. Düzdağ, *Şeyhülislām Ebu's-Su[c]ud*, Mesele no. 969, no. 970 and no. 971, 193; Mesele no. 967, 192; Mesele no. 353, 87.

109. Düzdağ, *Şeyhülislām Ebu's-Su^c ud*, Mesele no. 348, 85.
110. Necipoğlu, *Age of Sinan*, 48.
111. Necipoğlu, *Age of Sinan*, 52.
112. Düzdağ, *Şeyhülislam Ebu's-Su^c ud*, Mesele no. 481, 110–111.
113. Yılmaz, *Caliphate Redefined*, 257–259.
114. Necipoğlu, *Age of Sinan*, 47–57.
115. Nuran Koyuncu, *Osmanlı Devleti'nde Şia: Safevi Taraftarlarına Uygulanan Cezai Yaptırımlar: İran Tebaasıyla Evlenme Yasağı* (Konya: Çizgi Kitabevi, 2014), 117–120.
116. Stefan Winter, for instance, writes: 'The Bektaşis' association with the Janissary corps is perhaps the most striking case of the Ottomans' openness to Shiism or quasi-Shiism.' İdem, *The Shiites of Lebanon*, 12.
117. Imber, *Ebu's-Su'ud*, 92.
118. Imber, *Ebu's-Su'ud*, 91.
119. Düzdağ, *Şeyhülislam Ebu's-Su^c ud*, Mesele no. 479, 109.
120. For the different punishments, see, for example, BA.MD.7/754/2067; BA.MD.9/38/102; BA.MD.12/329–330/674; BA.MD.25/324/2983; BA.MD.29/209/488, published as documents no. 22, no. 30, no. 33, no. 42, and no. 57 in Savaş, *XVI. Asırda Anadolu'da Alevîlik*, Appendices. Also see ibid., 93–118.
121. BA.MD.36/280/734, published as document no. 80, in Savaş, *XVI. Asırda Anadolu'da Alevîlik*, 218.
122. Düzdağ, *Şeyhülislam Ebu's-Su^c ud*, Mesele no. 187, 62; Mesele no. 282, 73; Mesele no. 209, 62.
123. Necipoğlu, *Age of Sinan*, 48.
124. Fariba Zarinebaf-Shahr, 'Qizilbash "Heresy" and Rebellion in Ottoman Anatolia during the Sixteenth Century', *Anatolia Moderna/Yeni Anadolu* 7 (1977): 11.
125. See, for example, BA.MD.12/416/816; BA.MD.47/44/112; BA.MD.49/125/423, published as documents no. 30, no. 34, no. 97, no. 98 in Savaş, *XVI. Asırda Anadolu'da Alevîlik*, Appendices. For a well-studied case of neighbours accusing another neighbour of being Kizilbash, see Leslie Pierce, *Morality Tales: Law and Gender in the Ottoman Court of Aintab* (Berkeley: University of California Press, 2003).
126. BA.MD.27/177/403; BA.MD.35/153/390; BA.MD.35/366/931; BA.MD.58/349/893, published as documents no. 46, no. 72, no. 79, no. 102 in Savaş, *XVI. Asırda Anadolu'da Alevîlik*, 214.
127. BA.MD.47/44/112, published as document no. 97 in Savaş, *XVI. Asırda Anadolu'da Alevîlik*, 224–225.
128. BA.MD.46/146/300, published as document no. 95 in Savaş, *XVI. Asırda Anadolu'da Alevîlik*, 224. For further examples of false accusations, also see ibid., *XVI. Asırda Anadolu'da Alevîlik,* 118–122.
129. BA.MD.69/357/512, published as document no. 105 in Savaş, *XVI. Asırda Anadolu'da Alevîlik*, 228; an interesting *fetvā* by Ebu's-Su^c ud suggests that

such incidents were not infrequent. It concerns an incident whereby a mob attacks a group of Sufis, calling them Kizilbash. *Şeyhülislam Ebu's-Su*ᶜ*ud Efendi*, Mesele no. 340, 83.

130. Kent Schull, *Prisons in the Late Ottoman Empire: Microcosms of Modernity* (Edinburgh: Edinburgh University Press, 2014), 28.
131. BA.MD.12/302/619, published as document no. 32 in Savaş, *XVI. Asırda Anadolu'da Alevîlik*, 197–198.
132. BA.MD.52/99/239, published in Hezarfen and Şener, *Osmanlı Arşivi'nde*, 183.
133. See, for example, BA.MD.4/204/2143; BA.MD.36/294/779; and BA.MD. 42/77/332, published respectively as documents no. 5, no. 86 and no. 88 in Savaş, *XVI. Asırda Anadolu'da Alevîlik*, Appendices.
134. An important exception to this is Savaş, *XVI. Asırda Anadolu'da Alevîlik*, see esp. 163–167.
135. BA.MD.28/340/859 and BA.MD.28/340/860, published respectively as documents no. 50 and no. 51 in Savaş, *XVI. Asırda Anadolu'da Alevîlik*, 205.
136. Şener, *Osmanlı Belgeleri'nde*, 19. For other examples of timariots losing their land grants for being charged as Kizilbash, or because of their refusal to fight against the Safavids, see Savaş, *XVI. Asırda Anadolu'da Alevîlik*, 165–167.
137. Selahattin Tansel, *Yavuz Sultan Selim* (Ankara: Milli Eğitim Basımevi, 1969), 29. The original of the report is at TMA. E.3192.
138. Baki Öz, *Alevilikle İlgili Osmanlı Belgeleri* (Istanbul: Can Yayınları, 1995), Belge 40, 53.
139. Saim Savaş, *Bir Tekkenin Dini ve Sosyal Tarihi: Sivas Ali Baba Zaviyesi* (Istanbul: Dergah Yayınları, 1992), esp. 41–64.
140. BA.MD.7/120/312, published as document no. 16 in Savaş, *XVI. Asırda Anadolu'da Alevîlik*, 190.
141. BA.MD.3/562/1644, published as document no. 4 in Savaş, *XVI. Asırda Anadolu'da Alevîlik*, 184.
142. For a similar observation in connection to Bektashi-affiliated convents, see my 'Sinemilliler: Bir Alevi Ocağı ve Aşireti', *Kırkbudak* 2, no. 6 (Spring 2006): 19–59.
143. For examples of such documents, see my 'Sinemilliler: Bir Alevi Ocağı ve Aşireti', *Kırkbudak* 2, no. 6 (Spring 2006): 19–59.
144. Sam White, *The Climate of Rebellion in the Early Modern Empire* (Cambridge and New York: Cambridge University Press, 2011). For the general political and economic situation and the crisis of the seventeenth century in the Ottoman empire, see Suraiya Faroqhi, 'Crisis and Change, 1590–1699', in *An Economic and Social History of the Ottoman Empire, 1300–1914*, eds Halil İnalcık and Donald Quataert (Cambridge: Cambridge University Press, 1994), 413–622.
145. '*kizbleri zâhir olmayınca*.' Düzdağ, *Şeyhülislam Ebu's-Su*ᶜ*ud Efendi*, 111.

146. The latter point was made earlier in Üstün, 'Heresy and Legitimacy', 60–61.
147. Griffel, 'Toleration and Exclusion', 342–350. An underlining theological issue of these differing views concerned divergent conceptions of the relationship between external acts and inner belief; for the ways in which collective punishment of the Kizilbash was justified by earlier *fetvās* on the basis of the idea that acts were external signs of inner belief, see al-Tikriti, 'Kalam in the Service of the State', 136–149.
148. This appears to be especially true for earlier Kizilbash strongholds in western Anatolia, such as Teke. Imber, 'Persecution', 250.
149. Franz Babinger, 'Marino Sanuto's Tagebücher als Qwelle zur Geschichte der Safawijja', in *A Volume of Oriental Studies Presented to Edward G. Browne*, eds T. W. Arnold and Reynold A. Nicholson (Cambridge: Cambridge University Press, 1922), 34–35. Based on Venetian sources, Babinger elsewhere reports that three-quarters of the Anatolian population were followers of Shah Isma[c]il, see Franz Babinger and Fuad Köprülü, *Anadolu'da İslâmiyet*, trans. Ragıp Hulusi, ed. Mehmet Kanar (Istanbul: İnsan Yayınları, 2003), 20.
150. Hoca Sa[c]deddin, *Tācü't-Tevārīḫ*, II: 126.
151. BA.MD.33/204/413, published as document no. 71 in Savaş, *XVI. Asırda Anadolu'da Alevîlik*, 214.
152. BA.MD.31:142:52 (4 Cemaziye'l-evvel 985/1577), cited in Imber, 'Persecution', 246; also cited in Kütükoğlu, *Osmanlı-İran*, 11 n35.
153. Alexander H. Morton, 'The Chūb-i Ṭariq and Qizilbāsh Ritual in Safavid Persia', in *Études Safavide*, ed. Jean Calmard (Paris: Institut Français de Recherche en Iran, 1993), 225–245.
154. Chapter 2, n140.
155. Yusuf Ünal, 'More Than Mere Polemic: The Adventure of the *Risālah-i Ḥusniyah* in the Safavid, Ottoman, and Indian Lands' (MA thesis, Boğaziçi University, Istanbul, 2016).
156. For a study of the legends of Abu Muslim in the Turco-Iranian world, see Irène Mélikoff, *Abū Muslim: Le 'porte-hache' du Khorassan dans la tradition épique turco-iranienne* (Paris: A. Maisonneuve, 1962); the full text has been published in the Latin alphabet in Necati Demir et al., *Ebā Müslim-nāme*, 2 vols (Ankara: Destan Yayınları, 2007). For the systematic suppression of Abu Muslim's legends and memory in Safavid Iran, see Babayan, *Mystics, Monarchs, and Messiahs*, Chapter 5.
157. For details, see *ABS*, s.v. 'düşkün'.
158. Murat Borovalı and Cemil Boyraz, 'Türkiye'de Cemevleri Sorunu: Haklar ve Özgürlükler Bağlamında Eleştrel Bir Yaklaşım', *Mülkiye Dergisi* 40, no. 3 (2016): 55–85.
159. FD of Fethi Erdoğan, the *ocak* of Celal Abbas. A defected transliteration of this document and that of a later second copy of it have been published in 'Bir Ocağın Soy Şeceresi', n.a., *Hacı Bektaş Velî Araştırma Dergisi,* no. 19 (2001): 17–31.

Conclusion

A Protestant missionary in the Ottoman Empire relayed in his field report dated February 1855 some unusually exciting news about his 'discovery' of an 'obscure Muslim sect' in eastern Anatolia:

> There is a sect of nominal Moslems scattered through this region, of whom I think you have not heard. They bear the name Kuzulbash, which means, literally, 'red head.' But why this name has been given to them, I am not able as yet to determine . . . Though they are claimed by the Moslems, they are no followers of Mohammed. They believe in Christ, the Son of God, so far as they have a knowledge of him . . . They never, or almost never, go through the Moslem forms of prayer; nor do they keep their fast. They are a people by themselves, a peculiar people, and open to the gospel. Indeed they are very anxious to get it, and some have it already . . . The Turks seem to regard them very much as they do the Koords, as worthless heretics, and not worth caring for; and I think that no very serious trouble would come to them from that quarter, if they were all to embrace the truth openly.[1]

This report, most probably the earliest written record of the Kizilbash communities in modern times, was authored by Mr Dunmore, a missionary associated with the American Board of Commissioners for Foreign Missions, and it appeared in the board's bulletin, *The Missionary Herald*. With this report, Mr Dunmore laid the foundations of a hopeful vision regarding a possible Kizilbash conversion that the Protestant missionaries would maintain for about a decade, only to give it up when recognising its unlikely prospects. Two things led to the missionaries' disillusionment. First, the small group of Kizilbash whom Mr Dunmore believed were ready to embrace Protestantism were seeking from the missionaries a promise of formal protection similar to the one granted to the Protestant Armenians as a means of escaping the recently imposed requirement of military service, among other things. Such a move, however, would require the support of the British and American governments, which the latter had little interest in offering lest it would provoke an adverse reaction on the part of the Ottoman authorities who were hypersensitive to proselytisation among Muslims even after the relative expansion of religious freedoms in the empire by the 1856 Reform Edict (Islahat Fermanı). Equally frustrating for the missionaries was the reluctance of the Kizilbash with whom Mr Dunmore was in contact to build churches in their villages to formalise, as it were, their alleged conversion, despite all the lip service they paid to their love for Christ. As a result, we see a rapid decline both in numbers and in the optimistic tone of the missionaries' communications to the *Missionary Herald* concerning the Kizilbash, especially in the years following the departure from the field of Mr Dunmore, the initial and most enthusiastic advocate for the expansion of the Protestant mission beyond local 'heterodox' Christians.

The progressively diminishing prospects for the conversion of the Kizilbash would bring about a change in the missionaries' view of their religion itself in seemingly minor but significant ways. This shift first became apparent in a report from the year 1880 written by a certain Mr Perry. Unlike Mr Dunmore, Mr Perry emphasised paganism over alleged remnants of some ancient Christianity as the defining characteristic of the religion of the Kizilbash, while also conveying his scepticism about earlier, overly propitious assessments of their readiness to embrace the gospel. He wrote:

> Their religion is a relic of paganism molded by Mohammedan tradition and custom; but to me the special interest about it arises from what I consider to be a fact that, without knowing themselves the grounds on which they stand, they are a nation of pantheists. Their dishonesty, even in stating their belief, is pantheistic. For example, upon our arrival in their villages they throng about us, showing affection for our Bible, and listen to its teachings as long as we will preach to them; at the same time professing to accept the *three* sacred books (i.e. the Law, the Psalms, and the Gospels), and to reject the fourth or Koran; but it will often appear a day later that they not only accept the three books but one hundred and one more, which is equivalent to their accepting none at all. Assenting with us, also, to the doctrine of Christ's divinity, it will soon appear that they give a like reverence to Alee and others, even to the extent of regarding their own Sheik as divine.[2]

The report by Mr Perry would be one of the last ones about the Kizilbash before the latter would completely disappear from the Protestant missionaries' purview in the early 1880s. Although bearing no concrete results in the form of actual conversions, the missionaries' interest and speculations about the Kizilbash over the course of about three decades would have a lasting impact on the conception of Kizilbash origins by subsequent Western travellers and scholars who saw in them an extension of the ancient pagan and Christian populations of Anatolia.

Westerners' ascription of non-Muslim and non-Turkish origins to the Kizilbash would soon give rise to a reaction on the part of a group of (proto-)nationalist Ottoman/Turkish intellectuals who took it upon themselves to refute such claims. They tried to do so by explaining and normalising the Kizilbash difference as a factor of lingering pre-Islamic Turkish beliefs transmitted from Central Asia to Anatolia. They, thereby, hoped to counter not only the missionaries' speculations on the subject, but also substitute the extremely disparaging and exclusive religious framework of the traditional Ottoman discourse in respect of the Kizilbash communities with a more affirming and inclusive nationalist alternative. At some level, Fuad Köprülü's influential works published in the early twentieth century represented a scholarly refinement and expansion of these efforts, and it would soon eclipse all earlier theories, establishing itself as the new hegemonic knowledge of Kizilbashism in Turkish and international scholarship alike.

Despite their starkly opposing assertions and political implications, however, both the Christian-centric and Central Asia-centric narratives of Kizilbash/Alevi origins shared one important feature in common: they both relied on notions of syncretism and pre-Islamic survivals, with all of their connotations of impurity and historical anomaly, as their basic explanatory framework. The same ideas, albeit with more positive attributions, would also infiltrate and sway indigenous knowledge formation of Alevism in the wake of the Alevi cultural revival. The latter reignited and further complicated pertinent polemics by bringing into the conversation researchers of Alevi background, and stimulating the production of various new and competing narratives relying on the same conceptual parameters.[3]

The present work, above all, represents an objection against such decontextualised approaches that have remained a red herring in the treatment of the Kizilbashism/Alevism religion up to the present in both academic and public discussions. To counteract them in favour of a more historicising perspective, which also takes the Kizilbash/Alevi internal perspective seriously, I have endeavoured in this study to recover and re-insert the story of the communities in question into the broader narrative of the late medieval and early modern history of Anatolia and the neighbouring regions. Drawing on sources emanating from within the Kizilbash/Alevi communities themselves, I have argued that the seeds of Kizilbashism did not come from 'outside' but had their immediate origins within the social and religious milieu of Sufism, broadly defined with all of its marginal(ised) and contrary currents. Two developments in late medieval and early modern Islamdom were particularly relevant in paving the way for its emergence: the rise and dissemination of hereditary shaykh-hood and communal Sufi affiliations, and the convergence of enhanced ᶜAlid sentiments and renunciatory dervish currents. These two trends together formed the broader, pre-Safavid background against which Kizilbashism/Alevism took shape in terms of both its social organisation and its characteristic beliefs and rituals.

In a different but related vein, this study is directed at the conception of Kizilbashism/Alevism through the rubric of Shiᶜism. It more specifically pushes against its treatment as a reincarnation of what is called *Ghulāt* Shiᶜism that is associated with the initial party of ᶜAli prior to the solidification of the imamate after Jaᶜfar al-Sadiq. Without a doubt, one could identify several cogent parallels and overlaps between various early Shiᶜi ideas subsumed under *ghulūw* and a number of Kizilbash/Alevi beliefs, starting with the centrality of ᶜAli in Kizilbash/Alevi religious culture and devotional life. These would, however, be less than sufficient to make a case for historical continuity without verifiable venues of transmission or direct borrowing, such as the ones shown by other scholars in the case of the Nusayri-Alawites, for example.[4] Furthermore, most Shiᶜi elements within Alevism, infused as they are with a thoroughly esoteric system of beliefs, appear to have been mediated in large measure through Sufism. Whether or to what extent Sufism itself absorbed aspects of the early Shiᶜi tradition, while a legitimate and pertinent question, is nonetheless beyond the scope of this work. Suffice it to note here Marshall Hodgson's depiction of the Sufis as the 'evident successors' to the *Ghulāt* in respect to such broad questions as 'the spirituality of the soul and the possibility of its communion with God', despite the lack of any 'immediate connect[ion]' between the two.[5]

The embeddedness of Kizilbashism in the wider Muslim historical experience, as I have tried to demonstrate in this work, not only overturns its perception as a nebulous collection of semi-Islamised Turkmen tribes. This observation also facilitates its reconceptualisation as a coalition of Sufi and dervish circles, and related *sayyid* families, all with their own constituencies, who shared a 'family resemblance' on account of their pronounced ᶜAlid loyalty and opposition to the formalist juristic Islam. The broader Kizilbash milieu, to put it differently, was not simply a Safavid creation *ex nihilo* but had an autonomous and prior existence grounded in the cosmopolitan socio-religious Sufi and dervish landscape of the late medieval and early modern Middle East. A most tangible line of historical continuity in this regard is established by the Alevi documents that reveal certain Sufi and dervish circles and their lay following to be the antecedents of the various Alevi *ocak*s.

By the time Mr Dunmore 'discovered' the Kizilbash, the various *ocak*s had of course long forgotten their specific and heterogeneous pedigree in the wider Sufi milieu of earlier centuries, mainly due to the fermentation and consolidation of an overarching Kizilbash identity, and the accompanying process of *sayyid*-isation of the relevant shaykhly families. Fortunately, however, the documents in the *ocak*s' private archives preserve many traces of this past history that has long fallen into oblivion, as in the case of a network of Wafa'i affiliates in eastern Anatolia who emerge from these sources as one of the major building blocks of the historical Kizilbash movement. To be sure, not all of the Kizilbash/Alevi *ocak*s had a Wafa'i background, even though those with an evident Wafa'i connection formed the empirical focus of the present work. Further research into histories of individual Alevi *ocak*s is likely to reinforce and shed more light on various other suspected links of the Kizilbash movement, especially with the various Ahi circles, the followers of Şeyh Bedreddin in western Anatolia and the Balkans, and groups affiliated with the Nurbakhshi order, for which there already exists some strong evidence, as well as possible others that have hitherto remained unknown. However, the presence of a wide network of Wafa'i-cum-Kizilbash *ocak*s is in and of itself sufficient – in so far as Wafa'i affiliation points to an origin in Iraq and not Central Asia – to put into question the key premise of the Köprülü paradigm: that Kizilbashism in particular, and 'folk Islam' in Anatolia in general, was essentially an organic and direct extension of pre-Islamic Turkish tribal culture and religions.

The notion that Kizilbashism arose on the basis of a pre-Safavid infrastructure of some deeply entrenched Sufi and dervish networks does not, however, render irrelevant the role of the Safavids in the formation and consolidation of the Kizilbash movement and identity. The appeal of the Safavids, no doubt, lay in their being a politically triumphant ᶜAlid-*sayyid* family at a time of increased millenarian and messianic sensibilities, which rendered them an obvious vortex for the politically and religiously alienated segments of the Ottoman polity. The latter came together under the spiritual leadership of the Safavi household, while still maintaining their local hierarchies and characteristics, forming as such the backbone of the Kizilbash milieu. Safavid influence was also critical in solidifying this patchwork of related yet distinct groups into a permanent religious entity with a reinforced Shiᶜi colouring and greater internal homogenisation. At the same time, however, neither the rapid spread of the Kizilbash movement in the late fifteenth century and early sixteenth nor the striking resilience of it as a socio-religious collectivity to the present would have been conceivable had it not been for the critical role played by the local religious leaders, the *dede*s or *pir*s. These leaders continued to exert moral and religious authority over their disciple communities even as they came to accept the superior spiritual mandate of the Safavi family, and outlasted the demise of their *mürşid-i kamil*.

While *ocak* communities in Anatolia would turn progressively inward as their more palpable transregional lines of communication waned due to curtailed cross-regional mobility, a collective self-awareness transcending the boundaries of individual *ocak*s was retained through various mechanisms including, among other things, the circulation of texts, Alevi *dede*s, and minstrels and their poetry. Also important in the perpetuation of a sense of unity within an Alevi identity that steadily grew more centred on Anatolia was the renewed and growing import of Hacı Bektaş as a shared locus of devotion. The central Bektashi convent in Kırşehir, accordingly, came to function as an alternative site of pilgrimage, and as the new centre of religious authorisation for an increasing number Kizilbash/Alevi *ocak*s following the permanent disruption of contacts, first with Ardabil and later also with Karbala, even though the licensing authority of the Çelebi family was not universally recognised. The persistence and autonomy of *ocak* lineages, anchored as they were in an increasingly fading but nonetheless deeply rooted Sufi heritage of their own, also go a long way in explaining how the Safavids' Shiᶜitising influence over the Kizilbash communities was so effectively checked and filtered. This, no doubt, is what ensured the survival of a distinct Kizilbash identity in Anatolia despite the rapid absorption and assimilation of Kizilbashism into Imami Shiᶜism in Iran.

Notes

1. Mr Dunmore, 'Arabkir: Letter from Mr. Dunmore, October 24, 1854', *Missionary Herald* (February 1855): 55–56.
2. Mr Perry, 'Western Turkey Mission', *Missionary Herald* (May 1880): 185; emphasis in the original.
3. For the nineteenth-century missionary reports concerning the Kizilbash, and their effect on the emerging Turkish nationalist discourse, see my 'The Emergence of the Kızılbaş in Western Thought: Missionary Accounts and their Aftermath', in *Archaeology, Anthropology and Heritage in the Balkans and Anatolia: The Life and Times of F. W. Hasluck 1878–1920*, 2 vols, ed. David Shankland (Istanbul: ISIS Press, 2004), 1:329–353.
4. In the case of the Nusayri-Alawites, unlike with the Alevi-Bektashi communities, it is possible to trace their religious tradition to the inner circles of the

Tenth and the Eleventh Shiʿi Imams via specific historical figures and religious literature; for a recent work based on Nusayri-Alawi sources, and for further bibliography, see Yaron Friedman, *The Nuṣayrī-ʿAlawīs: An Introduction to the Religion, History and Identity of the Leading Minority in Syria* (Leiden: Brill, 2010).

5. Marshall G. S. Hodgson, 'How Did the Early Shi'a Become Sectarian?', *Journal of the American Oriental Society* 75, no. 1 (January–March 1955): 8.

Glossary

Ahl al-bayt	the family of the Prophet Muhammad, including his son-in-law, ᶜAli, and daughter, Fatima, and their descendants
aşçı	'chief cook', second highest rank at a Bektashi convent
baba	'father', honorific title for the elders of some dervish orders
bağlama	a long neck lute aka *saz,* considered sacred by the Alevis
cem	'gathering', the principal Alevi communal ritual
çerağ	candle, torch
çerağcı	'candle lighter', one who is assigned to light the candles in the *cem* (*q.v.*) ritual
dede	'grandfather; old man', honorific title for the elders of some dervish orders, and for the *ocakzade*s (*q.v.*)
defter	register
dergâh	dervish convent
fermān	imperial edict
*fetvā (*A. *fatwā*)	written answer to a legal question furnished by a *mufti* (*q.v.*)
futuwwa (Ot. *fütüvvet*)	'virtuous qualities of a young man', mystically orientated confraternities of young men and artisans
ġazāʾ (A. *ghazāʾ*)	frontier raids into non-Muslim territories
ġāzī (A. *ghāzī*)	frontier warrior fighting on behalf of Islam
Ghulāt	'those who overstep the bounds', used for certain Shiᶜi/ᶜAlid groups accused of heresy

ḫalīfe (A. *khalīfa*)	'successor', deputy of a Sufi master
ḫilāfetnāme	Sufi diploma granting one the title of *ḫalīfe* (*q.v.*)
ijāza (Ot. *icāzetnāme*)	Sufi diploma
khalīfat al-khulafā	representative of Safavi shahs in charge of Safavi *ḫalīfes* (*q.v.*)
ḳutb	'axis', head of the hiearchy of saints
madhab	a recognised school of Islamic jurisprudence
madrasa	institution of higher education for the study of Islamic sciences
masjid	small mosque
müderris	instructor in a madrasa (*q.v.*)
mufti	a jurist authorised to issue formal legal opinion
mühimme defterleri	registers of imperial orders sent to the provinces
mürşid (A. *murshid*)	'spiritual guide', Sufi master
mürşid-i kāmil	perfect spiritual guide
musahib	'companionship', an artifical kinship established between two Alevi couples
mütevellī	trustee of a pious endowment
naḳībü'l-eşrāf (A. *naqīb al-ashrāf*)	syndic of the descendants of the Prophet Muhammad
naqīb al-nuqabā	a *naqīb* in charge of a number of *naqīb*s in a certain area
nisba	epithet of origin or affiliation
ocak	'hearth', Alevi saintly lineage
ocakzade	member of an *ocak* (*q.v.*)
pir	same as *dede*
postnişīn	'one who sits on the skin', head of a dervish convent
ribāṭ	Sufi hospice
sālnāme	'yearbook', provincial almanac published by the Ottoman government
sayyid	descendant of the Prophet Muhammad
semah	Alevi ritual dance
şeyḫü'l-islām	*mufti* (*q.v.*) of Istanbul, top religious dignitary in the Ottoman Empire
shajara (Ot. *şecere*)	genealogical tree
silsila	Sufi's chain of initiation or spiritual genealogy
tabarrā	denouncing the enemies of ᶜAli and his descendants
talib	'seeker', hereditary disciple of an *ocak* (*q.v.*)

ṭarīqa	'way', an institutionalised order of mystics
tawallā	cherishing love for ᶜAli and his descendants
tımar	assignment of land revenues in return for military service
tımarlı sipahi/ timariot	a cavalry soldier holding a *tımar* (*q.v.*)
türbedār	keeper of a *türbe*, or mausoleum
waqf (Ot. *vaḳıf*)	pious endowment
*waqfiyya*s (Ot. *vaḳfiyye*, *vaḳıfnāme*)	deed of trust of a pious endowment
yatır	a site where a saint is buried
zāviye (A. *zāwiya*)	dervish convent
zāviyedār	keeper of a *zāviye* (*q.v.*)
ziyaret	'visit', the act or site of pilgrimage
ziyāretnāme	written testimony of one's visits to sites of pilgrimage

Selected Bibliography

Sources

Family Documents

Abuzer Güzel (d. 2013), member of the *ocak* of Ağuiçen from the village of Kurudere, Bulam-Adıyaman.

Ahmet Mutluay, member of the *ocak* of Ağuiçen from the village of Sün, Elazığ.

Ahmet Rıza Kargın (d. 2015), member of the *ocak* of Dede Kargın from the village of Dedekargın, Yazıhan-Malatya. [Originals currently in the Archive of Türk Kültürü ve Hacı Bektaş Veli Araştırma Merkezi in Ankara.]

Erhan Dede, member of the *ocak* of Derviş Çimli from the village of Dervişçimli, Elbistan-Maraş.

Fethi Erdoğan, member of the *ocak* of Celal Abbas (aka Şah Ali Abbas) from the village of Mığı (Sedeftepe), Elazığ.

Hasan Çevik (d. 2008?), member of the *ocak* of İmam Musa Kazim from Antep.

Hasan Hüseyin Gülbahar, member of the *ocak* of Şeyh Süleyman from the village of Gürge, Arguvan-Malatya. Documents received via Nurcemal Mola.

Hüseyin and Hayri Doğan, members of the *ocak* of Ağuiçen from the village of Böregenek, Adıyaman.

İsmail Doğan, member of the *ocak* of Seyyid Nuri Cemaleddin from the village of Delikan (Üçbudak), Karakoçan-Elazığ.

İzzettin Doğan, member of the *ocak* of Ağuiçen from the village of Kırlangıç, Hekimhan-Malatya.

Muharrem Ercan, member of the *ocak* of Sinemilli from the village of Bayındır, Keban-Elazığ.

Muharrem Naci Orhan (d. 2010), member of the *ocak* of İmam Zeynel Abidin from the village of Mineyik (Kuyudere), Arguvan-Malatya.

Mustafa Aygün, member of the *ocak* of Ağuiçen from the village of Şahlu-Yenimahalle in Göynücek-Amasya.

Mustafa İyidoğan, member of the *ocak* of Kızıl Deli from the village of Banaz, Yıldızeli-Sivas.
Mustafa Tosun and İhsan Gültekin (d. 2008?), members of the *ocak* of Şeyh Ahmed Dede from the village of Tabanbükü (Şeyh Hasan), Baskil-Elazığ. Documents received via Abdullah Bilgili and Can Delice.
Ocak of Şeyh Çoban, village of Nesimi Keşlik (Büyük Keşlik) in Alaca-Çorum. Documents from the FD of Nesimi Dede/Hüseyin Karaca, received via Levent Mete in Germany.
Tacim Bakır (d. 2013), member of the *ocak* of Sinemilli from the village of Kantarma, Elbistan-Kahramanmaraş.

Buyruk Copies

Bisâtî (?). *Menākıbü'l-Esrār Behcetü'l-Aḥrār.* MS, dated 1021/1612. Mevlânâ Museum Ferid Uğur Collection, no. 1172. Transcription and facsimile published in *Şeyh Sâfî Buyruğu*, edited by Ahmet Taşğın. Rheda-Wiedenbrück: Alevi Kültür Derneği Yayınları, 2003.
Buyruk. Edited by Sefer Aytekin. Ankara: Emek Basım-Yayınevi, 1958.
Buyruk: Alevî İnanç-İbâdet ve Ahlâk İlkeleri. Edited by Mehmet Yaman. Mannheim: Alevî Kültür Merkezi Dedeler Kurulu Yayınları, 2000.
Kitabü'l-Menakıb. Text published in appendix to Ahmad Hamid al-Sarraf, *al-Shabak*. Baghdad: Maṭba^cat al-Ma^cārif, 1954.
Macmū^ca (Şeyh Ṣāfī Buyruğu). MS, dated 1017/1608–1609. MMAK, no. 181.
Macmū^ca (Şeyh Ṣāfī Buyruğu). MS, undated. MMAK, no. 198.
Macmū^ca (Şeyh Ṣāfī Buyruğu). MS, undated. MMAK, no. 199.
(Şeyh Ṣāfī Buyruğu). MS, dated 1241/1825. Private library of Mehmet Yaman, member of the *ocak* of Hıdır Abdal from the village of Ocak in Kemaliye-Erzincan.
(Şeyh Ṣāfī Buyruğu). MS, dated 1261/1845. Private library of Hamza Özyıldırım, member of the *ocak* of Celal Abbas from the village of Kayabaşı in Kemah-Erzincan.
Şeyh Safi Buyruğu. Edited by Doğan Kaplan. Ankara: Diyanet Vakfı Yayınları, 2015.

Archival Sources

Ankara, VGMA:
Defter no. 166 (Esas 3/1)
Defter no. 419 (Erzurum Asker)
Defter no. 592 (Vakfiye-i Sadis)
Defter no. 816 (Tafsil-i Arabistan)
Defter no. 888 (Hülasa Defteri)
Istanbul, BA:
TT 64

İbnü'l-Emîn Evkaf, 2725
Cevdet Evkaf, 6210

PUBLISHED DOCUMENTS AND ARCHIVAL SOURCES

Ahmet, Refik. *On altıncı Asırda Rafızîlik ve Bektaşilik.* Istanbul: Muallim Ahmet Halit Kitabhanesi, 1932.

Akkiraz, Hasan. 'Sabahat Akkiraz'ın Hazırlattığı Alevi Raporu'. Alevi Enstitüsü [blog]. 19 December 2012. http://alevienstitusu.blogspot.com/2012/12/sabahat-akkirazn-hazrlattg-alevi-raporu.html.

Akkuş, Mehmet. '19. Asırdan Bir Bektaşî İcâzetnâmesi'. *Tasavvuf* 1, no. 1 (August 1999): 27–39.

Aşan, Muhammet Beşir. 'Fırat Havzasında Tespit Edilen Vefâi Silsile-nâmesi ve Bazı Düşünceler'. In *XIV. Türk Tarih Kongresi, Ankara: 9–13 Eylül 2002: Kongreye Sunulan Bildiriler,* 1,1517–1,524. 4 Vols. Vol. 2, part 2. Ankara: Türk Tarih Kurumu, 2005.

Barkan, Ömer Lûtfi and Enver Meriçli. *Hüdâvendigâr Livâsı Tahrir Defterleri.* Ankara: Türk Tarih Kurumu, 1988.

'Bir Ocağın Soy Şeceresi'. n.a., *Hacı Bektaş Velî Araştırma Dergisi,* no. 19 (2001): 17–31.

Düzdağ, Ertuğrul. *Kanuni Devri Şeyhülislam Ebussuud Efendi Fetvaları.* Istanbul: Kapı Yayınları, 2012.

Ebussu^{c}ud Efendi. *Ma^{c}rûzât: Şeyhülislâm Ebussuûd Efendi,* edited by Pehlul Düzenli. Istanbul: Klasik, 2013.

Eroğlu, Cengiz et al., Orhan, eds. *H. 1330/1912 Tarihli Musul Vilayet Salnamesi.* Ankara: ORSAM, 2012.

Fekete, L. 'İlk Safevî Şahlarının Türkçe Çıkartılmış İki Senedi'. *Philologia Orientalis* 3 (1973): 290–293.

Feridun Bey. *Münşeāt-ı Selāṭīn.* 2 Vols. Istanbul: n.p., 1274–1275/1858.

Gülsoy, Ersin and Mehmet Taştemir, eds. *1530 Tarihli Malatya, Behisni, Gerger, Kâhta, Husn-ı Mansur, Divriği ve Darende Kazâları: Vakıf ve Mülk Defteri.* Ankara: Türk Tarih Kurumu, 2007.

Hezarfen, Ahmet and Cemal Şener, eds. *Osmanlı Arşivi'nde Mühimme ve İrade Defterleri'nde Aleviler-Bektaşiler.* İstanbul: Karacaahmet Sultan Derneği Yayınları, n.d.

Ḫilāfetnāme dated Cemadiye's-sani 1242/1826. FD, Sivas branch of the *ocak* of Şah İbrahim Veli. A photocopy of the document in the private library of Mehmet Yaman. Location of the original unknown. Published in Karakaya-YK.

Ḫilāfetnāme dated Şevval 1089/1678. FD, Muharrem Naci Orhan. Published in Karakaya-YK.

'Kara Pir Bad'ın Soyağacı'. In Nejat Birdoğan, *Anadolu ve Balkanlar'da Alevi Yerleşmesi,* 223–235. Istanbul: Mozaik Yayınları, 1995.

Kökel, Coşkun. *Güvenç Abdal Ocakları.* 8 Vols. Vol. 2: *Tarihi Belgeler.* Istanbul: Güvenç Abdal Araştırma Eğitim Kültür ve Tanıtma Derneği Yayınları, 2013.

Mir-Ja‿fari, H. and M. Hashami Ardkani. 'Farman-i Shah Tahmāsp Ṣafavī ba Mavlānā Ražī al-Dīn Muḥammad'. *Barrasīhā-i tārīkhī* 9 (1352/1973): 95–110.
Musavi, T. M. *Orta-asr Azarbaijan Tarikhina Dair Fars-dilli Sanadlar (XVI–XVIII Asrlar)*. [In Cyrillic alphabet.] Baku: n.p., 1977.
Öz, Baki. *Alevilikle İlgili Osmanlı Belgeleri*. Istanbul: Can Yayınları, 1995.
Qaᵓim-maqami, Jahangir. *Muqaddama-ī bar shinākht-i asnād-i tārīkhī*. Tehran: Anjuman-i Āṣār-i Millī, 1350/1971.
Şahin, İlhan and Feridun Emecen, eds. *Osmanlılarda Dīvān-Bürokrasi-Ahkām. II. Beyazıd Dönemine Ait 906–1501 Tarihli Ahkām Defteri*. Istanbul: Türk Dünyası Araştırmaları Vakfı, 1994.
Şener, Cemal. *Osmanlı Belgelerinde Aleviler-Bektaşiler*. Istanbul: Karacaahmet Sultan Derneği Yayınları, 2002.
Şeyhülislam Feyzullah Efendi. *Fetâvâ-yı Feyziye*, edited by Süleyman Kaya. Istanbul: Klasik Yayınları, 2010.
Yalçın, Alemdar and Hacı Yılmaz. 'Kureyşan Ocağı Hakkında Bazı Bilgiler'. *Hacı Bektaş Velî Araştırma Dergisi* 23 (Autumn 2002): 9–24.
———. 'Bir Ocağın Tarihi Seyyid Hacı Ali Türâbî Ocağı'na Ait Yeni Bilgiler'. *Gazi Üniversitesi Türk Kültürü ve Hacı Bektaş Veli Araştırma Merkezi* 26 (Summer 2003): 121–140.
Yenişehirli Abdullah Efendi. *Behcetü'l-Fetâvâ*, edited by Süleyman Kaya, et al. Istanbul: Klasik Yayınları, 2012.
Yinanç, Refet and Mesut Elibüyük, eds. *Kanunî Devri Malatya Tahrir Defteri (1560)*. Ankara: Gazi Üniversitesi, 1983.
———. *Maraş Tahrir Defteri (1563)*. 2 Vols. Ankara: Ankara Üniversitesi, 1988.

CHRONICLES AND LITERARY SOURCES

ᶜAbd al-Wahhab al-Shaᶜrani, *al-Ṭabaqāt al-kubrā [or Lawāqiḥ al-anwār fī ṭabaqāt al-akhyār]*, 2 vols. Cairo: al-Maṭbaᶜa al-ᶜĀmira al-ᶜUthmānīyya, 1316/1898.
Abdal Mûsâ Velâyetnâmesi, edited by Abdurrahman Güzel. Ankara: Türk Tarih Kurumu, 1999.
ᶜAbdurrahman Cami. *Nefeḥātü'l-üns min haḍarāti'l-ḳuds*, translated by Lamiᶜi Çelebi. Istanbul: Marifet Yayınları, 1980.
Eflaki [al-Aflaki al-ᶜArifi, Shams al-Dīn Aḥmad]. *Manāḳib al-ᶜarifīn*, edited by Tahsin Yazıcı. Rev. 2nd edn. 2 Vols. Ankara: Türk Tarih Kurumu, 1976–1980.
———. *Ariflerin Menkıbeleri (Mevlânâ ve Etrafındakiler)*, translated by Tahsin Yazıcı. Rev. 4th edn. 2 Vols. Istanbul: Remzi Kitabevi, 1986.
A. Rıfki. *Bektaşī Sırrı*. Istanbul, 1325–1328/1907–1910.
Aḥmed Rıfᶜat. *Mirātü'l-maḳāṣıd fī defᶜi'l-mefāsid*. Istanbul: İbrāhīm Efendi Maṭbaᶜası, 1293/1876.
ᶜAli Suᶜad. *Seyāḥatlerim*. Istanbul: Ḳanāᶜat Maṭbaᶜası, 1332/1916.
———. *Seyahatlerim*, edited by N. Ahmet Özalp. Istanbul: Kitabevi Yayınları, 1996.

Âşık Virani Divanı, edited by M. Hâlid Bayrı. Istanbul: Maarif Kitaphanesi, 1959.

ᶜAşıkpaşazade Ahmed. *Die altosmanische Chronik des Āšıḳpašazāde*, edited by Friedrich Giese. Leipzig: O. Harrassowitz, 1929.

———. 'Menāḳıb ü tevārīḫ-i āl-i 'Os̱mān'. In *Osmanlı Tarihleri I: Osmanlı Tarihinin Anakaynakları Olan Eserlerin, Mütehassıslar Tarafından Hazırlanan Metin, Tercüme veya Sadeleştirilmiş Şekilleri Külliyatı*, edited by N. Atsız Çiftçioğlu, 79–329. Istanbul: Türkiye Yayınevi, 1949.

Bağdatlı İsmail Paşa. *Keşf-el-zunun zeyli: īżāḥ al-maknūn fī al- ẕayli ᶜalā kaşf al- ẓunūn ᶜan asāmī al-kutubi va'l funūn*. 2 Vols. Vol 1. İstanbul: Milli Eğitim Basımevi, 1945.

Başköylü Hasan Efendi. *Varlığın Doğuşu*, edited by Pirsultan Özcan. Istanbul: Anadolu Matbaası, 1992.

al-Basri, ᶜUthman bin Sanad al-Waᵓili. *Maṭaliᶜ al-Suᶜūd: Tārīkh al- ᶜIrāq min sanat 1188 ilā sanat 1242 h. / 1774–1826 m.*, edited by ᶜImad ᶜAbd al-Salam Raᵓuf and Suhayla ᶜAbd al-Majid al-Qaysi. Baghdad: al-Dār al-Waṭaniyya, 1991.

Battalname: Introduction, English Translation, Turkish Transcription, Commentary and Facsimile, edited by Yorgos Dedes. 2 Vols. Cambridge, MA: Harvard University, 1996.

Bursevi, Abdullah Veliyuddin. *Menâkıb-ı Eşrefzâde (Eşrefoğlu Rûmî'nin Menkıbeleri)*, edited by Abdullah Uçman. Istanbul: Kitabevi Yayınları, 2009.

Celâl-zâde Mustafa. *Selim-nâme*, edited by Ahmet Uğur and Mustafa Çuhadar. Ankara: Kültür Bakanlığı, 1990.

Das Vilâjet-nâme des Hâdschim Sultan, edited by Rudolf Tschudi. Berlin: Mayer & Müller, 1914.

Demir, Necati et al. *Ebā Müslim-nāme*. 2 Vols. Ankara: Destan Yayınları, 2007.

Elçin, Şükrü. 'Bir Seyh Sücâüddin Baba Velâyetnâmesi'. *Türk Kültürü Arastirmalari* 22, no. 1 (1984): 199–208.

Ergun, Sadeddin Nüzhet. *Bektaşi Edebiyatı Antolojisi: Bektaşi Şairleri ve Nefesleri.* Istanbul: Maarif Kitaphanesi, 1944.

———. *Hatayî Divanı: Şah İsmail-i Safevi, Hayatı ve Nefesleri.* Istanbul: Maarif Kitaphanesi, 1956.

Eskandar Beg Monshi. *History of Shah ᶜAbbas the Great (Tārīḵ-e ᶜĀlamārā-ye ᶜAbbāsī)*, edited by Roger Savory. 2 Vols. Boulder: Westview Press, 1978.

Eyüb Sabri. *Mir'ātü'l-Ḥarameyn.* 3 Vols. Istanbul: Bahriyye Matbaᶜası, 1306/1890.

Gelibolulu Mustafa ᶜAli. *Kitābü't- Tārīḫ-i Künhü'l-Aḫbar*, edited by Ahmet Uğur, et al. 2 Vols. Kayseri: Erciyes Üniversitesi, 1997.

Georgius de Ungaria. *Tractatus de moribus condictionibus et nequicia Turcorum/ Traktat über die Sitten, die Lebensverhältnisse und die Arglist der Türken*, edited and translated by R. Klockow. Köln: Böhlau Verlag, 1993.

Gö'çek Abdal. *Odman Baba Vilâyetnmesi: Vilâyetname-i Şâhî*, edited by Şevki Koca. [Istanbul]: Bektaşi Kültür Derneği, 2002.

Grey, Charles, trans. and ed. *A Narrative of Italian Travels in Persia, in the*

Fifteenth and Sixteenth Centuries. London: Printed for the Hakluyt Society, 1873.

Gümüşoğlu, Dursun, ed. *Tâcü'l-arifîn Es-Seyyid Ebu'l Vefâ Menakıbnāmesi: Yaşamı ve Tasavvufi Görüşleri*. Istanbul: Can Yayınları, 2006.

Hacı Bektaş-ı Veli Manzum Vilâyetnamesi, edited by Bedri Noyan. Istanbul: Can Yayınları, 1996.

Haririzade Mehmed Kemaleddin. *Tibyān wasā'il al-ḥaqā'iq fī bayān salāsil al-ṭarā'iq*. 3 Vols. 1876; reprint, Istanbul: n.p., 1949.

Hasan-ı Rumlu. *Ahsenü't-Tevārih*, abridged and translated into Turkish by Cevat Cevan. Ankara: Ardıç Yayınları, 2004.

Hoca Sa^cdeddin Efendi. *Tācü't-Tevārīḫ*. 2 Vols. Istanbul: Tab^cḫāne-i ^cĀmire, 1279–1280/1862–1863.

———. *Tacü't-Tevarih*, edited by İsmet Parmaksızoğlu. 5 Vols. Ankara: Kültür Bakanlığı, *c.*1992.

Hüseyin Hüsameddin. *Amasya Tārīḫi*. 4 Vols. Istanbul: Ḥikmet Maṭba^cası, 1327–1330/1911–1914.

İbn Kemâl. *Tevârîḫ-i Âl-i Os̱mân, VIII. Defter*, edited by Ahmet Uğur. Ankara: Türk Tarih Kurumu, 1997.

İdrîs-i Bidlîsî. *Selim Şah-nâme*, edited by Hicabi Kırlangıç. Ankara: Kültür Bakanlığı, 2001.

Jahn, Karl. *Geschichte Ġāzān-Ḫān's Aus Dem Ta'riḫ-i-mubārak-i-Ġāzānī Des Rašīd Al-Dīn Faḍlallāh B. İmād Al-Daula Abūl-Ḫair*. London: Luzac & Co., 1940.

Kaygusuz Abdal (Alâeddin Gaybî) Menâkibnâmesi, edited by Abdurrahman Güzel. Ankara: Türk Tarih Kurumu, 1999.

Khunji-Isfahani, Fadlullah b. Ruzbihan. *Tārīkh-i ^cĀlam-ārā-yi Amīnī,* edited by John E. Woods. Abridged English translation by Vladimir Minorsky. London: Royal Asiatic Society, 1992.

Koca, Turgut, ed. *Bektaşi Alevi Şairleri ve Nefesleri*. Istanbul: Maarif Kitaphanesi, 1990.

Koyun Baba Velâyetnamesi, edited by Muzaffer Doğanbaş. Istanbul: Dört Kapı, 2015.

Kreutel, Richard F. *Haniwaldanus Anonimi'ne Göre Sultan Bayezid-i Velî (1481–1512)*, translated into Turkish by Necdet Öztürk. Istanbul: Türk Dünyası Araştırmaları Vakfı, 1997.

Makâlât, edited by Esad Coşan. Ankara: T. C. Kültür Bakanlığı, 1996.

Mevlana Celalleddin Rumi. *The Mathnawi of Jalaluddin Rumi*, 5 Vols. Translated by A. Reynold Nicholson, compiled by Reza Nazari and Somayeh Nazari. 1925; reprint, Learn Persian Online Website, 2017.

Minorsky, Vladimir. *Tadhkirat Al-mulūk, a Manual of Ṣafavid Administration (circa 1137/1725) Persian Text in Facsimile (B. M. Or. 9496)*. London: Luzac & Co., 1943.

Mr Dunmore. 'Arabkir: Letter from Mr. Dunmore, October 24, 1854'. *Missionary Herald* (February 1855): 55–56.

Mr Perry. 'Western Turkey Mission'. *Missionary Herald* (May 1880): 185.
Nasuhü's-Silahi (Matrakçı). *Beyān-ı Menāzil-i Sefer-i ᶜIrāḳeyn-i Sulṭān Süleymān Ḫān,* edited by Hüseyin G. Yurdaydın. Ankara: Türk Tarih Kurumu, 1976.
Neşri, Mehmed. *Kitâb-ı Cihan-Nümâ: Neşri Tarihi,* edited by Faik Reşit Unat and Mehmed A. Köymen. 2 Vols. Ankara: Türk Tarih Kurumu, 1995.
Niebuhr, Carsten. *Reisebeschreibung nach Arabien und andern umliegenden Ländern.* 2 Vols. 1778. Reprint, *The Islamic World in Foreign Travel Accounts,* ser. ed. Fuad Sezgin. Vols 11–13. Frankfurt: Institut für Geschichte der Arabisch-Islamischen Wissenschaften, 1994.
Noyan, Bedri, ed. *Seyyid Ali Sultan (Kızıldeli Sultan) Vilayetnamesi.* Ankara: Ayyıldız Yayınları, n.d.
Özmen, İsmail, ed. *Alevi-Bektaşi Şiirleri Antolojisi.* 5 Vols. Ankara: Saypa Yayın, 1995.
Öztoprak, Halil. *Kurᵓan'da Hikmet Tarihte Hakikat ve Kurᵓan'da Hikmet İncil'de Hakikat.* 1956; reprint, Istanbul: Demos Yayınları, 2012.
Peçevi İbrahim. *Tārīh-i Peçevī,* edited by Fahri Ç. Derin and Vahit Çabuk. 2 Vols. Istanbul: Enderun Kitabevi, 1980.
al-Qazaruni, Husam Ibrahim b. Muhammad. *Ahmed er-Rifâî Menkıbeleri* [*Shifāᵓ al-asḳām fī sīrati ġavs̱ al-anām*], translated by Nurettin Bayburtlugil and Necdet Tosun. Istanbul: Vefa Yayınları, 2008.
Shah Ismaᶜil Hataᵓi. *Il Canzoniere di Šāh Ismāᶜīl Ḫaṭāᵓī,* edited by Tourkhan Gandjeï. Naples: Istituto Universitario Orientale, 1959.
———. *Şah İsmail Hatâ'î Külliyatı,* edited by Babek Cavanşir and Ekber N. Necef. İstanbul: Kaknüs Yayınları, 2006.
al-Shaᶜrani, 'Abd al-Wahhab. *al-Ṭabaqāt al-kubrā (or lawāqiḥ al-anwār fī ṭabaqāt al-akhyār).* 2 Vols. Vol. 1. Cairo: al-Maṭbaᶜa al-ᶜāmira al-ᶜUthmānīyya, 1316/1898.
Solak-zâde Mehmed Hemdemî Çelebî. *Solak-zâde Tarihi*, edited by Vahid Çabuk. 2 Vols. Ankara: Kültür Bakanlığı, 1989.
Şükrî-i Bitlisî. *Selîm-Nâme*, edited by Mustafa Argunşah. Kayseri: Erciyes Üniversitesi, 1997.
Tancî, Ebû Abdullah Muhammed İbn Battûta. *İbn Battûta Seyahatnâmesi*, edited by A. Sait Aykut. 2 Vols. Istanbul: Yapı Kredi Yayınları, 2002.
Taşköprizade Ebulhayr İsamüddin Ahmed Efendi. *Şaḳā'iḳ-i Nuᶜmāniyye ve Ẓeyilleri: Ḥadāᵓiḳu'ş-Şaḳāᵓik*, translated by Mecdi Mehmed Efendi, edited by Abdükadir Özcan. 5 Vols. Vol. 1. Istanbul: Çağrı Yayınları, 1989.
Tihranî, Abu Bekr-i. *Kitab-ı Diyarbekriyye*, translated by Mürsel Öztürk. Ankara: Kültür Bakanlığı, 2001.
Tulum, Mertol. *Tarihî Metin çalışmalarında Usul: Nâme-i Kudsî (Menâkıbu'l-Kudsiyye)'nin Yayımlanmış Metninden Derlenen Verilerle.* Konya: Çizgi Kitabevi, 2017.
Vahidi. *Vāḥidī's Menāḳıb-i Ḫvoca-i Cihān ve Netīce-i Cān*, edited by Ahmet T. Karamustafa. Sources of Oriental Languages and Literatures 17, ser. eds Şinasi Tekin and Gönül Alpay Tekin. Cambridge, MA: Harvard University, 1993.

Vilâyet-nâme: Manākıb-ı Hünkâr Hacı Bektâş-ı Velî, edited by Abdülbâkî Gölpınarlı. Istanbul: İnkılâp Kitapevi, 1990.

al-Wasiti, Taqi al-Din 'Abd al-Rahman b. 'Abd al-Muisin. *Tiryāq al-muḥibbīn fī ṭabaqāt khirqat al-mashāyikh al-ʿārifīn*. Cairo: Maṭba'at al-Miṣr, 1305/1887.

Yaqut b.ʿAbdu'llah al-Hamawi. *Muʿjam al-Buldān*. 5 Vols. Beirut: Dār al-Kuttāb al-ʿIlmiyya, 1955.

al-Zabidi, Murtada. *Rafʿ niqāb al-khafāʾ ʿan-man intahā ilā Wafā wa- Abī'l-Wafāʾ*. MS. Dār al-Kutup al-Miṣriyya, Tārīkh Taymūr, no. 2,323.

Zirke, Heidi, ed. *Ein hagiographisches Zeugnis zur persischen Geschichte aus der Mitte des 14. Jahrhunderts: Das achte Kapitel des Ṣafwat aṣ-ṣafā in kritischer Bearbeitung*. Berlin: Klaus Schwarz Verlag, 1987.

Studies

Abisaab, Rula Jurdi. *Converting Persia: Religion and Power in the Safavid Empire*. London: I. B. Tauris, 2004.

Abu Husayn, Abdulrahim. 'The Shiites in Lebanon and the Ottomans in the 16th and 17th Centuries'. In *Convegno sul tema La Shīʿa nell'impero ottomano: Roma, 15 aprile 1991*, 107–119. Rome: Accademia Nazionale Dei Lincei, 1993.

Acar, İsmail Hakkı. *Zara Folkloru*. Sivas: Emek Matbaa, 1975.

Adanır, Fikret. 'Religious Communities and Ethnic Groups under Imperial Sway: Ottoman and Habsburg Lands in Comparison'. In *The Historical Practice of Diversity: Transcultural Interactions from Early Mediterranean to the Postcolonial World*, edited by Dirk Hoerder, et al., 54–86. New York: Berghahn Books, 2003.

Ahmed Refik. *Bizans Karşısında Türkler*. 1927; reprint, Istanbul: Kitabevi Yayınları, 2005.

Akdağ, Mustafa. 'Tımar rejiminin bozuluşu'. *Ankara Üniversitesi Dil ve Tarih Coğrafya Fakültesi Dergisi* 4 (1945): 419–431.

———. *Türkiye Halkının Dirlik ve Düzenlik Kavgası: Celali İsyanları*. 1975; reprint, Istanbul: Cem Yayınevi, 1995.

———. *Türkiye'nin İktisadi ve İçtimai Tarihi*. 2 Vols. (1453–1559). 1959; reprint, Istanbul: Cem Yayınevi, 1995.

Aksüt, Hamza. *Anadolu Aleviliğinin Sosyal ve Coğrafi Kökenleri*. Ankara: Art Basın Yayın, 2002.

———. *Mezopotamya'dan Anadolu'ya Alevi Erenlerin İlk Savaşi (1240): Dede Garkın, Baba İshak, Baba İlyas*. Ankara: Yurt Kitap, 2006.

Algar, Hamid. 'Naqshbandīs and Safavids: A Contribution to the Religious History of Iran and Her Neigbors'. In *Safavid Iran and her Neighbors*, edited by Michel Mazzasoui, 7–48. Salt Lake City: University of Utah Press, 2003.

———. 'Review of *Hadji Bektach: un mythe et ses avatars. Genèse et évolution du soufisme populaire en Turquie*, by Irène Mélikoff'. *International Journal of Middle East Studies* 36, no. 4 (November 2004): 687–689.

Allouche, Adel. *The Origins and Development of the Ottoman–Ṣafavid Conflict (906–962/1500–1555)*. Berlin: Klaus Schwarz Verlag, 1983.

Ambraseys, Nicholas. *Earthquakes in the Mediterranean and the Middle East: A Multidisciplinary Study of Seismicity to 1900*. Cambridge and New York: Cambridge University Press, 2009.

Amir-Moezzi, Mohammad Ali. *The Divine Guide in Early Shi'ism: The Sources of Esotericism in Islam*, translated by David Streight. Albany: State University of New York Press, 1994.

Anthony, Sean W. *The Caliph and the Heretic: Ibn Saba and the Origin of Shiism*. Leiden and Boston: Brill, 2011.

Anzali, Ata. 'Safavid Shiᶜism, the Eclipse of Sufism and the Emergence of ᶜIrfān'. PhD diss., Rice University, Texas, 2012.

Adorjan, Imre. '"Mum Söndürme" İftirasının Kökeni ve Tarihsel Süreçte Gelişimiyle İlgili Bir Değerlendirme'. In *Alevilik*, edited by İsmail Engin and Havva Engin, 123–136. İstanbul: Kitap Yayınevi, 2004.

Arjomand, Said Amir. 'Religious Extremism (Ghuluww), Ṣūfısm and Sunnism in Safavid Iran: 1501–1722'. *Journal of Asian History* 15, no. 1 (1981): 1–35.

———. *The Shadow of God and the Hidden Imam: Religion, Political Order, and Societal Change in Shiᶜite Iran from the Beginning to 1890*. Chicago: The University of Chicago Press, 1984.

Arslanoğlu, İbrahim. *Şah İsmail Hatayî ve Anadolu Hatayîleri*. Istanbul: Der Yayınları, 1992.

Arslantaş, Yasin. 'Depicting the Other: Qizilbash Image in the 16th Century Ottoman Historiography'. PhD diss., Bilkent University, Ankara, 2013.

Asatryan, Mushegh. *Controversies in Formative Shiᶜi Islam: The Ghulat Muslims and their Beliefs*. London and New York: I. B. Tauris, 2017.

Aşkar, Mustafa. 'Reenkarnasyon (Tenasüh) Meselesi ve Mutasavvıfların Bu Konuya Bakışlarının Değerlendirilmesi'. *Tasavvuf* 1, no. 3 (April 2000): 85–100.

Atalay, Besim. *Bektaşilik ve Edebiyatı*. 1922; reprint, Istanbul: Ant Yayınları, 1991.

Atçıl, Abdurrahman. 'The Safavid Threat and Juristic Authority in the Ottoman Empire during the 16th Century'. *International Journal of Middle East Studies* 49 (2017): 295–314.

Aubin, Jean. 'La Politique religieuse des Safavides'. In *Le Shi'isme Imamite, Colloque de Strasbourg, 6–9 mai 1968*, edited by T. Fahd, 235–244. Paris: Presses Universitaires, 1970.

———. 'L'Avenèment des Safavides reconsidéré (Études Safavides III)'. *Moyen Orient et Océan Indien* 5 (1988): 1–130.

Avcı, A. Haydar. *Alevi Tarihinden Bir Kesit: Kalender Çelebi Ayaklanması*. Ankara: AAA Yayınları, 1998.Aytaş, Gıyasettin, ed. *Bingöl, Muş/Varto Yörelerinde Ocaklar, Oymaklar ve Boylarla İlgili Araştırma Sonuçları*. Ankara: Gazi Üniversitesi Türk Kültürü ve Hacı Bektaş Veli Araştırma Merkezi, 2010.

al-^{c}Azzawi, ^{c}Abbas. *Tārīkh al-^{c}Irāq bayna iḥtilālayn.* 5 Vols. Baghdad: Maṭba^{c}at Baghdād, 1935–1949.

Babayan, Kathryn. 'The Safavid Synthesis: From Qizilbash Islam to Imamite Shi^{c}ism'. *Iranian Studies* 27, nos 1–4 (1994): 135–161.

———. *Mystics, Monarchs, and Messiahs: Cultural Landscapes of Early Modern Iran.* Cambridge, MA: Harvard University Press, 2002.

Babinger, Franz. 'Der Islam in Kleinasien'. *Zeitschrift Der Deutschen Morgenländischen Gesellschaft* 1, no. 1 (1922): 126–152.

———. 'Marino Sanuto's Tagebücher als Qwelle zur Geschichte der Safawijja'. In *A Volume of Oriental Studies Presented to Edward G. Browne*, edited by T. W. Arnold and Reynold A. Nicholson, 28–50. Cambridge: Cambridge University Press, 1922.

Bacqué-Grammont, Jean-Louis. 'Études Turco-Safavides, III, Notes et documents sur la révolte de Şâh Veli b. Şeyh Celâl'. *Archivum Ottomanicum* 7 (1982): 5–69.

———. '1513 Yılında Rum Eyaletinde Şüpheli Tımar Sahiplerine Ait Bir Liste'. In Ord. Prof. Ömer Lütfi Barkan'a Armağan, *İstanbul Üniversitesi İktisat Fakültesi Mecmuası* 44, nos 1–2 (1985): 163–176.

———. 'Un rapport inédit sur la révolte anatolienne de 1527'. *Studia Islamica* 62 (1985): 155–171.

———. *Les Ottomans, les Safavides et leurs voisins (1514–1524).* Istanbul: Nederlands Historisch-Archaeologisch Instituut, 1987.

Balivet, Michel. *Şeyh Bedreddin: Tasavvuf ve İsyan.* Istanbul: Tarih Vakfı Yurt Yayınları, 2000.

Barkan, Ömer Lûtfi. 'Osmanlı İmparatorluğu'nda Bir İskân ve Kolonizatör Metodu Olarak Vakıflar ve Temlikler: I. İstilâ Devirlerinin Kolonizatör Dervişleri ve Zaviyeler'. *Vakıflar Dergisi* 2 (1942): 279–386.

Barkey, Karen. *Empire of Difference: The Ottomans in Comparative Perspective.* New York: Cambridge University Press, 2008.

Barthold, W. 'Tirmidh'. In *The Encyclopaedia of Islam*, 2nd edn. Leiden: Brill, 1960– .

———. *Turkestan Down to the Mongol Invasion.* 3rd edn. London: Luzac & Co., 1968.

Barzegar, Abbas. 'The Persistence of Heresy: Paul of Tarsus, Ibn Sabaʾ, and Historical Narrative in Sunni Identity Formation'. *Numen* 58 (2011): 207–231.

Bashir, Shahzad. *Messianic Hopes and Mystical Visions: The Nūrbakhshīya between Medieval and Modern Islam.* Columbia: University of South Carolina Press, 2003.

———. 'Messianism'. In *The Princeton Encyclopaedia of Islamic Political Thought*, edited by Gerhard Böwering, 338. Princeton: Princeton University Press, 2013.

———. 'The Origins and Rhetorical Evolution of the Term Qizilbāsh in Persianate Literature'. *Journal of the Economic and Social History of the Orient* 57 (2017): 364–391.

Basilov, V. N. 'Honour Groups in Traditional Turkmenian Society'. In *Islam in Tribal Societies: From the Atlas to the Indus,* edited by Akbar S. Ahmed and David M. Hart, 220–243. London: Routledge & Kegan Paul, 1984.

Bausani, A. 'Religion in the Post-Mongol Period'. In *The Cambridge History of Iran.* Vol. 5: *The Saljuq and Mongol Period,* edited by J. A. Boyle, 538–549. Cambridge: Cambridge University Press, 1968.

———. 'Religion in the Seljuq Period'. In *The Cambridge History of Iran.* Vol. 5: *The Saljuq and Mongol Period,* edited by J. A. Boyle, 283–302. Cambridge: Cambridge University Press, 1968.

Bayat, Fuzuli. 'Bektaşiyye Tarikatının Şekillenmesinde Yeseviyye ve Safeviyyenin Yeri'. In *Alevilik,* edited by İsmail Engin and Havva Engin, 171–189. Istanbul: Kitap Yayınevi, 2004.

Bayram, Mikâil. *Ahi Evren Ve Ahi Teşkilâtı'nın Kuruluşu.* Konya: n.p., 1991.

Beldiceanu-Steinherr, Irène. 'Le règne de Selīm ler: *Tournant* dans la vie politique et religieuse de l'Empire Ottoman'. *Turcica* 6 (1975): 34–48.

———. 'A propos des tribus Atčeken (XVe–XVIe siècles)'. *Journal of the Economic and Social History of the Orient* 30, no. 2 (1987): 122–195.

Berkey, Jonathan P. *The Formation of Islam: Religion and Society in the Near East, 600–1800.* New York: Cambridge University Press, 2003.

Bernheimer, Teresa. 'Genealogy, Marriage, and the Drawing of Boundaries among the ᶜAlids (Eighth–Twelfth Centuries)'. In *Sayyid and Sharifs in Muslim Societies: The Living Links to the Prophet*, edited by Morimoto Kazuo, 75–91. London: Routledge, 2012.

———. *The ᶜAlids: The First Family of Islam, 750–1200*. Edinburgh: Edinburgh University Press, 2013.

Beytullah, Mehmet. *Alevilik Keşmekeşliği ve Bulgaristan Kızılbaşlığı.* Sofia: Svetlik Yayınevi, 1999.

Birdoğan, Nejat. *Anadolu'nun Gizli Kültürü: Alevilik.* Hamburg: Hamburg Alevi Kültür Merkezi, 1990.

———. *Anadolu ve Balkanlar'da Alevi Yerleşimleri: Ocaklar-Dedeler-Soy Ağaçları.* Istanbul: Alev Yayınları, 1992.

———. *Alevi Kaynakları-1.* Istanbul: Kaynak Yayınları, 1996.

Birge, John K. *The Bektashi Order of Dervishes.* 1937; reprint, London: Luzac Oriental, 1994.

Borovalı Murat and Cemil Boyraz. 'Türkiye'de Cemevleri Sorunu: Haklar ve Özgürlükler Bağlamında Eleştrel Bir Yaklaşım'. *Mülkiye Dergisi* 40, no. 3 (2016): 55–85.

Bosbach, Franz. 'The European Debate on Universal Monarchy'. In *Theories of Empire, 1450–1800*, edited by David Armitage, 81–98. Aldershot: Ashgate, 1998.

Bosworth, Clifford Edmund. 'Bahāᵓ al-Dīn ᶜĀmilī in the Two Worlds of the Ottomans and Safavids'. In *Convegno Sul Tema La Shīᶜa Nell'impero Ottomano (Roma, 15 Aprile 1991)*, 85–105. Rome: Accademia Nazionale dei Lincei, 1993.

———. *The New Islamic Dynasties: A Chronological and Genealogical Manual*. New York: Columbia University Press, 1996.

Bozkurt, Fuat. *Aleviliğin Toplumsal Boyutları*. Istanbul: Yön Yayıncılık, 1990.

Böwering, Gerhard. *The Mystical Vision of Existence in Classical Islam: The Qurʾanic Hermeneutics of the Ṣūfī Sahl at-Tustarī (d. 283/896)*. Berlin: De Gruyter, 1980.

———. 'Early Sufism between Persecution and Heresy'. In *Islamic Mysticism Contested: Thirteen Centuries of Controversies and Polemics*, edited by Frederick De Jong and Bernd Radtke, 45–67. Leiden: Brill, 1999.

Brack, Jonathan. 'Was Ede Balı a Wafāʾī Shaykh? Sufis, Sayyids, and Genealogical Creativity in the Early Ottoman World'. In *Islamic Literature and Intellectual Life in Fourteenth-Century Anatolia*, edited by A. C. S. Peacock and Sara Nur Yıldız, 333–360. Würzburg: Ergon Verlag, 2016.

Brady, Thomas A., Jr, 'Confessionalization: The Career of a Concept'. In *Confessionalization in Europe, 1555–1700: Essays in Memory of Bodo Nischan*, edited by John M. Headley, et al., 1–20. Aldershot: Ashgate, 2004.

Brockelmann, C. *Geschichte der Arabischen Litteratur*. 2nd Supplementband. Leiden: Brill, 1938.

Browne, Edward G. *A Literary History of Persia*. Vol 4: *Modern Times (1500–1924)*. 1900; reprint, Cambridge: Cambridge University Press, 1930.

Bruinessen, Martin van. *Agha, Shaikh and State: The Social and Political Structures of Kurdistan*. London and New Jersey: Zed Books Ltd, 1978.

———. 'Kurds, Turks and the Alevi Revival in Turkey'. *Middle East Report* (July–September 1996): 6–9.

Brummett, Palmira. 'The Myth of Shah Ismail Safavi: Political Rhetoric and "Divine" Kingship'. In *Medieval Christian Perceptions of Islam: A Book of Essays*, edited by John V. Tolan, 331–359. New York: Garland, 1996.

Brüning, Alfons. 'Confessionalization in the *Slavia Orthodoxa* (Belorussia, Ukraine, Russia)? – Potential and Limits of a Western Historiographical Concept'. In *Religion and the Conceptual Boundary and Eastern Europe: Encounters of Faiths*, edited by T. Bremer, 66–97. London: Palgrave MacMillan, 2008.

Bülbül, Zekeriya. 'XVI. Yüzyılda Diyarbekir Beylerbeyliği'ndeki Yer İsimleri'. 2 Vols. PhD diss., Selçuk University, Konya, 1999.

Bulliet, Richard. *Islam: The View from the Edge*. New York: Columbia University Press, 1995.

Bumke, Peter J. 'The Kurdish Alevis – Boundaries and Perceptions'. In *Ethnic Groups in the Republic of Turkey,* edited by Peter A. Andrews, 510–519. Wiesbaden: L. Reichert, 1989.

Burak, Guy. 'Faith, Law and Empire in the Ottoman "Age of Confessionalization" (Fifteenth–Seventeenth Centuries): The Case of "Renewal of Faith"'. *Mediterranean Historical Review* 28, no. 1 (2013): 1–23.

Burbank, Jane and Frederick Cooper. *Empires in World History*. Princeton: Princeton University Press, 2010.

Busse, Heribert. *Chalif Und Grosskönig: Die Buyiden im Iraq (945–1055)*. Beirut and Wiesbaden: In Kommission bei F. Steiner, 1969.

Çakmak, Hüseyin. *Dersim Aleviliği: Raa Haqi: Dualar, Gülbengler, Ritüeller*. Ankara: Kalan Yayınları, 2013.

Çamuroğlu, Reha. 'Alevi Revivalism in Turkey'. In *Alevi Identity: Cultural, Religious and Social Perspectives,* ed. T. Olsson, et al., 79–84. Istanbul: Isis Press, 1998.

Canbakal, Hülya. 'An Exercise in Denominational Geography in Search of Ottoman Alevis'. *Turkish Studies* 6, no. 2 (June 2005): 253–271.

———. 'The Ottoman State and Descendants of the Prophet in Anatolia and the Balkans (c. 1500–1700)'. *Journal of the Economic and Social History of the Orient* 52 (2009): 542–578.

Carlson, Thomas A. 'Safavids before Empire: Two 15th-Century Armenian Perspectives'. *International Journal of Middle East Studies* 49, no. 2 (2017): 277–294.

Çıpa, H. Erdem. *The Making of Selim: Succession, Legitimacy, and Memory in the Early Modern Ottoman World.* Bloomington: Indiana University Press, 2017.

Clarke, Gloria L. *The World of the Alevis: Issues of Culture and Identity*. New York and Istanbul: AVS Publications, 1999.

Coffey, John. *Persecution and Toleration in Protestant England, 1559–1689.* Harlow and New York: Longman, 2000.

Connell, Michael Paul. 'The Nimatullahi Sayyids of Taft: A Study of the Evolution of a Late Medieval Iranian Sufi Tariqah'. PhD diss., Harvard University, Massachusetts, 2004.

Curry, John. *The Transformation of Muslim Mystical Thought in the Ottoman Empire: The Rise of the Halveti Order 1350–1650.* Edinburgh: Edinburgh University Press, 2010.

Dabashi, Hamid. 'Historical Conditions of Persian Sufism during the Seljuk Period'. In *The Heritage of Sufism.* Vol. 1: *Classical Persian Sufism from Its Origins to Rumi (700–1300),* edited by Leonard Lewisohnm, 137–174. Oxford: Oneworld Publications, 1999.

Daftary, Farhad. 'Ismaili–Sufi Relations in Post-Alamut Persia'. In *Ismailis in Medieval Muslim Societies: A Historical Introduction to an Islamic Community,* ed. Farhad Daftary, 183–213. London: I. B. Tauris, 2005.

Dağlı, Murat. 'The Limits of Ottoman Pragmatism'. *History and Theory* 52 (May 2013): 194–213.

Danişmend, İsmail Hami. *İzahlı Osmanlı Tarihi Kronolojisi.* 5 Vols. Istanbul: Türkiye Yayınevi, 1947–1961.

Danon, M. A. 'Un interrogatoire d'hérétiques Musulmans (1619)'. *Journal Asiatique* (April–June 1921): 281–293.

al-Darraji, Hamid Muhammad Hasan. *al-Rubuṭ wa al-takāyā al-Baghdādiyya fī al-ᶜahd al-ᶜUthmānī (941–1336 h./1534–1917 m.): Takhṭīṭuhā wa ᶜimāratuhā*. Baghdad: Dār al-Shuʾūn al-Thaqāfiyya al-ᶜĀmma, 2001.

Demirel, Ömer. *Osmanlı Vakıf-Şehir İlişkisine Bir Örnek: Sivas Şehir Hayatında Vakıfların Rolü*. Ankara: Türk Tarih Kurumu, 2000.

Denizli, Hikmet. *Sivas: Tarihi ve Anıtları*. Sivas: Özbelsan A.Ş. Kültür Hizmeti, 1995.

Dersimi, Nuri. *Kürdistan Tarihinde Dersim*. 1952; reprint, Diyarbakır: Dilan Yayınları, 1992.

DeWeese, Devin. *Islamization and Native Religion in the Golden Horde: Baba Tükles and Conversion to Islam in Historical and Epic Tradition*. Pennsylvania: Pennsylvania State University Press, 1994.

———. 'The Descendants of Sayyid Ata and the Rank of Naqīb in Central Asia'. *Journal of the American Oriental Society* 115, no. 4 (October–December 1995): 612–634.

———. 'Yasavī *Šayḫs* in the Timurid Era: Notes on the Social and Political Role of Communal Sufi Affiliations in the 14th and 15th Centuries'. *Oriente Moderno* 76, no. 2 (1996): 173–188.

———. 'The Yasavī Order and Persian Hagiography in Seventeenth-Century Central Asia: 'Ālim Sheikh of 'Alīyābād and his Lamaḥāt min nafaḥāt al-quds'. In *Heritage of Sufism-3*.

———. 'The Sayyid Atāʾī Presence in Khwārazm during the 16th and Early 17th Centuries'. In *Studies on Central Asian History in Honor of Yuri Bregel*, edited by Devin DeWeese, 245–291. Bloomington: Research Institute for Inner Asian Studies, 2001.

———. 'The Legitimation of Bahāʾ ad-Dīn Naqshband'. *Asiatische Studien/Études asiatiques* 60, no. 2 (2006): 261–305.

———. 'Intercessory Claims of Ṣūfī Communities during the 14th and 15th Centuries: "Messianic" Legitimizing Strategies on the Spectrum of Normativity'. In *Unity in Diversity: Mysticism, Messianism and the Construction of Religious Authority in Islam*, edited by Orkhan Mir-Kasimov, 197–221. Leiden: Brill, 2014.

Diani, Mario. 'The Concept of Social Movement'. *The Sociological Review* 40, no. 1 (1992): 1–25.

Donohue, John J. *The Buwayhid Dynasty in Iraq 334H/945 to 403H/1012: Shaping Institutions for the Future*. Leiden: Brill, 2003.

Dressler, Markus. 'Inventing Orthodoxy: Competing Claims for Authority and Legitimacy in the Ottoman-Safavid Conflict'. In *Legitimizing the Order: The Ottoman Rhetoric of State Power*, edited by Hakan T. Karateke and Maurus Reinkowski, 151–173. Leiden and Boston: Brill, 2005.

———. *Writing Religion: The Making of Turkish Alevi Islam*. New York: Oxford University Press, 2013.

Driedger, Michael. *Obedient Heretics: Mennonite Identities in Lutheran Hamburg and Altona during the Confessional Age*. Aldershot: Ashgate, 2002.

al-Durubi, Ibrahim ᶜAbd al-Ghani. *al-Baghdādiyūn: akhbāruhum wa majālisuhum*. Baghdad: Dār al-Shuʾūn al-Thaqāfiyya al-ᶜĀmma, 2001.

Eberhard, Elke. *Osmanische Polemik gegen die Safawiden im 16. Jahrhundert nach arabischen Handschriften*. Freiburg: Klaus Schwarz Verlag, 1970.

Ebstein, Michael. *Mysticism and Philosophy in al-Andalus: Ibn Masarra, Ibn al-Arabi and the Ismaili Tradition*. Leiden and Boston: Brill, 2013.

———. 'Spiritual Descendants of the Prophet: Al-Ḥakim al-Tirmidhī, Ibn al-ᶜArabī and Ikhwān al-Ṣafāᵓ on *Ahl al-Bayt*'. In *L'Esotérisme Shiᶜite L'Esotérisme Shiᶜite, ses racines et ses prolongements*, edited by M. A. Amir-Moezzi et al., 539–572. Turnhout: Brepols Publishers, 2016.

Edmonds, C. J. *Kurds, Turks, and Arabs*. London and New York: Oxford University Press, 1957.

Efendiyev, Oktay. 'Sultan II. Bayezid ve Şah İsmail'. In *XIII. Türk Tarih Kongresi: Ankara, 4–8 Ekim 1999: Kongreye Sunulan Bildiriler*, 89–95. Ankara: Türk Tarih Kurumu, 2002.

———. 'Çaldıran Savaşı'na Kadar Osmanlı-Safevi İlişkilerine Kısa Bir Bakış'. *Uluslararası Sosyal Araştırmalar Dergisi/The Journal of International Social Research* 26 (Winter 2009): 126–135.

Eisenstein, Herbert. 'Sunnite Accounts of the Subdivisions of the Shī'a'. In *Shī'a Islam, Sects and Sufism: Historical Dimensions, Religious Practice and Methdological Considerations*, edited by Frederick De Jong, 1–9. Utrecht: M. Th. Houtsma Stichting, 1992.

Emecen, Feridun M. *Osmanli Klasik Çağında Siyaset*. Istanbul: Timaş Yayınlar, 2009.

———. *İmparatorluk çağının Osmanlı Sultanları I: Bayezid II, Yavuz, Kanûnî*. Istanbul: İSAM Yayınlari, 2011.

———. *Yavuz Sultan Selim*. Izmir: Yitik Hazine Yayınları, 2011.

———. ''İhtilalci Bir Mehdilik' Hareketi mi? Şahkulu Baba Tekeli İsyanı Üzerine Yeni Yaklaşımlar'. In *Ötekilerin Peşinde Ahmet Yaşar Ocak's Armağan*, edited by Mehmet Öz and Fatih Yeşil, 521–534. Istanbul: Timaş Yayınları, 2015.

Engin, İsmail. *Tahtacılar: Tahtacıların Kimliğine ve Demografisine Giriş*. Istanbul: Ant Yayınları, 1998.

Ephrat, Daphna. *A Learned Society in a Period of Transition: The Sunni 'Ulema' of Eleventh-Century Baghdad*. Albany: State University of New York Press, 2000.

———. *Spiritual Wayfarers, Leaders in Piety: Sufis and the Dissemination of Islam in Medieval Palestine*. Cambridge: Cambridge University Press, 2008.

Ernst, Carl W. *Voices of Ecstasy in Sufism*. Albany: SUNY Press, 1985.

Eyice, Semavi. 'Çorum'un Mecidözü'nde Âşık Paşaoğlu Elvan Çelebi Zâviyesi'. *Türkiyât Mecmuası* 15 (1968): 211–246.

Farhat, May. 'Islamic Piety and Dynastic Legitimacy: The Case of the Shrine of Ali al-Rida in Mashhad (10th–17th Century)'. PhD diss., Harvard University, Massachusetts, 2002.

Faroqhi, Suraiya. 'XVI.–XVIII. Yüzyıllarda Anadolu'da Şeyh Aileleri'. In *Türkiye İktisat Tarihi Semineri: Metinler/Tartışmalar, 9–10 Haziran 1973*, edited by Osman Okyar, 197–229. Ankara: Hacettepe Üniversitesi Yayınları, 1975.

———. 'The Tekke of Hacı Bektaş: Social Position and Economic Activities'. *International Journal of Middle East Studies* 7 (1976): 183–208.

———. 'Seyyid Gazi Revisited: The Foundation as Seen through Sixteenth and Seventeenth-Century Documents'. *Turcica* 13 (1981): 90–122.

———. 'Conflict, Accommodation and Long-Term Survival: The Bektashi Order and the Ottoman State'. In *Bektachiyya: Études sur l'ordre mystique des Bektachis et les groupes relevant de Hadji Bektach*, edited by Alexandre Popovic and Gilles Veinstein, 171–184. Istanbul: Isis Press, 1995.

———. 'Sainthood as a Means of Self-Defence in Seventeenth-Century Ottoman Anatolia'. In *Coping with the State: Political Conflict and Crime in the Ottoman Empire 1550–1720*, 43–58. Istanbul: Isis Press, 1995.

———. 'The Bektashis: A Report on Current Research'. In *Bektachiyya: Études sur l'ordre mystique des Bektachis et les groupes relevant de Hadji Bektach*, edited by Alexandre Popovic and Gilles Veinstein, 9–28. Istanbul: Isis Press, 1995.

———. 'Crisis and Change, 1590–1699'. In *An Economic and Social History of the Ottoman Empire, 1300–1914*, edited by Halil İnalcık and Donald Quataert, 413–622. Cambridge: Cambridge University Press, 1994.

Al-Feel, Muhammad Rashid. *The Historical Geography of Iraq between the Mongolian and Ottoman Conquests, 1258–1534*. Najaf: Al-Adab Press, 1965.

Fırat, M. Şerif. *Doğu İlleri ve Varto Tarihi (Etimoloji–Din–Etnografya–Dil ve Ermeni Mezalimi)*. 5th edn. Ankara: Türk Kültürünü Araştırma Enstitüsü, 1983.

Fisher, Sydney N. *The Foreign Relations of Turkey 1481–1512*. Urbana: University of Illinois Press, 1948.

Fleischer, Cornell H. *Bureaucrat and Intellectual in the Ottoman Empire: The Historian Mustafa Âli (1541–1600)*. Princeton: Princeton University Press, 1986.

———. 'The Lawgiver as Messiah: The Making of the Imperial Image in the Reign of Süleymân'. In *Soliman le Magnifique et son temps: Actes du colloque de Paris, Galeries nationales du Grand palais, 7–10 mars 1990*, edited by Gillès Veinstein, 159–177. Paris: La Documentation française, n.d.

Flemming, Barbara. 'Sāhib-kırān und Mahdī: Türkische Endzeiterwartungen im ersten Jahrzehnt der Regierung Süleymāns'. In *Between the Danube and the Caucasus: A Collection of Papers concerning Oriental Sources on the History of the Peoples of Central and South-Eastern Europe*, edited by György Kara, 43–62. Budapest: Akadémiai Kiadó, 1987.

Floor, Willem. *The Persian Textile Industry in Historical Perspective: 1500–1925*. Paris: Éditions L'Harmattan, 1999.

———. 'The Khalifeh al-kholafa of the Safavid Sufi Order'. *Zeitschrift der Deutschen Morgenlandischen Gesellschaft* 153, no. 1 (2003): 51–86.

Fragner, Bert G. 'Farmān'. In *Encyclopaedia Iranica*. New York: Bibliotheca Persica Press, 1999.

Friedman, Yaron. *The Nusayri-'Alawis: An Introduction to the Religion, History and Identity of the Leading Minority in Syria.* Leiden and Boston: Brill, 2010.

Fuccaro, Nelida. 'The Ottoman Frontier in Kurdistan in the Sixteenth and Seventeenth Centuries'. In *The Ottoman World*, edited by Christine Woodhead, 237–250. London: Routledge, 2011.

Gellner, Ernest. *Saints of the Atlas*. London: Weidenfeld and Nicolson, 1969.

———. 'Doctor and Saint'. In *Islam in Tribal Societies: From the Atlas to the Indus,* edited by Akbar S. Ahmed and David M. Hart, 21–38. London and Boston and Melbourne and Henley: Routledge & Kegan Paul, 1984.

Gezik, Erdal. *Dinsel, Etnik ve Politik Sorunlar Bağlamında: Alevi Kürtler.* Ankara: Kalan Yayınları, 2000.

Glassen, Erika. 'Schah Ismāᶜīl, ein Mahdī der anatolischen Türkmenen?' *Zeitschrift der Deutschen Morgenländischen Gesellschaft* 121, no.1 (1971): 61–69.

Goertz, Hans-Jürgen. 'Kleruskritik, Kirchenzucht und Sozialdisziplinierung in den täuferischen Bewegungen der Frühen Neuzeit'. In *Kirchenzucht und Sozialdisziplinierung im frühneuzeitlichen Europa,* edited by Heinz Schilling, 183–198. Berlin: Duncker & Humblot, 1994.

Göğebakan, Göknur. *XVI. Yüzyılda Malatya Kazası (1516–1560).* Malatya: Malatya Belediyesi Kültür Yayınları, 2002.

Gökbilgin, M. Tayyib. 'XVI. Asır Başlarında Osmanlı Devleti Hizmetindeki Akkoyunlu Ümerâsı'. *Türkiyat Mecmuası* 9 (1951): 35–46.

Gölpınarlı, Abdülbâkî. *Yunus Emre: Hayatı.* Istanbul: Bozkurt Basımevi, 1936.-

-------. *İslam ve Türk İllerinde Fütüvvet Teşkilâtı ve Kaynakları.* Istanbul: Istanbul University, 1952.

———. 'Bektaşilik'. In *Türk Ansiklopedisi.* Ankara: Milli Eğitim Basımevi, 1953.

———. 'Kızılbaş'. In *İslâm Ansiklopedisi. İslâm Alemi Tarih, Coğrafya, Etnografya ve Biyografya Lugatı.* Istanbul: Milli Eğitim Basımevi, 1967.

———. *100 Soruda Türkiye'de Mezhepler ve Tarikatler.* Istanbul: Gerçek Yayınevi, 1969.

———. *Tasavvuf'tan Dilimize Geçen Deyimler ve Atasözleri.* Istanbul: İnkılâp ve Aka Kitabevleri, 1977.

———. *Alevî Bektâşî Nefesleri.* Istanbul: İnkılâp Kitabevi, 1992.

———. *Yunus Emre ve Tasavvuf.* 2nd edn. Istanbul: İnkılâp Kitabevi, 1992.

———. *Mevlânâ Müzesi Abdülbâkî Kütüphanesi Yazma Kitaplar Kataloğu.* Ankara: Türk Tarih Kurumu, 2003.

———. *Tarih Boyunca Islâm Mezhepleri ve Şîîlik.* İstanbul: Der Yayınları, 1987.

Gölpınarlı, Abdülbâkî and Pertev Nailî Boratav. *Pir Sultan Abdal.* Ankara: Türk Tarih Kurumu, 1943.

Goshgarian, Rachel. 'Futuwwa in Thirteenth-Century Rūm and Armenia: Reform Movements and the Managing of Multiple Allegiances on the Seljuk Periphery'. In *The Seljuks of Anatolia: Court and Society in the Medieval Middle East,* edited by A. C. S. Peacock and Sara Nur Yıldız, 227–263. London: I. B. Tauris, 2015.

Gösken, Urs and Nabil al-Tikriti. 'The 1502–1504 Correspondence between Şehzade Korkud and the Knights of St. John of Jerusalem'. *Mediterranea – Ricerche Storiche* 12, no. 34 (2015): 409–434.

Göyünç, Nejat. *XVI. Yüzyılda Mardin Sancağı*. Ankara: Türk Tarih Kurumu, 1991.

Graham, Terry. 'Abū Sa[c]īd ibn Abī'l-Khayr and the School of Khurāsān'. In *Heritage of Sufism-1*.

Grant, R. M. 'Charges of Immorality Against Religious Groups in Antiquity'. In *Studies in Gnosticism and Hellenistic Religions: Studies Presented to Gilles Quispel on the Occasion of his 65th Birthday,* edited by R. van den Broek and M. J. Vermaseren, 161–170. Leiden: Brill, 1997.

Green, Nile. *Sufism: A Global History*. Chichester and Malden, MA: Wiley-Blackwell, 2012.

Griffel, Frank. 'Toleration and Exclusion: Al-Shafi'i and al-Ghazali on the Treatment of Apostates'. *Bulletin of the School of Oriental and African Studies* 64, no. 3 (2001): 339–354.

Gültekin, Sadullah. 'Anadolu'da Bir Vefaî Şeyhi: Tahrir Defterleri Işığında Dede Karkın Hakkında Bir Değerlendirme'. *Türk Kültürü ve Hacı Bektaş Veli Araştırma Dergisi* 59 (2011): 147–158.

———. 'Osmanlı Devleti'nde Alevî Sözcüğünün Kullanımına Dair Bazı Değerlendirmeler'. *Alevilik Araştırmaları Dergisi* 6, no. 11 (2016): 27–41.

Gümüş, Burak. *Die Wiederkehr des Alevitentums in der Türkei und in Deutschland*. Konstanzer Schriften zur Sozialwissenschaft 73. Konstanz: Hartung-Gorre Verlag, 2007.

Halaçoğlu, Yusuf. *XVIII. Yüzyılda Osmanlı İmparatorluğu'nun İskân Siyaseti ve Aşiretlerin Yerleştirilmesi*. Ankara: Türk Tarih Kurumu, 1988.

Hammer-Purgstall, Joseph von. *Geschichte des Osmanischen Reiches*. 10 Vols. Vol. 3. 1828; reprint, Graz: Akademische Druck-u. Verlagsanstalt, 1963.

Haneda, M. Masashi, *Le châh et les Qizilbāš: le système militaire safavide*. Berlin: Klaus Schwarz, 1987.

Hanilçe, Murat and Melike Tepecik. 'Anadolu'nun Manevi Önderlerinden Bir Eren: Ahi Mahmud Veli (Keçeci Baba)'. *Alevilik Araştırmaları Dergisi/The Journal of Alevi Studies* 12, no. 12 (Winter 2016): 141–170.

Hanne, Eric J. *Putting the Caliph in His Place: Power, Authority, and the Late Abbasid Caliphate*. Madison and Teaneck: Fairleigh Dickinson University Press, 2007.

Hasluck, F. W. 'Geographical Distribution of the Bektashi'. *The Annual of the British School at Athens* 21 (1916): 84–124.

———. *Christianity and Islam under the Sultans*. 2 Vols. Oxford: Clarendon Press, 1929.

Headly, John M. 'The Habsburg World Empire and the Revival of Ghibellinism'. In *Theories of Empire, 1450–1800*, edited by David Armitage, 45–79. Aldershot: Ashgate, 1998.

Hınz, Walther. *Uzun Hasan ve Şeyh Cüneyd: XV. Yüzyılda İran'ın Millî Bir Devlet Haline Yükselişi*, translated by Tevfik Bıyıklıoğlu. Ankara: Türk Tarih Kurumu, 1992. Originally published under the title *Irans Aufstieg zum Nationalstaat im fünfzehnten Jahrhundert*. Berlin: Walter de Gruyter GmbH & Co., 1936.

Hodgson, Marshall G. S. 'How the Early Shî'a Became Sectarian'. *Journal of the American Oriental Society* 75, no. 1 (January–March 1955): 1–13.

———. 'Al-Darasî and Ḥamza in the Origin of the Druze Religion'. *Journal of American Oriental Society* 82, no. 1 (January–March 1962): 5–21.

———. *The Venture of Islam: Conscience and History in a World Civilization.* Chicago: The University of Chicago Press, 1977,

Imber, Colin Ḥ. 'The Persecution of the Ottoman Shīᶜites according to the *mühimme defterleri*, 1565–1585'. *Der Islam* 56, no. 2 (July 1979): 245–273.

———. 'The Ottoman Dynastic Myth'. *Turcica* 19 (1987): 7–27.

———. 'Canon and Apocrypha in Early Ottoman History'. In *Studies in Ottoman History in Honour of Professor V. L. Ménage,* edited by Colin Heywood and Colin Imber, 117–137. Istanbul: Isis Press, 1994.

———. 'Ideals and Legitimation in Early Ottoman History'. In *Süleyman the Magnificent and His Age: The Ottoman Empire in the Early Modern World,* edited by M. Kunt and C. Woodhead, 139–153. London and New York: Longman, 1995.

———. *Ebu's-Su'ud: The Islamic Legal Tradition.* Stanford: Stanford University Press, 2009.

———. 'Süleyman as Caliph of the Muslims: Ebû's-Suᶜûd's Formulation of Ottoman Dynastic Ideology'. In *Soliman le Magnifique et son temps: Actes du colloque de Paris, Galeries nationales du Grand palais, 7–10 mars 1990,* edited by Gillès Veinstein, 179–184. Paris: La Documentation française, n.d.

İnalcık, Halil. 'Mehmed the Conqueror and His Time'. *Speculum* 35, no. 3. (1960): 408–427.

———. 'Selim I'. *EI-2*.

———. 'Dervish and Sultan: An Analysis of the Otman Baba *Velāyetnāmesi*'. In *The Middle East and the Balkans under the Ottoman Empire: Essays on Economy and Society,* 19–36. Bloomington: Indiana University, 1993.

———. 'How to Read ᶜĀshıḳ Pasha-zāde's History'. In *Essays in Ottoman History,* 31–50. Istanbul: Eren Yayıncılık, 1998.

———. *Osmanlı İmparatorluğu Klâsik Çağ (1300–1600).* 1973; rev. edn. Istanbul: Yapı Kredi Yayınları, 2004.

Ivanow, W. *The Truth-Worshippers of Kurdistan: Ahl-i Haqq Texts.* The Ismaili Society Series A no. 7. Leiden: Brill, 1953.

İslamoğlu, Huricihan. *Osmanlı İmparatorluğu'nda Devlet ve Köylü.* 2nd edn. Istanbul: İletişim Yayınları, 2010.

Jacob, Georg. *Beiträge zur Kenntnis des Derwisch-Ordens der Bektaschis.* Berlin: Mayer & Müller, 1908.

———. *Die Bektaschijje in ihrem Verhältnis zu verwandten Erscheinungen.* Munich: Verlag der Königlich-bayerischen Akademie der Wissenschaften, 1909.

Jordan, Tim. 'The Unity of Social Movement'. *The Sociological Review* 43, no. 4 (1995): 675–692

Kabir, Mafizullah. *The Buwayhid Dynasty of Baghdad* (334/946–447/1055). Calcutta: Iran Society, 1964.

Kafadar, Cemal. *Between Two Worlds: The Construction of the Ottoman State*. Berkeley and Los Angeles: University of California Press, 1995.

Kaleli, Lütfü. *Kimliğini Haykıran Alevilik: Araştırma, Derleme*. Istanbul: Habora Kitabevi, 1990.

Kaplan, Doğan. 'Fuad Köprülü'ye Göre Anadolu Aleviliği'. *Marife* 3, no. 2 (Autumn 2003): 143–163.

———. 'Aleviliğin Yazılı Kaynaklarından Buyruklar ve Muhtevaları Üzerine'. Paper presented at the International Symposium on Bektashism and Alevism, 28–30 September 2005, Isparta.

———. 'Buyruklara Göre Kızılbaşlık'. PhD diss., Selçuk Üniversitesi, Konya, 2008.

Kaplan, Yosef. 'Confessionalization, Discipline and Religious Authority in the Early Modern Western Sephardic Diaspora'. In *Religious Movements and Transformations in Judaism, Christianity and Islam,* edited by Yohanan Friedmann, 83–108. Jerusalem: The Israel Academy of Sciences and Humanities, 2016.

Kara, Seyfullah. *Büyük Selçuklular ve Mezhep Kavgaları*. Istanbul: İz Yayıncılık, 2007.

Karakaya-Stump, Ayfer. 'Alevilik Hakkında 19. Yüzyıl Misyoner Kayıtlarına Eleştirel Bir Bakış ve Ali Gako'nun Öyküsü'. *Folklor/Edebiyat, Alevilik Özel Sayısı* 1, no. 29 (March 2002): 301–324.

———. 'The Emergence of the Kızılbaş in Western Thought: Missionary Accounts and their Aftermath'. In *Archaeology, Anthropology and Heritage in the Balkans and Anatolia: The Life and Times of F.W. Hasluck, 1878–1920*, edited by David Shankland, 329–353. 2 Vols. Istanbul: Isis Press, 2004.

———. 'Kızılbaş, Bektaşi, Safevi İlişkilerine Dair 17. Yüzyıldan Yeni Bir Belge (Yazı Çevirimli Metin-Günümüz Türkçesine Çeviri-Tıpkıbasım)'. In *Festschrift in Honour of Orhan Okay*, edited by Yücel Dağlı, et al., special issue of the *Journal of Turkish Studies/Türklük Bilgisi Araştırmaları* 30, no. II (2006): 117–130.

———. 'Sinemilliler: Bir Alevi Ocağı ve Aşireti'. *Kırkbudak* 2, no. 6 (Spring 2006): 19–59.

———. '16. Yüzyıldan Bir Ziyaretname (Yazı Çevirimli Metin-Günümüz Türkçesine Çeviri-Tıpkıbasım)'. In *In Memoriam Şinasi Tekin*, edited by George Dedes and Selim S. Kuru, special issue of the *Journal of Turkish Studies/Türklük Bilgisi Araştırmaları* 31, no. II (2007): 67–79.

———. 'Irak'taki Bektaşi Tekkeleri'. *Belleten* 71, no. 261 (August 2007): 689–720.

———. 'Documents and *Buyruk* Manuscripts in the Private Archives of Alevi *Dede* Families: An Overview'. *British Journal of Middle Eastern Studies* 37, no. 3 (2010): 273–286.

———. 'The Forgotten Dervishes: The Bektashi Convents in Iraq and Their Kizilbash Clients'. *International Journal of Turkish Studies* 16, nos 1 and 2 (2011): 1–24.

———. 'Alevi Dede Ailelerine Ait Buyruk Mecmuaları'. In *Eski Türk Edebiyatı Çalışmaları VII: Mecmûa: Osmanlı Edebiyatının Kırkambar*, edited by Hatice Aynur et al., 361–379. Istanbul: Turkuaz Yayınları, 2012.

———. 'The Wafā'iyya, the Bektashiyye and Genealogies of "Heterodox" Islam in Anatolia: Rethinking the Köprülü Paradigm'. *Turcica* 44 (2012–2013): 279–300.

———. *Vefailik, Bektaşilik, Kızılbaşlık: Alevi Kaynaklarını, Tarihini ve Tarihyazımını Yeniden Düşünmek.* Istanbul: Bilgi University Press, 2015.

Karamustafa, Ahmet T. '*Ḳalenders, Abdâls, Ḥayderî*s: The Formation of the *Bektâşîye* in the Sixteenth Century'. In *Süleymân the Second and his Time*, edited by Halil İnalcık and Cemal Kafadar, 121–129. Istanbul: Isis Press, 1993.

———. *God's Unruly Friends: Dervish Groups in the Islamic Later Middle Period 1200–1550.* Salt Lake City: University of Utah Press, 1994.

———. 'Early Sufism in Eastern Anatolia'. In *Heritage of Sufism-1.*

———. 'Yesevîlik, Melâmetîlik, Kalenderîlik, Vefâʾîlik ve Anadolu Tasavvufunun Kökenleri Sorunu'. In *Osmanlı Toplumunda Tasavvuf ve Sufiler: Kaynaklar–Doktrin–Ayin ve Erkan–Tarikatlar–Edebiyat–Mimari–İkonografi–Modernizm*, edited by Ahmed Yaşar Ocak, 61–88. Ankara: Türk Tarih Kurumu, 2005.

———. *Sufism: The Formative Period.* Berkeley: University of California Press, 2007.

———. 'Islamisation through the Lens of *Saltuk-name*'. In *Islam and Christianity in Mediaeval Anatolia*, edited by A. C. S. Peacock, Sara Nur Yıldız, and Bruno de Nicola, 349–364. Farnham: Ashgate, 2015.

———. 'In His Own Voice: What Hatayi Tells Us about Şah İsmail's Religious Views'. In *L'Ésotérisme Shiʿite: Ses Racines et Ses Prolongements/Shiʿi Esotericism: Its Roots and Developments*, edited by Mohammad Ali Amir-Moezzi, 608–609. Turnhout: Brepols Publishers, 2016.

'Karkın'. In *Türk Ansiklopedisi*. Ankara: Milli Eğitim Basımevi, 1974.

Karpat, Kemal and Yetkin Yıldırım, eds. *The Ottoman Mosaic.* Seattle: Cune Press, 2010.

Kaygusuz, İsmail. *Onar Dede Mezarlığı ve Adı Bilinmeyen Bir Türk Kolonizatörü Şeyh Hasan Oner*. Istanbul: Arkeoloji ve Sanat Yayınları, 1983.

Kehl-Bodrogi, Krisztina. 'Die 'Wiederfindung' des Alevitums in der Türkei: Geschichtsmythos und kollektive Identität'. *Orient* 34, no. 2 (1993): 267–281.

———. 'On the Significance of Musahiplik among the Alevis of Turkey: The Case of the Tahtacı'. In *Syncretistic Religious Communities in the Near East: Collected Papers of the Symposium, 'Alevism in Turkey and Comparable Syncretistic Religious Communities in the Near East in the past and Present', Berlin, 14–17 April 1995*, edited by K. Kehl-Bodrogi, et. al., 119–137. Leiden and New York and Köln: Brill, 1997.

Khadduri, Majid. *War and Peace in the Law of Islam*. Baltimore: The Johns Hopkins Press, 1955.

Kılıç, Rüya. *Osmanlıda Seyyidler ve Şerifler*. Istanbul: Kitap Yayınevi, 2005.

———. 'The Reflection of Islamic Tradition on Ottoman Social Structure: The Sayyids and the Sharīfs'. In *Sayyids and Sharifs in Muslim Societies: The Living Links to the Prophet*, edited by Morimoto Kazuo, 123–138. London and New York: Routledge, 2012.

Knysh, Alexander. '"Orthodoxy" and "Heresy" in Medieval Islam: An Essay in Reassessment'. *Muslim World* 83, no. 1 (January 1993): 43–67.

———. *Islamic Mysticism: A Short History*. Leiden and Boston and Köln: Brill, 2000.

Koerbin, Paul V. '"I am Pir Sultan Abdal": A Hermeneutical Study of the Self-Naming Tradition (*Mahlas*) in Turkish Alevi Lyric Song (*Deyiş*)'. PhD diss., University of Western Sydney, Sydney, 2011.

Köprülü, Fuad. 'Anadolu'da İslâmiyet'. İstanbul: İnsan Yayınları, 1996. First published in *Darü'l-fünūn Edebiyāt Mecmū'ası* 2 (1922): 281–311, 385–420, 457–486.

———. 'Bektaşiliğin Menşeleri: Küçük Asya'da İslâm Batınîliğinin Tekâmül-i Tarîhisi Hakkında Bir Tecrübe'. *Türk Yurdu* 7 (1341/1925): 121–140; reprint, Ankara, 2001, 9: 68–76. Originally published under the title 'Les origines du Bektachisme: Essai sur le développement historique de l'hétérodoxie musulmane en Asie Mineure'. In *Actes du congrès International d'histoire des religions*. Paris: n.p., 1923.

———. *Influence du chamanisme Turco-Mongol sur les ordres mystiques musulmans*. Istanbul: Imp. Zellitch frères, 1929.

———. 'Abbas (Abbas I)'. In *Türk Halk Edebiyatı Ansiklopedisi: Ortaçağ ve Yeniçağ Türklerinin Halk Kültürü Üzerine Coğrafya, Etnografya, Etmoloji, Tarih ve Edebiyat Lugatı*. Fasc. 1. Istanbul, Burhaneddin Basımevi, 1935.

———. 'Abdal'. In *Edebiyat Araştırmaları*, 362–417. 2 Vols. Vol. 2. Istanbul: Ötüken Yayınları, 1989. First published in *Türk Halk Edebiyatı Ansiklopedisi, Ortaçağ ve Yeniçağ Türklerinin Halk Kültürü Üzerine Coğrafya, Etnografya, Etnoloji, Tarih ve Edebiyat Lugatı*, fasc. 1 (Istanbul, 1935), 21–56.

———. 'Aḥmed Yesevī'. In *MIA*.

———. 'Bektaş: Hacı Bektaş Veli'. In *MIA*.

———. *Osmanlı Devleti'nin Kuruluşu*. 1959; reprint, Ankara: Türk Tarih Kurmu, 1991.

———. *Türk Edebiyatında İlk Mutasavvıflar*. 1919; reprint, Ankara: Türk Tarih Kurumu, 1993. Translated by Gary Leiser and Robert Dankoff under the title *Early Mystics in Turkish Literature*. London: Routledge, 2006.

Köprülü, Orhan F. 'Abdal Mûsâ'. In *DIA*.

Koyuncu, Nuran. *Osmanlı Devleti'nde Şia: Safevi Taraftarlarına Uygulanan Cezai Yaptırımlar: İran Tebaasıyla Evlenme Yasağı*. Konya: Çizgi Kitabevi, 2014.

Koz, M. Sabri. 'Cönk ve Mecmûa Yapraklarında Âşık Aramak'. In *Eski Türk*

Edebiyatı Çalışmaları VII: Mecmûa: Osmanlı Edebiyatının Kırkambar, edited by Hatice Aynur et al., 157–200. Istanbul: Turkuaz Yayınları, 2012.

Krstić, Tijana. *Contested Conversions to Islam: Narratives of Religious Change in the Early Modern Ottoman Empire*. Stanford: Stanford University Press, 2011.

Krupp, Alya. *Studien zum Menāqybnāme des Abu l-Wafā ᵓTāğ al-ᶜĀrifīn: Das historische Leben des Abu l-Wafāᵓ Tāğ al-ᶜĀrifīn*. München: Dr. Rudolf Trofenik, 1976.

Küçükdağ, Yusuf. 'Osmanlı Devleti'nin, Şah İsmail'in Şiî Propagandacılarına Halvetiyye ile Karşı Koyma Politikası'. In *XIII Türk Tarih Kongresi: Ankara: 4–8 Ekim 1999: Kongreye sunulan bildiriler*, 435–444. Vol. 3, part I. Ankara: Türk Tarih Kurumu, 2002.

Kütükoğlu, Bekir. *Osmanlı-İran Siyâsî Münâsebetleri (1578–1612)*. Istanbul: Istanbul Fetih Cemiyeti, 1993.

Le Strange, G. *Baghdad during the Abbasid Caliphate: From Contemporary Arabic and Persian Sources*. 1900; reprint, London: Curzon Press, 1990.

Leiser, Gary. 'The Madrasah and the Islamization of Anatolia before the Ottomans'. In *Law and Education in Medieval Islam: Studies in Memory of Professor George Makdisi*, edited by Joseph E. Lowry, et al., 174–191. Cambridge: E. J. W. Gibb Memorial Trust, 2004.

Lellouch, B. 'Osmanlı Sultanının İktidar ve Adaleti: Iran ve Mısır Cephelerinde Gerçekleştirilen Kıyımlar'. In *Bir Allame-i Cihan: Stefanos Yerasimos*, edited by Edhem Eldem, et al., 407–421. Vol. 1. Istanbul: Kitap Yayınevi, 2012.

Leopold, Anita Maria and Jeppe Sinding, eds. *Syncretism in Religion: A Reader*. New York: Routledge, 2004.

Lewis, Bernard. 'Some Observations on the Significance of Heresy in the History of Islam'. *Studia Islamica* 1 (1953): 43–63.

Lindner, Rudi Paul. *Nomads and Ottomans in Medieval Anatolia*. Bloomington: Research Institute for Inner Asian Studies, Indiana University, 1983.

Litvak, Meir. *Shiᶜi Scholars of Nineteenth-Century Iraq: The ᶜUlemaᵓ of Najaf and Karbalaᵓ*. Cambridge: Cambridge University Press, 1998.

Longrigg, Stephen Hemsley. *Four Centuries of Modern Iraq*. Oxford: Clarendon Press, 1925.

Luz, Nimrod. 'Aspects of Islamization of Space and Society in Mamluk Jerusalem and Its Hinterland'. *Mamluk Studies Review* 6 (2002): 133–154.

Mahjub, Muhammad Jaᶜfar. 'Chivalry and Early Persian Sufism'. In *Heritage of Sufism-1*.

Makdisi, George. 'Notes on Ḥilla and the Mazyadids in Medieval Islam'. *Journal of the American Oriental Society* 74 (1954): 249–262.

———. 'The Sunni Revival'. In *Islamic Civilization 950–1150*, edited by David S. Richards, 155–168. Oxford: Cassirer, 1973.

———. *History and Politics in Eleventh-Century Baghdad*. Aldershot: Variorum, 1990.

Markoff, Irene. 'Music, Saints, and Ritual: Samāᶜ and the Alevis of Turkey'. In

Manifestations of Sainthood in Islam, edited by Grace Martin Smith, 95–110. Istanbul: Isis Press, 1993.
Maroney, Eric. *Religious Syncretism*. London: SCM Press, 2006.
Martin, B. G. 'A Short History of the Khalwati Order of Dervishes'. In *Scholars, Saints, and Sufis: Muslim Religious Institutions in the Middle East since 1500*, edited by Nikkie R. Keddie, 275–305. Berkeley: University of California Press, 1972.
Mason, Herbert. 'Ḥallāj and the Baghdad School of Sufism'. In *Heritage of Sufism-1*.
Massignon, Louis. *The Passion of Al-Hallaj: Mystic and Martyr of Islam*. Princeton: Princeton University Press, 1994.
Matthee, Rudi. 'Iran's Ottoman Diplomacy during the Reign of Shāh Sulaymān I (1077–1105/1666–94)'. In *Iran and Iranian Studies: Essays in Honor of Iraj Afshar*, edited by Kambiz Eslami, 148–165. Princeton: Zagros Press, 1998.
———. 'The Safavid-Ottoman Frontier: Iraq-ı Arab as Seen by the Safavids'. In *Ottoman Borderlands: Issues, Personalities and Political Changes*, edited by Kemal H. Karpat and Robert W. Zens, 157–173. Madison: Center of Turkish Studies, University of Wisconsin, 2003.
Mazzaoui, Michel M. 'The Ghāzī Background of the Safavid State'. *Iqbāl Review* 12, no. 3 (1971): 79–90.
———. *The Origins of the Ṣafawids: Šī 'ism, Ṣūfism, and the Ġulāt*. Wiesbaden: Franz Steiner Verlag, 1972.
McGregor, Richard J. A. *Sanctity and Mysticism in Medieval Egypt: The Wafāʾ Sufi Order and the Legacy of Ibn ʿArabī*. Albany: State University of New York Press, 2004.
Melchert, Christopher. 'The Transition from Asceticism to Mysticism at the Middle of the Ninth Century C.E'. *Studia Islamica* 83 (1996): 51–70.
———. 'Ḥanābila and the Early Sufis'. *Arabica* XLVIII, no. 3 (2001): 352–367.
Mélikoff, Irène. *Abū Muslim: Le 'porte-hache' du Khorassan dans la tradition épique turco-iranienne*. Paris: A. Maisonneuve, 1962.
———. 'Le problème ḳızılbaş'. *Turcica* 6 (1975): 49–67.
———. 'Hatayî'. In *Uluslararası Folklor Ve Halk Edebiyatı Semineri Bildirileri: 27–29 Ekim, 1975*, 315–318. Konya: Konya Turizm Derneği Yayınları, 1976.
———. 'Recherches sur les composantes du syncrétisme Bektachi-Alevi'. In *Studia Turcologica Memoriae Alexii Bombaci dicata*, 379–395. Napoli: Instituto Universitario Orientale, 1982.
———. *Uyur İdik Uyardılar: Alevîlik-Bektaşîlik Araştırmaları*. Translated into Turkish by Turan Alptekin. Istanbul: Cem Yayınevi, 1993.
———. *Hacı Bektaş: Efsaneden Gerçeğe*. Translated into Turkish by Turan Alptekin. Istanbul: Cumhuriyet Kitapları, 1998. Originally published as *Hadji Bektach: un mythe et ses avatars. Genèse et évolution du soufisme populaire en Turquie*. Leiden: Brill, 1998.
Ménage, V. I. 'On the Recensions of Uruj's "History of the Ottomans"'. *Bulletin of the School of Oriental and African Studies* 30, no. 2 (1967): 314–322.

Mentzer, Raymond A. 'The Huguenot Minority in Early Modern France'. In *Religion and the Early Modern State: Views from China, Russia, and the West*, edited by James D. Tracey and Marguerite Ragnow, 185–206. Cambridge: Cambridge University Press, 2004.

Minorsky, Vladimir. 'The Poetry of Shāḥ Ismāᶜīl I'. *Bulletin of the School of Oriental and African Studies* 10 (1942): 1,006–1,053.

———. 'The Ahl-i Ḥaḳḳ'. In *Iranica: Twenty Articles*, 306–16. Tehran: n.p., 1964.

———. 'Sheikh Bālī-efendi on the Ṣafavids'. In *Medieval Iran and its Neighbours: Collected Studies*. London: Variorum Reprints, 1982. [Article XIV, originally published in *Bulletin of the School of Oriental and African Studies* 20 (1957): 437–450.]

———. 'The Gūrān'. In *Medieval Iran and its Neighbours*. London: Variorum Reprints, 1982. [Article XV, originally published in *Bulletin of the School of Oriental and African Studies* 11 (1943): 75–103.]

Mîrjafarî, Hüseyin. 'Sufism and Gradual Transformation in the Meaning of Ṣūfī in Safavid Period'. *IU Edebiyat Fakültesi Tarih Dergisi*, no. 32 (March 1979): 157–166.

Miroğlu, İsmet. *Kemah Sancağı ve Erzincan Kazası (1520–1566)*. Ankara: Türk Tarih Kurumu, 1990.

Mitchell, Colin P. *The Practice of Politics in Safavid Iran: Power, Religion, and Rhetoric*. London: I. B. Tauris, 2009.

Moin, A. Azfar. *The Millennial Sovereign: Sacred Kingship and Sainthood in Islam*. New York: Columbia University Press, 2012.

Momen, Moojan. *An Introduction to Shᶜi Islam: The History and Doctrines of Twelver Shiᶜsm*. New Haven and London: Yale University Press, 1985.

Moore, Robert I. *The Formation of a Persecuting Society: Authority and Deviance in Western Europe, 950–1250*. Oxford and New York: B. Blackwell, 1987.

Moosa, Matti. *Extremist Shiites: The Ghulat Sects*. Syracuse: Syracuse University Press, 1988.

Morimoto, Kazuo. 'The Formation and Development of the Science of Talibid Genealogies in the 10th & 11th Century Middle East'. *Oriente Moderno* 18, no. 1 (1999): 541–570.

———. 'Putting the *Lubāb al-ansāb* in Context: *Sayyid*s and *Naqīb*s in Late Saljuq Khurasan'. *Studia Iranica* 36, no. 2 (2007): 163–183.

———. 'The Earliest ᶜAlid Genealogy for the Safavids: New Evidence for the Pre-Dynastic Claim to *Sayyid* Status'. *Iranian Studies* 43, no. 4 (2010): 447–469.

———. 'An Enigmatic Genealogical Chart of the Timurids: A Testimony to the Dynasty's Claim to Yasavi-ᶜAlid Legitimacy?' *Oriens* 44, nos 1–2 (2016): 145–178.

———. 'Sayyid Ibn ᶜAbd Al-Ḥamīd: An Iraqi Shiᶜi Genealogist at the Court of Özbek Khan'. *Journal of the Economic and Social History of the Orient* 59, no. 5 (2016): 661–694.

Morrison, Elizabeth. *The Power of Patriarchs: Qisong and Lineage in Chinese Buddhism*. Leiden and Boston: Brill, 2010.

Morton, Alexander H. 'The Chūb-i Ṭariq and Qizilbāsh Ritual in Safavid Persia'. In *Études Safavide*, edited by Jean Calmard, 225–245. Paris: Institut Français de Recherche en Iran, 1993.

Movako, Muhammed. 'Arnavutluk'ta Bektaşi Edebiyatı', translated by Mürsel Öztürk. *Hacı Bektaş Veli Araştırma Dergisi* 10 (Summer 1999): 51–60.

Mulder, Stephennie. *The Shrines of the ᶜAlids in Medieval Syria: Sunnis, Shiᶜis and the Architecture of Coexistence*. Edinburgh: Edinburgh University Press, 2014.

Musalı, Namiq. 'Safevîler'in Diyarbakır Beylerbeyi Muhammed Han Ustaclu ve Anadolu'daki Faaliyetleri'. In *Uluslararası Diyarbakır Sempozyumu, 2–5 Kasım 2016*, edited by Ufuk Bircan, et al., 495–522. Diyarbakır: T. C. Diyarbakır Valiliği, 2017.

Nasr, Seyyed Hossein. 'Shiᶜism and Sufism: Their Relationship in Essence and in History'. *Religious Studies* 6, no. 3 (September 1970): 229–242.

Necipoğlu, Gülru. 'The Süleymaniye Complex in Istanbul: An Interpretation'. *Muqarnas* 3 (1985): 92–117.

———. *The Age of Sinan: Architectural Culture in the Ottoman Empire*. London: Reaktion, 2005.

Ne'met, Meshedikhanim. *Azerbaycan'da Pirler* (Sosyal-İdeolojik İktisadi-Siyasi Merkezler). [In Cyrillic alphabet.] Baku: Azerbaycan Dovlet Neşriyyatı Polikrafiya Birliyi, 1992.

Newman, Andrew J. "The Role of the Sadat in Safavid Iran: Confrontation or Accomoddation?' *Oriente Moderno* 18 (1999): 577–596.

———. *Safavid Iran: Rebirth of a Persian Empire*. London: I. B. Tauris, 2006.

Niewöhner-Eberhard, Elke. 'Machtpolitische Aspekte des Osmanisch-Safawidischen Kampfes um Bagdad im 16/17. Jahrhunderts'. *Turcica* VI (1975): 104–127.

Nöldeke, Arnold. *Das Heiligtum al-Husains zu Kerbela*. Berlin: Mayer & Müller, 1909.

Noyan, Bedri. *Bütün Yönleriyle Bektâşîlik ve Alevîlik*. 9 Vols. Ankara: Ardıç Yayınları, 1998–2011.

Ocak, Ahmet Yaşar. *Bektaşî Menâkıbnâmelerinde İslam Öncesi İnanç Motifleri*. Istanbul: Enderun Kitabevi, 1983.

———. *Osmanlı İmparatorluğunda Marjinal Sûfilik: Kalenderîler: XIV–XVII. Yüzyıllar*. Ankara: Türk Tarih Kurumu, 1992.

———. 'Din ve Düşünce'. In *Osmanlı Devleti ve Medeniyeti Tarihi*, edited by Ekmeleddin İhsanoğlu. Vol. 2. Istanbul: IRCICA, 1994.

———. *Babaîler İsyanı: Alevîliğin Tarihsel Altyapısı Yahut Anadolu'da İslâm-Türk Heterodoksisinin Teşekkülü*. Revised 2nd edn. Istanbul: Dergâh Yayınları, 1996.

———. *Osmanlı Toplumunda Zındıklar ve Mülhidler (15.–17. Yüzyıllar)*. Istanbul: Türk Tarih Vakfı Yurt Yayınları, 1998.

———. *Türk Sufiliğine Bakışlar*, 5th edn. Istanbul: İletişim Yayınları, 2002.

———. 'The Wafa'î tariqa (Wafâiyya) during and after the Period of the Seljuks of Turkey: A New Approach to the History of Popular Mysticism in Turkey'. *Mésogeios* 25–26 (2005): 209–248.

———. *Ortaçağ Anadolu'sunda İki Büyük Yerleşimci (Kolonizatör) Derviş Yahut Vefâiyye ve Yeseviyye Gerçeği: Dede Kargın ve Emîrci Sultan* (13. Yüzyıl). Ankara: Gazi Üniversitesi Yayınları, 2011.

Oestreich, Gerhard. *Neostoicism and the Early Modern State*. Cambridge: Cambridge University Press, 1982.

Oğuz, Mevlüt. *Malatya Tarihi ve Sosyoekonomik Durumu (M.Ö. 5500–M.S. 1920)*. İstanbul: n.p., 2000.

Orhonlu, Cengiz. *Osmanlı İmparatorluğu'nda Aşiretlerin İskanı*. Istanbul: Eren Yayıncılık, 1987.

Oytan, M. Tevfik. *Bektaşiliğin İçyüzü*. 1945; reprint, Istanbul: Demos Yayinları, 2007.

Özdoğan, Mehmet. *Aşağı Fırat Havzası 1977 Yüzey Araştırmaları*. İstanbul: Orta Doğu Teknik Üniversitesi Keban Ve Aşağı Fırat Havzası Projeleri Müdürlüğü, 1977.

Özel, Oktay. 'The Reign of Violence: The Celalis *c*. 1550–1700'. In *The Ottoman World*, edited by Christine Woodhead, 184–202. London: Routledge, 2012.

———. *The Collapse of Rural Order in Ottoman Anatolia: Amasya 1576–1643*. Leiden: Brill, 2015.

Özen, Kutlu. *Sivas Efsaneleri*. Sivas: K. Özen, 2001.

Parker, Geoffrey. 'Messianic Visions in the Spanish Monarchy, 1516–1598'. *Calíope: Journal of the Society for Renaissance and Baroque Hispanic Poetry* 8, no. 2 (2002): 5–24.

Peacock, A. C. S. and Sara Nur Yildiz. 'Introduction: Literature, Language and History in Late Medieval Anatolia'. In *Islamic Literature and Intellectual Life in Fourteenth- and Fifteenth-century Anatolia,* edited by A. C. S. Peacock and Sara Nur Yildiz, 19–45. Würzburg: Ergon Verlag Würzburg in Kommission, 2016.

Peacock, A. C. S. *The Great Seljuk Empire*. Edinburgh: Edinburgh University Press, 2015.

———. 'Islamisation in Medieval Anatolia'. In *Islamisation: Comparative Perspectives from History*, edited by A. C. S. Peacock, 134–155. Edinburgh: Edinburgh University Press, 2017.

Pehlivan, Battal. *Alevi-Bektaşi Fıkraları: Derleme*. Istanbul: Alev Yayınları, 1993.

Pfeiffer, Judith. 'Confessional Ambiguity vs. Confessional Polarization: Politics and the Negotiation of Religious Boundaries in the Ilkhanate'. In *Politics, Patronage and the Transmission of Knowledge in 13th–15th Century Tabriz,* edited by Judith Pfeiffer, 129–168. Leiden: Brill, 2013.

Pierce, Leslie. *Morality Tales: Law and Gender in the Ottoman Court of Aintab*. Berkeley: University of California Press, 2003.

Plokhy, Serhii. *The Cossacks and Religion in Early Modern Ukraine*. Oxford and New York: Oxford University Press, 2002.

Po-Chia Hsia, Ronnie. *Social Discipline in the Reformation: Central Europe 1550–1750*. London: Routledge, 1989.

al-Qadi, Wadad. 'The Development of the Term *Ghulāt* in Muslim Literature with Special Reference to Kaysāniyya'. In *Akten des VII. Kongresses für Arabistik und Islamwissenschaft Göttingen*, edited by Albert Dietrich, 295–319. Göttingen: Vandenhoeck & Ruprect, 1976.

al-Qasir, Muhammad 'Ali. *Buyūtāt Karbalāʾ al-qadīmah: wa-sharḥ wa-taḥqīq lum'ah tārīkhīyah fī buyūtāt Karbalāʾ wa-al-Ghāḍirīyah*. Beirut: Muʾassasat Al-Balāgh Lil-Ṭibāʾah Wa-al-Nashr Wa-al-Tawzīᶜ, 2011.

Quinn, Sholeh A. 'Rewriting Niᶜmatu'llāhī History in Safavid Chronicles'. In *Heritage of Sufism-3*.

Reid, James J. *Tribalism and Society in Islamic Iran 1500–1629*. Malibu: Undena Publications, 1983.

Reinhard, Wolfgang. 'Gegenreformation als Modernisierung? Prolegomena zu einer Theorie des konfessionellen Zeitalters'. *Archiv für Reformationgeschichte* 68 (1977): 226–252.

———. 'Reformation, Counter-Reformation, and the Early Modern State: A Reassessment'. *The Catholic Historical Review* 75 (1989): 383–404.

Renard, John. 'Abū Bakr in Tradition and Early Hagiography'. In *Tales of God's Friends: Islamic Hagiography in Translation*, edited by John Renard, 15–29. Berkeley: University of California Press, 2009.

Repp, R. C. *The Müfti of Istanbul: A Study in the Development of the Ottoman Learned Hierarchy*. London: Oxford University, 1986.

Ridgeon, Lloyd. 'ᶜAlī Ibn Abī Ṭālib in Medieval Persian Sufi-Futuwwat Treatises'. In *L'Esotérisme Shiᶜite, ses racines et ses prolongements*, edited by M. A. Amir-Moezzi, et. al., 665–685. Turnhout: Brepols Publishers, 2016.

Rizvi, Kishwar. 'Transformations in Early Safavid Architecture: The Shrine of Shaykh Safi al-din Ishaq Ardabili in Iran (1501–1629)'. Ph.D. diss., Massachusetts Institute of Technology, Massachusetts, 2000.

Roemer, Hans R. 'The Safavid Period'. In *Cambridge-Iran-6*.

———. 'The Qizilbash Turcomans: Founder and Victim of the Safavid Theocracy'. In *Intellectual Studies on Islam: Essays Written in Honor of Martin B. Dickson,* edited by Michel M. Mazzaoui and Vera B. Moreen, 27–39. Salt Lake City: University of Utah Press, 1990.

Ross, E. Denison. *The Early Years of Shāh Ismāᶜil: Founder of the Ṣafavī Dynasty*. London: Royal Asiatic Society of Great Britain and Ireland, 1896.

Şahin, Kaya. *Empire and Power in the Reign of Süleyman: Narrating the Sixteenth-Century Ottoman World.* Cambridge: Cambridge University Press, 2013.

Şahin, İlhan. 'Kırşehir'. In *D/A*.

Şahin, Şehriban. 'The Rise of Alevism as a Public Religion'. *Current Sociology* 53, no. 3 (May 2005): 465–485.

Salati, Marco. 'Toleration, Persecution and Local Realities: Observations on the Shiism in the Holy Places and the *Bilād al-Shām* (16th–17th Centuries)'. In *Convegno Sul Tema La Shīᶜa Nell'impero Ottomano (Roma, 15 Aprile 1991),* 121–148. Rome: Accademia Nazionale Dei Lincei, 1993.

———. 'An Act of Appointment to the Leadership of the Wafāᵓiyya Sufi Order from the Ottoman Court Records of Aleppo (1099/1687)'. *Eurasian Studies* XI (2013): 79–84.

Sanaullah, Mawlawi Fadil. *The Decline of the Saljūqid Empire.* Calcutta: University of Calcutta, 1938.

Şapolyo, Enver Behnan. *Mezhepler ve Tarikatlar Tarihi.* Istanbul: Türkiye Basımevi, 1964.

Sarwar, Ghulam. *History of Shah Ismail Safawi.* Aligarh: Muslim University, 1939.

Savaş, Saim. *Bir Tekkenin Dini ve Sosyal Tarihi: Sivas Ali Baba Zaviyesi.* Istanbul: Dergâh Yayınları, 1992.

———. *XVI. Asırda Anadolu'da Alevîlik.* Ankara: Vadi Yayınları, 2002.

Savory, Roger M. 'The Office of Khalīfat al-Khulafā under the Ṣafawids'. *Journal of American Oriental Society* 85, no. 4 (1965): 497–502.

———. *Iran under the Safavids.* Cambridge: Cambridge University Press, 1980.

———. 'A 15th-Century Ṣafavid Propagandist at Harāt'. In *Studies on the History of Ṣafawid Iran.* London: Variorum Reprints, 1987. [Article II, originally published in *American Oriental Society, Middle West Branch, Semi-Centennial Volume: A Collection of Original Essays*, edited by D. Sinor, 189–197. Bloomington: Indiana University Press, 1969.]

Scharfe, Patrick. *Portrayals of the Later Abbasid Caliphs: The Role of the Caliphate in Buyid and Saljūq-era Chronicles, 936–1180.* MA Thesis, The Ohio State University, Ohio, 2010.

Schilling, Heinz. *Konfessionskonflikt und Staatsbildung.* Gütersloh: Gütersloher Verlagshaus, 1981.

———. 'Confessionalization in the Empire: Religious and Societal Change in Germany between 1555 and 1620'. In *Religion, Political Culture and the Emergence of Early Modern Society: Essays in German and Dutch History,* edited by Heinz Schilling, 205–245. Leiden: Brill, 1992.

———. 'Confessional Europe'. In *Handbook of European History, 1400–1600: Late Middle Ages, Renaissance and Reformation,* edited by Thomas A. Brady, et al., 641–675. Leiden and New York: Brill, 1995.

———. 'Confessionalization: Historical and Scholarly Perspectives of a Comparative and Interdisciplinary Paradigm'. In *Confessionalization in Europe, 1555–1700: Essays in Memory of Bodo Nischan,* edited by John M. Headley, et al., 22–35. Aldershot: Ashgate, 2004.

Schimmel, Annemarie. 'Abū'l-Ḥusayn al-Nūrī: "Qibla of the Lights".' In *Heritage of Sufism-1.*

Schulze, Winfried. 'Gerhard Oestreichs Begriff "Sozialdisziplinierung in der frühen Neuzeit"'. *Zeitschrift für historische Forschung* 20 (1987): 265–302.

Selçuk, İklil. 'Suggestions on the Social Meaning and Functions of *Akhi* Communities and Their Hospices in Medieval Anatolia'. In *Architecture and Landscape in Medieval Anatolia, 1100–1500*, edited by Patricia Blessing and Rachel Goshgarian, 95–113. Edinburgh: Edinburgh University Press, 2017.

Şener, Cemal. *Alevilik Olayı: Bir Başkaldırının Kısa Tarihçesi*. Istanbul: Yön Yayıncılık, 1989.

Sevgen, Nazmi. 'Efsaneden Hakikate'. *Tarih Dünyası*, no. 21 (1951): 882–883.

Sezgin, Abdülkadir. 'Eren ve Evliya Kavramının Dini Tarihi Folklorik İzahı ve Eren İnancı Üzerine Düşünceler'. In *I. Uluslararası Türk Dünyası Eren ve Evliyalar Kongresi Bildirileri*, 457–508. Ankara: Anadolu Erenleri Kültür Ve Sanat Vakfı, 1998.

Shankland, David. *The Alevis in Turkey: The Emergence of a Secular Islamic Tradition*. London and New York: Routledge Curzon, 2003.

———. 'The Buyruk in Alevi Village Life? Thoughts from the Field of Rival Sources of Religious Inspiration'. In *Syncrétismes et hérésies dans l'Orient seldjoukide et ottoman (XIV–XVIII siècle), Actes du Colloque du Collège de France, octobre 2001*, edited by Gilles Veinstein, 311–323. Paris: Peeters, 2005.

Shaybi, Mustafa Kamil. *Sufism and Shi^{c}ism*. Surbiton: LAAM, 1991.

Shaw, Rosalind and Charles Stewart, eds. *Syncretism/Anti-Syncretism: The Politics of Religious Synthesis*. London: Routledge, 1994.

Shek, Richard. 'The Alternative Moral Universe of Religious Dissenters in Ming-Qing China'. In *Religion and the Early Modern State: Views from China, Russia, and the West*, edited by James D. Tracy and Marguerite Ragnow, 13–51. Reissue edn. Cambridge: Cambridge University Press, 2010.

Şimşek, Mehmet. *Doğu Anadolu'da Sosyal Ve Kültürel Yönleriyle örnek Bir Köyümüz: Hıdır Abdal Sultan Ocağı*. 3rd edn. Istanbul: Can Yayınları, 1991.

Slane, M. le Baron de. *Bibliothèque nationale, Département des manuscrits: Catalogue des manuscrits arabes*. Paris: Imprimerie nationale, 1883–1895.

Sohrweide, Hanna. 'Der Sieg der Ṣafaviden in Persien und seine Rückwirkungen auf die Schiiten Anatoliens im 16. Jahrhundert'. *Der Islam* 41 (1965): 95–223.

———. 'Dichter und Gelehrte aus dem Osten im osmanischen Reich'. *Der Islam* 46 (1970): 263–302.

Soileau, Mark. 'Conforming Haji Bektash: A Saint and His Followers between Orthopraxy and Heteropraxy'. *Die Welt Des Islams* 54 (2014): 423–459.

———. *Humanist Mystics: Nationalism and the Commemoration of Saints in Turkey*. Salt Lake City: The University of Utah Press, 2018.

Solak, İbrahim. *XVI. Asırda Maraş Kazası (1526–1563)*. Ankara: Akçağ Yayınları, 2004.

Sönmez, Ebru. *İdris-i Bidlisi: Ottoman Kurdistan and Islamic Legitimacy*. Istanbul: Libra Kitap, 2012.

Söylemez, Faruk. 'Anadolu'da Sahte Şah İsmail İsyanı'. *Sosyal Bilimler Enstitüsü* 17 (2004): 71–90.

Stewart, Devin J. *Islamic Legal Orthodoxy: Twelver Shiite Responses to the Sunni Legal System*. Salt Lake City: University of Utah Press, 1998.

Subrahmanyam, Sanjay. 'Turning the Stones Over: Sixteenth-Century Millenarianism from the Tagus to the Ganges'. *The Indian Economic and Social History Review* 40, no. 2 (April–June 2003): 129–161.

Sümer, Faruk. 'XVI. Asırda Anadolu, Suriye ve Irak'ta Yaşayan Türk Aşiretlerine Umumi Bir Bakış'. *İstanbul Üniversitesi İktisat Fakültesi Mecmuası* XI (1952): 509–523.

———. *Oğuzlar (Türkmenler): Tarihleri, Boy Teşkilato, Destanları*. Ankara: Ankara Üniversitesi, 1972.

———. *Çepniler: Anadolu'nun Bir Türk Yurdu Haline Gelmesinde Önemli Rol Oynayan Oğuz Boyu*. Istanbul: Türk Dünyası Araştırmaları Vakfı, 1992.

———. *Safevi Devletinin Kuruluşu ve Gelişmesinde Anadolu Türklerinin Rolü*. Ankara: Türk Tarih Kurumu, 1992.

Svendsen, Jonas. 'Bektaşi Demiş: Orthodox Sunni, Heterodox Bektasian Incongruity in Bektaşi Fıkraları'. PhD diss., The University of Bergen, Bergen, 2012.

Tambar, Kabir. *The Reckoning of Pluralism: Political Belonging and the Demands of History in Turkey*. Stanford: Stanford University Press, 2014.

Tanman, M. Baha. 'Hacı Bektāş-ı Velī Külliyesi'. In *DİA*.

Tansel, Selahattin. *Sultan II. Bâyezit'in Siyasî Hayatı*. Istanbul: Milli Eğitim Basımevi, 1966.

———. *Yavuz Sultan Selim*. Ankara: Milli Eğitim Basımevi, 1969.

Tapper, Richard. 'Holier Than Thou: Islam in Three Tribal Societies'. In *Islam in Tribal Societies: From the Atlas to the Indus*, edited by Akbar S. Ahmed and David M. Hart, 244–265. London and Boston and Melbourne and Henley: Routledge & Kegan Paul, 1984.

Tarım, Cevat Hakkı. *Tarihte Kirşehri-Gülşehri Ve Babailer-Ahiler-Bektaşler*. 3rd edn. Istanbul: Yeniçağ Matbaası, 1948.

Taştemir, Mehmet. *XVI. Yüzyılda Adıyaman (Behisni, Hısn-ı Mansur, Gerger, Kâhta) Sosyal ve İktisadî Tarihi*. Ankara: Türk Taih Kurumu, 1999.

Teber, Ömer Faruk. 'Osmanlı Belgelerinde Alevilik İçin Kullanılan Dinî-Siyasî Tanımlamalar'. *Dinî Araştırmalar* 10 (May–August 2007): 19–38.

Tekindağ, M. C. Şehabettin. 'Şah Kulu Baba Tekeli İsyanı'. *Belgelerle Türk Tarihi Dergisi* 3–4 (1967): 34–39, 54–59.

———. 'Yeni Kaynak ve Vesikaların Işığı altında Yavuz Sultan Selim'in İran Seferi'. *Tarih Dergisi* 17, no. 22 (1967): 49–86.

———. 'Selim-nâmeler'. *İÜEF Tarih Enstitüsü Dergisi* 1 (October 1970): 197–230.

Terzioğlu, Derin. 'Sufis in the Age of State-building and Confessionalization'. In *The Ottoman World*, edited by Christine Woodhead, 86–99. New York: Routledge, 2012.

———. 'How to Conceptualize Ottoman Sunnitization: A Historiographical Discussion'. *Turcica* 44 (2012–2013): 301–338.

———. 'Where ᶜ*İlm-i Ḥāl* Meets Catechism: Islamic Manuals of Religious Instruction in the Ottoman Empire in the Age of Confessionalization'. *Past and Present* 220 (2013): 79–114.

Tietze, Andreas. 'A Document on the Persecution of Sectarians in Early Seventeenth-Century Istanbul'. In *Bektachiyya: Études sur l'ordre mystique des Bektachis et les groupes relevant de Hadji Bektach*, edited by Alexandre Popovic and Gilles Veinstein, 165–170. Istanbul: Isis Press, 1995.

al-Tikriti, Nabil. 'Kalam in the Service of the State: Apostasy and the Defining of Ottoman Islamic Identity'. In *Legitimizing the Order: The Ottoman Rhetoric of State Power*, edited by Hakan T. Karateke and Maurus Reinkowski, 131–149. Leiden: Brill, 2005.

———. 'Ibn-i Kemal's Confessionalism and the Construction of an Ottoman Islam'. In *Living in the Ottoman Realm: Empire and Identity, 13th to 20th Centuries*, edited by Christine Isom-Verhaaren and Kent F. Schull, 95–107. Bloomington: Indiana University Press, 2016.

Togan, Ahmed Zeki Velidi. *Umumi Türk Tarihine Giriş*. Istanbul: İsmail Akgün Matbaası, 1946.

———. 'Londra ve Tahrandaki İslâmî yazmalardan bazılarına dair'. *İslâm Tetkikleri Enstitüsü Dergisi* 3, nos 1–2 (1959–1960): 132–160.

Trimingham, J. Spencer. *The Sufi Orders in Islam*. London: Oxford University Press, 1973.

Trouillot, Michel-Rolph. *Silencing the Past: Power and the Production of History*. Boston: Beacon Press, 1995.

Tucker, William F. 'The Kūfan Ghulāt and Millenarian (Mahdist) Movements in Mongol-Türkmen Iran'. In *Unity in Diversity: Mysticism, Messianism and the Construction of Religious Authority in Islam*, edited by Orkhan Mir-Kasimov, 177–194. Leiden: Brill, 2014.

Turan, Osman. *Doğu Anadolu Türk Devletleri Tarihi*. Istanbul: İstanbul Matbaası, 1973.

Türkdoğan, Orhan. *Alevi-Bektaşi Kimliği: Sosyo-antropolojik Araştırma*. Istanbul: Timaş Yayınları, 1995.

Uğur, Ahmet. *The Reign of Sultan Selīm I in the Light of the Selīm-nāme Literature*. Berlin: Klaus Schwarz Verlag, 1985.

(Ülken), Hilmi Ziya. 'Anadolu'da Dini Ruhiyat Müşahadeleri: Geyikli Baba'. *Mihrab Mecmuası* nos 13–14 (1340/1924): 434–448.

———. 'Anadolu'da Dini Ruhiyat Müşahedeleri: Hacı Bektaş-ı Velî'. *Mihrab* 1, nos 15–16 (1342/1924): 515–530.

Uluçam, Abdüsselâm. *Irak'taki Türk Mimari Eserleri*. Ankara: Kültür Bakanlığı, 1989.

Uluçay, Çağatay. 'Yavuz Sultan Selim Nasıl Padişah Oldu?' *İstanbul Üniversitesi Edebiyat Fakültesi Tarih Dergisi* 6, no. 9 (March 1954): 53–90; 7, no. 10 (September 1954): 117–142; 8, nos 11–12 (September 1955): 185–200.

Ulusoy, A. Celâlettin. *Hûnkar Hacı Bektaş Veli ve Alevî-Bektaşî Yolu*. 2nd edn. Hacıbektaş–Kırşehir: n.p., 1986.

Ünal, Mehmet Ali. *XVI. Yüzyılda Harput Sancağı (1518–1566)*. Ankara: Türk Tarih Kurumu, 1989.

———. *XVI. Yüzyılda Çemişgezek Sancağı*. Ankara: Türk Tarih Kurumu, 1999.

Ünal, Yusuf. 'More Than Mere Polemic: The Adventure of the *Risālah-i Ḥusniyah* in the Safavid, Ottoman, and Indian Lands'. MA thesis, Boğaziçi University, Istanbul, 2016.

Üstün, İsmail Safa. 'Heresy and Legitimacy in the Ottoman Empire in the Sixteenth Century'. PhD diss., University of Manchester, Manchester, 1991.

Uzunçarşılı, İsmail Hakkı. *Osmanlı Tarihi*. 6th edn. 4 Vols. Ankara: Türk Tarih Kurumu, 1995.

Uzunçarşılı, İsmail Hakkı and Rıdvan Nafiz. *Sivas Şehri*, edited by Recep Toparlı. Sivas: Sivas Ticaret Ve Sanayi Odası, 1997.

Veinstein, Gilles. 'Les premières mesures de Bâyezîd II contre les Kızılbaş'. In *Syncrétismes et hérésies dans l'Orient seldjoukide et ottoman (XIV–XVIII siècle), Actes du Colloque du Collège de France, octobre 2001,* 225–136. Paris: Peeters, 2005.

Vorhoff, Karin. 'Academic and Journalistic Publications on the Alevi and Bektashi of Turkey'. In *Alevi Identity: Cultural, Religious and Social Perspectives,* eds T. Olsson, et al., 23–50. Istanbul: Isis Press, 1998.

———. 'The Past in the Future: Discourses on the Alevis in Contemporary Turkey'. In *Turkey's Alevi Enigma: A Comprehensive Overview,* eds Paul J. White and Joost Jongerden, 93–108. Leiden: Brill, 2003.

Vryonis, Speros. *The Decline of Medieval Hellenism in Asia Minor and the Process of Islamization from the Eleventh through the Fifteenth Century.* Berkeley: University of California Press, 1971.

Walbridge, John. *The Wisdom of the Mystic East: Suhrawardī and Platonic Orientalism*. Albany: State University of New York, 2001.

Walsh, J. R. 'The Historiography of Ottoman–Safavid Relations in the Sixteenth and Seventeenth Centuries'. In *Historians of the Middle East*, edited by Bernard Lewis and P. M. Holt, 197–211. Oxford: Oxford University Press, 1962.

Walsham, Alexandra. *Charitable Hatred: Tolerance and Intolerance in England, 1500–1700.* Manchester: Manchester University Press, 2006.

Watenpaugh, Heghnar Zeitlian. 'Deviant Dervishes: Space, Gender, and the Construction of Antinomian Piety in Ottoman Aleppo'. *International Journal of Middle East Studies* 37 (2005): 535–565.

White, Sam. *The Climate of Rebellion in the Early Modern Empire*. Cambridge and New York: Cambridge University Press, 2011.

Winter, Michael. 'The *Ashrāf* and the *Naqīb Al-ashrāf* in Ottoman Egypt and Syria: A Comparative Analysis'. In *Sayyids and Sharifs in Muslim Societies: The Living Links to the Prophet*, edited by Morimoto Kazuo, 139–158. London and New York: Routledge, 2012.

Winter, Stefan. *The Shiites of Lebanon under Ottoman Rule, 1516–1788.* Cambridge and New York: Cambridge University Press, 2010.

Wolper, Ethel Sara. 'Khiḍr, Elwan Çelebi and the Conversion of Sacred Sanctuaries in Anatolia'. *Muslim World* 90, nos 3–4 (Autumn 2000): 309–322.

———. *Cities and Saints: Sufism and the Transformation of Urban Space in Medieval Anatolia*. University Park: Pennsylvania State University Press, 2003.

Woods, John E. *The Aqquyunlu: Clan, Federation, Empire*. 2nd edn. Salt Lake City: The University of Chicago Press, 1999.

Yalçın, Alemdar and Hacı Yılmaz. 'Kargın Ocaklı Boyu ile İlgili Yeni Belgeler'. *Hacı Bektaş Velî Araştırma Dergisi* 21 (Spring 2002): 13–87.

Yaman, Ali. *Alevilik-Bektaşilik Bibliyografyası*. Mannheim: Alevi-Bektaşi Kültür Enstitüsü, 1998.

———. *Kızılbaş Alevi Ocakları*. Istanbul: Şahkulu Sultan Külliyesi, 1998.

Yaman, Mehmet. *Alevilik: İnanç–Edeb–Erkân*. Istanbul, 1994; reprint, Istanbul: Demos Yayınları, 2012.

Yetkin, Çetin. *Türk Halk Hareketleri ve Devrimler*. Istanbul: Milliyet Yayınları, 1980.

Yıldırım, Abbas. *Seyit Şah İbrahim Veli Ocağı*. Ankara: n.p., 2006.

Yıldırım, Rıza. 'Turkomans between Two Empires: The Origins of the Qizilbash Identity in Anatolia (1447–1514)'. PhD diss., Bilkent University, Ankara, 2008.

Yılmaz, Hüseyin. 'İran'dan Sünnî Kaçışı ve Osmanlı Devleti'nde Safevî Karşıtı Propagandanın Yaygınlaşması: Hüseyin b. Abdullah el-Şirvânî'nin Mesiyanik Çağrısı'. In *Uluslararası Diyarbakır Sempozyumu, 2–5 Kasım 2016*, edited by Ufuk Bircan, et al., 299–310. Diyarbakır: T. C. Diyarbakır Valiliği, 2017.

———. *Caliphate Redefined: The Mystical Turn in Ottoman Political Thought*. Princeton: Princeton University Press, 2018.

Yılmaz, Meltem. 'Türkiye'de Cönkler Üzerine Yapılan Çalışmalara Dair'. *Tullis Journal*, 1, no. 1 (June 2016): 37–53.

Yinanç, Refet. *Dulkadir Beyliği*. Ankara: Türk Tarih Kurumu, 1989.

Yörükân, Yusuf Ziya. *Anadolu'da Alevîler ve Tahtacılar,* edited by Turhan Yörükân. Ankara: T. C. Kültür Bakanlığı, 2002.

Yorulmaz, Bülent. 'Kerbela ve Fuzuli'ye Dair'. In *I. Uluslararası Hacı Bektaş Veli Sempozyumu Bildirileri,* 371–401. Ankara: Hacı Bektaş Anadolu Kültür Vakfı, 2000.

Yücel, Sabri. *Keçeci Ahi Baba ve Zaviyesinde Yetişen Ünlü Kişiler*. Istanbul: Can Yayınları, 2003.

Yüksel, Hasan. 'Selçuklular Döneminden Kalma Bir Vefaî Zaviyesi (Şeyh Marzubân Zaviyesi)'. *Vakıflar Dergisi* 25 (1995): 235–250.

———. 'Ahi Vakıfları'. In *Uluslararası Kurluşunun 700. Yıl Dönümünde Bütün Yönleriyle Osmanlı Devleti Kongresi, 7–9 Nisan 1999*, edited by Alâaddin Aköz, et al., 157–168. Konya: Selçuklu Üniversitesi, 2000.

———. 'Bir Babaî (Vefaî) Şeyhi Zaviyesi (Şeyh Behlül Baba)'. *Osmanlı Araştırmaları* 21 (2001): 97–107.

Yürekli, Zeynep. *Architecture and Hagiography in the Ottoman Empire: The Politics of Bektashi Shrines in the Classical Age*. Farnham and Burlington: Ashgate, 2012.

Zarcone, Thierry. 'La mort initiatique dans l'alévisme et le Bektachisme: de la 'résurrection' de 'Alī à la pendaison de Ḥallāj'. In *L'Ésotérisme Shiᶜite, ses racines et ses prolongements*, edited by M. A. Amir-Moezzi, et al., 781–798. Turnhout: Brepols Publishers, 2016.

———. 'The Bektashi-Alevi "Dance of the Crane" in Turkey: A Shamanic Heritage?' In *Shamanism and Islam: Sufism, Healing Rituals and Spirits in the Muslim World*, 203–216. London and New York: I. B. Tauris, 2017.

Zarinebaf-Shahr, Fariba. 'Qizilbash "Heresy" and Rebellion in Ottoman Anatolia during the Sixteenth Century'. *Anatolia Moderna/Yeni Anadolu* 7 (1977): 1–15.

Zeeden, Ernst Walter. *Die Entstehung der Konfessionen: Grundlagen und Formen der Konfessionsbildung im Zeitalter der Glaubenskämpfe*. Munich: Oldenbourg, 1965.

———. *Konfessionbildung: Studien zu Reformation, Gegenreformation und katholischer Reform.* Stuttgart: Klett-Cotta, 1985.

Zelyut, Rıza. *Öz Kaynaklarına Göre Alevilik.* Istanbul: Anadolu Kültürü Yayınları, 1990.

Index

Note: *italics* indicates a figure

ᶜAbbas I, Shah, 191, 216n, 225, 230, 240, 242–3, 250, 254n
Abbasids
  Abbasid/Sunni orthodoxy, 48
  Mustansır bi-llah, 109
  revolution against the Umayyads, 158, 259, 298
  as usurpers, 116
ᶜAbd al-Hamid Sufi, 63
ᶜAbd al-Qadir al-Jilani, 50, 77n, 142n
ᶜAbd al-Rahman Tafsunji, 56, 59
Abdal Musa, 87n, 136n, 145, 157, 183n
Abdals of Rum
  association with the Karbala convent, 25, 171–7, 192, 194–6
  dervish community of, 91, 155–64
  emergence of the cult of Hacı Bektaş, 157, 164
  Hacı Bektaş's influence on, 161–2
  Hacı Bektaş's initial encounter with, 150, 151, 154–6, 160
  incorporation into the Bektashis, 9, 148, 157, 170–1, 173, 194–5
  incorporation into the Kizilbash/Alevi milieu, 173–4, 177–8
  links with the Babaᵓis, 148, 157, 159–60, 171–3
  links with the Wafaᵓiyya, 160–3
  origins of, 159
  pro-ᶜAlid-Shiᶜi character of, 158, 160–2
  as proto-Bektashis, 164–7
  relations with the Ottoman state, 168, 169–70
  rituals and traditions of, 158, 172
  and the Safavids, 173–6
  Seyyid Battal Gazi and, 162–4
ᶜAbdülhüseyin Dede, 195, 197, 210–11
ᶜAbdülmüᵓmin Dede, 193–7, 216n
Abu Bakr al-Siddiq, 69
Abu Bakr b. al-Hawwari, 66–9, 85n, 126
Abu Hamid al-Ghazali, 50, 279–80, 295
Abu Muhammad Talha al-Shunbuki, 49, 53, 61, 64–9
Abu Muslim Khorasani, 158, 298
Abu Saᶜid b. Abu'l-Khayr, 67
Abu'l-Faraj b. al-Jawzi, 51, 80n
Abu'l-Hasan al-Kharaqani, 67–8
Abu'l-Wafaᵓ al-Baghdadi
  in Alevi source documents, 45
  ᶜAlid orientation, 69–71, 74, 126
  asceticism of, 124
  association with Geyikli Baba, 94
  Bakri *silsila*, 69, 74
  celibacy of, 54–5, 172
  devotional practices, 72–3
  disciples of, 59–61, 103
  early life as a bandit, 53, 67–8
  as eponym of the Wafaᵓi Sufi tradition, 45, 73–4
  hagiography, 46, 48–50, 51–8, 63, 66–7, 70, 92
  heresy trial in Baghdad, 44, 51, 63, 68, 71–2
  initiatic chain, 63–5, 66
  initiation to Sufism, 53–4
  Kurdish identity, 52–3, 62
  lay followers of, 61–3
  life of, 48–52

Abu'l-Wafa° al-Baghdadi (*cont.*)
miracles of, 53, 73, 172
political involvement of, 63
populist outlook, 62–3
as a preacher-master, 61–2
provincial/tribal background, 67–8
relationship with °Adi b. Musafir, 59–60, 101
saintly powers of, 53, 59, 73
Sayyid Matar as spiritual heir to, 55–6, 58, 59
sayyid-ship of, 53
spiritual connection with Bayazid Bistami, 67, 75
spiritual legacy, 45–6, 172
spiritual lineage, 63–9, 73–4
spiritual successor(s), 55–9, 90
Sunni sectarian identity, 69, 70–2, 74
Sunni–Shi°i antagonism during the lifetime of, 48–9
this-worldly and renunciatory orientations, 54–5, 160
tomb-shrine of, 59, 172
written sources on, 46–7
see also Wafa°iyya
°Adi b. Musafir, 59–60, 101
Ağuiçen *ocak*
Alevi sources from, 18, *19*, 104
claim to the title of *mürşid*, 12, 106–8
*dede*s affiliated with, 105–6
in Eastern Anatolia, 104, 105
founding of, 104–5
tomb-shrine of, 105–7
Wafa°i *ijāza* sources, 111–13, 126–9, 138n, 144n, 240
Ahi
Ahis in Anatolia, 93, 123
connection of the Dede Kargın *ocak*, 122–3, 243
ijāza, 22, 93, 122–3
and the Kizilbash, 125, 227–8, 243, 324
see also Turabi Baba; Ahi Mahmud Veli
Ahi Evran, 122
Ahi Mahmud Veli (Keçeci Baba), 123
Ahi Ṭursan b. Habil, 122
Ahl al-bayt, 71, 161, 192, 286
Ahmad al-Rifa°i, 49, 50, 84n
Ahmed Yesevi, 9, 36n, 88n, 103, 105, 150–5, 180–1n, 210
Akdağ, Mustafa, 309n, 313n
Akhi *see* Ahi
Akkoyunlu, 222, 267–70, 272, 307n
Akyazılı Baba convent, 292
Aleppo, 47, 60, 97–8, 113, 123, 236
Alevi sources
Abu'l-Wafa° in, 45
on the adoptee sons of Abu'l-Wafa°, 56
Ahi *ijāza*, 93, 122–3
on Alevi–Bektashi relations, 147
copying and recopying of, 21–2
on *dedes*' visits to Iraq, 203
documents and manuscripts in private hands, 17–24
ḫilāfetnāmes, 231–2
from the Imam Husayn complex, 109, 111–12, 126, 203
from Iraq, 23, 188, 190
from the kadi courts, 293
manuscripts of literary religious works, 24
*ocak*s (family lineages) in, 299–301, *300*
of Safavi *ḫalīfe* network in, 231
Safavid-related documents, 23
sample Alevi documents, 20–1
sayyid genealogies, 23
*shajaras/şecere*s, 231–2
types of documents, 22–3
Wafa°i *ijāza*s, 22–3, 172–3
ziyāretnāmes, 5, 23, 125, 188, 203, *204*
see also Buyruk manuscripts
Alevi–Bektashi
Alevi–Bektashi relations, 145–8
Central Asian genealogy of, 11
the Köprülü paradigm, 8–12
as Turkmen phenomenon, 10
unity of Allah, Muhammad and °Ali, 75
the Wafa°i and, 25–6
Alevi–Bektashi mystical poetry, 33n, 34n
Alevis
bağlama (sacred lute), 1, 33n
community identity of, 2, 3–4
cultural revival of, 3, 13, 18, 322
as a dissentient religious community, 5–6
forefathers of, 2
within high/folk Islam dualism, 9, 10, 11
Kurdish-speaking Alevis, 12–13
musahiblik, 16, 75
oral tradition, 45
in relation to Islam, 5
in relation to Sufism, 5
semah (ritual dance), 75
shamanism in, 12
syncretism in, 12
teachings and beliefs, 4
term, 5
Zazaki-speaking Alevis, 12–13

Index

ᶜAli b. Abi Talib
initiatic chains and, 64, 69, 111–12, 122, 175, 235, 263
shrine of, 190, 196, 198
and the term Alevi, 4
ᶜAli b. Hayti, 56, 59, 69
Ali Baba convent, 291
ᶜAlidism
Abu'l-Wafaᵓ's ᶜAlid orientation, 69–71, 74, 126, 161
within Alevism, 5, 8, 297
ᶜAlid Sunnism, 70, 86n, 126, 143n, 161, 258, 286
of the Halvetis, 266, 285
of the Wafaᵓi tradition, 69–71, 74
Amasya, 105, 111, 266, 270, 276, 277, 281, 289

Anatolia
the Ahis in, 93, 123
heterodox tradition in, 148
Safavi deputies in, 231–8
socio-cultural landscape of, 89–90
in the thirteenth century, 149, 156
Wafaᵓi presence in, 90, 102–4
Antep, 121, 122, 228
antinomianism
of Abu'l-Wafaᵓ, 60, 71, 73, 74
of the Bektashi, 172
of Hacı Bektaş, 152
identification of Sufis through, 286
tensions with the Ottoman Empire, 90, 158, 169
Ardabil
communication with Anatolia, 211
convent in, 16, 147, 232, 238, 297, 325
decree against the Sufis of Ardabil, 262, 266, 292
the Safavids from, 220–1, 236
Sayyid Süleyman in, 236–8
the tradition of Ardabil, 26, 235–6, 244, 255n, 325
ᶜAşıkpaşazade (Aspz), 91–6, 134n, 136n, 150, 152, 157, 163, 307n, 310n
ᶜAskeri from Edirne (Edirneli Askeri), 201
ᶜAyna Khatun, 60, 172

Baba İlyas, 92–4, 98, 114, 121–2, 136n, 141n, 152, 154, 159, 163, 181n
Baba Samit, 174–5
Babaᵓi revolt, 9, 11, 93, 103, 114, 123, 148–9, 152, 159, 181n
Babas/Babagans
belief in the celibacy of Hacı Bektaş, 146, 165–7
bifurcation of the Bektashis, 166–7, 171, 177, 203
Karbala convent's significance for, 194–5
links with the Abdals, 148, 157, 159–60, 171–3
links with the Abdals and the Bektashis, 148, 157, 171–3
the station of celibacy, 171, 173
Badawiyya order, 60
Badri family, 60, 182n, 138n
Baghdad
Abu'l-Wafaᵓ's interrogation in, 44, 51, 63, 68, 71
Baghdad-centred normative Sufism, 46, 64
Bektashi convents in, 190–1, 196, 199–200, 201, 202, 211
kadi courts, 202
Kizilbash persecutions in, 189, 288, 296
as Kizilbash stronghold, 189–90
Madrasat al-Mustansiriyya, 109
Namık Paşa, 199
Safavids' victory in, 191
the Seljuk Turks in, 48
Shah ᶜAbbas's conquest of, 191, 211, 242
Bahlul Baba (Behlül Baba), 96–9, 121
Balım Sultan, 151, 167–9, 177, 186n, 266
Balkans
the Alevis in, 2, 19, 228, 244, 297, 299
the Bektashi of, 150, 173, 203
ġāzīs of, 150–1, 266–7
the Kizilbash in, 228, 230, 244, 282, 297, 299, 324
Şahkulu Revolt in, 264
see also Bedreddinis
Baqaᵓ b. Batu, 59, 77n
Bargini, village of, 105
Basra, 45, 49, 64, 65, 66, 70, 74
Battle of Çaldıran, 28, 228–31, 268, 272, 275–6, 277, 290
Bayazid Bistami, 67, 68, 75
Bayezid II, Sultan
appointment of Balım Sultan, 151, 167, 266
decree against the Sufis of Ardabil, 262, 265–6, 307n
internal consolidation policies, 267
Ottoman civil war, 260, 263, 269, 270, 272

Bayezid II, Sultan (*cont.*)
patronage of the Halveti Sufi order, 266
relations with the Safavids, 237, 265–7
Selim I's ascent to power, 263
Bedreddinis, 228, 279; *see also* Şahin Bedriddin
Behlül Semerkandi convent, 98–9
Bektaş Dede (an Alevi *dede* visiting Karbala), 205–8, *206*, *207*
Bektashi
Abdals and proto-Bektashis, 157–8, 163–7, 177, 266
Alevi–Bektashi relations, 3, 9, 98, 103, 117, 145–8, 240
assimilation into Sunni Islam, 170, 286
association with the Janissaries, 145, 146
bifurcation of into the Babagan and Çelebi branches, 151, 166–7, 171, 177, 214n
compared to Kizilbash/Alevi communities, 145–6
convents in Iraq, 16, 23, 190–203, 207–12, 217n, 218n, 286
Hacı Bektaş as eponym of, 9, 145, 152
hagiographies, 95, 150, 180n
heterodoxy of, 170
incorporation of the Abdals into, 9, 157, 170–1, 173, 194–5
links with the Babaʾis and the Abdals, 148, 157, 171–3
Najaf convent, 198–9
and the Ottoman state, 168–71
parallel ritual practices with the Wafaʾi Sufi tradition, 75, 172–3
promotion of by the Ottoman state, 177
rituals and traditions of, 154, 162, 172–3
and the Safavids, 174–6
see also Alevi–Bektashi; Babas/ Babagans; Çelebis
Binyılın Türküsü (*The Saga of the Millennium*), 1, 2
Bozok, 290
Burak (the mythical horse of the Prophet Muhammad), 5
Buyids, 48, 79n
Buyruk manuscripts
Alevi sources, 18, 21, 24
chronological evolution of, 239–40
Hacı Bektaş in, 240
İmam Cafer *Buyruk*s, 239, 240
Kitāb-ī Maḳām-ī, 244
Menāḳīb texts, 239
overview of, 24, 238–44, 252n, 254n
Safavids, 174, 228, 230, 255n, 296
Seyh Safi *Buyruk*s, 239, 240–3
and *futuwwa*-related literature, 123, 253n

Çandarlı Halil, 91–2
Celal Abbas *ocak* (aka Şah Ali Abbas), 18–19, 21, 235, 299, 300
Celalzade Mustafa, 269, 271
Çelebis
Alevi and (Çelebi) Bektashi identities, 146
authority over convents, 146, 147, 166, 170–1
bifurcation of the Bektashis, 151, 166–7, 177, 184n, 185n, 194–5, 214n
claims of supreme spiritual authority, 146–7
icāzetnāmes issued by, 23, 25, 209–10
influence on the Kizilbash/Alevi communities, 105, 178n, 238
Otman Baba's opposition to, 165–7
celibacy
of Abu'l-Wafaʾ, 54–5, 172
celibate Abdals/Babagans at the Karbạla convent, 194–5
of Hacı Bektaş, 146, 166–7
and radical dervishes, 51, 158
sexual abstinence of Otman Baba, 167
the station of celibacy, 171, 173
cem (Alevi ritual)
dar-ı Mansur, 5, 6, 7
görgü cemi, 16
of the Kizilbash/Alevis, 284, 296–7, 299
traditional form of, 1, 4–5, 16, 239, 299
Cemal Abdal *ocak*, 173
çerāğı (candle lighter), 195, 209–11, 219n, 220
communal Sufi affiliations *see* Sufism
confessional ambiguity, 10, 36n, 86n; *see also* ʿAlidism
confessionalisation
confessional homogeneity of the Safavids, 259
the confessional turn in the Ottoman state, 259–60, 262–3
confessionalisation theory, 256, 257–62, 302n
Selim I's confessional turn, 259, 263, 270–2
Sunni confessionalisation, 27, 29, 97, 257, 259–62, 274, 279–3, 285, 288, 290, 293, 301
see also Kizilbash confessionalisation

convents
  Akyazılı Baba convent, 292
  Ali Baba convent, 291
  in and around Kirkuk, 190, 201–3
  Behlül Semerkandi convent, 98–9
  Bektashi convents in Iraq, 190–2, 200–3, 286
  Çelebis authority over, 146, 147, 166, 170–1
  conversion into mosques, 290–1
  endowments for, 96–7, 98–9
  Gürgür Baba convent, 190, 201, 202
  Hızır İlyas convent, 190, 199–200, 203, 217n
  home convents, 298–9
  Merdan ᶜAli, 202–3
  Najaf convent, 190–1, 198–9
  ocak connections to, 16
  Qalminiyya convent, 52, 58–9
  Saruyatar convent, 292
  Seyh Çoban convent, 99–101, 130, 137n
  Seyyid Battal Gazi convent, 149, 158, 164, 169–71
  transfer to Sunni affiliates, 291–2, 298
  T-type convent mosques, 285
  see also Şahin Baba convent; Kırşehir convent; Karbala convent
Çorum, 92, 101, 121, 276, 277, 281

Daftari family, 202
Darraj family, 196, 216n
dede families
  Alevi documents and manuscripts in private hands, 17–24
  allegiance to *mürşid ocak*s, 15
  mobility of, 14–15
  ocak affiliations of, 16
  *shajaras/şecere*s, 205–8, 206, 207
  visits to Iraq, 203–10, 232
  visits to Karbala, 188, 191–2
  written *ḫilāfetnāmes* from Karbala convent, 208–10
  *see also ocak*s (family lineages)
Dede Kargın, 18, 42n, 104, 111, 114–15, 117
Dede Kargın *ocak*
  affinity with the Wafaʾi order, 114, 121–2
  Ahi connection, 122–3
  Ahi *ijāza*, 122–3, 243
  area of influence, 104
  in Bimare, Malatya province, 117–21
  burial site, Bahri, 119–20, 119, 120
  connection to Khorasan, 114, 115–16
  Çorum branch, 121
  letter on the Safavid victory in Baghdad, 191
  in Mardin, 116–17, 122
  name of, 114–15
  sayyid descent of, 115–16
  Wafaʾi *ijāza* sources, 111, 121–2, 126
Dersim/Tunceli, 54n, 101, 103–7, 112
Derviş Hasan b. Derviş ᶜAşık (a Wafaʾi-Kizilbash dervish in Anatolia), 125
dervishes
  aesthetic dervishes, 94, 158–9
  in Anatolia, 90
  Ede Balı, 91
  practice of celibacy and, 171
  renunciatory dervish piety, 158–9
  Sayyid–Sufi relations in Iraq, 210–11
  sedentary/itinerant in Wafaʾi, 94–5
  see also Abdals of Rum; Babas/Babagans; Çelebis
devir, 4, 33n, 158, 223, 283, 284
devşirme, 264, 271
DeWeese, Devin, 10, 62–3, 85n, 143n, 153, 179n
Dhu'l-Nun al-Misri, 64, 66, 68
dissentient religious communities, 5–7, 17
Dressler, Markus, 10, 34n
Dulkadirli, 117–18
Dunmore, Mr (American Protestant missionary), 41n, 320–1
düşkünlük, 298
Düzmece Shah İsmaᶜil uprising, 169, 282

Ebā Müslim-nāme, 298
Ebussuᶜud Efendi, 259, 260, 279, 283–8, 294–5
Ede Balı
  as an Ahi leader, 93, 122
  association with the Wafaʾi/ Babaʾi milieu, 90, 92–3, 134n, 160
  kinship ties, 91–2, 96
  name of, 133n
  relationship with the House of Osman, 91–2
Ednai (Alevi poet), 114, 140n
Eflaki (Shams al-Din Ahmad al-ᶜAflaki al-ᶜArifi), 149, 151–2
Egypt, 46–7, 49, 60–1, 68, 76n, 82n, 111, 140n, 172
Elazığ, 104–5, 126–8, 300
Elvan Çelebi
  on Ede Balı, 92

Elvan Çelebi (*cont.*)
on Hacı Bektaş, 148, 152
Menāḳıbü'l-ḳudsiyye, 148–9
mentions of Dede Kargın, 114
significance of, 94
Emecen, Feridun, 306n, 307n, 308n
Erdebil Sufileri *see* Sufis of Ardabil
Erdebil süreği, 26, 235
Erzincan, 21, 98, 104, 126, 128, 240–4, 267, 268, 269, 310n, 311n
Eskişehir, 149, 158, 163, 171
Euphrates River, 104–5, 130, 195
Evliya Çelebi
Abu'l-Wafaᵓ's tomb-shrine, 59, 82n
Behlül Semerkandi's convent, 98–9
on Bektashi convents in Anatolia, 286
on Bektashi convents in Iraq, 191, 201
on the Bektashi in Safavid lands, 175–6
on the Hızır İlyas convent, 199
reference to Geyikli Baba, 95–6, 154
on the Seyyid Battal Gazi convent, 170–1

Faroqhi, Suraiya, 170
Fatima Bacı, 155
Fazl-Allah b. Ruzbihan Khunji, 222–3
fetvās
against the Kizilbash, 260–1, 275–6, 277–8, 280, 283–6, 287, 288
as part of a vilifying discourse, 261, 278–9, 286, 314n, 319n
the punishment of the Kizilbash, 294–5, 306n
separation between canonical worship and Sufi rituals, 283–5
see also Ebussuᶜud Efendi
Fleischer, Cornell H., 273, 247n, 304n
futuwwa/fütüvvet, 93, 123, 134n, 143n, 243; *see also* Ahi
Fuzuli, 195, 297

Garkiniyya, 122
ġāzīs
activities in the Caucasus, 221–2, 226–7
the cult of Hacı Bektaş, 157
as frontier warlords, 168
Junayd's *ġazīs*, 221, 226–7
links with the Sufis and dervishes, 90, 95
within the new Ottoman state, 168
the Ottomans as, 270–1, 272, 273
and the Safavids, 174
George of Hungary, 93–4, 149
Geyikli Baba, 87n, 90, 94–6, 98, 154, 157, 160
Ghulāt see Shiᶜi Islam
Giyaseddin Keyhusrev III, 96, 98, 99
Gölpınarlı, Abdülbâkî, 24–5, 41n, 123, 132n, 135n, 178n, 180n, 181n, 182n, 186n, 244, 252n, 254n
Gürgür Baba convent, 190, 201–2

Hacı Bektaş
in *Buyruk* manuscripts, 240
Çelebi family as descendants of, 146
cult of, 157, 168
Dede Kargın *ocak* and, 117
Elvan Çelebi on, 148, 152
emergence of the cult of, 149–50, 157, 164
figure of, 9, 94, 95, 145
genealogy of, 151
heterodoxy of, 152–3, 170
Hızır İlyas convent, 190, 191, 199–200, 203
initial encounter with the Abdals, 150, 151, 154–6, 160
legacy of for the Safavids, 174–5
links with the Ottoman state, 150–1
Maḳālāt, 181n
miracles of, 172
narrative sources for, 148
Shiᶜitisation of the Abdals of Rum, 161–2
shrine as a site of pilgrimage, 149
as a Sufi within Sunnism, 286
tomb-shrine of, 150–1
in the *Velāyetnāme*, 105, 150, 151, 152–3, 154–6, 164
visit to burial site of Seyyid Battal, 165
Wafaᵓi/Babᵓi affiliation, 151–2, 154
Yesevi affiliation, 151, 152, 153–4
see also Bektashi
Hacı Hüseyin Mazlum Baba, 201, 202
Hacı Tuğrul, 155–6, 160
Haddadiyya, 49, 53
hair cutting
as initiatic rite, 173
miqrāḍ, 124–5
and the station of celibacy, 171, 173
hakullah (God's due), 113
Hallac-ı Mansur (Mansur al-Hallaj), 65, 68, 69, 284
as symbol in Alevi rituals, 5–7
Halveti Sufi order, 134n, 266, 285, 316n
Hanafi *madhab*, 97–8, 200
Hanbalism, 48, 51, 66, 79n
Haririzade Mehmed Kemaleddin, 47, 66, 85n

Hata°i (Hatayi), 34n, 174, 223, 244, 255n, 297
Hawwariyya, 66
Haydar, Shaykh, 221–2, 226
Haydaris, 157, 159, 176, 181n, 186n, 222
Hayran Abdal, 127–8, 173
Hazım Agah, 194, 198, 199, 200
Hıdır Abdal *ocak*, 173
Hilla, 48, 205
Hın-ı Mansur (Adıyaman), 103, 122
Hızır İlyas convent, 190, 191, 199–200, 203
Horasan Erenleri (Sufi saints of Khorasan), 154
ḥull (incarnationism), 66
Hüsameddin Çelebi, 90, 93, 122, 132n, 135n
Husayn b. °Abdullah al-Shirvani, 272, 285
Husayn Ra°i, 101, 172; *see also* Şeyh Çoban
Hüseyin Hüsameddin, 98
Husniyya (Abu°l-Wafa°'s wife), 54, 55, 57

Ibn °Aqil, 51
Ibn Battuta, 194, 198, 199
Ibn Taymiyya, 279, 295
*ijāza/icāzetnāme*s
  of the Ağuiçen *ocak*, 111–12
  Ahi, 93, 122–3
  among Alevi sources, 22, 45
  of the Dede Kargın *ocak*, 121–3
  of the İmam Zeynel Abidin *ocak*, 108–11
  from the Karbala convent, 125
  the Wafa°i *ijāzas*, 56, 67, 103, 107–9, 111–12, 123–8, 131, 172, 297
Illuminationist (*Ishrāqi*) philosophy *see* Shihab al-Din Suhrawardi
Imam Hasan al-°Askari, shrine of, 190, 201
Imam Husayn
  descent from, 97, 111
  figure of, 126, 282
  shrine of, 109–12, 126, 147, 190, 192–7, 203, 209–11, 212n, 216n
  see also Karbala convent
Imam Ja°far al-Sadiq, 65, 67, 115, 239–41, 323
Imam Musa al-Kazim, shrine of, 190, 200, 202, 210
İmam Musa Kazım *ocak*, 228
Imam Rida°, 175, 176
İmam Zeynel Abidin *ocak* (*dede*s of Mineyik)
  archives of, 18–19, 129
  claim to the title of *mürşid*, 18, 19, 106–7, 108
  in Eastern Anatolia, 104, 106, 209
  ḫilāfetnāmes, 232–4, 233
  Wafa°i *ijāza* sources, 108–11, 128, 211, 231
  Wafa°i/Iraqi origins of, 104, 107, 113, 139n
Imber, C. H., 133n, 141n, 212n, 249n
Iraq
  al-Batiha region, 49
  Alevi sources from, 188, 190
  Bektashi convents in, 190–2, 200–3
  caliph al-Qadir bi-illah, 48
  dede families' visits to, 188, 191–2, 199, 203–10, 232
  Najaf convent, 198–9
  within Ottoman–Safavid rivalry, 188–9
  Safavid governors of Baghdad, 189–90
  Sayyid–Sufi relations in, 210–11
  shrine cities of, 189, 196
  Sunni political dominance, 48
  see also Karbala convent
Islam
  Alevism in relation to, 5
  dissentient religious communities from, 5–7
  High Islam/folk Islam distinction, 8–9, 10
  see also Shi°i Islam; Sunni Islam
Isma°il, Shah
  and the Akkoyunlu territories, 267, 268, 269–70, 272
  Düzmece Shah İsma°il uprising, 169
  on the *ġazīs*, 227
  hereditary shaykh of the Safavi, 2
  involvement in the Nur Ali Halife revolt, 268–9
  messianism in the poetry of, 223, 225
  pen name Hata°i, 174
  plans to conquer Rum, 268
  poetry of, 34n, 40n, 174, 223, 224
  proclamation of Twelver Shi°ism, 229
  Selim I's policy towards, 267–8, 269–70, 275
  treatment of his followers, 264
  uprisings by his followers, 263–5, 266, 268
istiḫāre, 54, 57

Janissaries, 145–6, 275
Junayd, Shaykh, 221–2, 226–7, 229, 235–6, 249n, 310n
Junayd al-Baghdadi, 61, 64–7

ka°aba (*ka°be*), 164
Kadıncık Ana, 166–7
Kafadar, Cemal, 10, 27, 36n, 47
Kalender Çelebi uprising, 168–9
Kara Pir Bad *ocak*, 18, 95n
Karakoyunlu, 221, 226, 227
Karamustafa, Ahmet T., 10–11, 25, 132n, 153–4, 157–8, 159
Karbala convent
  Abdals of Rum association with, 25, 171–2, 192, 194–5
  ᶜAbdülhüseyin Dede, last *postnişīn* of, 197, 216n
  Alevi sources from, 23, 192, 196, 197
  association with Alevi *ocaks*, 16, 25–6
  as Bektashi affiliated, 147, 171–2, 194–5, 197
  Darraj family, 196
  dede families' visits to, 188, 191–2
  endowment deed, 192–4
  founding of by ᶜAbdülmü°min Dede, 195
  image of, late nineteenth century, *193*
  in the nineteenth century, 197–8
  production of *shajaras*/*şeceres*, 205, 206
  significance of to the Babagan Bektashis, 194–5
  the tomb complex of Imam Husayn, 192
  the Wafa°i *ijāzas*, 125
  the Wafa°i-cum-Kizilbash *ocak*s and, 171–2
  written *ḫilāfetnāmes* from, 208–10
Katil (Kattal?) Gazi Kargıni, 115
Kazimiyya, 189, 190, 200, 201, 205
Keçeci Baba, *see* Ahi Mahmud Veli
Kerbela Dergâhı *see* Karbala convent
khalīfat al-khulafā°, 231
Kharijis, 61
Khawaja Mulla Isfahani, 272
khirqa (Sufi robe), 69, 124, 173
Khorasan
  Abu'l-Wafa°'s affiliates in, 60
  Hacı Bektaş in, 154, 155, 156, 157
  the *ocaks* from, 104, 114, 115–16, 121, 130, 149, 236
  School of Khorasan, 67
  Sufi saints of, 154, 157, 162
Khwarazm, 117, 149
Khwarazm-Shahs, 116
Kirkuk, 190, 201, 202–3
Kırşehir convent
  Alevi sources from, 22, 23, 147
  anti-Ottoman activities and, 169
  under Balım Sultan, 151, 167, 266
  the Çelebi family and, 146, 147, 166, 170–1
  as focal point of Alevi accreditation, 16
  as pilgrimage site, 149
Kızıl Deli *ocak*, 18–19, 209
Kızılbaş āyīni, 284, 296; *see also cem*
Kizilbash
  the Abdals of Rum within, 173–4, 177–8
  absence of from Ottoman archives, 292–3
  in Anatolia, 227–9, 230
  the Bektashi compared to, 145–6
  Çelebi influence on, 105
  cems, 296–7, *299*
  communal Sufi affiliation in, 26–7
  conservative Imami Shiᶜi doctrines, 234
  cultural and symbolic codes, 297
  decline of within the Safavid Empire, 229–30
  distinct identity of, 7–8
  early Turkish scholarship on, 322
  emergence of, 322–3
  evolution of, 323
  as the forefathers of the Alevis, 2
  gender-mixed rituals, 72–3, 74, 282, 296–7
  Kizilbash military elite, 222–3, 230
  links with the pro-Safavid and Sufi circles of Iraq, 188–9
  messianic expectations within, 226
  name, 29n, 222
  *ocak*s (family lineages) within, 3, 14, 16–17
  origins of, contemporary debates, 12
  parallel ritual practices with the Wafa°i Sufi tradition, 75
  pre-Safavid identity, 220–1, 322–3
  Protestant missionaries and, 320–2
  as religio-political movement, 2–3, 7
  rituals and traditions of, 284–5
  Safavi *ḫalīfe* network in, 231–8
  Safavid influence on, 161, 324–5
  within the Safavid Kizilbash movement, 7–8
  and the Safavid rise to power, 220–4
  Safavid ties, post-Çaldıran period, 229–31
  scholarship on, 8–11
  Selim I's anti-Kizilbash agenda, 272
  and Shiᶜi Islam, 323
  syncretism of, 13, 322
  tāj, 222, 269, 288
  teachings and beliefs, 8

term, 320
traditional community organisation, 14
transformation into a closed religious order, 3, 7–8
transmission of religious texts from the Safavids, 238–44
within Turkish folk Islam, 2–3, 8
Turkmen tribes in, 26
the Wafaᵓi *ocaks* in, 125–9
Wafaᵓi Sufi tradition in the history of, 18, 24–5, 27, 176–7
Kizilbash confessionalisation
concept of, 256, 257–8
home convents, 298–9, *299*
homogenisation of belief and ritual practices, 296–8
in response to persecution, 27, 257, 259–62, 295–6
Safavid influence, 297–8
Shiᶜi/ᶜAlid sentiments, 297
socio-religious organisation, 298
Kizilbash persecutions
accusations of heresy (*fetvās*), 260–1, 275–6, 277–8, 280, 283–5, 287, 288
after Selim I, 281–2
as collective obligation, 278–9, 288–9
demographic impact of, 295–6
informal accommodation policies, 293–5
in Iraq, 189
and Ottoman pragmatism, 260, 261
and the Ottoman-Safavid conflict, 168, 260
in relation to Sunni confessionalisation, 27, 257, 259–62, 280–1, 282–3, 285, 293
under Selim I, 275–81
socio-economic implications of, 289–92
within a wider Ottoman state-formation process, 289
Kizilbash uprisings, 2, 11, 225, 263–5, 266, 268
Konya, 93, 311n, 312n
Köprülü, Fuad
on the Abdals of Rum, 148, 159, 164, 176
on Baba İlyas, 181n
on the Bektashi–Kizilbash/Alevi relationship, 25, 145–7, 176
on Hacı Bektaş, 152, 153, 154, 181n, 182n
on Halveti Sufi order, 134n
incorporation of the Abdals into the Bektashi order, 170, 171
influence of, 322
Köprülü paradigm, 8–12, 24, 36n, 37n, 48n, 135n, 115, 324
Sufism and the Alevis, 26, 31n, 35n
Kufa, 49, 205
Kul Himmet, 297
Kurds
Abu'l-Wafaᵓ's Kurdish heritage, 52–3, 62
Kurdish-speaking Alevis, 12–13
Kureyşan *ocak*, 18

Little Ice Age, 293

Madrasat al-Mustansiriyya, 109
Mahmud Çelebi, 166, 167
Majid Kurdi, 52, 59
Maḳālāt, 181n
Malatya, 117–21, 125, 126, 163, 209, 211, 236, 282; *see also* Hısn-ı Mansur
Mamluks, 103, 118, 263
Mansur al-Bataᵓihi, 49
Maraş
kadi courts, 206, 207, 208
*ocak*s in, 105, 117, 126, 128, 205
Mardin, 116–17, 119, 121, 122
Mehmed II, 92, 259, 267, 271
Mehmed Taki Dede, 197–8
Mélikoff, Irène, 11–12
messianism
early modern Eurasia, 274
before the first Islamic millennium, 224
of Junayd, 221
in Sufism, 220, 222–6
Mesᶜud, Sultan, 48, 71
metadoxy, 47, 266; *see also* ᶜAlidism; confessional ambiguity
meydan (ritual space), 4–5
Minorsky, V., 223, 252n
Miᶜrāj/Miraç, 4, 5, 35n, 67
miyān al-basta (waistband), 125, 173
Mongols/Ilkhanids, 70, 99
mosques, 285, 286, 290–1
Muhammad b. Salim *see* Tustari-Salimiyya
Muhammad ibn Idris al-Shafiᶜi, 295
Muhammad Tapar, Sultan, 71
Muhammad Turkmani (Abuᵓl-Wafaᵓ's disciple), 60
Muharrem Naci Orhan, 20
Murad (nephew of Selim I), 269, 275, 276
mürşid-i kāmils, 225, 325
Murtada al-Musawi al-Husayni, 205

Murtada al-Zabidi
on Abu'l-Wafa°, 80n
on the adoptee sons of Abu'l-Wafa°, 56, 57
Raf^c niqāb, 47
on Wafa°i sayyids outside Iraq, 60, 97–8, 113
Mustafa ^cÂli, 114
al-Mustazhir bi-llah, Caliph, 63

Nād-i ^cAlī, prayer of, 109
Najaf, convent of, 198–9
Namık Paşa (governor of Baghdad), 199
naqīb al-ashrāf, 22, 111–12, 116, 129, 189, 192
Naqshbandi Sufi order, 152, 153, 169, 197–8, 202, 266
nazr (pious donation), 60, 172
Necipoğlu, Gülru, 280, 285
Niebuhr, Carsten, 191
Ni^cmatullahi Sufi order, 161; *see also* Shah Ni^cmatullahi Wali
Nu^cmaniyya, 49, 51
Nur Ali Halife, 265, 268–9
nūr Muḥammadī (the Muhammadan light), 4, 65, 75
Nurbakhshi Sufi order, 228
Nusayri Alawites, 6, 279, 323

Ocak, Ahmet Yaşar, 11–12, 25, 31n, 41n, 140n, 164, 180n
*ocak*s (family lineages)
and Alevi identity, 325
Çelebis claims of supreme spiritual authority, 146–7
convents of, 16
dede family model of, 14–15, 16, 146–7
in Eastern Anatolia, 104
evolution of, 26, 298, 299–301, *300*, 323–4
family archives, 3–4
integration of the Abdals into, 173
in the Kizilbash milieu, 125–9
within Kizilbash/Alevi communities, 3, 14, 16–17
parameters of, 14–15
regional hierarchies, 15
relations with the Karbala convent, 25–6
Sayyid Ghanim's lineage and, 107–13
*sayyid*isation of the shaykyly families, 126–7, 128–9
sayyid-ship claims, 129–30, 205–8, 206–7, 323–4
Şeyh Ahmed Dede *ocak*, 18, 103
Şeyh Çoban *ocak*, 18, 101
Şeyh Delil Berhican *ocak*, 18, 112–13, 118
shajaras/şeceres, 205–8
spiritual and hereditary transmission lines, 111, 112
Wafa°i backgrounds, 324
the Wafa°i *ijāzas*, 123–30
see also İmam Zeynel Abidin *ocak*; Ağuiçen *ocak*; *dede* families; Dede Kargın *ocak*; Sinemilli *ocak*
*ocakzade*s, 14–15
oniki hizmet (twelve services), 296; *see also cem*
Orhan Beg, 94
Osman (eponym of the Ottoman empire), 91–2, 150
Otman Baba
as great master of the Abdals, 158, 161, 162, 164
opposition with the Çelebis, 166, 167
sexual abstinence of, 167
Ottoman state
absence of Kizilbash from Ottoman archives, 292–3
Amasya Treaty, 274, 282–3
centralisation of, 168, 257
civil war, 260, 263, 269, 272
confessional homogeneity, 259
the confessional turn in, 259–60, 262–3
decree against the Sufis of Ardabil, 262, 265–6
founding myths, 91
House of Osman's ties with Wafa°i, 91–4, 95–6
legitimacy claims of, 272–4
oppositional political activism towards, 168–9
the Ottomans as *ġāzī*s, 270–1, 272, 273
Ottoman–Safavid conflict, xxi, 27, 168, 188–9, 203, 257, 258–60, 273–4
policies towards Iraq, 188–9
policy towards Bektashis, 168
promotion of Friday mosques, 285, 286
promotion of the Bektashi order, 177
relations with the Abdals of Rum, 168, 169–70
religious persecution by, 279–80
response to the rise of the Safavids, 168
Şeyh Bedreddin's uprising against, 279
socio-economic benefits of territorial expansion, 270–1

state-building project, 150
state-formation within Kizilbash persecution, 289
state/religion interrelationship, 285–7
Sunni normativity, 257, 260–1, 262, 274, 280–1, 282–3, 285, 286–8, 293
verification of *sayyid*-ships, 207–8
the Zeyniyye in, 96
see also Bayezid II; Kizilbash persecutions; Selim I (Yavuz Selim)

Pir Sultan Abdal, 291, 297
poetry
Alevi–Bektashi mystical poetry, 33n, 34n
cannonisation of Alevi sacred poetry, 297–8
of Shah Isma^cil, 34n, 40n, 174, 223, 224
poverty (*faqr*)
of Abu'l-Wafa^ɔ, 54
Sufi absolute poverty (*faḳr*), 91, 94, 95, 124–5
and Wafa^ɔi Sufi tradition, 95, 176–7
Prince Ahmed, 269, 270, 271, 275, 276
Prince Korkud, 276
Prince Murad, 269, 275, 276
Protestant missionaries, 320–2

al-Qadir bi-llah, Caliph, 48
Qadiri creed, 48
Qadiri Sufi order, 47, 48, 66, 291
al-Qa^ɔim bi-Amrillah, Caliph, 44, 72
Qalandari (Kalenderi), 61, 152, 157, 159, 176
Qalminiyya, Abu^ɔl-Wafa^ɔ's convent in, 58–9
Qur^ɔan
Abu'l-Wafa^ɔ's use of, 63
esoteric approach to, 65
Qadiri creed and, 48
Qusan, 44, 49, 51, 52, 63, 67, 70, 71, 74

Rāfẓ, 49, 71
Ramadan Majnun (Abu'l-Wafa^ɔ's disciple), 60
raqṣ/raḳṣ (dance), 61
Rifa^ɔi Sufi order, 47, 49, 52, 66
Risale-i Hüsniyye, 297
Rıza Tevfik (Bölükbaşı), 32n
Rükneddin Kılıçarslan IV, Sultan, 99
Rum, lands of, 89, 150, 151, 157, 161, 269, 295; *see also* Anatolia
Rum Abdalları *see* Abdals of Rum
Rum Erenleri (Sufi saints of Rum), 154
Rumi, Mevlana Celaleddin, 90

Sadık Dede, 194, 195–6
Safavids
and the Abdals of Rum, 173–6
Amasya Treaty, 274, 282–3
association with the ideology and practice of *ġazā^ɔ*, 226–7
Bayezid II relations with, 265–7
Bayezid II's decree against and approach to the Sufis of Ardabil, 262, 265–6
and the Bektashis, 175–6
Buyruk manuscripts, 174
confessional homogeneity, 259
decline of the Kizilbash within, 229–30
dervish/Sufi coalition of, 221
and the Düzmece Shah İsma^cil uprising, 169
emergence of, 220
ḫalīfe appointments, 231–8
impact of the Ottoman civil war, 269
involvement in Kizilbash uprisings, 263–5
Kizilbash ties, post-Çaldıran period, 229–31
and the Kizilbash/Alevis, 324–5
legacy of Hacı Bektaş, 174–5
links with the Nurbakhshi Sufi order, 228
messianism of, 222–6
Ottoman–Safavid conflict, *xxi*, 27, 168, 188–9, 203, 257, 258–60, 273–4
policies towards Iraq, 188–9
rise to power, 221–4
Safavid governors of Baghdad, 189–90
Sayyid Süleyman's genealogy with, 235–8
Selim I's anti-Safavid policies, 267–8, 269–70, 275
Shi^citisation in Iran, 256–7
transmission of religious texts to the Kizilbash milieu, 238–44
and the Turkmen tribes, 227–8
see also Isma^cil, Shah
Şah İbrahim Veli, *ocak* of, 18, 19, 28, 231, 235–6, 238
Şahin Baba convent
Alevi sources from, 196, 199, 205, 209
co-identity with Hızır İlyas convent, 199–200
dede families' visits to, 191, 199, 211
endowment deed, 192–4
functionaries of, 210, 218–19n
location of, 190, 199, 200
Şahkulu Uprising, 263–5, 266, 268
Sahl al-Tustari, 64–6, 68, 70, 74–5

Salman Farisi, 122
Samarra, 189, 190, 201, 203
Sarı Gürz Hamza Efendi, 260, 277–80, 294
Saruyatar convent, 291
Sayf al-Dawla (Sadaqa b. Mansur, Shiᶜi Mazyadid amir), 48–9, 71, 78n
Sayyid ᶜAli b. Sayyid Khamis, 56–7
Sayyid Ghanim
  as the brother of Sayyid Matar, 56
  İmam Zeynel Abidin as a descendant of, 108–9, 110
  kinship ties to Abu'l-Wafaᵓ, 56, 82n, 107
  kinship ties to Sayyid ᶜAli b. Sayyid Khamis, 57, 58, 111–13, 121, 124, 130
  silsila (lineage of), 107–9
  Wafaᵓi-Kizilbash *ocak*s lineages from and, 107–13
Sayyid Khamis (nephew of Abu'l-Wafaᵓ), 56–7, 107–8, 111–13, 121, 124–5, 127, 130
Sayyid Matar (Abuᵓl-Wafaᵓ's disciple)
  descendants as administrators of the Qalminiyya convent, 58–9, 116
  Sayyid Ghanim as the brother of, 56
  as the spiritual heir to Abu'l-Wafaᵓ, 55–6, 58–9, 81n, 82n, 138n
Sayyid Mir Nizam Erdebili, 238
Sayyid Muhammad b. Sayyid Ibrahim (last Wafaᵓi shaykh in Anatolia), 125
Sayyid Pir Hayat al-Din (Seyyid Velayet's great ancestor), 56–7, 113, 133n
Sayyid Salim (Abuᵓl-Wafaᵓ's brother), 56, 58
Sayyid Shihab al-Din Ahmad al-Husayni al-Wafaᵓi, 111–13; *see also* Shihab al-Din Ahmad
Selçuki Hatun, *ribāṭ* of, 199
Selim I (Yavuz Selim), Sultan
  Akkoyunlu émigrés support for, 272
  anti-Safavid policies, 267–8, 269–70, 275
  ascent to power, 260, 263, 270, 275
  confessional turn of, 259, 263, 271–2
  conversion of dervish convents into mosques, 290–1
  expansionist aims of, 269–71
  Ottoman civil war, 260, 263, 269, 272
  persecution of opponents of, 276–7
  persecution of the Kizilbash, 169, 272, 275–81
  raids in Georgia, 270, 271
  religious legitimisation for the rule of, 272–3, 274
  titles of, 225, 263
  use of the term 'Kizilbash', 262
Seljuks of Anatolia
  ᶜAlaᵓeddin, Sultan, 98
  arrival of, 17
  Babaᵓi revolt against, 9, 149
  in Baghdad, 48
  Battle of Mantzikert, 89
  Giyaseddin Keyhusrev III, Sultan, 96
  Kılıçarslan I, Sultan, 199
  Muhammed Tapar, 48, 49, 78n
  Nizam al-Mulk, 280
  political activism and, 63
  socio-economic conditions, 312n
  the Sufis and
  Wafaᵓi relations with, 27, 102, 130
  *waqfiyya*s, 96
Selman Cemali Baba, 201
Selman Kufi, 123
serçeşme (fountainhead), 164, 238
Şeyh Ahmed Dede (Shaykh Ahmed-i Tavil), *ocak* of, 18, 102–3, 103
Şeyh Bedreddin, 228, 279, 284, 324
Şeyh Çoban *ocak*, 18, 101
Şeyh Delil Berhican *ocak*, 18, 112–13, 118
Şeyh Hasanlu, village of, 102–3
Şeyh Süleyman *ocak*, 18, 125, 203
Seyyid ᶜAbbas (*postnişīn* of the Karbala convent), 197
Seyyid ᶜAli Sultan, 18; *see also* Kızıl Deli
Seyyid Baki (sender of letter to Dede Kargıns), 191, 242
Seyyid Battal Gazi
  and the Abdals, 162–3, 164–5, 173
  figure of, 94
  Hacı Bektaş's visit to the tomb of, 165
Seyyid Battal Gazi convent, 149, 158, 169–71
Seyyid Hüseyin (*postnişīn* of the Karbala convent), 197
Seyyid İbrahim (Alevi *dede* visiting Iraqi shrine cities), 211
Seyyid Mehmed Taki (*postnişīn* of the Karbala convent), 197
Seyyid Muhammad Tahir (Safavi *ḥalīfe* in Anatolia), 232–4
Seyyid Süleyman (Alevi *dede*), 235–8
Seyyid Velayet, 56, 60, 92, 95, 96, 113
Shah Niᶜmatullah Wali, 228
shamanism, 11, 12
Shaykh (ᶜAli) ᶜAjami, 54–5
Shaykh Ahmad al-Jammi, 103, 113
Shaykh ᶜAskari Shuli, 56, 59

Shaykh Çoban (Şeyh Çoban)
convent of, 99–101, 130, 137n
Wafa'i identity, 100–2
Shaykh Marzuban (Şeyh Merzuban)
endowment for the convents of, 96–102
Wafa'i identity, 97–8, 113
Shaykh Muhammad b. Hasan el-Kargıni, 111
Shaykhavand, clan of, 236
Shihab al-Din Ahmad, 97–8, 113
Shihab al-Din al-Wasiti (Shihab al-Din Abu'l-Huda Ahmad b. ʿAbd al-Munʿim al-Shabrisi al-Wasiti), 46
Shihab al-Din Suhrawardi, 68
Shiʿi Islam
in and around Qusan, 70–1
in Ebussudʿud Efendi's *fetvās*, 286
Ghulāt sects, 2, 11, 31n, 35n, 36n, 323
Imami Shiʿism, 2, 230, 234, 304n, 325n
influence on Sahl al-Tustari's teachings, 65
and the Kizilbash/Alevis, 323
Shiʿitisation by the Safavids, 256–7
tensions with Sufism, 258–9
Twelver Shiʿism, 222, 229
Shirvan (Azerbaijan), 46, 61, 174–5, 311n
Siirt, 103
silsila (initiatic chains), 65–8, 69, 74, 107–8
Sinemilli *ocak*
Ağuiçens as their *mürşid*, 105, 126
Alevi sources from, 18
Bektaş Dede, 205–9
genealogy of, 127–9
link to Derviş Çimli ocak, 144n
(presumed) tomb-shrine of Sultan Sinemil(li), 127
the *shajara* of, 126–9
Wafa'i affiliation, 126–7
see also Hayran Abdal
Sivas
Alevis in, 208
Ali Baba convent, 291
the Kizilbash in, 96
*ocak*s in, 104
Wafa'i convents, 96–7, 99–100, 101
Sufis of Ardabil, 262, 265–6, 310n
Sufis of Teke, 265–6
Sufism
Alevi discourse in relation to, 5, 26
in Anatolia, 90
communal Sufi affiliations, 26–7, 62–3
early history of, 75
formulation of a normative Sufism, 50
legitimate vs heretical in *fetvās*, 283–5, 286
notion of absolute poverty (*faḳr*), 91, 94, 95, 124–5
Nurbakhshi Sufi order, 228
popular and elite versions of, 68–9
popularisation of, 26, 49–50, 62–3, 73–4
preacher-masters, 61–2
significance of al-Batiha region, 49
Sufi–Ottoman relations under Bayezid II, 267
tariqa Sufism, 61, 90, 159, 166, 177
tensions with Shiʿi Islam, 258–9
tensions with Sunni Islam, 50–1, 72, 258–9
this-worldly and renunciatory orientations, 54–5, 160, 166–7
T-type convent mosques, 285
see also Wafa'iyya
Şükri Bidlisi, 269
Sükuti Baba, 199, 202
Sulayman, Shah, 228, 232, 234, 244
Süleyman I (Kanuni (the Lawgiver)), 194, 195–6, 198, 225, 259, 274, 282
Süleymaniye complex, Istanbul, 280–1
Sultan ʿAla'eddin (Keykubat I), 98, 99, 114
Sultan ʿAla'eddin Keykubat II, 102
Sultan Yusuf (patriarch of the Dede Kargıns in Malatya), 119
Sün, village of, 105, 126
Sunni confessionalisation, 27, 257, 259–62, 274, 280–1, 282–3, 285, 293
Sunni Islam
Abu'l-Wafa''s Sunni identity, 69, 70–2, 74
adherence to the shariʿa, 286–7
in and around Qusan, 70–1
the Bektashi order within, 170, 286
Qadiri creed, 48
recentering of, 77n
Sunni normativity in the Ottoman state, 257, 260–1, 262, 274, 280–1, 282–3, 285, 286–8, 293
Sunni-Shiʿi antagonism, 48, 258, 285–6
tensions with Sufism, 50–1, 72, 258–9
sürhser defteri (Kizilbash register), 277
Suşehri, 96, 98
syncretism
in Alevism, 12
as an explanatory model, 13–14
of the Kizilbash/Alevis, 13, 322
of Turkish folk Islam, 9

Taceddin-i Kurdi, 92
Tahmasp, Shah
  appointment of *ḫalīfe*s, 231
  Buyruk manuscripts from the reign of, 240, 242, 243–4
  cauldron of, 175
  as Şāh Dehmān b. Seyyid Şāh İsmāᶜī l, 241
  Süleyman's campaign against, 280
Tāj al-ᶜĀrifīn (Crown of the Gnostics), 50, 53
*talib*s, 14–15, 16
Taptuk Emre, 156
Taqi al-Din ᶜAbd al-Rahman al-Wasiti, 46–7
taqiyya (religious dissimulation), 86n, 170
tarik (sacred stick), 66, 297
*ṭarīḳ-i evliyā*ᵓ (order of the saints), 209
ṭarīqat al-faqr (order of poverty), 124; *see also* poverty
tawallā tabarrā, 86n, 161, 286
timar holders (timariots), 264, 271, 290
Tirmidh, Sayyids of, 116, 122
Tokat, 123, 268, 269, 277, 291
Trebizond (Trabzon), 221, 267, 270, 282
Trouillot, Michel-Rolph, 1
Turabi Baba, 123, 243
Turkish folk Islam, 9
Türkistan Erenleri (Sufi saints of Turkistan), 154
Turkmen baba, model of, 9, 115, 153
Turkmen tribes, 9, 10–11, 26, 115, 221, 227–8
Tustari-Salimiyya, 66

Üryan Hızır *ocak, 15*

Vahidi, 157–8, 164, 165
Velāyetnāme, 150, 151, 152–3, 154–6, 164, 165, 172
Virani Baba, 198

Wafaᵓi-Kizilbash *ocak*s
  in Eastern Anatolia, 104
  Sayyid Ghanim's lineage and, 107–13
  spiritual and hereditary transmission lines, 111, 112
  see also İmam Zeynel Abidin *ocak*; *Ağuiçen ocak*; Dede Kargın *ocak*
Wafaᵓiyya
  Abu'l-Wafaᵓ as eponym of, 45, 73–4
  in Anatolia, 90, 102–4
  connection to Sahl al-Tustari, 65–6
  connection with Anatolian Sufism, 25–6
  connections with the Ahis, 93, 123
  initiation rituals, 125
  within Kizilbash/Alevi history, 18, 24–5, 27, 176–7
  links with the Abdals, 160–3
  metadoxic outlook of, 47, 266
  notions of poverty, 95
  within Ottoman history, 91–4, 95–6
  parallel ritual practices with Kizilbash/ Alevi communities, 75
  parallel ritual practices with the Bektashi, 172–3
  *samā*ᵓ (ritual dance), 75, 172
  *sayyid*s and/ or dervishes outside Iraq, 60–1
  silsila, 65–8
  the Wafaᵓi *ijāzas*, 123–30
Walsh, J. R., 311–12n
waqfiyya (endowment deeds), 96–7, 98–9, 192–4
Wasit, 46, 47, 49, 51, 70, 82n
women
  in Alevi ritual life, 4
  gender-mixed rituals, 72–3, 74, 282, 296–7

Yazidis, 6
Yemini, 297
Yesevi Sufi order, 9, 153, 36n
Yüksel, Hasan, 99
Yunus Emre, 153, 156, 284

Zara, 96, 98
zāwiya (dervish convent), 44, 60, 61, 93, 99, 193–4
Zazas, 12–13
Zeynal Dede (*türbedār* of the Şahin Baba convent), 200, 210
Zeyniyye, 96

EU representative:
Easy Access System Europe
Mustamäe tee 50, 10621 Tallinn, Estonia
Gpsr.requests@easproject.com

www.ingramcontent.com/pod-product-compliance
Lightning Source LLC
Chambersburg PA
CBHW061704300426
44115CB00014B/2555

* 9 7 8 1 4 7 4 4 3 2 6 9 6 *